BARGAIN FINDER

THE ENCYCLOPEDIC
MONEY SAVING GUIDE
TO NEW YORK CITY
FOR RESIDENTS/FOR TOURISTS

3rd edition

by Eric Zuesse

The author of this book Eric Zuesse, is available to address your organization or group concerning any of the subjects covered in BARGAIN FINDER. He also serves as a consultant to book publishers and self-publishers in saving money on producing and publicizing books. He may be reached at 242-0041.

He further holds monthly seminars on bargain-finding, as well as on the city's greatest bargain restaurants, and conducts periodic guided bargain finder's walking tours. For information regarding either of these seminars, or regarding the walking tour, contact The Learning Annex at 956-8800.

Research: Eric Zuesse
Writing: Eric Zuesse
Graphic Design: Eric Zuesse
Production: Eric Zuesse
Publicity: Golden-Lee Books

A Consumers' Alliance book, published by Golden-Lee Books, Brooklyn, NY.

© 1983 by Eric Zuesse

ISBN 0-9608950-0-0-495

CONTENTS

GETTING THE GOODS

1:	Appliances	5
2:	Autos & Supplies	14
3:	Bikes	22
4:	Cameras & Optical Eqt.	25
5:	Clothing—Children's	31
6:	Clothing—Men's	33
7:	Clothing—Women's	41
8:	Dinnerware & Cookware	72
9:	Fabrics, Yarns & Notions	79
10:	Flowers & Plants	84
11:	Foods	86
12:	Furnishings	104
13:	Health & Beauty Aids	118
14:	High Fidelity	131
15:	Home-Improvement Items	139
16:	Housewares	150
17:	Jewelry & Gifts	157
18:	Linens	168
19:	Liquors, Wines, Beers, Sodas	171
20:	Musical Instruments	183
21:	Office Equipment	185
22:	Personal Accessories	193
23:	Pets	200
24:	Publications	203
25:	Recordings & Tapes	208
26:	Smoking Supplies	213
27:	Sporting Goods	220
28:	Stationery & Art Supplies	224
29:	Toys, Games & Hobbies	230
30:	Warehouse Salvage Job-Lot	233
xx:	Geographical Directory of Stores:	See Ch. 47.

THE HUMAN TOUCH

31:	Services	238
32:	Personal Finance	242

ESPECIALLY FOR <u>NEW</u> NEW YORKERS

33:	N.Y.C. Neighborhoods	253
34:	Apartment Bargains	257
35:	Where to Go When Things Go Wrong	260
36:	AM-FM-TV Stations	265

ESPECIALLY FOR TOURISTS

37: NYC's 40 Bargain-Hotels 267
38: Travel Services 273
xx: Restaurants, Fun, & Tours: See below.

RESTAURANTS

39: The 146 Bargain-Restaurants 278
40: The 3 Culinary Honor-Rolls 292
41: The 17 Types of Cuisine Served 294
42: The Restaurants by Location 296

ENJOYING NEW YORK

43: The 40 Free-Or-Cheap Entertainments 300
44: Bargain Finder Walking Tours 305

GETTING AROUND

45: Maps 317
46: Best Free Maps 323
47: Geographical Directory 324

INDEX 340

1:
APPLIANCES
Expect 20-50% discounts.

Depending on how experienced a comparison-shopper you are, you'll be pleased, amazed, or even shocked, once you've found out how much you can slice off those "list" and department-store prices. Some people have even asked me whether the places I recommend are selling "hot" merchandise! Rest assured, they are not. Full manufacturers' warranties apply, and many of these stores in fact have better return-policies than do the full-priced retailers. How can they do it? They're extremely efficient, working without huge showrooms or large sales-staffs. Many are located in low-rent parts of town. Characteristically, these shops are jammed floor-to-ceiling with merchandise in factory-sealed cartons. That, too, cuts down costs. But most importantly of all, these places have simply made the basic decision to gear their entire operations so that they can work on a miniscule retail mark-up. This is in contrast to most stores, which aim to attract customers not on the basis of offering outstanding value, but rather by expensive promotion and advertising, or by high-rent retail locations which draw a lot of off-the-street traffic. Sometimes it's amazing how much difference just one flight of stairs can make—perhaps $100 in the cost of a television set, for example!

Don't feel shy about phoning stores for comparison-prices. If one doesn't cooperate, just call the next. Almost all will quote prices over the phone. But you must specify the make and model number of what you want.

Most of the recommended outlets sell thousands of items besides what they stock. So if a store doesn't have what you're looking for, then ask them "Can you get it?" and "What would the price be?" In many instances, they'll be able to answer both questions immediately; sometimes, however, they'll have to place a phone-call to their distributor (which may very well be another one of these recommended stores. These discounters often work together that way.)

In any case, it's best if you know ahead of time precisely what items you're interested in, by make and model number. *Consumer Reports* is one major source of advice to help you select; but frankly they're not, in my opinion, any better than less-well-known similar publications, such as *Consumer Guide*. If you don't have the time to read several such product-rating magazines or books, the best thing to do is to seek the opinion of a major appliance-repair facility which represents many manufacturers. The problem here is that it's usually difficult to get the personnel to comment. They won't want to jeopardize their standing with the manufacturers, so they'll be cautious. Don't expect them to say, "Brand X is junk, and will conk out after a couple of years," even if they believe it to be so. They're much more likely to comment, "Brand X is all right. But Brand Y doesn't seem to come in very often for repair." Read between the lines. Sometimes you won't have anything more to go on than a facial expression. And keep in mind that this is one instance where the manager is usually not the best person to speak with. The best fellow to get an informed and unbiased opinion from is usually the guy up front at the repair-counter, who takes defective appliances in all day, and writes out the repair-tickets. He generally knows which appliances break down most often, and in which way, because all this information goes onto the repair-ticket. Furthermore, he's not subject to the same constraints as the manager. He won't necessarily feel that his informed personal opinion will be interpreted as an official company position, since he's not an official of the company.

Although I've found *Consumer Reports*' product-ratings to be in some instances rather unreliable, that magazine occasionally publishes frequency-of-repair records for various makes of appliances—especially of televisions, refrigerators, washers, and other big-ticket items. These records are extremely valuable—perhaps the shopper's best single source of comparative product-information. In the product-recommendations below, I've relied on this resource going back several years, plus on product-ratings appearing in the various consumer-magazines, plus on repairmen's comments. I also have personally tested out the performance of practically every brand of electric shaver, including the terribly overrated (in *Consumer Reports*) and very popular Norelco models (which I've found to be bad in many ways: the flat shape of the triple-rotary head is especially a monstrosity which doesn't fit the face or any curve or crevice thereof—it must have been designed for shaving table-tops; and the unit is bad and slow on fast-growing or long or thick hairs, requiring supplementation with a blade-shaver on these); and the one that I found to be outstanding—the Remington Microscreen—can be sampled by anyone who simply walks into the Remington Service Center, 7 E. 46th St., 687-4881, and requests to try out the machine. All the major brands of canister vacuum-cleaners and electric blenders were also personally tested, and here my findings were not substantially at variance with those of Consumers' Union. Finally, I checked out the performance of all the available brands of "Walkman"-like portable stereos, and also of free-standing headphone-sets that plug into them.

RECOMMENDED PRODUCTS:

Televisions, Color: Sony, Zenith. **Televisions, B/W:** Sanyo, Panasonic, GE, Quasar. **Video Tape Recorders:** Panasonic, Sony. **Refrigerators, Freezers, Washers, Dishwashers:** Whirlpool, Maytag. **Air Conditioners:** Friedrich. **Blenders:** Hamilton Beach. **Electric Shavers:** Remington Microscreen. **Vacuum-Cleaners, Canister:** Sunbeam, Sanyo. **Small Cassette Recorders:** Panasonic. **Walkmen, FM:** Sonora = Thomas = Omnitron (all identical), Unisef TR. **Walkmen, Cassette-Play, FM:** Accona MCS-33, Unisef TU (but the Unisef's headphones are tinny, and should be replaced with the below-listed headsets). **Walkmen, Cassette Record-Play, FM:** Unics UP-207 (but the headphones are poor and should be replaced with those listed below), Ambassador = Continental = Vela (all identical). Know that the record function in all makes is low-fidelity from the radio, and good only from the microphones. **Walkmen headphones:** Sporty Walkabout FM Radio (dirt-cheap, and the headset alone is worth the price), Altek AK-1500. **Typewriters, Desk-Top:** See text introducing Chapter 21, "Office Equipment." **Typewriters, Portable:** the smallest, cheapest, model by Olympia and by Olivetti.

RECOMMENDED STORES:
large appliances

(examples: clothes washers and dryers, dish washers, dryers, freezers, microwave ovens, ovens, range hoods, ranges, refrigerators, stoves, televisions, washing machines)

⁺Kaufman Electric** (475-8313); ****Abe's Radio** (Brooklyn, 257-4900); ****Adco Distributing** (Brooklyn, 788-5916); ****A&Z Appliances** (267-1176); ****Benny's Impex** (925-7535); ****Dial-A-Brand** (978-4400); ****Eichler Bros.** (925-5750); ****Happy Buying Center** (695-0456); ****Home Sales** (241-3272); ****Lewi Supply** (777-6910); ****L&J Audio** (425-2530); ****Price Watchers** (337-6633); ****Sona Electrical** (233-1010); ****Townie Merchandise** (929-8060); ****World Wide Discount** (477-5441); *⁺**ABC Trdg.** (228-5080); ***Bryce** (575-8600); ***Columbia Appliances** (Queens, 358-1600); ***Drake Bros.** (964-8450); ***Focus Electronics** (Brooklyn, 871-7600); ***Harry's Discounts** (Brooklyn, 236-3507); ***Hazy Electronics** (736-8614); ***Joann's Variety Store** (Brooklyn, 648-8517); ***Queens Discount Appliances** (Queens, 639-5070); ***Saverite Photo Elec.** (966-6655); ***STL Electronics** (849-7627); ***Top Value Appliance** (Brooklyn, 236-5355); ⁺**Dial Appliance** (253-8100); **Argus Appliances** (794-1705); **Bernie's Discount** (564-8582); **Columbia Radio** (849-6189); **Co-op Sales** (Brooklyn, 384-2443); **DRA Buying** (523-7700); **EBA Associates** (Brooklyn, 252-3400); **Essex Camera/Electronics** (677-6420); **Greater NY Trdg.** (226-2808); **Gutierrez Trdg.** (697-7582); **Harron Distributors** (685-6285); **M.A.Z. Trdg.** (Queens, 478-5661); **R.K. Trdg.** (Queens, 639-2881); **Savemart Clearance** (Bronx, 292-6700); **Sona Appliances** (Queens, 446-8448).

small appliances

(examples: adders, air conditioners, air purifiers, answering machines, bean pots, blank recording tapes—major brands only, blenders, broilers, buffet ranges, bun warmers, calculators, car stereos, carpet sweepers, cassettes and players, clocks, coffee grinders, computer games, corn poppers, Corning ware, dehumidifiers, disposers, electric brooms, electric can-openers, electric spoons, electric toothbrushes, facial saunas, fans, floor-polishers, food-processors, frypans, garbage-disposers, griddles, grills, grinders, hair-cutters and dryers, heaters, hi- fis, hot plates, humidifiers, ice-crushers, intercoms, irons, juicers, knife sharpeners, knitting machines, luggage—Samsonite and American Tourister, manicure-sets, massagers, meat-grinders, mixers, pens—Parker & Schaeffer & Cross, percolators, phones, polishers, popcorn-makers, pots—Farberware, pressure-cookers, purifiers, radios, record-players, recording tapes, rotisseries, rug shampooers, sewing machines, shavers, slicers, smoke detectors, stereos, sun-lamps, tapes for recording, telephones, televisions, Thermos bottles made of stainless steel, toasters, trash-compactors, typewriters, vacuum cleaners, vaporizers, vibrators, video-tape recorders, waffle-irons, walkie talkies, warmers, waste-disposers, watches—Seiko and Citizen, water piks)

⁺Kaufman Electric** (475-8313); ****Abe's Radio** (Brooklyn, 257-4900);

1: APPLIANCES

Annex Outlet (964-8661); ****A&Z Appliances (267-1176); ****Benny's Impex** (925-7535); ****Bondy Export** (925-7785); ****Camera World Clearance** (intermittent stock, 563-8328); ****Eichler Bros.** (925-5750); ****Happy Buying Center** (695-0456); ****Kunst Sales** (966-1909); ****Lewi Supply** (777-6910); ****L&J Audio** (425-2530); ****Sona Electrical** (233-1010); ****S&W Electronics** (966-2950); ****Townie Merchandise** (929-8060); ****Triest Export** (246-1548.); ****World Wide Discount** (477-5441); ***+ABC Trdg.** (228-5080); ***Baby Site Electronics** (564-5349); ***BCA Dept. Store** (227-4770); ***Biphonic Elec.** (Queens, 274-9888); ***Columbia Appliances** (Queens, 358-1600); ***Drake Bros.** (964-8450); ***Eighth Av. Electronics** (279-5195); ***Focus Electronics** (Brooklyn, 871-7600); ***Fourteenth St. Audio** (989-5329); ***Garment Hi-Fi** (944-2120); ***Golden Appliances** (Brooklyn, 853-5782); ***Harmony Video** (Brooklyn, 627-8960); ***Harry's Discounts** (Brooklyn, 236-3507); ***Hazy Electronics** (736-8614); ***Joann's Variety Store** (648-8517); ***Live Wire Electronics** (Queens, 544-6145); ***M.&B. Appliances** (Queens, 699-1462); ***National Video Discount** (Queens, 268-0062); ***Queens Discount Appliances** (Queens, 639-5070); ***Sam & Raj Appliances** (Queens, 446-1004); ***Saverite Photo Elec.** (966-6655); ***Stereo King** (354-1492); ***U.S.A. Electronics** (221-1354); **Adding Machine Service** (684-6168); **Advance Sewing Machine** (226-5621); **Beaver Electronic** (344-3420); **Bernie's Discount** (564-8582); **Columbia Radio** (849-6189); **Co-op Sales** (Brooklyn, 384-2443); **Crown Sewing Machines** (663-8968); **Essex Camera/Electronics** (677-6420); **E.Z. Stereo** (Brooklyn, 383-0150); **Greater NY Trdg.** (226-2808); **Guild Sewing Machines** (267-1938); **Gutierrez Trdg.** (697-7582); **International Solgo** (895-6996); **Kingsway Video** (Brooklyn, 645-4700); **M.A.Z. Trdg.** (Queens, 478-5661); **M.S. Distribution** (685-5085); **R.K. Trdg.** (Queens, 639-2881); **Rose Distributors** (246-2359); **Sona Appliances** (Queens, 446-8448); **Vendome Trdg.** (691-7500); **Yair Import** (687-5540).

irons/blenders/clocks (& SEE ABOVE)

***Vercesi Hardware (475-1883); ****Ashreh Supply** (925-9507); ****Dollar Bills** (867-0212); ****Romano Trdg.** (581-4248); ***Lou-Mark Trdg.** (242-9440); ***Top Value Appliance** (Brooklyn, 236-5355); **Lee-Or Discount** (Brooklyn, 377-1010).

off-brand budget appliances

(examples: $10 portable transistor radios, tinny-sounding portable record players, cheap cassettes and players, cheap car stereos, cheap walkmen)

+Mills Sales (477-1000); ****Ashreh Supply (925-9507); ****Dynamite** (689-8908); ****Olympic Electronics** (564-0567); ****R&F Electronics** (679-5962); ****The City Dump** (431-1670); ***Ed-El Electronics** (255-7082); ***Hazy Electronics** (736-8614); ***Hunter Audio** (986-1540); ***MCB Trdg.** (741-0848); ***Mecca** (679-9336); ***Newport of Japan** (686-1320); ***Stereo King** (354-1492); ***Susan Trdg.** (431-8529); **+Atlantic Export** (Queens, 274-7900); **Cohen's Electronics** (571-1392); **Global Mktg.** (924-3888); **Grand Stereo** (689-5808); **Norman's House of Deals** (683-4772); **R.K. Trdg.** (Queens, 639-2881); **Sunbright** (889-1995); **Warren St. Merchandise** (227-8330).

STORES-DIRECTORY

Phone a store before you go out of your way to visit it. Especially do this during July and August, when most establishments reduce or eliminate weekend-hours.

In the listings below, "*" means especially recommended, "+" means that the store offers a bonus discount to BF readers, "ch."

1: APPLIANCES

and "c.c." mean respectively checks and credit cards, and "exch." and "rfd." mean respectively exchange and refund. Nearest subway-stops are shown. For example, "B-D-F to 47" means to take the B, D, or F train to 47th Street. Store-hours are also indicated, with days of the week abbreviated, like "M-S 8-6."

*+ **ABC Trdg.**, 31 Canal St. (Ludlow), 228-5080, F to E. Broadway, Sun-Th 9-6, F 9-2, c.c., no ch., exch., no rfd. Often very crowded. Bonus discount to BF readers: 0% to 2%. Sells: **Large Appliances, Small Appliances.**

** **Abe's Radio**, Brooklyn, 1396 Rockaway Pkwy. (Farragut), 257-4900, no subway stop nearby, M-S 10-7, all cash, no exch. or rfd. Sells: **Large Appliances, Small Appliances.**

** **Adco Distributing**, Brooklyn, 571 3rd Av. (15), 788-5916, N-RR to Prospect Av., M-S 8:30-5, c.c., no ch., exch., no rfd. No TV sets, but good selection of large appliances; also some plumbing supplies. Sells: **Large Appliances, Home-Improvement Items.**

Adding Machine Service, 59 W. 30 (6th Av.), 684-6168, B-D-F-N-QB-RR to 34, M-F 8:30-5:30, S 9:30-3:30, ch., no c.c., exch., no rfd. Small store. Small selection. Only small typewriters, calculators, and radios. Sells: **Small Appliances.**

Advance Sewing Machine, 521 Broadway (Spring), 226-5621, N-RR to Prince St., 6 to Spring, M-F 8:30-6, S 8:30-4, ch., c.c., no exch. or rfd. Sells: **Small Appliances, Fabrics, Yarns & Notions.**

** **Annex Outlet**, 43 Warren St. (Church), 964-8661, A-CC-1-2-3 to Chambers, MTTh 8-6, W 8-9, F 8-3:30, Sun 9-5, all cash, 7-day exch. or rfd. Sells: **Small Appliances, Recordings & Tapes.**

Argus Appliances, 507 E. 80 (York-E.River), 794-1705, 6 to 77, plus a long walk, M-F 9-5:45, ch., c.c., exch. or rfd. No exch. or rfd. without box in undamaged condition. Sells: **Large Appliances.**

** **Ashreh Supply**, 473 Broadway (Grand), 3rd floor, 925-9507, J-M-N-QB-RR-6 to Canal, Sun-Th 11-7, all cash, no exch. or rfd. Basically a wholesaler who accomodates retail-trade. Sells: **Irons/Blenders/Clocks, Off-Brand Budget Appliances, Cameras & Optical Eqt., Jewelry & Gifts, Personal Accessories, Smoking Supplies, Stationery & Art Supplies.**

\+ **Atlantic Export**, Queens, 25-98 Steinway St., Astoria, 274-7900, RR to Astoria Blvd., M-W 11-7:30, ThF 11-9, Sun 12-6, c.c., no ch., exch., no rfd. Bonus discount to BF readers: 10% to 25%. Sells: **Off-Brand Budget Appliances, Dinnerware & Cookware, Jewelry & Gifts.**

** **A&Z Appliances**, 34 Canal St. (Ludlow), 267-1176, F to E. Broadway, 7 days 11-7, c.c. +5%, no ch., exch., no rfd. Will special-order. Sells: **Large Appliances, Small Appliances.**

* **Baby Site Electronics**, 269 W. 34 (8th Av.), 564-5349, A-AA-CC-E to 34, M-S 9:30-7:30, c.c., no ch., 7-day exch., no rfd. Sells: **Small Appliances.**

* **BCA Dept. Store**, 49 E. Broadway (Catherine), 227-4770, J-M-RR-4-5-6 to Chambers & Bkln. Bridge, F to E. Broadway, 7 days 10-7, all cash, no exch. or rfd. Sells: **Small Appliances.**

Beaver Electronic, 20 Beaver St. (B'wy), 344-3420, 4-5 to Bowling Green, M-F 7:30-5:30, c.c., no ch., exch., no rfd. Will special-order. Small store. Sells: **Small Appliances.**

** **Benny's Impex**, 51 Canal St. (Orchard), 925-7535, F to E. Broadway, Sun-Th 9:30-5:30, F 9:30-2; Brooklyn, 4717 13th Av., 853-8888, B to 50th St., Sun-Th 10-7, F 10-2. Both stores: ch., c.c. $75 up (+4% on some), 10-day exch. or rfd. Sells: **Large Appliances, Small Appliances.**

** **Bernie's Discount**, 821 6th Av. (28-9), 564-8582&8758, B-D-F-N-QB-RR to 34, M-F 9-5:30, S 10:30-2:30, ch., c.c. +3%, exch., no rfd. Sells: **Large Appliances, Small Appliances.**

* **Biphonic Elec.**, Queens, 28-13 Steinway St., Astoria, 274-9888, F-GG-N to Steinway St., RR to 30th Av., M-F 10:30-7, S 10:30-6, c.c., no ch., 7-day exch., no rfd. Sells: **Small Appliances.**

** **Bondy Export**, 40 Canal St. (Ludlow), 925-7785, F to E. Broadway, Sun-Th 10-6, F 10-3, ch., c.c., no exch. or rfd. Sells: **Small Appliances.**

* **Bryce**, 115 W. 40 (6th-B'wy), 575-8600, B-D-F to 42, M-F 9-5:45, S 9-4, ch., c.c., exch., no rfd. Has audio showroom. Sells: **Large Appliances, High Fidelity, Office Equipment.**

** **Camera World Clearance**, 100 W. 32 (6th Av.), 563-8328, B-D-F-N-

10 **1: APPLIANCES**

QB-RR to 34, 3, c.c., no ch. Sometimes there are great bargains, basically hi-fi and small electronics items. Sells: **Small Appliances.**

    Cohen's Electronics, 182 Church St. (Reade-Duane), 571-1392, A-CC-1-2-3 to Chambers, 1 to Franklin, 7 days 9-6, all cash, exch., no rfd. Sells: **Off-Brand Budget Appliances, Recordings & Tapes.**

✳   **Columbia Appliances**, Queens, 42-41 Main St., Flushing, 358-1600, 7 to Main St., T-Sun 10-7, ch., c.c., exch., no rfd. Sells: **Large Appliances, Small Appliances.**

    Columbia Radio, 1237 Amsterdam Av. (121), 849-6189, 1 to 116, M-S 10-6, all cash, no exch. or rfd. Sells: **Large Appliances, Small Appliances.**

    Co-op Sales, Brooklyn, 232 Broadway (Roebling-Havemeyer), 384-2443, J-M to Marcy, M-F 10-5:30, Sun 10-4, c.c., no ch., exch., no rfd. Will special-order. Sells: **Large Appliances, Small Appliances, Furnishings, Jewelry & Gifts.**

    Crown Sewing Machines, 2792 Broadway (108), 663-8968, 1 to 110, M-S 10-6, c.c., no ch., exch., no rfd. Good only on sewing machines, Singers. Sells: **Small Appliances.**

+   **Dial Appliance**, 253-8100, Bonus discount to BF readers: 0% to 2%. Sells: **Large Appliances.**

✳✳   **Dial-A-Brand**, 978-4400 & 1-516-352-4447 & 1-201-653-6727. Sells: **Large Appliances.**

✳✳   **Dollar Bills**, 99 E. 42 (Park Av.), 867-0212, 4-5-6-7 to Grand Central, M-W 8-6:30, ThF 8-7, S 10-6, ch., c.c., 7-day exch. or rfd. A small department store that's best on toiletries, housewares, and cigarettes, but good also on men's wear. Same owner: J. Chuckles, Strawberry, Sunshine, Zoom stores. Sells: **Irons/Blenders/Clocks, Clothing—Men's, Housewares, Smoking Supplies.**

    DRA Buying, 523-7700 & 1-516-482-8686. Sells: **Large Appliances.**

✳   **Drake Bros.**, 114 Fulton St. (B'wy), up 1 flight, 964-8450, A-CC-J-M-RR-2-3-4-5 to B'wy-Nassau & Fulton, M-F 8:30-5:30, ch., c.c., no exch. or rfd. Sells: **Large Appliances, Small Appliances.**

✳✳   **Dynamite**, 1165 Broadway at 27th St., 689-8908, N-RR to 28th St., 7-days 9-6, c.c., no ch., exch., no rfd. Usually carries the best off-brands. Also cheap movie-rentals. Sells: **Off-Brand Budget Appliances, Recordings & Tapes.**

    EBA Associates, Brooklyn, 2329 Nostrand Av. (I), 252-3400, 3-4 to Flatbush Av., MTTh 9-8:15, WFS 9-6, all cash, no exch. or rfd. Bonus discount to BF readers: 5% to 10%. Sells: **Large Appliances, High Fidelity.**

✳   **Ed-El Electronics**, 62 W. 14 (6th Av.), 255-7082, B-F-LL to 14th St. & 6th Av., 7 days 10-7, c.c., no ch., exch., no rfd. Sells: **Off-Brand Budget Appliances.**

✳✳   **Eichler Bros.**, 70 Canal at Allen, 925-5750, F to E. Broadway, B-D to Grand, M-Th 9-6, Sun 9-5, F 9-3, all cash, exch., no rfd. Sells: **Large Appliances, Small Appliances.**

✳   **Eighth Av. Electronics**, 520 8th Av. (36-7), 279-5195, A-AA-CC-E to 34, 7 days 10-8, all cash, no exch. or rfd. Sells: **Small Appliances.**

    Essex Camera/Electronics, 17 Essex St. (Canal), 677-6420, F to E. Broadway, irregular hours, ch., no c.c., 10-day exch. or rfd. Sells: **Large Appliances, Small Appliances, Cameras & Optical Eqt.**

    E.Z. Stereo, Brooklyn, 892 Manhattan Av. (Greenpoint Av.), 383-0150&0168, GG to Greenpoint Av., MTFS 10-7, W 10-6, Th 10-8, c.c., no ch., exch., no rfd. Sells: **Small Appliances, High Fidelity.**

✳   **Focus Electronics**, Brooklyn, 4523 13th Av., 871-7600, B to Ft. Ham. Pkwy., M-Th 10-9, F 10-2, Sun 10-6, ch., c.c., 10-day exch., no rfd. Sells: **Large Appliances, Small Appliances, Cameras & Optical Eqt.**

✳   **Fourteenth St. Audio**, 46 W. 14 (5th-6th), 989-5329, B-F-LL to 14th St. & 6th Av., 7 days 10-7, all cash, exch., no rfd. Sells: **Small Appliances.**

✳   **Garment Hi-Fi**, 55 W. 39 (5th-6th), 944-2120, B-D-F to 42, M-F 9-7, S 10-4, c.c., no ch., 14-day exch., no rfd. Full audio showroom. Very nice people. Low-key atmosphere. Sells: **Small Appliances, High Fidelity.**

✳   **Global Mktg.**, 49 W. 23 (5th-6th), 924-3888, B-F to 23, N-RR to 23rd St., M-Th 8-6, F 8-2, Sun 10-3, ch., no ch., exch., no rfd. Sells: **Off-Brand Budget Appliances, Jewelry & Gifts.**

✳   **Golden Appliances**, Brooklyn, 4103 13th Av., 853-5782, B to Ft. Ham. Pkwy., M-Th 10-6, F 10-1, Sun 10-5, c.c., no ch., no exch. or rfd. Sells: **Small Appliances.**

    Grand Stereo, 1175 Broadway (28), 689-5808, N-RR to 28th St., M-F

1: APPLIANCES

9-6, S 9-12, all cash, no exch. or rfd. No retail when too busy with wholesale. Sells: **Off-Brand Budget Appliances.**

Greater NY Trdg., 81 Canal St. (Eldridge-Allen), 226-2808&8850, F to E. Broadway, Sun-Th 10-5:30, F 10-3, ch., no c.c., 7-day exch. or rfd. Sells: **Large Appliances, Small Appliances, Dinnerware & Cookware, Jewelry & Gifts.**

Guild Sewing Machines, 139 E. Broadway (Pike-Canal), 267-1938, F to E. Broadway, M-F 9-5, Sun 9-2, all cash, no exch. or rfd. Only sewing machines, Singer. Sells: **Small Appliances.**

Gutierrez Trdg., 149 Madison Av. at 32, 697-7582, 6 to 33, by appointment, all cash, no exch. or rfd. Phone with specific model or style number. Sells: **Large Appliances, Small Appliances.**

✷✷ **Happy Buying Center**, 22 W. 32 (5th-6th), 7th floor, 695-0456, B-D-F-N-QB-RR to 34, M-F 9-6, S 9-5, ch., c.c. +8%, (only cert. chs.), exch., no rfd. Sells: **Large Appliances, Small Appliances, Furnishings.**

✷ **Harmony Video**, Brooklyn, 2357 Con. Is. Av. (T-U), 627-8960 & 1-800-221-8927, D-M-QB to Av. U, M-Th 9-6, F 9-2, Sun 10-4, c.c., no ch., no exch. or rfd. Only VTR's, video tapes, and answering machines. Sells: **Small Appliances, Recordings & Tapes.**

Harron Distributors, 352 3rd Av. (25), 685-6285, 6 to 23, M-S 9:30-6:30, ch., c.c., exch., no rfd. Sells: **Large Appliances.**

✷ **Harry's Discounts**, Brooklyn, 8701 18th Av., 236-3507&5150, B to 18th Av., M-F 8-6, S 8-5, ch., c.c. +5%, exch. or rfd. Will special-order. Sells: **Large Appliances, Small Appliances.**

✷ **Hazy Electronics**, 358 7th Av. (29-30), 736-8614 & 244-8056, 1 to 28, M-S 10-6:30, c.c., no ch., 7-day exch. or rfd. Sells: **Large Appliances, Small Appliances, Off-Brand Budget Appliances.**

✷✷ **Home Sales**, 241-3272. Sells: **Large Appliances.**

✷ **Hunter Audio**, 507 5th Av. (42), concession in rear of Record Hunter store, 986-1540, B-D-F to 42, 7 to 5th Av., M-S 9-6, ch., c.c., 5-day exch., no rfd. Sells: **Off-Brand Budget Appliances.**

✷ **International Solgo**, 77 W. 23 (6th), 895-6996 & 675-3555 & 1-516-354-8815, B-F to 23, M-F 9-6, S 9-4, ch., c.c., 5-day exch. or rfd. Sells: **Small Appliances.**

✷ **Joann's Variety Store**, Brooklyn, 2209 Av. X, 648-8517, D-M-QB to Neck Rd., M-S 9-6, ch., c.c., exch. or rfd. But no returns if package is opened. Sells: **Large Appliances, Small Appliances, Health & Beauty Aids, Home-Improvement Items, Housewares.**

✷✷+ **Kaufman Electric**, 365 Grand St. (Essex), 475-8313 & 228-4160, F-J-M to Delancey & Essex, Sun-Th 10-5, F 10-1, ch., no c.c., exch., no rfd. Will special-order. Very cooperative. Bonus discount to BF readers: 2% to 5%. Sells: **Large Appliances, Small Appliances, Dinnerware & Cookware.**

Kingsway Video, Brooklyn, 1690 E. 15th St., 645-4700, D-M-QB to Kings Hwy., M-S 10:30-7, all cash, exch., no rfd. Sells: **Small Appliances.**

✷✷ **Kunst Sales**, 45 Canal St. (Orchard), 966-1909, F to E. Broadway, Sun-Th 9-6:30, F 9-12, c.c., no ch., exch., no rfd. Has stereo showroom. Sells: **Small Appliances.**

Lee-Or Discount, Brooklyn, 1113 Av. J (Coney Is. Av.), 377-1010, D-M-QB to Av. J, Sun-Th 9:30-7, F 9:30-3, all cash, exch., no rfd. Sells: **Irons/Blenders/Clocks, Housewares, Toys, Games & Hobbies.**

Lewi Supply, 15 Essex St. (Canal), 777-6910, F to E. Broadway, Sun-Th 10-6, F 10-1, all cash, exch., no rfd. Sells: **Large Appliances, Small Appliances.**

✷ **Live Wire Electronics**, Queens, 107-21 Continental Av., Forest Hills, 544-6145, E-F-GG-N to 71-Continental Avs., M-F 9:30-6:30, Sun 10:30-4, c.c., no ch., no exch. or rfd. Video, TV, and Commodore computers. Sells: **Small Appliances, Office Equipment, Recordings & Tapes.**

✷✷ **L&J Audio**, 3 Hanover Sq. (Wm.-Pearl), 425-2530, J-M-RR-2-3 to Wall & Broad Sts., M-F 8-6, Sun 10-3, c.c. +5%, no ch., no exch. or rfd. Will special-order. Takes mail-orders. Sells: **Large Appliances, Small Appliances, High Fidelity.**

✷ **Lou-Mark Trdg.**, 13 E. 17 (5th Av.), 242-9440, LL-N-QB-RR-4-5-6 to Union Sq., M-F 9-6, S 9-4, Sun 9-12, all cash, exch., no rfd. Sells: **Irons/Blenders/Clocks, Health & Beauty Aids, Jewelry & Gifts.**

M.A.Z. Trdg., Queens, 81-19 Broadway, Elmhurst, 478-5661, F-GG-N to Elmhurst Av., 7 days 10-9, all cash, 5-day exch., no rfd. Sells: **Large Appliances, Small Appliances.**

1: APPLIANCES

* **M.&B. Appliances**, Queens, 83-15 Broadway, Elmhurst, 699-1462, F-GG-N to Elmhurst Av., W-M 10-8, ch., c.c., exch., no rfd. Sells: **Small Appliances**.

* **MCB Trdg.**, 25 W. 23 (5th-6th Avs.), 741-0848, N-RR to 23rd St., B-F to 23, M-F 8-6:30, ch., c.c., exch., no rfd. Sells: **Off-Brand Budget Appliances, Cameras & Optical Eqt.**

* **Mecca**, 1167 Broadway (27), 679-9336, N-RR to 28th St., M-F 10-5, all cash, no exch. or rfd. Sells: **Off-Brand Budget Appliances, Recordings & Tapes**.

+ **Mills Sales, 889 Broadway at 19th St., 477-1000, LL-N-QB-RR-4-5-6 to Union Sq., N-RR to 23rd St., M-F 9-5, S 9-2, all cash, no exch. or rfd. No retail sales (wholesale only) Labor Day through Xmas. A specialty here is steel ball-point pens super-cheap by the dozen. Bonus discount to BF readers: 5%. Sells: **Off-Brand Budget Appliances, Dinnerware & Cookware, Home-Improvement Items, Jewelry & Gifts, Personal Accessories, Stationery & Art Supplies, Toys, Games & Hobbies**.

M.S. Distribution, 76 Madison Av. at 28th, 685-5085, 6 to 28, M-F 12-7, S 1-6, ch., no c.c., exch., no rfd. Sells: **Small Appliances**.

* **National Video Discount**, Queens, 107-08 70th Rd. at Austin St., Forest Hills, 268-0062 & 1-800-645-5414, E-F-GG-N to 71-Continental Avs., M-W 10-8, Th 10-9, S 10-6, Sun 12-5, ch., c.c. +5%, no exch. or rfd. Specializes in TV and video. Sells: **Small Appliances**.

* **Newport of Japan**, 1201 Broadway (28-9), 686-1320, N-RR to 28th St., M-F 9-6, S 10-2, all cash, no exch. or rfd. Sells: **Off-Brand Budget Appliances, Recordings & Tapes**.

Norman's House of Deals, 1164 Broadway (27-8), 683-4772, N-RR to 28th St., M-F 8-5, SSun 8-1, all cash, no exch. or rfd. Sells: **Off-Brand Budget Appliances**.

** **Olympic Electronics**, 123 W. 30 (6th-7th Avs.), 564-0567, B-D-F-N-QB-RR to 34, 1 to 28, M-S 9-6, c.c., no ch., exch. or rfd. Sells: **Off-Brand Budget Appliances**.

** **Price Watchers**, 337-6633 & 1-516-239-3800. Sells: **Large Appliances**.

* **Queens Discount Appliances**, Queens, 40-16 82nd St. (Roosevelt), Jackson Hts., 639-5070 & 429-0620, 7 to 82nd St., 7 days 11-7, all cash, 3-day exch. or rfd. Sells: **Large Appliances, Small Appliances**.

** **R&F Electronics**, 36 W. 29 (B'wy), 679-5962, N-RR to 28th St., M-Th 9-6, SunF 9-4:30, all cash, no exch. or rfd. Sells: **Off-Brand Budget Appliances, Dinnerware & Cookware, Home-Improvement Items, Jewelry & Gifts**.

R.K. Trdg., Queens, 60-15 Roosevelt Av., Woodside, 639-2881 & 779-5144, 7 to 61st St., M-S 10-7, c.c., no ch., exch. or rfd. Sells: **Large Appliances, Small Appliances, Off-Brand Budget Appliances**.

** **Romano Trdg.**, 628 W. 45th St. on 12th Av., 581-4248, A-AA-CC-E to 42, plus a long walk, M-F 8-5:30, S 8-5, all cash, exch. or rfd. Very cooperative. A little bit of everything, designer-name and major brand items. Sells: **Irons/Blenders/Clocks, Clothing—Men's, Jewelry & Gifts, Office Equipment, Personal Accessories, Stationery & Art Supplies, Toys, Games & Hobbies**.

Rose Distributors, 247 W. 46 (7th-8th), 246-2359, A-AA-CC-E to 50, 1 to 50, M-S 9-7, all cash, exch., no rfd. Very busy. Good prices, but they bargain too. Sells: **Small Appliances**.

* **Sam & Raj Appliances**, Queens, 37-12 74th St., Jackson Hts., 446-1004, E-F-GG-N-7 to 74th-B'way & Roosevelt-Jack.Hts., W-M 10:30-6, all cash, exch. or rfd. No exch. or rfd. if unit is in working condition. Sells: **Small Appliances, Dinnerware & Cookware**.

Savemart Clearance, Bronx, 317 E. 149, 292-6700, no subway stop nearby, M-S 10-6, ch., c.c., no exch. or rfd. Mostly Zenith TV and Fisher audio. Sells: **Large Appliances**.

* **Saverite Photo Elec.**, 46 Canal St. (Orchard), 966-6655, F to E. Broadway, Sun-Th 10-6, F 10-2, ch., no c.c., 10-day exch., no rfd. Sells: **Large Appliances, Small Appliances, Cameras & Optical Eqt.**

Sona Appliances, Queens, 37-42 74th St., Jackson Hts., 446-8448, E-F-GG-N-7 to 74th-B'wy & Roosevelt-Jack.Hts., W-M 10-7, c.c., no ch., 1-day exch. or rfd. Sells: **Large Appliances, Small Appliances**.

** **Sona Electrical**, 135 Division St. at Canal, 233-1010, F to E. Broadway, W-M 11-6, all cash, 7-day exch. or rfd. Will special-order. Takes mail-orders. Sells: **Large Appliances, Small Appliances**.

* **STL Electronics**, 849-7627&7571. For phone-quote, leave model num-

1: APPLIANCES

ber and your phone on their answering machine. Sells: **Large Appliances, High Fidelity.**

* **Stereo King**, 550 8th Av. (37-8), 354-1492, A-AA-CC-E to 34, A-AA-CC-E to 42, c.c., no ch., exch., no rfd. Sometimes it pays to bargain here; on other items, their first price is sensational. Sells: **Small Appliances, Off-Brand Budget Appliances.**

Sunbright, 1153 Broadway (25-6), 889-1995, N-RR to 28th St., Sun-F 10-6, all cash, exch., no rfd. Sells: **Off-Brand Budget Appliances.**

* **Susan Trdg.**, 300 Canal St. (B'wy), 431-8529, J-M-N-QB-RR-6 to Canal, 7 days 10-6, ch., c.c., exch., no rfd. Sells: **Off-Brand Budget Appliances, Furnishings, Home-Improvement Items, Personal Accessories.**

** **S&W Electronics**, 50 Canal S. (Orchard), 966-2950, F to E. Broadway, irregular hours, usually Sun-Th 10-6, ch., no c.c., 7-day exch. or rfd. Sells: **Small Appliances, Cameras & Optical Eqt.**

** **The City Dump**, 334 Canal St. (Greene), 431-1670, A-AA-CC-E-1 to Canal, J-M-N-QB-RR-6 to Canal, 7 days 10-6, all cash, exch., no rfd. Outstanding values only on the items for which the store is here recommended. Otherwise uneven. Sells: **Off-Brand Budget Appliances, Jewelry & Gifts, Sporting Goods.**

* **Top Value Appliance**, Brooklyn, 1867 86th St., 236-5355, B to 20th Av., MTTh 9:30-9, WFS 9:30-6, all cash, exch., no rfd. Sells: **Large Appliances, Irons/Blenders/Clocks.**

** **Townie Merchandise**, 212 W. 14 (7th Av), 929-8060 & 675-6662, 1-2-3 to 14, A-AA-CC-E-LL to 14 St. & 8 Av., M-S 10-6, all cash, exch., no rfd. Will special-order. Popular among seamen and Latin American tourists. Sells: **Large Appliances, Small Appliances, Clothing—Men's, Clothing—Women's, Health & Beauty Aids.**

** **Triest Export**, 560 12th Av. (44), 246-1548., A-AA-CC-E to 42, plus a long walk, Sun-F 7-6, all cash, no exch. or rfd. Very busy. Expect long wait on line. Popular with seamen and foreign tourists. Sells: **Small Appliances, Cameras & Optical Eqt., Clothing—Men's, Personal Accessories, Toys, Games & Hobbies.**

* **U.S.A. Electronics**, 125 W. 45 (6th-7th), 221-1354, B-D-F to 47, M-S 10-6, c.c., no ch., 14-day exch., no rfd. Sells: **Small Appliances.**

Vendome Trdg., 69 W. 23 (6th Av.), 691-7500, B-F to 23, M-F 9-5:45, S 10-3, ch., c.c., 7-day exch. or rfd. Sells: **Small Appliances.**

*** **Vercesi Hardware**, 152 E. 23 (Lex.-3rd), 475-1883, 6 to 23, M-F 8-7:30, S 9-5:30, ch., no c.c., exch., no rfd. Only paint-brand stocked is Red Devil. Sells: **Irons/Blenders/Clocks, Home-Improvement Items.**

Warren St. Merchandise, 32 Warren St. (Church), 227-8330, A-CC-1-2-3 to Chambers, N-RR to City Hall, M-S 9-6, ch., no c.c., exch. or rfd. Only ball-point pens, small off-brand walkman-type radios etc., car-radios, and brand-name blank cassettes. Street-stand, extends indoors. Sells: **Off-Brand Budget Appliances, Recordings & Tapes, Stationery & Art Supplies.**

** **World Wide Discount**, 37 Canal St. at Ludlow, 477-5441, F to E. Broadway, Sun-Th 9:30-6, F 9:30-1, ch., no c.c., no exch. or rfd. Will special-order. Sells: **Large Appliances, Small Appliances.**

Yair Import, 17 E. 45 (5th-6th), 687-5540, 7 to 5th Av., B-D-F to 47, 4-5-6-7 to Grand Central, M-F 9-7, S 10-4, all cash, exch., no rfd. Sells: **Small Appliances.**

2:
AUTOS & SUPPLIES
Discounts vary.

Which are the best cars? Which are the best cars for the money? The more that you read *Consumer Reports*, the studies by the Federal Government, and actuarial data on personal injury and collision claims compiled nationwide by the Insurance Institute for Highway Safety—these three being the only sources of objective information available on the subject of how safe, economical, and good, the various makes of cars really are—the more you realize that your selection of an automobile is going to have to be highly subjective in the final analysis. Sometimes, the contradictory findings of these three authorities are nothing else than appalling. For example, the Dodge Omni/Plymouth Horizon (the identical car by different names) passed the U.S. Department of Transportation's crash-tests with flying colors. Yet the 2-door Dodge Omni has one of the worst insurance injury claims records of any automobile. There's nothing in any of the Federal Government's tests which would explain this discrepancy.

Furthermore, if you have the U.S. Dept. of Transportation's famous former freebie, *The Car Book*, you'll note under "Insurance and Accident Costs" on page 41, that the Volkswagen Rabbit 2-door has an extraordinarily low "Average Loss Payment Per Insured Vehicle Year"—in fact, one of the lowest of any car, large or small. Yet you'll also note in the very next column, that the insurance industry tacks on a surcharge to policies covering this same car. They don't offer a discount for insuring it, as you might expect; instead they do the reverse. Why? Could it be because the Rabbit failed two of the Government's crash-tests (which it did—see page 14 of *The Car Book*)? No—the insurance industry gives discounts or assesses surcharges not on the basis of government crash-tests, but rather because of actuarial experience. How can one account for such a boldfaced discrepancy?

Or consider, for example, the most objective and meaningful automobiles-data published by Consumers' Union in *Consumer Reports*: the Frequency-of-Repair Records for past model-years. According to these figures, the Omni and Horizon have scored only fair. And on the line that shows average cost of repairs, they've scored only slightly better than average. Yet this isn't what *The Car Book* indicates. According to that, the Omni and Horizon are among the most outstandingly inexpensive of all cars from the standpoint of maintenance-costs. The most consistently and impressively inexpensive-to-maintain cars of all are the Toyota Celica, Corolla, and Corona, according to C.U.'s records, which year-after-year have shown both low frequency-of-repair and low average cost-of-repair, for every operating system in each of these models. But *The Car Book* tells quite a different story. According to the

2: AUTOS & SUPPLIES

equally detailed figures presented there, the Celica, Corolla, and Corona, have had only average annual maintenance-costs.

Who can make sense out of such contradictions? They're typical of what the careful automobile-buyer is likely to run into regardless what car he's considering to buy.

I've worn myself out trying to make sense of them. So I'll instead summarize the little that I've found that can be said without contradiction on the subjects of maintenance-costs and safety for various makes and models of automobiles:

• Two-door models are consistently more dangerous to the safety of the driver and passengers than are four-door models of the same car. This applies regardless what the size of the automobile is. For some makes, you double your safety just by buying a four-door rather than a two-door model.

• Your costs of repairing a car that's been in a collision are going to be far lower if you've got a four-door rather than the equivalent two-door model.

• The likelihood of theft—and this has to be considered equivalent to a major maintenance-expense, especially in NYC—is twice as high for the two-door car than for the same four-door model. Small non-sport autos also are far less preferred by the thieves, who go after the jazzier and larger cars.

• The heavier an automobile is, the likelier it is to be relatively safe (but the more fuel it'll consume). In fact, small cars are twice as fatal as large ones.

• Japanese cars (with the possible exception of Toyota) tend to be slightly less safe than American automobiles of the same size and weight.

That's about it. The most important thing is to get a four-door car. How about that now?

Why didn't *Consumer Reports* tell us this? Because they've never broken their data down that way. Neither has the Federal Government. Only the Insurance Institute for Highway Safety has. And this has been their strongest and most consistent finding, for years, and even decades. The press, to my knowledge, has never picked up on it, though the news-media have well publcized I.I.H.S.'s other findings, such as the slightly worse safety-records of Japanese cars as compared to American makes of comparable size.

The mass of generally contradictory data about autos doesn't permit any specific recommendations about "all-around good cars" (except the legendary Dodge Dart, which certainly must have been the all-time high scorer in practically every field and from every objective rating-source during its time) or even about selecting this or that American carmaker's products over its competition's, either for safety or for maintenance or for both. One can't say, for example, that a Mercedes is generally superior to a Honda or to a Toyota or to a Plymouth or to a Chevy, or even to a Cadillac (which could just as well be the worst as the best of these, depending on the viewpoint and on the source of the data). So why pay for the more expensve car? Even if your main concern is safety, there are some four-door intermediates that cost far less than a Mercedes or even than a Cadillac. And some rather luxurious automobiles sell for substantially less than either. So why pay more?

Going The Second-Hand Route

Here's what I'd do if I were going to buy an automobile: I'd first visit the lots displaying reconditioned used rental and leased cars. Several such places are listed in the recommendations below. One advantage of doing this is that such dealers have national reputations to uphold, not merely local. Another is that the warranties these places offer are better than what you'll usually find—or than you'll ever be able to wrangle through *Buy Lines* or otherwise with a private person trying to dump his latest lemon. In fact, some of these dealers—as individually indicated—offer 24,000-mile, 2-year warranties, that cover more than just the power-train. In any case, each offers a strong enough warranty so that I trust them when they say—as I've heard them all say—that the associated car-rental and leasing companies don't retail the lemons out of their fleets, but rather wholesale them at auction (mostly to other used-car dealers). Furthermore, most of these places keep on file, and will show you, the repair-records of each car on their lots. Such information simply isn't available at other used-car dealers, because they're not selling what they themselves bought new and have owned since. Finally, most of these cars have had fairly low mileage. Some were even bought late in a model-year, and were thus soon replaced. You can, in fact, find some current model-year cars on these lots. I'd rather buy them here, used, than at a regular dealer, new. The warranty is as good or better; the price is lower; the initial bugs have been shaken out of the car so that the buyer won't have to deal with them; and the chance of getting a lemon is far less.

I've so far mentioned nothing about price. Obviously, I've found these dealers to be selling below-market; otherwise, I wouldn't recommend them. However, the lots that sell used *lease*-cars charge more than the ones specializing in second-hand *rental* autos, since the former category of cars normally have had lower mileage. But both are equally good value.

If you're hankering for a brand-new car, that, too, will be found in the listings below, via auto-brokers.

Tire-Shopping

It's well-known that a safe car with unsafe tires is not a safe car. Therefore, your periodic purchase of tires is important not only because hundreds of dollars will be involved, but also because your physical well-being may be affected. (Also your gas-mileage, because radial tires mean more m.p.g.) In 1973, *Consumer Reports* gave their top rating to the Firestone Steel-Belted Radial 500's. In light of the subsequent scandalous safety problems with that tire—the many accidents and deaths—and the subsequent headline-making recall of it, one wonders what one ought to think of the next top-rated tire in that magazine. In fact, this Consumers'

2: AUTOS & SUPPLIES

Union top-rated tire was so good it came near to bankrupting Firestone, and produced nearly $2 billion in lawsuits against the company.

However, there is one serious source of information available to the public on the question of tire-quality. The U.S. Department of Transportation, National Highway Traffic Safety Administration, 400 7th St. N.W., Washington, D.C. 20590, publishes free of charge something called *Tire Grading System Information*, which includes standardized test-ratings of all makes and models of tires. This reference-source is distributed only as a sheaf of barely-legible Xeroxes, about 40 sheets held together with a single staple. But if you're going to buy a new set of tires, there's nothing else that can be nearly as helpful. I've heard that the Reagan Administration is planning to cease this publication. Therefore, highlights from it will be summarized below.

Keep in mind that these tests were not carried out by the Government, but rather by the manufacturers themselves, who supposedly adhered to strict test-requirements dictated by the Government. The system tests and grades tires on three scales:

Treadwear. This indicates how much mileage you can expect. A "90"-rated tire is supposed to last half as many miles as a "180." The Montgomery Ward Bias Ply Runabout—shown in the Government publication to be made by Kelly Springfield—scored the lowest: 40. The Goodyear Eagle Radial Ply 390 topped the list at 240; supposedly, this tire can be expected to last as long as 6 installations and replacements of the Ward Runabout.

Traction. This tells you the tire's ability to stop on wet surfaces. The scale is simply A, B, and C, with A being best, C being worst.

Temperature-Resistance. Also graded A, B, and C. The lowest ("C") rating here signals a hot-running tire susceptible to blowouts or tread-separations on long trips at highway-speeds.

Basically, the first scale rates a tire's longevity; the other two show its safety under the two conditions of slippery surfaces and extended highway-driving.

There's been much criticism of the accuracy of the treadwear-ratings. For example, Uniroyal scores some of its tires 220; Michelin rates its at only 140; yet Michelin's are generally conceded, by those knowledgeable on the subject, to last about 30% longer than the best Uniroyals. Some manufacturers were far more conservative than others in assigning ratings to their tires. It appears that this was less of a problem with the two safety-tests (traction and temperature-resistance) than with the longevity-test (treadwear). Even the very conservative Michelin safety-rated its tires A, A for its TRX, XAS, and XVS models; and A, B for its XAWW, XWW, XZX, and ZX lines. If there was less fudging on the safety-tests than on the ones for longevity, the reason is probably that liability and insurance factors provide an incentive for manufacturers to keep to the straight-and-narrow when making safety-related claims.

The top-scoring tires on this standardized system were generally the radial ply's, next the bias-belted ply's, and last the bias ply's. Of course the last group is also usually the cheapest. Therefore, I'll summarily list the highest-rated tires in each of the three classes. (That means radial ply's scoring 180, B, B, or better; bias-belted ply's scoring 150, B, B, or better; and bias ply's rated 100, B, B, or better.):

RADIAL PLY: Alliance Steel-Belted Radial 118 14, 118 15, 120 13, 120 14, 129 14, & 129 15. **Bridgestone** Steel-Belted 108V, 111V, 112V, 113V, 116V, 123V, 170V2, 207V, 212V, 604V, 702P, & 703V. **Centennial** Radial 60, Radial 70, & Tradition 70 Radial. **Co-op** Mark 70 Steel-Belted Radial. **Continental** 165, 195, & 205. **Dunlop** Elite Radial, & GT Qualifier Radial. **Fulda** Diadem Stahl SR Series, & Rasant Steel HR Series. **Goodrich** Lifesaver Radial (but not "all-season"), & Pursuit Radial. **Goodyear** Blue Streak Rayon, Customguard GT 14 & 15, Eagle 390, & Imported Grand Prix Sr. E & S. **Ohtsu. Phoenix. Remington** Society 70 Radial All-Season, & RT 120 Radial. **Riken. Toyo** Steel-Belted 712, 714, & 784. **Uniroyal** Fastrak Fiberglass Belted Radial.

BIAS-BELTED PLY: Centennial Belted 60, & 70. **Dunlop GT Qualifier Belted** 60, & 70. **Remington XT-120 Belted** 60, & 70.

BIAS PLY: Armstrong Maxi-Trac Super 60, & Tru-Trac 60. **Co-op** SPD Poly. **Dunlop** Gold Seal RS Patrol. **Formula** I Super Stock 50 M50-15. **Global. M&M. Pos-A-Traction.**

Of all the above-listed tires, the safest (double-A) were: Dunlop Elite RS Patrol Radial 70 Series (which also scored a super-high 210 for treadwear), Fulda Rasant Steel HR Series, Phoenix 3011, Riken Black Belt, Riken Professor Ace 70 Series Radial (which, in addition, scored an astoundingly high 230 for treadwear), and Toyo Steel-Belted 714. All are radial-ply type. However, one tire indicated to be a bias ply (not even bias-belted ply) and to have scored an amazingly high (for this category) 140 treadwear-rating, also scored double-A safe: Formula I Super Stock 50 M50-15.

Of all the tires I showed listed under Radial Ply, the following had the highest treadwear-ratings (210 or above): Centennial Radial 70, Centennial Tradition 70 Radial All-Season, Co-op Mark 70 Steel-Belted Radial, Dunlop Elite RS Patrol Radial 70 Series (which scored an all-around superb 210, A, A), Dunlop Elite 70 Radial All-Season, Dunlop GT Qualifier Radial 70 Series, Goodrich Lifesaver Radial, Goodrich Pursuit Radial, Remington Society 70 Radial All-Season, Remington RT120 Radial 70 Series, and Riken Professor Ace 70 Series Radial (whose all-around score was the highest of all, at 230, A, A).

Incidentally, Remington and Centennial tires are made by Dunlop. The various gas-station and chain-store brands all scored medium-to-poor, and were made by generally low-rated manufacturers.

Among those people with whom I've spoken whom I consider to be most expert on the subject of tires, **Michelin**—which as I'd mentioned, scores itself only medium on the longevity-test, but excellent on the two safety-tests—is almost universally referred to as the best tire-manufacturer, with Dunlop and Bridgestone coming in not far behind. One of these tire-experts also happens to be vice president of a dealer I recommend for tires, Benni Jakubovic, of Northeastern Tire, in Brooklyn, a place whose specialty is that they will special-order any make they don't carry. They're a good place to check out if you're having trouble finding a particular brand, and I've found that Mr. Jakubovic gives an honest and informed opinion on the merits and demerits even of brands he doesn't carry in regular stock.

Auto Insurance

Here, too, is a major recurring expense for car-owners. So I'm listing below the least costly auto-insurers that provide decent service.

First, however, two important things should be noted: Assigned-risk coverage is always far more expensive than any that's written with an individual company, and so should be avoided; and most of the insurers who are recommended in auto-insurance shopping-guides for offering low rates, are not available—they do not write such policies. I list only companies which I have verified, as of the time of this writing, actually to be writing personal auto insurance.

United Community Insurance Co. Available only through membership in groups. One way is by joining Workmen's Circle (phone 889-6800). Their dues are cheap, and are returned manyfold merely by the auto-insurance savings alone; but WC has other benefits as well: life insurance, health insurance, credit union, etc. United Community has by far the lowest available auto-rates of anyone.

*American Consumer Insurance Co.** Available only to preferred drivers. Phone 895-0036 or 1-516-364-2700.

GEICO. 423-9000.

Aetna Casualty. Jacob Marrus Agency, 685-4676; Campbell Agency, 227-3320.

RECOMMENDED PRODUCTS:
See above.

RECOMMENDED STORES:

autos—used

Budget Used Rental Cars (Queens, 478-5056); **National Car Rental Used Cars** (476-5941); **Avis Used Rental Cars** (Queens, 381-1740); **Hertz Used Cars** (595-4608).

autos—new

Associated Bank Card Holders; Fraternal organizations; Purchase Power (outside NYC, 1-800-526-4380).

autos—rent/lease: CH. 38

auto parts

Expect 30-50% discounts.
(examples: batteries, mufflers, shock absorbers, spark plugs)

G.T. & Sons Auto Parts (Brooklyn, 377-6306); **Kalat & Jenmar Auto Parts** (925-8151); **Saw Mill Auto Wreckers** (298-5600); **Worth Auto Parts** (777-5920); *+**Ganin Tire** (Brooklyn, 253-9800); *Adelman Automotive (Brooklyn, 377-9545); *Mil Auto Parts (Queens, 779-6020); **All-Brands Auto Parts** (925-9455); **Essex Auto Parts** (673-8170); **Jobber Joe Auto Parts** (Queens, 458-0770).

auto supplies

Expect 15-40% discounts.

(examples: polishes, waxes)

*+**Ganin Tire** (Brooklyn, 253-9800); ***Adelman Automotive** (Brooklyn, 377-9545).

tires

Expect 40-60% discounts.

***+**Liben-Hansel Tire** (Bronx, 299-1000); ****Atlantic Tire Shop** (Brooklyn, 827-7373); ****Major Tires** (Brooklyn, 375-0080); ****Saw Mill Auto Wreckers** (298-5600); ***Adelman Automotive** (Brooklyn, 377-9545); ***Northeastern Tire Service** (Brooklyn, 633-7301); +**Midway Tire** (Brooklyn, 339-6200); **Automotive City** (Brooklyn, 469-9012).

insurance: SEE TEXT ABOVE

STORES-DIRECTORY

Phone a store before you go out of your way to visit it. Especially do this during July and August, when most establishments reduce or eliminate weekend-hours.

In the listings below, "*" means especially recommended, "+" means that the store offers a bonus discount to BF readers, "ch." and "c.c." mean respectively checks and credit cards, and "exch." and "rfd." mean respectively exchange and refund. Nearest subway-stops are shown. For example, "B-D-F to 47" means to take the B, D, or F train to 47th Street. Store-hours are also indicated, with days of the week abbreviated, like "M-S 8-6."

*   **Adelman Automotive**, Brooklyn, 1539 Coney Is. Av. (L), 377-9545 (tires), 258-1605 (parts), D-M-QB to Av. M, M-S 8-6, ch., c.c. Manufacturer's warranty. This place is often very busy. Sells: **Auto Parts, Auto Supplies, Tires.**

   All-Brands Auto Parts, 15 Laight St. at Canal, 925-9455&69, A-AA-CC-E-1 to Canal, M-F 9-6, S 10-5, all cash, exch. or rfd. 15% charge on returns. Sells: **Auto Parts.**

   Associated Bank Card Holders, 2 Executive Campus, room 322, Cherry Hill NJ 08002. $15/yr. membership for group-buying discounts on cars and auto-insurance. Write for details. Sells: **Autos—New.**

**   **Atlantic Tire Shop**, Brooklyn, 2765 Atlantic Av. at Miller Av., 827-7373, J to Van Siclen, M-F 7-6, S 7-3, ch., c.c. Manufacturer's warranty. This place is usually extremely busy. Sells: **Tires.**

   Automotive City, Brooklyn, 555 Coney Is. Av. (Beverly Rd.), 469-9012, D-M-QB to Beverly, M-W 8:30-6:30, Th 8:30-8, F 8:30-3, c.c., no ch. Manufacturer's warranty. Sells: **Tires.**

   Avis Used Rental Cars, Queens, 48-05 Grand Av., Maspeth, 381-1740, no subway stop nearby, M-F 9-8, S 9-6, all cash. Standard 12/12,000 warranty. Repair-record shown upon request. Sells: **Autos—Used.**

**   **Budget Used Rental Cars**, Queens, 91-01 Northern Blvd., Jackson Hts., 478-5056, 7 to 90th St., hours by appointment, all cash. Strong warranty 12 months or 12,000 miles Sells: **Autos—Used.**

*   **Consumers Distributing**, Queens, 107-18 70th Rd., Forest Hills, 268-2091, E-F-GG-N to 71-Continental Avs.; Queens, 39-20 Bell Blvd., Bayside, 225-0253, no subway stop nearby; Queens, 156-16 Northern Blvd., Flushing, 961-5024, no subway stop nearby; Queens, 97-10 Queens Blvd., Rego Park, 896-7250, F-GG-N to 63rd Dr.; Brooklyn, Av. U at Mill Av. (nr. Kings Plaza), 241-7633, D-M-QB to Av. M; Queens, 54-30 Myrtle Av., Ridgewood, 386-2809, LL-M to Myrtle & Wyckoff. All stores: M-F 10-9 (Ridgewood 10-6), S 10-6, Sun 12-5, ch., c.c. during banking hours,

2: AUTOS & SUPPLIES

30-day exch. or rfd. Large selection. A catalog-showroom chain. Sells: **Bikes, Dinnerware & Cookware, Home-Improvement Items, Housewares, Jewelry & Gifts, Sporting Goods.**

    Essex Auto Parts, 5 Av. A at Houston, 673-8170&8898, F to 2nd Av., M-S 8:30-6, Sun 8:30-1, c.c. over $20, no ch., no exch. or rfd. Sells: **Auto Parts.**

    Fraternal organizations, like Workmen's Circle (listed in text above, under 'Auto Insurance'). (Also see list under 'Insurance' in Ch. 32.) Membership brings access to group-buying discounts on cars. Sells: **Autos—New.**

*+ **Ganin Tire**, Brooklyn, 2360 Flatbush Av. (T), 253-9800, no subway stop nearby; Brooklyn, 6502 Bay Pkwy., 236-8400, N to Bay Pkwy. Both stores: M-F 8-7, S 8-6, ch., c.c. Manufacturer's warranty. No phone-quotes. Another store in Lawrence, L.I. Bonus discount to BF readers: 5%. Sells: **Auto Parts, Auto Supplies.**

** **G.T. & Sons Auto Parts**, Brooklyn, 1219 McDonald Av. (J), 377-6306, F to Av. I, M-F 8-5:30, S 8-2, all cash, exch., no rfd. Sells: **Auto Parts.**

    Hertz Used Cars, 210 W. 77 at Amsterdam (used rental cars at this location), 595-4608, 1 to 79; Queens, 31-08 Northern Blvd., L.I.C. (for used leased cars), 786-2133, F-GG-N to 36th St. Both stores: M-F 9-6, S 10-4, ch., no c.c. Average 12/12,000 warranty. Strong warranty +$95. Repair-record shown upon request. Sells: **Autos—Used.**

    Jobber Joe Auto Parts, Queens, 69-05 Northern Blvd., Jackson Hts., 458-0770, F-GG-N to 65th St., M-F 8-5:30, S 8-1, all cash, no exch. or rfd. Sells: **Auto Parts.**

** **Kalat & Jenmar Auto Parts**, 141 Chrystie St. (Kenmare), 925-8151, J-M to Bowery, M-F 9-5, all cash, exch., no rfd. Sells: **Auto Parts.**

+ **Liben-Hansel Tire, Bronx, 1732 Webster Av. (174th St. off Cross-Bronx Expwy.) (main store), 299-1000, CC-D to 174, M-F 8:30-5:30, S 8:30-1:30; Queens, 44-10 Little Neck Pkwy. at Northern Blvd. nr. NYC line, 631-5400, no subway stop nearby, M-F 8-5, S 8-1. Both stores: ch., c.c. Manufacturer's warranty. No phone-quotes. Installations at main store only. Bonus discount to BF readers: 10% to 20%. Sells: **Tires.**

** **Major Tires**, Brooklyn, 2489 MacDonald Av. (W-X), 375-0080, F to Av. X, M-F 8-6, S 8-4, c.c., no ch. Manufacturer's warranty. Sells: **Tires.**

+ **Midway Tire**, Brooklyn, 1755 Coney Is. Av. (N-O), 339-6200&3700, D-M-QB to Av. M, M-F 8-6, S 8-5, ch., c.c. Manufacturer's warranty. No phone-quotes. Bonus discount to BF readers: 5% to 10%. Sells: **Tires.**

* **Mil Auto Parts**, Queens, 37-65 88th St., Jackson Hts., 779-6020, 7 to 90th St., M-F 8:30-6, S 8:30-5, c.c. $10+, no ch., no exch. or rfd. Sells: **Auto Parts.**

** **National Car Rental Used Cars**, 25 W. Old Country Rd., Hicksville, NY 11801, 476-5941 & 1-516-935-0500, M-F 9-9, S 9-6, ch., no c.c. All cars come with strong 2-yr. warranty. Repair-record shown upon request. Sells: **Autos—Used.**

* **Northeastern Tire Service**, Brooklyn, 451 Dahill Rd. (39th St., 16th Av., Cortelyou), 633-7301, F to Ditmas, M-Th 7:30-6, Sun 7:30-5, F 7:30-4, ch., c.c. Manufacturer's warranty. Sells: **Tires.**

    Purchase Power, 623 Warburton Av., Hastings-on-Hudson, NY, 1-800-526-4380, $15/yr. membership gives you group-buying car-discounts at cooperating local dealers. Sells: **Autos—New.**

** **Saw Mill Auto Wreckers**, 12 Worth St., Yonkers, near the NYC line, 298-5600 & 1-914-968-5300, M-F 8-5:30, S 8-1, c.c., no ch., exch., no rfd. Everything is from wrecked cars; none is new 'from the box.' Sells: **Auto Parts, Tires.**

** **Worth Auto Parts**, 27 Cooper Sq. at 5th St. & Bowery, 777-5920, 6 to Astor, B-D-F-6 to B'wy-Laf. & Bleecker; 232 W. Broadway (N. Moore), 226-5016, 1 to Franklin. Both stores: M-F 8:30-6, S 8:30-5, ch., c.c. $15 minimum, exch. or rfd. Sells: **Auto Parts.**

3:
BIKES
Expect 5-30% discounts.

All the recommended stores will quote prices by phone.

This chapter was one of the most frustrating for me to research, simply because there are no steep discounts on bicycles anywhere. I've never been able to understand why this is so. The bike-shops I'm recommending have around a 5-10% competitive edge on bikes, and a 15-30% advantage on parts and accessories. That's all. Your real savings will come in the selection of the proper brand.

American-made bikes constitute 80% of the domestic market, but offer vastly inferior value compared with the European and Japanese imports. Except for Taiwan, every country that makes bicycles produces superior ones to those manufactured here. That's just an unfortunate fact, acknowledged by virtually all serious cyclists, and even by *Consumer Reports*. The only American brand that presents a glimmer of quality-competition for the European and Japanese products is Schwinn, but in terms of value, there's no contest at all. Still, Americans, by the overwhelming ratio of 80% to 20%, evidently prefer to slip clunkers between their legs. Who will ever be able to explain why?

10-speeds have 70% of the U.S. market; 3-speeds almost all the rest. Each style has its own advantages. Women often find the 3-speed models more comfortable, because these bikes are designed with a more congenial "feel" and ride: The gear-shifting is easier; the touring-style handlebars are sometimes more convenient; and the wider seats are more comfortable if the cyclist rides sitting up rather than crouched over in racing-position. Nonetheless, most cyclists find that once they've ridden a 10-speed, they're hooked. The peddling is much easier, and once one has become accustomed to riding in the crouched-over position, one usually doesn't want to go back to the more-relaxed and so less safe kiddie-bike riding-style.

When shopping for a bike, the key things to look for are that the frame be fully lugged (any bike-shop will point out to you what this means); and that the weight, exclusive of accessories, be between 27-32 pounds. (Heavier is unnecessary from the standpoint of both price and ruggedness, and tends to indicate that the frame is crudely made. Lighter bikes cost a heavy premium, and are usually very finicky—you'll pray that you won't ride over a nail or pothole.) Almost invariably, the brakes should be center-pull. But in any case, try out the brakes on the stationary bike. Do both right and left brake-pads approach the wheel-rims at the same rate and simultaneously? They should. Also, when you squeeze the brake-levers, and when the rubber pads then contact the wheel-rims, do the brake-levers now offer firm or rather mushy resistance to further squeezing? It should feel as if you're squeezing a rock. Your life may eventually depend on that "rock."

Decide what features you want, and then look for the cheapest, lightest, lugged-frame European or Japanese bike that fulfills these requirements and that has brakes which pass the tests I just described. That's it in a nutshell.

I've looked through all the standard consumer-publications that rate the competing brands of bikes; and the lack of consensus among these authorities is quite striking. However, each brand listed below has found ardent supporters in at least one of these publications, and no ardent detractors in any of them; and all the makes seem to be generally well-regarded by the cyclists I've spoken with. In addition, there are two brands which seem to be highly regarded by cyclists, but where the opinion is far from unanimous among the rating-magazines: Raleigh and Atala. In any case, since there is so little agreement among the "experts," you'll probably do best to make the judgment on your own, if you just look for the things I described above. But for what it's worth, here's that list of generally well-rated brands, which may serve—if nothing else—as a starting-point for your search.

RECOMMENDED PRODUCTS:

Bikes: Centurion, Kobe, Fuji, Mercier, Gitane, Peugeot, Joannou, Panasonic, Nishiki, Kabuki, Windsor, Bertin, Vista Espada.

RECOMMENDED STORES:

bicycles & supplies

*JBJ Discount Pets (982-5310); **Bikes By George** (533-0203); **Brooklyn Bicycle** (Brooklyn, 941-9095); **Bruno-Sam's Bikes** (Brooklyn, 858-2957); **Frank's Bike Shop** (533-6332); **Roberts Bicycle** (Queens, 353-5432); **Stuyvesant Bicycle** (254-5200).

kids' bikes

Jack's Bargain Stores (924-5322); **Toys 'R' Us (Brooklyn, 258-2061); *Consumers Distributing (Queens, 268-2091); **Valco Discount (Queens, 274-1200).

motorscooters

*Camrod Cycle (582-7444); *Hillside Cycle (Queens, 739-2750); *King Motorcycle (Brooklyn, 773-2279).

STORES-DIRECTORY

Phone a store before you go out of your way to visit it. Especially do this during July and August, when most establishments reduce or eliminate weekend-hours.

In the listings below, "*" means especially recommended, "+" means that the store offers a bonus discount to BF readers, "ch." and "c.c." mean respectively checks and credit cards, and "exch." and "rfd." mean respectively exchange and refund. Nearest subway-stops are shown. For example, "B-D-F to 47" means to take the B, D, or F train to 47th Street. Store-hours are also indicated, with days of the week abbreviated, like "M-S 8-6."

Bikes By George, 351 E. 12 (1st Av.), 533-0203, LL to 1st Av., M-S 9-6, all cash, exch., no rfd. Sells: **Bicycles & Supplies**.

3: BIKES

Brooklyn Bicycle, Brooklyn, 715 Coney Is. Av. (C), 941-9095, D-M-QB to Cortelyou, M-S 10-6, c.c., no ch., exch., no rfd. Sells: **Bicycles & Supplies.**

Bruno-Sam's Bikes, Brooklyn, 91 Court St. (Schermerhorn), 858-2957, M-RR-2-3-4-5 to Borough Hall & Court St., M-F 1-6, S 9-6, c.c., no ch., exch., no rfd. Sells: **Bicycles & Supplies.**

* **Camrod Cycle**, 610 W. 57 (11th Av.), 582-7444&7435, A-AA-B-CC-D-1 to 59, M-F 9-7, ch., c.c. Mfr.'s warranty. Sells: **Motorscooters.**

* **Consumers Distributing**, Queens, 107-18 70th Rd., Forest Hills, 268-2091, E-F-GG-N to 71-Continental Avs.; Queens, 39-20 Bell Blvd., Bayside, 225-0253, no subway stop nearby; Queens, 156-16 Northern Blvd., Flushing, 961-5024, no subway stop nearby; Queens, 97-10 Queens Blvd., Rego Park, 896-7250, F-GG-N to 63rd Dr.; Brooklyn, Av. U at Mill Av. (nr. Kings Plaza), 241-7633, D-M-QB to Av. M; Queens, 54-30 Myrtle Av., Ridgewood, 386-2809, LL-M to Myrtle & Wyckoff. All stores: M-F 10-9 (Ridgewood 10-6), S 10-6, Sun 12-5, ch., c.c. during banking hours, 30-day exch. or rfd. Large selection. A catalog-showroom chain. Sells: **Kids' Bikes, Autos & Supplies, Dinnerware & Cookware, Home-Improvement Items, Housewares, Jewelry & Gifts, Sporting Goods.**

Frank's Bike Shop, 553 Grand St. (FDR Drive), 533-6332, F to E. Broadway, plus a long walk, F-T 9-7, c.c., no ch., exch., no rfd. Sells: **Bicycles & Supplies.**

* **Hillside Cycle**, Queens, 139 Hillside Av., Jamaica, 739-2750, E-F to Sutphin Blvd., M-Th 9-9, FS 9-6, c.c. +5%, no ch. Mfr.'s warranty. Sells: **Motorscooters.**

** **Jack's Bargain Stores**, 2 W. 14 at 5th Av., 2nd floor, 924-5322, B-F-LL to 14th St. & 6th Av.; 142 W. 34 (6th-7th), 947-4135, B-D-F-N-QB-RR to 34, 1-2-3 to 34. Both stores: 9:30-7 M-S, all cash, 25-day exch. or rfd. Other stores in Newark. Specializes in clothing. Other items: small selection. Sells: **Kids' Bikes, Clothing—Children's, Clothing—Women's, Furnishings.**

* **JBJ Discount Pets**, 151 E. Houston St. at Eldridge, 982-5310, F to 2nd Av., M-S 11-6, Sun 11-3, all cash, no exch. or rfd. Only 1 bike; many pets. Sells: **Bicycles & Supplies, Pets.**

* **King Motorcycle**, Brooklyn, 657 Utica Av. (Clarkson), 773-2279, 2 to Utica, M-F 9-7:30, S 9-5, c.c. +6%, no ch. Mfr.'s warranty. Sells: **Motorscooters.**

Roberts Bicycle, Queens, 33-13 Francis Lewis Blvd., Bayside, 353-5432, no subway stop nearby, M-F 9-8, ch., c.c., exch., no rfd. Sells: **Bicycles & Supplies.**

Stuyvesant Bicycle, 349 W. 14 (8th-9th), 254-5200, A-AA-CC-E-LL to 14 St. & 8 Av., M-S 9:30-5:30, c.c., no ch., exch., no rfd. Sells: **Bicycles & Supplies.**

** **Toys 'R' Us**, Brooklyn, 2875 Flatbush Av. (Belt Pkwy.), 258-2061, no subway stop nearby, M-S 10-9, Sun 11-5, ch., c.c., 90-day exch. or rfd. Large selection. Other stores nationwide. Sells: **Kids' Bikes, Toys, Games & Hobbies.**

Valco Discount, Queens, 32-40 & 32-62 Steinway St., Astoria, 274-1200 & 545-8443, F-GG-N to Steinway St., M-W 10-7, ThF 10-8, SSun 10:30-5:30, ch., no c.c., exch. or rfd. Large selection. Sells: **Kids' Bikes, Housewares, Sporting Goods, Stationery & Art Supplies, Toys, Games & Hobbies.**

4:
CAMERAS & OPTICAL EQT.
Expect 25-60% discounts.

Here's another area where the savings can easily amount to hundreds of dollars. The stores I'm recommending are an outstanding lot not just for value, though, but also because they're honest. The sad fact is that crookedness is common in the camera-trade. I've disqualified from consideration all stores, such as Grand Central Camera, Cambridge Camera Exchange, and others well-known and not so well-known, which have been cited in legal proceedings by consumer-agencies, or otherwise publicly exposed (or which I've verified on my own) to have been engaging in such practices as false advertising, false packaging, phony "list" prices, selling the right box with wrong and inferior merchandise in it, stripping camera-boxes of some of their contents—like straps, batteries, and lens-caps—and then charging extra for these accessories, etc. A genuine discount-store does not do such things, and I've often been gratified to find that most of the places that do—and that promote their "specials" in huge ads in the *New York Times* or other media—are usually advertising prices higher than what's normally charged at the stores I recommend below.

Practically every shop recommended here will quote prices by phone.

Informed camera-shopping entails five stages: First, you find out what you want the camera to do, what features you need. The best aid for this is the paperback book, *The Joy of Photography*, by Eastman Kodak Co. (Addison Wesley Publishers, $12 current list-price), a phenomenal course in photography, showing by example what each gadget, function, and control-knob does, and how to use it. Then you determine what brands-and-models fulfill these requirements. Camera-store salesmen can generally answer this kind of question; but don't rely on only one store, or else you'll know only about the cameras they sell or specialize in. Thirdly, you narrow the field of competing models by eliminating those which fail to meet your quality-requirements. Here's where the camera-rating magazines discussed below—especially *Popular Photography*—can be very helpful. Next, you inform yourself as to how the remaining contenders come factory-packaged—whether or not the case, standard lens, batteries, full factory warranty, etc., are included in the standard box, or whether they're boxed (and thus charged) separately. (Some "grey market" cameras do not include any manufacturer's warranty, so watch out for that!) The key thing here is that whenever you discuss or inquire about a specific camera at any store, you should ask what—if any—lens, accessories and manufacturer's warranties come in the same box with the camera-body. And finally, you phone the recommended camera-stores for prices, specifying for each camera the boxed and optional accessories you want. Only then will you be able to get comparison-prices that can really be compared, and that relate to a camera-package which you might actually want to buy. Only then can you avoid wasting both your own time and that of camera-salesmen. Never hesitate to ask these salesmen precisely what's included in a camera-package they're quoting on. This, after all, is one of the two questions they're most competent to answer—the other being camera-features. They usually know little about the quality of various cameras, though they may speak much upon the subject. Finally, before you pay for your camera, look inside every box you're buying, and make sure that you're getting exactly what you're paying for. This is less important with the stores I'm recommending than it is with other camera-shops, since I've checked these ones out; but it should be done nonetheless, just in case someone slips up—and who knows, but maybe an honest store may be bought out by one that's not so honest!

So how do you select what make-and-model of camera to buy? Of all camera-rating magazines, *Popular Photography* is by far the best. *Modern Photography* is tolerably good at rating lenses, but not much else. *Consumer Reports* is poor all-around. Only *Popular Photography* does a total mechanical stripdown of cameras, and reports on the appropriateness of materials used and on the general construction, including ease of repair-access, seal against dirt, and other important factors. And only this magazine rates Single Lens Reflex cameras for vibration. When the mirror inside an SLR goes up so that the picture can be taken, a certain amount of camera-shake inevitably happens; and often this vibration will blur the picture even more than would an inferior lens. It's ridiculous to rate SLR's for lens-quality, and then to ignore shake, which may affect picture-quality even more; yet this is what all the other magazines do.

There are, however, some problems even with *Popular Photography*'s camera-ratings. Both the meaning and significance of the technical charts are poorly explained. Nowhere, for example, is lens "contrast" related to picture-clarity, for which this parameter is so important—in some cases as important as vibration. And nothing is said about the respective effects that vibration, flare, and the other tested parameters, have on picture-quality. The charts are written by technicians for technicians; the magazine is terribly edited. But nonetheless, this is the only publication where the necessary information is given, even if poorly.

My brand-recommendations below are based primarily on the technical charts in *Popular Photography*, and on conversations with camera-repairmen. Also, with regard to camera-lenses, I've consulted, in addition, *Modern Photography*. But keep in mind that the picture-taking quality of practically all brands of SLR's is at such a high level that even professional photographers can't tell the difference between "good" and "bad." Indeed, Nikons and Leicas have long been overpriced simply because they've been popular among pros—these are snob-cameras (especially Leicas), but every thorough and objective examination shows them not to be superior in any way (and often to be inferior) to other, more

4: CAMERAS & OPTICAL EQT.

moderately-priced, cameras. If you ask a pro about his Nikon, he'll tell you that the body is more rugged, and the lens superior. In fact, Pentax usually scores higher in both departments, while costing far less. And when something does go wrong with a Pentax, the camera is designed so that the repair will usually also be less expensive. I should point out, however, that Nikon is in the process of upgrading its value, especially with the EM model, which was introduced with a list price of $357.50 in 1979, but which could routinely be had for $130 two years later at BARGAIN FINDER stores, and which at that price represented the best value among automatic SLR's, its only problem being a fragile rewind mechanism (something you never encounter with Pentax). However, not all of the snob-cameras are similarly upgrading. For example, Leicas continue to maintain a prestige-image by virtue of their absurdly and utterly unjustifiedly high price alone, and as a result, retain a much higher proportion of their resale-value than does any other camera-make, Pentax included. Poor value, as so often happens, makes good investment, because a lot of ignorant people have more money than they know how to throw.

RECOMMENDED PRODUCTS:

Cameras: Pentax (usually the best value of all being their cheapest models, but Pentax is good in all price-ranges; what you get for a higher price is more features, not more quality). Other Japanese makers also offer good value, but not as consistently.
Lenses: Pentax has a very slight edge here; sometimes, other Japanese lenses are better. Best values of all are usually closeouts of previous years' models, and also the very carefully selected private-label Japanese-made lens-line sold at Spiratone.

RECOMMENDED STORES:

cameras, lenses, supplies

(includes: editors, enlargers, exposure-meters, light-meters, movie eqt., projectors)

***+**C.O.M.B. Co.** (intermittent stock, outside NYC, 1-800-328-0609, catalog is free if you mention this book); ****Bi-Rite Photo & Electronics** (685-2130); ****S&W Electronics** (966-2950); ****Triest Export** (246-1548); ***Adorama Camera** (564-4465); ***Camera Discount Ctr.** (226-1014); ***Focus Electronics** (Brooklyn, 871-7600); ***Midtown Foto** (575-1633); ***Olden Camera** (226-3727); ***Prestige Photo** (683-6715); ***Saverite Photo Elec.** (966-6655); ***Sharp Photo** (532-1809); ***Spiratone Lenses/Accessories** (594-5267); ***Tri-State Camera** (349-2555); **Essex Camera/Electronics** (677-6420); **Warren Camera** (Brooklyn, 336-0418).

photo film and paper

****Ashreh Supply** (925-9507); ****D&M Film & Paper** (620-9100); ****Fairstryk Film & Paper** (757-4755); ***Adorama Camera** (564-4465); ***Camera Discount Ctr.** (226-1014); ***Olden Camera** (226-3727); ***Prestige Photo** (683-6715).

photo chemicals

***Adorama Camera** (564-4465); ***Bomze-Jaybee** (777-5577); ***Camera Discount Ctr.** (226-1014); ***Olden Camera** (226-3727); ***Prestige Photo**

4: CAMERAS & OPTICAL EQT.

(683-6715).

scopes & binoculars

**Ashreh Supply (925-9507); **S&W Electronics (966-2950); *Adorama Camera (564-4465); *Camera Discount Ctr. (226-1014); *MCB Trdg. (741-0848); *Michael C. Fina (869-5050); *Midtown Foto (575-1633); *Olden Camera (226-3727); *Prestige Photo (683-6715); *Pushcart (962-4142); *Tri-State Camera (349-2555); Essex Camera/Electronics (677-6420); Warren Camera (Brooklyn, 336-0418).

film-developing

***Custom Quality Studio; **15-Cent Photo (outside NYC, 1-201-226-2285); **Clark Color; **Finest Foto; **Master Color Labs; *T.R. Color (564-9119).

photos copied

Atlas Photo (683-6590); Franklin Photo (246-4255); Hopkins Photo (929-0800); Master Photo (757-0277).

STORES-DIRECTORY

Phone a store before you go out of your way to visit it. Especially do this during July and August, when most establishments reduce or eliminate weekend-hours.

In the listings below, "*" means especially recommended, "+" means that the store offers a bonus discount to BF readers, "ch." and "c.c." mean respectively checks and credit cards, and "exch." and "rfd." mean respectively exchange and refund. Nearest subway-stops are shown. For example, "B-D-F to 47" means to take the B, D, or F train to 47th Street. Store-hours are also indicated, with days of the week abbreviated, like "M-S 8-6."

** **15-Cent Photo**, Clifton, NJ 07015, 1-201-226-2285, ch., no c.c., exch. or rfd. Phone or write for their current prices (which you'll also find much advertised on late-night TV). Sells: **Film-Developing**.

* **Adorama Camera**, 138 W. 34 (6th-7th), 2nd floor, 564-4465, B-D-F-N-QB-RR to 34, 1-2-3 to 34, M-Th 9:30-6, F 9:30-1, Sun 10-4, ch., c.c., 14-day exch. or rfd. Sells: **Cameras, Lenses, Supplies, Photo Film And Paper, Photo Chemicals, Scopes & Binoculars**.

** **Ashreh Supply**, 473 Broadway (Grand), 3rd floor, 925-9507, J-M-N-QB-RR-6 to Canal, Sun-Th 11-7, all cash, no exch. or rfd. Basically a wholesaler who accomodates retail-trade. Sells: **Photo Film And Paper, Scopes & Binoculars, Appliances, Jewelry & Gifts, Personal Accessories, Smoking Supplies, Stationery & Art Supplies**.

Atlas Photo, 45 W. 27, 2nd floor, 683-6590&7640, N-RR to 28th St., M-F 8-5, ch., no c.c., exch. or rfd. Sells: **Photos Copied**.

** **Bi-Rite Photo & Electronics**, 15 E. 30 (5th Av.), 685-2130 & 1-800-223-1970, N-RR to 28th St., M-Th 9-6, F 9-1, Sun 10:30-3:30, ch., c.c., 15-day exch. or rfd. Sells: **Cameras, Lenses, Supplies**.

* **Bomze-Jaybee**, 7 E. 19 (5th Av.), 777-5577, B-F-LL to 14th St. & 6th Av., N-RR to 23rd St., M-S 9-5:30, ch., c.c., exch., no rfd. Good only on chemicals. Sells: **Photo Chemicals**.

* **Camera Discount Ctr.**, 89A Worth St. (Church-B'wy), 226-1014, A-CC-1-2-3 to Chambers, 1 to Franklin, M-F 8:30-5:30, Sun 10-3, ch., c.c., 14-day exch. or rfd. Sells: **Cameras, Lenses, Supplies, Photo Film And Paper, Photo Chemicals, Scopes & Binoculars**.

** **Clark Color**, G.P.O. Box 3240, NY, NY 10116, ch., no c.c., exch. or rfd. Takes mail-orders. Sells: **Film-Developing**.

***+ **C.O.M.B. Co.**, 6850 Wayzata Blvd., Minneapolis, MN 55426, 1-800-328-0609, catalog is free if you mention this book, ch., c.c., exch., no rfd. Takes mail-orders. Catalog. Very cooperative. Catalog is free only if you mention Bargain Finder.

4: CAMERAS & OPTICAL EQT.

Sells: **Cameras, Lenses, Supplies, Home-Improvement Items, Jewelry & Gifts, Personal Accessories, Warehouse Salvage Job-Lot.**

*** **Custom Quality Studio**, Box 4838, Chicago, IL 60680. More consistently good quality than most of the other places. Sells: **Film-Developing.**

** **D&M Film & Paper**, 508 W. 26 (10th Av.), 9th floor, 620-9100, A-AA-CC-E to 23, plus a long walk, M-F 9-4:30, ch., no c.c., exch., no rfd. Mostly mail-order. Phone for price-list. Sells: **Photo Film And Paper.**

Essex Camera/Electronics, 17 Essex St. (Canal), 677-6420, F to E. Broadway, irregular hours, ch., no c.c., 10-day exch. or rfd. Sells: **Cameras, Lenses, Supplies, Scopes & Binoculars, Appliances.**

** **Fairstryk Film & Paper**, 445 W. 50 (9th-10th), 757-4755, A-AA-CC-E to 50, M-F 10:30-2, ch., no c.c. Exch. or rfd. if defective. Primarily mail-order. phone for price-list. Sells: **Photo Film And Paper.**

* **Finest Foto**, 482 Sunrise Hwy., Rockville Ctr., NY 11571, no subway stop nearby, ch., no c.c. Takes mail-orders. Sells: **Film-Developing.**

* **Focus Electronics**, Brooklyn, 4523 13th Av., 871-7600, B to Ft. Ham. Pkwy., M-Th 10-7, F 10-2, Sun 10-6, ch., c.c., 10-day exch., no rfd. Sells: **Cameras, Lenses, Supplies, Appliances.**

Franklin Photo, 353 W. 48 (9th Av.), 246-4255, A-AA-CC-E to 50, M-F 9-5, ch., no c.c., exch. or rfd. Sells: **Photos Copied.**

Hopkins Photo, 56 W. 22 (5th-6th), 3rd floor, 929-0800, B-F to 23, N-RR to 23rd St., M-F 9-5:30, all cash, exch. or rfd. Sells: **Photos Copied.**

** **Master Color Labs**, GPO Box 30, Newark, NJ 07101, ch., no c.c., exch. or rfd. Write for current prices (which you'll also find advertised in newspapers). Sells: **Film-Developing.**

Master Photo, 165 W. 46 (6th-7th), 757-0277, N-RR to 49th St., B-D-F to 47, M-F 9-5, ch., no c.c., exch. or rfd. Sells: **Photos Copied.**

* **MCB Trdg.**, 25 W. 23 (5th-6th Avs.), 741-0848, N-RR to 23rd St., B-F to 23, M-F 8-6:30, ch., c.c., exch., no rfd. Sells: **Scopes & Binoculars, Appliances.**

* **Michael C. Fina**, 580 5th Av. at 47th, 2nd floor, 869-5050, B-D-F to 47, M-F 9-5:30, ch., c.c., exch. or rfd. Takes mail-orders. Catalog. Sells: **Scopes & Binoculars, Dinnerware & Cookware, Jewelry & Gifts, Personal Accessories.**

* **Midtown Foto**, 21 W. 47, up 1 flight, 575-1633, B-D-F to 47, M-Th 9-6, F 9-2, Sun 10-4, ch., c.c., 15-day exch., no rfd. Sells: **Cameras, Lenses, Supplies, Scopes & Binoculars.**

* **Olden Camera**, 1265 Broadway (32), up 1 flight, 226-3727, B-D-F-N-QB-RR to 34, MTWFS 9-6, Th 9-8, ch., c.c. 10-day rfd., 30-day exch. Huge selection. Extremely busy. Sells: **Cameras, Lenses, Supplies, Photo Film And Paper, Photo Chemicals, Scopes & Binoculars.**

* **Prestige Photo**, 373 5th Av. at 35th, up 1 flight, 683-6715, B-D-F-N-QB-RR to 34, M-Th 10-6, F 10-2, Sun 11-4:30, ch., c.c., 15-day exch., no rfd. Sells: **Cameras, Lenses, Supplies, Photo Film And Paper, Photo Chemicals, Scopes & Binoculars.**

* **Pushcart**, 140 Church St. (Warren-Chambers), 962-4142, A-CC-1-2-3 to Chambers; 412 5th Av. (37-8), 398-9210, B-D-F to 42. Both stores: M-F 8-5:30, S 8-4:30, all cash, 15-day exch. or rfd. This is the same store as the Job Lot Trdg. Co., but the relative values in these merchandise-categories aren't as terrific; and most isn't even job-lot, but regular. Sells: **Scopes & Binoculars, Health & Beauty Aids, Home-Improvement Items.**

* **Saverite Photo Elec.**, 46 Canal St. (Orchard), 966-6655, F to E. Broadway, Sun-Th 10-6, F 10-2, ch., no c.c., 10-day exch., no rfd. Sells: **Cameras, Lenses, Supplies, Appliances.**

* **Sharp Photo**, 1225 Broadway (30), rm. 502, 532-1809, N-RR to 28th St., M-F 9-5:30, Sun 10-2, ch., c.c., 7-day exch. or rfd. Sells: **Cameras, Lenses, Supplies.**

* **Spiratone Lenses/Accessories**, 130 W. 31 (6th-7th), 594-5267, B-D-F-N-QB-RR to 34; Queens, 135-06 Northern Blvd., Flushing, 886-2000, 7 to Main St. Both stores: M-F 9-5:45, S 9-4:45, ch., c.c., exch. or rfd. Takes mail-orders. Catalog. No cameras; only their house-brand of Japanese-made lenses and accessories--many of which have received very favorable technical reviews. Sells: **Cameras, Lenses, Supplies.**

** **S&W Electronics**, 50 Canal S. (Orchard), 966-2950, F to E. Broadway, irregular hours, usually Sun-Th 10-6, ch., no c.c., 7-day exch. or rfd. Sells: **Cameras, Lenses, Supplies, Scopes & Binoculars, Appliances.**

4: CAMERAS & OPTICAL EQT.

* **T.R. Color**, 5 W. 30 (5th Av.), 2nd floor, 564-9119, N-RR to 28th St., B-D-F-N-QB-RR to 34, M-F 9a.m.-10p.m., S 11-6, ch., no c.c., exch., no rfd. Only Ektachrome, only transparencies. Sells: **Film-Developing.**

** **Triest Export**, 560 12th Av. (44), 246-1548, A-AA-CC-E to 42, plus a long walk, Sun-F 7-6, all cash, no exch. or rfd. Very busy. Expect long wait on line. Popular with seamen and foreign tourists. Sells: **Cameras, Lenses, Supplies, Appliances, Clothing—Men's, Personal Accessories, Toys, Games & Hobbies.**

* **Tri-State Camera**, 179 Broadway (John), up 1 flight, 349-2555, A-CC-J-M-RR-2-3-4-5 to B'wy-Nassau & Fulton, 4-5 to Wall St., M-Th 9-6, F 9-2, Sun 10-3, ch., c.c., exch. or rfd. Sells: **Cameras, Lenses, Supplies, Scopes & Binoculars.**

Warren Camera, Brooklyn, 1721 Kings Hwy., 336-0418, D-M-QB to Kings Hwy., M-F 10-7, S 10-6, Sun 11-5, c.c., no ch., exch. or rfd. Exceptionally objective recommendations of equipment. They don't try to sell you up to something no better quality but more expensive. Sells: **Cameras, Lenses, Supplies, Scopes & Binoculars.**

5:
CLOTHING—CHILDREN'S
Expect 20-50% discounts.

There used to be two price-ranges for children's clothing: the expensive domestic stuff, and the cheap Korean and other Oriental imports. Now, there's also a third, and super-expensive, category: the designer-labels, most of which are produced in the same countries—and factories—that manufacture the cheap kiddie-clothes. No longer are people saying that the foreign-made garments are junk, because that'd usually be condemning the designer-wear as well, and price-snobs wouldn't want to do that. But still, there are lots of people who would rather pay $20 for a pair of child's designer-jeans than $6 for the very same pair of pants without the designer-name sewn onto the back pocket. And some of the stores recommended below specialize in offering precisely this overpriced merchandise at hefty discounts.

Actually, the whole question of quality is rather less important with regard to children's wear than it is with adults' clothing, simply because kids grow so fast that sometimes they don't even have a chance to wear things out. That's why outstanding values can often be found at the several stores I recommend that specialize in recycled kids' wear.

If you're nonetheless determined to obtain the most reliably well-made (new) clothing for your kids, some of the domestically manufactured garments usually have a slight edge. For example, the best-constructed jeans tend to be two old traditional American standbys—Wranglers (or "Mavericks"), and Lees—but I wouldn't recommend them, because the foreign-made off-brands offer better value.

RECOMMENDED PRODUCTS:
See above.

RECOMMENDED STORES:

Numbers which precede store-names show the price-categories of the clothing sold:

"2" represents designer children's wear.
"3" indicates top name-brand offerings.
"4" means off-brand children's clothing.

kids' clothing

(examples: babies' clothes, coats, dresses, dungarees, jackets, jeans, layettes, shirts, skirts, suits, ties, underwear)

3&4 ***Frankel's Discount Clothing (intermittent stock, Brooklyn, 768-9788); 4&5 **Cayne's 2 (244-8761); 4&5 **Cayne's 4 (560-9212); 2&3 **Century 21 (227-9092); 4 **Earl's (intermittent stock, Queens, 894-6406); 4&5 **Eleven West (695-7537); 2&3 **Fabulous Julie's

(Queens, 526-9892); **4 **Jack's Bargain Stores** (924-5322); **3&4 **Jay's Bargain Store** (691-7142); **2 **Little Rascals** (226-1680); **3 **Quiltex Factory Outlet** (Brooklyn, 788-3158); **3&4 **William Wiesner** (Brooklyn, 384-0649); **2&3 *A&G Children's Wear** (966-3775); **4 *C&C Bargains** (Brooklyn, 625-9210); **4 *C&S Variety** (Brooklyn, 259-5290); **4 *Major Dept. Store** (Brooklyn, 875-6924); **4 *Youngworld** (852-7890); **3&4 B. Kaminsky** (226-5856); **4 Bohrer's Children's Wear** (254-6988); **4 Broadway Fashion** (431-4134); **4&5 First Cost** (intermittent stock, 697-0244); **3 Lester's Children's Wear** (Brooklyn, 375-7337); **3&4 Most's Dept. Store** (Queens, 225-3455); **3 Natan Borlam** (Brooklyn, 782-0108).

kids' shoes

(includes sneakers)

3&4 ***Frankel's Discount Clothing (intermittent stock, Brooklyn, 768-9788); **4&5 **Alee Discount** (intermittent stock, 619-2980); **4 **Earl's** (intermittent stock, Queens, 894-6406); **3&4&5 **Manufacturer's Shoe Outlet** (226-6266); **2&3 **Richie's Shoes** (228-5442); **2&3&4 *Pat's Shoes** (intermittent stock, Brooklyn, 647-0664); **4&5 *Shoe Giant Outlets** (Queens, 728-9284); **4&5 First Cost** (intermittent stock, 697-0244); **4 Hamer's Shoes** (Brooklyn, 871-3766); **3 Lester's Children's Wear** (Brooklyn, 375-7337); **4 Shoe Arcade** (Brooklyn, 436-1106).

used clothing for kids

Frugal Frog (876-5178); **Once Upon A Time** (831-7619); **Replay** (942-4142); **Second Act** (988-2440); **Second Cousin** (929-8048); **Thrifty Threads** (Brooklyn, 336-8037).

STORES-DIRECTORY

See unified clothing-stores-directory at the end of Chapter 7.

6:
CLOTHING—MEN'S
Expect 30-70% discounts.

New York is heaven for this. Our town has exported some of its local grandeur—native bargain-haunts like Sym's have by now expanded with branches in many towns and states—but for sheer selection, and even for the best values, still no place anywhere can compare with New York. This city is the dumping-ground for everybody's overproduction and bankrupt stock—occasionally including even superb and current-styled European-made garments, like $300 suits which are a good value for that money, being discounted to $30. (But note: In the past ten years, I've encountered this sort of thing only at four stores on four different occasions. One of these clearances went on for more than a year; but still, sales like this are far from a routine occurrence. And when they do happen, don't expect to hear about them from ads or from consumer-reporters. None of the four, to my knowledge, was promoted anywhere. Your best chance of finding such super-bargains is at the places listed in the chapter on Warehouse Job-Lots and which are shown there to carry men's clothing. These stores are usually indicated in the present chapter by the qualifier "intermittent stock" in parentheses after the name under the merchandise-category headings.)

One reason for Manhattan's wealth of discount clothing-offerings is that this town is America's clothing-trades center (though much of the actual manufacturing is now done out-of-town). Some makers here sell direct from their trade-showrooms or factories. Some have built up such a booming retail-business offering their own stock at about 40-50% discount, that the local department-stores no longer carry their clothing—only the out-of-town ones do—and yet the manufacturers' profits from local sales are nonetheless way up. Most of the operations that function this way are located on the upper floors of office-buildings along 5th Avenue, between 14th and 22nd Streets. This strip has also become home to many regular multi-brand discounters of men's clothing, where the markdowns are usually about the same as at the genuine showrooms. In any case, for both kinds of places, I've not recommended all discounters, but only the best ones. There are quite a number (especially of factory-outlets) which give only a 30-40% break on suits and coats, and that's not good enough to qualify for a recommendation here.

The clothing-quality rating-system I use is a key to interpreting the store-recommendations. When I say, "'1' is hand-tailored wear," I'm referring to the standards applied in the clothing-trades, though I happen to disagree with these criteria. A man's suit, for example, is usually considered top quality only if it has hand-stitching behind the lapels, inside the cuffs, or at other points such as the button-holes. Now, this has nothing to do with either styling or durability, and I therefore don't consider the standard a rational one; but yet suits constructed this way do cost much more to make, and so one can't really fairly compare their prices with what's being charged for fully machine-made suits even of the best quality. I break the latter kind of garment into two categories: "'2' refers to dressy designer clothing," and, "'3' is good quality with no designer-tag." Suits in these categories are well-put-together, with fine fabrics; in fact, they're usually better-made than the ones I've rated "1." In order of value, I'd suggest "3" as best, "2" next, and "1" last; but of course there will be other people with different priorities than mine—you make your own judgment. The remaining two quality-rating categories are relatively straightforward, so I'll say nothing more about them: "'4' represents medium quality clothing," and "'5' indicates cheap quality merchandise."

If you're a shopper determined to get nothing "less" than a "1" suit (which technically is called a "#6" in the trade), then you should really go to one of the custom-tailors I'm recommending; especially to Stanley Slacks and Simon Klinger, but the others are worth checking out also. This way, you'll have a fully custom-tailored suit for half the regular price of the off-the-rack equivalent. The non-Hong-Kong custom tailors will even copy and custom-fit any very expensive rack-suit—and at a small fraction of the price. So why buy the original?

I've used the same quality-grading system for other clothing-categories than just suits, and the meaning is generally the same in each case.

RECOMMENDED PRODUCTS:
See above.

RECOMMENDED STORES:

> **Numbers which precede store-names show quality and fashionableness of clothing sold:**
>
> **"1" is hand-tailored wear, or top shoes.**
> **"2" refers to dressy designer clothing.**
> **"3" is good quality with no designer-tag.**
> **"4" represents medium quality clothing.**
> **"5" indicates cheap quality merchandise.**

---

men's belts

3&4 ***Frankel's Discount Clothing (intermittent stock, Brooklyn, 768-9788); **4&5 **Alee Discount** (intermittent stock, 619-2980); **3&4 **Ben Freedman** (674-0854); **2 **BFO Plus** (673-9026); **2&3 **Century 21** (227-9092); **2 **Dollar Bills** (867-0212); **3&4&5 **Fleetwood Market** (intermittent stock, 766-9766); **2&3&4 **Fowad** (222-7000); **2 **Sym's** (791-1199); **3 *+Canal Jean Co.** (431-4765); **2 *Gucci on 7** (intermittent stock, 826-2600); **2 *Mern's** (371-9195); **2&3 *National Brands Outlet** (Queens, 459-0300); **1&2&3 *Rothman** (777-7400); **3&4 *Superior Merchandising** (intermittent stock, 233-4615); **3 +Worker's Quarters** (Brooklyn, 331-4833); **2&3&4&5 Alexander's at World Trade Ctr** (466-1414); **4&5 First Cost** (intermittent stock, 697-0244); **3&4&5 Gabay's Outlet** (intermittent stock, 254-3180); **2&3 Lewis & Clark**

6: CLOTHING—MEN'S

(255-4686); **2 Moe Ginsburg** (242-3482); **4 Sofia Sam Milich** (475-9312).

men's coats—dressy

(includes raincoats)

1&2&3 ***M.C. Corner (265-4151); **4&5 **Alee Discount** (intermittent stock, 619-2980); **1&3 **Aurora Design Tailor** (687-1259); **3&4 **Ben Freedman** (674-0854); **3&4 **Canal Bargain** (intermittent stock, 227-8040); **2&3&4 **Fowad** (222-7000); **3 **Hampshire Clothes** (675-7806); **2 **L.S. Men's Clothing** (575-0933); **3 **M&M Tailors** (475-8312); **2&3 **The Townsman** (755-6660); **2&3 *Atlantic Clothing** (227-8918); **3 *Borislaw Clothier** (242-8134); **1&3 *Catania Clothing** (255-5510); **2&3&4 *Cedrick's** (Staten Island, 987-3577); **2&3 *De Silva Ltd.** (586-1316); **2 *Gucci on 7** (intermittent stock, 826-2600); **2&3 *Louis Barall & Son** (226-6195); **2&3 *National Brands Outlet** (Queens, 459-0300); **3&4 *Park Kenny Clothes** (477-1948); **1&2&3 *Rothman** (777-7400); **2&3 *Schaer Bros.** (Brooklyn, 282-5653); **2&3&4 *Trend Quality Job Lot** (intermittent stock, 889-4686); **3 *Turnpike Clothing Outlet** (Queens, 776-2547); **3&4&5 ⁺Lever & Greenberg** (226-1023); **2&3&4&5 Alexander's at World Trade Ctr** (466-1414); **3&4&5 Gabay's Outlet** (intermittent stock, 254-3180); **3 L.B.C. Clothing** (226-1620); **4&5 Mansfield Clothes** (228-1410); **2 Moe Ginsburg** (242-3482); **3 Parkway** (267-1296); **3 Royal Fashion** (475-3540); **3 The Individual Man** (924-2157).

coats—quilted & parkas

2&3 ***⁺S&A Clothing (966-5354); **3&4 ***Frankel's Discount Clothing** (intermittent stock, Brooklyn, 768-9788); **4 ***Job Lot Trdg.** (intermittent stock, 962-4142); **1&2&3 ***M.C. Corner** (265-4151); **3&4 **Ben Freedman** (674-0854); **3&4 **Canal Bargain** (intermittent stock, 227-8040); **3&4 **China Mall** (226-4720); **2&3&4 **Fowad** (222-7000); **3 **Fred Krupnik** (226-2778); **3&4 **Lucky Gift** (233-0960); **2 **Sym's** (791-1199); **2&3 **The Townsman** (755-6660); **4 **United Salvage Alka Seltzer** (intermittent stock, 962-5567); **3 *⁺Canal Jean Co.** (431-4765); **2&3 **Down In The Village** (260-2330); **4 *⁺Mr. Excitement** (intermittent stock, Queens, 847-3600); **2&3 *Colony** (924-8815); **2&3 *De Silva Ltd.** (586-1316); **3 *Hong Kong Import** (753-5340); **2 *Mern's** (371-9195); **2&3 *National Brands Outlet** (Queens, 459-0300); **3&4 *United Chambers Trdg.** (267-0488); **4 *Wallach's Outlet** (Brooklyn, 339-0192); **3 *W.M. Men's Wear** (674-1823); **3 ⁺Worker's Quarters** (Brooklyn, 331-4833); **2&3&4&5 Alexander's at World Trade Ctr** (466-1414); **4&5 Dee & Dee Stores** (243-5620); **4&5 First Cost** (intermittent stock, 697-0244); **2&3 Lewis & Clark** (255-4686); **2 Moe Ginsburg** (242-3482); **4 So Cheap** (intermittent stock, 982-7918).

coats—leather & sheepskin

2 **European Liquidators (879-9140); **2&3&4 **Fowad** (222-7000); **2&3 **Jeans 'N Things** (677-7158); **2&3 **Parezio II** (233-3942); **2&3&4 **Romano Trdg.** (581-4248); **3 **Sheepskin Market** (564-8874); **2&3 **The Townsman** (755-6660); **4 *Alex Leather City** (869-0666); **2 *Gucci on 7** (intermittent stock, 826-2600); **4 *Kalga Leather Sportswear** (594-932); **2 *Mern's** (371-9195); **2&3 *National Brands Outlet** (Queens, 459-0300); **3 Bridge Merchandise** (674-6320); **5 I&Z Leather** (673-1796); **3&4 Mitchell's Leather Wear** (925-6757).

men's formals & tuxedos

2 **Sym's (791-1199); **2 *Gucci on 7** (intermittent stock, 826-2600); **1&2&3 *Rothman** (777-7400); **2 Moe Ginsburg** (242-3482).

6: CLOTHING—MEN'S

men's gloves

3&4 ***Frankel's Discount Clothing (intermittent stock, Brooklyn, 768-9788); 4 ***Job Lot Trdg. (intermittent stock, 962-4142); 2 **BFO Plus (673-9026); 2&3 **Century 21 (227-9092); 2 **Dollar Bills (867-0212); 2 **Sym's (791-1199); 4 **United Salvage Alka Seltzer (intermittent stock, 962-5567); 4 *+Mr. Excitement (intermittent stock, Queens, 847-3600); 2&3 *Colony (924-8815); 2 *Gucci on 7 (intermittent stock, 826-2600); 2 *Mern's (371-9195); 2&3 *National Brands Outlet (Queens, 459-0300); 1&2&3 *Rothman (777-7400); 3&4 *Superior Merchandising (intermittent stock, 233-4615); 2&3&4&5 Alexander's at World Trade Ctr (466-1414); 3&4 Bernard Krieger (226-1929); 4&5 Dee & Dee Stores (243-5620); 4&5 First Cost (intermittent stock, 697-0244); 2&3 Lewis & Clark (255-4686); 3&4 Most's Dept. Store (Queens, 225-3455); New York Watches (924-4516); 4&5 Robbins Men's Wear (691-2573).

men's hats

3&4 ***Frankel's Discount Clothing (intermittent stock, Brooklyn, 768-9788); 4 **Cho's Variety (349-7544); 3 *+Canal Jean Co. (431-4765); 2 *Gucci on 7 (intermittent stock, 826-2600); 2 *Mern's (371-9195); 1&2&3 *Rothman (777-7400); 3 *Young's Hats (964-5693); 2&3&4&5 Alexander's at World Trade Ctr (466-1414); 4&5 Central Hat (254-4170); 4&5 First Cost (intermittent stock, 697-0244); 3&4&5 Gabay's Outlet (intermittent stock, 254-3180); Kol-Bo Discount (473-7829); 4&5 Robbins Men's Wear (691-2573).

jeans (FOR DESIGNERS', SEE CH. 7)

3&4 ***Frankel's Discount Clothing (intermittent stock, Brooklyn, 768-9788); 1&2&3 ***M.C. Corner (265-4151); 4&5 **Alee Discount (intermittent stock, 619-2980); 4&5 **Cayne's 1 (695-8451); 4&5 **Cayne's 4 (560-9212); 4&5 **Eleven West (695-7537); 3 **Fred Krupnik (226-2778); 2&3&4 **Romano Trdg. (581-4248); 3 **Townie Merchandise (929-8060); 3 **Triest Export (246-1548.); 4 **United Salvage Alka Seltzer (intermittent stock, 962-5567); 3 *+Canal Jean Co. (431-4765); 3 *Dave's Army/Navy (989-6444); 3 *Fiedler's (475-8372); 3 *Nathan Kurtz (475-6550); 3 *N&L Corp. (982-8514); 2&3 *Slep (677-5328); 3&4 *Superior Merchandising (intermittent stock, 233-4615); 3 *W.M. Men's Wear (674-1823); 3 *Z&L Import (475-6240); 3&4 Better Wear Mfg. (966-0619); 3&4 Brown's Army-Navy (Queens, 429-8508); 4&5 Dee & Dee Stores (243-5620); 4&5 First Cost (intermittent stock, 697-0244); 3 H. Tenzer (473-6082); 3 Luso Sales (563-4180); 3 M&M Menswear (982-9188); 4 Regent's Wear (226-3255); 3 Sam Popper (226-9752); 4&5 Silt Sportuar (966-3479); 4 So Cheap (intermittent stock, 982-7918); 4&5 Three Star Tailoring (925-0495).

men's pants/slacks

3&4 ***Frankel's Discount Clothing (intermittent stock, Brooklyn, 768-9788); 4 ***Job Lot Trdg. (intermittent stock, 962-4142); 1&2&3 ***M.C. Corner (265-4151); 4&5 **Alee Discount (intermittent stock, 619-2980); 3&4 **Ben Freedman (674-0854); 3&4 **Canal Bargain (intermittent stock, 227-8040); 2&3&4 **Fowad (222-7000); 3 **Fred Krupnik (226-2778); 2&3 **Jeans 'N Things (677-7158); 2&3 **Parezio II (233-3942); 2 **Sym's (791-1199); 2&3 **The Townsman (755-6660); 4 **United Salvage Alka Seltzer (intermittent stock, 962-5567); 3 *+Canal Jean Co. (431-4765); 4 *+Mr. Excitement (intermittent stock, Queens, 847-3600); 3&4 *BFO Suits (254-0059); 2&3&4 *Cedrick's (Staten Island, 987-3577); 2&3 *Colony (924-8815); 2&3 *De Silva Ltd. (586-1316);

6: CLOTHING—MEN'S

2 *Gucci on 7 (intermittent stock, 826-2600); 2 *Mern's (371-9195); 2&3 *National Brands Outlet (Queens, 459-0300); 1&2&3 *Rothman (777-7400); 3&4 *Superior Merchandising (intermittent stock, 233-4615); 3&4&5 +Lever & Greenberg (226-1023); 2&3&4&5 Alexander's at World Trade Ctr (466-1414); 4 Broadway Fashion (431-4134); 4&5 Dee & Dee Stores (243-5620); 4&5 First Cost (intermittent stock, 697-0244); 3 L.B.C. Clothing (226-1620); 2&3 Lewis & Clark (255-4686); 2 Moe Ginsburg (242-3482); 3&4 Most's Dept. Store (Queens, 225-3455); 2&3&4 Phantom (243-7910); 4 Regent's Wear (226-3255); 4&5 Robbins Men's Wear (691-2573); 4 So Cheap (intermittent stock, 982-7918).

shirts

3&4 ***Frankel's Discount Clothing (intermittent stock, Brooklyn, 768-9788); 4 ***Job Lot Trdg. (intermittent stock, 962-4142); 1&2&3 ***M.C. Corner (265-4151); 3&4 ***Odd Job Trdg. (intermittent stock, 686-6825); 2 ***Runway Fashions (686-8502); 1&3 **Aurora Design Tailor (687-1259); 3&4 **Ben Freedman (674-0854); 2 **BFO Plus (673-9026); 3&4 **Canal Bargain (intermittent stock, 227-8040); 4&5 **Cayne's 1 (695-8451); 4&5 **Cayne's 4 (560-9212); 2&3 **Century 21 (227-9092); 2 **Dollar Bills (867-0212); 4&5 **Eleven West (695-7537); 3&4&5 **Fleetwood Market (intermittent stock, 766-9766); 2&3&4 **Fowad (222-7000); 3 **Fred Krupnik (226-2778); 2&3 **Jeans 'N Things (677-7158); 2&3 **Parezio II (233-3942); 2&3 **S. Sosinsky & Son (475-9784); 2 **Sym's (791-1199); 2&3 **The Townsman (755-6660); 4 **United Salvage Alka Seltzer (intermittent stock, 962-5567); 3 **Canal Jean Co. (431-4765); 4 *+Mr. Excitement (intermittent stock, Queens, 847-3600); 3 *+Rukico Tailors (832-0725); 2 *Antony (477-0592); 2&3 *Baretta Fashions 1 (Queens, 275-0638); 2&3&4 *Cedrick's (Staten Island, 987-3577); 2&3 *Colony (924-8815); 2&3 *De Silva Ltd. (586-1316); 2 *Gucci on 7 (intermittent stock, 826-2600); 2 *Mern's (371-9195); 3 *Mohan's Custom Tailor (697-0050); 2&3 *National Brands Outlet (Queens, 459-0300); 3&4 *No Name (766-9766); 2&3 *Slep (677-5328); 2&3&4 *Trend Quality Job Lot (intermittent stock, 889-4686); 3 *Turnpike Clothing Outlet (Queens, 776-2547); 2&3&4&5 Alexander's at World Trade Ctr (466-1414); 3&4 Bayard International (594-6658); 3 Bridge Merchandise (674-6320); 4 Broadway Fashion (431-4134); 4&5 First Cost (intermittent stock, 697-0244); 2&3 Lewis & Clark (255-4686); 2 Moe Ginsburg (242-3482); 3&4 Most's Dept. Store (Queens, 225-3455); 3 Parkway (267-1296); 2&3&4 Phantom (243-7910); 3 Premier Textile (966-1984); 4&5 Robbins Men's Wear (691-2573); 4 So Cheap (intermittent stock, 982-7918).

shoes—bedroom & slippers

4 ***Job Lot Trdg. (intermittent stock, 962-4142); 3&4 ***Odd Job Trdg. (intermittent stock, 686-6825); 3&4&5 ***+John Cipriano Shoes (477-5858); 2 **Sym's (791-1199); 2 *Gucci on 7 (intermittent stock, 826-2600); *Mitsu (947-7892); 4 *Ray Variety (736-2547); 4 *S&A Future (924-3873); 2&3&4&5 Alexander's at World Trade Ctr (466-1414); 3&4 Bok Lei Bo (233-0935); 4&5 Dee & Dee Stores (243-5620); Dems Bargain Stores (243-9416); 4 East Village Variety (674-8300); Kol-Bo Discount (473-7829).

men's shoes—dress

1&2&3 ***Irving's Shoes (265-8286); 1&2&3 ***M.C. Corner (265-4151); 3&4&5 ***+John Cipriano Shoes (477-5858); 1 **Adamici Outlet (924-6087); 2&3 **American Arion (766-8514); 2&3&4 **Baretta Fash-

6: CLOTHING—MEN'S

ions 2 (921-2979); 3&4 **Bob's Discount (intermittent stock, 674-4296); 4&5 **Eighth Av. Bargain King (594-4049); 2&3&4 **Fowad (222-7000); 3&4 **John's Shoe Outlet (255-7035); 3&4&5 **Manufacturer's Shoe Outlet (226-6266); 3&4 **Odd Lot Shoes (687-8810); 3 **Shoes-N-Things (intermittent stock, 254-4860); 2 **Sym's (791-1199); 3&4 *+Interstate Footwear (227-1886); 2&3 *Baretta Fashions 1 (Queens, 275-0638); 2 *Baretta Fashions Midtown (687-2853); 1&2 *Fabulous Find (242-9474); 2 *Gucci on 7 (intermittent stock, 826-2600); 2 *Mern's (371-9195); 2&3&4 *Pat's Shoes (intermittent stock, Brooklyn, 647-0664); 4&5 *Shoe Giant Outlets (Queens, 728-9284); 2&3&4 *Trend Quality Job Lot (intermittent stock, 889-4686); 2&3&4&5 Alexander's at World Trade Ctr (466-1414); 4 Del Pino Shoes (757-6853); 3&4&5 Gabay's Outlet (intermittent stock, 254-3180); 2 Gatrimone Shoes (695-4124); 3 Genao's Shoes (673-9811); 4 Hamer's Shoes (Brooklyn, 871-3766); 2&3 J. Sherman Shoes (233-7898).

men's shoes—sports/work (JOGGERS: CH. 27)

3&4 ***Frankel's Discount Clothing (intermittent stock, Brooklyn, 768-9788); 4 ***Job Lot Trdg. (intermittent stock, 962-4142); 3&4 ***Odd Job Trdg. (intermittent stock, 686-6825); 3&4&5 ***+John Cipriano Shoes (477-5858); 3&4 **Bob's Discount (intermittent stock, 674-4296); 4&5 **Eighth Av. Bargain King (594-4049); 3&4&5 **Manufacturer's Shoe Outlet (226-6266); 3 **Shoes-N-Things (intermittent stock, 254-4860); 3 *+Canal Jean Co. (431-4765); 2&3 *Colony (924-8815); 2 *Gucci on 7 (intermittent stock, 826-2600); 2&3&4 *Pat's Shoes (intermittent stock, Brooklyn, 647-0664); 4&5 *Shoe Giant Outlets (Queens, 728-9284); 3&4 *United Chambers Trdg. (267-0488); 3 +Worker's Quarters (Brooklyn, 331-4833); 3&4 Brown's Army-Navy (Queens, 429-8508); 4&5 First Cost (intermittent stock, 697-0244); 3&4&5 Gabay's Outlet (intermittent stock, 254-3180); 4 Hamer's Shoes (Brooklyn, 871-3766); 2&3 J. Sherman Shoes (233-7898); 3&4&5 Peck & Chase Shoes (674-8860); 4&5 Robbins Men's Wear (691-2573); 4 Shoe Arcade (Brooklyn, 436-1106); 4 Shoes, Boots, Etc. (285-9750).

socks

3&4 ***Frankel's Discount Clothing (intermittent stock, Brooklyn, 768-9788); 4 ***Job Lot Trdg. (intermittent stock, 962-4142); 3&4 **Ben Freedman (674-0854); 2&3 **Century 21 (227-9092); 2 **Dollar Bills (867-0212); 3 **Jacob Young & Son (225-9232); 3&4 **Joe's Bargain Center (phoneless); 2&3&4 **Romano Trdg. (581-4248); 2 **Sym's (791-1199); 2&3 **The Townsman (755-6660); 3 **Canal Jean Co. (431-4765); 4 *+Mr. Excitement (intermittent stock, Queens, 847-3600); 3 *Dave's Army/Navy (989-6444); 4 *Klein's (intermittent stock, 475-9804); 3 *M. Friedman Hosiery (674-3292); 2 *Mern's (371-9195); 4 *Milton Siegel (925-9519); 2&3 *National Brands Outlet (Queens, 459-0300); 1&2&3 *Rothman (777-7400); 3 *William Rosengarten (674-2310); 3 +Wingdale Hosiery (684-4291); 3 +Worker's Quarters (Brooklyn, 331-4833); 4 Cheap Charlie's (intermittent stock, Brooklyn, 252-4932); 3&4 I. Tuschman & Sons (226-4318); 3 Lismore Hosiery (674-3440); 2 Moe Ginsburg (242-3482).

men's suits—new

(includes blazers)

2&3 ***+S&A Clothing (966-5354); 1&2&3 ***M.C. Corner (265-4151); 2 ***Runway Fashions (686-8502); 3&4 **Ben Freedman (674-0854); 3&4 **Canal Bargain (intermittent stock, 227-8040); 2 **Dollar Bills (867-0212); 2&3&4 **Fowad (222-7000); 3 **Hampshire Clothes (675-7806); 2 **L.S. Men's Clothing (575-0933); 3 **M&M Tailors (475-8312); 2

6: CLOTHING—MEN'S

Sym's (791-1199); **2&3 **The Townsman (755-6660); **2 *Antony** (477-0592); **2&3 *Atlantic Clothing** (227-8918); **2&3 *Baretta Fashions 1** (Queens, 275-0638); **3&4 *BFO Suits** (254-0059); **3 *Borislaw Clothier** (242-8134); **1&3 *Catania Clothing** (255-5510); **2&3&4 *Cedrick's** (Staten Island, 987-3577); **2&3 *De Silva Ltd.** (586-1316); **2 *Gucci on 7** (intermittent stock, 826-2600); **2&3 *Louis Barall & Son** (226-6195); **2 *Mern's** (371-9195); **2&3 *National Brands Outlet** (Queens, 459-0300); **3&4 *Park Kenny Clothes** (477-1948); **1&2&3 *Rothman** (777-7400); **2&3 *Samuel Zimbler** (255-6699); **2&3 *Schaer Bros.** (Brooklyn, 282-5653); **2&3&4 *Trend Quality Job Lot** (intermittent stock, 889-4686); **3 *Turnpike Clothing Outlet** (Queens, 776-2547); **3&4&5 +Lever & Greenberg** (226-1023); **2&3&4&5 Alexander's at World Trade Ctr** (466-1414); **3 Arthur Richards** (247-2300); **4&5 Gino Napoli** (73-8220); **3 L.B.C. Clothing** (226-1620); **4 Lesh Clothing** (255-6893); **4&5 Mansfield Clothes** (228-1410); **3 Modak Apparel** (267-5145); **2 Moe Ginsburg** (242-3482); **3 Parkway** (267-1296); **2&3&4 Phantom** (243-7910); **3 Royal Fashion** (475-3540); **3 The Individual Man** (924-2157).

men's suits—used

2&3 *Council Thrift Shop (757-6132); **2&3 *Girls Club Thrift Shop** (535-8570); **1&2&3 *Second Time Around** (685-2170); **3 *Super-Thrift Shop** (988-6399); **3 Call Again Thrift Shop** (831-0845); **1&2&3 Irvington House Thrift** (879-4555).

suits—custom-tailored

1&3 **Aurora Design Tailor (687-1259); **1&2 **Dorson Clothes** (924-7676); **3 **Felipito's Place** (947-2079); **3 **M&M Tailors** (475-8312); **1 **Simon Klinger** (255-2650); **1 **Stanley Goncher** (989-4900); **3 *+Rukico Tailors** (832-0725); **3 *Mohan's Custom Tailor** (697-0050); **1&3 *Mr. Tony** (255-8585).

men's sweaters

3&4 ***Frankel's Discount Clothing (intermittent stock, Brooklyn, 768-9788); **4 ***Job Lot Trdg.** (intermittent stock, 962-4142); **1&2&3 ***M.C. Corner** (265-4151); **3&4 **Ben Freedman** (674-0854); **2 **BFO Plus** (673-9026); **2&3 **Century 21** (227-9092); **2 **Dollar Bills** (867-0212); **2&3&4 **Fowad** (222-7000); **2 **Sym's** (791-1199); **2&3 **The Townsman** (755-6660); **3 *+Canal Jean Co.** (431-4765); **4 **Mr. Excitement** (intermittent stock, Queens, 847-3600); **2&3 *Colony** (924-8815); **2 *Gucci on 7** (intermittent stock, 826-2600); **2 *Mern's** (371-9195); **2&3 *National Brands Outlet** (Queens, 459-0300); **1&2&3 *Rothman** (777-7400); **3&4 *Superior Merchandising** (intermittent stock, 233-4615); **3 +Worker's Quarters** (Brooklyn, 331-4833); **2&3&4&5 Alexander's at World Trade Ctr** (466-1414); **4 Bally Weave** (Queens, 726-7219); **2&3 Lewis & Clark** (255-4686); **2 Moe Ginsburg** (242-3482).

men's swimsuits

3&4 **Ben Freedman (674-0854); **2&3 **Century 21** (227-9092); **2 **Dollar Bills** (867-0212); **2&3 **The Finals** (431-1414); **2&3 **The Townsman** (755-6660); **2 *Gucci on 7** (intermittent stock, 826-2600); **2 *Mern's** (371-9195); **2&3 *National Brands Outlet** (Queens, 459-0300); **2&3&4&5 Alexander's at World Trade Ctr** (466-1414).

ties

1&2&3 ***M.C. Corner (265-4151); **3&4 **Ben Freedman** (674-0854); **2 **BFO Plus** (673-9026); **2&3 **Century 21** (227-9092); **2 **Dollar Bills** (867-0212); **2 **Sym's** (791-1199); **2&3 **The Townsman** (755-6660);

6: CLOTHING—MEN'S

2&3 *De Silva Ltd.** (586-1316); **2** *Gucci on 7** (intermittent stock, 826-2600); **2** *Mern's** (371-9195); **2&3** *National Brands Outlet** (Queens, 459-0300); **1&2&3** *Rothman** (777-7400); **3&4** *Superior Merchandising** (intermittent stock, 233-4615); **2&3&4&5 Alexander's at World Trade Ctr** (466-1414); **2 Moe Ginsburg** (242-3482).

underwear

3&4 **Ben Freedman** (674-0854); **4&5** **Cayne's 1** (695-8451); **4&5** **Cayne's 4** (560-9212); **2** **Dollar Bills** (867-0212); **4&5** **Eleven West** (695-7537); **3** **Jacob Young & Son** (225-9232); **3&4** **M. Frankel ('Moe's')** (673-4590); **2&3&4** **Romano Trdg.** (581-4248); **2** **Sym's** (791-1199); **3** **Townie Merchandise** (929-8060); **3** **Triest Export** (246-1548.); **4** **United Salvage Alka Seltzer** (intermittent stock, 962-5567); **3** *Dave's Army/Navy** (989-6444); **3** *Ideal Hosiery** (226-4792); **4** *Klein's** (intermittent stock, 475-9804); **3** *M. Friedman Hosiery** (674-3292); **3** *Nathan Kurtz** (475-6550); **2&3** *National Brands Outlet** (Queens, 459-0300); **1&2&3** *Rothman** (777-7400); **3** *S&G Hosiery** (925-2044); **3** *William Rosengarten** (674-2310); **3** *Young's** (226-4333); **3** +Worker's Quarters** (Brooklyn, 331-4833); **3&4 Brown's Army-Navy** (Queens, 429-8508); **4 Cheap Charlie's** (intermittent stock, Brooklyn, 252-4932); **4&5 First Cost** (intermittent stock, 697-0244); **3 H. Tenzer** (473-6082); **3&4 I. Tuschman & Sons** (226-4318); **3 Odds & Ends Sundries** (Brooklyn, 854-1453); **3&4&5 Pennywise Sales** (226-7065); **3 Premier Textile** (966-1984); **4&5 Robbins Men's Wear** (691-2573).

bathrobes & p.j.'s

2&3 **Century 21** (227-9092); **2&3** **S. Sosinsky & Son** (475-9784); **2** *Gucci on 7** (intermittent stock, 826-2600); **3** *Nathan Kurtz** (475-6550); **2&3&4&5 Alexander's at World Trade Ctr** (466-1414); **4&5 Robbins Men's Wear** (691-2573).

antique & military clothing

4 **Cheap Jack's Clearance Store** (674-9718); **3** *+Canal Jean Co.** (431-4765); **4 So Cheap** (intermittent stock, 982-7918).

STORES-DIRECTORY

See unified clothing-stores-directory at the end of Chapter 7.

# 7:
CLOTHING—WOMEN'S
Expect 25-65% discounts.

There's certainly no shortage of discount-outlets for this. The problem is rather one of winnowing down the number of recommended shops to something manageable, so that only those with the steepest discounts are listed. Consequently, there's no place here for chains or stores like Labels For Less, which has only modest discounts; or Bolton's, whose claimed "bargains" usually don't even qualify above the normal run of department-store values; or Mr. Ephram's, which barely missed because of both selection and value; or so many other shops which might rate in Peoria, but not here in the super-competitive Big Apple. Such retailers occasionally have impressive "sale" items; but then so too do department-stores, and so do most stores everywhere.

Whether you're looking to pay $3,000 for a $5,000 couturier dress, $350 for a $700 designer gown, or $6 for a $20 skirt—or anything in between—you're bound to find it here, any day of the year. And if you're a really careful shopper, you'll probably be stunned when you find that current $300 French-made designer-name fully lined wool suit selling without the label for only $50. But it's important that you recognize in advance which stores specialize in which price-and-quality range, so that you'll quickly find what you want, rather than what you don't. The numerical merchandise-grades that are explained below, preceding the store-names, serve this purpose. If you're looking for a specific item and make, you should phone the shops listed as selling garments of that specific type and merchandise-grade, to find out who carries precisely what you're seeking. Some of the shops will quote prices over the phone.

One thing that you won't find in the list below is furs. Fake furs, yes, in quality-ranges from top to bottom; but no tortured and dead animals. Most fur-trapping employs the leg-hold trap, which slams shut on the animal's leg, and breaks his bone, while the creature bleeds to death over an average 15-hour period, in indescribable agony. (Some bite off the broken leg, only to stumble off and bleed to death in the bush, lost to the trapper, except for the useless foot-and-leg segment left behind.) In box-traps set for beaver, muskrat and other water-species, the animal suffers about 15 minutes of terror and struggle before it drowns. Seals are killed by clubbing, followed often by skinning alive—all under the watchful eye, and amidst the screams of, mother-seals. But the worst of it all is that for every target fur-bearing animal caught and killed, an average of 3 non-target creatures are trapped and die—"trash" animals, in trapper-parlance: eagles, cats, dogs, small bears, turtles, etc. The mindless, promo-hyped vain "glamour" of each such full-length coat is lined with the following amounts of real-world horror:

7: CLOTHING—WOMEN'S

	Target Animals	Trash Animals	Hours of Agony
Coyote	16	48	960
Lynx	18	54	1080
Mink	60	180	3600
Opossum	45	135	2700
Otter	20	60	1200
Red Fox	42	126	2520
Raccoon	40	120	2400
Sable	50	150	3000
Muscrat	50	150	1500
Beaver	15	45	225

Some people try to justify the wearing of furs from ranch-raised animals, and the entire institution of mink-ranches etc., by saying that these animals were "raised for their furs." Well, "slaves were raised for their labor." (That used to be the justification, you know.) Some rationale! It's interesting how individuals who have deficiencies of conscience and compassion identify automatically with the oppressor, as if victims don't count. To buy a fur coat is to be a financier for a vast animal-Gulag of pain and suffering. It would be fairer if the furriers were trapped and skinned; the people who finance the industry by wearing furs should be mugged and their coats stolen, as the lives were stolen from the animals. Some people will sink to any level for stupid vanity or greed. Would they wear cat- or dog-skins?

Fur-industry ads condition the mindless to admire and envy individuals who are clad in furs. People who can be sold on that idea will buy anything. There must be a lot of fools: The fur-industry is booming like never before.

Sometimes I wonder who are the real "beasts."

The wearing of sheepskin, however, belongs in a different class, because sheep are killed for their meat. But one doesn't have to be a vegetarian to realize that raising and killing animals merely to wear their skins for vanity is barbaric cruelty. The arguments about vegetarianism are another question entirely. Must one murder in order to live? Maybe not. Must one murder in order to flaunt? Decidedly no. No!

RECOMMENDED PRODUCTS:
See above.

RECOMMENDED STORES:

Numbers which precede store-names show quality and fashionableness of clothing sold:

"1" is couturier-wear, or supreme shoes.
"2" refers to dressy designer clothing.
"3" is good quality but often casual.
"4" represents medium quality clothing.
"5" indicates cheap quality merchandise.

ladies' belts

7: CLOTHING—WOMEN'S 43

4&5 ***Carter Leather (475-3537); 3&4 ***Frankel's Discount Clothing (intermittent stock, Brooklyn, 768-9788); 4&5 **Alee Discount (intermittent stock, 619-2980); 3 *⁺Canal Jean Co. (431-4765); 2 *Gucci on 7 (intermittent stock, 826-2600); 2&3&4&5 Alexander's at World Trade Ctr (466-1414).

bridals

⁺Holiday Bridal (564-0316); Charming Bridal (594-7066).

chinese jackets, robes

3&4 **Canal St. Market (226-9142); 3&4 **China Mall (226-4720); 3&4 *G.H. Tailor (732-0368); 2&3&4&5 Alexander's at World Trade Ctr (466-1414); 3&4 Bok Lei Bo (233-0935); 4 Leung Trdg. (431-4474); 3&4 Pearl River (966-1010); 3 Wah Fun (227-1672).

ladies' coats (ALSO SEE CH. 6)

2 ***Abe J. Geller (736-8077); 2 ***Azriel Altman (889-0782); 3&4 ***Frankel's Discount Clothing (intermittent stock, Brooklyn, 768-9788); 4&5 ***Fredwin (661-2766); 4&5 ***Scott's Dress (982-2131); 4&5 ***Stuart's (928-9691); 4&5 ***Winfred (874-8465); 3&4 ***Zoom (964-4111); 4&5 **Alee Discount (intermittent stock, 619-2980); 1&3 **Aurora Design Tailor (687-1259); 2&3 **Century 21 (227-9092); 3&4 **Cheap Charlie's (Queens, 353-2603); 3&4 **D&E Outlet (Queens, 392-5677); 3 **Designers Choice (406-1090); 4 **Earl's (intermittent stock, Queens, 894-6406); 4&5 **Eighth Av. Bargain King (594-4049); 2&3&4 **Fowad (222-7000); 2 **Lea's (677-2043); 1&2&3 **Loehmann's (Bronx, 295-4100); 3 **M&M Tailors (475-8312); 3 *⁺Main St. Fashion World (Queens, 544-3254); 2 *A. Altman (982-7722); 2&3 *Aaron's Dress (Brooklyn, 768-5400); 3&4&5 *Bee Hive (354-2857); 3 *Benny's (Brooklyn, 438-9437); 3 *Benny's Loft (Brooklyn, 851-2086); 3 *Designers Below (619-2147); 3&4 *Discount Fashions (Brooklyn, 643-0490); 3 *FitzPatrick's for Coats (349-2424); 2 *Forman's Basement (228-2500); 4&5 *Goodfriend's (686-6910); 2 *Gucci on 7 (intermittent stock, 826-2600); 2&3 *Harris's Women's Apparel (989-9765); 3 *Hong Kong Import (753-5340); 4 *I. Margulis (Queens, 263-5052); 3&4 *J. Chuckles (867-3771); *J.B.Z. Unlimited (473-8550); 2&3 *Judy Better Dresses (719-2999); 2 *Max's Better Dress (755-2434); 3&4 *Mintzer Mercantile (intermittent stock, 226-5413); 3 *New Store (741-1077); 3&4&5 *One Block Over (564-7035); 3 *Spitzer's Corner Store (477-4088); 3&4 *Strawberry (986-7030); 2 *Sue's Discount Dress (752-5574); *Sunshine (697-5192); 2&3 ⁺Fashion Delight (533-4840); 3 ⁺Fun Fox Ltd. (944-6520); . 2&3&4&5 Alexander's at World Trade Ctr (466-1414); 4&5 Blooming (594-2429); Bonnie J (Queens, 261-7538); 3 Cozy Boutique (535-3128); 2&3 Designer Liquidators (751-4353); 2 Empire (684-8359); 4&5 First Cost (intermittent stock, 697-0244); 3&4&5 Gabay's Outlet (intermittent stock, 254-3180); 3 Jeff's Boutique (533-8222); 2 Lupu's (Brooklyn, 377-3793); 4&5 Lynn's (929-9030); 3 Merri-Jean's Factory Outlet (Bronx, 654-1900); 1&2 Ms. Miss or Mrs. (736-0557); 3&4 Normie's (Brooklyn, 338-1229); 3 Rainbarrel Factory Outlet (964-0210); 2 Ruth Brooks (744-5412); 2 S.K. Friedman (777-3593); 4&5 Smart Size (Queens, 932-3185); 4 S&S Fashion (362-1674); 2&3 S&W Fashions (924-6656).

ladies' coats—fake fur

5 **A&M Textile (982-1906); 3 **Chateau Creations (244-6722); 1&2&3 **Loehmann's (Bronx, 295-4100); 2&3&4&5 Alexander's at World Trade Ctr (466-1414); 2 S.K. Friedman (777-3593); 2&3 S&W Fashions

7: CLOTHING—WOMEN'S

(924-6656).

hand-knit sweaters, gloves, etc.

2 **Manos Del Uruguay (564-6115); 3 **Pacific Traders (475-5838).

dresses, skirts, slacks

2 ***Abe J. Geller (736-8077); 2 ***Azriel Altman (889-0782); 4&5 ***Fredwin (661-2766); 4 ***Parkay Designs (683-0058); 4&5 ***Scott's Dress (982-2131); 4&5 ***Stuart's (928-9691); 4&5 ***Winfred (874-8465); 3&4 ***Zoom (964-4111); 4&5 **Alee Discount (intermittent stock, 619-2980); 3 **Boni Knitwear (226-3305); 4&5 **Casa International (226-3180); 4&5 **Cayne's 1 (695-8451); 2&3 **Century 21 (227-9092); 3&4 **Cheap Charlie's (Queens, 353-2603); 3&4 **Crown Mercandise (966-7583); 3&4 **D&E Outlet (Queens, 392-5677); 3 **Designers Choice (406-1090); 5 **D&S Dresses (473-3363); 4 **Earl's (intermittent stock, Queens, 894-6406); 4&5 **Eighth Av. Bargain King (594-4049); 4&5 **Eleven West (695-7537); 2 **European Liquidators (879-9140); 3&4&5 **Fleetwood Market (intermittent stock, 766-9766); 2&3&4 **Fowad (222-7000); 4 **FRSG Quality Knitwear (475-8585); 4&5 **Helen Walters Sportswear (Brooklyn, 743-9167); 4 **Jack's Bargain Stores (924-5322); 2 **Lea's (677-2043); 1&2&3 **Loehmann's (Bronx, 295-4100); 4&5 **M.C.W. Apparel (966-0280); 3 **Pacific Traders (475-5838); 4 **What's New Discount (532-9226); 4&5 **Worthmore (594-8998); 3 *⁺Main St. Fashion World (Queens, 544-3254); 2 *A. Altman (982-7722); 2&3 *Aaron's Dress (Brooklyn, 768-5400); 4&5 *American Boutique (594-3428); 3&4&5 *Bee Hive (354-2857); 3 *Benny's (Brooklyn, 438-9437); 3&4 *Brands For Less (Brooklyn, 266-6440); 5 *Carol-Ann Shoppes (243-8727); 2&3 *Colony (924-8815); 4 *C&S Variety (Brooklyn, 259-5290); 3 *Designers Below (619-2147); 3&4 *Discount Fashions (Brooklyn, 643-0490); *E.N.S. Shop (663-1029); 2 *Forman's Basement (228-2500); 2&3 *French Connection (737-1900); 4&5 *Goodfriend's (686-6910); 2 *Gucci on 7 (intermittent stock, 826-2600); 2&3 *Harris's Women's Apparel (989-9765); 3 *Hong Kong Import (753-5340); 4 *I. Margulis (Queens, 263-5052); 3&4 *J. Chuckles (867-3771); 1&2 *Jay's Advance (239-1166); *J.B.Z. Unlimited (473-8550); 2&3 *Judy Better Dresses (719-2999); 4 *Kazootie (964-4218); 3&4 *Lebanon Fashions (686-4636); 4&5 *Leon (intermittent stock, 254-1880); 2 *Max's Better Dress (755-2434); 2 *Mern's (371-9195); 4 *Michelle Imports (889-3620); 3&4 *Mintzer Mercantile (intermittent stock, 226-5413); 3 *Nam Nam Boutique (533-9642); 3 *New Store (741-1077); 3&4&5 *One Buck Over (564-7035); 4 *Park Av. Job Lot (intermittent stock, 673-7536); 3&4 *Que Linda (925-6565); 4 *Sam's Knitwear (966-0390); 3&4 *Savannah Warehouse (989-5096); 4&5 *Sol's (226-0355); 3 *Spitzer's Corner Store (477-4088); 3&4 *Strawberry (986-7030); 2 *Sue's Discount Dress (752-5574); *Sunshine (697-5192); 2 *The Loft (736-3358); 4 *Wearhouse (254-4550); 2&3 ⁺Al's Sample Nook (Queens, 591-6035); 2&3 ⁺Fashion Delight (533-4840); 3 ⁺Fun Fox Ltd. (944-6520); 4 ⁺Prima Impex (679-9066); .. 2&3 A&A Distributors (Bronx, 829-9515); 2&3&4&5 Alexander's at World Trade Ctr (466-1414); 4&5 Ariel Fashions (947-0107); 4&5 Blooming (594-2429); Bonnie J (Queens, 261-7538); 4 Broadway Fashion (431-4134); 3&4 Budget Boutique (221-1982); 3 Cozy Boutique (535-3128); 2&3 Designer Liquidators (751-4353); 4 Dress Shoppe (260-4963); 2 Empire (684-8359); 5 Factory Outlet (Brooklyn, 624-0321); 4 Fashions Aloft (724-9815); 4&5 Galleria International (431-6320); 4&5 Goldstone Sportswear (966-6077); 4 India Malaysia Imports (869-9995); 3 Jeff's Boutique (533-8222); 4&5 Jerri's Ltd. (Brooklyn, 871-0955); 3 Kaymore (475-3854); 3&4 Lord's Ex-Imp. (398-0346); 2

7: CLOTHING—WOMEN'S

Lupu's (Brooklyn, 377-3793); **4&5 Lynn's** (929-9030); **3 Merri-Jean's Factory Outlet** (Bronx, 654-1900); **4&5 M&J Sportswear** (925-3145); **3&4 Most's Dept. Store** (Queens, 225-3455); **5 M&R Fashions** (226-3535); **1&2 Ms. Miss or Mrs.** (736-0557); **4 Pier 333** (752-3174); **3&4 Round House Fashions** (966-5951); **2 Ruth Brooks** (744-5412); **4&5 Seamar** (947-0443); **4 Shelgo Factory Outlet** (675-6455); **2 S.K. Friedman** (777-3593); **4&5 Smart Size** (Queens, 932-3185); **2 Sophisticate Seconds** (Queens, 672-0005); **4 S&S Fashion** (362-1674); **2&3 S&W Fashions** (924-6656); **3 The Grab Bag** (666-4230); **4&5 Three Star Tailoring** (925-0495).

ladies' gloves

3&4 ***Frankel's Discount Clothing (intermittent stock, Brooklyn, 768-9788); **3&4 ***Zoom** (964-4111); **2&3 **Century 21** (227-9092); **4&5 **Eighth Av. Bargain King** (594-4049); **2&3 *Colony** (924-8815); **2 *Gucci on 7** (intermittent stock, 826-2600); **3&4 *J. Chuckles** (867-3771); **3&4 *Strawberry** (986-7030); **2&3&4&5 Alexander's at World Trade Ctr** (466-1414); **4&5 First Cost** (intermittent stock, 697-0244); **2&3 S&W Fashions** (924-6656).

hosiery

(examples: body-suits, hose, panty-hose, stockings)

3&4 ***Zoom (964-4111); **4&5 **Alee Discount** (intermittent stock, 619-2980); **3 **Buy Well Hosiery** (666-5757); **4&5 **Cayne's 1** (695-8451); **2&3 **Century 21** (227-9092); **4&5 **Eighth Av. Bargain King** (594-4049); **4&5 **Eleven West** (695-7537); **3 **Towne Merchandise** (929-8060); **3 **Ultra Smart Hosiery** (686-1564); **4&5 **Worthmore** (594-8998); **3 *Ideal Hosiery** (226-4792); **3&4 *J. Chuckles** (867-3771); **3 *M. Friedman Hosiery** (674-3292); **3 *M. Steuer Hosiery** (563-0052); **3&4 *Mintzer Mercantile** (intermittent stock, 226-5413); **3 *Nathan Kurtz** (475-6550); **3 *S&G Hosiery** (925-2044); **3&4 *Strawberry** (986-7030); ***Sunshine** (697-5192); **3 *Wingdale Hosiery** (684-4291); **2&3&4&5 Alexander's at World Trade Ctr** (466-1414); **4&5 Dee & Dee Stores** (243-5620); **4&5 First Cost** (intermittent stock, 697-0244); **3&4 I. Tuschman & Sons** (226-4318); **3 Lismore Hosiery** (674-3440); **4&5 Lynn's** (929-9030); **3 Madeline's Hosiery** (Queens, 721-4338); **3 Ronald's Hosiery** (584-3121); **3 Value Hosiery** (243-7243).

jeans—designer

4&5 **Casa International (226-3180); **4&5 **Cayne's 1** (695-8451); **3&4 **China Mall** (226-4720); **3&4 **Crown Mercandise** (966-7583); **4&5 **Eighth Av. Bargain King** (594-4049); **3 **Jeans & Things** (964-9428); **3 **Jeans 'N Things** (677-7158); **3 **Parezio II** (233-3942); **4&5 **Worthmore** (594-8998); **3 *Alma Llanera** (966-3910); **3&4&5 *Bee Hive** (354-2857); **3&4 *Brands For Less** (Brooklyn, 266-6440); **3&4 *Lebanon Fashions** (686-4636); **3&4 *Mintzer Mercantile** (intermittent stock, 226-5413); **3&4&5 *One Block Over** (564-7035); **3&4 *Que Linda** (925-6565); **3&4 *Saab International** (889-6591); **3 *Slep** (677-5328); **4&5 Ariel Fashions** (947-0107); **3&4 Bayard International** (594-6658); **3 Bridge Merchandise** (674-6320); **4 Broadway Fashion** (431-4134); **3&4 Lord's Ex-Imp.** (398-0346); **4 Manufacturer's Outlet** (Brooklyn, 336-5123); **3 Premier Textile** (966-1984); **2 Traffico** (477-2722); **3&4 V.I.M. Stores** (Brooklyn, 693-4600).

lingerie

(examples: body-suits, braziers, corsets, girdles, slips)

4&5 **Alee Discount (intermittent stock, 619-2980); **3 **Buy Well Hosiery**

7: CLOTHING—WOMEN'S

(666-5757); **4&5 **Cayne's 1** (695-8451); **2&3 **Century 21** (227-9092); **3&4 **Crown Mercandise** (966-7583); **4 **Earl's** (intermittent stock, Queens, 894-6406); **4&5 **Eighth Av. Bargain King** (594-4049); **4&5 **Eleven West** (695-7537); **3&4&5 **Fleetwood Market** (intermittent stock, 766-9766); **2&3 **Goldman & Cohen** (966-0737); **4&5 **Worthmore** (594-8998); **4** ***⁺Ever Ready Lingerie** (925-5125); **2 *A. Rosenthal** (473-5428); **4&5 *Goodfriend's** (686-6910); **3&4 *J. Chuckles** (867-3771); **3 *M. Steuer Hosiery** (563-0052); **3&4 *Mintzer Mercantile** (intermittent stock, 226-5413); **3&4 *Strawberry** (986-7030); **3 *Wyse Wear** (226-2658); **2&3&4&5 Alexander's at World Trade Ctr** (466-1414); **4&5 Dee & Dee Stores** (243-5620); **2&3 Designer Liquidators** (751-4353); **4&5 Lynn's** (929-9030); **3&4 Most's Dept. Store** (Queens, 225-3455); **5 M&R Fashions** (226-3535); **3 Value Hosiery** (243-7243).

loungewear

(examples: bathrobes, house-dresses, night gowns, pajamas)

2&3 **Century 21 (227-9092); **3&4 **Crown Mercandise** (966-7583); **4 **Earl's** (intermittent stock, Queens, 894-6406); **4&5 **Eighth Av. Bargain King** (594-4049); **2&3 **Goldman & Cohen** (966-0737); **4&5 *Goodfriend's** (686-6910); **3&4 *J. Chuckles** (867-3771); **3&4 *Mintzer Mercantile** (intermittent stock, 226-5413); **3 *Nathan Kurtz** (475-6550); **3&4 *Strawberry** (986-7030); **2&3&4&5 Alexander's at World Trade Ctr** (466-1414); **4&5 Lynn's** (929-9030); **3 Odds & Ends Sundries** (Brooklyn, 854-1453); **3&4&5 Pennywise Sales** (226-7065); **4&5 Smart Size** (Queens, 932-3185).

maternity-wear

4 *⁺H.E.R. Maternity (594-8580); **3 *Discount Maternity** (Brooklyn, 253-0578); **2&3 Expectations** (997-1570).

millinery, hats

4&5 ***Bag Man (560 8952); **4 **Cho's Variety** (349-7544); **2 *Gucci on 7** (intermittent stock, 826-2600); **3&4 *J. Chuckles** (867-3771); **3&4 *Strawberry** (986-7030); **2&3&4&5 Alexander's at World Trade Ctr** (466-1414); **3 Arden** (391-6968); **3&4 Bernard Krieger** (226-1929); **4&5 Lynn's** (929-9030); **4 Wai Lee** (840-2720); **3&4 William Tannenbaum** (840-3796).

ladies' shoes & boots (&: CH. 6)

3&4 ***Frankel's Discount Clothing (intermittent stock, Brooklyn, 768-9788); **4&5 **Alee Discount** (intermittent stock, 619-2980); **2&3 **Anbar Shoes** (227-0253); **2&3 **Century 21** (227-9092); **4&5 **Eighth Av. Bargain King** (594-4049); **4 **Lucky Rose Shoes** (phoneless); **3&4&5 **Manufacturer's Shoe Outlet** (226-6266); **3 **Olaf Daughters Outlet**; **3&4 **Shoe Steal** (964-4017); **4 **The Shoe Rack** (924-6859); **3&4 **Yoav Shoes** (391-1275); **2&3 *⁺Eti-Quette** (398-1460); **2&3 *⁺F.M. Handbags & Shoes** (673-3230); **2 *Gucci on 7** (intermittent stock, 826-2600); **2 *Helen Perl Shoes** (752-2543); **3&4 *J. Chuckles** (867-3771); **4 *Lynn's Shoes** (674-2840); **2&3&4 *Pat's Shoes** (intermittent stock, Brooklyn, 647-0664); **3&4 *Pina Colada** (475-9372); **3&4 *Que Linda** (925-6565); **4&5 *Shoe Giant Outlets** (Queens, 728-9284); **2&3&4 *S&T Women's Shoes** (861-9470); **3&4 *Strawberry** (986-7030); **3 *Wendy's Footwear** (233-4596); **3&4 *Zoom** (964-4111); **4 ⁺Don Ricardo Shoes** (866-9492); **4 ⁺The Sophisticate** (865-8622); **2&3&4&5 Alexander's at World Trade Ctr** (466-1414); **3 Feet** (245-0436); **4&5 First Cost** (intermittent stock, 697-0244); **4&5 Garo Leather** (Queens, 793-3743); **3 Genao's Shoes** (673-9811); **4 High Fashion** (674-8273); **2**

7: CLOTHING—WOMEN'S

Jerri's Shoes (866-2820); **4 Joli Madame Boutique** (477-2471); **2 Lace Up** (475-8040); **1 Linea Garbo** (687-4139); **3&4 Metro Shoe Mart** (254-5188); **3&4 Sabra Shoes** (349-3494); **4 Shoe Arcade** (Brooklyn, 436-1106); **4 Shoe Mart** (425-5594); **3&4 Shoe Town** (Queens, 830-9820); **4&5 Step Inn Shoes** (226-5844); **3&4&5 Step 'N Style Shoes** (269-0149); **3&4 The Foot Lot** (223-0235).

ladies' suits & blazers

2 ***Abe J. Geller (736-8077); **2 ***Azriel Altman** (889-0782); **4&5 ***Fredwin** (661-2766); **4&5 ***Scott's Dress** (982-2131); **4&5 ***Stuart's** (928-9691); **4&5 ***Winfred** (874-8465); **3&4 ***Zoom** (964-4111); **4&5 **Alee Discount** (intermittent stock, 619-2980); **3 **Boni Knitwear** (226-3305); **2&3 **Century 21** (227-9092); **3&4 **Cheap Charlie's** (Queens, 353-2603); **3&4 **D&E Outlet** (Queens, 392-5677); **3 **Designers Choice** (406-1090); **4&5 **Eighth Av. Bargain King** (594-4049); **2&3&4 **Fowad** (222-7000); **4 **FRSG Quality Knitwear** (475-8585); **2 **Lea's** (677-2043); **1&2&3 **Loehmann's** (Bronx, 295-4100); **4&5 **M.C.W. Apparel** (966-0280); **4 **What's New Discount** (532-9226); **3 *⁺Main St. Fashion World** (Queens, 544-3254); **2 *A. Altman** (982-7722); **2&3 *Aaron's Dress** (Brooklyn, 768-5400); **4&5 *American Boutique** (594-3428); **3 *Benny's** (Brooklyn, 438-9437); **3 *Designers Below** (619-2147); **3&4 *Discount Fashions** (Brooklyn, 643-0490); ***E.N.S. Shop** (663-1029); **2 *Forman's Basement** (228-2500); **2&3 *French Connection** (737-1900); **2 *Gucci on 7** (intermittent stock, 826-2600); **2&3 *Harris's Women's Apparel** (989-9765); **4 *I. Margulis** (Queens, 263-5052); **3&4 *J. Chuckles** (867-3771); **1&2 *Jay's Advance** (239-1166); **2&3 *Judy Better Dresses** (719-2999); **2 *Max's Better Dress** (755-2434); **2 *Mern's** (371-9195); **3 *New Store** (741-1077); **3&4 *Park Kenny Clothes** (477-1948); **4 *Sam's Knitwear** (966-0390); **3&4 *Savannah Warehouse** (989-5096); **4&5 *Sol's** (226-0355); **3&4 *Strawberry** (986-7030); **2 *Sue's Discount Dress** (752-5574); ***Sunshine** (697-5192); **2 *The Loft** (736-3358); **2&3 ⁺Fashion Delight** (533-4840); **2&3 A&A Distributors** (Bronx, 829-9515); **2&3&4&5 Alexander's at World Trade Ctr** (466-1414); **4&5 Blooming** (594-2429); **Bonnie J** (Queens, 261-7538); **2&3 Designer Liquidators** (751-4353); **2 Empire** (684-8359); **3 Jeff's Boutique** (533-8222); **3 Kaymore** (475-3854); **2 Lupu's** (Brooklyn, 377-3793); **2 Merri-Jean's Factory Outlet** (Bronx, 654-1900); **1&2 Ms. Miss or Mrs.** (736-0557); **3&4 Normie's** (Brooklyn, 338-1229); **2 Ruth Brooks** (744-5412); **2 S.K. Friedman** (777-3593); **4&5 Smart Size** (Queens, 932-3185); **2 Sophisticate Seconds** (Queens, 672-0005); **2&3 S&W Fashions** (924-6656); **3 The Grab Bag** (666-4230).

ladies' suits—custom-tailored

1&3 **Aurora Design Tailor (687-1259); **3 **Felipito's Place** (947-2079); **1 **Simon Klinger** (255-2650); **3 *⁺Rukico Tailors** (832-0725); **1&3 *Mr. Tony** (255-8585); **3&4&5 Gabay's Outlet** (intermittent stock, 254-3180).

ladies' swimsuits

3&4 ***Zoom (964-4111); **2&3 **Century 21** (227-9092); **3&4 **Crown Mercandise** (966-7583); **4&5 **Eighth Av. Bargain King** (594-4049); **2&3 **The Finals** (431-1414); **2 *Gucci on 7** (intermittent stock, 826-2600); **3&4 *J. Chuckles** (867-3771); **3&4 *Mintzer Mercantile** (intermittent stock, 226-5413); **3&4 *Strawberry** (986-7030); **2&3&4&5 Alexander's at World Trade Ctr** (466-1414); **4&5 Lynn's** (929-9030); **4 Rosalie Fashions** (431-6345); **3&4 Round House Fashions** (966-5951); **2&3 S&W Fashions** (924-6656).

tops, sweaters, blouses

7: CLOTHING—WOMEN'S

2 ***Azriel Altman (889-0782); 4&5 ***Fredwin (661-2766); 4 ***Parkay Designs (683-0058); 4&5 ***Scott's Dress (982-2131); 4&5 ***Stuart's (928-9691); 4&5 ***Winfred (874-8465); 4&5 ***Zoom (964-4111); 4&5 **Alee Discount (intermittent stock, 619-2980); 3 **Boni Knitwear (226-3305); 4&5 **Casa International (226-3180); 4&5 **Cayne's 1 (695-8451); 2&3 **Century 21 (227-9092); 3&4 **Cheap Charlie's (Queens, 353-2603); 3&4 **Crown Mercandise (966-7583); 3&4 **D&E Outlet (Queens, 392-5677); 5 **D&S Dresses (473-3363); 4 **Earl's (intermittent stock, Queens, 894-6406); 4&5 **Eighth Av. Bargain King (594-4049); 4&5 **Eleven West (695-7537); 2 **European Liquidators (879-9140); 3&4&5 **Fleetwood Market (intermittent stock, 766-9766); 2&3&4 **Fowad (222-7000); 4 **FRSG Quality Knitwear (475-8585); 4&5 **Helen Walters Sportswear (Brooklyn, 743-9167); 4 **Jack's Bargain Stores (924-5322); 1&2&3 **Loehmann's (Bronx, 295-4100); 4&5 **M.C.W. Apparel (966-0280); 3 **Pacific Traders (475-5838); 4 **What's New Discount (532-9226); 4&5 **Worthmore (594-8998); 3 *+Main St. Fashion World (Queens, 544-3254); 2&3 *Aaron's Dress (Brooklyn, 768-5400); 4&5 *American Boutique (594-3428); 3&4&5 *Bee Hive (354-2857); 3 *Benny's (Brooklyn, 438-9437); 3&4 *Brands For Less (Brooklyn, 266-6440); 5 *Carol-Ann Shoppes (243-8727); 2&3 *Colony (924-8815); 4 *C&S Variety (Brooklyn, 259-5290); 3 *Designers Below (619-2147); 3&4 *Discount Fashions (Brooklyn, 643-0490); *E.N.S. Shop (663-1029); 2 *Forman's Basement (228-2500); 2&3 *French Connection (737-1900); 3&4 *G.H. Tailor (732-0368); 4&5 *Goodfriend's (686-6910); 2 *Gucci on 7 (intermittent stock, 826-2600); 2&3 *Harris's Women's Apparel (989-9765); 3 *Hong Kong Import (753-5340); 3&4 *J. Chuckles (867-3771); 1&2 *Jay's Advance (239-1166); *J.B.Z. Unlimited (473-8550); 2&3 *Judy Better Dresses (719-2999); 4 *Kazootie (964-4218); 3&4 *Lebanon Fashions (686-4636); 4&5 *Leon (intermittent stock, 254-1880); 2 *Max's Better Dress (755-2434); 4 *Michelle Imports (889-3620); 3&4 *Mintzer Mercantile (intermittent stock, 226-5413); 3 *Nam Nam Boutique (533-9642); 3 *New Store (741-1077); 3&4&5 *One Block Over (564-7035); 4 *Park Av. Job Lot (intermittent stock, 673-7536); 4 *Sam's Knitwear (966-0390); 3&4 *Savannah Warehouse (989-5096); 4&5 *Sol's (226-0355); 3 *Spitzer's Corner Store (477-4088); 3&4 *Strawberry (986-7030); 2 *Sue's Discount Dress (752-5574); *Sunshine (697-5192); 4 *Wearhouse (254-4550); 3 +Fun Fox Ltd. (944-6520); 4 +Prima Impex (679-9066); . 2&3 A&A Distributors (Bronx, 829-9515); 2&3&4&5 Alexander's at World Trade Ctr (466-1414); 4&5 Ariel Fashions (947-0107); 4 Bally Weave (Queens, 726-7219); 4&5 Blooming (594-2429); Bonnie J (Queens, 261-7538); 3 Bridge Merchandise (674-6320); 4 Broadway Fashion (431-4134); 3&4 Budget Boutique (221-1982); 3 Cozy Boutique (535-3128); 2&3 Designer Liquidators (751-4353); 4 Dress Shoppe (260-4963); 2 Empire (684-8359); 5 Factory Outlet (Brooklyn, 624-0321); 4 Fashions Aloft (724-9815); 4&5 Galleria International (431-6320); 4&5 Goldstone Sportswear (966-6077); 4 India Malaysia Imports (869-9995); 4&5 Jerri's Ltd. (Brooklyn, 871-0955); 3&4 Lord's Ex-Imp. (398-0346); 2 Lupu's (Brooklyn, 377-3793); 4&5 Lynn's (929-9030); 4 Manufacturer's Outlet (Brooklyn, 336-5123); 3 Merri-Jean's Factory Outlet (Bronx, 654-1900); 4&5 M&J Sportswear (925-3145); 3&4 Most's Dept. Store (Queens, 225-3455); 5 M&R Fashions (226-3535); 1&2 Ms. Miss or Mrs. (736-0557); 3 Paula Knitwear (925-2520); 4 Pier 333 (752-3174); 4 Rosalie Fashions (431-6345); 3&4 Round House Fashions (966-5951); 2 Ruth Brooks (744-5412); 4&5 Seamar (947-0443); 4 Shelgo Factory Outlet (675-6455); 2 S.K. Friedman (777-3593); 4&5 Smart Size (Queens, 932-3185); 4 So Cheap (intermittent stock, 982-7918); 4 S&S Fashion (362-1674); 2&3 S&W Fashions (924-6656);

7: CLOTHING—WOMEN'S

3 The Grab Bag (666-4230); **4&5 Three Star Tailoring** (925-0495); **2 Traffico** (477-2722).

uniforms for nurses

Mfr.'s Uniform Outlet (Queens, 335-3900); **3 Premier Textile** (966-1984).

used clothing for women

2&3 *Council Thrift Shop (757-6132); **2&3 *Girls Club Thrift Shop** (535-8570); **1&2&3 *Second Time Around** (685-2170); **3 *Super-Thrift Shop** (988-6399); **3 Call Again Thrift Shop** (831-0845); **1&2&3 Irvington House Thrift** (879-4555).

slightly used designer-wear

2&3 A Second Spring (787-7426); **1&2 Encore Resale Dress** (879-2850); **1&2 Michael's Resale Dress** (737-7273); **2&3 Reprise** (260-0896); **2 Sophisticate Seconds** (Queens, 672-0005).

antique clothing & cheap-chic

4 **Cheap Jack's Clearance Store (674-9718); ***+Buen Dia** (673-1910); **3 *+Canal Jean Co.** (431-4765); **3&4 *Pina Colada** (475-9372); **2&3 A Second Spring** (787-7426); **4 So Cheap** (intermittent stock, 982-7918).

STORES-DIRECTORY

Phone a store before you go out of your way to visit it. Especially do this during July and August, when most establishments reduce or eliminate weekend-hours.

In the listings below, "*" means especially recommended, "+" means that the store offers a bonus discount to BF readers, "ch." and "c.c." mean respectively checks and credit cards, and "exch." and "rfd." mean respectively exchange and refund. Nearest subway-stops are shown. For example, "B-D-F to 47" means to take the B, D, or F train to 47th Street. Store-hours are also indicated, with days of the week abbreviated, like "M-S 8-6."

* **A. Altman**, 182 Orchard St. (Stanton-Houston), 982-7722, F to 2nd Av., 7 days 9-5, ch., c.c., no exch. or rfd. French fashion emphasis. But better is the affiliated store Azriel Altman. (Bigger and better selection there.) Sells: **Ladies' Coats, Dresses, Skirts, Slacks, Ladies' Suits & Blazers.**

* **A. Rosenthal**, 92 Orchard St. (Broome-Delancey), 473-5428, F-J-M to Delancey & Essex, Sun-Th 9-6, F 9-3, c.c. $20+, no ch., exch., no rfd. (But no returns if tried on.) 25-33% off current styles, top designers and brands. Beats the 20% average discount on such items on Orchard St. Sells: **Lingerie.**

A Second Spring, 353 Amsterdam Av. (77), 787-7426, 1 to 79, T-S 12-7, Sun 1-6, ch., c.c., no exch. or rfd. Sells: **Slightly Used Designer-Wear, Antique Clothing & Cheap-Chic.**

A&A Distributors, Bronx, 1978 Williamsbridge Rd. (Neil Av.), 829-9515, 5 to Pelham Pkwy., TW 10-6, ThFS 10-7, Sun 12-4, c.c., no ch., exch., no rfd. Sells: **Dresses, Skirts, Slacks, Ladies' Suits & Blazers, Tops, Sweaters, Blouses.**

* **Aaron's Dress**, Brooklyn, 627 5th Av. (17th St.), 768-5400, N-RR to Prospect Av., MTWFS 9:30-6, Th 9:30-9, ch., c.c., 7-day exch. or rfd. Sells: **Ladies' Coats, Dresses, Skirts, Slacks, Ladies' Suits & Blazers, Tops, Sweaters, Blouses.**

*** **Abe J. Geller**, 491 7th Av. (36-7), 5th floor, 736-8077 & 560-9652, A-AA-CC-E to 34, M-F 10-5, S 10-3, ch., no c.c., no exch. or rfd. Will phone-quote. Will special-order. Takes mail-orders. Very cooperative. City's lowest prices on top designers. Even lower than Azriel Altman, though Altman has better-value items to begin with, + sensational sales, so is usually preferable. Sells: **Ladies' Coats, Dresses, Skirts, Slacks, Ladies' Suits & Blazers.**

** **Adamici Outlet**, 88 7th Av. (15-6), 924-6087, 1-2-3 to 14, MTWFS 10-8,

7: CLOTHING-DIRECTORY

Th 10-9, ch., c.c., exch., no rfd. Clearance outlet for the Adamici store at 7th Av. & 17th St. Sells: **Men's Shoes—Dress.**

* **A&G Children's Wear**, 261 Broome St. (Orchard-Allen), 966-3775, F-J-M to Delancey & Essex, B-D to Grand, Sun-Th 10-5, F 10-3, all cash, exch., no rfd. Sells: **Kids' Clothing.**

** **Alee Discount**, 85 Chambers St. (B'wy-Church), 619-2980, A-CC-1-2-3 to Chambers, N-RR to City Hall, M-F 9-6, S 10-5, ch., c.c., 10-day exch. or rfd. Sells: **Kids' Shoes, Men's Belts, Men's Coats—Dressy, Jeans, Men's Pants/Slacks, Ladies' Belts, Ladies' Coats, Dresses, Skirts, Slacks, Hosiery, Lingerie, Ladies' Shoes & Boots, Ladies' Suits & Blazers, Tops, Sweaters, Blouses, Linens, Warehouse Salvage Job-Lot.**

* **Alex Leather City**, 526 7th Av. (38), 3rd floor, 869-0666, N-QB-RR-1-2-3-7 to 42 & Times Square, 1-2-3 to 34, M-F 9-5, S 9-4, c.c., no ch., no exch. or rfd. Prices low to begin with, but if the owner is there he practically invites bargaining, and will sell most items for 50% of the tagged price. I don't know how. Sells: **Coats—Leather & Sheepskin.**

Alexander's at World Trade Ctr, 4 WTC, 466-1414, AA-E to World Trade Ctr., M-F 8-6:45, S 10-5, ch., c.c., 7-day exch. or rfd. Large selection. Uneven values, some terrific, some blah. Not the other branches because this one sells only clothing; the chain is bad on other items. Still, NYC's best dept. stores. Sells: **Men's Belts, Men's Coats—Dressy, Coats—Quilted & Parkas, Men's Gloves, Men's Hats, Men's Pants/Slacks, Shirts, Shoes—Bedroom & Slippers, Men's Shoes—Dress, Men's Suits—New, Men's Sweaters, Men's Swimsuits, Ties, Bathrobes & P.J.'s, Ladies' Belts, Chinese Jackets, Robes, Ladies' Coats, Ladies' Coats—Fake Fur, Dresses, Skirts, Slacks, Ladies' Gloves, Hosiery, Lingerie, Loungewear, Millinery, Hats, Ladies' Shoes & Boots, Ladies' Suits & Blazers, Ladies' Swimsuits, Tops, Sweaters, Blouses.**

* **Alma Llanera**, 482 Broadway (Broome), 966-3910, J-M-N-QB-RR-6 to Canal, Sun-F 9:30-5:30, all cash, exch., no rfd. No try-ons. Sells: **Jeans—Designer.**

+ **Al's Sample Nook**, Queens, 179-05 Union Tnpk., Utopia, 591-6035, no subway stop nearby, M-S 10-6, Sun 12-4, ch., c.c., 3-day exch., no rfd. Bonus discount to BF readers: 5%. Sells: **Dresses, Skirts, Slacks.**

** **A&M Textile**, 185 E. Houston St. at Orchard, 982-1906, F to 2nd Av., 7 days 11-5, ch., c.c., exch. or rfd. Sells: **Ladies' Coats—Fake Fur.**

** **American Arion**, 149 Church St. (Chambers), 766-8514, A-CC-1-2-3 to Chambers, M-F9:30-6, S 10-5, c.c., no ch., exch., no rfd. Affiliated with Baretta 1 & 2. Sells: **Men's Shoes—Dress.**

* **American Boutique**, 470 7th Av. (36), 4th floor, 594-3428, A-AA-CC-E to 34, M-S 8:30-4:30, all cash, exch., no rfd. Sells: **Dresses, Skirts, Slacks, Ladies' Suits & Blazers, Tops, Sweaters, Blouses.**

** **Anbar Shoes**, 97 Reade St. (Church-W.B'wy), 227-0253, A-CC-1-2-3 to Chambers, M-F 8-5:30, S 10-4, ch., no c.c., 7-day exch. or rfd. Affiliated with Shoe Steal. Sells: **Ladies' Shoes & Boots.**

* **Antony**, 106 Orchard St. (Delancey), 477-0592, F-J-M to Delancey & Essex, Sun-F 10-6, c.c., no ch., 7-day exch., no rfd. Small store. Small selection. An Italian designer, current styles and merchandise. Sells: **Shirts, Men's Suits—New.**

Arden, 1014 6th Av. (37-8), 391-6968, B-D-F to 42, B-D-F-N-QB-RR to 34, M-F 9:30-6, S 10-5, ch., no c.c., 1-day exch., no rfd. Sells: **Millinery, Hats.**

Ariel Fashions, 30 W. 32, 947-0107, B-D-F-N-QB-RR to 34, M-F 8-5:30, S 8-2, c.c., no ch., exch., no rfd. Sells: **Dresses, Skirts, Slacks, Jeans—Designer, Tops, Sweaters, Blouses.**

Arthur Richards, 91 5th Av. at 17th St., 2nd floor, 247-2300, B-F-LL to 14th St. & 6th Av., LL-N-QB-RR-4-5-6 to Union Sq., MTWFS 9-6, Th 9-7:30, ch., c.c., 7-day exch. or rfd. (But only if unaltered.) Not generally recommended for women's wear (which they also carry). Sells: **Men's Suits—New.**

* **Atlantic Clothing**, 1 Allen St. at Division, 227-8918, F to E. Broadway, M-Th 9-5, F 9-2, Sun 9-4, ch., no c.c., exch. or rfd. Especially good on raincoats. Sells: **Men's Coats—Dressy, Men's Suits—New.**

** **Aurora Design Tailor**, 104 E. 40 (Park Av.), rm. 908, 687-1259, 4-5-6-7 to Grand Central, M-S 10-7, ch., c.c. Everything is custom-made. Raw-canvas fitting is optional. A Hong Kong custom tailor. Sells: **Men's Coats—Dressy, Shirts, Suits—Custom-Tailored, Ladies' Coats, Ladies' Suits—Custom-Tailored.**

*** **Azriel Altman**, 204 5th Av. (25), 889-0782, N-RR to 23rd St., 7 days 10-6, ch., c.c., no exch. or rfd. Very cooperative. Large selection. Astounding values often

7: CLOTHING-DIRECTORY 51

hidden in obscure corners. Many underpriced new designers all discounted. Much clothing from France. Get on mailing list for sensational sales. Sells: **Ladies' Coats, Dresses, Skirts, Slacks, Ladies' Suits & Blazers, Tops, Sweaters, Blouses.**

B. Kaminsky, 18 Orchard St. (Canal), 226-5856, F to E. Broadway, Sun-Th 9-5:30, F 9-5, all cash, no exch. or rfd. Sells: **Kids' Clothing.**

*** **Bag Man**, 261 W. 34 (8th Av.), 560 8952, A-AA-CC-E to 34, M-S 10-7, all cash, exch., no rfd. One in the DAC Jewelry group. Sells: **Millinery, Hats, Home-Improvement Items, Jewelry & Gifts, Personal Accessories.**

Bally Weave, Queens, 31-01 30th Av., Astoria, 726-7219, RR to 30th Av., M-S 10-6, all cash, exch., no rfd. Sells: **Men's Sweaters, Tops, Sweaters, Blouses.**

* **Baretta Fashions 1**, Queens, 96-50 Queens Blvd., Rego Park, 275-0638, F-GG-N to 63rd Dr., M-Th 10-7, F 10-8, c.c., no ch., exch., no rfd. Affiliated with Baretta 2 and American Arion. Sells: **Shirts, Men's Shoes—Dress, Men's Suits—New.**

** **Baretta Fashions 2**, 642 8th Av. (41-2), 921-2979, A-AA-CC-E to 42, M-S 10-7, ch., c.c., exch., no rfd. Affiliated with Baretta 1 and American Arion. Sells: **Men's Shoes—Dress.**

* **Baretta Fashions Midtown**, 22 E. 43 (Mad.), 687-2853, 7 to 5th Av., 4-5-6-7 to Grand Central, M-S 10-7, c.c., no ch., exch., no rfd. Sells: **Men's Shoes—Dress.**

Bayard International, 35 W. 32 (5th-6th), 594-6658, B-D-F-N-QB-RR to 34, M-F 9-6, all cash, exch., no rfd. Salesmen can be rather curt. Sells: **Shirts, Jeans—Designer.**

* **Bee Hive**, 55 W. 42 (6th Av.), 354-2857, B-D-F to 42, 7 to 5th Av., M-F 9-7, S 9:30-6; 75 Nassau St. (John-Fulton), 732-1990, A-CC-J-M-RR-2-3-4-5 to B'wy-Nassau & Fulton, M-F 8-6; Brooklyn, 400 Fulton St. (Gallatin), 834-0031, 2-3 to Hoyt, B-D-M-N-QB-RR to DeKalb, MTWFS 10-7, Th 10-8, Sun 12-5; Bronx, 2912 3rd Av. (151), 585-1330, 2-5 to 3rd Av., M-S 10-7, Sun 11:30-5. All stores: all cash, exch., no rfd. Sells: **Ladies' Coats, Dresses, Skirts, Slacks, Jeans—Designer, Tops, Sweaters, Blouses.**

** **Ben Freedman**, 137 Orchard St. (Delancey), 674-0854, F-J-M to Delancey & Essex, 7 days 9-6, ch., no c.c., exch. or rfd. Some superb values in irregulars of London Fog, Arrow, and Jantzen. Sells: **Men's Belts, Men's Coats—Dressy, Coats—Quilted & Parkas, Men's Pants/Slacks, Shirts, Socks, Men's Suits—New, Men's Sweaters, Men's Swimsuits, Ties, Underwear.**

* **Benny's**, Brooklyn, 3804 13th Av., 438-9437, B to 9th Av., plus a long walk, Sun-Th 10-6, F 10-4, ch., no c.c., 7-day exch., no rfd. Some seconds. Sells: **Ladies' Coats, Dresses, Skirts, Slacks, Ladies' Suits & Blazers, Tops, Sweaters, Blouses.**

* **Benny's Loft**, Brooklyn, 5012 New Utrecht Av., up 1 flight, 851-2086, B to 50th St., Sun-Th 11-5, F 11-2, ch., no c.c., 7-day exch., no rfd. Large selection. Seconds. Sells: **Ladies' Coats.**

Bernard Krieger, 316 Grand St. (Orchard), 226-1929&4927, B-D to Grand, F-J-M to Delancey & Essex, Sun-Th 9-4:30, F 9-3, ch., no c.c., exch., no rfd. Sells: **Men's Gloves, Millinery, Hats, Personal Accessories.**

Better Wear Mfg., 500 Broadway (Broome), 966-0619, 6 to Spring, N-RR to Prince St., Sun-Th 9:30-5, F 9:30-3, all cash, exch., no rfd. Sells: **Jeans.**

** **BFO Plus**, 149 5th Av. at 21st St., 2nd floor, 673-9026, N-RR to 23rd St., 7 days 9:30-5, ch., c.c., 7-day exch. or rfd. Large selection of shirts. Sells: **Men's Belts, Men's Gloves, Shirts, Men's Sweaters, Ties.**

* **BFO Suits**, 149 5th Av. at 21st St., 6th floor, 254-0059, N-RR to 23rd St., 7 days 9-5, ch., c.c., 7-day exch. or rfd. Sells: **Men's Pants/Slacks, Men's Suits—New.**

Blooming, 23 W. 34 (5th-6th), 594-2429, B-D-F-N-QB-RR to 34, M-S 9:30-8:30, Sun 11-6, c.c., no ch., 10-day exch., no rfd. Boutique sportswear. Sells: **Ladies' Coats, Dresses, Skirts, Slacks, Ladies' Suits & Blazers, Tops, Sweaters, Blouses.**

** **Bob's Discount**, 109 Ludlow St. (Delancey), 674-4296, F-J-M to Delancey & Essex, W-M 10-5, all cash, exch., no rfd. Sells: **Men's Shoes—Dress, Men's Shoes—Sports/Work, Personal Accessories, Sporting Goods, Warehouse Salvage Job-Lot.**

Bohrer's Children's Wear, 139 1st Av. (8-9), 254-6988, LL to 1st Av., 6 to Astor, M-S 10-6:30, c.c., no ch., 5-day exch. or rfd. Sells: **Kids' Clothing.**

Bok Lei Bo, 78 Bayard St. (Mott), 233-0935, J-M-N-QB-RR-6 to Canal, J-

7: CLOTHING-DIRECTORY

M-RR-4-5-6 to Chambers & Bkln. Bridge, B-D to Grand, 7 days 10-7:30, all cash, exch., no rfd. Sells: **Shoes—Bedroom & Slippers, Chinese Jackets, Robes, Clothing—Women's.**

** **Boni Knitwear**, 93 Allen St. (Broome), 226-3305, F-J-M to Delancey & Essex, Sun-Th 8-5, F 8-4, all cash, exch., no rfd. No try-ons. Sells: **Dresses, Skirts, Slacks, Ladies' Suits & Blazers, Tops, Sweaters, Blouses.**

** **Bonnie J**, Queens, 71-07 Austin St., Forest Hills, 261-7538, E-F-GG-N to 71-Continental Av., M-S 9:45-6, ch., c.c., exch., no rfd. Sells: **Ladies' Coats, Dresses, Skirts, Slacks, Ladies' Suits & Blazers, Tops, Sweaters, Blouses.**

* **Borislaw Clothier**, 2 E. 17 at 5th Av., 242-8134, LL-N-QB-RR-4-5-6 to Union Sq., M-F 8-6, S 8-5, ch., c.c., exch., no rfd. Sells: **Men's Coats—Dressy, Men's Suits—New.**

* **Brands For Less**, Brooklyn, 2615 W. 13th St. (one block E. of Stillwell & Av. Z), 266-6440, B to Bay 50th, M-F 10-5, S 10-6, Sun 11-5, all cash, exch., no rfd. Sells: **Dresses, Skirts, Slacks, Jeans—Designer, Tops, Sweaters, Blouses.**

** **Bridge Merchandise**, 74 Orchard St. (Grand), 674-6320, F to E. Broadway, F-J-M to Delancey & Essex, Sun-Th 9-5, F 9-3, ch., c.c., exch., no rfd. Sells: **Coats—Leather & Sheepskin, Shirts, Jeans—Designer, Tops, Sweaters, Blouses.**

** **Broadway Fashion**, 581 Broadway (Prince), 431-4134, N-RR to Prince St., M-Th 9:30-5:30, SunF 9:30-3, all cash, no rfd. No try-ons. Sells: **Kids' Clothing, Men's Pants/Slacks, Shirts, Dresses, Skirts, Slacks, Jeans—Designer, Tops, Sweaters, Blouses.**

Brown's Army-Navy, Queens, 83-18 37th Av., Jackson Hts., 429-8508, 7 to 82nd St.; Queens, 74-17 Roosevelt Av., Jackson Hts., 476-8447, E-F-GG-N-7 to 74th-B'wy & Roosevelt-Jack.Hts. Both stores: M-S 9-8, ch., c.c., exch. or rfd. Sells: **Jeans, Men's Shoes—Sports/Work, Underwear, Sporting Goods.**

Budget Boutique, 1 W. 42 (5th Av.), 221-1982, B-D-F to 42, 7 to 5th Av., M-F 9-6, S 10-5, c.c., no ch., exch., no rfd. Small store. Small selection. Sells: **Dresses, Skirts, Slacks, Tops, Sweaters, Blouses.**

*+ **Buen Dia**, 108 W. Houston St. at Thompson, 673-1910, A-AA-B-CC-D-E-F to 4, M-S 12-7, Sun 2-6; 201 W. 11 at 7th Av., 673-1910, 1-2-3 to 14, M-S 12-7. Both stores: c.c., no ch., exch., no rfd. Very cooperative. Everything is knit in Latin America. Bonus discount to BF readers: 5% to 8%. Sells: **Antique Clothing & Cheap-Chic, Jewelry & Gifts, Personal Accessories.**

** **Buy Well Hosiery**, 2592 Broadway (98), 666-5757, 1-2-3 to 96, M-S 10-6, ch., no c.c., exch., no rfd. (But no returns if package opened.) Sells: **Hosiery, Lingerie.**

Call Again Thrift Shop, 1735 2nd Av. (89-90), 831-0845, 4-5-6 to 86, M-S 10-4:15, all cash, no exch. or rfd. Excellent condition. Sells: **Men's Suits—Used, Used Clothing For Women.**

** **Canal Bargain**, 121 Chambers St. (W. B'wy), 227-8040, A-CC-1-2-3 to Chambers, M-S 9-7, ch., c.c., exch., no rfd. Occasionally, but very rarely, some astounding bargains. For a while, they were selling thousands of exquisite $400 suits for $30. Sells: **Men's Coats—Dressy, Coats—Quilted & Parkas, Men's Pants/Slacks, Shirts, Men's Suits—New.**

*+ **Canal Jean Co.**, 504 Broadway (Spring-Broome) (huge store), 304 Canal (B'wy) (large store), 431-4765&8439, J-M-N-QB-RR-6 to Canal, 7 days 10:30-7, ch., c.c., 10-day exch., no rfd. Bargains range from fairly good to sensational. Store's buyers are very value-conscious; they select well. Entire stock is casual wear, including military cheap-chic. Bonus discount to BF readers: 5% to 20%. Sells: **Men's Belts, Coats—Quilted & Parkas, Men's Hats, Jeans, Men's Pants/Slacks, Shirts, Men's Shoes—Sports/Work, Socks, Men's Sweaters, Antique & Military Clothing, Ladies' Belts, Antique Clothing & Cheap-Chic.**

** **Canal St. Market**, 234 Canal St. (Baxter), basement, 226-9142, J-M-N-QB-RR-6 to Canal, 7 days 10:30-7, all cash, exch., no rfd. Several independent retailers, all good. Sells: **Chinese Jackets, Robes.**

* **Carol-Ann Shoppes**, 142 W. 14 (6th-7th), 243-8727, B-F-LL to 14th St. & 6th Av., 1-2-3 to 14; 22 W. 14 (5th-6th), 221-3138, B-F-LL to 14th St. & 6th Av.; 44 E. 23 (Mad.), 473-5354, N-RR to 23rd St., 6 to 23; 55 W. 42 (6th Av.), 221-3138, B-D-F to 42, 7 to 5th Av.; 429 Lexington Av. (43), 687-8824, 4-5-6-7 to Grand Central; 129 E. 45 (Lex.), 687-8890, 4-5-6-7 to Grand Central; 712 3rd Av. (45), 661-6995, 4-5-6-7 to Grand Central; 37-01 Main St., Flushing, 886-4655, 7 to Main St.; 37-11 Main St., Flushing, 359-8205, 7 to Main St.; Queens, 56-47 Myrtle Av., Ridgewood, 497-5532,

7: CLOTHING-DIRECTORY 53

LL-M to Myrtle & Wyckoff. All stores: M-S 10-6, all cash, no exch. or rfd. Sells: **Dresses, Skirts, Slacks, Tops, Sweaters, Blouses.**

** **Carter Leather**, 41 E. 11 (University), 5th floor, 475-3537, LL-N-QB-RR-4-5-6 to Union Sq., N-RR to 8th St., M-F 9-5 (for other hours, phone first), all cash, exch., no rfd. Very-good-quality leather wallets; medium-quality belts for women. An authentic factory-outlet. Sells: **Ladies' Belts, Personal Accessories.**

** **Casa International**, 595 Broadway (Houston), 226-3180, N-RR to Prince St., Sun-F 8-5, all cash, exch., no rfd. No try-ons. Sells: **Dresses, Skirts, Slacks, Jeans—Designer, Tops, Sweaters, Blouses.**

* **Catania Clothing**, 85 5th Av. at 16th St., 7th floor, 255-5510, B-F-LL to 14th St. & 6th Av., LL-N-QB-RR-4-5-6 to Union Sq., M-F 9-5:30, S 9-4, c.c., no ch., no exch. or rfd. There are 1's only in the suits, not in the other stuff. Sells: **Men's Coats—Dressy, Men's Suits—New.**

** **Cayne's 1**, 1345 Broadway (36), 695-8451, B-D-F-N-QB-RR to 34, M-S 10-6:30, c.c., no ch., 25-day exch. or rfd. One in the Cayne group. Sells: **Jeans, Shirts, Underwear, Dresses, Skirts, Slacks, Hosiery, Jeans—Designer, Lingerie, Tops, Sweaters, Blouses, Linens, Sporting Goods.**

** **Cayne's 2**, 225 W. 34 (7th-8th), basement downstairs, 244-8761, 1-2-3 to 34, A-AA-CC-E to 34, M-S 10-6:30, c.c., no ch., 25-day exch. or rfd. One in the Cayne group. Sells: **Kids' Clothing, Health & Beauty Aids, Linens.**

** **Cayne's 4**, 247 W. 34 (7th-8th), 560-9212, A-AA-CC-E to 34, 1-2-3 to 34, M-S 10-6:30, c.c., no ch., 25-day exch. or rfd. One in the Cayne group. Sells: **Kids' Clothing, Jeans, Shirts, Underwear.**

* **C&C Bargains**, Brooklyn, 400 Fulton St. at Gallatin Place, 625-9210, B-D-M-N-QB-RR to DeKalb, 2-3 to Hoyt, 2-3-4-5 to Nevins, M-S 9:30-7, Sun 11:30-5, all cash. 21-day exch. or 5-day rfd. Sells: **Kids' Clothing.**

* **Cedrick's**, Staten Island, 342 New Dorp (Hylan Blvd.), 987-3577, S.I. Rapid Transit to New Dorp, M 9:30-8, TWS 9:30-6, ThF 9:30-9, Sun 11-3, ch., c.c., exch., no rfd. An odd mixture, includes many closeouts of outdated fashions. Uneven values. Sells: **Men's Coats—Dressy, Men's Pants/Slacks, Shirts, Men's Suits—New.**

Central Hat, 144 Orchard St. (but sign says '140 Orchard') (Rivington), 254-4170, F-J-M to Delancey & Essex, Sun-Th 9-5:30, F 9-2, all cash, no exch. or rfd. Sells: **Men's Hats.**

** **Century 21**, 12 Cortlandt St. (B'wy), 227-9092, A-CC-J-M-RR-2-3-4-5 to B'wy-Nassau & Fulton, 4-5 to Wall St., M-F 8-6; Brooklyn, 472 86th St (4th-5th Avs.), 748-3266, RR to 86th St., M-S 9-9. Both stores: ch., c.c., 5-day exch. or rfd. Not good on appliances. But this small department-store has good prices in every other department. It's much like Dollar Bill's, which has more men's-wear emphasis. Sells: **Kids' Clothing, Men's Belts, Men's Gloves, Shirts, Socks, Men's Sweaters, Men's Swimsuits, Ties, Bathrobes & P.J.'s, Ladies' Coats, Dresses, Skirts, Slacks, Ladies' Gloves, Hosiery, Lingerie, Loungewear, Ladies' Shoes & Boots, Ladies' Suits & Blazers, Ladies' Swimsuits, Tops, Sweaters, Blouses, Health & Beauty Aids.**

Charming Bridal, 254 W. 35 (8th Av.), 5th floor, 594-7066, A-AA-CC-E to 34, S 9-12:30, by appt. M-W 9-3, ch., no c.c., no exch. or rfd. Sells: **Bridals.**

** **Chateau Creations**, 114 W. 26 (6th Av.), 9th floor, 244-6722, B-F to 23, 1 to 28, M-F 8:30-4, S by appt. (phone, speak with Harry Hessel), ch., no c.c., exch. or rfd. An authentic factory outlet. Fake furs that look real (but they don't feel real). A way to avoid being a rich creep who subsidizes the wanton torture of animals. Sells: **Ladies' Coats—Fake Fur.**

** **Cheap Charlie's**, Queens, 41-01 162nd St., Flushing, 353-2603, no subway stop nearby, MTWFS 10-6, Th 10-8, c.c., no ch., exch., no rfd. Sells: **Ladies' Coats, Dresses, Skirts, Slacks, Ladies' Suits & Blazers, Tops, Sweaters, Blouses.**

Cheap Charlie's, Brooklyn, 1362 Coney Is. Av. (J-K), 252-4932, D-M-QB to Av. J, M-Th 9:30-12 & 1-6, FS 9:30-5, all cash, exch., no rfd. Small store. Sells: **Socks, Underwear.**

** **Cheap Jack's Clearance Store**, 151 1st Av. (9-10), 674-9718, LL to 1st Av., M-S 11-8, Sun 12-6, all cash, no exch. or rfd. First phone to make sure that this is still a clearance-store, because when it wasn't, the prices were not good; and so if it isn't, the prices probably aren't good. Sells: **Antique & Military Clothing, Antique Clothing & Cheap-Chic.**

** **China Mall**, 234 Canal St. (Baxter), 226-4720, J-M-N-QB-RR-6 to Canal,

7 days 10:30-7, all cash, exch., no rfd. Several independent retailers inside, all good. Sells: **Coats—Quilted & Parkas, Chinese Jackets, Robes, Jeans—Designer.**

** **Cho's Variety**, 121 Chambers St. (Church-W. B'wy), 349-7544, A-CC-1-2-3 to Chambers, M-S 11-6, all cash, exch., or rfd. Small store. Street-stand. Sells: **Men's Hats, Millinery, Hats, Personal Accessories, Toys, Games & Hobbies.**

* **Colony**, 56 7th Av. (13-4), 924-8815, 1-2-3 to 14, M-F 10-7:30, S 11-7, Sun 1-5, c.c., no ch., exch., no rfd. Well-selected current-fashion sportswear, at discounts good for the latest stuff. Sells: **Coats—Quilted & Parkas, Men's Gloves, Men's Pants/Slacks, Shirts, Men's Shoes—Sports/Work, Men's Sweaters, Dresses, Skirts, Slacks, Ladies' Gloves, Tops, Sweaters, Blouses.**

* **Council Thrift Shop**, 842 9th Av. at 55th St., 757-6132, A-AA-B-CC-D-1 to 59, M-F 9:30-4, all cash, no exch. or rfd. Sells: **Men's Suits—Used, Used Clothing For Women.**

Cozy Boutique, 200 E. 86 (3rd Av.), 535-3128, 4-5-6 to 86, MTWS 11-7:30, ThF 11-8, Sun 1-6, c.c., no ch., 7-day exch., no rfd. Small store. Sells: **Ladies' Coats, Dresses, Skirts, Slacks, Tops, Sweaters, Blouses.**

** **Crown Mercandise**, 543 Broadway (Prince), 966-7583, N-RR to Prince St., Sun-F 8-6, all cash, exch., no rfd. Sells: **Dresses, Skirts, Slacks, Jeans—Designer, Lingerie, Loungewear, Ladies' Swimsuits, Tops, Sweaters, Blouses.**

* **C&S Variety**, Brooklyn, 2237 & 2271 86th St., 259-5290, B to Bay Pkwy., M-S 9:30-7, all cash, 20-day exch. or rfd. Sells: **Kids' Clothing, Dresses, Skirts, Slacks, Tops, Sweaters, Blouses.**

* **Dave's Army/Navy**, 779 6th Av. (26-7), 989-6444, N-RR to 28th St., B-F to 23, M-F 7:30-5:45, S 9-4:30, all cash, 30-day exch. or rfd. Sells: **Jeans, Socks, Underwear.**

** **D&E Outlet**, Queens, 32-02 Queens Blvd., Woodside, 392-5677, 7 to 33rd St., M-F 9-5, S 9-4, all cash, no exch. or rfd. Sells: **Ladies' Coats, Dresses, Skirts, Slacks, Ladies' Suits & Blazers, Tops, Sweaters, Blouses.**

* **De Silva Ltd.**, 32 W. 46 (5th-6th), 586-1316, B-D-F to 47, M-F 10-6:30, S 9:30-6, ch., c.c., exch. or rfd. Small selection. Sells: **Men's Coats—Dressy, Coats—Quilted & Parkas, Men's Pants/Slacks, Shirts, Men's Suits—New, Ties.**

Dee & Dee Stores, 22 W. 14 (5th-6th), 243-5620, B-F-LL to 14th St. & 6th Av., M-S 9:30-7, Sun 11-6; Brooklyn, 777 Manhattan Av. (Meserole), 389-0181, GG to Greenpoint Av., M-S 9:30-7; Brooklyn, 8515 5th Av., 836-3146, RR to 86th St., M-S 9:30-9; Brooklyn, 534 5th Av. (14th St.), 499-4372, N-RR to Prospect Av., F-N-RR to 9th St. & 4th Av., M-S 9:30-6; Brooklyn, 2159 86th St., 996-7903, B to Bay Pkwy., M-S 9:30-6; Brooklyn, 5008 5th Av., 492-1751, N-RR to 53rd St., M-S 9:30-6. All stores: all cash, 21-day exch. or rfd. Other stores: Bayonne, Perth Amboy, Plainfield, in NJ. Sells: **Coats—Quilted & Parkas, Men's Gloves, Jeans, Men's Pants/Slacks, Shoes—Bedroom & Slippers, Hosiery, Lingerie.**

Del Pino Shoes, 1871 Broadway (61-2), 757-6853, A-AA-B-CC-D-1 to 59, M-S 9-6, ch., c.c., exch. or rfd. (But only if unworn.) Sells: **Men's Shoes—Dress.**

Dems Bargain Stores, 146 W. 14 (6th-7th), 243-9416, 1-2-3 to 14, B-F-LL to 14th St. & 6th Av., M-S 9-7, Sun 12-5, all cash, exch., no rfd. Sells: **Shoes—Bedroom & Slippers, Dinnerware & Cookware.**

Designer Liquidators, 127 E. 57 (Lex.), 751-4353, N-RR-4-5-6 to 59th & Lex., MTh 10-8, TWFS 10-7, Sun 12-5; 2045 Broadway (71), 787-3955, 1-2-3 to 72, M-S 10-8, Sun 12-6. Both stores: ch., no c.c., no exch. or rfd. Sells: **Ladies' Coats, Dresses, Skirts, Slacks, Lingerie, Ladies' Suits & Blazers, Tops, Sweaters, Blouses.**

* **Designers Below**, 150 Fulton St. (B'wy), subway arcade, 619-2147, A-CC-J-M-RR-2-3-4-5 to B'wy-Nassau & Fulton, M-Th 10-6:30, F 10-4, ch., c.c., 7-day exch., no rfd. Sells: **Ladies' Coats, Dresses, Skirts, Slacks, Ladies' Suits & Blazers, Tops, Sweaters, Blouses.**

** **Designers Choice**, 46 Warren St. (W. B'wy-Church), 406-1090, A-CC-1-2-3 to Chambers, M-F 10-6, Sun 12-5, ch., c.c., exch. or rfd. Sells: **Ladies' Coats, Dresses, Skirts, Slacks, Ladies' Suits & Blazers.**

* **Discount Fashions**, Brooklyn, 129 Livingston St. (Boerum), 643-0490, M-RR-2-3-4-5 to Borough Hall & Court St., M-Th 10:30-6, F 10:30-4, ch., c.c., 7-day exch. or rfd. Sells: **Ladies' Coats, Dresses, Skirts, Slacks, Ladies' Suits & Blazers, Tops, Sweaters, Blouses.**

* **Discount Maternity**, Brooklyn, 2663 Nostrand Av. at M, 253-0578, D-M-QB to Av. M, plus a long walk, M-S 10-6, Sun 12-5, ch., c.c., no exch. or rfd. Factory

7: CLOTHING-DIRECTORY

outlet for a top-name mfr. which prefers not to be identified. Sells: **Maternity-Wear.**

** **Dollar Bills**, 99 E. 42 (Park Av.), 867-0212, 4-5-6-7 to Grand Central, M-W 8-6:30, ThF 8-7, S 10-6, ch., c.c., 7-day exch. or rfd. A small department store that's best on toiletries, housewares, and cigarettes, but good also on men's wear. Same owner: J. Chuckles, Strawberry, Sunshine, Zoom stores. Sells: **Men's Belts, Men's Gloves, Shirts, Socks, Men's Suits—New, Men's Sweaters, Men's Swimsuits, Ties, Underwear, Appliances, Housewares, Smoking Supplies.**

+ **Don Ricardo Shoes**, 2691 Broadway (102-3), 866-9492, 1 to 103, M-S 10:30-7, ch., c.c., exch., no rfd. (But no exchange on boots.) Bonus discount to BF readers: 10%. Sells: **Ladies' Shoes & Boots.**

** **Dorson Clothes**, 87 5th Av. (16-7), 2nd floor, 924-7676, B-F-LL to 14th St. & 6th Av., LL-N-QB-RR-4-5-6 to Union Sq., M-S 8:30-5, c.c., no ch., no exch. or rfd. Free alterations. Also stocks off-the-rack suits. Sells: **Suits—Custom-Tailored.**

*+ **Down In The Village**, 652 Broadway (Bleecker), 260-2330, B-D-F-6 to B'wy-Laf. & Bleecker, M-S 10-6, Sun 12-5, ch., c.c., exch., no rfd. Specializes in carrying practically every name in down clothing. Bonus discount to BF readers: 10%. Sells: **Coats—Quilted & Parkas, Sporting Goods.**

Dress Shoppe, 70 E. 9 (B'wy), 260-4963, N-RR to 8th St., 6 to Astor, c.c., no ch., no exch. or rfd. Tiny store. India-made garments. Sells: **Dresses, Skirts, Slacks, Tops, Sweaters, Blouses.**

** **D&S Dresses**, 80 Essex St., in NYC market, first entrance south of Delancey St., 473-3363, F-J-M to Delancey & Essex, M-S 9-5, all cash, exch., no rfd. No try-ons. Small selection. A stand. Sells: **Dresses, Skirts, Slacks, Tops, Sweaters, Blouses.**

** **Earl's**, Queens, 78-25 Metropolitan Av., Middle Village, 894-6406, no subway stop nearby, M-S 11-6, all cash, exch. or rfd. Bonus discount to BF readers: 10% to 20%. Sells: **Kids' Clothing, Kids' Shoes, Ladies' Coats, Dresses, Skirts, Slacks, Lingerie, Loungewear, Tops, Sweaters, Blouses, Furnishings.**

East Village Variety, 186 1st Av. (11-12), 674-8300, LL to 1st Av., 7 days 9-8, all cash, exch., no rfd. Sells: **Shoes—Bedroom & Slippers, Personal Accessories.**

** **Eighth Av. Bargain King**, 306 W. 36 at 8th Av., 594-4049, A-AA-CC-E to 34, M-F 9-7, Sun 10:30-4, ch., c.c., exch., no rfd. Sells: **Men's Shoes—Dress, Men's Shoes—Sports/Work, Ladies' Coats, Dresses, Skirts, Slacks, Ladies' Gloves, Hosiery, Jeans—Designer, Lingerie, Loungewear, Ladies' Shoes & Boots, Ladies' Suits & Blazers, Ladies' Swimsuits, Tops, Sweaters, Blouses.**

** **Eleven West**, 11 W. 34 (5th Av.), 695-7537, B-D-F-N-QB-RR to 34, M-S 10-6:30, c.c., no ch., 25-day exch. or rfd. One in the Cayne group. Sells: **Kids' Clothing, Jeans, Shirts, Underwear, Dresses, Skirts, Slacks, Hosiery, Lingerie, Tops, Sweaters, Blouses.**

Empire, 469 2nd Av. (27), 684-8359, 6 to 28, M-S 11-6, Sun 11-5; 1206 2nd Av. (63), 752-7174, N-RR-4-5-6 to 59th & Lex., MTWF 11-7, Th 11-8, S 11-6, Sun 11-5; Queens, 72-44 Austin St., Forest Hills, 268-9471, E-F-GG-N to 71-Continental Avs., M-S 10-5:30, Sun 11-5; Bronx, 3765 Riverdale Av. (237), 548-9662, 1 to 238, M-S 10-5:30, Sun 11-5. All stores: ch., c.c., no exch. or rfd. Other stores: suburban L.I., N.J., and Norwalk Ct. Sells: **Ladies' Coats, Dresses, Skirts, Slacks, Ladies' Suits & Blazers, Tops, Sweaters, Blouses.**

* **E.N.S. Shop**, 690 Columbus Av. (93-4), 663-1029, A-AA-B-CC to 96, MWThFS 10-7, T 1-7, ch., c.c., exch., no rfd. Small store. Very nice people. Sells: **Dresses, Skirts, Slacks, Ladies' Suits & Blazers, Tops, Sweaters, Blouses.**

Encore Resale Dress, 1132 Madison Av. (84), 879-2850, 6 to 68, M-S 10:30-6, Sun 12:30-6, ch., no c.c., no exch. or rfd. Sells: **Slightly Used Designer-Wear.**

*+ **Eti-Quette**, 20 W. 38 (5th-6th), 398-1460, B-D-F to 42, M-F 8:30-7, S 11-6; 860 Lexington Av. (64-5), 288-5419, 6 to 68, N-RR-4-5-6 to 59th & Lex., M-F 10-7, S 11-6. Both stores: ch., c.c., exch., no rfd. Good selection. Bonus discount to BF readers: 5% to 10%. Sells: **Ladies' Shoes & Boots.**

** **European Liquidators**, 1404 2nd Av. (73), 879-9140, 6 to 68, 6 to 77, M-F 11-7:45, S 11-6:45, Sun 12-6, ch., c.c., no exch. or rfd. Boutique styles. Sells: **Coats—Leather & Sheepskin, Dresses, Skirts, Slacks, Tops, Sweaters, Blouses.**

*+ **Ever Ready Lingerie**, 568 Broadway (Prince), 925-5125, N-RR to Prince St., T-Th 9:30-5:30, SunF 9:30-5, ch., no c.c., exch., no rfd. Large selection. Bonus discount to BF readers: 5% to 10%. Sells: **Lingerie.**

Expectations, 1027 6th Av. (38), 997-1570, B-D-F to 42, B-D-F-N-QB-

7: CLOTHING-DIRECTORY

RR to 34, M-S 10-7; Queens, 20-10 Steinway St., Astoria, 274-8154, RR to Ditmars, plus a long walk; Queens, 71-28 Main St., Flushing, 261-9877, no subway stop nearby; Bronx, 24 Westchester Sq., 597-6318, 6 to E. Tremont; Brooklyn, 2038 86th St., 996-3938, B to 20th Av. All stores: ch., c.c., exch., no rfd. Sells: **Maternity-Wear.**

* **Fabulous Find**, 25 E. 17 (B'wy-5th), 242-9474, LL-N-QB-RR-4-5-6 to Union Sq., B-F-LL to 14th St. & 6th Av., M-F 9-6, S 9-4:30, ch., c.c., exch. or rfd. Good selection. Sells: **Men's Shoes—Dress.**

** **Fabulous Julie's**, Queens, 77-40 164th St., Flushing, 526-9892, E-F to Parsons Blvd., plus a long walk, M-S 9:30-5, ch., $15+, c.c. $75+, 5-day exch., no rfd. 11 other stores in Byram and Fairfield Ct., Miami and Sunrise Fl., Pleasantville NY, and throughout Long Island. Sells: **Kids' Clothing.**

Factory Outlet, Brooklyn, 176 Livingston St. at Smith, 624-0321, 2-3 to Hoyt, ThF 7-6, S 6-3, ch., no c.c., exch., no rfd. Sells: **Dresses, Skirts, Slacks, Tops, Sweaters, Blouses.**

\+ **Fashion Delight**, 131 3rd Av. (14-5), 533-4840, LL to 3rd Av., M-Th 10-7, F 10-5, Sun 11-6, ch., c.c., 1-day exch., no rfd. Bonus discount to BF readers: 10% to 20%. Sells: **Ladies' Coats, Dresses, Skirts, Slacks, Ladies' Suits & Blazers.**

Fashions Aloft, 208 W. 72 (B'wy), up 1 flight, 724-9815, 1-2-3 to 72, MTWFS 11-6, Th 11-8, Sun 12-5, ch., c.c., 5-day exch. or rfd. Sells: **Dresses, Skirts, Slacks, Tops, Sweaters, Blouses.**

Feet, 1841 Broadway (60-1), 245-0436, A-AA-B-CC-D-1 to 59, M-F 10-7, S 11-7, ch., c.c., no exch. or rfd. Sells: **Ladies' Shoes & Boots.**

** **Felipito's Place**, 314 W. 36 (8th Av.), 947-2079, A-AA-CC-E to 34, M-F 9-6, S by appt., ch., no c.c., exch. or rfd. Also has a small selection of medium-quality fashion-show samples at less than half price—mostly dresses. Sells: **Suits—Custom-Tailored, Ladies' Suits—Custom-Tailored.**

* **Fiedler's**, 140 Orchard St. (Delancey-Rivington), 475-8372, F-J-M to Delancey & Essex, Sun-F 10-6, all cash, exch., no rfd. Sells: **Jeans.**

First Cost, 90 E. 42nd St. at Park Av., 697-0244, 4-5-6-7 to Grand Central, M-F 8-7, SSun 10-5; Queens, 46-20 108 St., Corona, 271-1121, 7 to 111, ThS 9-6, F 9-9. Both stores: all cash, 7-day exch. or rfd. Sells: **Kids' Clothing, Kids' Shoes, Men's Belts, Coats—Quilted & Parkas, Men's Gloves, Men's Hats, Jeans, Men's Pants/Slacks, Shirts, Men's Shoes—Sports/Work, Underwear, Ladies' Coats, Ladies' Gloves, Hosiery, Ladies' Shoes & Boots, Dinnerware & Cookware, Foods, Health & Beauty Aids, Home-Improvement Items, Housewares, Jewelry & Gifts, Sporting Goods, Toys, Games & Hobbies, Warehouse Salvage Job-Lot.**

* **Fitzpatrick's for Coats**, 51 Murray St., 349-2424, 2-3 to Park Place, M-F 9:15-5:15, S 9:15-4, ch., c.c., exch., no rfd. Takes mail-orders. Catalog. Small selection. Sells nuns' garb, but their women's black dress coat is a terrific value for anyone, and their closeout items (lingerie, etc.) are also excellent bargains. Sells: **Ladies' Coats.**

** **Fleetwood Market**, 28 & 30 Warren St. (Church), 766-9766, A-CC-1-2-3 to Chambers, N-RR to City Hall, M-S 8-6, c.c., no ch., 7-day exch., no rfd. Has irregulars of Arrow shirts. Sells: **Men's Belts, Shirts, Dresses, Skirts, Slacks, Lingerie, Tops, Sweaters, Blouses.**

*\+ **F.M. Handbags & Shoes**, 126 Ludlow St. (Rivington), 673-3230, F-J-M to Delancey & Essex, Sun-F 10-6, ch., c.c., exch., no rfd. Bonus discount to BF readers: 5% to 10%. Sells: **Ladies' Shoes & Boots.**

* **Forman's Basement**, 82 Orchard St. (Broome), inside store downstairs, 228-2500, F-J-M to Delancey & Essex, F to E. Broadway, Sun-Th 9-6, F 9-4, ch., c.c., 10-day exch. or rfd. Half price in clearance-basement. Sells: **Ladies' Coats, Dresses, Skirts, Slacks, Ladies' Suits & Blazers, Tops, Sweaters, Blouses.**

** **Fowad**, 2554 Broadway at 96th St., 222-7000 & 8000 & 9000, 1-2-3 to 96, M-S 9:30-7:30, ch., c.c., 3-day exch. or rfd. Damaged, irregulars, and firsts; past-seasons' fashions. Sells: **Men's Belts, Men's Coats—Dressy, Coats—Quilted & Parkas, Coats—Leather & Sheepskin, Men's Pants/Slacks, Shirts, Men's Shoes—Dress, Men's Suits—New, Men's Sweaters, Ladies' Coats, Dresses, Skirts, Slacks, Ladies' Suits & Blazers, Tops, Sweaters, Blouses.**

** **FRSG Quality Knitwear**, 333 Park Av. S. (24-5), 475-8585, 6 to 23, M-F 7-5, c.c., no ch., exch. or rfd. Sells: **Dresses, Skirts, Slacks, Ladies' Suits & Blazers, Tops, Sweaters, Blouses.**

*** **Frankel's Discount Clothing**, Brooklyn, 3924 3rd Av. at 40th St., 768-9788 & 788-9402, B-N-RR to 36th St., W-S 10-7, Sun 10-5, c.c., no ch., exch. or rfd. Large selection. Especially good on Frye boots. This place is basically an army-

7: CLOTHING-DIRECTORY

navy type store with casual-clothing job lots. Sells: **Kids' Clothing, Kids' Shoes, Men's Belts, Coats—Quilted & Parkas, Men's Gloves, Men's Hats, Jeans, Men's Pants/Slacks, Shirts, Men's Shoes—Sports/Work, Socks, Men's Sweaters, Ladies' Belts, Ladies' Coats, Ladies' Gloves, Ladies' Shoes & Boots, Sporting Goods, Warehouse Salvage Job-Lot.**

** **Fred Krupnik**, 29 Orchard St. (Canal-Hester), 226-2778, F to E. Broadway, Sun-Th 8-4:30, F 8-2, all cash, exch. or rfd. Sells: **Coats—Quilted & Parkas, Jeans, Men's Pants/Slacks, Shirts.**

*** **Fredwin**, 130 E. 44 (Lex), 661-2766, 4-5-6-7 to Grand Central; 77 New St. (Wall), 269-9130, J-M-RR-2-3 to Wall & Broad Sts., 4-5 to Wall St., N-RR-1 to Rector. Both stores: M-F 8-6, all cash, 5-day exch. or rfd. Affiliated with Winfred, Scott's Dress, and Stuart's. All merchandise sells for below its original wholesale—at least two-thirds discount. Sells: **Ladies' Coats, Dresses, Skirts, Slacks, Ladies' Suits & Blazers, Tops, Sweaters, Blouses, Warehouse Salvage Job-Lot.**

* **French Connection**, 1091 Lexington Av. (76-7), 737-1900, 6 to 77; Madison at 87th, 348-4990, 4-5-6 to 86. Both stores: MTWFS 10-5:45, Th 10-7:45, ch., c.c., no exch. or rfd. Boutique fashions. Sells: **Dresses, Skirts, Slacks, Ladies' Suits & Blazers, Tops, Sweaters, Blouses.**

Frugal Frog, 1707 2nd Av. (88), 876-5178, 4-5-6 to 86, MTWThS 11-5, F 1-5, ch., no c.c., no exch. or rfd. Sells: **Used Clothing For Kids.**

+ **Fun Fox Ltd.**, 512 7th Av. (37-8), 41st St., 944-6520 x. 501, 1-2-3 to 34, M-F 9-4:45, S 9-12:45, ch., no c.c., exch., no rfd. Small selection. Factory outlet for Fox Run, which is headquartered on another floor. Bonus discount to BF readers: 5%. Sells: **Ladies' Coats, Dresses, Skirts, Slacks, Tops, Sweaters, Blouses.**

Gabay's Outlet, 225 1st Av. (13-4), 254-3180, LL to 1st Av., M-S 9-6, Sun 10-4, all cash, exch., no rfd. Defectives mostly from department stores. Sells: **Men's Hats, Men's Shoes—Dress, Men's Shoes—Sports/Work, Ladies' Coats, Ladies' Suits—Custom-Tailored, Men's Belts, Men's Coats—Dressy.**

Galleria International, 542 Broadway (Broome), 431-6320, J-M-N-QB-RR-6 to Canal, Sun-F 9-5, all cash, exch., no rfd. Sells: **Dresses, Skirts, Slacks, Tops, Sweaters, Blouses.**

Garo Leather, Queens, 98-18 Metropolitan Av. (Herrick), Forest Hills, 793-3743, no subway stop nearby, M-F 10-5:30, S 11-5, all cash, no exch. or rfd. Sells: **Ladies' Shoes & Boots.**

Gatrimone Shoes, 371 7th Av. (30-1), 695-4124, 1 to 28, M-F 10-6:30, S 11-5:30, ch., c.c., exch., no rfd. Sells: **Men's Shoes—Dress.**

Genao's Shoes, 95 Rivington St. (Orchard), 673-9811, F-J-M to Delancey & Essex, 7 days 10-6, ch., c.c., exch., no rfd. Sells: **Men's Shoes—Dress, Ladies' Shoes & Boots.**

* **G.H. Tailor**, 18B Doyers (Pell), 732-0368, J-M-N-QB-RR-6 to Canal, J-M-RR-4-5-6 to Chambers & Bkln. Bridge, B-D to Grand, 7 days 10-7, all cash, exch. or rfd. Sells: **Chinese Jackets, Robes, Tops, Sweaters, Blouses.**

Gino Napoli, 141 5th Av. at 21st St., 6th floor, 73-8220, N-RR to 23rd St., 7 days 9:30-5:30, c.c. $50+, no ch., exch., no rfd. Sells: **Men's Suits—New.**

* **Girls Club Thrift Shop**, 202 E. 77th at 3rd Av., 535-8570, 6 to 77, M-S 10-4:45, all cash, no exch. or rfd. Sells: **Men's Suits—Used, Used Clothing For Women.**

** **Goldman & Cohen**, 54 Orchard St. (Grand), 966-0737, F-J-M to Delancey & Essex, F to E. Broadway, Sun-Th 9-5:30, F 9:3:30, ch., c.c., no exch. or rfd. Large selection. Continual specials and sales that are often terrific values. Regular merchandise is not quite as good value as the other nearby stores recommended for lingerie. Sells: **Lingerie, Loungewear.**

Goldstone Sportswear, 533 Broadway (Spring), 966-6077, N-RR to Prince St., 6 to Spring, M-Th 10-6, F 10-2, Sun 10-5, all cash, exch., no rfd. No try-ons. Sells: **Dresses, Skirts, Slacks, Tops, Sweaters, Blouses.**

* **Goodfriend's**, 381 Park Av. S. at 27th St., 686-6910, 6 to 28, M-F 8-5:30, S 11-5, ch., no c.c., 7-day exch. or rfd. Sells: **Ladies' Coats, Dresses, Skirts, Slacks, Lingerie, Loungewear, Tops, Sweaters, Blouses.**

* **Gucci on 7**, 699 5th Av. (54-5), 1 flight up inside store, 826-2600 (ask for Gucci on 7), E-F to 5th Av., M-S 9:30-6, ch., c.c., no exch. or rfd. Clearance outlet for the stuff downstairs—all Gucci. Sells: **Men's Belts, Men's Coats—Dressy, Coats—Leather & Sheepskin, Men's Formals & Tuxedos, Men's Gloves, Men's Hats, Men's Pants/Slacks, Shirts, Shoes—Bedroom & Slippers, Men's Shoes—Dress, Men's Shoes—Sports/Work, Men's Suits—New, Men's Sweaters, Men's Swim-**

7: CLOTHING-DIRECTORY

suits, Ties, Bathrobes & P.J.'s, Ladies' Belts, Ladies' Coats, Dresses, Skirts, Slacks, Ladies' Gloves, Millinery, Hats, Ladies' Shoes & Boots, Ladies' Suits & Blazers, Ladies' Swimsuits, Tops, Sweaters, Blouses.

H. Tenzer, 49 1st Av. at 3rd St., 473-6082, F to 2nd Av., Sun-F 9-5, all cash, exch. or rfd. Sells: **Jeans, Underwear.**

Hamer's Shoes, Brooklyn, 5102 12th Av., 871-3766, B to 50th St., Sun-Th 10:30-7, F 10:30-3, c.c., no ch., no exch. or rfd. Sells: **Kids' Shoes, Men's Shoes—Dress, Men's Shoes—Sports/Work.**

** **Hampshire Clothes**, 85 5th Av. at 16th, 4th floor, 675-7806, LL-N-QB-RR-4-5-6 to Union Sq., B-F-LL to 14th St. & 6th Av., M-F 9-5, S 9-3, ch., c.c., exch., no rfd. Sells: **Men's Coats—Dressy, Men's Suits—New.**

* **Harris's Women's Apparel**, 275 7th Av. (25-6), 989-9765, 1 to 28, M-S 10-5:45, Sun 10-5; Queens, 70-44 Austin St., Forest Hills, 263-1057, E-F-GG-N to 71-Continental Avs., M-S 10-5:45, Sun 12-5. Both stores: ch., c.c., no exch. or rfd. Another store in Hempstead. Sells: **Ladies' Coats, Dresses, Skirts, Slacks, Ladies' Suits & Blazers, Tops, Sweaters, Blouses.**

*+ **H.E.R. Maternity**, 213 W. 35 (7th Av.), 13th floor, 594-8580, A-AA-CC-E to 34, M-F 9-4:30, all cash, exch., no rfd. Bonus discount to BF readers: 5% to 10%. Sells: **Maternity-Wear.**

* **Helen Perl Shoes**, 692 Lexington Av. (57), 752-2543, N-RR-4-5-6 to 59th & Lex., MTWFS 10:30-6:30, Th 10:30-8, ch., c.c., no exch. or rfd. Sells: **Ladies' Shoes & Boots.**

** **Helen Walters Sportswear**, Brooklyn, 2686 Coney Island Av. (Desmond Court), 743-9167, D-M-QB to Neck Rd., M-S 9:30-5, Sun 12-4, ch., no c.c., exch., no rfd. Mostly polyester sportswear, very large sizes. Sells: **Dresses, Skirts, Slacks, Tops, Sweaters, Blouses.**

* **High Fashion**, 149 Orchard St. (Rivington), 674-8273, F-J-M to Delancey & Essex, F to 2nd Av., 7 days 10-6, ch., c.c., exch., no rfd. Sells: **Ladies' Shoes & Boots.**

+ **Holiday Bridal**, 120 W. 37 (B'wy), 2nd floor, 564-0316, B-D-F-N-QB-RR to 34, 1-2-3 to 34, M-F 8:30-4, all cash, no exch. or rfd. Both off-the-rack and custom-fitted. Bonus discount to BF readers: 2% to 10%. Sells: **Bridals.**

* **Hong Kong Import**, 252 A E. 51 (3rd Av.), 753-5340, E-F to Lex. Av., M-S 11-7, ch., c.c., exch., no rfd. Very small store. Sells: **Coats—Quilted & Parkas, Ladies' Coats, Dresses, Skirts, Slacks, Tops, Sweaters, Blouses.**

* **I. Margulis**, Queens, 114-49 Queens Blvd. (77th Av.), Forest Hills, 263-5052, E-F to Union Tnpk., E-F to 75th Av., MTWFS 10-6, Th 10-8, ch., c.c., no exch. or rfd. Sells: **Ladies' Coats, Dresses, Skirts, Slacks, Ladies' Suits & Blazers.**

I. Tuschman & Sons, 61 Orchard St. (Grand), 226-4318, F to E. Broadway, B-D to Grand, Sun-F 9-5:30, ch., no c.c., exch. or rfd. (But only if new.) Sells: **Socks, Underwear, Hosiery.**

* **Ideal Hosiery**, 339 Grand St. (Ludlow), 226-4792, F-J-M to Delancey & Essex, Sun-F 9-6, all cash, exch., no rfd. Sells: **Underwear, Hosiery.**

India Malaysia Imports, 28 W. 46 (5th-6th), 869-9995, B-D-F to 47, M-F 9:30-6, S 9:30-1, c.c., no ch., exch., no rfd. Sells: **Dresses, Skirts, Slacks, Tops, Sweaters, Blouses.**

*+ **Interstate Footwear**, 152 Duane St. at W. B'way, 227-1886, A-CC-1-2-3 to Chambers, 1 to Franklin, M-F 8-4:30, c.c., no ch., exch., no rfd. Bonus discount to BF readers: 10%. Sells: **Men's Shoes—Dress.**

*** **Irving's Shoes**, 752 9th Av. (51), 265-8286, A-AA-CC-E to 50, T-S 10-5, all cash, exch. or rfd. Closeouts, department-store irregulars, etc. Examine shoes carefully before buying, and you can get incredible steals here on some exquisite footwear. Sells: **Men's Shoes—Dress.**

Irvington House Thrift, 1534 2nd Av. at 80th, 879-4555, 6 to 77, MTThFS 9:30-6, W 9:30-8, all cash, no exch. or rfd. Large selection. Sells: **Men's Suits—Used, Used Clothing For Women.**

I&Z Leather, 191 Orchard St. (Stanton), 673-1796, F to 2nd Av., F-J-M to Delancey & Essex, 7 days 9:30-5, c.c., no ch., exch., no rfd. Sells: **Coats—Leather & Sheepskin.**

* **J. Chuckles**, 321 Madison Av. at 42nd St., 867-3771, 4-5-6-7 to Grand Central, M-F 10-7, S 10-6; 1290 6th Av. (52), 757-6240, B-D-F to 47, M-F 10-7, S 10-6, Sun 12-6. Both stores: ch., c.c., exch., no rfd. Large selection. Boutique styles. Listed 'regular' prices are about 15% below competition on most items; 80% of stock is discounted 25-50% off that. Zoom is clearance-store for chain. Sells: **Ladies' Coats,**

7: CLOTHING-DIRECTORY

Dresses, Skirts, Slacks, Ladies' Gloves, Hosiery, Lingerie, Loungewear, Millinery, Hats, Ladies' Shoes & Boots, Ladies' Suits & Blazers, Ladies' Swimsuits, Tops, Sweaters, Blouses, Personal Accessories.

    J. Sherman Shoes, 121 Division St. (Orchard), 233-7898, F to E. Broadway, Sun-Th 8-4:30, F 8-3, c.c., no ch., no exch. or rfd. Sells: **Men's Shoes—Dress, Men's Shoes—Sports/Work.**

**   **Jack's Bargain Stores**, 2 W. 14 at 5th Av., 2nd floor, 924-5322, B-F-LL to 14th St. & 6th Av.; 142 W. 34 (6th-7th), 947-4135, B-D-F-N-QB-RR to 34, 1-2-3 to 34. Both stores: 9:30-7 M-S, all cash, 25-day exch. or rfd. Other stores in Newark. Specializes in clothing. Other items: small selection. Sells: **Kids' Clothing, Dresses, Skirts, Slacks, Tops, Sweaters, Blouses, Bikes, Furnishings.**

**   **Jacob Young & Son**, 329 Grand St. (Orchard), 225-9232, F-J-M to Delancey & Essex, Sun-Th 9-5, F 9-3, all cash, no exch. or rfd. Sells: **Socks, Underwear.**

*   **Jay's Advance**, 491 7th Av. at 37th St., 9th floor, 239-1166, A-AA-CC-E to 34, M-F 9-5, S 10-3, ch., no c.c., no exch. or rfd. Sells: **Dresses, Skirts, Slacks, Ladies' Suits & Blazers, Tops, Sweaters, Blouses.**

**   **Jay's Bargain Store**, 40 W. 14 (5th-6th), 691-7142, B-F-LL to 14th St. & 6th Av., M-S 9:30-7, Sun 10:30-5:30, c.c., no ch., 21-day exch. or rfd. Huge selection. Sells: **Kids' Clothing.**

*   **J.B.Z. Unlimited**, 121 Orchard St. (Delancey), 473-8550, F-J-M to Delancey & Essex, Sun-F 9-6, ch., c.c., no exch. or rfd. Sells: **Ladies' Coats, Dresses, Skirts, Slacks, Tops, Sweaters, Blouses.**

**   **Jeans & Things**, 197 Madison Street (E. B'wy), 964-9428, F to E. Broadway, M-S 9-7, all cash, exch., no rfd. Sells: **Jeans—Designer.**

**   **Jeans 'N Things**, 140 W. 4 (6th-MacDougal), 677-7158, A-AA-B-CC-D-E-F to 4, M-S 11-8, ch., c.c., exch., no rfd. 7 Sells: **Coats—Leather & Sheepskin, Men's Pants/Slacks, Shirts, Jeans—Designer.**

    Jeff's Boutique, 122 Orchard St. (Delancey), 533-8222, F-J-M to Delancey & Essex, 7 days 9-6, ch., c.c., exch., no rfd. Sells: **Ladies' Coats, Dresses, Skirts, Slacks, Ladies' Suits & Blazers.**

    Jerri's Ltd., Brooklyn, 312 Ditmas Av., 871-0955 & 435-5832, F to Ditmas, 7 days 10-5:45, ch., no c.c., 7-day exch. or rfd. Sells: **Dresses, Skirts, Slacks, Tops, Sweaters, Blouses.**

    Jerri's Shoes, 2611 Broadway (98-9), 866-2820, 1-2-3 to 96, M-F 10:30-6:45, S 10:30-6:15, ch., c.c., exch., no rfd. Sells: **Ladies' Shoes & Boots.**

***   **Job Lot Trdg.**, 140 Church St. (Warren-Chambers), 962-4142, A-CC-1-2-3 to Chambers; 412 5th Av. (37-8), 398-9210, B-D-F to 42. Both stores: M-F 8-5:30, S 8-4:30, all cash, 15-day exch. or rfd. Both are huge stores, with terrific selections. Sells: **Coats—Quilted & Parkas, Men's Gloves, Men's Pants/Slacks, Shirts, Shoes—Bedroom & Slippers, Men's Shoes—Sports/Work, Socks, Men's Sweaters, Dinnerware & Cookware, Foods, Home-Improvement Items, Housewares, Jewelry & Gifts, Linens, Personal Accessories, Sporting Goods, Stationery & Art Supplies, Toys, Games & Hobbies, Warehouse Salvage Job-Lot.**

**   **Joe's Bargain Center**, 123 1st Av. (7-8), phoneless, LL to 1st Av., F to 2nd Av., M-F 10-6, all cash, no exch. or rfd. Irregulars. Sells: **Socks, Personal Accessories.**

+   **John Cipriano Shoes, 148 Orchard St. (Rivington), 477-5858, F-J-M to Delancey & Essex, W-Sun 7:30-5:30, all cash, exch., no rfd. Much of the stock is job lots, so it's best to phone first to ask what they've got, just to make sure they've got what you want. Bonus discount to BF readers: 5% to 15%. Sells: **Shoes—Bedroom & Slippers, Men's Shoes—Dress, Men's Shoes—Sports/Work.**

**   **John's Shoe Outlet**, 204 W. 14 (7th), 255-7035, 1-2-3 to 14, M-S 10:30-7, all cash, exch., no rfd. Good selection. Sells: **Men's Shoes—Dress.**

    Joli Madame Boutique, 145 Orchard St. (Rivington), 477-2471, F-J-M to Delancey & Essex, F to 2nd Av., 7 days 10-6, c.c., no ch., exch., no rfd. Sells: **Ladies' Shoes & Boots, Personal Accessories.**

*   **Judy Better Dresses**, 20 W. 43 (5th-6th), 719-2999, B-D-F to 42, 7 to 5th Av., Sun-Th 0-6, F 10-4, ch., c.c., exch., no rfd. Sells: **Ladies' Coats, Dresses, Skirts, Slacks, Ladies' Suits & Blazers, Tops, Sweaters, Blouses.**

*   **Kalga Leather Sportswear**, 245 W. 29 (7th-8th), 11th floor, 594-932, 1 to 28, M-F 8-6, all cash, no exch. or rfd. An authentic factory-outlet. Sells: **Coats—Leather & Sheepskin.**

    Kaymore, 92 Orchard St. (Broome), 475-3854, F-J-M to Delancey &

Essex, Sun-Th 9-6, F 9-4, ch., c.c., 10-day exch. or rfd. Sells: **Dresses, Skirts, Slacks, Ladies' Suits & Blazers.**

❋ **Kazootie**, 59 Nassau St. (Maiden-John), 964-4218, A-CC-J-M-RR-2-3-4-5 to B'wy-Nassau & Fulton, M-F 8-6:30; 303 Park Av. S. at 23rd St., 674-1967, 6 to 23, M-F 9:30-6:30; 136 E. 57 at Lex., 826-0859, N-RR-4-5-6 to 59th & Lex., M-F 9:30-8. All stores: ch., c.c., exch., no rfd. Sells: **Dresses, Skirts, Slacks, Tops, Sweaters, Blouses.**

❋ **Klein's**, 199 Orchard St. (Houston), 475-9804, F to 2nd Av., Sun-F 10-5, all cash, exch., no rfd. Small stand. Closeouts. Sells: **Socks, Underwear.**

Kol-Bo Discount, 611 Broadway at Houston, 473-7829, N-RR to 8th St., B-D-F-6 to B'wy-Laf. & Bleecker, M-F 7:30-6, SSun 10-4, all cash, exch., no rfd. In the recommended categories, carries: earmuffs, cheap small backpacks, berets, Chinese bedroom-shoes. Sells: **Men's Hats, Shoes—Bedroom & Slippers, Sporting Goods.**

Lace Up, 119 Orchard St. (Delancey), 475-8040, F-J-M to Delancey & Essex, Sun-F 9:30-5:30, ch., c.c., 7-day exch., no rfd. Sells: **Ladies' Shoes & Boots.**

L.B.C. Clothing, 337 Grand St. (Ludlow-Orchard), 226-1620, F-J-M to Delancey & Essex, M-F 10-6, S 9-6, F 9-4, ch., no c.c., 7-day exch. or rfd. Sells: **Men's Coats—Dressy, Men's Pants/Slacks, Men's Suits—New.**

❋❋ **Lea's**, 81 Rivington St. (Orchard), 677-2043, F-J-M to Delancey & Essex, Sun-Th 10-5:30, F 10-3, ch., c.c., 10-day exch., no rfd. The steepest top-designer discounts on Orchard St., and one of the best three NYC designer-wear discount stores, along with Abe Geller and Azriel Altman. Sells: **Ladies' Coats, Dresses, Skirts, Slacks, Ladies' Suits & Blazers.**

❋ **Lebanon Fashions**, 1179 Broadway (28), 2nd floor, 686-4636, N-RR to 49th St., M-F 8-6, S 8-4, all cash, exch., no rfd. Sells: **Dresses, Skirts, Slacks, Jeans—Designer, Tops, Sweaters, Blouses.**

❋ **Leon**, 1 Essex (Canal), 254-1880, F to E. Broadway, Sun-F 11:30-6, ch., no c.c., 5-day exch. or rfd. Sportswear closeouts. Sells: **Dresses, Skirts, Slacks, Tops, Sweaters, Blouses, Warehouse Salvage Job-Lot.**

Lesh Clothing, 100 5th Av. at 15th St., 9th floor, 255-6893, B-F-LL to 14th St. & 6th Av., LL-N-QB-RR-4-5-6 to Union Sq., M-F 9-6, S 9-4, ch., no c.c., exch., no rfd. Sells: **Men's Suits—New.**

Lester's Children's Wear, Brooklyn, 1110 Av. U. at Con. Is. Av., & 2411 Coney Is. Av. at U, 375-7337 & 339-1131, D-M-QB to Av. U, MWFS 10-6, TTh 10-9, ch., c.c., exch., no rfd. Sells: **Kids' Clothing, Kids' Shoes.**

Leung Trdg., 44 E. Broadway (Market), 431-4474, F to E. Broadway, B-D to Grand, J-M-RR-4-5-6 to Chambers & Bkln. Bridge, 7 days 10-7, ch., no c.c., exch. or rfd. Sells: **Chinese Jackets, Robes.**

+ **Lever & Greenberg**, 271 Canal St. (B'wy-Lafayette), 226-1023, J-M-N-QB-RR-6 to Canal, 7 days 9-6, ch., c.c., exch., no rfd. Mostly closeouts of outdated fashions. Uneven values, but some are excellent. Sells: **Men's Coats—Dressy, Men's Pants/Slacks, Men's Suits—New.**

Lewis & Clark, 228 7th Av. (23-4), 255-4686, 1 to 23, M-F 9:30-6, S 10-4, ch., c.c., 7-day exch. or rfd. Sells: **Men's Belts, Coats—Quilted & Parkas, Men's Gloves, Men's Pants/Slacks, Shirts, Men's Sweaters.**

Linea Garbo, 109 E. 42 (Lex.), 687-4139, 4-5-6-7 to Grand Central, MTWFS 11-6, Th 11-7; 620 5th Av. (49-50), Rockefeller Ctr. Promenade, 246-1938, B-D-F to 47, MTWFS 10-6, Th 10-7. Both stores: ch., c.c., exch. or rfd. Classically elegant styles, extravagantly high quality shoes and boots. No narrow widths. Prices are high, but unusually low for this quality. Affil. with Loradan. Sells: **Ladies' Shoes & Boots.**

Lismore Hosiery, 334 Grand St. (Ludlow), 674-3440, F-J-M to Delancey & Essex, Sun-Th 8-5:30, ch., c.c., 4 Sells: **Socks, Hosiery.**

❋❋ **Little Rascals**, 101 Orchard St. (Delancey), 226-1680, F-J-M to Delancey & Essex, irregular hours, usually Sun-F 11-6, ch., c.c., exch., no rfd. Much European-made wear. Sells: **Kids' Clothing.**

❋❋ **Loehmann's**, Bronx, W. Fordham Rd. at Jerome Av., 295-4100, 4 to Fordham Rd., M-S 10-9:30; Brooklyn, 19 Duryea Place (Flatbush), MTThFS 10-5:30, W 10-9:30, D-M-QB to Beverly; Queens, 60-06 99th St., Rego Park, 271-4000, F-GG-N to 63rd Dr., MTThFS 10-5:30, W 10-9:30. All stores: ch., no c.c., no exch. or rfd. Large selection. 54 stores nationwide, including suburbs. Sells: **Ladies' Coats, Ladies' Coats—Fake Fur, Dresses, Skirts, Slacks, Ladies' Suits & Blazers, Tops, Sweaters, Blouses.**

Lord's Ex-Imp., 73 W. 38 (6th Av.), 398-0346, B-D-F-N-QB-RR to 34, B-

7: CLOTHING-DIRECTORY

D-F to 42, M-F 10-5:30, S 11-4, all cash, exch., no rfd. Sells: **Dresses, Skirts, Slacks, Jeans—Designer, Tops, Sweaters, Blouses.**

* **Louis Barall & Son**, 58 Lispenard St., 226-6195, J-M-N-QB-RR-6 to Canal, M-F 9:30-6, S 9:30-5, ch., no c.c., exch. or rfd. Exceptionally good on raincoats. Sells: **Men's Coats—Dressy, Men's Suits—New.**

** **L.S. Men's Clothing**, 23 W. 45 (5th-6th), 2nd floor, 575-0933, B-D-F to 47, M 10-7, T-Th 10-6, F 10-5, Sun by appt., ch., c.c., exch. or rfd. (But only if unaltered.) Emphasis on natural-shoulder styles. Sells: **Men's Coats—Dressy, Men's Suits—New.**

** **Lucky Gift**, 20 Bowery at Pell, 233-0960 & 962-9793, J-M-RR-4-5-6 to Chambers & Bkln. Bridge, F to E. Broadway, 7 days 10-8, all cash, no exch. or rfd. Small store. Chinese-made items. Sells: **Coats—Quilted & Parkas, Linens.**

** **Lucky Rose Shoes**, 501 W. 125 (Amsterdam), phoneless, A-AA-B-CC-D to 125, 1 to 125, usually open T-S 10-5, all cash, no exch. or rfd. Sells: **Ladies' Shoes & Boots.**

** **Lupu's**, Brooklyn, 1494 Coney Island Av. (K-L), 377-3793&5733, D-M-QB to Av. J, MTThFS 10-6, W 10-9, ch., no c.c., no exch. or rfd. Sells: **Ladies' Coats, Dresses, Skirts, Slacks, Ladies' Suits & Blazers, Tops, Sweaters, Blouses.**

Luso Sales, 63 W. 36, 563-4180, B-D-F-N-QB-RR to 34, M-F 9:30-6, S 9:30-2, ch., no c.c., exch., no rfd. Sells: **Jeans.**

Lynn's, 103 W. 14 (6th Av.), 929-9030, B-F-LL to 14th St. & 6th Av.; Brooklyn, 545 Fulton St. (DeKalb), 834-9368, 2-3 to Hoyt, B-D-M-N-QB-RR to DeKalb; Brooklyn, 5710 5th Av., 492-3414, N-RR to 59th St.; Queens, 5609 Catalpa Av., Ridgewood, 497-4164, M to Fresh Pond Rd.; Queens, 40-17 31st Av., Astoria, 932-8661, F-GG-N to Steinway St.; Queens, 162-11 & 162-19 Jamaica Av., Jamaica, 523-5855, E-F to Parsons Blvd.; Bronx, 305 E. Fordham Rd. (Kingsbridge), 584-1847, CC-D to Fordham Rd.; 579 W. 181 (St. Nicholas), 927-8476, 1 to 181; Bronx, 380 E. 150 (3rd), 665-7565, 2-5 to 3rd Av. All stores: M-S 10-5:30, c.c., no ch., 5-day exch. or rfd. Sells: **Ladies' Coats, Dresses, Skirts, Slacks, Hosiery, Lingerie, Loungewear, Millinery, Hats, Ladies' Swimsuits, Tops, Sweaters, Blouses.**

* **Lynn's Shoes**, 163 Orchard St. (Rivington-Stanton), 674-2840, F-J-M to Delancey & Essex, F to 2nd Av., 7 days 9-6, c.c., no ch., exch., no rfd. Sells: **Ladies' Shoes & Boots.**

** **M. Frankel ('Moe's')**, 39 1st Av. (3), 673-4590, F to 2nd Av., M-S 9-6, Sun 11-5, all cash, exch. or rfd. Irregulars of top-brand underwear. Sells: **Underwear.**

* **M. Friedman Hosiery**, 326 Grand St. (Orchard), 674-3292, F to E. Broadway, F-J-M to Delancey & Essex, B-D to Grand, Sun-F 9-5, ch., no c.c., exch., no rfd. Sells: **Socks, Underwear, Hosiery.**

* **M. Steuer Hosiery**, 31 W. 32 (5th-6th), 563-0052, B-D-F-N-QB-RR to 34, M-F 8-5, S 10-2, ch., $15+, no c.c., no exch. or rfd. Factory outlet for the Value Hosiery chain. No purchase only of a single pair of hosiery—only 3+. But lingerie singly. Sells: **Hosiery, Lingerie.**

Madeline's Hosiery, Queens, 30-14 Steinway St., Astoria, 721-4338, F-GG-N to Steinway St., RR to 30th Av., MS 9:30-7, TW 9:30-6:30, ThF 9:30-7:30, all cash, no exch. or rfd. Sells: **Hosiery.**

*+ **Main St. Fashion World**, Queens, 67-09 Main St., Flushing, 544-3254, no subway stop nearby, Sun-Th 10:30-6, ch., c.c., 7-day exch., no rfd. Some seconds. Bonus discount to BF readers: 10%. Sells: **Ladies' Coats, Dresses, Skirts, Slacks, Ladies' Suits & Blazers, Tops, Sweaters, Blouses.**

* **Major Dept. Store**, Brooklyn, 386 Fulton St. (Jay), 875-6924, A-CC-F to Jay St. & Boro Hall, M-S 9:30-7, c.c., no ch., 7-day exch. or rfd. Sells: **Kids' Clothing.**

** **Manos Del Uruguay**, 35 W. 36 (5th-6th), 12th floor, 564-6115, B-D-F-N-QB-RR to 34, open only 3rd Monday after Thanksgiving through Dec. 23, M-F 11-7, ch., c.c., no exch. or rfd. Beautiful multi-tonal sweaters, hats, scarves, ties, jackets, capes, and mittens. Wool is hand-spun and kettle-dyed. 50% off. No retail at other times than indicated. Sells: **Hand-Knit Sweaters, Gloves, Etc., Jewelry & Gifts, Personal Accessories.**

Mansfield Clothes, 141 5th Av. at 21st St., 7th floor, 228-1410, N-RR to 23rd St., M-F 9-5, Sun 9-4, c.c., no ch., exch., no rfd. Sells: **Men's Coats—Dressy, Men's Suits—New.**

Manufacturer's Outlet, Brooklyn, 1224 Av. U, 336-5123, D-M-QB to Av. U, M-S 11-6, c.c., no ch., exch., no rfd. Sells: **Jeans—Designer, Tops, Sweaters, Blouses.**

** **Manufacturer's Shoe Outlet**, 537 Broadway (Spring-Broome),

226-6266, N-RR to Prince St., M-F 9-6, S 9-2, Sun 10-5, all cash, exch., no rfd. (But no exch. SSun.) The premier outlet-store for the Shoe Town chain of shoe-discounters. The other outlets are called 'Shoe Giant' (recommended elsewhere). Sells: **Kids' Shoes, Men's Shoes—Dress, Men's Shoes—Sports/Work, Ladies' Shoes & Boots.**

* **Max's Better Dress**, 510 Madison Av. (52-3), 755-2434, E-F to 5th Av., irregular hours, usually M-F 8-6, Sun 11-5, c.c., exch., no rfd. Small store. Sells: **Ladies' Coats, Dresses, Skirts, Slacks, Ladies' Suits & Blazers, Tops, Sweaters, Blouses.**

*** **M.C. Corner**, 240 Central Park South at Broadway on Columbus Circle, 265-4151, A-AA-B-CC-D-1 to 59, M-S 9-7:30, Sun 10-6, ch., c.c., exch., no rfd. Much is last season's merchandise. Some of the bargains are mind-blowing; others are just very good. Sells: **Men's Coats—Dressy, Coats—Quilted & Parkas, Jeans, Men's Pants/Slacks, Shirts, Men's Shoes—Dress, Men's Suits—New, Men's Sweaters, Ties.**

** **M.C.W. Apparel**, 546 Broadway (Spring-Prince), 966-0280, N-RR to Prince St., M-F 10-6, S 10-3, Sun 9-5, all cash, exch., no rfd. No try-ons. Sells: **Dresses, Skirts, Slacks, Ladies' Suits & Blazers, Tops, Sweaters, Blouses.**

* **Mern's**, 525 Madson Av. (54), 371-9195, E-F to 5th Av.; 75 Church St. at Vesey, 227-5471, AA-E to World Trade Ctr. Both stores: M-F 9:30-6:30, S 9:30-6, ch., c.c., 7-day exch. or rfd. Mad. Av. store is much larger. No women's wear at Church St. Note: Mern's sometimes shows 'list' prices that are lower than actual. Then values are better than appear. Sells: **Men's Belts, Coats—Quilted & Parkas, Coats—Leather & Sheepskin, Men's Gloves, Men's Hats, Men's Pants/Slacks, Shirts, Men's Shoes—Dress, Socks, Men's Suits—New, Men's Sweaters, Men's Swimsuits, Ties, Dresses, Skirts, Slacks, Ladies' Suits & Blazers.**

Merri-Jean's Factory Outlet, Bronx, 3261 White Plains Rd. (Burke), 654-1900, 2-5 to Burke Av., M-S 10-5, ch., no c.c., exch., no rfd. Sells: **Ladies' Coats, Dresses, Skirts, Slacks, Ladies' Suits & Blazers, Tops, Sweaters, Blouses.**

Metro Shoe Mart, 339 Park Av. S. (24-5), 254-5188, 6 to 23, M-F 7:30-5:30, all cash, no exch. or rfd. Sells: **Ladies' Shoes & Boots.**

Mfr.'s Uniform Outlet, Queens, 69-28 Queens Blvd., Woodside, 335-3900, 7 to 69th St., M-F 9:30-8, S 9:30-6, Sun 11-5, ch., c.c., 10-day exch. or rfd. Also uniforms for waitresses, beauticians, barbers. Sells: **Uniforms For Nurses.**

Michael's Resale Dress, 1041 Madison Av. (79-80), 2nd floor, 737-7273, 6 to 77, T-S 9:30-6, ch., no c.c., no exch. or rfd. Sells: **Slightly Used Designer-Wear.**

* **Michelle Imports**, 1187 Broadway (28-9), 889-3620, N-RR to 28th St., M-F 9:30-8, S 10-5, all cash, no exch. or rfd. All cotton garments from India. Sells: **Dresses, Skirts, Slacks, Tops, Sweaters, Blouses.**

* **Milton Siegel**, 14 Orchard St. (Canal), 925-9519, F to E. Broadway, Sun-Th 9-5, F 9-3, all cash, no exch. or rfd. By the dozen only. Some irregulars at about 70% discount. Sells: **Socks.**

* **Mintzer Mercantile**, 313 Church St. (Lispenard), 226-5413&5344&5428, A-AA-CC-E-1 to Canal, M-F 9-5:30, S 9-2:30, ch., no c.c., 3-day exch. or rfd. Sometimes some excellent bargains here. 40-70% off. Sells: **Ladies' Coats, Dresses, Skirts, Slacks, Hosiery, Jeans—Designer, Lingerie, Loungewear, Ladies' Swimsuits, Tops, Sweaters, Blouses.**

Mitchell's Leather Wear, 33 Orchard St. (Hester), 925-6757, F to E. Broadway, Sun-Th 9-5, F 9-4, c.c., no ch., exch., no rfd. Sells: **Coats—Leather & Sheepskin.**

* **Mitsu**, 25 W. 35 (5th-6th), 947-7892, B-D-F-N-QB-RR to 34, M-S 10-6, all cash, exch., no rfd. Carries some of the same stuff as Azuma, but for about 20% less. Sells: **Shoes—Bedroom & Slippers, Home-Improvement Items, Jewelry & Gifts.**

M&J Sportswear, 486 Broadway at Broome, 925-3145&48&89, J-M-N-QB-RR-6 to Canal, M-F 10-6, Sun 10-5, all cash, no rfd. 6 or more items, slightly better discount. Sells: **Dresses, Skirts, Slacks, Tops, Sweaters, Blouses.**

M&M Menswear, 167 Orchard St. (Stanton), 982-9188, F to 2nd Av., 7 days 9-6, all cash, exch., no rfd. Sells: **Jeans.**

** **M&M Tailors**, 105 Av. A (7), 475-8312, 6 to Astor, M-F 8-7, S 8-4, all cash, exch., no rfd. Ready-made and to-order men's suits; only small stock of women's wear, all ready-made. Sells: **Men's Coats—Dressy, Men's Suits—New, Suits—Custom-Tailored, Ladies' Coats.**

Modak Apparel, 29 John St. (B'wy-Nassau), 267-5145, A-CC-J-M-

7: CLOTHING-DIRECTORY

RR-2-3-4-5 to B'wy-Nassau & Fulton, M-S 9-6, c.c., no ch., exch., no rfd. Sells: **Men's Suits—New.**

    Moe Ginsburg, 162 5th Av. at 21st, 7th & 2nd floors, 242-3482 & 982-5254, N-RR to 23rd St., 7 days 9:30-5:30, ch., c.c., 7-day exch. or rfd. Large selection. Sells: **Men's Belts, Men's Coats—Dressy, Coats—Quilted & Parkas, Men's Formals & Tuxedos, Men's Pants/Slacks, Shirts, Socks, Men's Suits—New, Men's Sweaters, Ties.**

*   **Mohan's Custom Tailor**, 60 E. 42 (Park-Lex.), rm. 1762, 697-0050, 4-5-6-7 to Grand Central, M-S 10:30-8, ch., c.c. Everything is custom-made. Sells: **Shirts, Suits—Custom-Tailored.**

    Most's Dept. Store, Queens, 210-15 Horace Harding Blvd., Bayside, 225-3455, no subway stop nearby, T-S 9:30-6, all cash, no exch. or rfd. Sells: **Kids' Clothing, Men's Gloves, Men's Pants/Slacks, Shirts, Dresses, Skirts, Slacks, Lingerie, Tops, Sweaters, Blouses, Linens.**

    M&R Fashions, 596 Broadway (Houston), 226-3535, N-RR to Prince St., M-F 7-5:30, all cash, exch., no rfd. Sells: **Dresses, Skirts, Slacks, Lingerie, Tops, Sweaters, Blouses.**

*+   **Mr. Excitement**, Queens, 81-53 Lefferts Blvd. at Cuthbert, 847-3600, E-F to Union Tnpk., TThFS 11-6, ch., c.c., exch. or rfd. Small store. Bonus discount to BF readers: 10% to 20%. Sells: **Coats—Quilted & Parkas, Men's Gloves, Men's Pants/Slacks, Shirts, Socks, Men's Sweaters, Warehouse Salvage Job-Lot.**

*   **Mr. Tony**, 134 5th Av. (18-19), 3rd floor, 255-8585, N-RR to 23rd St., B-F-LL to 14th St. & 6th Av., LL-N-QB-RR-4-5-6 to Union Sq., M-F 8:30-5:30, S 8:30-1; 120 W. 37 (B'wy), 594-0930, B-D-F-N-QB-RR to 34, M-F 9-6. Both stores:, no exch. or rfd. Request raw-canvas fitting. Sells: **Suits—Custom-Tailored, Ladies' Suits—Custom-Tailored.**

    Ms. Miss or Mrs., 462 7th Av. (35), 8th floor, 736-0557, A-AA-CC-E to 34, MTWF 9-6, Th 9-8, S 9-4, ch., no c.c., no exch. or rfd. Will phone-quote. Will special-order. Takes mail-orders. Very cooperative. Large selection. Very crowded, yet personalized attention. Sells: **Ladies' Coats, Dresses, Skirts, Slacks, Ladies' Suits & Blazers, Tops, Sweaters, Blouses.**

*   **Nam Nam Boutique**, 303 Park Av. S. (23), 533-9642, 6 to 23, M-F 9-7, S 11-5, c.c., no ch., exch., no rfd. Sells: **Dresses, Skirts, Slacks, Tops, Sweaters, Blouses.**

    Natan Borlam, Brooklyn, 157 Havemeyer St., 782-0108 & 387-2983, J-M to Marcy, Sun-Th 10-5, F 10-2, ch., no c.c., 14-day exch. or rfd. Very cooperative. Tough neighborhood. Sells: **Kids' Clothing.**

*   **Nathan Kurtz**, 27 Canal St. (Essex-Ludlow), 475-6550, F to E. Broadway, Sun-Th 9-5, F 9-3, ch., no c.c., exch. or rfd. Sells: **Jeans, Underwear, Bathrobes & P.J.'s, Hosiery, Loungewear.**

*   **National Brands Outlet**, Queens, 95-24 63rd Rd., Rego Park, 459-0300, F-GG-N to 63rd Dr., M-S 10-10, Sun 11-5, ch., c.c., 7-day exch. or rfd. Large selection. Other stores throughout the suburbs. Sells: **Men's Belts, Men's Coats—Dressy, Coats—Quilted & Parkas, Coats—Leather & Sheepskin, Men's Gloves, Men's Pants/Slacks, Shirts, Socks, Men's Suits—New, Men's Sweaters, Men's Swimsuits, Ties, Underwear.**

*   **New Store**, 289 7th Av. (26-7), 741-1077, 1 to 28, M-F 10-8, SSun 10-6:30, ch., c.c., exch., no rfd. Large selection. Sells: **Ladies' Coats, Dresses, Skirts, Slacks, Ladies' Suits & Blazers, Tops, Sweaters, Blouses.**

*   **N&L Corp.**, 163 Orchard St. (Stanton-Rivington), 982-8514, F to 2nd Av., 7 days 9-5, all cash, exch., no rfd. Sells: **Jeans.**

*   **No Name**, 28 and 30 Warren St. (Church), 766-9766, A-CC-1-2-3 to Chambers, N-RR to City Hall, M-S 8-6, all cash, exch., no rfd. Arrow shirts, thirds and damaged. Other closeouts and odd lots. Sells: **Shirts, Warehouse Salvage Job-Lot.**

    Normie's, Brooklyn, 2102 Flatbush Av. (P), 338-1229, no subway stop nearby, M-F 9:30-8, S 10-6, Sun 12-4, ch., c.c., no exch. or rfd. Sells: **Ladies' Coats, Ladies' Suits & Blazers.**

***   **Odd Job Trdg.**, 7 E. 40 (Mad.), 686-6825, B-D-F to 42, 7 to 5th Av.; 66 W. 48 (6th Av.), 575-0477, B-D-F to 47. Both stores: M-Th 8-5:30, F 8-3, Sun 10-5, ch., no c.c., 15-day exch. or rfd. Sells: **Shirts, Shoes—Bedroom & Slippers, Men's Shoes—Sports/Work, Dinnerware & Cookware, Foods, Health & Beauty Aids, Home-Improvement Items, Housewares, Linens, Personal Accessories, Stationery & Art Supplies, Toys, Games & Hobbies, Warehouse Salvage Job-Lot.**

**   **Odd Lot Shoes**, 6 E. 46 (5th Av.), 687-8810, B-D-F to 47, M-F 9-5:45, S

9-5, c.c., no ch., exch. or rfd. The outlet-store for Adler, Weyenberg-Massagic, Nunn Bush, and Stacey Adams. Sells: **Men's Shoes—Dress.**

Odds & Ends Sundries, Brooklyn, 4809 New Utrecht Av., 854-1453, B to 50th St., Sun-Th 10-6, F 10-1, ch., no c.c., exch. or rfd. Sells: **Underwear, Loungewear, Personal Accessories, Toys, Games & Hobbies.**

** **Olaf Daughters Outlet**, 34 W. 17 (5th-6th), B-F-LL to 14th St. & 6th Av., usually open M-F 1-5, all cash, no exch. or rfd. Phoneless, so call 696-2595 or 929-7957, and ask if the 17th Street outlet store is open today. Sells: **Ladies' Shoes & Boots.**

Once Upon A Time, 171 E. 92 (3rd Av.), 831-7619, 6 to 96, T-S 11-5, ch., no c.c., no exch. or rfd. Sells: **Used Clothing For Kids.**

* **One Block Over**, 131 W. 35 (6th-7th), 564-7035, B-D-F-N-QB-RR to 34, 1-2-3 to 34, M-F 9-6, S 10:30-6, all cash, exch., no rfd. Large selection. Sells: **Ladies' Coats, Dresses, Skirts, Slacks, Jeans—Designer, Tops, Sweaters, Blouses.**

** **Pacific Traders**, 742 Broadway (Astor), 475-5838, N-RR to 8th St., M-S 11-7, c.c., no ch., exch., no rfd. Sells: **Hand-Knit Sweaters, Gloves, Etc., Dresses, Skirts, Slacks, Tops, Sweaters, Blouses.**

** **Parezio II**, 77 Chambers St. (B'wy), 233-3942, A-CC-1-2-3 to Chambers, N-RR to City Hall, M-S 10-6:30, ch., c.c., exch., no rfd. Small store. Sells: **Coats—Leather & Sheepskin, Men's Pants/Slacks, Shirts, Jeans—Designer.**

* **Park Av. Job Lot**, 270 Park Av. S. (21), 673-7536, 6 to 23, M-S 9-6, all cash, 7-day exch., no rfd. Many Slavic gift items. Sells: **Dresses, Skirts, Slacks, Tops, Sweaters, Blouses, Health & Beauty Aids, Jewelry & Gifts, Warehouse Salvage Job-Lot.**

* **Park Kenny Clothes**, 141 5th Av. at 21st St., 2nd floor, 477-1948, N-RR to 23rd St., M-F 9-5, S 9-4, Sun 9-3, ch., c.c., exch. or rfd. Sells: **Men's Coats—Dressy, Men's Suits—New, Ladies' Suits & Blazers.**

*** **Parkay Designs**, 14 W. 29 (5th-B'wy), 683-0058, N-RR to 28th St., M-F 10-6, S by appt. (phone), ch., no c.c., exch. or rfd. Cotton garments from India. Wholesalers who sell at same price retail. 50-80% discounts. Sells: **Dresses, Skirts, Slacks, Tops, Sweaters, Blouses.**

Parkway, 52 Fulton St. at Cliff, 267-1296, A-CC-J-M-RR-2-3-4-5 to B'wy-Nassau & Fulton, M-F 10-6, S 10-5, Sun 10-4, ch., c.c., exch., no rfd. Sells: **Men's Coats—Dressy, Shirts, Men's Suits—New.**

* **Pat's Shoes**, Brooklyn, 1226 Liberty Av. (Drew), 647-0664, A-CC to 80th St.; Queens, 104-28 Jamaica Av., Richmond Hill, 846-0155, J to 102. Both stores: M-Th 8:30-6:30, F 8:30-7:30, S 8:30-6, c.c., no ch., 7-day exch., no rfd. Clearance or cancellation shoes. Sells: **Kids' Shoes, Men's Shoes—Dress, Men's Shoes—Sports/Work, Ladies' Shoes & Boots.**

Paula Knitwear, 37 Orchard St. (Hester), 925-2520, F to E. Broadway, Sun-Th 10-4:30, F 10-1, ch., no c.c., exch., no rfd. Sells: **Tops, Sweaters, Blouses.**

Pearl River, 13 Elizabeth St. (Bayard), 966-1010, J-M-N-QB-RR-6 to Canal, J-M-RR-4-5-6 to Chambers & Bkln. Bridge, B-D to Grand, 7 days 10-8, c.c. $20+, no ch., exch., no rfd. Sells: **Chinese Jackets, Robes, Dinnerware & Cookware.**

Peck & Chase Shoes, 161 Orchard St. (Rivington-Stanton), 674-8860, F-J-M to Delancey & Essex, 7 days 9-6, c.c., no ch., exch., no rfd. Sells: **Men's Shoes—Sports/Work.**

Pennywise Sales, 99 Allen St. (Delancey), 226-7065, J-M to Bowery, Sun-Th 9-4:30, F 9-3, all cash, exch., no rfd. No exch. if package has been opened. Sells: **Underwear, Loungewear.**

Phantom, 315 7th Av. (28), 243-7910, 1 to 28; 185 Church St. (Reade), 964-1173, A-CC-1-2-3 to Chambers; 323 Park Av. S. (24), 777-8299, 6 to 23; 207 W.38 (7th Av.), 921-2669, A-AA-CC-E to 34, A-AA-CC-E to 42; 954 8th Av. (57), 757-9303, A-AA-B-CC-D-1 to 59; 180 Varick St. (King), 924-0328, 1 to Houston. All stores: M-F 10-6, S 10-4, c.c., no ch., 7-day exch., no rfd. Closeouts of previous seasons' fashions. Uneven values, but some terrific bargains. Sells: **Men's Pants/Slacks, Shirts, Men's Suits—New.**

Pier 333, 511 Lexington Av. at 48th St. (Lex. Hotel), rm. 333, 752-3174, 6 to 51, M-S 9a.m.-10p.m., ch., no c.c., exch. or rfd. Sells: **Dresses, Skirts, Slacks, Tops, Sweaters, Blouses.**

* **Pina Colada**, 145 4th Av. (13-4), 475-9372, LL-N-QB-RR-4-5-6 to Union Sq., M-F 12-7, S 12-6, c.c., no ch., exch., no rfd. Small store. Some punk, some boutique, styles. Dresses, zoot-suits, and especially shoes. Sells: **Ladies' Shoes &**

7: CLOTHING-DIRECTORY

Boots, Antique Clothing & Cheap-Chic.

Premier Textile, 512 Broadway (Spring-Broome), 966-1984&4733 & 226-6667, 6 to Spring, M-F 9-5:30, Sun 10-4, all cash, exch., no rfd. No try-ons. Sells: **Shirts, Underwear, Jeans—Designer, Uniforms For Nurses.**

+ **Prima Impex**, 1185 Broadway (28), 679-9066, N-RR to 49th St., M-S 9-7, all cash, no exch. or rfd. Bonus discount to BF readers: 5% to 7%. Sells: **Dresses, Skirts, Slacks, Tops, Sweaters, Blouses.**

* **Que Linda**, 594 Broadway (Prince), 925-6565, N-RR to Prince St., M-F 7-6, S 9-4:30, Sun 8-5, c.c., no ch., exch., no rfd. Sells: **Dresses, Skirts, Slacks, Jeans—Designer, Ladies' Shoes & Boots.**

** **Quiltex Factory Outlet**, Brooklyn, 168 39th St., 3rd floor, 788-3158, B-N-RR to 36th St., M-Th 10-3, all cash, no exch. or rfd. An authentic factory outlet. A major brand of children's clothing. Sells: **Kids' Clothing.**

Rainbarrel Factory Outlet, 116 John St. at Pearl, 964-0210, A-CC-J-M-RR-2-3-4-5 to B'wy-Nassau & Fulton, M-F 10-6; Brooklyn, 4610 13th Av., 435-7942, B to 50th St., Sun-Th 10-6, F 10-3; Brooklyn, 1504 Coney Is. Av. (K-L), 377-4703, D-M-QB to Av. M, MTW 10-6, Th 10-8, F 10-3, Sun 10-5. All stores: ch., c.c., 7-day exch., no rfd. Sells: **Ladies' Coats.**

* **Ray Variety**, 539 9th Av. at 40th, 736-2547, A-AA-CC-E to 42, M-S 9:30-6:30, all cash, exch. or rfd. Sells: **Shoes—Bedroom & Slippers, Health & Beauty Aids, Linens.**

Regent's Wear, 34 Orchard St. (Hester), 226-3255, F to E. Broadway, Sun-Th 9:30-5, F 9:30-1, c.c., no ch., 14-day exch., no rfd. Sells: **Jeans, Men's Pants/Slacks.**

Replay, 664 W. 204 (B'wy), 942-4142, A to 207, T-S 11-5, ch., no c.c., no exch. or rfd. Sells: **Used Clothing For Kids.**

Reprise, 14 5th Av. (8-9), 260-0896, A-AA-B-CC-D-E-F to 4, N-RR to 8th St., M-S 12-7, Sun 1-6, ch., c.c., no exch. or rfd. Sells: **Slightly Used Designer-Wear.**

** **Richie's Shoes**, 183 Av. A (11-12), 228-5442, LL to 1st Av., MTThFS 10-5, ch., c.c., exch. or rfd. Sells: **Kids' Shoes.**

Robbins Men's Wear, 48 W. 14 (5th-6th), 691-2573, B-F-LL to 14th St. & 6th Av.; 146 E. 14 (3rd Av.), 260-0456, LL to 3rd Av.; 1265 Broadway (32), 684-5429, B-D-F-N-QB-RR to 34; 519 8th Av. (35), 564-3756, A-AA-CC-E to 34; 609 8th Av. (41), 564-1194, A-AA-CC-E to 42; 1717 Broadway (55), 581-7033, A-AA-B-CC-D-1 to 59; Queens, 38-17 Main St., Flushing, 445-7301, 7 to Main St.; Queens, 37-42 Junction Blvd., Corona, 424-0377, 7 to Junction Blvd.; Queens, 30-88 Steinway St., Astoria, 626-7180, F-GG-N to Steinway St.; Queens, 57-33 Myrtle Av. (Seneca), Ridgewood, 497-4489, M to Seneca; Brooklyn, 1213 Kings Hwy., 375-4133, D-M-QB to Kings Hwy.; Bronx, 279 E. Fordham Rd. (Kingsbridge Rd.), 367-2499, CC-D to Fordham Rd. All stores: M-S 9-7:30, all cash, exch. or rfd. No try-ons. Somewhat uneven values, but worth recommending for the things I'm recommending the chain for. Other stores in Long Island. Sells: **Men's Gloves, Men's Hats, Men's Pants/Slacks, Shirts, Men's Shoes—Sports/Work, Underwear, Bathrobes & P.J.'s, Health & Beauty Aids, Sporting Goods.**

** **Romano Trdg.**, 628 W. 45th St. on 12th Av., 581-4248, A-AA-CC-E to 42, plus a long walk, M-F 8-5:30, S 8-5, all cash, exch. or rfd. Very cooperative. A little bit of everything, designer-name and major brand items. Sells: **Coats—Leather & Sheepskin, Jeans, Socks, Underwear, Appliances, Jewelry & Gifts, Office Equipment, Personal Accessories, Stationery & Art Supplies, Toys, Games & Hobbies.**

Ronald's Hosiery, 2431 Grand Concourse (188), 584-3121, CC-D to Fordham Rd., M-S 10-5:45, c.c., no ch., exch., no rfd. Sells: **Hosiery.**

Rosalie Fashions, 32 Orchard St. (Hester), 431-6345, F to E. Broadway, Sun-F 10-5, ch., c.c., 7-day exch., no rfd. Sells: **Ladies' Swimsuits, Tops, Sweaters, Blouses.**

* **Rothman**, 111 5th Av. at 18th St., 777-7400, LL-N-QB-RR-4-5-6 to Union Sq., B-F-LL to 14th St. & 6th Av., TWFS 9:30-6, MTh 10-7, ch., c.c., 14-day exch. or rfd. Extremely conservative styles (mostly last season's stuff, but these styles don't change that fast anyway), all American-cut. Sells: **Men's Belts, Men's Coats—Dressy, Men's Formals & Tuxedos, Men's Gloves, Men's Hats, Men's Pants/Slacks, Socks, Men's Suits—New, Men's Sweaters, Ties, Underwear.**

Round House Fashions, 41 Orchard St. (Hester), 966-5951, F to E. Broadway, Sun-F 9:30-5, ch., no c.c., exch., no rfd. Sells: **Dresses, Skirts, Slacks, Ladies' Swimsuits, Tops, Sweaters, Blouses.**

Royal Fashion, 915 Broadway (21), 15th floor, 475-3540, N-RR to 23rd

7: CLOTHING-DIRECTORY

St., MTWF 9-6, Th 9-8, S 9-5, Sun 10-4, ch., c.c., no exch. or rfd. Sells: **Men's Coats—Dressy, Men's Suits—New.**

*+ **Rukico Tailors**, 511 Lex. Av. at 48th St., Hotel Lexington, rm. 338, 832-0725, 6 to 51, M-S 10-7, ch., c.c. A Hong Kong custom tailor. Bonus discount to BF readers: 20% to 30%. Sells: **Shirts, Suits—Custom-Tailored, Ladies' Suits—Custom-Tailored.**

*** **Runway Fashions**, 418 Park Av. S. at 29th St., 686-8502, 6 to 28, M-F 10-6, S 11-4, c.c., no ch., exch., no rfd. Small store. Specializes in exquisite European-made designer suits underpriced even at list, then discounted 50%. (Same suits seen at Sym's costing 5% more.) Sells: **Shirts, Men's Suits—New.**

Ruth Brooks, 1138 3rd Av. (66), 744-5412, 6 to 68, M-S 10:30-6, ch., c.c., no exch. or rfd. Sells: **Ladies' Coats, Dresses, Skirts, Slacks, Ladies' Suits & Blazers, Tops, Sweaters, Blouses.**

** **S. Sosinsky & Son**, 143 Orchard St. (Rivington), 475-9784, F-J-M to Delancey & Essex, M 10-5, TWTh 9:30-5, F 10-3:30, Sun 9-5, ch., no c.c., 30-day exch. or rfd. Small store. Mostly irregulars at two-thirds discount. Sells: **Shirts, Bathrobes & P.J.'s.**

***+ **S&A Clothing**, 95 Canal St. (Eldridge-Forsyth), 966-5354, F to E. Broadway, J-M-N-QB-RR-6 to Canal, M-F 10-5, Sun 10-3, ch., no c.c., exch. or rfd. Small store. Some irregulars that are terrific values. Even the firsts are comparable value to Sym's' norm, though of course the selection here is puny by comparison. Bonus discount to BF readers: 10% to 20%. Sells: **Coats—Quilted & Parkas, Men's Suits—New.**

* **S&A Future**, 108 W. 14 (6th Av.), 924-3873, B-F-LL to 14th St. & 6th Av., 7 days 10-6, all cash, exch. or rfd. Sells: **Shoes—Bedroom & Slippers, Dinnerware & Cookware.**

* **Saab International**, 34 W. 28 (B'way), 889-6591, N-RR to 28th St., M-S 8-6, all cash, exch., no rfd. Large selection. Sells: **Jeans—Designer.**

Sabra Shoes, 1 John St. (B'way), 349-3494, A-CC-J-M-RR-2-3-4-5 to B'wy-Nassau & Fulton, M-F 8-6, c.c., no ch., exch., no rfd. Sells: **Ladies' Shoes & Boots.**

Sam Popper, 87 Orchard St. at Broome, 226-9752, F-J-M to Delancey & Essex, Sun-Th 9-5, F 9-3, c.c., no ch., exch., no rfd. Sells: **Jeans.**

* **Sam's Knitwear**, 93 Orchard St. (Broome-Delancey), 966-0390, F-J-M to Delancey & Essex, Sun-F 9:30-5:30, ch., c.c., exch., no rfd. Samples. Sells: **Dresses, Skirts, Slacks, Ladies' Suits & Blazers, Tops, Sweaters, Blouses.**

* **Samuel Zimbler**, 176 5th Av. (22-3), 255-6699, N-RR to 23rd St., M-S 9:30-6, ch., c.c., exch. or rfd. Sells: **Men's Suits—New.**

* **Savannah Warehouse**, 229 10th Av. (23), 989-5096, A-AA-CC-E to 23, SSun 11-6, all cash, no exch. or rfd. Sells: **Dresses, Skirts, Slacks, Ladies' Suits & Blazers, Tops, Sweaters, Blouses.**

* **Schaer Bros.**, Brooklyn, 2602 Snyder Av. at Veronica Place, 282-5653, 3-4 to Church, M-F 9-6, S 9-5, ch., no c.c., exch. or rfd. But only if unaltered. Sells: **Men's Coats—Dressy, Men's Suits—New.**

*** **Scott's Dress**, 30 E. 23 (Mad.), 982-2131, N-RR to 23rd St., 6 to 23; 179 Broadway (Dey), 962-9926, N-RR-1 to Cortlandt. Both stores: M-F 8-6, all cash, 5-day exch. or rfd. Affiliated with Winfred, Fredwin's and Stuart's. All merchandise sells for below its original wholesale price—at least two-thirds discount. Sells: **Ladies' Coats, Dresses, Skirts, Slacks, Ladies' Suits & Blazers, Tops, Sweaters, Blouses, Warehouse Salvage Job-Lot.**

Seamar, 25 W. 32 (5th-6th), 3rd floor, 947-0443, B-D-F-N-QB-RR to 34, M-F 8-6, S 9-5, all cash, exch. or rfd. Sells: **Dresses, Skirts, Slacks, Tops, Sweaters, Blouses.**

Second Act, 1046 Madison Av. (80), 2nd floor, 988-2440, 6 to 77, irregular hours, usually T-S 10-5, ch., no c.c., no exch. or rfd. Sells: **Used Clothing For Kids.**

Second Cousin, 142 7th Av. S. (10), 929-8048, 1 to Christopher St., M-S 11-6, all cash, no exch. or rfd. Sells: **Used Clothing For Kids.**

* **Second Time Around**, 220 E. 23 (3 Av.), 685-2170, 6 to 23, M-S 10-4:45, all cash, no exch. or rfd. Sells: **Men's Suits—Used, Used Clothing For Women.**

* **S&G Hosiery**, 263 Broome St. (Orchard), 925-2044, F-J-M to Delancey & Essex, B-D to Grand, Sun-Th 9-4:30, F 9-2, all cash, exch., no rfd. Sells: **Underwear, Hosiery.**

** **Sheepskin Market**, 218 W. 29 (7th Av.), 564-8874, 1 to 28, M-F 10-5:30, SSun 11-4:30, ch., c.c., 7-day exch. or rfd. Sells: **Coats—Leather & Sheepskin.**

7: CLOTHING-DIRECTORY

Shelgo Factory Outlet, 641 6th Av. (20), 2nd floor, 675-6455, B-F to 23, M-F 9-5, S 9-12, all cash, exch. or rfd. Small selection. Sells: **Dresses, Skirts, Slacks, Tops, Sweaters, Blouses.**

Shoe Arcade, Brooklyn, 4801 New Utrecht Av., 436-1106, B to 50th St., Sun-Th 11-6, F 11-3, ch., no c.c., exch., no rfd. Sells: **Kids' Shoes, Men's Shoes—Sports/Work, Ladies' Shoes & Boots.**

* **Shoe Giant Outlets**, Queens, 31-13 Steinway St., Astoria, 728-9284, F-GG-N to Steinway St., MTWS 10-7, ThF 10-9, Sun 11-5; Queens, 166-25 Jamaica Av., Jamaica, 526-9650, E-F to 169th St., MTWS 9:30-6:30, ThF 9:30-8, Sun 11-5. Both stores: ch., c.c., exch. or rfd. Outlets for the Shoe Town discount chain. But the best is called 'Manufacturer's Shoe Outlet,' recommended separately here. (Latter has better selection.) Sells: **Kids' Shoes, Men's Shoes—Dress, Men's Shoes—Sports/Work, Ladies' Shoes & Boots.**

Shoe Mart, 69 New St. (Exchange Place), 425-5594, J-M-RR-2-3 to Wall & Broad Sts., 4-5 to Wall St., N-RR-1 to Rector, M-F 9-6, ch., c.c., 1-day exch. or rfd. Small store. Sells: **Ladies' Shoes & Boots.**

** **Shoe Steal**, 116 Duane St. (B'wy-Church), 964-4017, A-CC-1-2-3 to Chambers, 1 to Franklin, M-F 8-5:30, S 10-4, ch., no c.c., 7-day exch. or rfd. Affiliated with Anbar Shoes. Sells: **Ladies' Shoes & Boots.**

Shoe Town, Queens, 95-10 63rd Drive, Rego Park, 830-9820, F-GG-N to 63rd Dr., MTW 10-7, ThFS 10:8, Sun 11-5, ch., c.c., 14-day exch. or rfd. More than 100 stores in this chain, many in the suburbs. Outlet-stores for the chain are called Shoe Giant and Manufacturer's Shoe Outlet, elsewhere recommended here. Sells: **Ladies' Shoes & Boots.**

Shoes, Boots, Etc., 63 Warren St. at W. B'wy, 285-9750, A-CC-1-2-3 to Chambers, M-S 10-6, all cash, exch., no rfd. Small store. Many irregulars of military-surplus-type clothing and camping gear. Sells: **Men's Shoes—Sports/Work, Sporting Goods, Warehouse Salvage Job-Lot.**

** **Shoes-N-Things**, 131 Allen St. (Rivington), 254-4860, F-J-M to Delancey & Essex, J-M to Bowery, irregular hours, phone first, all cash, no exch. or rfd. Odd lots. Sells: **Men's Shoes—Dress, Men's Shoes—Sports/Work.**

Silt Sportuar, 487 Broadway at Broome, 966-3479, 6 to Spring, M-F 10:30-5:30, Sun 10-4, all cash, exch. or rfd. No try-ons. Sells: **Jeans.**

** **Simon Klinger**, 144 5th Av. (19-20), 255-2650, N-RR to 23rd St., B-F-LL to 14th St. & 6th Av., LL-N-QB-RR-4-5-6 to Union Sq., M-F 9-5:30, S 9-5, ch., c.c. Guaranteed fit. Raw-canvas fitting. Sells: **Suits—Custom-Tailored, Ladies' Suits—Custom-Tailored.**

S.K. Friedman, 740 Broadway at Astor Place, 777-3593, N-RR to 8th St., M-F 9-6:30, S 9-6, ch., c.c., exch. or rfd. Large selection. Sells: **Ladies' Coats, Ladies' Coats—Fake Fur, Dresses, Skirts, Slacks, Ladies' Suits & Blazers, Tops, Sweaters, Blouses.**

* **Slep**, 132 Orchard St. (Delancey-Rivington), 677-5328, F-J-M to Delancey & Essex, F to 2nd Av., 7 days 9-6, all cash, exch. no rfd. No try-ons. Small store. Sells: **Jeans, Shirts, Jeans—Designer.**

Smart Size, Queens, 30-41 Steinway St., Astoria, 932-3185, F-GG-N to Steinway St.; Queens, 89-48 165th St., Jamaica, 291-1700, E-F to 169th St.; Brooklyn, Albee Sq. Mall, 855-2400, 2-3 to Hoyt, B-D-M-N-QB-RR to DeKalb; Brooklyn, Bed-Sty Mall, 636-0600, ; Bronx, 111 E. Fordham Rd., 367-5404, CC-D to Fordham Rd. All stores: MTW 10-6, ThFS 10-7, Bx.-Steinway-Albee Sun 12-5, ch., c.c., 7-day exch. or rfd. Outlet division of Lane Bryant. For large sizes only. Other stores: Newark, Valley Stream, and Carle Place. Sells: **Ladies' Coats, Dresses, Skirts, Slacks, Loungewear, Ladies' Suits & Blazers, Tops, Sweaters, Blouses.**

So Cheap, 704 Broadway (4), 982-7918, B-D-F-6 to B'wy-Laf. & Bleecker, M-F 11-6:30, S 10:30-6, all cash, no exch. or rfd. Uneven values, occasionally terrific. Many damaged items. Sells: **Coats—Quilted & Parkas, Jeans, Men's Pants/Slacks, Shirts, Antique & Military Clothing, Tops, Sweaters, Blouses, Antique Clothing & Cheap-Chic, Warehouse Salvage Job-Lot.**

Sofia Sam Milich, 177 E. Houston St. (Allen-Orchard), 475-9312, F to 2nd Av., W-M 8:30-4:30, all cash, no exch. or rfd. Outstanding on medium quality men's belts, but not good on other things. Sells: **Men's Belts.**

* **Sol's**, 535 Broadway (Spring), 226-0355, N-RR to Prince St., 6 to Spring, Sun-F 10-6, all cash, exch. no rfd. No try-ons. Sells: **Dresses, Skirts, Slacks, Ladies' Suits & Blazers, Tops, Sweaters, Blouses.**

Sophisticate Seconds, Queens, 83-07 37th Av., 672-0005, 7 to 82nd

St., M-F 11-7, S 11-6, all cash, no exch. or rfd. Sells: **Dresses, Skirts, Slacks, Ladies' Suits & Blazers, Slightly Used Designer-Wear.**

   *   **Spitzer's Corner Store**, 101 Rivington St. at Ludlow, 477-4088, F-J-M to Delancey & Essex, Sun-Th 9:30-5:30, F 9:30-3, c.c., c.c., 7-day exch. or rfd. Sells: **Ladies' Coats, Dresses, Skirts, Slacks, Tops, Sweaters, Blouses.**

      S&S Fashion, 2496 Broadway (93), 362-1674, 1-2-3 to 96, M-S 10:30-8, ch., c.c., exch., no rfd. Sells: **Ladies' Coats, Dresses, Skirts, Slacks, Tops, Sweaters, Blouses.**

   *   **S&T Women's Shoes**, 1467 2nd Av. (76), 861-9470, 6 to 77; 1043 Lexington Av. (74), 988-0722, 6 to 77. Both stores: M-S 10:30-6, ch., c.c., no exch. or rfd. Sells: **Ladies' Shoes & Boots.**

  **   **Stanley Goncher**, 12 W. 19 (5th Av.), up 1 flight, 989-4900, N-RR to 23rd St., B-F-LL to 14th St. & 6th Av., LL-N-QB-RR-4-5-6 to Union Sq., M-S 9:30-4:30, ch., c.c. Suit guaranteed to fit. He'll copy and custom-tailor any top suit for half the off-the-rack price of the original. Price includes raw-canvas fitting. Sells: **Suits—Custom-Tailored.**

      Step Inn Shoes, 257 Canal St. (Lafayette), 226-5844, J-M-N-QB-RR-6 to Canal, M-F 8-6:30, S 9-6:30, Sun 11-6:30, c.c., no ch., exch., no rfd. Sells: **Ladies' Shoes & Boots.**

      Step 'N Style Shoes, 1 New York Plaza (near Battery Park), 269-0149, N-RR-1 to South Ferry, M-F 8-5:30; 84 Chambers St. (Broadway), 962-7020, A-CC-1-2-3 to Chambers, N-RR to City Hall, M-F 8-5:30; 30 Rockefeller Plaza, lower concourse, 757-6690, B-D-F to 47, M-F 8-5:30; Brooklyn, 138 Montague St., 643-0706, M-RR-2-3-4-5 to Borough Hall & Court St., M-S 10-7. All stores: c.c., no ch., exch. or rfd. Sells: **Ladies' Shoes & Boots.**

   *   **Strawberry**, 129 E. 42 at Lex., 986-7030, 4-5-6-7 to Grand Central, M-F 10-7, S 10-6, Sun 12-6; 80 Broad St. (Stone-Beaver), 425-6627, 4-5 to Bowling Green, J-M-RR-2-3 to Wall & Broad Sts., M-F 9:30-6:30; 501 Madison Av. (51), 753-5008, 6 to 51, E-F to 5th Av., M-F 8:30-7, S 10-6; 120 W. 49 (6th Av.), 391-8718, B-D-F to 47, N-RR to 49th St., M-F 9:30-6:45, S 10-6; 14 W. 34 (Empire State Bldg.), 279-8664, B-D-F-N-QB-RR to 34, MTWS 10-7, ThF 10-8:30, Sun 12-6; 147 E. 86 (Lex.), 427-1318, 4-5-6 to 86, M-F 10-9, S 10-7, Sun 12-6; 880 3rd Av. (53-4), 888-6666, E-F to Lex. Av., M-F 10-7, S 10-6; Brooklyn, 490 Fulton St. (Hoyt-Bond), 858-8984, 2-3 to Hoyt, M-S 10-7, Sun 12-6. All stores: ch., c.c., exch., no rfd. Large selection. Boutique styles. Listed 'regular' prices are about 15% below competition on most items; 80% of stock is discounted 25-50% off that. Zoom is clearance-store for chain. Sells: **Ladies' Coats, Dresses, Skirts, Slacks, Ladies' Gloves, Hosiery, Lingerie, Loungewear, Millinery, Hats, Ladies' Shoes & Boots, Ladies' Suits & Blazers, Ladies' Swimsuits, Tops, Sweaters, Blouses, Personal Accessories.**

 *** **Stuart's**, 1420 St. Nicholas Av. (181), 928-9691, 1 to 181, M-S 10-6, all cash, 5-day exch. or rfd. Affiliated with Winfred, Fredwin, and Scott's Dress. All merchandise sells for below its original wholesale price—at least two-thirds discount. Sells: **Ladies' Coats, Dresses, Skirts, Slacks, Ladies' Suits & Blazers, Tops, Sweaters, Blouses, Warehouse Salvage Job-Lot.**

   *   **Sue's Discount Dress**, 638 Lexington Av. (54), 752-5574, E-F to Lex. Av., M-F 8:30-6:30, Sun 11-5, ch., c.c., 10-day exch., no rfd. Small store. Sells: **Ladies' Coats, Dresses, Skirts, Slacks, Ladies' Suits & Blazers, Tops, Sweaters, Blouses.**

   *   **Sunshine**, 110 5th Av. (16), 697-5192, B-F-LL to 14th St. & 6th Av., LL-N-QB-RR-4-5-6 to Union Sq., M-F 9:30-6, S 9:30-5:30; 396 Madison Av. (45-6), 697-5192, 4-5-6-7 to Grand Central, M-F 9-6, S 9:30-5:30; 10 Maiden Lane (B'wy), 349-2525, A-CC-J-M-RR-2-3-4-5 to B'wy-Nassau & Fulton, M-F 8-6. All stores: ch., c.c., exch., no rfd. Boutique styles. Listed 'regular' prices are about 15% below competition on most items; 80% of stock is discounted 25-50% off that. Zoom is clearance-store for chain. Sells: **Ladies' Coats, Dresses, Skirts, Slacks, Hosiery, Ladies' Suits & Blazers, Tops, Sweaters, Blouses.**

   *   **Superior Merchandising**, 12 Warren St. (B'wy-Church), 233-4615, A-CC-1-2-3 to Chambers, N-RR to City Hall, M-S 7-6, all cash, no exch. or rfd. Very uneven. Some sensational bargains. Some not good. Sells: **Men's Belts, Men's Gloves, Jeans, Men's Pants/Slacks, Men's Sweaters, Ties, Recordings & Tapes.**

   *   **Super-Thrift Shop**, 1437 2nd Av. (75), 988-6399, 6 to 77, M-S 10-4:30, all cash, no exch. or rfd. Most is in excellent condition. Sells: **Men's Suits—Used, Used Clothing For Women.**

      S&W Fashions, 283, 287, & 291 7th Av. (26), and 165 W. 26 (7th Av.), 924-6656, 1 to 28, Sun-Th 10-6:30, F 10-4; Brooklyn, 4217 13th Av., 438-9679, B to

7: CLOTHING-DIRECTORY 69

Ft. Ham. Pkwy., Sun-Th 10-6, F 10-3. Both stores: ch., c.c., exch., no rfd. Sells: **Ladies' Coats, Ladies' Coats—Fake Fur, Dresses, Ladies' Suits & Blazers, Tops, Sweaters, Blouses.**

** **Sym's**, 45 Park Place, 791-1199, 2-3 to Park Place, M-F 9-7, S 9-6, c.c., no ch., exch., no rfd. This is the giant. But some irregulars are not marked, so check throrougly. Sale items are stunning bargains. Other stores throughout the suburbs and elsewhere. Sells: **Men's Belts, Coats—Quilted & Parkas, Men's Formals & Tuxedos, Men's Gloves, Men's Pants/Slacks, Shirts, Shoes—Bedroom & Slippers, Men's Shoes—Dress, Socks, Men's Suits—New, Men's Sweaters, Ties, Underwear.**

** **The Finals**, 149 Mercer St. (Prince), 431-1414 & 1-800-431-9111, N-RR to Prince St., T-S 10-6, Sun 11-6, ch., c.c., $25+, exch., no rfd. Takes mail-orders. Catalog. Sells own brand competitive with Adidas & Speedo, but half the price. Sells: **Men's Swimsuits, Ladies' Swimsuits, Sporting Goods.**

The Foot Lot, 70 Fulton St. at Ryders Alley, 223-0235, A-CC-J-M-RR-2-3-4-5 to B'wy-Nassau & Fulton, M-F 8-7, S 12-5, ch., c.c., exch., no rfd. Small store. Sells: **Ladies' Shoes & Boots.**

The Grab Bag, 2610 Broadway (98-9), 666-4230, 1-2-3 to 96, M-S 10-8, c.c., no ch., exch., no rfd. Small store. Small selection. Sells: **Dresses, Skirts, Slacks, Ladies' Suits & Blazers, Tops, Sweaters, Blouses.**

The Individual Man, 85 5th Av. at 16th St., 8th floor, 924-2157, B-F-LL to 14th St. & 6th Av., LL-N-QB-RR-4-5-6 to Union Sq., M-F 9-5, S 9-3, c.c., no ch., exch. or rfd. (But only if unaltered and with tags.) Sells: **Men's Coats—Dressy, Men's Suits—New.**

* **The Loft**, 491 7th Av. (37), 19th floor, 736-3358, A-AA-CC-E to 34, M-F 9:30-5:30, S 10-4, ch., no c.c., no exch. or rfd. Ann and Calvin Klein here—nothing else. Sells: **Dresses, Skirts, Slacks, Ladies' Suits & Blazers.**

** **The Shoe Rack**, 150 W. 28 (6th-7th), 924-6859, 1 to 28, M-F 8-6, phone S, all cash, no exch. or rfd. Casual, not dressy, styles. The outlet store for Shoe Shack and Village East Bootery. Sells: **Ladies' Shoes & Boots.**

\+ **The Sophisticate**, 2618 Broadway at 99th St., 865-8622, 1-2-3 to 96, M-S 10:30-7, ch., c.c., exch., no rfd. Bonus discount to BF readers: 10%. Sells: **Ladies' Shoes & Boots.**

** **The Townsman**, 666 Lexington Av. (55-6), 755-6660, E-F to Lex. Av., M-F 9:30-7, S 9-6, ch., c.c., exch., no rfd. Sells: **Men's Coats—Dressy, Coats—Quilted & Parkas, Coats—Leather & Sheepskin, Men's Pants/Slacks, Shirts, Socks, Men's Suits—New, Men's Sweaters, Men's Swimsuits, Ties.**

Three Star Tailoring, 561 Broadway (Prince), 925-0495, N-RR to Prince St., 7 days 9-5:30, all cash, exch., no rfd. No try-ons. Sells: **Jeans, Dresses, Skirts, Slacks, Tops, Sweaters, Blouses.**

Thrifty Threads, Brooklyn, 2082 E. 13, 336-8037, D-M-QB to Av. U, T-S 10-5, ch., no c.c., no exch. or rfd. Sells: **Used Clothing For Kids.**

** **Townie Merchandise**, 212 W. 14 (7th Av), 929-8060 & 675-6662, 1-2-3 to 14, A-AA-CC-E-LL to 14 St. & 8 Av., M-S 10-6, all cash, exch., no rfd. Will special-order. Popular among seamen and Latin American tourists. Sells: **Jeans, Underwear, Hosiery, Appliances, Health & Beauty Aids.**

Traffico, 722 Broadway (Waverly), 477-2722, N-RR to 8th St., M-S 11-7, ch., c.c., exch., no rfd. Sells: **Jeans—Designer, Tops, Sweaters, Blouses.**

* **Trend Quality Job Lot**, 40 E. 41, 889-4686, 4-5-6-7 to Grand Central, 7 to 5th Av., M-F 11-7, ch., no c.c., exch. or rfd. Sells: **Men's Coats—Dressy, Shirts, Men's Shoes—Dress, Men's Suits—New.**

** **Triest Export**, 560 12th Av. (44), 246-1548., A-AA-CC-E to 42, plus a long walk, Sun-F 7-6, all cash, no exch. or rfd. Very busy. Expect long wait on line. Popular with seamen and foreign tourists. Sells: **Jeans, Underwear, Appliances, Cameras & Optical Eqt., Personal Accessories, Toys, Games & Hobbies.**

* **Turnpike Clothing Outlet**, Queens, 192-11 Union Tnpk., Utopia, 776-2547 & 465-9472, no subway stop nearby, T-F 10-8:45, Sun 10-4:45, SM 10-5:45, ch., c.c., exch. or rfd. Often has some sensational values in slight irregulars and in closeouts. Sells: **Men's Coats—Dressy, Shirts, Men's Suits—New.**

** **Ultra Smart Hosiery**, 15 E. 30 (Mad.), 4th floor, 686-1564, 6 to 28, N-RR to 28th St., M-Th 8-5, F 8-3, all cash, exch., no rfd. Large selection. Sells: **Hosiery.**

* **United Chambers Trdg.**, 83 Chambers St. (B'wy-Church), 267-0488, A-CC-1-2-3 to Chambers, N-RR to City Hall, M-F 9-6, S 9-5, c.c. $15+, no ch., 10-day exch. or rfd. Often has some sensational values in slight irregulars and in closeouts.

7: CLOTHING-DIRECTORY

Sells: **Coats—Quilted & Parkas, Men's Shoes—Sports/Work, Sporting Goods.**

** **United Salvage Alka Seltzer**, 7 E. Broadway (Catherine), 962-5567, J-M-N-QB-RR-6 to Canal, J-M-RR-4-5-6 to Chambers & Bkln. Bridge, M-Th 10-5:30, Sun 9:30-3:30, all cash, no exch. or rfd. Small store. Small selection. Sells: **Coats—Quilted & Parkas, Men's Gloves, Jeans, Men's Pants/Slacks, Shirts, Underwear, Warehouse Salvage Job-Lot.**

Value Hosiery, 255 W. 23 (8th Av.), 243-7243, A-AA-CC-E to 23; 1653 2nd Av. (86), 628-5140, 4-5-6 to 86; 4930 Broadway (207), 569-2250, A to 207; 4225 Broadway (179), 795-1680, A to 181; Bronx, 271A W. 231 (Corlear), 548-2161, 1 to 231; Queens, 107-10 Continental Av., Forest Hills, 544-3699, E-F-GG-N to 71-Continental Avs.; Brooklyn, 4615 13th Av., 853-4296, B to 50th St. All stores: M-S 10-6 (except Bkln. is M-F 10-6, Sun 10-5), ch., no c.c., exch. or rfd. (But no returns on undergarments.) Sells: **Hosiery, Lingerie.**

V.I.M. Stores, Brooklyn, 1316 Flatbush Av. (Church), 693-4600, D-M-QB to Church; Brooklyn, 428 Knickerbocker Av. (Myrtle), 453-3313, M to Knickerbocker; Brooklyn, 5414 5th Av., 439-7944, N-RR to 53rd St.; Brooklyn, 511 Fulton St. (Hoyt), phoneless, 2-3 to Hoyt; Queens, 165-05 Jamaica Av., Jamaica, 297-2515, E-F to 169th St., plus a long walk. All stores: M-S 9:30-7, Sun 11-5:30, c.c., no ch., 21-day exch. or rfd. Large selection. Sells: **Jeans—Designer.**

Wah Fun, 43A Mott St. (Bayard), 227-1672, J-M-N-QB-RR-6 to Canal, J-M-RR-4-5-6 to Chambers & Bkln. Bridge, B-D to Grand, 7 days 11-8, all cash, exch. or rfd. Sells: **Chinese Jackets, Robes.**

Wai Lee, 1026 6th Av. (38-9), 840-2720, B-D-F to 42, B-D-F-N-QB-RR to 34, M-F 9-6, S 10-6, ch., c.c., exch., no rfd. Sells: **Millinery, Hats.**

* **Wallach's Outlet**, 1417 Kings Hwy., Brooklyn, 339-0192, D-M-QB to Kings Hwy., MTThFS 10-7, W 10-6, Sun 12-5, ch., no c.c., 7-day exch., no rfd. Most is India-made. Sells: **Coats—Quilted & Parkas.**

* **Wearhouse**, 687A Broadway (3), 254-4550, B-D-F-6 to B'wy-Laf. & Bleecker, M-S 11-6:30, ch., c.c., exch., no rfd. Most is India-made. Sells: **Dresses, Skirts, Slacks, Tops, Sweaters, Blouses.**

* **Wendy's Footwear**, 123 Nassau St. (Fulton), 233-4596, A-CC-J-M-RR-2-3-4-5 to B'wy-Nassau & Fulton, J-M-RR-4-5-6 to Chambers & Bkln. Bridge, M-F 9-6, S 11-4, ch., c.c., 7-day exch. or rfd. Sells: **Ladies' Shoes & Boots.**

** **What's New Discount**, 166 Madison Av. (32-3), 532-9226, 6 to 33; 122 E. 42 (Lex. Av. subway, subway level), 867-0574, 4-5-6-7 to Grand Central; 405 Lexington Av. (42nd St., subway level), 986-5645, 4-5-6-7 to Grand Central; 1525 York Av (80-1), 988-4215, 6 to 77, plus a long walk. All stores: M-F 10-6, c.c., exch., no rfd. Sells: **Dresses, Skirts, Slacks, Ladies' Suits & Blazers, Tops, Sweaters, Blouses.**

* **William Rosengarten**, 326 Grand St. (Orchard), 674-2310, F-J-M to Delancey & Essex, Sun-Th 9-5, F 9-2, ch., no c.c., exch. or rfd. Sells: **Socks, Underwear.**

William Tannenbaum, 39 W. 38 (5th-6th), 840-3796, B-D-F to 42, M-F 9-5, S 9-3, all cash, no exch. or rfd. Large selection. Sells: **Millinery, Hats.**

** **William Wiesner**, Brooklyn, 312 Roebling St. (Broadway), 384-0649, J-M to Marcy, Sun-Th 11-6:30, F 11-3, ch., no c.c., exch. or rfd. Mostly closeouts and seconds. Sells: **Kids' Clothing.**

*** **Winfred**, 2183 Broadway (77-8), 874-8465, 1 to 79, M-S 10-6, all cash, 5-day exch. or rfd. Affiliated with Fredwin, Scott's Dress, and Stuart's. All merchandise sells for below its original wholesale price—at least two-thirds discount. Sells: **Ladies' Coats, Dresses, Skirts, Slacks, Ladies' Suits & Blazers, Tops, Sweaters, Blouses, Warehouse Salvage Job-Lot.**

+ **Wingdale Hosiery**, 34 W. 30 (5th-6th), 684-4291, N-RR to 28th St., B-D-F-N-QB-RR to 34, M-F 7-4, all cash, exch. or rfd. Bonus discount to BF readers: 5% to 10%. Sells: **Hosiery, Socks.**

* **W.M. Men's Wear**, 145 Orchard St. (Rivington), 674-1823, F-J-M to Delancey & Essex, F to 2nd Av., Th-T 9-5, all cash, exch. or rfd. Sells: **Coats—Quilted & Parkas, Jeans.**

+ **Worker's Quarters**, Brooklyn, 1940 86th St., 331-4833, B to 20th Av., MTS 11-7, W 11-6, Th 11-9, F 11-8, c.c., no ch., exch., no rfd. Bonus discount to BF readers: 5%. Sells: **Men's Belts, Coats—Quilted & Parkas, Men's Shoes—Sports/Work, Socks, Men's Sweaters, Underwear.**

** **Worthmore**, 245 W. 34 (7th-8th), 594-8998, A-AA-CC-E to 34, M-S 10-7, c.c., no ch., exch. or rfd. No try-ons. One in the Cayne group. Sells: **Dresses, Skirts,**

7: CLOTHING-DIRECTORY

Slacks, Hosiery, Jeans—Designer, Lingerie, Tops, Sweaters, Blouses.

* **Wyse Wear**, 266 Broome St. at Allen, 226-2658, F-J-M to Delancey & Essex, B-D to Grand, J-M to Bowery, Sun-Th 9-4:30, F 9-3, all cash, no exch. or rfd. They're 25% off, whereas the standard bra-discount in this neighborhood is 20%. Sells: **Lingerie**.

** **Yoav Shoes**, 252 W. 40 (8th Av.), 391-1275, A-AA-CC-E to 42, M-F 8-6:30, S 11-5, c.c., exch., no rfd. Sells: **Ladies' Shoes & Boots**.

* **Young's**, 319 Grand St. at Orchard, 226-4333&4309, F-J-M to Delancey & Essex, Sun-F 9-4:30, all cash, exch. or rfd. Sells: **Underwear**.

* **Young's Hats**, 139 Nassau St. at Beekman, 964-5693, A-CC-J-M-RR-2-3-4-5 to B'wy-Nassau & Fulton, M-F 9-5, S 12-3, ch., no c.c., exch., no rfd. Stetson and other popular makes, casual and dress. Sells: **Men's Hats**.

* **Youngworld**, 452 Fulton St. (Hoyt), 852-7890, B-D-M-N-QB-RR to DeKalb, 2-3 to Hoyt, 2-3-4-5 to Nevins, MTWFS 9:30-7, Th 9:30-9, Sun 11:30-5, c.c., no ch. 21-day exch., 7-day rfd. Sells: **Kids' Clothing**.

* **Z&L Import**, 159 Orchard St. (Stanton-Rivington), 475-6240, F to 2nd Av., 7 days 9-5:30, all cash, 7-day exch., no rfd. Sells: **Jeans**.

*** **Zoom**, 79 Nassau St. (John), 964-4111, A-CC-J-M-RR-2-3-4-5 to B'wy-Nassau & Fulton, MTW 8-6, ThF 8-6:30, ch., c.c., exch., no rfd. Clearance-store for Strawberry, J. Chuckles, and Sunshine, all in the A&E Stores group (as is Dollar Bill's, which however sells men's wear, and no ladies' wear). Sells: **Ladies' Coats, Dresses, Skirts, Slacks, Ladies' Gloves, Hosiery, Ladies' Shoes & Boots, Ladies' Suits & Blazers, Ladies' Swimsuits, Tops, Sweaters, Blouses.**

8:
DINNERWARE & COOKWARE
Expect 30-50% discounts

You can get all the brand-names at the discounts indicated above, or else pay at least two-thirds less than the name-brand discount-price by going to off-brands which are only a very slight—if any—compromise in quality. Then, too, as I discuss at the end of these comments, where I deal with restaurant-supply houses, you can buy exquisite and famous-brand restaurant-china at a per-piece cost which is about 75% less than that of department-store-bought equivalents; but in order to do it, you'll need space to keep a full china-service for 30 people—or else you'll have to find friends who are willing to split the set and the cost.

First, the off-brand route: A top-name set of "Queen's-Lace style" dishes that lists for $320, and that sells for $189 at one store I recommend, $192 at another, and $220 at all the rest, can be matched almost indistinguishably by an off-brand copy which sells for $59-$79 at the shops I recommend for off-brands. This way, you'll pay less than one-quarter of the list (and regular department-store) price for virtually the same dishes. Most of the off-brands come from mainland China—they're the real "china"! But others are made in Poland or Japan. (Of course, some of the over-priced top brands also come from Japan. If you recognize the brand-name, rest assured, the make is overpriced.) The major problem with shopping the off-brand-dishes route is the limited selection of styles, most of which are obviously Chinese, not at all similar to the big-brand-name patterns. However, one should at least be open-minded to the attractiveness of the authentic Chinese patterns. With time, these may come to be highly valued, even as antiques. The single store with probably the largest selection of off-brand, basically just Chinese, china, is Kam Kuo, 7 Mott St., 349-3098, located in Chinatown. Upstairs on the second floor, especially in locked display-cases, you'll find the "Western-style" dishes. This outfit is primarily a Chinese foods-store, and they don't discount. Thus, they're not a recommended BF store. Still, their china is good value, for the reason I indicated: It's off-brand, and so you don't pay an inflated price for a big name underneath the plate. The places in the recommended-stores listings below, under "China—Off-Brand," generally have slightly lower prices on the same dinnerware sets, but the selections are smaller.

If you're looking for a specific major brand and style-name of dishes or flatware, don't hesitate to phone the stores I recommend for top brands; most will phone-quote.

With pots and pans, the copies—virtually all Korean—are usually produced to look like Revere ware (which is the best. Copper is twice as conductive as aluminum, and so spreads the heat more evenly. Stainless steel is better for the insides, both because it's

8: DINNERWARE & COOKWARE

more durable than any other metal, and because aluminum insides become pitted by any acidic food, and contaminate that food with traces of aluminum—a mild but cumulative poison having no positive nutritive value.) If you choose carefully, you can get Revere-ware copies that are only moderately inferior to the originals, and that cost 80% less than the normal price of Revere. When shopping for a copy, these are the things to check for: First, how thick is the copper-layer on the bottom? Examine several pans of the make you're considering to buy. If the copper on any of these samples is so thin anywhere that the steel shows through, then this is an inferior make. Second, check the attachment of the handle to the pot, and test it gently to see if the unit acts like a unit or rather like two weakly welded parts. Finally, the weight should be fairly hefty. Thicker metal walls are both more durable and somewhat more conductive. Even if these tests are met, however, you should realize that the quality of the steel will never be quite as good in these Korean copies as you'll find in the domestic equivalents. Run your finger over the inside of the pot. If any grey stuff comes off, this is shedding metal. Washing the pot won't stop that shedding. Best avoid such pots.

If you insist on the very best cookware, the Job Lot Trading Company often sells very slight seconds of Revere ware for half the regular price of firsts. Phone them at 398-9210 or 962-4142, to check if these are now in.

Aluminum-bottomed cookware, such as Farberware (which actually has an aluminum-core bottom), can also be good if the aluminum layer is very thick. It would have to be twice as thick as an equivalent amount of copper in order to approach copper-bottomed pans in conductivity. A brand of aluminum-core bottomed ware which meets this requirement is now being imported from the Orient, under the "Sammisa" name, and it's first-rate, with stainless steel that's as fine quality as any from any country, and it's much less expensive than Farberware. But by all means avoid the aluminum pots with Teflon or other non-stick fluorinated plastic coatings inside. These are so dangerous that in other countries, such as Switzerland, such items are required to bear labels warning that it has been determined that cancer-causing gases arise from them when heated. The loss of these poisons, in the form of gases, results in the gradual inactivation of the non-stick feature, so that you're left ultimately with a worthless pan which may have planted in you the seeds of a cancer ten years hence. This stuff is as bad news as the Food and Drug Administration (which is the agency that's supposed to protect us Americans against such things).

Restaurant-grade cookware is also available, at the places specifically listed for that; and here is a whole other world of terrific bargains for the home-chef. The stores I recommend are those with the steepest discounts on these items.

Another source of incredible savings on dishes, as I mentioned at the beginning, is restaurant-china suppliers, some of which will sell by the piece, but most of whom will deal only in sets serving 30 people. You can buy beautiful top-quality china this way, paying only slightly more than the list price of an inferior top-brand service for 8; and you'll never again need to worry about breaking a dish! On top of that, there are restaurant-china places I recommend which will supply dishes by the dozen, and others selling by the piece—but these are far from exquisite dishes; they're strictly utilitarian.

RECOMMENDED PRODUCTS:
See above.

RECOMMENDED STORES:

cups

*****Job Lot Trdg.** (intermittent stock, 962-4142); *****Odd Job Trdg.** (intermittent stock, 686-6825); ****Odds & Ends Job-Lots** (intermittent stock, Queens, 441-6878); ****Weber's Job Lot** (intermittent stock, 564-7668); ***Eighty-Eight Cent Shops** (753-6969); **Dr. Schlock's** (intermittent stock, 766-8627); **First Cost** (intermittent stock, 697-0244); **Murray's Pottery** (Brooklyn, 376-6002); **Odd Lot Trdg.** (intermittent stock, 736-5243).

china—off-brand

*****Odd Job Trdg.** (intermittent stock, 686-6825); ***Consumers Distributing** (Queens, 268-2091); ***Glenwood Gift** (Brooklyn, 649-3296); ***Sam & Raj Appliances** (Queens, 446-1004); ***Variety Store** (Brooklyn, 336-1100); +**Atlantic Export** (Queens, 274-7900); **Auction Al** (Brooklyn, 336-2597); **Dems Bargain Stores** (243-9416); **H.M. Discount** (675-8171); **Pearl River** (966-1010); **Sasson** (929-7070); **Sofsan** (989-7292).

china—brand-name

*****Eastside China** (Brooklyn, 633-8672); *****Odd Job Trdg.** (intermittent stock, 686-6825); ***+**Kaufman Electric** (475-8313); ****J.J.G. Warehouse** (intermittent stock, 243-0632); ***Glenwood Gift** (Brooklyn, 649-3296); ***Michael C. Fina** (869-5050); ***S&A Future** (924-3873); **A. Benjamin** (226-6013); **East Side Gifts** (982-7200); **F&A Trdg.** (929-9354); **Greater NY Trdg.** (226-2808); **Jerry Samuels** (246-2887); **Jompole** (594-0440); **Lanac Sales** (226-8925); **Rainbow China** (Queens, 225-9547).

china—restaurant

****Dishes & Auction Goods** (966-1891); ****King Glassware** (226-9651); ****Standard China** (475-2750); ***Empire Food Service** (226-4447); ***Sang Kung Kitchen Supplies** (226-4527).

pots, pans, jugs

*****Job Lot Trdg.** (intermittent stock, 962-4142); *****Odd Job Trdg.** (intermittent stock, 686-6825); ****Odds & Ends Job-Lots** (intermittent stock, Queens, 441-6878); ****R&F Electronics** (679-5962); ****Weber's Job Lot** (intermittent stock, 564-7668); ****Zabars Upstairs** (787-2000); ***S&A Future** (924-3873); **First Cost** (intermittent stock, 697-0244); **Odd Lot Trdg.** (intermittent stock, 736-5243).

pots—top-brand (& SEE CH. 1, "SMALL")

*****Job Lot Trdg.** (intermittent stock, 962-4142); ****Zabars Upstairs** (787-2000).

professional cookware

(examples: carving boards, cutlery, dishes, fondues, frypans, grills, ice buck-

8: DINNERWARE & COOKWARE 75

ets, kettles, knives, ladles, pots, skillets)
King Glassware (226-9651); **Zabars Upstairs** (787-2000); *Empire Food Service** (226-4447); *Sang Kung Kitchen Supplies** (226-4527); **K-O Restaurant Eqt.** (925-4643).

cutlery, knives

***Alexander's Hardware** (intermittent stock, 267-0336); ***Job Lot Trdg.** (intermittent stock, 962-4142); ***Odd Job Trdg.** (intermittent stock, 686-6825); **+Mills Sales** (477-1000); **Odds & Ends Job-Lots** (intermittent stock, Queens, 441-6878); **R&F Electronics** (679-5962); **Weber's Job Lot** (intermittent stock, 564-7668); **Zabars Upstairs** (787-2000); *Robin Imports* (753-6475); **Dr. Schlock's** (intermittent stock, 766-8627); **First Cost** (intermittent stock, 697-0244); **Odd Lot Trdg.** (intermittent stock, 736-5243).

all flatware

(includes: forks, knives, ladles, spoons, silverware)
***Eastside China** (Brooklyn, 633-8672); ***+Kaufman Electric** (475-8313); **Investment Rarities**; *Glenwood Gift** (Brooklyn, 649-3296); *Michael C. Fina** (869-5050); *Robin Imports** (753-6475); **A. Benjamin** (226-6013); **Greater NY Trdg.** (226-2808); **Jerry Samuels** (246-2887); **Jompole** (594-0440).

silverware

(includes: candle snuffers, candle sticks, caraffs, casseroles, chafing dishes, coasters, coffee and tea sets, cuspidors, decanters, double boilers, flatware, goblets, lazy suzans, pewter-ware, punchbowls, steins, tankards, trivets, urns, vases)
***Eastside China** (Brooklyn, 633-8672); **A. Benjamin** (226-6013); **Eastern Silver** (226-5708); **Greater NY Trdg.** (226-2808); **Jerry Samuels** (246-2887); **Jompole** (594-0440); **Lanac Sales** (226-8925).

corelle wear: CH. 1, "SMALL"

thermos: CH.'S 1, 16

food processors: CH. 1, "SMALL"

blenders: CH. 1, "SMALL"

crystal ware: CH.17

STORES-DIRECTORY

Phone a store before you go out of your way to visit it. Especially do this during July and August, when most establishments reduce or eliminate weekend-hours.

In the listings below, "*" means especially recommended, "+" means that the store offers a bonus discount to BF readers, "ch." and "c.c." mean respectively checks and credit cards, and "exch." and "rfd." mean respectively exchange and refund. Nearest subway-stops are shown. For example, "B-D-F to 47" means to take the B, D, or F train to 47th Street. Store-hours are also indicated, with days of the week abbreviated, like "M-S 8-6."

A. Benjamin, 80 Bowery (Canal) (in Manhattan Diamond Ctr.), 226-6013, J-M-N-QB-RR-6 to Canal, M-S 8:30-4, ch., c.c., exch. or rfd. (Except on special orders.) Sells: **China—Brand-Name, All Flatware, Silverware, Jewelry & Gifts.**
    *** **Alexander's Hardware**, 60 Reade St. (B'wy), 267-0336, N-RR to City

8: DINNERWARE & COOKWARE

Hall, A-CC-1-2-3 to Chambers, M-F 8:30-6, S 8:30-5, ch., c.c., exch. or rfd. Large selection. Merits a long time browsing. Has great bargains in some obscure corners. Often has top quality cutlery at incredibly low prices. Much furniture-hardware. Abrasives. Sells: **Cutlery, Knives, Home-Improvement Items, Stationery & Art Supplies, Warehouse Salvage Job-Lot.**

    * **Atlantic Export**, Queens, 25-98 Steinway St., Astoria, 274-7900, RR to Astoria Blvd., M-W 11-7:30, ThF 11-9, Sun 12-6, c.c., no ch., exch., no rfd. Bonus discount to BF readers: 10% to 25%. Sells: **China—Off-Brand, Appliances, Jewelry & Gifts.**

    Auction Al, Brooklyn, 1221 Av. U, 336-2597, D-M-QB to Av. U, M-S 10-5:30, all cash, no exch. or rfd. Small store. Sells: **China—Off-Brand.**

    * **Consumers Distributing**, Queens, 107-18 70th Rd., Forest Hills, 268-2091, E-F-GG-N to 71-Continental Avs.; Queens, 39-20 Bell Blvd., Bayside, 225-0253, no subway stop nearby; Queens, 156-16 Northern Blvd., Flushing, 961-5024, no subway stop nearby; Queens, 97-10 Queens Blvd., Rego Park, 896-7250, F-GG-N to 63rd Dr.; Brooklyn, Av. U at Mill Av. (nr. Kings Plaza), 241-7633, D-M-QB to Av. M; Queens, 54-30 Myrtle Av., Ridgewood, 386-2809, LL-M to Myrtle & Wyckoff. All stores: M-F 10-9 (Ridgewood 10-6), S 10-6, Sun 12-5, ch., c.c., during banking hours, 30-day exch. or rfd. Large selection. A catalog-showroom chain. Sells: **China—Off-Brand, Autos & Supplies, Bikes, Home-Improvement Items, Housewares, Jewelry & Gifts, Sporting Goods.**

    Dems Bargain Stores, 146 W. 14 (6th-7th), 243-9416, 1-2-3 to 14, B-F-LL to 14th St. & 6th Av., M-S 9-7, Sun 12-5, all cash, exch., no rfd. Sells: **China—Off-Brand, Clothing—Men's.**

    ** **Dishes & Auction Goods**, 280 Bowery (Houston), 966-1891, F to 2nd Av., M-F 9-4:30, S 9-2, all cash, exch., no rfd. Pieces, not sets, by the dozen. Sells: **China—Restaurant.**

    Dr. Schlock's, 19 Warren St. (B'wy-Church), 766-8627, A-CC-1-2-3 to Chambers, N-RR to City Hall, M-F 8-6, S 8:30-5, all cash, exch. or rfd. Small store. Sells: **Cups, Cutlery, Knives, Fabrics, Yarns & Notions, Foods, Warehouse Salvage Job-Lot.**

    East Side Gifts, 351 Grand St. (Ludlow-Essex), 982-7200, F-J-M to Delancey & Essex, Sun-F 9:30-5:30, ch., c.c., no exch. or rfd. Sells: **China—Brand-Name, Jewelry & Gifts.**

    Eastern Silver, 54 Canal St. (Orchard) 3rd floor, 226-5708, F to E. Broadway, M-Th 8:30-6, F 8:30-2, Sun 9:30-6, ch., no c.c., exch., no rfd. Sells: **Silverware.**

    *** **Eastside China**, Brooklyn, 5002 12th Av., 633-8672, B to 50th St., Sun-Th 10-6, F 10-2, ch., no c.c., exch., no rfd. Terrific discounts on current lines, and even more amazing closeout-specials. Huge selection of dishes. Phone for prices. Sells: **China—Brand-Name, All Flatware, Silverware, Jewelry & Gifts.**

    * **Eighty-Eight Cent Shops**, 591 Lexington Av. (52), 753-6969, E-F to Lex. Av., M-F 9:30-6; 1457 Broadway (41), 354-0111, N-QB-RR-1-2-3-7 to 42 & Times Square, M-F 7:15-6, Sun 12-6; 33 W. 8 (5th-6th), 475-6951, A-AA-B-CC-D-E-F to 4, Sun-F 11-10, S 11-12; 89 Chambers St. (B'wy-Church), 267-6722, A-CC-1-2-3 to Chambers, N-RR to City Hall, M-F 7:30-6; 144 Fulton St. (B'wy), 964-2142, A-CC-J-M-RR-2-3-4-5 to B'wy-Nassau & Fulton, M-F 7:30-6. All stores: all cash, exch. or rfd. Everything in store is 88 cents; only the Fulton and Chambers stores have areas set aside for more expensive merchandise. Sells: **Cups, Foods, Health & Beauty Aids, Home-Improvement Items, Housewares, Stationery & Art Supplies, Toys, Games & Hobbies.**

    * **Empire Food Service**, 114 Bowery (Grand), 226-4447, J-M to Bowery, B-D to Grand, M-F 8-5, all cash, exch. or rfd. Dirt-cheap china-service for 12. Sells: **China—Restaurant, Professional Cookware.**

    F&A Trdg., 114 W. 14 (6th Av.), 929-9354, B-F-LL to 14th St. & 6th Av., M-S 9:30-6:45, Sun 10-4, all cash, exch., no rfd. Sells: **China—Brand-Name.**

    First Cost, 90 E. 42nd St. at Park Av., 697-0244, 4-5-6-7 to Grand Central, SSun 10-5; Queens, 46-20 108 St., Corona, 271-1121, 7 to 111, ThS 9-6, F 9-9. Both stores: all cash, 7-day exch. or rfd. Sells: **Cups, Pots, Pans, Jugs, Cutlery, Knives, Clothing—Children's, Clothing—Men's, Clothing—Women's, Foods, Health & Beauty Aids, Home-Improvement Items, Housewares, Jewelry & Gifts, Sporting Goods, Toys, Games & Hobbies, Warehouse Salvage Job-Lot.**

    * **Glenwood Gift**, Brooklyn, 118 Conklin Av., 649-3296, LL to Rockaway Pkwy., TWFS 10:30-6:30, Th 10:30-8, c.c., exch. or rfd. Takes phone-orders. Sells: **China—Off-Brand, China—Brand-Name, All Flatware, Jewelry & Gifts.**

8: DINNERWARE & COOKWARE 77

Greater NY Trdg., 81 Canal St. (Eldridge-Allen), 226-2808&8850, F to E. Broadway, Sun-Th 10-5:30, F 10-3, ch., no c.c., 7-day exch. or rfd. Sells: **China—Brand-Name, All Flatware, Silverware, Appliances, Jewelry & Gifts.**

H.M. Discount, 112 W. 14 (6th Av.), 675-8171, B-F-LL to 14th St. & 6th Av., M-S 9:30-7, Sun 11-6, all cash, exch., no rfd. Sells: **China—Off-Brand.**

✣✣ **Investment Rarities**, 1 Appletree Sq., Minneapolis, MN 55420, 1-800-328-1928, worth phoning if you're looking for sterling only, since they carry most patterns by single pieces (for replacement), or in complete sets. These are the finest-condition pieces culled from sets acquired for melt-down, and these pieces are then sold singly or matched into sets, at c. 70% discount off new. Sells: **All Flatware.**

Jerry Samuels, 48 W. 47, 246-2887&2906, B-D-F to 47, M-F 10-4, ch., c.c., exch., no rfd. Sells: **China—Brand-Name, All Flatware, Silverware.**

✣✣ **J.J.G. Warehouse**, 36 W. 25 (B'wy), 243-0632, N-RR to 23rd St., M-F 10-5, SSun 10-4, ch., c.c., no exch. or rfd. Constantly changing stock, always giftwares, but sometimes crystal, sometimes Limoges and Wedgewood closeouts, sometimes earthenware. Mostly 40-60% off. Up to 70%. Sells: **China—Brand-Name, Jewelry & Gifts.**

✣✣✣ **Job Lot Trdg.**, 140 Church St. (Warren-Chambers), 962-4142, A-CC-1-2-3 to Chambers; 412 5th Av. (37-8), 398-9210, B-D-F to 42. Both stores: M-F 8-5:30, S 8-4:30, all cash, 15-day exch. or rfd. Both are huge stores, with terrific selections. Sells: **Cups, Pots, Pans, Jugs, Pots—Top-Brand, Cutlery, Knives, Clothing—Men's, Foods, Home-Improvement Items, Housewares, Jewelry & Gifts, Linens, Personal Accessories, Sporting Goods, Stationery & Art Supplies, Toys, Games & Hobbies, Warehouse Salvage Job-Lot.**

Jompole, 330 7th Av. at 29th St., 3rd floor, 594-0440&2, 1 to 28, MTWF 10-4, Th 10-7, S 10-3, ch., no c.c., exch. or rfd. (But only if defective.) Sells: **China—Brand-Name, All Flatware, Silverware, Jewelry & Gifts.**

✣✣+ **Kaufman Electric**, 365 Grand St. (Essex), 475-8313 & 228-4160, F-J-M to Delancey & Essex, Sun-Th 10-5, F 10-1, ch., no c.c., exch., no rfd. Will special-order. Very cooperative. Bonus discount to BF readers: 2% to 5%. Sells: **China—Brand-Name, All Flatware, Appliances.**

✣✣ **King Glassware**, 112 Bowery (Grand), 226-9651&5967, J-M to Bowery, B-D to Grand, M-F 8-4:45, ch., no c.c., exch., no rfd. Sells: **China—Restaurant, Professional Cookware.**

K-O Restaurant Eqt., 99 Bowery (Grand), 925-4643 & 226-9409, J-M to Bowery, B-D to Grand, M-F 9-5:30, S 10-3, all cash, no exch. or rfd. Especially woks. Sells: **Professional Cookware.**

Lanac Sales, 63 Canal St. at Allen, 226-8925 & 925-6422, F to E. Broadway, B-D to Grand, M-Th 10-6, F 10-2, Sun 9-5, ch., no c.c., no exch. or rfd. Large selection of dishes. Sells: **China—Brand-Name, Silverware, Jewelry & Gifts.**

✣ **Michael C. Fina**, 580 5th Av. at 47th, 2nd floor, 869-5050, B-D-F to 47, M-F 9-5:30, ch., c.c., exch. or rfd. Takes mail-orders. Catalog. Sells: **China—Brand-Name, All Flatware, Cameras & Optical Eqt., Jewelry & Gifts, Personal Accessories.**

✣✣+ **Mills Sales**, 889 Broadway at 19th St., 477-1000, LL-N-QB-RR-4-5-6 to Union Sq., N-RR to 23rd St., M-F 9-5, S 9-2, all cash, no exch. or rfd. No retail sales (wholesale only) Labor Day through Xmas. A specialty here is steel ball-point pens super-cheap by the dozen. Bonus discount to BF readers: 5%. Sells: **Cutlery, Knives, Appliances, Home-Improvement Items, Jewelry & Gifts, Personal Accessories, Stationery & Art Supplies, Toys, Games & Hobbies.**

Murray's Pottery, Brooklyn, 802 Kings Hwy., 376-6002, D-M-QB to Kings Hwy., MWFS 11-6:30, TTh 11-9:30, ch., no c.c., exch., no rfd. Sells: **Cups, Jewelry & Gifts.**

✣✣✣ **Odd Job Trdg.**, 7 E. 40 (Mad.), 686-6825, B-D-F to 42, 7 to 5th Av.; 66 W. 48 (6th Av.), 575-0477, B-D-F to 47. Both stores: M-Th 8-5:30, F 8-3, Sun 10-5, ch., no c.c., 15-day exch. or rfd. Sells: **Cups, China—Off-Brand, China—Brand-Name, Pots, Pans, Jugs, Cutlery, Knives, Clothing—Men's, Foods, Health & Beauty Aids, Home-Improvement Items, Housewares, Linens, Personal Accessories, Stationery & Art Supplies, Toys, Games & Hobbies, Warehouse Salvage Job-Lot.**

Odd Lot Trdg., 33 W. 34 (5th-6th Avs.), 736-5243, B-D-F-N-QB-RR to 34; Queens, 19-40 37th St., Astoria, 932-3534, RR to Ditmars; Queens, 28-32 Steinway St., Astoria, 545-5604, RR to 30th Av., F-GG-N to Steinway St.; Queens, 103-54 94th St., Forest Hills, 263-5608, E-F to 75th Av.; Queens, 162-03 Jamaica Av., Jamaica, 657-4242, E-F to Parsons Blvd.; Queens, 103-54 94th St., Ozone Park, 738-2944, A-

CC to Rockaway Blvd.; Brooklyn, 503 Fulton St., 625-7926, 2-3 to Hoyt; Brooklyn, 1166 E. 92nd St., 272-1482, LL to Rockaway Pkwy. All stores: MTWS 10-6, ThF 10-8, Sun 11-5, c.c., no ch., 7-day exch. or rfd. Other stores throughout the greater metropolitan area. Sells: **Cups, Pots, Pans, Jugs, Cutlery, Knives, Health & Beauty Aids, Stationery & Art Supplies, Warehouse Salvage Job-Lot.**

** **Odds & Ends Job-Lots**, Queens, 88-09 Jamaica Av., Woodside, 441-6878, J to Woodhaven Blvd., M-S 9-6, Sun 9-3; Queens, 57-60 Woodside Av., Woodside, phoneless, 7 to 61st St., M-Th 10-7, F 10-9, S 9-6, Sun 9-5. Both stores: all cash, exch. or rfd. Sells: **Cups, Pots, Pans, Jugs, Cutlery, Knives, Health & Beauty Aids, Home-Improvement Items, Housewares, Jewelry & Gifts, Recordings & Tapes, Toys, Games & Hobbies, Warehouse Salvage Job-Lot.**

Pearl River, 13 Elizabeth St. (Bayard), 966-1010, J-M-N-QB-RR-6 to Canal, J-M-RR-4-5-6 to Chambers & Bkln. Bridge, B-D to Grand, 7 days 10-8, c.c. $20+, no ch., exch., no rfd. Sells: **China—Off-Brand, Clothing—Women's.**

Rainbow China, Queens, 253-16 Northern Blvd., Bayside, 225-9547, no subway stop nearby, TWThS 9:30-6, F 9:30-9, ch., no c.c., exch., no rfd. Sells: **China—Brand-Name.**

** **R&F Electronics**, 36 W. 29 (B'wy), 679-5962, N-RR to 28th St., M-Th 9-6, SunF 9-4:30, all cash, no exch. or rfd. Sells: **Pots, Pans, Jugs, Cutlery, Knives, Appliances, Home-Improvement Items, Jewelry & Gifts.**

* **Robin Imports**, 510 Madison Av. (52-3), 753-6475, E-F to 5th Av., M-F 9-6, S 10-5, ch., c.c., exch., no rfd. Sells: **Cutlery, Knives, All Flatware, Linens.**

* **S&A Future**, 108 W. 14 (6th Av.), 924-3873, B-F-LL to 14th St. & 6th Av., 7 days 10-6, all cash, exch. or rfd. Sells: **China—Brand-Name, Pots, Pans, Jugs, Clothing—Men's.**

* **Sam & Raj Appliances**, Queens, 37-12 74th St., Jackson Hts., 446-1004, E-F-GG-N-7 to 74th-B'wy & Roosevelt-Jack.Hts., W-M 10:30-6, all cash, exch. or rfd. No exch. or rfd. if unit is in working condition. Sells: **China—Off-Brand, Appliances.**

Sang Kung Kitchen Supplies, 108 Bowery (Grand), 226-4527 & 925-3059, J-M to Bowery, B-D to Grand, M-F 9-6, all cash, no exch. or rfd. Large selection of woks. Sells: **China—Restaurant, Professional Cookware.**

Sasson, 154 W. 14 (7th Av.), 929-7070, 1-2-3 to 14, 7 days 9-8, all cash, no exch. or rfd. Sells: **China—Off-Brand, Sporting Goods.**

Sofsan, 2 W. 14 (5th Av.), 989-7292 & 255-4367, B-F-LL to 14th St. & 6th Av.; Queens, 159-29 Jamaica Av., Jamaica, 526-0514, E-F to Parsons Blvd. Both stores: M-S 10:30-7, c.c., no ch., no exch. or rfd. Sells: **China—Off-Brand, Linens.**

** **Standard China**, 231 Bowery (Stanton), 475-2750, F to 2nd Av., M-F 9-5, all cash, no exch. or rfd. Some exquisite china-services for 30 people—no more expensive than a department-store-bought equivalent for 8 people. Sells: **China—Restaurant.**

* **Variety Store**, Brooklyn, 1402 Av. U, 336-1100, D-M-QB to Av. U, M-S 10-6, all cash, no exch. or rfd. Large selection of kitchen cabinets and off-brand Chinese dishes, and that's practically the whole store. Sells: **China—Off-Brand, Housewares.**

** **Weber's Job Lot**, 505 8th Av. at 35th, 564-7668, A-AA-CC-E to 34, M-F 10-6:30, S 10-6; 136 Church St. at Warren, 564-7668, A-CC-1-2-3 to Chambers, M-S 8-6; 2064 Broadway at 71st, 787-1644, 1-2-3 to 72, M-F 9-9, S 9-6, Sun 12-6. All stores: c.c., no ch., 7-day exch. or rfd. Some terrific values; others not good. Some prices wrongly marked on items each time I was there; checkout counter said 'It's an error.' Sells: **Cups, Pots, Pans, Jugs, Cutlery, Knives, Health & Beauty Aids, Home-Improvement Items, Jewelry & Gifts, Linens, Personal Accessories, Stationery & Art Supplies, Warehouse Salvage Job-Lot.**

** **Zabars Upstairs**, 2245 Broadway (80), 787-2000, 1 to 79, M-Th 8-7:30, F 8a.m.-10p.m., S 9a.m.-12mdnt., Sun 9-7:30, ch., c.c., exch. or rfd. Large selection. Their values on these things are generally even better than their food-bargains. And the place is mobbed, so be prepared for crowds and long lines. Sells: **Pots, Pans, Jugs, Pots—Top-Brand, Professional Cookware, Cutlery, Knives.**

9:
FABRICS, YARNS & NOTIONS
Expect 40-90% discounts.

Practically every store listed in this chapter will quote prices over the phone.

Though Manhattan has several neighborhoods which specialize in these things, the bargains aren't concentrated solely in that borough. It's material to note that fabrics are the substance of Manhattan's strong suit (if you'll pardon the triple pun), but Brooklyn's the place to go if you're into yarns. (Oops, there it happened again.)

Manhattan has four distinct discount-fabric-districts: Broadway from about Franklin Street northward eight blocks to about Spring Street (but the most highly advertised, popular, and crowded store along this strip, the Fabric Warehouse, has the least discounts, and is not recommended); Eldridge Street on the Lower East Side, along the one block from Grand to Broome (this block being about a 7-minute walk away from the Broadway strip just mentioned, which is directly westward); 38th, 39th, and 40th Streets, off 8th Avenue (mostly between 7th and 8th Avenues); and (mainly for designers' fabrics) the south side of 57th Street between 6th and 7th Avenues (specifically, the two neighboring stores, Poli and Paron). The four best yarn-shops, however, are all spread around Brooklyn. And about half the shops listed in this chapter aren't in any of these "districts."

With imagination, you can save even more than the customary 50% on fabrics by looking in unorthodox places. Some famous actors and actresses dress in style for peanuts by shopping at outlets that specialize in exotic upholstery, drapery and slipcover fabrics, rather than the usual dress fabrics. In fact, sometimes the same material which costs $25 a yard at a fancy dress-fabric store can be found at this type of outlet for only $1-a-yard. But these are not the shops to go to for polyesters or other common dress goods.

There's a hardware store in midtown which has long had an incredible bargain-offer on plastic buttons: Simon Greenspan, at 261 W. 35, 244-3496. It seems that one of their customers, who was a button-dealer, went bankrupt, and that this hardware-store then ended up with his whole stock, which was millions of buttons. The last I saw, these useful little plastic things were being offered there in 4-pound bags for only $1. Sensational! If you're interested, phone first to ask if they've still got any left.

RECOMMENDED STORES:
drapery & upholstery fabrics

***Jacob Wiesenfeld (431-6010); ***Leratex Fabrics (925-3678); ***Louis Bargain Center (Brooklyn, 854-1003); **+Inter Coastal Textile

80   9: FABRICS, YARNS & NOTIONS

(925-9235); **Frontier Fabrics (925-3000); **Gurian Fabrics (689-9696); **Shalom Export (226-8466); *⁺Sutter Textile (398-0248); *The Yardstick Fabrics (924-7131); *W.M. Textile (226-5115); Silk Surplus Scalamandre (753-6511).

designer dress fabrics

(especially imported woolens and silks)

***J.&A. Stelzer Fabrics (391-4988); **Diamond Discount Fabric (228-8189); *⁺B&A Textile (925-8343); *The Yardstick Fabrics (924-7131); Modlin Fabrics (391-4830); Paron Fabrics (247-6451); Poli Fabrics (245-7589).

common dress fabrics

(including synthetics and fabrics for shirts and lingerie)

***⁺Abe Bloom & Sons (924-2560); ***Arzee Fabrics (730-7054); ***J.&A. Stelzer Fabrics (391-4988); ***Jacob Wiesenfeld (431-6010); ***Louis Bargain Center (Brooklyn, 854-1003); ***Monezel Textiles (431-3939); **Bergos Fabrics (Brooklyn, 768-0419); **Budlee Fabrics (226-070n); **Dana Fabrics (966-4948); **David Fabrics (964-7130); **Diamond Discount Fabric (228-8189); **Frontier Fabrics (925-3000); **Peerless Fabrics (964-3588); **Relatex Fabrics (226-1534); **Shalom Export (226-8466); *⁺Sutter Textile (398-0248); *Aberdeen Fabrics (695-2233); *Flo-Ann Textiles (564-8769); *Fran's Fabrics Bargains (564-1560); *Margaret's Fabrics (925-8483); *The Yardstick Fabrics (924-7131); *W.M. Textile (226-5115); Paron Fabrics (247-6451); Poli Fabrics (245-7589); Rainbow Textiles (226-0895).

suit fabrics

(especially heavy woolens, includes coat fabrics)

***⁺Abe Bloom & Sons (924-2560); ***J.&A. Stelzer Fabrics (391-4988); ***Jacob Wiesenfeld (431-6010); ***Louis Bargain Center (Brooklyn, 854-1003); ***Monezel Textiles (431-3939); **Diamond Discount Fabric (228-8189); **Max Eagle Fabrics (431-4745); **M.Recht Textile (966-7373); **Shalom Export (226-8466); *⁺B&A Textile (925-8343).

scissors, sewing-aids

*Kirsch Drapery Hardware (966-6690); Advance Sewing Machine (226-5621); C.K.&L. Surplus (966-1745); Mitchell Mogal (226-8378).

yarns

***Marboro Yarns (Brooklyn, 256-6675); **Carlton Yarn (Brooklyn, 331-8250); *Barkow's Yarn (Brooklyn, 253-3369); *Peter Pan Yarns (Brooklyn, 232-9001); Bell Yarn (674-1030); B&M Yarn (475-6380); Dr. Schlock's (intermittent stock, 766-8627); Sunray Yarn (475-0062).

buttons

***⁺Abe Bloom & Sons (924-2560); ***David Jackendoff (255-9025); **Gordon Button (921-1684); **Harry Grunberg (226-4721); **Reliable Button Works (869-0560); *K Trimming (431-8929); Harry Kantrowitz (563-1610).

ribbons

****Superior Ribbon (689-3280); ***David Jackendoff (255-9025).

zippers

***David Jackendoff (255-9025); **Harry Grunberg (226-4721); *K Trimming (431-8929); Breitman's (924-7114); Harry Kantrowitz (563-1610);

M.E. (260-2060).

trimmings & threads

***David Jackendoff (255-9025); **Harry Grunberg (226-4721); *K Trimming (431-8929); **M.E.** (260-2060); **Tinsel Trdg.** (730-1030).

STORES-DIRECTORY

Phone a store before you go out of your way to visit it. Especially do this during July and August, when most establishments reduce or eliminate weekend-hours.

In the listings below, "*" means especially recommended, "+" means the store offers a bonus discount to BF readers, "ch." and "c.c." mean respectively checks and credit cards, and "exch." and "rfd." mean respectively exchange and refund. Nearest subway-stops are shown. For example, "B-D-F to 47" means to take the B, D, or F train to 47th Street. Store-hours are also indicated, with days of the week abbreviated, like "M-S 8-6."

***+ **Abe Bloom & Sons**, 6 W. 19 (5th Av.), 924-2560, B-F-LL to 14th St. & 6th Av., LL-N-QB-RR-4-5-6 to Union Sq., N-RR to 23rd St., M-F 7-4:30, ch., no c.c., exch., no rfd. Small store. Small selection. Bonus discount to BF readers: 10%. Sells: **Common Dress Fabrics, Suit Fabrics, Buttons.**

* **Aberdeen Fabrics**, 250 W. 39 (7th-8th), 695-2233, A-AA-CC-E to 42, N-QB-RR-1-2-3-7 to 42 & Times Square, M-F 9-5, all cash, no exch. or rfd. Sells: **Common Dress Fabrics.**

Advance Sewing Machine, 521 Broadway (Spring), 226-5621, N-RR to Prince St., 6 to Spring, M-F 8:30-6, S 8:30-4, ch., c.c., no exch. or rfd. Sells: **Scissors, Sewing-Aids, Appliances.**

*** **Arzee Fabrics**, 270 W. 38 (8th Av.), 730-7054, A-AA-CC-E to 42, A-AA-CC-E to 34, M-Th 9-5, F 9-2, all cash, no exch. or rfd. Small selection. Sells: **Common Dress Fabrics.**

*+ **B&A Textile**, 430 Broadway (Howard-Canal), 925-8343, J-M-N-QB-RR-6 to Canal, M-F 9-5, all cash, no exch. or rfd. Bonus discount to BF readers: 10%. Sells: **Designer Dress Fabrics, Suit Fabrics.**

* **Barkow's Yarn**, Brooklyn, 2636 Nostrand Av. (M), 253-3369, D-M-QB to Av. M, plus a long walk, M-S 10:30-7, Sun 10:30-6, all cash, exch., no rfd. They hung up the phone on me three times when I asked their hours. Sells: **Yarns.**

Bell Yarn, 75 Essex St. (Broome), 674-1030, F-J-M to Delancey & Essex, Sun-F 9-5:30; Queens, 95-16 63rd Rd., Rego Park, 459-1134, F-GG-N to 63rd Dr., MThF 9-8:45, TWS 9-6:45. Both stores: ch., no c.c., exch. or rfd. Sells: **Yarns.**

** **Bergos Fabrics**, Brooklyn, 637 5th Av. (18), 768-0419, N-RR to Prospect Av.; Brooklyn, 8022 5th Av. (81), 748-2274, RR to 77th St. Both stores: M-S 10-6, all cash, no exch. or rfd. Sells: **Common Dress Fabrics.**

B&M Yarn, 151 Essex St. (Rivington), 475-6380, F-J-M to Delancey & Essex, Sun-F 9-5, all cash, no exch. or rfd. Sells: **Yarns.**

Breitman's, 671 6th Av. (21), 924-7114, B-F to 23, M-F 9-4, all cash, exch., no rfd. Sells: **Zippers.**

** **Budlee Fabrics**, 458 Broadway (Grand), 226-070n, J-M-N-QB-RR-6 to Canal, 7 days 10-5, all cash, exch., no rfd. (But only if uncut.) Sells: **Common Dress Fabrics.**

** **Carlton Yarn**, Brooklyn, 1311 W. 7th St. (Bay Pkwy.), 331-8250, N to Bay Pkwy., MTh 9:30-7:30, TWFS 9:30-6, all cash, exch. or rfd. Sells: **Yarns.**

C.K.&L. Surplus, 307 Canal St. (B'wy-Mercer), 966-1745, J-M-N-QB-RR-6 to Canal, M-S 9-6, Sun 10-6, ch. $20+, no c.c., exch., no rfd. Carries a very good Italian line of scissor, cheaper but comparable to Wiss. Also metal parts and surplus, etc. Sells: **Scissors, Sewing-Aids, Furnishings, Home-Improvement Items.**

** **Dana Fabrics**, 113 Eldridge St. (Broome), 966-4948, B-D to Grand, Sun-Th 7-4, F 7-3, all cash, no exch. or rfd. Sells: **Common Dress Fabrics.**

** **David Fabrics**, 168 William St. at Beekman, 964-7130, J-M-RR-4-5-6 to Chambers & Bkln. Bridge, phone for hours, ch., no c.c., exch. or rfd. (But only on uncut goods.) Tiny store. Sells: **Common Dress Fabrics.**

9: FABRICS, YARNS & NOTIONS

*** **David Jackendoff**, 763 6th Av. (25-6), 255-9025, B-F to 23, N-RR to 28th St., M-F 6-4, all cash, no exch. or rfd. Job lots. Small stock. Sells: **Buttons, Ribbons, Zippers, Trimmings & Threads.**

** **Diamond Discount Fabric**, 165 1st Av. (10), 228-8189 & 674-9612, LL to 1st Av., 6 to Astor, M-S 10:30-8, Sun 11-7, ch., no c.c., no exch. or rfd. Large selection. Sells: **Designer Dress Fabrics, Common Dress Fabrics, Suit Fabrics.**

* **Dr. Schlock's**, 19 Warren St. (B'wy-Church), 766-8627, A-CC-1-2-3 to Chambers, N-RR to City Hall, M-F 8-6, S 8:30-5, all cash, exch. or rfd. Small store. Sells: **Yarns, Dinnerware & Cookware, Foods, Warehouse Salvage Job-Lot.**

* **Flo-Ann Textiles**, 300 W. 39 (8th Av.), 564-8769, A-AA-CC-E to 42, M-F 8-5:30, S 9-4, all cash, no exch. or rfd. Sells: **Common Dress Fabrics.**

* **Fran's Fabrics Bargains**, 369 W. 34 (9th Av.), 564-1560, A-AA-CC-E to 34, M-F 10-6:30, ch., no c.c., no exch. or rfd. Sells: **Common Dress Fabrics.**

** **Frontier Fabrics**, 251 Church St. (Leonard), 925-3000, 1 to Franklin, MTThFS 10-6, W 10-7, all cash, no exch. or rfd. Sells: **Drapery & Upholstery Fabrics, Common Dress Fabrics.**

** **Gordon Button**, 142 W. 38 (6th-7th), 921-1684, N-QB-RR-1-2-3-7 to 42 & Times Square, B-D-F to 42, M-F 8:30-5:30, all cash, no exch. or rfd. Huge selection. Sells: **Buttons.**

** **Gurian Fabrics**, 6 W. 30 (5th Av.), 689-9696, N-RR to 28th St., B-D-F-N-QB-RR to 34, M-F 9-5, ch., c.c., no exch. or rfd. Vast selection. Sells: **Drapery & Upholstery Fabrics.**

** **Harry Grunberg**, 118 Eldridge (Broome), 226-4721, B-D to Grand, Sun-F 10:30-4, all cash, exch. or rfd. Sells: **Buttons, Zippers, Trimmings & Threads.**

Harry Kantrowitz, 555 8th Av. (38), 563-1610, A-AA-CC-E to 42, M-F 8:15-5:15, ch., no c.c., no exch. or rfd. Sells: **Buttons, Zippers.**

***+ **Inter Coastal Textile**, 480 Broadway (Broome), 925-9235, J-M-N-QB-RR-6 to Canal, M-Th 9-6, F 9-5, ch., no c.c., exch. or rfd. Large selection. Speak only to David, Pedro, Harvey, or Abe. Some of the others give wrong prices. Bonus discount to BF readers: 3% to 5%. Sells: **Drapery & Upholstery Fabrics.**

*** **J.&A. Stelzer Fabrics**, 239 W. 39 (7th-8th), 391-4988, N-QB-RR-1-2-3-7 to 42 & Times Square, A-AA-CC-E to 42, M-Th 9-5, F 9-3, ch., no c.c., no exch. or rfd. Sells: **Designer Dress Fabrics, Common Dress Fabrics, Suit Fabrics.**

*** **Jacob Wiesenfeld**, 450 Broadway (Grand), 431-6010, J-M-N-QB-RR-6 to Canal, Sun-F 8-5, all cash, no exch. or rfd. Sells: **Drapery & Upholstery Fabrics, Common Dress Fabrics, Suit Fabrics.**

* **K Trimming**, 519 Broadway (Spring), 431-8929 & 226-3539, N-RR to Prince St., 6 to Spring, Sun-Th 10-5:30, F 10-2, all cash, exch. or rfd. Sells: **Buttons, Zippers, Trimmings & Threads.**

* **Kirsch Drapery Hardware**, 105 Eldridge St. (Grand), 966-6690, B-D to Grand, Sun-F 9-5, c.c., no ch., exch., no rfd. Wiss scissors were here cheaper than anywhere else I had seen. Sells: **Scissors, Sewing-Aids.**

*** **Leratex Fabrics**, 110 Eldridge St. (Grand-Broome), 925-3678, B-D to Grand, Sun-Th 8:30-5, F 8:30-4, ch., no c.c., exch., no rfd. (But only if uncut.) Sells: **Drapery & Upholstery Fabrics.**

*** **Louis Bargain Center**, Brooklyn, 4216 13th Av., 854-1003, B to Ft. Ham. Pkwy., Sun-Th 9:30-6, F 9:30-3, all cash, no exch. or rfd. Often very busy. Carries many job lots and roll-ends at savings of 60-85%. Sells: **Drapery & Upholstery Fabrics, Common Dress Fabrics, Suit Fabrics.**

*** **Marboro Yarns**, Brooklyn, 2178 Bay Ridge Av., 256-6675, N to Bay Pkwy., M-S 10-5, all cash, no exch., no rfd. Sells: **Yarns.**

* **Margaret's Fabrics**, 430 Broadway (Howard), 925-8483, J-M-N-QB-RR-6 to Canal, M-F 9-5, Sun 11-4, all cash, no exch. or rfd. Sells: **Common Dress Fabrics.**

** **Max Eagle Fabrics**, 61 Delancey St. (Allen), 431-4745, F-J-M to Delancey & Essex, J-M to Bowery, Sun-F 10-3, all cash, no exch. or rfd. Sells: **Suit Fabrics.**

M.E., 177 E. Houston St. (Orchard), 260-2060, F to 2nd Av., Sun-F 8:30-5, all cash, no exch. or rfd. Sells: **Zippers, Trimmings & Threads.**

Mitchell Mogal, 440 Broadway (Grand), 226-8378, J-M-N-QB-RR-6 to Canal, M-F 9-5, all cash, no exch., no rfd. Terrific on Wiss scissors; also on miniature cap-guns. Sells: **Scissors, Jewelry & Gifts, Personal Accessories, Toys, Games & Hobbies.**

9: FABRICS, YARNS & NOTIONS

Modlin Fabrics, 240 W. 40 (7th-8th), 391-4830, N-QB-RR-1-2-3-7 to 42 & Times Square, A-AA-CC-E to 42, M-F 8-6, S 9-5, ch., c.c., exch., no rfd. Sells: **Designer Dress Fabrics**.

*** **Monezel Textiles**, 470 Broadway (Grand), 431-3939, J-M-N-QB-RR-6 to Canal, Sun-F 9-5, all cash, no exch. or rfd. Sells: **Common Dress Fabrics, Suit Fabrics**.

** **M.Recht Textile**, 118 Eldridge St. (Broome), 966-7373, B-D to Grand, Sun-Th 9-4, F 9-2, all cash, no exch. or rfd. Sells: **Suit Fabrics**.

Paron Fabrics, 140 W. 57 (6th-7th), 247-6451, B to 57, N-QB-RR to 57th St., M-S 9-6, ch., no c.c., no exch. or rfd. Sells: **Designer Dress Fabrics, Common Dress Fabrics**.

** **Peerless Fabrics**, 88 Franklin St. (Church), 964-3588, 1 to Franklin, M-F 9-3, all cash, no exch. or rfd. Rolls only. Pieces not cut to order. Sells: **Common Dress Fabrics**.

* **Peter Pan Yarns**, Brooklyn, 7609 18th Av., 232-9001, B to 79th St.; Brooklyn, 2347 86th St., 372-1166, B to 25th Av. Both stores: hours usually M-F 9-6, S 9-5, all cash, exch., no rfd. Sells: **Yarns**.

Poli Fabrics, 130 W. 57 (6th-7th), 245-7589, B to 57, N-QB-RR to 57th St., M-S 9-6, ch., no c.c., no exch. or rfd. Sells: **Designer Dress Fabrics, Common Dress Fabrics**.

** **Rainbow Textiles**, 414 Broadway (Canal), 226-0895, J-M-N-QB-RR-6 to Canal, M-F 9-6, SSun 10-5, all cash, no exch. or rfd. Sells: **Common Dress Fabrics**.

** **Relatex Fabrics**, 360 Broadway (Franklin), 226-1534, 1 to Franklin, M-F 9-5, ch., no c.c., exch. or rfd. Sells: **Common Dress Fabrics**.

** **Reliable Button Works**, 65 W. 37 at 6th Av., 2nd floor, 869-0560, B-D-F-N-QB-RR to 34, M-F 8-5:30, ch., no c.c., no exch. or rfd. Fabric-covered buttons made here to match garment--you supply fabric. Sells: **Buttons**.

** **Shalom Export**, 513 Broadway (Broome-Spring), 226-8466&3844, N-RR to Prince St., 6 to Spring, M-F 9-5, ch., no exch. or rfd. Sometimes reluctant to sell retail. Sells: **Drapery & Upholstery Fabrics, Common Dress Fabrics, Suit Fabrics**.

Silk Surplus Scalamandre, 223 E. 58 (3rd Av.), 753-6511, N-RR-4-5-6 to 59th & Lex.; 843 Lexington Av. (64), 879-4708, 6 to 68, N-RR-4-5-6 to 59th & Lex. Both stores: M-F 10-5:15, S 11-3:45, ch., no c.c., no exch. or rfd. Also Westbury and Paramus locations. Closeout stores for Scalamandre. Discounted about half, but still ridiculously expensive. Some over $100/yard. Sells: **Drapery & Upholstery Fabrics**.

Sunray Yarn, 349 Grand St. (Essex), 475-0062, F-J-M to Delancey & Essex, Sun-F 9:30-5:30, ch., no c.c., exch. or rfd. Sells: **Yarns**.

**** **Superior Ribbon**, 48 W. 27 (5th-6th), 689-3280, N-RR to 28th St., M-F 8:30-4, ch., no c.c., exch., no rfd. Large selection. Ribbon manufacturer who sells 50&100-yard rolls cheaper than you'll pay for a few yards at a department-store. Sells: **Ribbons**.

*+ **Sutter Textile**, 257 W. 39 (7th-8th), 398-0248, A-AA-CC-E to 42, N-QB-RR-1-2-3-7 to 42 & Times Square, M-F 9:15-5:45, S 10-4:45, ch., c.c., no exch. or rfd. Huge selection. Sells: **Drapery & Upholstery Fabrics, Common Dress Fabrics**.

* **The Yardstick Fabrics**, 54 W. 14 (5th-6th Avs.), 924-7131, B-F-LL to 14th St. & 6th Av., 7 days 9-7, c.c., no ch., no exch. or rfd. Sells: **Drapery & Upholstery Fabrics, Designer Dress Fabrics, Common Dress Fabrics**.

Tinsel Trdg., 47 W. 38 (5th-6th), 730-1030, B-D-F to 42, B-D-F-N-QB-RR to 34, M-F 10:30-5, S 12-5, ch., c.c., no exch. or rfd. Specialty is braids. Sells: **Trimmings & Threads**.

* **W.M. Textile**, 108 Eldridge St. (Grand-Broome), 226-5115, B-D to Grand, Sun-Th 9-5, F 9-3, all cash, no exch. or rfd. Sells: **Drapery & Upholstery Fabrics, Common Dress Fabrics**.

10:
FLOWERS & PLANTS
Expect 20-60% discounts.

RECOMMENDED PRODUCTS:
Indoor Plants:

HARDIEST LOW-LIGHT PLANTS:
WATER LIGHTLY: Dracaena Marginata, Corn Plant, Philodendron Cordatum, Philodendron Pertusum, Snake Plant. **WATER MODERATELY:** Chinese Evergreen, Aspidistra, Neanthe Bella Palm, Nephthytis. **WATER HEAVILY:** Spathiphyllum.

HARDIEST MEDIUM-LIGHT PLANTS:
WATER LIGHTLY: Schefflera, Ploemele, Rubber Plant. **WATER MODERATELY:** Bamboo Palm (erumpens or seifritzii).

HARDIEST HEAVY-LIGHT PLANTS:
WATER LIGHTLY: Polyscias. **WATER MODERATELY:** Ficus Exotica. **WATER HEAVILY:** Chrysanthemum.

Other types of indoor plants are not recommended, as they are not as hardy (usually not even nearly as hardy).

RECOMMENDED STORES:
flowers
(includes: arrangements, bouquets, carnations, roses, wreaths)

***Superior Florists** (679-4065); ****Stulbaum's Florist** (684-8927); *****York Floral** (686-2070); **Public Flower Mkt.** (684-2850).

plants

***Farmer Grey's** (564-2316); *****Bonsai Plants** (255-2187); *****Plant Connection** (564-0474); *****Plant Shed** (249-7404); *****Sixth Av. Wholesale Greenery** (243-0341); **NYC Outdoor Greenmarkets**; **Plant World** (861-6282); **Sixth Av. Greenery** (255-1117); **Third Av. Greenery** (679-7243).

STORES-DIRECTORY

Phone a store before you go out of your way to visit it. Especially do this during July and August, when most establishments reduce or eliminate weekend-hours.

In the listings below, "*" means especially recommended, "+" means that the store offers a bonus discount to BF readers, "ch." and "c.c." mean respectively checks and credit cards, and "exch." and "rfd." mean respectively exchange and refund. Nearest subway-stops are shown. For example, "B-D-F to 47" means to take the B, D, or F train to 47th Street. Store-hours are also indicated, with days of the week abbreviated, like "M-S 8-6."

*   **Bonsai Plants**, 777 6th Av. (26-7), 255-2187, N-RR to 28th St., B-F to 23, 7 days 10-6, ch., c.c., no exch. or rfd. This time, a name can be deceiving. They don't

10: FLOWERS & PLANTS

sell bonsais. Sells: **Plants**.

*** **Farmer Grey's**, 327 10th Av. at 29th St., 564-2316, A-AA-CC-E to 34, M-F 9-6, SSun 10-7, ch., c.c., no exch. or rfd. Sells: **Plants**.

NYC Outdoor Greenmarkets, Phone 477-3220 for the location of the one nearest you. They're functioning during only summer and fall. Sponsored by NYC Council on The Environment. Sells: **Plants, Foods**.

* **Plant Connection**, 823 6th Av. (28), and 106A W. 28 (6th Av.), 564-0474 & 924-5025, N-RR to 28th St., M-F 9-6, SSun 10-6, ch., c.c., no exch. or rfd. Sells: **Plants**.

* **Plant Shed**, 515 E. 72 (York-E.River), 249-7404, 6 to 68, plus a long walk, T-F 9-7, SSun 9-6, c.c., no ch., no exch. or rfd. Large selection. Sells: **Plants**.

Plant World, 3rd Av. at 77th, 861-6282, 6 to 77, M-S 9-7, all cash, no exch. or rfd. Small selection. Sells: **Plants**.

Public Flower Mkt., 796 6th Av. at 27th St., 684-2850, N-RR to 28th St., M-S 8-6, Sun 8-2, ch., no c.c., no exch. or rfd. Sells: **Flowers**.

Sixth Av. Greenery, 355 6th Av. (Wash. Pl. - 3rd St.), 255-1117, A-AA-B-CC-D-E-F to 4, M-Th 9-8, FS 9-10, Sun 10-6, ch., no c.c., exch., no rfd. Sells: **Plants**.

* **Sixth Av. Wholesale Greenery**, 771 6th Av. (26), 243-0341, B-F to 23, N-RR to 28th St., M-F 9-6, SSun 11-5, ch., c.c., no exch. or rfd. Sells: **Plants**.

** **Stulbaum's Florist**, 810 6th Av. (28), 684-8927, N-RR to 28th St., 7 days 8-6, ch., no c.c., no exch. or rfd. Sells: **Flowers**.

*** **Superior Florists**, 828 6th Av. (28-9), 679-4065 & 684-2595, N-RR to 28th St., 7 days 9-6, c.c., no ch., no exch. or rfd. Very cooperative. Large selection. Sells: **Flowers**.

Third Av. Greenery, 557 3rd Av. at 37th, 679-7243, 4-5-6-7 to Grand Central, 6 to 33, 7 days 8-8, ch., c.c., exch., no rfd. Sells: **Plants**.

* **York Floral**, 804 6th Av. (27), 686-2070, N-RR to 28th St., M-F 8:30-6, S 9-6, ch., c.c. $15+, no exch. or rfd. Sells: **Flowers**.

11:
FOODS
Expect 20-60% discounts.

Whatever you're looking for, from candies to caviars, you can find it in New York City for less; but unless you know where to shop, you'll end up paying more—not less—here than elsewhere.

This town is best on specialty-foods. The recommended shops include many that specialize in Indian, Chinese and Arabic gourmet delicacies. However, there are also a few full-line regular-brand discount supermarkets; and you'll also find a good number of places that sell such stand-by items as meat, fish, and cheese. Practically everything that's edible is available at discount at the recommended outlets.

If you don't happen to live near one of the endorsed stores, here are the least expensive local supermarket-chains, in order: C-Town, Key, Waldbaum's, Pathmark, Associated, E&B. The most expensive is Sloan's. All others are in-between.

Viable Vegetarianism

One can greatly increase food-savings by taking an imaginative and informed approach to nutrition. For example, there was a 1977 book, *Eating for Life*, by a certain Nathaniel Altman, which gave comparative longevity and disease data for vegetarians versus meat-eaters; and what it claimed to show—and did so, I think, convincingly—is that vegetarians live longer and have less disease than flesh-eaters (also that an extraordinarily high percentage of Olympic athletes are vegetarians). Perhaps one reason which would help explain this is that vegetarians are lower on the food-chain, which of course means that they consume far less agricultural insecticides. This might account for the lower cancer-rates for vegetarians. But the biggest health-difference between the two groups has to do with heart-disease; and here the lower cholesterol-consumption and the higher intake of dietary fiber by vegetarians must be major factors.

There can no longer be any question about the deadly effects of consumption of animal-fats. The definitive study concerning cholesterol appeared early in 1982 in the British medical journal, *The Lancet*, carried out by the Oslo (Norway) Department of Health, and the Life Insurance Companies' Institute for Medical Statistics, under the direction of Dr. I. Hjermann. It showed a 40% reduction in heart-attack risk associated with a reduction in animal-fat intake. The study also indicated that this dietary change had an even bigger positive health-impact than did reduced cigarette-smoking, and that the lowered heart-attack rate was not accompanied by any increase in deaths from other causes, such as cancer.

Some people are concerned about the possibility that a vegetarian diet might not provide a full nutritional complement, especially of proteins. However, Soybeans have more protein than beef, and of equivalently high quality; and the 3-to-1-combination of soybeans (or soy flour) with sesame seeds (or sesame butter, which is the whole seeds ground) provides a more complete and well-balanced protein than does any animal food-source—even than egg-white (which offers the best-balanced protein of any single food). But sesame seeds, and especially soybeans, must be cooked in order for the protein to be assimilable by the body. Cooking deactivates things like trypsin-inhibitor and phytic acid which are found in these seeds and which otherwise would block digestion not only of the protein, but also of the calcium and zinc with which soy and sesame are so generously endowed. (Sesame seeds, in fact, have more calcium than does any other food, including much more than cheese—but without the cholesterol. Sesame tahini, however, which is made by grinding sesame seeds that have been stripped of their hulls, has only one-tenth the calcium, and also far less of other nutrients.) Furthermore, these grains are loaded with additional valuable nutrients either lacking or scarce in meats: fiber, lecithin, vitamin E, B-vitamins, and trace-minerals. And of course, their dry-weight cost is about 10% that of beef. One more thing: Legumes such as soybeans contain a certain type of protein which decreases the body's absorbtion of starch. In a controlled scientific test recently, it was found that this results in weight-loss. Because less starch from bread, potatoes, etc., is digested, even a high-calorie diet just passes through the body. If you're interested in further information about soy, you can write to two places. First: The Book Publishing Company, The Farm, Summertown, Tennessee 38483. Ask for a copy of their free booklet, *Yay, Soybeans!*, which has some excellent soybean recipies (but without sesame seeds). Also request information about—and current prices of—*The Farm Vegetarian Cookbook* and their other publications. Then: The Soyfoods Center, P.O. Box 234, Lafayette, CA 94549. Request a free catalog of their publications. (Another equally marvelous food-source, which promises to become the soybean of the tropics, and which may soon be made available in the U.S. as well, is the winged bean. For free information about this extraordinary plant, write to the Commission on International Relations, National Research Council, 2101 Constitution Av. N.W., Washington, D.C. 24018, and request their free report, "The Winged Bean: A High Protein Crop for The Tropics.")

One of the dining-spots I recommend in the restaurants-section (Chapters 39-42), the Dojo, at 24 St. Marks Place, in East Greenwich Village (674-9821), offers a terrific introduction to soy-cuisine in the form of their "soyburger dinner," which is just about the cheapest and most nutritious entre served anywhere. Quite filling and delicious. Chapter 40 contains a list or "Honor-Roll" of all the recommended bargain-dining establishments that have good offerings for vegetarians.

Soybeans and sesame seeds can be most cheaply obtained from the stores listed for "Grains and Beans," and at the health-food stores. Soy flour and sesame butter can be found at some of the recommended health-food stores—sometimes only on special-order.

One final point about soybeans: this plant has an extraordinary agricultural property which some authorities speculate might be able to help prevent global famines in the coming decades, and also to reduce petroleum-consumption here in the U.S.: Unlike other plants which consume nitrogen from the soil—thus depleting it, and so causing a need for heavier use of petroleum-based fertilizers—soy plants are nitrogen-fixating: They transfer some of the abundant nitrogen from the air into the soil, thus restoring and fertilizing topsoil without the use of petroleum. Greater cultivation of soybeans could help reverse the escalating world-wide trend toward the depletion of topsoil and the consequent loss of farmable land, which is progressing in the U.S. alone at the alarming rate of a million lost farmable acres yearly. Third-world countries are in even worse shape—and so would be even more benefited by increased soy-cropping. In contrast, other food-sources—including the traditional farming of animals such as cows or chickens—speed the world ultimately toward increasing food-and-petroleum shortages.

Beef & Chicken

Many people don't realize that the higher grades of beef have more fat—and cholesterol—than do the cheaper ones. Also, the most expensive meats are aged, and this increases the amount of malenaldehyde—a potent carcinogen found in all dead flesh. Chicken usually has the highest malenaldehyde content of all meats. The malenaldehyde, in conjunction of course with the high insecticide-residues found in animal-fats, may help account for the generally higher cancer-rates of meat-eaters as compared to vegetarians. However, there's another poison which may also partly explain this carcinogenicity of meats: Diethylstilbestrol (DES). This is added to animal-feed in the United States in order to fatten the livestock, which it does by increasing the creature's watery tissue. A proven carcinogen, it's banned outright in Sweden, France, Australia, Argentina, Canada, and 15 other countries. Canada at one time banned all imports of beef, mutton, and lamb from the U.S., because of the DES. Then, to regain this lost business, U.S. meat-producers agreed to raise DES-free meat, but only for export to Canada—we don't get it.

Nearly 90% of all commercially raised American chickens eat feed which contains arsenic—another known carcinogen, and one which in larger quantities becomes an instant poison. This is done so as to stimulate growth and egg-production, and to give chickens the yellower skin that consumers prefer. Chicken livers contain especially high levels of arsenic, a cumulative poison.

Fish and Radioactivity

The chief health-threat in eating fish stems from the 89,000 barrels of nuclear wastes which the U.S. Government has so far admitted having dumped off the Atlantic and Pacific coasts between 1946 and 1970. For example, one typical Atomic Energy Commission report reveals an incident in 1955, in which 740 drums of "high-level solid wastes" were trucked to Earle, N.J., and dumped into the Atlantic. Congressional testimony in 1958 disclosed that the University of California Radiation Laboratory at Berkeley disposed of its "high-level large volume aqueous waste" by dumping off the Pacific coast. The military refuses to make public its own list of past dumping operations, but knowledgeable authorities estimate that hundreds of thousands of barrels of defense-related radioactive wastes have been disposed of at sea. One retired Navy pilot testified that in three separate missions, he flew a total of six to eight tons of nuclear wastes out off the coast of New Jersey, where he dropped them into the Atlantic. Divers have occasionally stumbled upon ruptured, glowing radioactive drums in shallow coastal areas 150 feet deep. Nonetheless, there has never been any systematic attempt to monitor known dump-sites for radioactive contamination. Nor have studies been done of, for example, the plutonium content of fish. However, it seems reasonable to assume that as increasing numbers of the dumped drums rupture, sharply escalating quantities of intensely carcinogenic elements will enter the food-chain through fish. Some of these elements are so poisonous that only a few molecules are enough to kill a man; and I wouldn't want to eat a fish that had those few molecules. (Note: Japan has announced plans to dump 100,000 barrels of radioactive wastes into the Pacific this year alone. Britain began dumping 250 tons of the stuff off its own coasts in late 1981.)

Studies done many years ago showed that the food with the highest naturally-occuring radioactivity is brazil nuts, which turned out to be a whopping 30-times as radioactive as the second-most-radioactive food. It seems that brazil nuts tend to serve as a vacuum-cleaner for radioactive elements in the soil.

Miso, a very high-protein product of fermented soybeans, possesses a substance called "zybicolin" or "dipicolinic acid," which has been found to be a magnet which attracts, absorbs, and discharges from the body, radioactive elements such as strontium. In fact, a prominent Japanese physician noted that Nagasaki-victims who regularly ate miso soup exhibited far fewer ill effects from the bomb than did those who consumed little or no miso. So if you're going to eat fish or brazil nuts, you might as well take them with miso. This fermented soy-product, which is loaded with valuable nutrients (including the lactobacillus that makes yogurt so healthy), can be obtained at the stores listed for "Health Foods."

Breakfast Cereals

Many scientific studies have been done of the nutritional adequacy of breakfast cereals, and almost all of them have reported that oatmeal is best. Fraudulent ads about "the *Total* difference" notwithstanding, unmodified whole-grain cereals score far higher than do processed cereals having 100% supplementation of a few isolated vitamins (and a total lack of other essential nutrients). Rats fed the (depleted and then) "enriched" cereals die; those fed whole-grain cereals—especially oatmeal—live. But if you buy Quaker Oats or the other brands, you'll be paying more than twice as much as you need to. Most of the stores I recommend under the categories "Grains, Beans, Flours," and "Health Foods," sell the same stuff loose, by the pound, as "rolled oats," at less than half the brand-name price.

Candies

If you're a candy-freak, the tastiest and cheapest candies that have no preservatives, artificial colorings, or coconut (the only vegetarian source of cholesterol), are three from the Mars Candy Co.: Mars (with almonds), Snickers (with peanuts), and Three Musketeers. They all have a delicious malted-chocolate base. Snickers has as much protein as do the super-expensive "high-protein" health-food-store candy-brands, and tastes much better. ("Health-food sweets" are frauds, and even a contradiction in terms.) Each in its own way is as yummy as the best of the imported and specialty candies—and many of the latter have preservatives or other poisons which these don't. The cheapest place in the City to get them is at Wolf's Wholesale, at Atlantic and Court in Brooklyn. The best of the imported specialty candies are two by Perugina: Bacci, and Gianduja, both of which are chocolate-hazelnut delights, and again without any garbage in the ingredients. These can be most inexpensively obtained at Piemonte Ravioli, in Little Italy. The boxes are terrific gift-items.

Coffees & Substitutes

Many studies have shown that you add approximately 100% to your probability of getting lethal pancreatic cancer for every cup-a-day of coffee-intake. So if you consume, for example, 2 cups daily, your chance of getting pancreatic cancer is about 3 times normal. Decaffeinated coffees are the same. One of the hypothesized reasons for these findings is the fact that insecticides which are illegal in the U.S. are used legally and profusely on coffee crops in Latin America; and according to the General Accounting Office of the Congress, nearly half the coffee beans coming into this country contain measurable amounts of pesticides that are banned in the United States. Yet despite this commonplace illegal contamination, FDA inspectors rarely seize shipments or refuse them entry. After all, how could the vast American coffee industry then survive? (Most of these illegal pesticides, ironically, are made by U.S. firms for use abroad. The coffee-growers are a major market for these products. So our domestic chemical industry also has a lot at stake in this. In fact, the chemicals are sprayed so abundantly that the peasants who harvest the crops are commonly sick from acute pesticide-poisoning and have extraordinarily high cancer-rates. Then we drink the coffee.)

I've tried all 14 coffee-substitutes available in the New York area, and three clearly stand out as best. For hot coffee, the Swiss instant product, Pionier, has the best taste and is the most coffee-like—almost as coffee-like as a regular instant coffee. However, it's very expensive. For iced or very cold coffee, the Polish instant product, Inka, is as coffee-like as a regular instant—and makes the tastiest and most refreshing of all coffee-substitutes, hot or cold. It also has the virtue of being inexpensive—cheaper than real instant-coffees. (Incidentally, ignore the package-directions on both Pionier and Inka. They say to use one teaspoonful per cup. I think you'll find that you actually need one heaping tablespoonful.) The non-instant American product, Comtessa, which looks like ground espresso, is also worth mentioning, because while it isn't as good an imitation of coffee as the products just mentioned, it makes a beverage which wears well with repeated use—quite hearty and toasty. The price is moderate. All of these coffee-substitutes are made of highly roasted grains, and are nutritionally safe and innocuous—just pure flavor and aroma. They're available at health-food stores; and if a particular dealer doesn't carry these brands, then tell the shopkeeper that these were the top-rated brands in *Bargain Finder*, and ask him if he'll order them in. But there's also one tea which can be especially attractive to died-in-the-wool coffee-lovers: the smoked tea known as Lapsang Souchong. Also, many Japanese consider miso soup to be a substitute for coffee.

Except for the very expensive Swiss water-process decaffeinated coffees, all decaffeinated brands use acknowledgedly cancer-causing petroleum solvents to remove the caffein. The most popular such solvent used to be trichloroethylene—the same stuff that's employed by drycleaners and that causes them to have an astronomical leukemia-rate. I found out about this in the early 1960's when I wrote to the makers of Sanka, asking them how they removed the caffein; and I never drank decaffeinated coffee after that. (They even told me how much of the trichloroethylene remained in the Sanka!) In the late 1970's, for some inexplicable reason, consumerists suddenly became exercized over this use of trichloroethylene; and so most of the manufacturers switched to methylene chloride instead. Then, for some equally inexplicable reason, consumerists quieted down again. (It's since been established that methylene chloride causes cancer in rats.) Decaffeinated instant coffee is useless, anyway, because the two instantized coffee-substitutes mentioned above are just as coffee-like without the poisons.

If you're intent on taking real coffee, you might as well enjoy it to the fullest. One brand of espresso available in the New York area is both inexpensive and extraordinarily good, having a distinctive earthy aroma and nutty taste: Cafe Caribe, available at some supermarkets. You can brew it the same way you brew your regular coffee, and it'll taste great; it doesn't need to be made in an espresso-pot.

Most coffees have a slight bitterness to the taste, and a way to eliminate this is to add about 5-10 particles of garlic-powder per cup of hot water, before or during brewing. This is not enough to produce a garlicky flavor, but it is a sufficient amount to eliminate the bitterness and produce a richer coffee.

Herbal Teas

Several common spices make delicious herbal teas, at a small fraction of the cost of the branded packaged stuff. Each of the following thrown into water that's been freshly boiled (and where needed, sifted through a fine-meshed strainer) makes a very tasty non-stimulant brew: savory, spearmint, wintergreen, winterberry, celery seed, lemon-grass, and basil. Generally, use about a teaspoonful per cup (or if powdered—which is far more economical—then about one-quarter that). In addition, the following powder-blend makes a quart of a scrumptious instant tea—one-and-one-eighth teaspoonsful of cinnamon-powder, one-eighth teaspoonful of clove-powder, and one-twenty-fourth teaspoonful of ginger powder. (Or you can blend the following, which will be enough to make ultimately 24 quarts: 9 tablespoons cinnamon, 1 tablespoon clove, 1 teaspoon ginger—all powders, as before.) (If you want to transform this into a perky lemon-spice tea, just add a drop of lemon-extract to the cup and stir before drinking.) These spices can be obtained at the places I recommend for "Spices & Herbs." (Purity Maid, in Queens, which sells a huge selection of spices, both mail-order and pick-up, for about 75% discount—plus a bonus-BF-discount—would be the best.) Phone ahead to find which places sell or can get the herbs or spices you're looking for. If you're interested in exploring the medicinal effects of these and other herbs and spices, the best—and by far the cheapest—source to consult is John Lust's *The Herb Book*, available in a Bantam paperback.

Stimulant Teas

As for real teas, of the forty or so that I've tried, the following have been both outstanding and reasonably priced: Lipton's (regular tea), San Francisco Cinnamon-Orange (available reasonably priced only at a store I list especially for teas: Porto Rico on Bleecker St.), Apple (ditto), Twining's (orange-) Spiced Tea, Bigelow's Constant Comment (orange-spice tea), Bigelow's Lemon Lift (lemon-spice tea, the perkiest of them all), Lipton's Instant Lemon-Flavored Tea (for a superb iced tea), Twining's Earl Grey (bergamot-spice tea), China Rose Congou (rose-spice tea, also called "Le The Noir Rose" in French on the other side of the round tin found at the stores I list for "Chinese Specialties"), The Au Jasmin in the square gold-yellow tin (Jasmine Tea, as it's called on the other side of the tin, also found at the "Chinese Specialties" stores. The same-named tea in the square red tin isn't quite as good. The jasmine I mentioned is the best—and a very cheap—jasmine tea.) **NOTE:** It's always best to buy tea loose, not in bags. The price is much cheaper, and the tea brews faster. After steeping, simply pour the tea into the cup through the finest-meshed strainer you can find. The 88-Cent Shops, recommended in the Housewares Chapter, have fairly fine-meshed strainers. One of the tea-specialty stores I list, Porto Rico, sells loose all the teas I've mentioned, except for Lipton's. Zabar's carries the Bigelow teas.

Vegetable Oils

The same types of petroleum-solvents that are used to remove the caffein from decaffeinated coffees are also employed to isolate vegetable-oils from grains like corn, sunflower seeds, etc. The only exceptions are oils removed by pressing rather than by solvent-extraction; and pressed oils are sold only at health-food stores. In fact, these pressed oils—most especially if they're drawn from safflower, sunflower, soybean, and corn—have shown a remarkable ability to reduce the arterial plaque that leads to clogged blood-vessels and finally to heart-attacks. But to be maximally wholesome, it's not enough that a vegetable-oil be press-extracted; it should also be unpasteurized and unrefined, because studies have repeatedly shown that refined or highly heated vegetable-oils often have a greater tendency to form arterial plaque than they do to dissolve it. So how do you recognize such unprocessed oils? First by there being a sediment at the bottom of the bottle. Second by the aroma when you open the container. Refined oils have the aromatic natural essences removed along with the vitamin E and other nutrients. The vitamin E is then sold separately to vitamin-supply houses as natural vitamin E. The lecithin—especially valuable in preventing heart-attacks—is sold primarily to other food-processors for use as an emulsifier. The oil that's left has no smell.

Two types of vegetable-oil should always be avoided: coconut, because it's a saturated fat, virtually like animal-fat; and cotton-seed, because it contains potent inherent and added poisons: malvalic acid, gossypol, and others naturally occuring in the cottonseed; and high insecticide-residues resulting from the especially intense spraying of cottonfields. Studies have shown that cottonseed-oil causes extensive arterial plaque and also cancer in a wide variety of test-animals. It should never be used in food. The unhealthfulness of animal-fats has previously been mentioned, so their similarity to coconut-oil obviously doesn't reflect well on the latter. Also, if the oil listed on an ingredients-label says "hydrogenated," then part of the oil's unsaturated (good) component has been transformed into a saturated, animal-fat-like material; and this makes it about as undesirable as if it had come from coconuts. The very nutritious oils, to summarize, are those press-extracted from unrefined safflower, sunflower, soybean, and corn. Other press-extracted unrefined oils that I haven't mentioned—such as those from peanuts, olives, and sesame seeds, to name a few—are nutritionally neutral.

The Federal Deception Agency

Some people mistakenly think that the U.S. Food and Drug Administration exists to protect the public against the kinds of poisons I've been speaking of, but the FDA is if anything even more corrupt than other governmental regulatory agencies. The American Medical Association has defended its stand against increased nutritional concern among physicians and the general public by saying that poisonous and carcinogenic chemicals "are promptly excluded from processed foodstuffs by the Food and Drug Administration, which takes no chances" with the public's health. But speaking more honestly in an unusually candid moment, a former FDA Commissioner himself once admitted, "The people think the FDA is protecting them—it isn't. What the FDA is doing and what the public thinks it's doing are as different as night and day." It surprises many people, for example, to learn that the FDA accepts one pellet of rodent-excreta per pint of wheat. But if you find that amount, don't complain to the Federal Deception Agency. They also tolerate 50 insect-fragments or 2 rodent-hairs per 100 grams

(3.5 ounces) of peanut butter. 150 insect-fragments and four rat-hairs are the limit set for eight ounces of chocolate dessert. Uncle Sam also says that tomato juice is "clean" when it has less than 25 fruit-fly larvae per cupful. An executive of one of the largest breakfast-cereal manufacturers regulated by the FDA, frankly acknowledged that his firm "couldn't make" its products "out of flour that dirty." A Ralph-Nader organization study showed furthermore that in the FDA's other area of authority, drugs, the agency doesn't even fulfill its congressionally obligatory mandate to keep off the market ineffective prescription-medications: 1 out of every 8 prescriptions filled in this country is for a drug that the FDA has found to be ineffective but has nonetheless failed its mandate to ban. (Nader himself, however, has surprised me with how ill-informed he personally is about some of the things that this chapter covers. On NBC's Donahue Show aired March 1, 1981, questioners from the studio-audience who were concerned about the use of potent poisons to fatten chickens, and to remove caffein from coffee, drew blanks from him on both issues, although he tried to appear knowledgeable by addressing his answers to other questions. He evidently was less informed than some of the housewives were, regarding the respective long-established commercial uses of arsenic and trichloroethylene in foods. Also, when he was asked about natural versus synthetic vitamins, he unwittingly supported the common health-food industry fraud by saying, blanketly, that "the two are not exactly identical," and that the natural are superior to the synthetic; when, actually, each statement is either wholly or partly false, and grossly misleading in any case. The facts about those issues are presented in Chapter 13.) And despite the Delaney Amendment which gives the FDA authority to prohibit carcinogens from entering the food-supply, carcinogenic drugs—which the agency also can outlaw—are now so common that no one was surprised when a lab-building at Rutgers University was ordered closed recently on account of a component of common birth-control pills found to have been permeating the air. The synthetic female hormone, estradiol benzoate, is an established animal carcinogen related to the supplement that's used to fatten beef-cattle, and a suspected human cancer-causer as well; and it's thought to have been responsible for the extraordinarily high number of cancers that had been discovered among the Rutgers lab-workers, which is why the lab was closed down. But millions of women who take birth-control pills are routinely subjected to this same chemical every day in their contraceptives. Consumer-protection in the U.S. is even worse than in many other lands. For example, France, another industrialized country known for its corrupt government, permits only one two-hundredth the number of chemical food-additives that ours does. But be that as it may, the consumer's only effective defense against filthy or poisonous foods certainly is not government. It's simply extreme caution informed by rigorous self-education.

Basic Nutrition-Library

This educational process requires some good books. Two pa-

11: FOODS

perbacks in addition to the three previously mentioned, are strongly recommended for a basic nutrition-library: U.S. Dept. of Agriculture, *Composition of Foods—Agriculture Handbook #8*, U.S. Govt. Prtg. Ofc.; and: Nutrition Search Inc., *Nutrition Almanac*, McGraw-Hill. The first gives tables showing some of the most important nutrient-contents of 2,500 common foods; the second describes the importance and function of each of the known nutrients. Both are reasonably priced. There is unfortunately no equally good volume that deals with the major natural and added poisons in various foods, but I've tried to cover here some of the highlights of this important subject.

Incidentally, Nature Food Center food stores throughout the City offer free of charge a fairly good monthly nutrition-magazine, *Today's Living*. Not quite as excellent as *Prevention*, but a darned good freebie.

RECOMMENDED PRODUCTS:
See above.

RECOMMENDED STORES:

baked goods

(examples: breads, buns, cakes, cookies, croissants, pies)

Argento Bakery (Brooklyn, 745-8761); ****Bakery Thrift (Queens); ****Carini Pastry** (Brooklyn, 438-9216); ****G. Malko** (Brooklyn, 624-7659); ****Malko Karkanni** (Brooklyn, 834-0845); ****Modern Bakery** (Brooklyn, 851-7402); ****Mona Lisa Bakery** (Brooklyn, 256-7706); ****Scala Bros. Pastry** (Brooklyn, 836-1844); ****Scotto's Bakery** (Brooklyn, 438-0889); ****V Discount Bakery** (Brooklyn, 531-2396); ****Oriental Pastry & Grocery** (Brooklyn, 875-7687); ***Black Forest Bakery** (254-8181); ***Bleecker St. Pastry** (242-4959); ***Elias Malko** (858-4230); ***Hammond's Bakery** (Brooklyn, 284-7666); ***Jo Misa Cookie Factory** (Bronx, 379-6223); ***Lafayette French Pastry** (242-7580); ***Piemonte Ravioli** (226-0475); ***Rocco's Pastry Shop** (242-6031); ***The People's Bakery** (Brooklyn, 774-215); **Benkert's Bakery** (Queens, 728-7630); **Cafe Galleria Bakery** (Brooklyn, 625-7883); **Damaskus Bakery** (Brooklyn, 855-1457); **Fairway Foods** (595-1888); **Mary Bakery** (533-7780); **Mike's Bakery** (Brooklyn, 256-6546); **Olsen's Bakery** (Brooklyn, 439-6673); **Vaccaro Bakery** (Queens, 278-6818).

candies

***Anything & Everything (Brooklyn, 332-1508); *****Job Lot Trdg.** (intermittent stock, 962-4142); *****Julius The Candy King** (473-5329); *****Wolf's Wholesale** (Brooklyn, 522-5651); ****Kadouri Import** (677-5441); ****Sahadi Importing** (Brooklyn, 624-4550); ***Court Wholesale** (Brooklyn, 625-2421); ***Eighty-Eight Cent Shops** (753-6969); ***J. Wolsk** (475-7946); ***Mutual Dried Fruit** (673-3489); ***Piemonte Ravioli** (226-0475); **Dr. Schlock's** (intermittent stock, 766-8627); **First Cost** (intermittent stock, 697-0244); **Zabar's for Foods** (787-2000).

nuts, dried fruits

G. Malko (Brooklyn, 624-7659); ****Kadouri Import (677-5441); ****Malko Karkanni** (Brooklyn, 834-0845); ****Sahadi Importing** (Brooklyn, 624-4550); ****Shammas** (Brooklyn, 855-2455); ***Elias Malko** (858-4230); ***J. Wolsk** (475-7946); ***Mutual Dried Fruit** (673-3489).

11: FOODS

cheeses

**Adolf Kusy Meats (242-4755); **Basior-Schwartz (929-5368); *Cheese of All Nations (732-0752); *East Village Cheese (477-2601); *Murray's Cheese (243-3289); Fairway Foods (595-1888); Omaha Food Discount (Brooklyn, 638-5400).

chinese foods

*Chinese American Trdg. (267-5224); China Brilliance (431-9194); Kam Fook (227-5305); Wing Lee Lung Food Fair (431-9879).

indian foods

*Yassin International (684-1188); Annapurna (889-7540); Bharat Indian Foods (Queens, 445-4231); Ganesh Groceries (Queens, 458-7100); House of Spices (Queens, 476-1577); India Spice (686-8955); K. Kalustyan (685-3416); Little India (683-1691); Sinha Trdg. (683-4419).

mid-eastern foods

**G. Malko (Brooklyn, 624-7659); **Malko Karkanni (Brooklyn, 834-0845); **Sahadi Importing (Brooklyn, 624-4550); **Shammas (Brooklyn, 855-2455); *+Oriental Pastry & Grocery (Brooklyn, 875-7687); *Elias Malko (858-4230); *Le Baklava (751-1377).

fruits & vegetables

**Meat-N-Foods Warehouse (243-9183); Essex Fruiterers (phoneless); Fairway Foods (595-1888); NYC Outdoor Greenmarkets.

grains, beans, flours

**G. Malko (Brooklyn, 624-7659); **International Grocery (279-5514); **Malko Karkanni (Brooklyn, 834-0845); **Sahadi Importing (Brooklyn, 624-4550); **Shammas (Brooklyn, 855-2455); *+Oriental Pastry & Grocery (Brooklyn, 875-7687); *Churchill Int'l Grocery (997-9195); *Elias Malko (858-4230); *Le Baklava (751-1377); Annapurna (889-7540); Ganesh Groceries (Queens, 458-7100); House of Spices (Queens, 476-1577); Integral Yoga Foods (243-2642); K. Kalustyan (685-3416); Wholefoods (673-5388).

health foods

(includes peanut and sesame butters)
*Quality Health Foods (Brooklyn, 435-4333); General Nutrition Center (GNC). Integral Yoga Foods (243-2642); Original Health Food (866-0212); Prana Foods (228-3632); Wholefoods (673-5388).

spices & herbs

****+Purity Maid Spices (Queens, 326-1610); **G. Malko (Brooklyn, 624-7659); **International Grocery (279-5514); **Kadouri Import (677-5441); **Malko Karkanni (Brooklyn, 834-0845); **Sahadi Importing (Brooklyn, 624-4550); **Shammas (Brooklyn, 855-2455); *+Oriental Pastry & Grocery (Brooklyn, 875-7687); *Churchill Int'l Grocery (997-9195); *Elias Malko (858-4230); *Murray's Cheese (243-3289); *Yassin International (684-1188); Annapurna (889-7540); Bharat Indian Foods (Queens, 445-4231); Dr. Schlock's (intermittent stock, 766-8627); Ganesh Groceries (Queens, 458-7100); House of Spices (Queens, 476-1577); India Spice (686-8955); K. Kalustyan (685-3416); Little India (683-1691); Sinha Trdg. (683-4419).

teas

11: FOODS

*Chinese American Trdg. (267-5224); *Ming Hing (925-7410); +Porto Rico Importing (477-5421); China Brilliance (431-9194); Kam Fook (227-5305); Schapira Coffee (675-3733); Wing Lee Lung Food Fair (431-9879).

coffees

**G. Malko (Brooklyn, 624-7659); *+Oriental Pastry & Grocery (Brooklyn, 875-7687); +Porto Rico Importing (477-5421); Schapira Coffee (675-3733); Zabar's for Foods (787-2000).

gourmet specialties

**Brite Glo (569-3390); **International Gourmet (569-2611); Zabar's for Foods (787-2000).

meats & fowl

(includes: bacon, beef, chicken, franks, hams, lamb, pork, salamis, sausages, steak, turkey, veal)

**Adolf Kusy Meats (242-4755); **Cut-Well Beef (989-8240); **Cuzins Meat (736-5737); **Meat-N-Foods Warehouse (243-9183); *Allen Ruhalter Meat (475-6521); *Old Bohemian Meat (989-2870); *SML Meat Warehouse (Brooklyn, 272-1405); *Universal Foods (691-4600); *Washington Beef (563-0200); Omaha Food Discount (Brooklyn, 638-5400).

seafoods

(includes: fish, clams, smoked fish)

**Rego Smoked Fish (Queens, 894-1400); *Harry Julius (S&G Stanley) (475-8365); Central Fish (279-2317); Sea Breeze Fish (563-7537); Sea-Tide Fish Markets (Queens, 426-7786); The Fish Factory (369-7744).

caviars

**Beluga Caviar Corp. (675-2100); **Rego Smoked Fish (Queens, 894-1400); **Russ & Daughters (475-4880); Caviarteria (759-7410); Zabar's for Foods (787-2000).

pickled foods

The Pickleman (533-8448).

supermarket-foods (WIDE VARIETY)

***Anything & Everything (Brooklyn, 332-1508); **Meat-N-Foods Warehouse (243-9183); **Plus Discount Foods (Queens); Consumer Food Outlet (Brooklyn, 257-9727); Fairway Foods (595-1888).

packaged/canned foods

***Anything & Everything (Brooklyn, 332-1508); ***Odd Job Trdg. (intermittent stock, 686-6825); **Meat-N-Foods Warehouse (243-9183); *SML Meat Warehouse (Brooklyn, 272-1405); Fairway Foods (595-1888); First Cost (intermittent stock, 697-0244).

bean-curds & sprouts

****Fong Inn (962-5196).

beverages: CH. 19

pet-foods: CH.23

STORES-DIRECTORY

Phone a store before you go out of your way to visit it. Especially do this during July and August, when most establishments reduce or eliminate weekend-hours.

In the listings below, "*" means especially recommended, "+" means that the store offers a bonus discount to BF readers, "ch." and "c.c." mean respectively checks and credit cards, and "exch." and "rfd." mean respectively exchange and refund. Nearest subway-stops are shown. For example, "B-D-F to 47" means to take the B, D, or F train to 47th Street. Store-hours are also indicated, with days of the week abbreviated, like "M-S 8-6."

** **Adolf Kusy Meats**, 861 Washington St. (13), 242-4755, A-AA-CC-E-LL to 14 St. & 8 Av., M-F 4-2, all cash, exch. or rfd. Doesn't sell in units as small as only a single pound, but rather larger quantities. Sells: **Cheeses, Meats & Fowl.**

* **Allen Ruhalter Meat**, 104 Essex St. (Delancey-Rivington) in market across fm. NYC Traffic Dept., 475-6521, F-J-M to Delancey & Essex, M-S 8-5, all cash, exch. or rfd. Sells: **Meats & Fowl.**

Annapurna, 127 E. 28 (Lex.), 889-7540, 6 to 28, 7 days 10:30-7, all cash, exch. or rfd. Sells: **Indian Foods, Grains, Beans, Flours, Spices & Herbs.**

*** **Anything & Everything**, Brooklyn, 2930 Av. X (Nostrand), 332-1508, no subway stop nearby, MTWF 10-6, Th 10-9, S 10-6, Sun 12-5, all cash, exch. or rfd. Large selection. Practically a super-discount supermarket, but specializing in packaged non-perishable foods, etc., no fresh produce. Sells: **Candies, Supermarket-Foods, Packaged/Canned Foods, Housewares, Pets, Warehouse Salvage Job-Lot.**

** **Argento Bakery**, Brooklyn, 7114 Ft. Ham. Pkwy., 745-8761, N to Ft. Ham. Pkwy., plus a long walk, M-S 7a.m.-9p.m., Sun 7-7, all cash, no exch. or rfd. Italian. Sells: **Baked Goods.**

** **Bakery Thrift**, Queens, 168-23 Douglas Av., Jamaica; Queens, 60-06 37th Av., Woodside; Queens, 89-19 Atlantic Av., Ozone Park; Queens, 51-02 Roosevelt Av., Jackson Hts.; Brooklyn, 1505 Albany Av., All stores: 526-3184 (the central office), M-S 10-5, all cash, no exch. or rfd. Day-old Wonder Bread and Hostess cakes, etc., from ITT Continental Baking Co. Sells: **Baked Goods.**

** **Basior-Schwartz**, 421 W. 14 (9th-10th), 929-5368, A-AA-CC-E-LL to 14 St. & 8 Av., M-F 5a.m.-12:30p.m., all cash, exch., no rfd. Doesn't sell in units as small as only one pound, but only larger quantities. Their non-cheese values aren't so good. Sells: **Cheeses.**

** **Beluga Caviar Corp.**, 180 Varick St. (Charlton-King), 11th floor, 675-2100, 1 to Houston, M-F 9-3:30, all cash, no exch. or rfd. An extremely wide selection, all types and grades, not only Beluga but others, all very fresh. This is the best caviar-place in the City, probably in the country. Sells: **Caviars.**

Benkert's Bakery, Queens, 28-30 Steinway St., Astoria, 728-7630, F-GG-N to Steinway St., RR to 30th Av., W-M 6a.m.-8p.m., all cash, no exch. or rfd. German & Czech. Sells: **Baked Goods.**

Bharat Indian Foods, Queens, 42-71 Main St., Flushing, 445-4231, 7 to Main St., ThF 5-8, SSun 12-6, all cash, exch. or rfd. Sells: **Indian Foods, Spices & Herbs.**

* **Black Forest Bakery**, 177 1st Av. at 11th St., 254-8181, LL to 1st Av., 6 to Astor, M-F 8-8, S 8-7, all cash, exch. or rfd. Sells: **Baked Goods.**

* **Bleecker St. Pastry**, 245 Bleecker St. (6th Av.), 242-4959, A-AA-B-CC-D-E-F to 4, M-Th 7:30-7, FS 7:30-7:30, Sun 7:30-4, all cash, no exch. or rfd. Italian. Sells: **Baked Goods.**

** **Brite Glo**, 66 Nagle Av. (193), 569-3390, 1 to 191, A to 200-Dyckman, M-Th 9-6, F 9-2, Sun 9-4, all cash, exch. or rfd. Sells: **Gourmet Specialties.**

Cafe Galleria Bakery, Brooklyn, 174 Montague St. (Court-Clinton), 625-7883, M-RR-2-3-4-5 to Borough Hall & Court St., 7 days 8a.m.-11p.m., all cash, no exch. or rfd. Eclectic: German, Swiss, Italian, French, baked goods. Sells: **Baked Goods.**

** **Carini Pastry**, Brooklyn, 3801 13th Av., 438-9216, B to 9th Av.; Brooklyn, 6213 Ft. Ham. Pkwy., 833-3645, N to Ft. Ham. Pkwy. Both stores: 7 days 8-8, all cash, no exch. or rfd. Italian. Sells: **Baked Goods.**

11: FOODS

Caviarteria, 29 E. 60 (Mad.), 759-7410 & 1-800-221-1020, N-RR-4-5-6 to 59th & Lex., M-S 9-6, Oct.-Mar.: Sun 10-5, ch., c.c., exch. or rfd. Takes mail-orders. Catalog. Very cooperative. Small store. Very wide selection. Sells: **Caviars.**

Central Fish, 527 9th Av. (39-40), 279-2317 & 560-8163, A-AA-CC-E to 42, M-F 8-6:30, S 8-5, all cash, exch. or rfd. Sells: **Seafoods.**

* **Cheese of All Nations**, 153 Chambers St. (Hudson), 732-0752, A-CC-1-2-3 to Chambers, M-S 8-5:30, c.c., no ch., exch. or rfd. Takes mail-orders. Large selection. Sells: **Cheeses.**

China Brilliance, 32 E. Broadway (Market-Catherine), 431-9194, F to E. Broadway, B-D to Grand, J-M-N-QB-RR-6 to Canal, 7 days 10:30-7:30, all cash, exch. or rfd. Sells: **Chinese Foods, Teas.**

* **Chinese American Trdg.**, 91 Mulberry St. (Canal), 267-5224, J-M-N-QB-RR-6 to Canal, 7 days 9-8, all cash, exch., no rfd. Large selection. Often very crowded and busy. Sells: **Chinese Foods, Teas.**

* **Churchill Int'l Grocery**, 519 9th Av. (38-9), 997-9195, A-AA-CC-E to 42, M-S 8-6:30, all cash, exch. or rfd. Most things here are very good bargains, but a few are not. Sells: **Grains, Beans, Flours, Spices & Herbs.**

Consumer Food Outlet, Brooklyn, 937 E. 107 at Flatlands, 257-9727, LL to E. 105, M-S 8a.m.-9p.m., Sun 9-6, all cash, exch. or rfd. Sells: **Supermarket-Foods.**

* **Court Wholesale**, Brooklyn, 244 Court St. (Baltic), 625-2421, F-GG to Bergen St., M-S 9-6:30, all cash, exch. or rfd. Small selection. Main business is supplying toiletries, brand-name candies, etc., to local housewares-stores. Sells: **Candies, Housewares.**

** **Cut-Well Beef**, 426 W 13 (Washington), 989-8240 & 8155, A-AA-CC-E-LL to 14 St. & 8 Av., M-F 6-4, S 8-4, all cash, exch. or rfd. Sells: **Meats & Fowl.**

** **Cuzins Meat**, 515 9th Av. (38-9), 736-5737, A-AA-CC-E to 42, M-S 7-6, all cash, exch. or rfd. Sells: **Meats & Fowl.**

Damaskus Bakery, Brooklyn, 195 Atlantic Av. (Court), 855-1457, M-RR-2-3-4-5 to Borough Hall & Court St., 7 days 8a.m.-9p.m., all cash, no exch. or rfd. Arabic. Sells: **Baked Goods.**

Dr. Schlock's, 19 Warren St. (B'wy-Church), 766-8627, A-CC-1-2-3 to Chambers, N-RR to City Hall, M-F 8-6, S 8:30-5, all cash, exch. or rfd. Small store. Sells: **Candies, Spices & Herbs, Dinnerware & Cookware, Fabrics, Yarns & Notions, Warehouse Salvage Job-Lot.**

* **East Village Cheese**, 239 E. 9 (2nd Av.), 477-2601, 6 to Astor, LL to 3rd Av., M-S 9-7, Sun 11-6, all cash, no exch. or rfd. Sells: **Cheeses.**

* **Eighty-Eight Cent Shops**, 591 Lexington Av. (52), 753-6969, E-F to Lex. Av., M-F 9:30-6; 1637 Broadway (41), 354-0111, N-QB-RR-1-2-3-7 to 42 & Times Square, M-F 7:15-6, Sun 12-6; 33 W. 8 (5th-6th), 475-6951, A-AA-B-CC-D-E-F to 4, Sun-F 11-10, S 11-12; 89 Chambers St. (B'wy-Church), 267-6722, A-CC-1-2-3 to Chambers, N-RR to City Hall, M-F 7:30-6; 144 Fulton St. (B'wy), 964-2142, A-CC-J-M-RR-2-3-4-5 to B'wy-Nassau & Fulton, M-F 7:30-6. All stores: all cash, exch. or rfd. Everything in store is 88 cents; only the Fulton and Chambers stores have areas set aside for more expensive merchandise. Sells: **Candies, Dinnerware & Cookware, Health & Beauty Aids, Home-Improvement Items, Housewares, Stationery & Art Supplies, Toys, Games & Hobbies.**

* **Elias Malko**, 150 Atlantic Av. (Clinton), 858-4230, M-RR-2-3-4-5 to Borough Hall & Court St., 7 days 9-9, all cash, exch. or rfd. Arabic. Sells: **Baked Goods, Nuts, Dried Fruits, Mid-Eastern Foods, Grains, Beans, Flours, Spices & Herbs.**

Essex Fruiterers, Essex at Canal, phoneless, F to E. Broadway, M-F 9-5, Sun 9-2, all cash, exch. or rfd. Sells: **Fruits & Vegetables.**

Fairway Foods, 2127 Broadway (74-5), 595-1888, 1-2-3 to 72, M-F 8-9:45, SSun 8-8:45, on \$10 or less, no c.c., exch. or rfd. Everything except meats. Sells: **Baked Goods, Cheeses, Fruits & Vegetables, Supermarket-Foods, Packaged/Canned Foods.**

First Cost, 90 E. 42nd St. at Park Av., 697-0244, 4-5-6-7 to Grand Central, M-F 8-7, SSun 10-5; Queens, 46-20 108 St., Corona, 271-1121, 7 to 111, ThS 9-6, F 9-9. Both stores: all cash, 7-day exch. or rfd. Sells: **Candies, Packaged/Canned Foods, Clothing—Children's, Clothing—Men's, Clothing—Women's, Dinnerware & Cookware, Health & Beauty Aids, Home-Improvement Items, Housewares, Jewelry & Gifts, Sporting Goods, Toys, Games & Hobbies, Warehouse Salvage Job-Lot.**

**** **Fong Inn**, 46 Mott St. (Bayard), 962-5196, J-M-N-QB-RR-6 to Canal, J-M-

11: FOODS

RR-4-5-6 to Chambers & Bkln. Bridge, B-D to Grand, 7 days 8-7, all cash, no exch. or rfd. They manufacture their own. An authentic factory-outlet, with the lowest prices in the country on these things. Their 'dry bean curd' is super, less watery than others. Sells: **Bean-Curds & Sprouts.**

** **G. Malko**, Brooklyn, 176 Atlantic Av. (Clinton-Court), 624-7659, M-RR-2-3-4-5 to Borough Hall & Court St., 7 days 9-7, all cash, exch. or rfd. Ships nationwide. Arabic baked specialties. Sells: **Baked Goods, Nuts, Dried Fruits, Mid-Eastern Foods, Grains, Beans, Flours, Spices & Herbs, Coffees.**

Ganesh Groceries, Queens, 72-26 37th Av., Jackson Hts., 458-7100, E-F-GG-N-7 to 74th-B'wy & Roosevelt-Jack.Hts., W-M 10-7, all cash, exch., no rfd. Sells: **Indian Foods, Grains, Beans, Flours, Spices & Herbs.**

General Nutrition Center (GNC), about 20 stores in the 5 boroughs, ch., c.c., exch. or rfd. Their many specials are terrific, and even their regular prices aren't bad. A nationwide chain, excellent for mail-order vitamins, GNC, listed separately here. Sells: **Health Foods, Health & Beauty Aids.**

* **Hammond's Bakery**, Brooklyn, 1436 Nostrand Av. (Church), 284-7666, 3-4 to Church, 7 days 10-9, all cash, no exch. or rfd. Jamaican. Sells: **Baked Goods.**

* **Harry Julius (S&G Stanley)**, 120 Essex St. (Delancey-Riv.) in market across from NYC Dept. of Traffic, 475-8365, F-J-M to Delancey & Essex, M-F 8-6, S 8-5, all cash, exch. or rfd. Sells: **Seafoods.**

House of Spices, Queens, 76-17 Broadway, Jackson Hts., 476-1577, E-F-GG-N-7 to 74th-B'wy & Roosevelt-Jack.Hts., T-S 10-8, all cash, exch. or rfd. Takes mail-orders. Sells: **Indian Foods, Grains, Beans, Flours, Spices & Herbs.**

India Spice, 110 Lexington Av. (27-8), 686-8955, 6 to 28, 7 days 10:30-7, all cash, exch. or rfd. Sells: **Indian Foods, Spices & Herbs.**

Integral Yoga Foods, 250 W. 14 (8th Av.), 243-2642, A-AA-CC-E-LL to 14 St. & 8 Av., M-F 10-8:30, S 10-7, Sun 12-6, all cash, exch. or rfd. Large selection. Sells: **Grains, Beans, Flours, Health Foods.**

** **International Gourmet**, 4791 Broadway (200), 569-2611, A to 200-Dyckman, Sun-Th 9-6, F 9-3, all cash, exch. or rfd. Sells: **Gourmet Specialties.**

** **International Grocery**, 529 9th Av. (39-40), 279-5514, A-AA-CC-E to 42, M-S 8-6, all cash, exch. or rfd. Sells: **Grains, Beans, Flours, Spices & Herbs.**

* **J. Wolsk**, 87 Ludlow (Broome), 475-7946, F-J-M to Delancey & Essex, Sun-Th 8-7, F 8-2, ch., no c.c., no exch. or rfd. Small store. Good selection of branded and unbranded, packaged and loose, candies, especially chocolates. Crowded and cramped space; otherwise like Mutual Dried Fruit. Sells: **Candies, Nuts, Dried Fruits.**

* **Jo Misa Cookie Factory**, Bronx, 1844 Givan Av. (Ely), 379-6223, 5 to Baychester, M-F 8-5, S 9-5, all cash, no exch. or rfd. Sells: **Baked Goods.**

*** **Job Lot Trdg.**, 140 Church St. (Warren-Chambers), 962-4142, A-CC-1-2-3 to Chambers; 412 5th Av. (37-8), 398-9210, B-D-F to 42. Both stores: M-F 8-5:30, S 8-4:30, all cash, 15-day exch. or rfd. Both are huge stores, with terrific selections. Sells: **Candies, Clothing—Men's, Dinnerware & Cookware, Home-Improvement Items, Housewares, Jewelry & Gifts, Linens, Personal Accessories, Sporting Goods, Stationery & Art Supplies, Toys, Games & Hobbies, Warehouse Salvage Job-Lot.**

*** **Julius The Candy King**, Essex St. Market immediately north of Delancey (first stand inside), 473-5329, F-J-M to Delancey & Essex, M-S 9-5:30, all cash, no exch. or rfd. Low-quality chocolates, hard candies, etc., some mixed with nuts, all at far lower price than other stores selling same goods, all sold loose. Sells: **Candies.**

K. Kalustyan, 123 Lexington Av. (28-9), 685-3416, 6 to 28, 7 days 10-7:30, all cash, exch. or rfd. Takes mail-orders. Sells: **Indian Foods, Grains, Beans, Flours, Spices & Herbs.**

** **Kadouri Import**, 51 Hester St. at Essex, 677-5441, F to E. Broadway, Sun-F 9-5, all cash, no exch. or rfd. Sometimes different prices same item different parts of the store. Not recommended for grains and beans. Candy-selection is small. Sells: **Candies, Nuts, Dried Fruits, Spices & Herbs.**

Kam Fook, 101 E. Broadway (Pike), 227-5305, F to E. Broadway, 7 days 10-8, all cash, no exch. or rfd. Sells: **Chinese Foods, Teas.**

* **Lafayette French Pastry**, 298 Bleecker St. (7th Av.), 242-7580, A-AA-B-CC-D-E-F to 4, 1 to Christopher St., 7 days 7a.m.-11p.m., all cash, no exch. or rfd. French. Sells: **Baked Goods.**

* **Le Baklava**, 325 E. 48 (1st-2nd), 751-1377, 6 to 51, M-F 11:30-7, S 12-5, ch., no c.c., exch. or rfd. Sells: **Mid-Eastern Foods, Grains, Beans, Flours.**

Little India, 128 E. 28 (Lex.), 683-1691, 6 to 28, M-S 10-8, Sun 11-6, all

11: FOODS

cash, exch. or rfd. Sells: **Indian Foods, Spices & Herbs.**

** **Malko Karkanni**, Brooklyn, 199 Atlantic Av. (Court), 834-0845, M-RR-2-3-4-5 to Borough Hall & Court St., 7 days 9-9, all cash, exch. or rfd. Arabic. Sells: **Baked Goods, Nuts, Dried Fruits, Mid-Eastern Foods, Grains, Beans, Flours, Spices & Herbs.**

Mary Bakery, 224 Av. B (13-4), 533-7780, LL to 1st Av., 7 days 7:30a.m.-9p.m., all cash, no exch. or rfd. Italian. Sells: **Baked Goods.**

** **Meat-N-Foods Warehouse**, 403A W. 14 (9th Av.), 243-9183, A-AA-CC-E-LL to 14 St. & 8 Av., 7 days 9-6, all cash, exch. or rfd. Sells: **Fruits & Vegetables, Meats & Fowl, Supermarket-Foods, Packaged/Canned Foods.**

Mike's Bakery, Brooklyn, 7005 13th Av., 256-6546, N to Ft. Ham. Pkwy., plus a long walk, 7 days 5a.m.-6:30p.m., all cash, no exch. or rfd. Italian. Sells: **Baked Goods.**

* **Ming Hing**, 82 Walker St. (Lafayette), 925-7410, J-M-N-QB-RR-6 to Canal, M-S 8-6, all cash, exch. or rfd. Chinese teas--not a large selection, but the City's lowest prices on them. Sells: **Teas.**

** **Modern Bakery**, Brooklyn, 3905 13th Av., 851-7402, B to 9th Av., 7 days 6a.m.-9p.m., all cash, no exch. or rfd. Italian. Sells: **Baked Goods.**

** **Mona Lisa Bakery**, Brooklyn, 7713 13th Av., 256-7706, B to 79th St., plus a long walk, 7 days 8-7, all cash, no exch. or rfd. Italian. Sells: **Baked Goods.**

* **Murray's Cheese**, 42 Cornelia St. (Bleecker, 6th Av.), 243-3289, A-AA-B-CC-D-E-F to 4, M-S 8-6, ch., no c.c., no exch. or rfd. Sells: **Cheeses, Spices & Herbs.**

Mutual Dried Fruit, 127 Ludlow St. (Rivington), 673-3489, F-J-M to Delancey & Essex, Sun-F 9-5, all cash, no exch. or rfd. Good selection of branded and non-branded, packaged and loose, candies, especially chocolates. Similar to J. Wolsk, but not cramped space here. Sells: **Candies, Nuts, Dried Fruits.**

NYC Outdoor Greenmarkets, Phone 477-3220 for the location of the one nearest you. They're functioning during only summer and fall. Sponsored by NYC Council on The Environment. Sells: **Fruits & Vegetables, Flowers & Plants.**

*** **Odd Job Trdg.**, 7 E. 40 (Mad.), 686-6825, D-F to 42, 7 to 5th Av.; 66 W. 48 (6th Av.), 575-0477, B-D-F to 47. Both stores: M-Th 8-5:30, F 8-3, Sun 10-5, ch., no c.c., 15-day exch. or rfd. Sells: **Packaged/Canned Foods, Clothing—Men's, Dinnerware & Cookware, Health & Beauty Aids, Home-Improvement Items, Housewares, Linens, Personal Accessories, Stationery & Art Supplies, Toys, Games & Hobbies, Warehouse Salvage Job-Lot.**

* **Old Bohemian Meat**, 425 W. 13 (Washington), 989-2870, A-AA-CC-E-LL to 14 St. & 8 Av., MTW 6-11:30 & 12:30-3:30, ThF 6-11:30 & 12:30-6, all cash, exch. or rfd. Sells only in multi-pound units. Sells: **Meats & Fowl.**

Olsen's Bakery, Brooklyn, 5722 8th Av., 439-6673, N to 8th Av., M-S 5a.m.-8p.m., all cash, no exch. or rfd. Scandanavian. Sells: **Baked Goods.**

Omaha Food Discount, Brooklyn, 197 Ft. Greene Place (off Hanson St., nr. Atlantic & Flatbush), 638-5400, B-N-RR-D-M-QB-1-2-3-4-5 to Pacific-Atlantic, WTh 9-5, S 8-4, all cash, exch. or rfd. Sells: **Cheeses, Meats & Fowl.**

*+ **Oriental Pastry & Grocery**, Brooklyn, 170 Atlantic Av. (Clinton), 875-7687 & 624-9506, M-RR-2-3-4-5 to Borough Hall & Court St., 7 days 10-8:30, all cash, exch. or rfd. Arabic. Bonus discount to BF readers: 2% to 5%. Sells: **Baked Goods, Mid-Eastern Foods, Grains, Beans, Flours, Spices & Herbs, Coffees.**

Original Health Food, 2530 Broadway (94-5), 866-0212, 1-2-3 to 96, 7 days 10-9, all cash, exch. or rfd. Sells: **Health Foods.**

* **Piemonte Ravioli**, 190 Grand St. (Mulberry), 226-0475, B-D to Grand, J-M-N-QB-RR-6 to Canal, T-S 8-6, Sun 8-3, all cash, no exch. or rfd. Top-brand imported Italian chocolates and cookies; also packaged noodles they make there themselves. They've got a super-high protein kind, as well as regular types. Sells: **Baked Goods, Candies.**

** **Plus Discount Foods**, Queens, 144-29 Northern Blvd., Flushing, 7 to Main St.; Queens, 72-15 Kissena Blvd., Flushing, no subway stop nearby; Brooklyn, 1230 Neptune Av., B-D-F-M-N-QB to Coney Island; Brooklyn, 2320 Ralph Av., no subway stop nearby; Bronx, 831 Rosedale Av. (Soundview), 6 to Morrison, plus a long walk; Staten Island, 1933 Victory Blvd., no subway stop nearby. All stores:. Large selection. For information (which they wouldn't give to me), try phoning 1-800-257-5711, or the Kissena Blvd. supermarket at 526-9505 (the only one with a published phone number). Sells: **Supermarket-Foods.**

+ **Porto Rico Importing**, 201 Bleecker St. (6th-MacDougal), 477-5421, A-

11: FOODS

AA-B-CC-D-E-F to 4, MTW 10-7, ThFS 10-9, Sun 12-5, ch., c.c., exch. or rfd. Takes mail-orders. Catalog. Very cooperative. Large selection. Tea: try San Francisco Cinnamon-Orange. Coffee: try blend: Venezuelan, Colombian, French Mocha, all in equal one-third parts. But the tea-values are best here. Bonus discount to BF readers: 10%. Sells: **Teas, Coffees.**

Prana Foods, 145A 1st Av. at 9th St., 228-3632, LL to 1st Av., 6 to Astor, M-S 10-8, Sun 12-6, all cash, exch. or rfd. Sells: **Health Foods.**

****+**Purity Maid Spices**, Queens, 56-70 58th St. (Maurice), Maspeth, 326-1610, no subway stop nearby, M-Th 8-5, F 7:30-3:30, ch., no c.c., exch., no rfd. Will phone-quote. Will special-order. Takes mail-orders. Catalog. Very cooperative. Large selection. Both by the jar and in bulk. Price list; or phone for prices. Send check; they'll ship UPS same day. Bonus-discount also applies if you mention BF on phone. Astounding! Bonus discount to BF readers: 10%. Sells: **Spices & Herbs.**

* **Quality Health Foods**, Brooklyn, 4923 13th Av., 435-4333, B to 50th St., Sun-Th 11-6:30, F 11-3, all cash, no exch. or rfd. Small store. Small selection. Sells: **Health Foods.**

** **Rego Smoked Fish**, Queens, 69-80 75th St. Middle Village, 894-1400, no subway stop nearby, M-S 8-4, Sun 8-11a.m., all cash, no exch. or rfd. Their caviar is the lowest quality, but half the regular discount price for such stuff. Sells: **Seafoods, Caviars.**

* **Rocco's Pastry Shop**, 243 Bleecker St. (6th Av.), 242-6031, A-AA-B-CC-D-E-F to 4, 7 days 8a.m.-11p.m., all cash, no exch. or rfd. Italian. Sells: **Baked Goods.**

** **Russ & Daughters**, 175 E. Houston St. (Orchard), 475-4880, F to 2nd Av., W-M 8-6:30, ch., no c.c., no exch. or rfd. Many types, good selection, including double-zero and triple-zero grades of Beluga. Sells: **Caviars.**

** **Sahadi Importing**, Brooklyn, 187 Atlantic Av. (Court-Clinton), 624-4550&5762, M-RR-2-3-4-5 to Borough Hall & Court St., M-S 9-7, all cash, exch. or rfd. Sells: **Candies, Nuts, Dried Fruits, Mid-Eastern Foods, Grains, Beans, Flours, Spices & Herbs.**

** **Scala Bros. Pastry**, Brooklyn, 7017 Ft. Ham. Pkwy., 836-1844, N to Ft. Ham. Pkwy., plus a long walk, T-Sun 8-8, all cash, no exch. or rfd. Italian. Sells: **Baked Goods.**

Schapira Coffee, 117 W. 10 (6th Av.), 675-3733, A-AA-B-CC-D-E-F to 4, M-F 9-6:30, S 9-5, ch., no c.c., exch. or rfd. Sells: **Teas, Coffees.**

** **Scotto's Bakery**, Brooklyn, 3807 13th Av., 438-0889, B to 9th Av., 7 days 7a.m.-8p.m., all cash, no exch. or rfd. Italian. Sells: **Baked Goods.**

Sea Breeze Fish, 541 9th Av. at 40th St., 563-7537, A-AA-CC-E to 42, M-F 7:30-6, S 7:30-5, all cash, exch. or rfd. Sells: **Seafoods.**

Sea-Tide Fish Markets, Queens, 95-31 Roosevelt Av., Jackson Hts., 426-7786, 7 to Junction Blvd.; Queens, 75-11 Roosevelt Av., Jackson Hts., 424-9208, E-F-GG-N-7 to 74th-B'wy & Roosevelt-Jack.Hts. Both stores: M-S 7-7, all cash, exch. or rfd. Sells: **Seafoods.**

** **Shammas**, Brooklyn, 197 Atlantic Av. (Court), 855-2455, M-RR-2-3-4-5 to Borough Hall & Court St., 7 days 9:30-9:30, all cash, exch. or rfd. Sells: **Nuts, Dried Fruits, Mid-Eastern Foods, Grains, Beans, Flours, Spices & Herbs.**

Sinha Trdg., 120 Lexington Av. at 28th St., up 1 flight, 683-4419, 6 to 28, 7 days 11-7, all cash, exch. or rfd. Sells: **Indian Foods, Spices & Herbs.**

* **SML Meat Warehouse**, Brooklyn, Linden Blvd. & Ashford St., 272-1405, 2 to New Lots, M-F 10-7, S 8-5, Sun 9-3, all cash, exch., no rfd. Sells: **Meats & Fowl, Packaged/Canned Foods.**

The Fish Factory, 1825 2nd Av. (94-5), 369-7744, 6 to 96, M-F 9-3:30, S 9-2, all cash, exch. or rfd. Mainly a wholesaler. Sells: **Seafoods.**

* **The People's Bakery**, Brooklyn, 734 Nostrand Av. (Park Place), 774-215, A-CC to Nostrand, M-S 8-9:30, all cash, no exch. or rfd. Jamaican. Sells: **Baked Goods.**

The Pickleman, 27 Essex St. (Hester), 533-8448&0062, F-J-M to Delancey & Essex, F to E. Broadway, Sun-F 8-6, all cash, no exch. or rfd. The City's largest selection of pickles. Sells: **Pickled Foods.**

* **Universal Foods**, 408 W. 14 (9th Av.), 691-4600, A-AA-CC-E-LL to 14 St. & 8 Av., M-S 6-6, all cash, exch. or rfd. Sells: **Meats & Fowl.**

** **V Discount Bakery**, Brooklyn, 2430 Ralph Av. (N-O), 531-2396, no subway stop nearby, M-S 8-6, all cash, exch. or rfd. Top supermarket-store brands of bread and cake, many at half price. Sells: **Baked Goods.**

11: FOODS

Vaccaro Bakery, Queens, 22-03 Astoria Blvd., 278-6818, RR to Ditmars, 7 days 7-6, all cash, no exch. or rfd. Italian. Sells: **Baked Goods.**

* **Washington Beef**, 575 9th Av. (42), 563-0200, A-AA-CC-E to 42, MTWS 6-5:30, ThF 6-6:30, all cash, exch. or rfd. Often extremely crowded. Sells: **Meats & Fowl.**

Wholefoods, 117 Prince St. (Wooster-Greene), 673-5388, N-RR to Prince St., A-AA-CC-E to Spring, M-S 10-8:45, Sun 10-8, all cash, exch. or rfd. Large selection. Large store. Sells: **Grains, Beans, Flours, Health Foods.**

Wing Lee Lung Food Fair, 50 E. Broadway (Market-Catherine), 431-9879, F to E. Broadway, J-M-RR-4-5-6 to Chambers & Bkln. Bridge, J-M-N-QB-RR-6 to Canal, 7 days 10-8, all cash, exch. or rfd. Sells: **Chinese Foods, Teas.**

*** **Wolf's Wholesale**, Brooklyn, 126 Court St. at Atlantic, 522-5651, M-RR-2-3-4-5 to Borough Hall & Court St., M-F 6:30-6, S 7-6, all cash, exch. or rfd. Regular brand-name items only. (For pipes and lighters, though, also check out the values at the Barney's at 76 Court St.) Sells: **Candies, Smoking Supplies.**

* **Yassin International**, 132 E. 26 (Lex.), 684-1188, 6 to 28, M-S 10-7, ch., no c.c., exch. or rfd. Small store. Small selection. Sells: **Indian Foods, Spices & Herbs.**

Zabar's for Foods, 2245 Broadway (80), 787-2000, 1 to 79, M-Th 8-7:30, F 8a.m.-10p.m., S 9a.m.-12mdnt., Sun 9-7:30, ch., c.c., exch. or rfd. Large selection. Uneven values, but never bad. Anyone who likens the place to Balducci's in the Village, has never compared prices. Zabar's is mobbed, and deserves to be. Sells: **Candies, Coffees, Gourmet Specialties, Caviars.**

12:
FURNISHINGS
Expect 33-60% discounts.

Included among the recommended stores below, you'll find furnishings for every pocketbook and taste. The heaviest coverage is of the well-known American makers, since these are the producers that account for the biggest chunk of the market. But you'll also find furniture, lamps, and carpets, from lesser-known—and usually better-value—makers, both domestic and foreign. There's even a fairly strong representation of designer-original furniture at steep discounts. However, since these things are wildly overpriced to begin with, I personally can't get too enthusiastic about them. To each his own—the stuff is there if you want it.

Practically every store recommended in this chapter will phone-quote prices.

For famous-name American furniture that's made in North Carolina, such as Drexel, Heritage, and Henredon, and several others, there are also discounters in that state which ship furniture into New York (and elsewhere). However, I don't include these dealers in my listings of recommended stores for the simple reason that it would have been just too much for me to do anything more than to check their prices, and so I don't know how well they handle customer-complaints (a big thing in the furniture-business, where scratches, dents, and cracks "fresh from the crate" can practically ignite a war). Furthermore, many of the North Carolina dealers I checked out quoted me prices that were just too high. On the other hand, the following few not only quoted very low prices, but from what I can tell about them over the phone and via their sales-literature, it does at least *seem* that they are probably reliable: Murrow Furniture, 1-800-334-1614 & 1-919-799-4010, 3514 S. College Rd., Wilmington, NC 28406; Sobol House, 1-704-669-8031, Richardson Blvd., Black Mountain, NC 28711; and Nite Furniture, 1-704-437-1491, 611 S. Green St., Morganton, NC 28655. If you decide to do business with one of these, make sure in advance that the furniture will be delivered in a two-or-three-man truck, and not to your doorstep in a crate, but rather into your house where it should be uncrated and set up by the deliverers. Murrow uses its own truck, which is good (the van comes up to NYC about once a month); some other distributors use common carriers, which is not. Also, when you get a price-quote, inquire in advance how much the delivery will cost, what kind of delivery it will be, whether the delivery-charge includes set-up in your home, and whether your only recourse if things go sour is the furniture-maker's warranty.

Besides the traditional famous-name furniture-makers, there are, of course, many others; and often you'll get better value by looking into these less well-known alternatives. On the low-priced

12: FURNISHINGS

end is pillow, foam, and unpainted furniture, and also some very stylish and well-made "lifestyle" or casual pieces, as well as clearance items. But the less-renowned manufacturers also offer some of the best values at the higher-priced end, as you'll quickly see when you comparison-shop.

For example, let's say you're looking simply for cheap, attractive, well-made furniture, and you're willing to wait until the right things come along at the right price. Where to go first? Why, to the Door Store Clearance Outlet, which sells comfortable, modern, handsomely constructed pieces (some slightly damaged, others not) routinely at 60-70% discount.

Or on the other hand, suppose you've got a taste for exquisite elegance, and a budget to match, but you want to save 60% no-sweat, or 70% by filling out a tedious form and perhaps waiting a week or so. Well, then you'll find things like a magnificent $8,000 Oriental hand-carved rosewood dining-room set for 8 people, selling for $3,300 the no-sweat way at East Art Center, or for $2,300 if you file the necessary papers required by Dragon Gate Import. Both the respective stores sell pretty much the same items, but on a different basis. Then, perhaps you'll need a $4,000 hand-made Oriental rug upon which to place your hand-made Oriental dining-room set. Where to go? Any day of the year, you'll find a huge selection of these at the half-dozen upper-floor wholesalers-retailers I list for such things. But it won't cost you $4,000. Your price: $1,500.

Getting back to more down-to-earth carpeting, furniture, and such: If you're looking for wall-to-wall carpeting, the smallest discount you'll be able to find on the famous-brand stuff is only 25%; but take heart, you can easily increase that to 40% or even more, simply by shopping the off-brands, or by going to remnants. The latter route is troublesome only if you want more of a particular color-and-pattern of carpet than a certain store happens to carry. But then you could always order the remaining few yards custom-cut from a roll, unless that style has been discontinued. In any case, the stores-listings make special note of which carpet-outlets carry the largest remnant-selections, both in the higher and lower quality-ranges.

The only well-promoted carpeting-place that I recommend is Kalfian's in Brooklyn—both for the huge size and the huge selection of their remnants, but not for carpeting cut from rolls. The not-recommended but overwhelmingly-advertised chain, Kaufman Carpets, is a good example of why one should always be suspicious of stores (or indeed, products, for that matter) which advertise a lot in the major media. Not only did I not find their prices to be good on the standard items I was using for comparison, but this outfit has been cited repeatedly by the City's Department of Consumer Affairs and by other agencies, for false advertising, dreadful installations, non-response to complaints, and such-like. Sometimes their ads blanket all the major TV stations at the same time that the TV news is reporting the consumer agencies' actions (which never amount to anything anyway); and everything goes on as before, later if not immediately. Two other non-recommended stores should also be mentioned, simply because they've been praised for their "bargains" by consumer reporters all over the city—TV, radio, newspapers, books, you name it—and every time I check prices at these places, I just can't figure out why: ABC Carpet, and The Rug Warehouse. I've repeatedly found that prices at the stores I recommend below are 40% less on Oriental carpets, and usually about 10-20% less on the other types of carpeting.

Perhaps one problem here is that throughout the whole furnishings-field, quality is something understood usually only by those within the profession itself. This is especially the case with Oriental rugs, so I ought to summarize the features which determine quality of these sometimes-works-of-art. To get meaningful comparison-prices, you first have to know what kind of rug it is; and this usually—but not always—is associated with where it was woven. For example, Isfahans always come from the Isfahan region of Iran, but Bukharas are produced in both Pakistan (better quality) and India (at a much lower price). You can't compare the price of an Isfahan with that of even a Pakistani Bukhara; the former is a finer and more difficult rug to produce, and can be expected to cost about 10 times the price. The Bukhara may, perhaps, be more—or less—beautiful; but it shouldn't be nearly as expensive as the Isfahan. If you're purchasing for long-term investment, the more expensive rugs do tend to appreciate better in value. But if you're looking for something that's just as beautiful at a fraction of the price, you're shopping virtually a different market.

After you've determined the kinds, and the rug-nationalities, that you find attractive, you make note of the following: 1) Knot-count, which is the number of knots per square-inch. The dealer—if he's at all knowledgeable—will be able to tell you this instantly. But if you want to check for yourself, don't hesitate to pick up the edge of the rug, and to ask him kindly to supply you with a ruler. (Better yet, bring your own.) Reputable rug-merchants will be pleased to cooperate with what in their trade is a routine request. The higher the knot-count, the more expensive the rug. The next thing to check for is, 2) The kind or kinds of materials of which the carpet is woven, both the tuft, and the backing. Sometimes the tuft will be composed of two fabrics; for example, Isfahans often have woolen tuft, with silk tuft used to highlight parts of the design, and this will usually add slightly to the price. Then, 3) You'll want to examine the fineness of workmanship, by lifting up the edge of the rug and having a look at the underside. Irregularities that show up in this way tend to depreciate the value of a carpet; the finest look perfect from underneath. Finally, 4) Consider the complexity of the pattern: The more packed it is with detail, the more expensive the rug will tend to be. But the most important questions are: What country is the rug from? What kind of rug is it? What is its knot-count? Usually, with just these three questions, you've got a sufficient basis to do informed comparison-shopping. Note that I've not discussed antique rugs, nor antiques in general. Frankly, I'm simply not competent to offer even rudimentary advice in such highly specialized fields. I had enough to do just learning the basics for comparison-pricing the new merchandise.

12: FURNISHINGS

The field of regular machine-made carpeting is much simpler. The chief thing determining cost here is weight—how many ounces the carpeting is rated at. The second thing is knot-count, which again can easily be measured with a ruler. Finally, you should consider what kind of fiber the carpeting is made of. Of course, if you're shopping for a major brand of carpet, it's enough for you to know simply the maker and the style-name, because this will enable you to comparison-shop different dealers on precisely the same item. (The big-name carpet-chains, however, like Allen Carpet, use their own concocted style-names, thus making comparison-shopping them very difficult. The same trick is used by some of the department stores. But worry not: Their prices aren't good anyway, as you'll find out if you get one of the salesmen at these places to tell you their own house-name and price for a particular standard-brand carpet-style.)

Since I've made so much comment upon heavily advertised retailers that fail to deliver the bargains, I should also point out one very extraordinary exception to this general rule: James Roy Furniture. Their late-night-TV ads speak only the truth: Virtually all major brands of furniture are sold there at a minimum of 33% discount. They started their ad-blitz after they were recommended in the 2nd edition of *Bargain Finder*, but they're just the same today as they ever were. The only difference is that now I recommend a lot more stores that are similar to James Roy, even if these other places advertise less, or not at all. You've now got a much larger number of great furniture-discounters to comparison-price. This means also a larger number of furniture-showrooms to look through, to find exactly what you want for immediate delivery—and perhaps at a clearance-price which is only 40% of (or 60% off) list. If you do find a showroom-sample that you want delivered, first ask to see a picture of the item in the manufacturer's catalog. You'll want to verify what the item is, then its list-price, before you settle firmly on where to buy it. If any salesman tries to rush you, or otherwise to prevent you from comparison-shopping the item, it's usually best to walk out and not come back—but not until you've first gone to the store-owner or manager to tell him why. With this book, you've got a very powerful bargaining-chip in your hand. The recommended places all know that they're competing against the very best—other recommended stores. But you've also got one other potent bargaining-tool: the phone. Most of these stores will phone-quote. If one doesn't, just forget about the place, and go on to the next one on the list. Once you've found what you want, by manufacturer, grouping-name, and item-number (and fabric, if upholstered), you can phone around for prices, and you might be well-advised to do so, since we're talking here about big-ticket expenses where only 5% might amount to hundreds of dollars.

But keep in mind, before you shop the name-brands, that a less orthodox approach to furniture-buying will usually save you about 50% off even the discounted brand-name price. For example, with bedding, places like Dixie Foam, or for cheaper quality and prices Economy Foam or ABC Foam, can offer you mattresses superior to the spring-variety, but at a very small fraction of the price. (In fact,

Dixie offers a special "carbamate" foam mattress which they confidently guarantee for 15 years because its life-expectancy is about three times that.) And a box-spring is a total waste, whose only function is to boost the sales of Serta, Sealy, Simmons, and such. A platform-bed is superior, and permits you to store things in drawers underneath, rather than wasting all the volume a box-spring consumes. A loft-bed is, in some circumstances, even better. And if you're considering a convertible, the brand-name kind with the clunky steel fold-out frame is now virtually an expensive outdated relic. Other types, such as pillow or foam, may suit your needs far better, yet cost far less. Or suppose you're looking for shelving. The ruggedest and least expensive kind is steel shelving—the type that's listed in Chapter 21, "Office Equipment." If you order this shelving in beige, it's both attractive and versatile, fitting into practically any home's color-scheme. And these units are so strong that you can store practically anything—or any quantity of things—on them. That makes them especially marvelous for New York's small apartments, where space is so limited. But whatever it is you're looking for, you should find it here.

I close with a caution, which pertains primarily to brand-name sofas, but which occasionally applies also to other types of upholstered furniture: The upholstery-fabric commonly known as "Haitian cotton" (but which is usually made in India) is practically uncleanable. If it has a rubberized backing of any sort (and most of them do), you'll probably end up having to reupholster the entire sofa once it's gotten dirty. So best keep it continually covered—or better yet, not get stuck in the first place with this the most popular of all sofa upholstery-fabrics.

RECOMMENDED PRODUCTS:
See above.

RECOMMENDED STORES:

better-quality furniture-brands

(of: bars, bassinets, beds, bedstands, benches, book-cases, bridge-tables, buffets, bunks, cabinets, card-tables, carpets, carts, chair pads, chairs, chests, chimes, commodes, convertibles, couches, credenzas, cushions, desks, dinettes, dressers, floor-coverings, garden-furniture, hammocks, hassocks, headboards, lamps, lavabos, lawn-furniture, lights, mattresses, mirrors, ottomans, plaques, plexiglas furniture, recliners, rockers, room-dividers, rugs, sofas, stools, tables, tiffany shades, tiles, valets)

***+**Foremost Furniture** (889-6347); ***+**Furniture Tree** (532-7633); ***+**New York Furniture Ctr.** (679-8866); ****Albert Furniture** (594-3993); ****American Bedding & Furniture** (Queens, 843-9210); ****Consumers Furniture** (473-1865); ****Happy Buying Center** (695-0456); ****James Roy Furniture** (679-2565); ****JDS Furniture** (677-7226); ****Siromo Furniture** (Bronx, 295-0464); ***A-One Furniture** (473-8188).

medium/low-quality furniture

***+**Foremost Furniture** (889-6347); ***+**Furniture Tree** (532-7633); ***+**Furniture Wholesale Co-op** (876-5838); ****American Bedding & Furniture** (Queens, 843-9210); ****Consumers Furniture** (473-1865); ****Happy Buying Center** (695-0456); ****James Roy Furniture** (679-2565); ****OK Furniture & Carpeting** (628-5864); ****S. Redisch Furniture** (962-0700);

**Siromo Furniture (Bronx, 295-0464); *A-One Furniture (473-8188); *M&M Furniture Discount (677-6820); +Metro Interiors (Brooklyn, 252-4292); Best Housekeeping (677-8808); Co-op Sales (Brooklyn, 384-2443).

designers' furniture

**Design World (929-5559); **International Home Clearance (phoneless); *Palazzetti (684-1199); Decorators' Warehouse (757-1106); International Home (895-5595); Viaventi (242-4051).

fine hand-carved furniture

***Dragon Gate Import (532-6383); ***East Art Center (685-5370).

unpainted, & platform-beds

**Design World (929-5559); Rodos 104th St. (663-3551).

beds—foam

***+Dixie Foam (777-3626); *ABC Foam (431-9485); *Economy Foam (473-4462).

beds—loft-

*Gemini Loftbeds (674-6193); *Serenade Loftbeds (947-1840); LumberSmith (852-4434).

convertible sofas

***+Dixie Foam (777-3626); ***+Foremost Furniture (889-6347); ***+Furniture Tree (532-7633); ***+New York Furniture Ctr. (679-8866); **Albert Furniture (594-3993); **American Bedding & Furniture (Queens, 843-9210); **Consumers Furniture (473-1865); **Convertible Connection (620-0177); **Happy Buying Center (695-0456); **James Roy Furniture (679-2565); **JDS Furniture (677-7226); **OK Furniture & Carpeting (628-5864); **S. Redisch Furniture (962-0700); **Siromo Furniture (Bronx, 295-0464); *A-One Furniture (473-8188); *Klein Decorators (Brooklyn, 331-6363); *M&M Furniture Discount (677-6820); Berkshire House Convertibles (246-4770); Best Housekeeping (677-8808); Jennifer House Convertibles (532-4697); John Harley (736-1644); Plumbline Design (477-2074).

carpeting—better quality

***+Fishler Floors (689-0355); ***+Northeast Floor Coverings (988-5326); **Carpet Discount House (Queens, 456-7111); **Crescent Carpet (684-0778); **Geremia Carpeting (686-9065); **Kingsway Carpet (Brooklyn, 339-9000); **Padawer Carpets & Remnants (777-4114); **Quality Broadloom & Remnant (Brooklyn, 941-4200); *Baskin Floors (564-3476); *Carpet Display (563-3399); *JBJ Carpet Remnants (924-0348); Carpet Bazaar & Remnants (Queens, 358-9459); D. Kalfian for Remnants (Brooklyn, 875-2222); Leonard St. Carpet Warehouse (226-0274); Queens Floor Covering (Queens, 721-6900); Redi-Cut Carpets (695-6759).

carpeting—cheaper brands

**Carpet Discount House (Queens, 456-7111); **OK Furniture & Carpeting (628-5864); **+Roosevelt Rug & Linoleum (Queens, 728-4693); *Bergen Tile (Brooklyn, 789-9000); *Jay's Rug Shop (Brooklyn, 266-6656); Carpet Bazaar & Remnants (Queens, 358-9459); Queens Floor Covering (Queens, 721-6900); Superior Floor Covering (673-

12: FURNISHINGS

0637).

oriental rugs

**Ahdout Oriental Rugs (684-5672); **Bella Oriental Rugs & Antiques (684-0107); **Farsh International (889-2090); **Noury & Sons (889-6701); *+Taj International (889-7697); *Sasson Imports (889-4646); *Torange Rugs (689-2538); Palisades International (686-6262); Parviz Shenassa (684-6449).

linoleum, tiles, vinyl

**+Northeast Floor Coverings (988-5326); *+Roosevelt Rug & Linoleum (Queens, 728-4693); *Bergen Tile (Brooklyn, 789-9000); Superior Floor Covering (673-0637).

closeouts, etc.

***Door Store Clearance (889-5491); ***Kahan National Furniture (intermittent stock, Brooklyn, 782-2760); **P&G Trdg. (Brooklyn, 745-0730); Decor Arts (691-8156); Great North Woods (889-0983); Two-Morrow (intermittent stock, 254-0820).

marble-top tables

**Sun Lighting (Queens, 291-3456); *Empress Gift Shop (475-8395); *Weinstock Lamp (Queens, 727-4848); Rainbow Mirror (Brooklyn, 438-0332).

lamps (LAMP-PARTS: CH. 15)

****Woodware (outside NYC, 1-802-388-6297); ***Galdi Industries (Brooklyn, 522-5395); ***Kahan National Furniture (intermittent stock, Brooklyn, 782-2760); ***Sherrill Closeouts Warehouse (674-4430); **Brass Loft Factory Outlet (226-5467); **Chandelier Warehouse (Brooklyn, 388-800); **Lamp Warehouse (Brooklyn, 436-2207); **NY Ceiling Fan Ctr. (254-6720); **Sun Lighting (Queens, 291-3456); *Empress Gift Shop (475-8395); *Weinstock Lamp (Queens, 727-4848); DAC Lighting (966-7062); International Fluorescent (966-1096); Nat Skop (Brooklyn, 256-4913); Plumbline Design (477-2074); Rainbow Mirror (Brooklyn, 438-0332); Tri-Surplus (intermittent stock, 964-9237).

clip-on lighting fixtures

**Chandelier Warehouse (Brooklyn, 388-800); *Susan Trdg. (431-8529); C.K.&L. Surplus (966-1745).

track-lighting

**Chandelier Warehouse (Brooklyn, 388-800); **Lamp Warehouse (Brooklyn, 436-2207); **NY Ceiling Fan Ctr. (254-6720); Plumbline Design (477-2074).

chandeliers

**Chandelier Warehouse (Brooklyn, 388-800); **Lamp Warehouse (Brooklyn, 436-2207); **Sun Lighting (Queens, 291-3456); *Empress Gift Shop (475-8395); *Weinstock Lamp (Queens, 727-4848); DAC Lighting (966-7062); International Fluorescent (966-1096); Rainbow Mirror (Brooklyn, 438-0332).

plexiglass furniture

*+Perplexity Lucite (688-3571); *Art Plastics (255-7917).

wicker furniture

Earl's (intermittent stock, Queens, 894-6406); ***Hang Ups Wicker.

nursery/children's furniture

(examples: baby furniture, carriages, cribs, high chairs, playpens, strollers)
Jack's Bargain Stores (924-5322); **Ben's Babyland (674-1360); **Klein's Kiddy Korner** (Brooklyn, 435-8400); **Schneider's** (228-3540); **Yeedl's Juvenile Furniture** (Brooklyn, 435-5900).

pillow-furniture

Design Collective (242-3967); ***Easy Look Pillow Furn. (732-3026); ***Pillow Furniture** (929-9858); **Plumbline Design** (477-2074).

brass beds

*Elegante Brass Beds (Brooklyn, 256-8988); **Brass Bed Factory** (594-8777).

STORES-DIRECTORY

Phone a store before you go out of your way to visit it. Especially do this during July and August, when most establishments reduce or eliminate weekend-hours.

In the listings below, "*" means especially recommended, "+" means that the store offers a bonus discount to BF readers, "ch." and "c.c." mean respectively checks and credit cards, and "exch." and "rfd." mean respectively exchange and refund. Nearest subway-stops are shown. For example, "B-D-F to 47" means to take the B, D, or F train to 47th Street. Store-hours are also indicated, with days of the week abbreviated, like "M-S 8-6."

* **ABC Foam**, 77 Allen St. at Grand, 431-9485, B-D to Grand, Sun-F 9-5:30, S 10-3, all cash, exch., no rfd. Small selection, no better-quality foams. Sells: **Beds—Foam**.

** **Ahdout Oriental Rugs**, 220 5th Av. at 26th St., rm. 607, 684-5672, N-RR to 28th St., M-F 10:30-4, ch., no c.c., exch. or rfd. Will special-order. Sells: **Oriental Rugs**.

** **Albert Furniture**, 22 W. 34 (5th-6th), 4th floor, 594-3993, B-D-F-N-QB-RR to 34, M-S 10-5, Thursday evening by appt., ch., no c.c. 1 yr. free service. Sells: **Better-Quality Furniture-Brands, Convertible Sofas**.

** **American Bedding & Furniture**, 109-03 Liberty Av., Richmond Hill, 843-9210, A to 111th St., MTWFS 9-6, Th 9-9, c.c., no ch., exch., no rfd. Stocks only medium-lower quality, but will special-order the better stuff, also at excellent savings. Sells: **Better-Quality Furniture-Brands, Medium/Low-Quality Furniture, Convertible Sofas**.

* **A-One Furniture**, 45 E. 20 (B'wy), 473-8188, N-RR to 23rd St., M-S 10-5, ch., c.c. 1 yr. free service. Sells: **Better-Quality Furniture-Brands, Medium/Low-Quality Furniture, Convertible Sofas**.

* **Art Plastics**, 359 Canal St. (W. B'wy), 255-7917, A-AA-CC-E-1 to Canal, 7 days 9-5:30, ch., c.c., exch., no rfd. Sells: **Plexiglass Furniture**.

* **Baskin Floors**, 320 W. 37 (8th Av.), 564-3476, A-AA-CC-E to 42, A-AA-CC-E to 34, irregular hours, usually M-F 9-5:30, all cash, no exch. or rfd. Sells: **Carpeting—Better Quality**.

* **Bella Oriental Rugs & Antiques**, 281 5th Av. on E. 30th St., 684-0107, N-RR to 28th St., M-F 11-5, ch., no c.c., exch. or rfd. Small store. Small selection. Sells: **Oriental Rugs**.

Ben's Babyland, 87 Av. A (6), 674-1360, F-J-M to Delancey & Essex, 6 to Astor, plus a long walk, M-F 9-6, SSun 9-5, ch., c.c., exch., no rfd. Sells: **Nursery/Children's Furniture**.

* **Bergen Tile**, Brooklyn, 215 Flatbush Av. (Dean), 789-9000, 2-3-4 to Bergen; Brooklyn, 242 Flatbush Av. (6th Av.), 789-5818, 2-3-4 to Bergen; Queens,

12: FURNISHINGS

31-70 Steinway St., Astoria, 721-0890, F-GG-N to Steinway St.; Queens, 153-05 Jamaica Av., Jamaica, 523-4240, E-F to Parsons Blvd.; Queens, 153-19 Jamaica Av., Jamaica, 297-2077, E-F to Parsons Blvd.; Queens, 37-27 Junction Blvd., Jackson Hts., 429-1740, 7 to Junction Blvd. All stores: MTh 8:30-8:30, TWFS 8:30-6, ch., c.c., no exch. or rfd. Especially large selection of vinyl-asbestos tiles, especially at 215 Flatbush. Sells: **Carpeting—Cheaper Brands, Linoleum, Tiles, Vinyl.**

Berkshire House Convertibles, 242 W. 27 (7th-8th), 246-4770, 1 to 28, MTW 12-7, Th 12-8, ch., c.c., no exch. or rfd. Sells: **Convertible Sofas.**

Best Housekeeping, 17 Av. A (1), 677-8808, F to 2nd Av., Sun-F 8:30-6, c.c., no ch., exch. or rfd. Sells: **Medium/Low-Quality Furniture, Convertible Sofas.**

Brass Bed Factory, 15 W. 36 (5th Av.), 3rd floor, 594-8777, B-D-F-N-QB-RR to 34, M-F 10-6, SSun 12-5, ch., no c.c. 5 yrs. free service. Good quality. Sells: **Brass Beds.**

** **Brass Loft Factory Outlet**, 20 Greene St. (Canal), 3rd floor, 226-5467, J-M-N-QB-RR-6 to Canal, A-AA-CC-E-1 to Canal, TWThSSun 10:30-5:30, ch., no c.c., 14-day exch., no rfd. If it's made of brass, they sell it, for 30-60% less than normal. Sells: **Lamps, Home-Improvement Items, Jewelry & Gifts.**

Carpet Bazaar & Remnants, Queens, 136-16 Northern Blvd. (Main St.), Flushing, 358-9459, 7 to Main St., MTh 9-8:45, TWFS 9-5:45, Sun 11-4:30, ch., c.c., no exch. or rfd. Large selection. Sells: **Carpeting—Better Quality, Carpeting—Cheaper Brands.**

** **Carpet Discount House**, Queens, 61-01 Myrtle Av., Ridgewood, 456-7111, M to Fresh Pond Rd., MThF 10-7:30, TWS 10-5:30, ch., c.c., no exch. or rfd. Sells: **Carpeting—Better Quality, Carpeting—Cheaper Brands.**

* **Carpet Display**, 129 W. 35 (6th-7th), 563-3399, B-D-F-N-QB-RR to 34, 1-2-3 to 34, M-F 9:30-5, ch., no c.c., no exch. or rfd. Good for remnants. Sells: **Carpeting—Better Quality.**

** **Chandelier Warehouse**, Brooklyn, 40 Withers St. (Lorimer), 388-800, GG-LL to Lorimer & Metropolitan, 7 days 10-4, ch., c.c., exch., no rfd. Large selection. Their prices are low enough to qualify for two stars; then they'll bargain even 10% lower. Unusual. Their fans are Hunter ceiling, special-order. Sells: **Lamps, Clip-On Lighting Fixtures, Track-Lighting, Chandeliers, Home-Improvement Items.**

C.K.&L. Surplus, 307 Canal St. (B'way-Mercer), 966-1745, J-M-N-QB-RR-6 to Canal, M-S 9-6, Sun 10-6, ch. $20+, no c.c., exch., no rfd. Carries a very good Italian make of scissor, cheaper but comparable to Wiss. Also metal parts and surplus, etc. Sells: **Clip-On Lighting Fixtures, Fabrics, Yarns & Notions, Home-Improvement Items.**

** **Consumers Furniture**, 45 E. 20 (B'way), 5th floor, 473-1865, N-RR to 23rd St., MTWFS 9-4:30, Th 9-7:30, ch., c.c. 1 yr. free service. Sells: **Better-Quality Furniture-Brands, Medium/Low-Quality Furniture, Convertible Sofas.**

** **Convertible Connection**, 666 6th Av. (20-1), 620-0177, B-F to 23, M-S 9:30-6:30, Sun 12-4, ch., c.c., no exch. or rfd. Sells: **Convertible Sofas.**

Co-op Sales, Brooklyn, 232 Broadway (Roebling-Havemeyer), 384-2443, J-M to Marcy, M-F 10-5:30, Sun 10-4, c.c., no ch., exch., no rfd. Will special-order. Sells: **Medium/Low-Quality Furniture, Appliances, Jewelry & Gifts.**

** **Crescent Carpet**, 29 W. 26 (B'way), 684-0778, N-RR to 28th St., M-F 8-5, ch., no c.c., no exch. or rfd. Sells: **Carpeting—Better Quality.**

D. Kalfian for Remnants, Brooklyn, 475 Atlantic Av. (Nevins), 875-2222, A-AA-B to 163, B-N-RR to Pacific, MTh 9-7, WFSSun 9-5, c.c., no ch., no exch. or rfd. Vast selection of terrific remnants, and sometimes several of the same carpeting, so you can buy really big coverage. But custom-cut prices here aren't outstanding. Sells: **Carpeting—Better Quality.**

DAC Lighting, 164 Bowery (Delancey), 966-7062, J-M to Bowery, B-D to Grand, 7 days 9:30-5:30, c.c., no ch., 7-day exch. or rfd. Sells: **Lamps, Chandeliers.**

Decor Arts, 25 W. 14 (7th-8th), 691-8156, 1-2-3 to 14, A-AA-CC-E-LL to 14 St. & 8 Av., M-F 10-6, S 10-5, ch., c.c., exch., no rfd. Directors chairs, Mexican chess sets, and other stuff, in an odd melange. Sells: **Closeouts, Etc., Jewelry & Gifts.**

Decorators' Warehouse, 665 11th Av. (48), 757-1106, A-AA-CC-E to 50, M-S 10-6, Sun 12-5, ch., c.c., no exch. or rfd. Large selection. Sells: **Designers' Furniture.**

** **Design Collective**, 13 W. 18 (5th Av.), 242-3967, B-F-LL to 14th St. & 6th Av., N-RR to 23rd St., 7 days 11-6, c.c., exch., no rfd. Sells: **Pillow-Furniture.**

** **Design World**, 55 W. 21 (5th-6th), 929-5559, N-RR to 23rd St., MTWF

12: FURNISHINGS

9-6:30, Th 9-9, S 9-6, Sun 12-5, ch., no c.c., no exch. or rfd. Top designs and quality, a great bargain only in comparison to the usually ridiculously overpriced world of designer-furniture; in contrast, this is reasonably priced. Sells: **Designers' Furniture, Unpainted, & Platform-Beds.**

☆☆+ **Dixie Foam**, 20 E. 20 (B'way), 777-3626, N-RR to 23rd St., MTWFS 10-6, Th 10-8, Sun 12-5, ch., c.c., exch. or rfd. Unlike competitors, Dixie doesn't lie about the quality or density of their foam--it's actually true. Better quality than the other recommended stores. Long warranty. Bonus discount to BF readers: 10%. Sells: **Beds—Foam, Convertible Sofas.**

☆☆☆ **Door Store Clearance**, 191 Lexington Av. at 32nd St., 889-5491, 6 to 33, M-S 10-6, ch., c.c., no exch. or rfd. Small store. Floor samples and closeouts from main branches; e.g.: chair $65 elsewhere, $49 at Door Store, $20 here. Some slightly damaged. Tables, chairs, stools, bookcases, sofas. Sells: **Closeouts, Etc..**

☆☆☆ **Dragon Gate Import**, 1115 B-wy (25), 532-6383 & 691-8600, N-RR to 28th St., 7 days 12-5, c.c. +5%, no exch. or rfd. Speak to Leo Chin. Here you'll be buying wholesale; he'll tell you what forms to fill out, and where they can be obtained. Then you'll save about 70%. Sells: **Fine Hand-Carved Furniture.**

☆☆ **Earl's**, Queens, 78-25 Metropolitan Av., Middle Village, 894-6406, no subway stop nearby, M-S 11-6, all cash, exch. or rfd. Bonus discount to BF readers: 10% to 20%. Sells: **Wicker Furniture, Clothing—Children's, Clothing—Women's.**

☆☆☆ **East Art Center**, 455 3rd Av. (31), 685-5370, 6 to 33, M-S 11-6, ch., no c.c., no exch. or rfd. Sells: **Fine Hand-Carved Furniture, Jewelry & Gifts.**

☆ **Easy Look Pillow Furn.**, 62 Thomas St. (Church-W.B'wy), 732-3026, 1 to Franklin, A-CC-1-2-3 to Chambers, M-S 10-6, ch., no c.c., exch., no rfd. Sells: **Pillow-Furniture.**

☆ **Economy Foam**, 173 E. Houston St. at Allen, 473-4462, F to 2nd Av., Sun-F 9:30-5:30, c.c., no ch., exch., no rfd. Small selection. No high quality foams. Sells: **Beds—Foam.**

☆ **Elegante Brass Beds**, Brooklyn, 1460 65th St., 256-8988, B-N to 62nd St. & New Utrecht Av., MTWSun 9-5, Th 9-9, ch., c.c., exch., no rfd. Will custom-make any quality, including the junky dept.-store quality, for 50% off; but specializes in good quality. Sells: **Brass Beds.**

☆ **Empress Gift Shop**, 332 Grand St. (Ludlow), 475-8395, F-J-M to Delancey & Essex, Sun-F 10-5, ch., c.c., exch. or rfd. Sells: **Marble-Top Tables, Lamps, Chandeliers.**

☆☆ **Farsh International**, 245 5th Av. (28), 2nd floor, 889-2090, N-RR to 28th St., M-F 9:30-5:30, ch., no c.c., no exch. or rfd. Large selection. Sells: **Oriental Rugs.**

☆☆+ **Fishler Floors**, 34 E. 29 (Mad.), 689-0355, N-RR to 28th St., 6 to 28, M-F 9-5, ch., no c.c., no exch. or rfd. Bonus discount to BF readers: 5%. Sells: **Carpeting—Better Quality.**

☆☆+ **Foremost Furniture**, 8 W. 30 (5th Av.), 10th floor, 889-6347 & 242-3354, N-RR to 28th St., MTWF 9-5, Th 9-7:30, S 9-4, ch., no c.c. 5 yrs. free service and parts. Former name was 'Harold Berman.' Get on mailing list for announcements of terrific clearances to 75% off. Large showroom. Bonus discount to BF readers: 10% to 15%. Sells: **Better-Quality Furniture-Brands, Medium/Low-Quality Furniture, Convertible Sofas.**

☆☆+ **Furniture Tree**, 192 Lexington Av. at 32nd St., 9th floor, 532-7633, 6 to 33, M-S 9-5, Th 9-7, ch., no c.c. Free service. Bonus discount to BF readers: 10% to 20%. Sells: **Better-Quality Furniture-Brands, Medium/Low-Quality Furniture, Convertible Sofas.**

☆☆+ **Furniture Wholesale Co-op**, 1326 Madison Av. at 94th St., 876-5838, 6 to 96, Th-Sun 12-6, MT 12-7, ch., no c.c. Free service. Bonus discount to BF readers: 10%. Sells: **Medium/Low-Quality Furniture.**

☆☆☆ **Galdi Industries**, Brooklyn, 290 Court St. at Douglass, 522-5395, F-GG to Bergen St., M-F 8-4:30, S 12-2, all cash, exch. or rfd. Only Capodimonte, a huge selection, which they import direct. Sells: **Lamps, Jewelry & Gifts.**

☆ **Gemini Loftbeds**, 674-6193. They set it up in your home. Sells: **Beds—Loft.**

☆☆ **Geremia Carpeting**, 418 Park Av. S., 2nd floor, 686-9065, 6 to 28, M-F 9-5, ch., no c.c., no exch. or rfd. Sells: **Carpeting—Better Quality.**

Great North Woods, 425 5th Av. (38-9), 889-0983, B-D-F to 42, 7 to 5th Av.; 683 Lexington Av. (56-7), 593-0423, N-RR-4-5-6 to 59th & Lex., E-F to Lex. Av.; 160 E. 86 (Lex.), 369-6555, 4-5-6 to 86. All stores: M-S 10-6:30, Sun 12-5:30, ch.,

114 **12: FURNISHINGS**

c.c., exch., no rfd. Butcher block. Almost continual sales. Usually the cheapest and best in town for this. Sells: **Closeouts, Etc..**

* **Hang Ups Wicker**, Canal at W. Broadway, A-AA-CC-E-1 to Canal, SSun 10-7; 39th St. at 9th Av., A-AA-CC-E to 42, WThF 10-7. Both stores: ch., no c.c. Sells: **Wicker Furniture, Jewelry & Gifts.**

** **Happy Buying Center**, 22 W. 32 (5th-6th), 7th floor, 695-0456, B-D-F-N-QB-RR to 34, M-F 9-6, S 9-5, ch., c.c. +8%, (only cert. chs.), exch., no rfd. Sells: **Better-Quality Furniture-Brands, Medium/Low-Quality Furniture, Convertible Sofas, Appliances.**

International Fluorescent, 135 Bowery (Grand), 966-1096, B-D to Grand, J-M to Bowery, M-F 8-5, SSun 9:30-5, ch., c.c., exch. or rfd. Sells: **Lamps, Chandeliers, Home-Improvement Items.**

International Home, 440 Park Av. S. (29-30), 895-5595, 6 to 28, M-F 10-6, SSun 11-5, ch., no c.c. 1 year free service. Other stores in Roslyn Heights and (clearance) Carle Place, Long Island. Sells: **Designers' Furniture.**

** **International Home Clearance**, Carle Place, L.I., 100 Voice Rd. (Glen Cove Rd.) at Macy's last bldg. on l., phoneless (for info.: 895-5595 & 1-516-484-4414), SSun 11-5, ch., no c.c., no exch. or rfd. The values are good enough to warrant going outside the City. Sells: **Designers' Furniture.**

** **Jack's Bargain Stores**, 2 W. 14 at 5th Av., 2nd floor, 924-5322, B-F-LL to 14th St. & 6th Av.; 142 W. 34 (6th-7th), 947-4135, B-D-F-N-QB-RR to 34, 1-2-3 to 34. Both stores: 9:30-7 M-S, all cash, 25-day exch. or rfd. Other stores in Newark. Specializes in clothing. Other items: small selection. Sells: **Nursery/Children's Furniture, Bikes, Clothing—Children's, Clothing—Women's.**

** **James Roy Furniture**, 15 E. 32 (Mad.), 5th floor, 679-2565, N-RR to 28th St., 6 to 33, M-S 10-5, ch., c.c. 1 yr. free service. Sells: **Better-Quality Furniture-Brands, Medium/Low-Quality Furniture, Convertible Sofas.**

* **Jay's Rug Shop**, Brooklyn, 1968 86th St., 266-6656, B to 20th Av., MTh 10-7, TWFS 10-5, ch., no c.c., no exch. or rfd. Small stock of remnants. Sells: **Carpeting—Cheaper Brands.**

* **JBJ Carpet Remnants**, 233 W. 14 (7th-8th), 924-0348, 1-2-3 to 14, A-AA-CC-E-LL to 14 St. & 8 Av., irregular hours, usually M-F 9-6, S 10-3, ch., no c.c., no exch. or rfd. Very cooperative. Specializes in commercial carpeting. Sells: **Carpeting—Better Quality.**

** **JDS Furniture**, 45 E. 20 (B'wy), 5th floor, 677-7226, N-RR to 23rd St., MTWFS 10-5, Th 10-8, ch., c.c. 1 yr. free service. At first, they low-balled me, but then when they finally got around to giving me their real price, that turned out to be low enough. Sells: **Better-Quality Furniture-Brands, Convertible Sofas.**

Jennifer House Convertibles, 404 Park Av. S. at 28th St., 532-4697, 6 to 28; 1014 2nd Av. (54), 751-1720, E-F to Lex. Av.; 1530 2nd Av. (79-80), 535-1242, 6 to 77; 1770 Broadway (57), 581-1559, A-AA-B-CC-D-1 to 59. All stores: M-Th 10-8, FS 10-6, Sun 12-5, ch., c.c. 1 yr. free service. Sells: **Convertible Sofas.**

John Harley, 54 W. 33 (5th-6th), 736-1644, B-D-F-N-QB-RR to 34, M-F 10-6, S 10-5, c.c., no ch. 5 years free service. Sells: **Convertible Sofas.**

*** **Kahan National Furniture**, Brooklyn, 60 Broadway (Wythe), 782-2760, J-M to Marcy, then take free bus B24 back towards river, phone first, but hours usually M-Th 10-5 and Sun by appt., ch., no c.c., no exch. or rfd. Large selection. Hotel-furniture liquidators. When major hotels change the furniture (including office-) every 3 yrs. or so, it ends up here, selling at 70-80% discount, good condition. Sells: **Closeouts, Etc., Lamps, Office Equipment.**

** **Kingsway Carpet**, Brooklyn, 907 Kings Hwy., 339-9000, D-M-QB to Kings Hwy., M-Th 9-7, F 9-2, Sun 11-5, ch., c.c., no exch. or rfd. Sells: **Carpeting—Better Quality.**

* **Klein Decorators**, Brooklyn, 1910 86th St., 331-6363, B to 20th Av., M-Th 10-6, F 10-2, Sun 10-4, ch., c.c., no exch. or rfd. Sells: **Convertible Sofas.**

Klein's Kiddy Korner, Brooklyn, 4501 New Utrecht Av., 435-8400, B to Ft. Ham. Pkwy., Sun-Th 9:30-6:30, F 9:30-3, all cash, no exch. or rfd. Sells: **Nursery/Children's Furniture.**

** **Lamp Warehouse**, Brooklyn, 1073 39th St. at Ft. Ham. Pkwy., 436-2207, B to 9th Av., B to Ft. Ham. Pkwy., MTF 9-5:30, Th 9-9, SSun 10-5, ch., c.c., exch., no rfd. Large selection. Their fans are Casablanca and Hunter ceiling fans. Sells: **Lamps, Track-Lighting, Chandeliers, Home-Improvement Items.**

Leonard St. Carpet Warehouse, 14 Leonard St. (W.B'wy-Hudson), 226-0274, 1 to Franklin, M-S 10-6, Sun 12-5, ch., no c.c., no exch. or rfd. Sells:

12: FURNISHINGS

Carpeting—Better Quality.
    LumberSmith, 852-4434. They set it up in your home. Sells: **Beds—Loft**.
+   **Metro Interiors**, Brooklyn, 3700 Nostrand Av. (X), 252-4292, no subway stop nearby, M-S 11-5, c.c., no ch., exch. or rfd. Only dinettes, home bars, room dividers, giftware. Bonus discount to BF readers: 2% to 5%. Sells: **Medium/Low-Quality Furniture, Jewelry & Gifts**.
*   **M&M Furniture Discount**, 303 Park Av. S. at 23rd St., up 1 flight, 677-6820, 6 to 23, MTW 10-6, ThF 10-6:45, S 10-4, ch., c.c. Free service. Sells: **Medium/Low-Quality Furniture, Convertible Sofas**.
    Nat Skop, Brooklyn, 1942 86th St., 256-4913&6700, B to 20th Av., MTWS 7:30-6, ThF 7:30-9, c.c., no ch., no exch. or rfd. Limited housewares and lamps: only toilet seats and wall- and hanging-lamps. Sells: **Lamps, Home-Improvement Items, Housewares**.
+   **New York Furniture Ctr., 41 E. 31 (Mad), 679-8866, N-RR to 28th St., 6 to 33, MTWFS 10-4:30, Th 10-8, ch., c.c. 1 yr. service free. Bonus discount to BF readers: 4%. Sells: **Better-Quality Furniture-Brands, Convertible Sofas**.
+   **Northeast Floor Coverings, 1492 1st Av. (78), 988-5326, 6 to 77, M-F 8-6, S 10-5, ch., c.c., no exch. or rfd. Has some remnants. Bonus discount to BF readers: 10%. Sells: **Carpeting—Better Quality, Linoleum, Tiles, Vinyl**.
**   **Noury & Sons**, 440 Park Av. S. at 30th St., 2nd floor, 889-6701 & 1-800-223-1110, 6 to 28, M-F 9-5, all cash, no exch. or rfd. Large selection. Branch in Westbury is named 'Peykar.' Sells: **Oriental Rugs**.
**   **NY Ceiling Fan Ctr.**, 620-4 Broadway (Houston), 254-6720, B-D-F-6 to B'wy-Laf. & Bleecker, N-RR to Prince St., MTF 9:30-5:30, Th 9:30-9, SSun 10-5, ch., c.c., exch., no rfd. Affiliated with Lamp Warehouse, just smaller stock; but will special-order. Their fans are Casablanca and Hunter ceiling fans. Sells: **Lamps, Track-Lighting, Home-Improvement Items**.
**   **OK Furniture & Carpeting**, 1504 1st Av. at 79th St., 628-5864, 6 to 77; Queens, 54-05 Northern Blvd., Woodside, 728-5220, F-GG-N to Northern Blvd.; Queens, 210-06 Jamaica Av., Queens Village, 454-5900, no subway stop nearby; Brooklyn, 1475 Flatbush Av. (Glenwood), 859-8995, 3-4 to Flatbush Av.; Bronx, 536 E. Fordham Rd. (Lorillard), 733-0800, CC-D to Fordham Rd., plus a long walk. All stores: MThF 10-9, TWS 10-6, Sun 12-6, ch., c.c. Free service. Sells: **Medium/Low-Quality Furniture, Convertible Sofas, Carpeting—Cheaper Brands**.
**   **Padawer Carpets & Remnants**, 112 4th Av. (12), 777-4114, LL-N-QB-RR-4-5-6 to Union Sq., M-F 8-5, S 10-5, ch., (but a wait to clear) no c.c., no exch. or rfd. Very cooperative. Extremely nice people. Huge selection. Samples arranged by graduated colors, especially helpful for interior decoration. In all ways the best place for self-installers. Sells: **Carpeting—Better Quality**.
*   **Palazzetti**, 461 Park Av. S. (31), 9th floor, 684-1199, 6 to 33, M-F 10-5, ch., c.c. (but only AE), exch., no rfd. Only tables and chairs, Bauhaus (van der Rohe, Breuer) and Le Corbusier. Sells: **Designers' Furniture**.
    Palisades International, 245 5th Av. (28), rms. 1902-5, 686-6262 & 679-1384, N-RR to 28th St., M-F 10-5, ch., no c.c., exch., no rfd. Sells: **Oriental Rugs**.
    Parviz Shenassa, 220 5th Av. at 26, rm. 1506, 684-6449, N-RR to 28th St., M-F 11-6, ch., c.c., exch. or rfd. Sells: **Oriental Rugs**.
*+   **Perplexity Lucite**, 237 E. 53 (3rd-2nd Avs.), 688-3571, E-F to Lex. Av., M-S 10:30-6:30, Sun 12-5, ch., c.c. (only c.c. is AE), exch., no rfd. Another store in Carle Place, Long Island. Bonus discount to BF readers: 5%. Sells: **Plexiglass Furniture, Jewelry & Gifts, Stationery & Art Supplies**.
**   **P&G Trdg.**, Brooklyn, 241 Bay Ridge Av. (=69th St.), 745-0730, RR to Bay Ridge Av., MTW 8-5:30, ThF 8-8:30, S 8-5, ch., no c.c., no exch. or rfd. Large selection. No lamps or lighting fixtures. No phone-quotes. No phone-information (too bad, going out of your way to get here is just a gamble). Items change constantly. Sells: **Closeouts, Etc.**.
*   **Pillow Furniture**, 144 5th Av. (19), up 1 flight, 929-9858, N-RR to 23rd St., M-S 11-7, Sun 1-6, all cash, exch. or rfd. Sells: **Pillow-Furniture**.
    Plumbline Design, 654 Broadway (Bond-Bleecker), 477-2074, B-D-F-6 to B'wy-Laf. & Bleecker, M-S 11-6, Sun 1-6, ch., c.c. 1 yr. service. Sells: **Convertible Sofas, Lamps, Track-Lighting, Pillow-Furniture**.
**   **Quality Broadloom & Remnant**, Brooklyn, 814 Coney Island Av. (Ditmas), 941-4200, D-M-QB to Cortelyou; Brooklyn, 4403 13th Av., 871-6272, B to Ft. Ham. Pkwy. Both stores: MT 10-7, W 10-6, Th 10-8, F 10-3, Sun 10-5, ch., c.c., no exch. or rfd. Many remnants at Coney Is. Av. store--strongly recommended. Sells:

12: FURNISHINGS

Carpeting—Better Quality.

Queens Floor Covering, Queens, 30-74 Steinway St., Astoria, 721-6900, F-GG-N to Steinway St., MTWS 9:30-6, ThF 10-8, c.c., no ch., no exch. or rfd. Sells: **Carpeting—Better Quality, Carpeting—Cheaper Brands**.

Rainbow Mirror, Brooklyn, 4805 New Utrecht Av., 438-0332&4416, B to 50th St., M-S 8-4, ch., no c.c. Free service. Sells: **Marble-Top Tables, Lamps, Chandeliers, Home-Improvement Items.**

Redi-Cut Carpets, 471 W. 42 (10th Av.), 695-6759, A-AA-CC-E to 42; 1833 1st Av. (94-5), 831-2644, 6 to 96; Bronx, 3545 Webster Av. (Gunhill Rd.), 547-1410&1825, 2-5 to Gun Hill Rd. All stores: MThF 10-9, TWS 10-6, ch., c.c., no exch. or rfd. Large selection of remnants at each location. Very good for that. Sells: **Carpeting—Better Quality.**

Rodos 104th St., 2717 Broadway at 104th, 663-3551, 1 to 103, M-F 10-7, S 10-6, ch., c.c. Free service. Sells: **Unpainted, & Platform-Beds.**

*+ **Roosevelt Rug & Linoleum**, Queens, 31-74 Steinway St., Astoria, 728-4693, F-GG-N to Steinway St., MTW 9-6, ThF 9-7:30, S 9-5:30, ch., c.c., no exch. or rfd. Bonus discount to BF readers: 5% to 10%. Sells: **Carpeting—Cheaper Brands, Linoleum, Tiles, Vinyl.**

** **S. Redisch Furniture**, 27 E. Broadway (Catherine-Market), 962-0700, F to E. Broadway, J-M-RR-4-5-6 to Chambers & Bkln. Bridge, MTWF 9-6, Th 9-8, S 9-4, Sun 10-4, ch., c.c., exch., no rfd. Sells: **Medium/Low-Quality Furniture, Convertible Sofas.**

* **Sasson Imports**, 244 5th Av. (28), 2nd floor, 889-4646, N-RR to 28th St., M-F 10-5, all cash, exch., no rfd. Sells: **Oriental Rugs.**

* **Schneider's**, 20 Av. A. at 2nd St., 228-3540, F to 2nd Av., F-J-M to Delancey & Essex, MTh 10-8, TWFSSun 10-6, ch., no c.c., exch. or rfd. Sells: **Nursery/Children's Furniture.**

* **Serenade Loftbeds**, 947-1840. They set in up in your home. Sells: **Beds—Loft.**

*** **Sherrill Closeouts Warehouse**, 12 E. 22 (B'way), 674-4430, N-RR to 23rd St., 6 to 23, M-F 10-6, SSun 10-6, ch., c.c., no exch. or rfd. Oriental items, mostly hand-carved or hand-painted, 50-60% off. Sells: **Lamps, Jewelry & Gifts.**

** **Siromo Furniture**, Bronx, 190 E. Mosholu Pkwy. S., 295-0464, M-F 9-5, ch., no c.c. Free service. No showroom. Must know make. Sells: **Better-Quality Furniture-Brands, Medium/Low-Quality Furniture, Convertible Sofas.**

** **Sun Lighting**, Queens, 84-60 Parsons Blvd., Jamaica, 291-3456, E-F to Parsons Blvd.; Brooklyn, 331 Rockaway Av. (NY Av.), 342-7175&9800, A-CC to Rockaway Av., plus a long walk. Both stores: M-F 8-5:30, S 8-4:30, ch., c.c., no exch. or rfd. Sells: **Marble-Top Tables, Lamps, Chandeliers.**

Superior Floor Covering, 155 Essex St. (Stanton), 673-0637, F-J-M to Delancey & Essex, M-F 9-6, Sun 9:30-4:30, ch., no ch., exch. or rfd. (But only on uncut goods.) Sells: **Carpeting—Cheaper Brands, Linoleum, Tiles, Vinyl.**

* **Susan Trdg.**, 300 Canal St. (B'way), 431-8529, J-M-N-QB-RR-6 to Canal, 7 days 10-6, ch., c.c., exch., no rfd. Sells: **Clip-On Lighting Fixtures, Appliances, Home-Improvement Items, Personal Accessories.**

*+ **Taj International**, 255 5th Av. (28-9), 2nd floor, 889-7697, N-RR to 28th St., M-F 9-5, ch., no c.c., exch., no rfd. Large selection. Bonus discount to BF readers: 10%. Sells: **Oriental Rugs.**

* **Torange Rugs**, 220 5th Av. at 26th St., rm. 1610, 689-2538, N-RR to 28th St., M-F 9-6, ch., no c.c., exch. or rfd. Sells: **Oriental Rugs.**

Tri-Surplus, 63 Reade St. (B'wy-Church), 964-9237, A-CC-1-2-3 to Chambers, M-F 9-5:30, S 9-4:30, ch., no c.c., exch. or rfd. Small store. Small selection. Sells: **Lamps, Warehouse Salvage Job-Lot.**

Two-Morrow, 111 Rivington (Essex), 254-0820, F-J-M to Delancey & Essex, 7 days 10-6, all cash, exch., no rfd. Defectives from department stores. Sells: **Closeouts, Etc..**

Viaventi, 171 7th Av. at 20th St., 242-4051, 1 to 18, M-F 10:30-6, S 11:30-5, ch., c.c., no exch. or rfd. Sells: **Designers' Furniture.**

* **Weinstock Lamp**, Queens, 34-30 Steinway St., Astoria, 727-4848, F-GG-N to Steinway St., M-Th 9-5, F 9-2, ch., no c.c., exch. or rfd. Sells: **Marble-Top Tables, Lamps, Chandeliers.**

**** **Woodware**, Rt. 7 S., Middlebury, Vt., 1-802-388-6297. Such incredible value that I break the rules here. $20-25 for hand-carved wood lamps; other hand-made wooden items, gifts, clocks. He even cuts down the trees himself. Sells: **Lamps,**

12: FURNISHINGS

Jewelry & Gifts.
Yeedl's Juvenile Furniture, Brooklyn, 4301 13th Av., 435-5900, B to Ft. Ham. Pkwy., M-Th 11-7, F 11-2, Sun 10:30-6, ch., no c.c., no exch. or rfd. Sells: **Nursery/Children's Furniture.**

13:
HEALTH & BEAUTY AIDS
Expect 25-80% discounts.

The biggest savings here are on perfumes and colognes, where actually "80% off" can be a conservative figure. There are a half-dozen local perfumer-retailers who make house knock-offs of top brand frangrances; and the places that I recommend are those whose copies I find to be indistinguishable from the originals, and whose prices are also the most reasonable. Thus, for example, I don't list Tuli-Latus in Queens, as they're too expensive; and I also refrain from endorsing Jon Paul in Manhattan, because I'm not persuaded by their copies. Two of the outlets that I do recommend—Chem-Arom, and Classique—carry as well floral and other natural scents at 80-90% off the prices charged for the same stuff at the Perfumer's Workshop counters of Macy's and Bloomingdales; and some people find these natural fragrances more appealing than anything Aramis, Chanel, Givenchy, and such, have come up with; but that's a matter of personal taste. What's not a question of taste, but just a simple fact, is that the best discounters can and do routinely sell the same perfumes and colognes—in each instance having the same smell and lasting-power as the famous-name original—at prices 80-95% lower, and yet they still can make a profit. That gives you an idea of what the traditional manufacturers' and retailers' markups are in this trade. So when you buy one of the traditional brands, just think of all those television ads you're paying for at $5,000 per second; and can anybody smell that?

Vitamins

Another area where rather impressive savings are possible is health-food supplements, vitamins and minerals. Here it's easy to pay 50% less without any compromise in quality. Again, the most ridiculously overpriced items are the well-known brand-name supplements, like Geritol, Theragran, One-A-Day, etc.; of which, again, copies—with exactly the same formulations as the originals—are available for 50-85% less than the cost of the promo-puffed brands. RVP, Nutrition Headquarters, and GNC, are the recommended outfits that specialize in such copies, and their free mail-order catalogs list the top brands and prices next to their own copies and prices.

When shopping for food-supplements, keep in mind that the ratings I've given the various outlets are based on comparisons of prices on 35 different items; and that in this field, the comparative ratings with regard to prices on a specific item may occasionally vary substantially from these broader-based ratings. For example, although Freeda is recommended without stars, no store offers better values in the field of multivitamin-mineral one-per-day-type

13: HEALTH & BEAUTY AIDS

supplements—Freeda's real specialty.

The most popular confusion in the field of nutritional supplements, and a major source of wasted money for consumers, concerns the question of whether natural vitamins are superior to synthetic ones. Rest assured, there's absolutely no advantage to be had from buying the much more expensive "natural" kind. For example, pure natural vitamin C is not available except as a very rare laboratory curiosity; it costs more than $100 per pound, and any vitamin-outlet that advertises "natural vitamin C" is not telling things quite as they are (and that unfortunately includes some of the places I recommend—an indication of how commonplace misleading advertising really is, despite the alleged efforts of the Federal Trade Commission). A little bit of natural vitamin C is mixed in with a lot of the synthetic, so that the label "natural"— and a much higher price—can be tacked on. But no problem; the synthetic vitamin C (which is actually derived by chemical modification of sugar) is chemically identical to the natural—they're both the same ascorbic acid (sometimes buffered to an ascorbate by adding an alkalai)—so there's no way that it's going to make the slightest bit of difference which one you buy, except that you'll pay a lot less for the acknowledgedly "synthetic" than for the allegedly "natural."

Another prime example is vitamin E. In this case, there's a slight chemical difference between the natural (which really exists, and is sold, as advertised) and the synthetic. "Natural" vitamin E is the stuff that's removed in the processing and refining of supermarket-brand vegetable-oils to make them cheaper—and unfortunately somewhat carcinogenic without this natural antioxidant which prevents the formation of cancer-causing free-radicals in oils. The removed vitamin E is then sold separately to the vitamin-manufacturers; and this is one reason those junky commercial food-oils cost less than the unrefined health-food brands (which doesn't include all health-food brands, however. You can recognize the unrefined ones by two things: They've got a solid sediment at the bottom of the bottle; and they have a fragrance to them, whereas the refined ones have no smell at all.) So when you buy the natural vitamin E, you're paying a heavy surcharge for what you've probably been robbed of in your vegetable-oil.

The question remains: Is there an advantage to the higher-priced natural vitamin E? There's none at all. Although the synthetic is less potent for its weight and volume, vitamin E is not sold by either weight or volume. It's sold by lab-tested and proven potency, as measured by something called "International Units" or "I.U." So, for example, 400 I.U. of vitamin E is equally potent and effective, regardless whether it's natural or synthetic. The only difference is the price: The natural costs twice as much. One of the recommended outlets, RVP, doesn't even sell the synthetic kind. Fortunately, the other recommended places do. RVP also doesn't sell the cheapest form of vitamin C. But again, the other outlets I list do. (The least expensive form is the best to buy. For example, "vitamin C, plus bioflavonoids, rutin and hesperidin complex" adds only marginally to the effectiveness of the vitamin C alone, but greatly hikes the cost. You do better simply by purchasing the next-higher potency of the pure vitamin.)

One of the top-recommended food-supplement suppliers specializes in only a single nutrient: lecithin. Many studies have shown that diets rich in corn or safflower oil (especially if of the unrefined variety), and with supplemental lecithin, greatly reduce the probability of heart-attacks, even if the individual is otherwise consuming an unhealthy diet. The cheapest lecithin-source probably anywhere in the country, is American Lecithin Co., which sells by mail-order from their warehouse in Queens. Lecithin comes in two commercial forms: the processed granular, and the natural gooey liquid, the latter of which costs only 20% as much as the former. The liquid also has another use: It's marvelous to rub on the inside of a pan to prevent cooked food from sticking. However, the liquid is so gooey that it should be diluted with about five parts of your cooking-oil to one part of lecithin, and used this way in recipies, as part of the cooking-oil. To order from American Lecithin, phone them at 274-4350, and ask the per-pound price of Alcolec S liquid lecithin in the 8-pound tin, or of their granular lecithin in the 4-pound bag, and also the cost of shipping the package to you U.P.S. Then ask for the total price, including shipping; and send them a money-order for that sum. (For repeat-purchases after the first, a personal check may be accepted; but not on the first order.) They're extremely conscientious people, and they always ship on the same day they receive payment. You'll be surprised at how fast the package arrives. Incidentally, lecithin keeps indefinitely without being refrigerated, so there's no storage-problem.

Drugs & Toiletries

Other things covered in this chapter include toiletries and both prescription- and non-prescription-drugs. Price-comparisons on pharmaceuticals can be somewhat deceptive if one goes only by the N.Y.-State-required posted drug-store prices, which are for set quantities usually of 100 tablets. Some pharmacies post excellent prices on the mandatorily listed quantity; but woe to the patient who comes in with a prescription for 50 or 150 tablets. I've taken this into account in my ratings of drug stores; and I recommend only those who have good prices across the board and on non-standard quantities, not just on the officially posted prices.

Most drugstores will phone-quote prices if you tell them that you've got a prescription for a specific drug.

Whenever you get a prescription, always ask your doctor if the same drug is available without the brand-name—i.e., as a "generic." Even the Food and Drug Administration has acknowledged that "generics" are as effective as the vastly more expensive "proprietaries" (which are really only the same drugs with highly advertised brand-names). Then, if Doc says "no," don't give up; ask your pharmacist the same question when you hand him the prescription to price. You may be surprised to find that Doc was wrong. Such physicians are fairly common, but decidedly not worth patronizing again, although it might make sense to see such

13: HEALTH & BEAUTY AIDS

a doctor just one more time to have him re-write the last prescription he'll ever give you.

The very same overpricing of the brand-name product is to be found in the field of non-prescription drugs. Just look at the ingredients-label on the package, where you'll find the real identity of what you're buying. For example, if you're shopping for Tylenol, you'll find that the same potency of the same active ingredient—acetaminophen—is available for less money under the Datril name. (Incidentally, acetaminophen-based pain relievers, taken in quantity, cause severe liver-damage; aspirins, on the other hand, cause ulcers, but taken in quarter-tablet units will greatly reduce the risk of heart-attacks.) And all aspirins are the same; only Bayer costs more. Often, the overpriced top-brands add innocuous and ineffective chemicals to avoid comparison with the cheaper products. Bufferin, for example, does this. There's no evidence that the alkalai it adds to the aspirin is effective in protecting the user from ulcers. Another trick is exemplified in the Anacin ads, which claim "more pain-reliever" as measured by milligrams, and which then falsely compare Anacin with Tylenol, the latter of which is based on a different active ingredient and so therefore not directly comparable in terms of milligrams at all. We pay heavily for these deceptive ads. The active ingredient in Anacin can be purchased for a fifth the price as off-brand aspirin. The major pharmaceutical houses play both doctors and the general public for suckers; and as a consequence they historically have had higher profit/sales ratios than any other industry. It evidently pays handsomely to assume that the public is passive and willing to be conned, and that the FDA will be just as passive.

The best nutshell-descriptions of the relative merits and demerits, and dangers, of various prescription and non-prescription drugs, are to be found in Joe Graedon's book *The People's Pharmacy* (but not *The People's Pharmacy #2*). He sticks his neck out, makes recommendations from among competing medications, and tells which drugs don't work. *The Physicians' and Pharmacists' Guide to Your Medicines*, by the U.S. Pharmacopeial Convention (published by Ballantine), is more formal, and in some ways more thorough—a virtual drug-encyclopedia, and certainly the best of its kind. Both books are relatively inexpensive quality paperbacks, strongly recommended; and both are slightly discounted on the third floor of Barnes & Noble's main store at 5th avenue and 18th Street. There's only one good herbalist encyclopedia, John Lust's *The Herb Book*; and fortunately it's available very cheaply as a pulp Bantam paperback. It tells the medical effects of over 500 different herbs, how to use them, and which of them can be dangerous; also, it's cross-indexed both by diseases and by symptoms. The best-value medical encyclopedia is certainly the *Merck Manual*, which can be compared with others costing three times the price, and which is also sometimes discounted at Barnes & Noble. The *Merck* is written for physicians, but it's nonetheless generally comprehensible by the average layman, and much more information-packed, and far better indexed, than the popularly written Morris-Fishbein-type of medical encyclopedia for scared-to-death lamebrains.

Eyeglasses & Contact-Lenses

Finally, one other merchandise-category that's covered in this chapter is eyeglasses and contact-lenses. Manufacturers' overpricing on frames for prescription glasses is simply monumental. Non-prescription ready-made sunglasses which use the same frames will list for half the price (or less) complete, and will be found at *BARGAIN FINDER* stores for less than $5. (See Chapter 22 for this.) Better to buy the sunglasses just for the frames alone, rather than to pay perhaps 10 times the price for the same frames at an optician. The recommended local NYC opticians, Unique Eyewear and the SUNY Optometric Center, will tell you honestly which sunglass-frames will, and which won't, be suitable for fitting to your prescription-lenses—not all are. Generally, if the frames appear to be of good quality, and if your prescription isn't terribly strong, they'll do OK. So it might pay to buy a few pairs of good, attractive, and fashionable non-prescription sunglasses with the objective in mind that ultimately one or more of them will be made into regular prescription eyeglasses, at a cost of perhaps $15 for the lenses and $4 for the frames.

It's not recommended that you have your eyes examined at a traditional commercial eyeglass- or contact-lens place. A proper eye-exam takes at least 50 minutes—usually longer—and when the exam is part of an all-inclusive price, you can be sure that the time spent with you will be far less than that (sometimes less than 10 minutes). Not only may the resulting eyeglasses be less than the best for your eyes, but diseases that you may be developing and which can be found at a very early stage by a proper eye-exam will then likely go unnoticed, and may later be discovered at a stage too late—or too expensive—to treat. The place I recommend for the eye-exam—SUNY's College of Optometry in Manhattan—does the most reliably thorough and reasonably priced (at present, no more than $25) eye-exam I know of anywhere in the City. Ask the optometrist to mark your optometric centers onto the prescription he writes up. (More on that later.) Once you've had the prescription filled, the SUNY facility will check the glasses free of charge to make sure that the prescription has been correctly executed. The SUNY eye-clinic is only a 12-minute walk away from Unique Eyewear, which fortunately makes the two a convenient match. You ought to have the lenses checked, because a substantial proportion of lenses turn out to be incorrectly ground.

Different places are recommended if you wear contacts. But still, it's advised here, too, that you follow the same procedure of having the initial exam done at the SUNY optometric facility, and of having the lenses ground elsewhere but then checked by SUNY.

During an eye-exam, it's routine that the optometrist measure how far apart your eyes are—what in optometry is called the "centers," because the centers of your lenses should be exactly as far apart as are your irises. However, this crucial figure is stupidly not written onto eyeglass-prescriptions, and as a result many prescriptions are filled off-center, producing headaches and sometimes

13: HEALTH & BEAUTY AIDS

distorted vision. It's therefore strongly, indeed emphatically, suggested, that **when you have your eyes examined, ask the optometrist to write the centers onto the prescription.**

Roughly 20% of all eyeglass-prescriptions aren't filled properly. The sloppiness in the opticians' trade is a major scandal. Yet optometrists are continually amazed that patients who are wearing wrongly ground lenses usually either don't know or don't care. If you're among the small minority who won't accept botchwork, then you'll want to be cautious about this, in which case the following procedure is for you:

FOR EYEGLASS-WEARERS: First, select the frames you want. If these are sunglass-frames as per the preceding, the sunglasses should be purchased first. Then, go to the SUNY College of Optometry, and have your eyes examined. As mentioned before, you should routinely **ask the optometrist to write your centers onto the prescription.** Next, visit the dispensary in the same eye-clinic. The problems with this dispensary are that the frames are not discounted, and the frames-selection is poor. The advantages have to do with the lenses, which are ground accurately, within much tighter than normal tolerances; and which are reasonably priced. Therefore, it's suggested that you ask the dispenser, first if you've brought sunglasses with you for the frames, whether those sunglass-frames are suitable for the lenses you need; and second if you didn't bring such frames with you (or if the answer to the preceding question is "no"), what kinds of frames you should look for elsewhere and bring to the SUNY Optometric Center so that they can grind and fit lenses according to your prescription. Then, once you've been instructed as to what types of frames are suitable, go to Unique Eyewear or to the recommended mail-order optician, to buy those frames at discount, and return to the SUNY eye-clinic dispensary to have the lenses ground and fitted to those frames.

FOR CONTACT-LENS WEARERS: Here the problems are simpler, because there's no problem with frames. Have the eye-exam at the SUNY facility, fill the prescription at the places recommended for contact-lenses, and return to the SUNY eye-clinic to have those lenses checked and verified.

The above procedures may seem too much of a bother to some people, but the alternatives may turn out to be even worse: a botched prescription, botched execution of the prescription, a poor selection of frames to choose from, and overpaying for it all. In any event, there is always the other option available: taking your chances with lenses which almost certainly will be less-accurately—though probably within acceptable tolerances—fitted to your eyes.

Under the category of toiletry-items, I have only one recommendation: I personally find the best shampoo to be Ivory Dishwashing Detergent, which is highly concentrated yet extremely mild, and which costs far less per application than anything advertised as a "shampoo." Since it's used to wash dishes that people eat from, it's also very safe. Perhaps you'll find this unorthodox "shampoo" worth a try.

13: HEALTH & BEAUTY AIDS

RECOMMENDED PRODUCTS:
See above.

RECOMMENDED STORES:

beauty supplies

(examples: cosmetics, creams, curlers, hairsprays, lashes, lotions, shampoos)

Citi Cosmetics (752-3505); **Royal Beauty Supply** (Brooklyn, 339-0700); **Sweetheart Discount** (766-4537); **Ultra Cosmetics** (582-3510); **United Beauty Supply** (582-2324).

perfumes & colognes

*****+**Classique Perfumes** (392-1650); ***Chem-Arom** (Queens, 843-2216); **Essential Products** (344-4288); **Odds & Ends Job-Lots** (intermittent stock, Queens, 441-6878); **Townie Merchandise** (929-8060); *Lou-Mark Trdg.** (242-9440); *Park Av. Job Lot** (intermittent stock, 673-7536); *Pushcart** (962-4142); **Citi Cosmetics** (752-3505); **Sweetheart Discount** (766-4537); **The Bargain Lot** (intermittent stock, 736-1346).

wigs & lashes

+**Lawrence Fashions** (391-6693).

prescription drugs

Barney's Cut-Rate Brooklyn (Brooklyn, 643-0643); **Central Prescription Pharmacy** (260-4430); **Duane Reade Drugs** (541-9708); **Elm Drugs** (267-4142); **Kings Houston Drugs** (254-0066); *Barney's Cut-Rate Pharmacy** (719-1940); *Barney's** (732-3799); *Milshap Pharmacy** (674-7007); *Pathmark Pharmacies** (826-0670); *Roosevelt Drugs** (Queens, 424-1291); **Gallery Drugs** (838-6765); **Genovese** (Queens, 278-1901); **King's Pharmacy** (Brooklyn, 253-0200); **LeRoy Pharmacy Prescriptions** (222-2300); **Midtown East Pharmacy** (986-7111); **Prescription Headquarters** (Queens, 886-4550).

non-prescription, & toiletries

(examples: antacids, aspirins, colognes, condoms, creams, denture-cleaners, deodorants, deodorizers, diapers, disinfectants, foot-pads, hairsprays, lotions, powders, razors, shampoos, tampons, thermometers, toothbrushes, toothpastes)

***Odd Job Trdg.** (intermittent stock, 686-6825); **Abehill Stores** (Queens, 335-2116); **Cayne's 2** (244-8761); **Century 21** (227-9092); **Duane Reade Drugs** (541-9708); **Elm Drugs** (267-4142); **Kings Houston Drugs** (254-0066); **Odds & Ends Job-Lots** (intermittent stock, Queens, 441-6878); **Weber's Job Lot** (intermittent stock, 564-7668); *Eighty-Eight Cent Shops** (753-6969); *F&G Discount** (866-7830); *Joann's Variety Store** (Brooklyn, 648-8517); *Milshap Pharmacy** (674-7007); *Morris Discount** (Brooklyn, 375-2529); *Pushcart** (962-4142); *Ray Variety** (736-2547); *Roosevelt Drugs** (Queens, 424-1291); **First Cost** (intermittent stock, 697-0244); **G & Sons Dept. Store** (Brooklyn, 438-2604); **H&E Stores** (Brooklyn, 376-3163); **JRPS Discount** (874-7828); **King's Pharmacy** (Brooklyn, 253-0200); **Odd Lot Trdg.** (intermittent stock, 736-5243); **Pay Less Brooklyn** (Brooklyn, 449-2678); **Pay Less** (344-1084); **Phil's** (688-4144); **Robbins Men's Wear** (691-2573); **S&J Stores** (Brooklyn, 266-7837); **Tight End** (Brooklyn, 627-9765).

13: HEALTH & BEAUTY AIDS

vitamins (& MINERALS)

*****Sundown Vitamins**; ****Nutrition Headquarters**; ****RVP Vitamins**; ****Vital Foods**; ***CVV Vitamins**; ***GNC Vitamins** (outside NYC, 1-800-245-6562); ***Pushcart** (962-4142); **Freeda Vitamins** (685-4980); **General Nutrition Center (GNC)**; **Nature Food Centers**; **Stur-Dee Vitamins**.

lecithin

*****American Lecithin Co.** (Queens, 274-4350).

medical, surgical, rehab. eqt.

***Arista Surgical** (679-3694); **Medco Surgical** (Queens, 740-9100).

optometrics

(measuring you for eyeglasses or contact-lenses, and writing optical prescriptions)

SUNY Optometric Center (477-7900).

eyeglasses

Prism Optical; **Unique Eyewear** (947-4977).

contact-lenses

+**American Vision Centers** (580-1600); +**Group National Contact Lens** (787-0733); **Professional Contact Lens** (883-0995).

STORES-DIRECTORY

Phone a store before you go out of your way to visit it. Especially do this during July and August, when most establishments reduce or eliminate weekend-hours.

In the listings below, "*" means especially recommended, "+" means that the store offers a bonus discount to BF readers, "ch." and "c.c." mean respectively checks and credit cards, and "exch." and "rfd." mean respectively exchange and refund. Nearest subway-stops are shown. For example, "B-D-F to 47" means to take the B, D, or F train to 47th Street. Store-hours are also indicated, with days of the week abbreviated, like "M-S 8-6."

** **Abehill Stores**, Queens, 74-21 37th Av., 335-2116, E-F-GG-N-7 to 74th-B'wy & Roosevelt-Jack.Hts., M-F 9:30-7:45, S 9:30-7, ch., no c.c., 35-day exch. or rfd. Sells: **Non-Prescription, & Toiletries**.

*** **American Lecithin Co.**, Queens, 32-34 61st St. (Northern Blvd.), Woodside, 274-4350, F-GG-N to Northern Blvd., M-F 9-5. Very cooperative. Takes mail-orders. Phone; specify liquid (8-lb. tin) or granulated (4-lb. bag), or dog-diet supplement, UPS-shipped; send M.O. (or a check on subsequent orders); they ship pronto. Nice! Sells: **Lecithin, Pets**.

+ **American Vision Centers**, 2301 Broadway (83), 580-1600, 1 to 86; 93 Nassau St. (Fulton), 349-5063, A-CC-J-M-RR-2-3-4-5 to B'wy-Nassau & Fulton; 1276 Lexington Av. at 86th St., 427-3600, 4-5-6 to 86; Penn Sta., LIRR Concourse, 594-5110, A-AA-CC-E to 34; Brooklyn, 1302 Kings Hwy., 627-8900, D-M-QB to Kings Hwy.; Brooklyn, Albee Sq., DeKalb at Fulton, 522-3737, B-D-M-N-QB-RR to DeKalb, 2-3 to Hoyt. All stores: hours vary according to location (phone for hours), ch., c.c., 60-day exch. or rfd. Other locations: Carle Place, Valley Stream, Smithhaven, Huntington, Poughkeepsie, Ithaca, Auburn, Elmira, Utica. Plus: Mass., Md, Mo., Pa., Tx., Ga., Ill. Bonus discount to BF readers: 10% to 20%. Sells: **Contact-Lenses**.

* **Arista Surgical**, 67 Lexington Av. (25-6), 679-3694, 6 to 23, M-F 8:15-4:45, ch., no c.c., no exch. or rfd. Closeouts and job lots at special reductions. Sells: **Medical, Surgical, Rehab. Eqt.**.

* **Barney's**, 41 John St. (Nassau), 732-3799 (pharmacy), 372-7271 (to-

13: HEALTH & BEAUTY AIDS

baccos), A-CC-J-M-RR-2-3-4-5 to B'wy-Nassau & Fulton, M-F 9-5, ch., no c.c., exch. or rfd. Not affiliated with the other Barney's stores. Sells: **Prescription Drugs, Smoking Supplies.**

** **Barney's Cut-Rate Brooklyn**, Brooklyn, 76 Court St. at Livingston, 643-0643 (pharmacy), 875-8355 (tobacco), M-RR-2-3-4-5 to Borough Hall & Court St., M-S 8-6, ch., no c.c., exch. or rfd. Sells: **Prescription Drugs, Smoking Supplies.**

* **Barney's Cut-Rate Pharmacy**, 25 W. 42 (5th-6th), 719-1940, 7 to 5th Av., B-D-F to 42, M-F 8-6, ch., no c.c., exch. or rfd. Sells: **Prescription Drugs, Smoking Supplies.**

** **Cayne's 2**, 225 W. 34 (7th-8th), basement downstairs, 244-8761, 1-2-3 to 34, A-AA-CC-E to 34, M-S 10-6:30, c.c., no ch., 25-day exch. or rfd. One in the Cayne group. Sells: **Non-Prescription, & Toiletries, Clothing—Children's, Linens.**

** **Central Prescription Pharmacy**, 145A 4th Av. (13-4), 2nd floor, 260-4430, LL-N-QB-RR-4-5-6 to Union Sq., M-F 9-5:45, ch., no c.c., exch. or rfd. Their special strength is on non-standard quantities, though they're good also for the regular 100-tablet (or whatever) prescriptions. Sells: **Prescription Drugs.**

** **Century 21**, 12 Cortlandt St. (B'wy), 227-9092, A-CC-J-M-RR-2-3-4-5 to B'wy-Nassau & Fulton, 4-5 to Wall St., M-F 8-6; Brooklyn, 472 86th St (4th-5th Avs.), 748-3266, RR to 86th St., M-S 9-9. Both stores: ch., c.c., 5-day exch. or rfd. Not good on appliances. But this small department-store has good prices in every other department. It's much like Dollar Bill's, which has more mens'-wear emphasis. Sells: **Non-Prescription, & Toiletries, Clothing—Children's, Clothing—Men's, Clothing—Women's.**

*** **Chem-Arom**, Queens, 103-15 101st St. (Liberty), Ozone Park, 843-2216, A-CC to Rockaway Blvd., M-F 8:30-5:30, ch., no c.c., exch. or rfd. Will phone-quote. Takes mail-orders. Copies. Will send free samples. Specify which brand-name perfumes you want copies of. No floral scents available here. Sells: **Perfumes & Colognes.**

Citi Cosmetics, 643 Lexington Av. (54-5), 752-3505, E-F to Lex. Av., M-F 9-8, S 9-6, ch., c.c., exch., no rfd. All the top (and overpriced) designer-names, at the small discounts that are possible for this stuff. Make-up demonstrations. Licensed cosmetician. Sells: **Beauty Supplies, Perfumes & Colognes.**

****+ **Classique Perfumes**, 245 Columbus Av. at 71st St., 787-8652, AA-B-CC to 72, M-S 9-8; Queens, 10-22 44th Dr. L.I.C., 392-1650, E-F to 21st St. & Ely, M-F 9-6. Both stores: c.c., no ch., exch. or rfd. Will phone-quote. Takes mail-orders. Catalog. Very cooperative. Large selection. Copies. Free samples. Specify which brand you want a copy of, or which floral scent you want. The store is also very nice, and welcomes walk-in customers. Great! Great! Bonus discount to BF readers: 10%. Sells: **Perfumes & Colognes.**

* **CVV Vitamins**, 860 Grand Blvd., P.O. Box T, Deer Park, NY 11729. Write for catalog. Sells: **Vitamins.**

** **Duane Reade Drugs**, 224 W. 57 at Broadway, 541-9708, B-D-E to 7th Av., A-AA-B-CC-D-1 to 59; 144 E. 44 (Lex.), 370-0327, 4-5-6-7 to Grand Central; 1412 Broadway (39-40), 354-2554, N-QB-RR-1-2-3-7 to 42 & Times Square; 304 Madison Av. (41-2), 687-3878, 4-5-6-7 to Grand Central; 1150 6th Av. (44-5), 221-3588, B-D-F to 47; 20 E. 46 (Mad.), 682-2448, 4-5-6-7 to Grand Central; 485 Lexington Av. at 47th St., 682-5338, 6 to 51; 370 Lexington Av. (40-1), 683-9704, 4-5-6-7 to Grand Central; 360 Park Av. S. at 26th St., 685-6717, 6 to 28; 300 Park Av. S. at 22nd St., 533-7580, 6 to 23; 1 World Trade Ctr., Bank Mall, 775-0005, AA-E to World Trade Ctr.; 19 Park Place (Church), 349-5175, 2-3 to Park Place; 37 Broadway (Morris), 425-8460, 4-5 to Bowling Green; 40 Beaver St. (William), 943-3690, J-M-RR-2-3 to Wall & Broad Sts.; 50 Pine St. (William), 425-3720, J-M-RR-2-3 to Wall & Broad Sts.; 90 John St. (Gold), 349-1285, A-CC-J-M-RR-2-3-4-5 to B'wy-Nassau & Fulton; 51 W. 51 (5th-6th), 582-8525, B-D-F to 47; 299 Broadway (Duane-Reade), 227-6168, A-CC-1-2-3 to Chambers, N-RR to City Hall. All stores: M-F 8-6, S (above Canal St. only) 9-5, ch., c.c., exch. or rfd. Obviously, success hasn't spoiled them. Sells: **Prescription Drugs, Non-Prescription, & Toiletries.**

* **Eighty-Eight Cent Shops**, 591 Lexington Av. (52), 753-6969, E-F to Lex. Av., M-F 9:30-6; 1457 Broadway (41), 354-0111, N-QB-RR-1-2-3-7 to 42 & Times Square, M-F 7:15-6, Sun 12-6; 33 W. 8 (5th-6th), 475-6951, A-AA-B-CC-D-E-F to 4, Sun-F 11-10, S 11-12; 89 Chambers St. (B'wy-Church), 267-6722, A-CC-1-2-3 to Chambers, N-RR to City Hall, M-F 7:30-6; 144 Fulton St. (B'wy), 964-2142, A-CC-J-M-RR-2-3-4-5 to B'wy-Nassau & Fulton, M-F 7:30-6. All stores: all cash, exch. or rfd. Everything in store is 88 cents; only the Fulton and Chambers stores have areas set aside for more expensive merchandise. Sells: **Non-Prescription, & Toiletries, Din-**

13: HEALTH & BEAUTY AIDS

ery & Art Supplies, Toys, Games & Hobbies.
** **Elm Drugs**, 114 Liberty St. (across from WTC), up 1 flight, 267-4142, N-RR-1 to Cortlandt, M-F 7-6, ch., c.c., exch. or rfd. Sells: **Prescription Drugs, Non-Prescription, & Toiletries.**
** **Essential Products**, 90 Water St. (Wall), 344-4288, J-M-RR-2-3 to Wall & Broad Sts., M-F 9-6, ch., no c.c., exch. or rfd. Takes mail-orders. Catalog. Very cooperative. Good copies. No floral fragrances. Sells: **Perfumes & Colognes.**
* **F&G Discount**, 2531 Broadway (94-5), 866-7830, 1-2-3 to 96, M-S 9-6, Sun 10-6, c.c., no ch., exch., no rfd. Sells: **Non-Prescription, & Toiletries.**
 First Cost, 90 E. 42nd St. at Park Av., 697-0244, 4-5-6-7 to Grand Central, M-F 8-7, SSun 10-5; Queens, 46-20 108 St., Corona, 271-1121, 7 to 111, ThS 9-6, F 9-9. Both stores: all cash, 7-day exch. or rfd. Sells: **Non-Prescription, & Toiletries, Clothing—Children's, Clothing—Men's, Clothing—Women's, Dinnerware & Cookware, Foods, Home-Improvement Items, Housewares, Jewelry & Gifts, Sporting Goods, Toys, Games & Hobbies, Warehouse Salvage Job-Lot.**
 Freeda Vitamins, 36 E. 41 (Mad.), 685-4980, 4-5-6-7 to Grand Central, M-Th 8:30-6:30, F 8:30-4, ch., c.c., exch., no rfd. Write or phone for catalog. Sells: **Vitamins.**
 G & Sons Dept. Store, Brooklyn, 4806 New Utrecht Av., 438-2604, B to 50th St., MTTh 10-9, WSun 10-6, F 10-4, ch., c.c., exch. or rfd. Sells: **Non-Prescription, & Toiletries, Housewares, Sporting Goods, Stationery & Art Supplies, Toys, Games & Hobbies.**
 Gallery Drugs, 131 E. 60 (Lex.), basement, 838-6765, N-RR-4-5-6 to 59th & Lex., M-F 8-6:30, S 9-4:30, ch., c.c., exch. or rfd. Not nearly as good as one would expect from a basement-place, but it just barely makes the listings here. Non-prescription items are generally not bargains here. Sells: **Prescription Drugs.**
 General Nutrition Center (GNC), about 20 stores in the 5 boroughs, ch., c.c., exch. or rfd. Their many specials are terrific, and even their regular prices aren't bad. A nationwide chain, excellent for mail-order vitamins, GNC, listed separately here. Sells: **Vitamins, Foods.**
 Genovese, Queens, 30-14 30th Av., L.I.C., 278-1901, RR to 30th Av.; Queens, 21-25 Broadway, L.I.C., 932-9200, RR to Broadway; Queens, 31-09 Ditmars Blvd., Astoria, 721-8666, RR to Ditmars; Queens, 30-09 Steinway St., Astoria, 274-6600, F-GG-N to Steinway St., RR to 30th Av.; Queens, 37-32 82nd St., Jackson Hts., 478-0700, 7 to 82nd St.; Queens, 136-51 Roosevelt Av., Flushing, 886-5280, 7 to Main St.; Queens, 46-02 Greenpoint Av., Sunnyside, 784-0070, 7 to 46th St.; Queens, 153-65 Cross Is. Pkwy., Whitestone, 767-6000, no subway stop nearby; Queens, 43-20 Bell Blvd., Bayside, 631-8200, no subway stop nearby. All stores: M-F 9-8, S 9-7, Sun 9-5, for later hours call individual store, ch., c.c., exch. or rfd. Not good prices on small housewares, stationery, candies. Generally not good on toiletries either. Inconsistent on toys. Only the prescription-department's recommended. Sells: **Prescription Drugs.**
* **GNC Vitamins**, 418 Wood St., Pittsburgh, PA 15222, 1-800-245-6562. Write or phone for catalog. Sells: **Vitamins.**
+ **Group National Contact Lens**, 1995 Broadway (67-8), rm. 605, 787-0733, 1 to 66, by appt.: M-F 10:30-6:30, S 9:30-2, c.c. +$4, no ch., exch. or rfd. Bonus discount to BF readers: 10%. Sells: **Contact-Lenses.**
 H&E Stores, Brooklyn, 1918 Kings Hwy., 376-3163, D-M-QB to Kings Hwy., M-S 9:30-7, all cash, 25-day exch. or rfd. Sells: **Non-Prescription, & Toiletries.**
* **Joann's Variety Store**, Brooklyn, 2209 Av. X, 648-8517, D-M-QB to Neck Rd., M-S 9-6, ch., c.c., exch. or rfd. But no returns if package is opened. Sells: **Non-Prescription, & Toiletries, Appliances, Home-Improvement Items, Housewares.**
 JRPS Discount, 2431 Broadway (89-90), 874-7828, 1 to 79, M-S 9-8, Sun 10-4, ch., c.c., exch. or rfd. Sells: **Non-Prescription, & Toiletries.**
** **Kings Houston Drugs**, 201 E. Houston St. (Orchard-Ludlow), 254-0066, F to 2nd Av., W-Sun 10-6:30, all cash, exch. or rfd. Especially strong on non-standard quantities, but also close to the best on the normal 100-tablet (or whatever) prescriptions. Sells: **Prescription Drugs, Non-Prescription, & Toiletries.**
 King's Pharmacy, Brooklyn, 2474 Flatbush Av. (U), 253-0200, no subway stop nearby; Brooklyn, 1928 Kings Hwy., 339-3500, D-M-QB to Kings Hwy.; Brooklyn, 1110 Kings Hwy., 375-5700, D-M-QB to Kings Hwy.; Brooklyn, 472 Kings Hwy., 336-5400, F to Kings Hwy.; Brooklyn, 3082 Ocean Av. (Voorhies), 891-8201, D-

M-QB to Sheepshead Bay; Queens, 93-17 63rd Dr., Rego Park, 459-3564, F-GG-N to 63rd Dr. All stores: M-S 9-10:45, Sun 10-9, ch., c.c., exch. or rfd. Sells: **Prescription Drugs, Non-Prescription, & Toiletries, Smoking Supplies.**

    ✝ **Lawrence Fashions**, 1000 6th Av. (37-8), 391-6693, B-D-F to 42, M-S 10-5, all cash, exch. or rfd. Also has eyelashes. Bonus discount to BF readers: 10% to 20%. Sells: **Wigs & Lashes.**

    LeRoy Pharmacy Prescriptions, 2507 Broadway (93), 222-2300, 1-2-3 to 96; 1294 Lexington Av. (87), 410-3510, 4-5-6 to 86; Queens, 61-28 Springfield Blvd., Bayside, 225-7660, no subway stop nearby; Bronx, 1448 Metropolitan Av., 823-4344, 6 to E. 177. All stores: M-S 9-7, Sun 10-5, ch., c.c., exch. or rfd. Although very good on prescriptions, they're definitely not recommended for anything else in the store—very uneven on toiletries, etc. Sells: **Prescription Drugs.**

    ✱ **Lou-Mark Trdg.**, 13 E. 17 (5th Av.), 242-9440, LL-N-QB-RR-4-5-6 to Union Sq., M-F 9-6, S 9-4, Sun 9-12, all cash, exch., no rfd. Sells: **Perfumes & Colognes, Appliances, Jewelry & Gifts.**

    Medco Surgical, Queens, 220-30 Jamaica Av., Queens Village, 740-9100, no subway stop nearby, M-F 9-6, all cash, exch. or rfd. Sells: **Medical, Surgical, Rehab. Eqt..**

    Midtown East Pharmacy, 725 3rd Av. (45-6), 986-7111, 4-5-6-7 to Grand Central, M-F 8-6:30, S 10-6, ch., c.c., exch. or rfd. Sells: **Prescription Drugs.**

    Milshap Pharmacy, 114 E. 16 (Irving Place), 674-7007, LL-N-QB-RR-4-5-6 to Union Sq., M-F 9-5:45, all cash, no exch. or rfd. Sells: **Prescription Drugs, Non-Prescription, & Toiletries, Housewares.**

    ✱ **Morris Discount**, Brooklyn, 1620 Av. U, 375-2529, D-M-QB to Av. U, M-F 9-7:30, S 10-6, all cash, exch. or rfd. Sells: **Non-Prescription, & Toiletries, Housewares.**

    Nature Food Centers, about 10 stores in the 5 boroughs, ch., c.c., exch. or rfd. Sells: **Vitamins.**

    ✱✱ **Nutrition Headquarters**, 104 W. Jackson St., Carbondale, IL 62901. Send for catalog. Sells: **Vitamins.**

    ✱✱✱ **Odd Job Trdg.**, 7 E. 40 (Mad.), 686-6825, B-D-F to 42, 7 to 5th Av.; 66 W. 48 (6th Av.), 575-0477, B-D-F to 47. Both stores: M-Th 8-5:30, F 8-3, Sun 10-5, ch., no c.c., 15-day exch. or rfd. Sells: **Non-Prescription, & Toiletries, Clothing—Men's, Dinnerware & Cookware, Foods, Home-Improvement Items, Housewares, Linens, Personal Accessories, Stationery & Art Supplies, Toys, Games & Hobbies, Warehouse Salvage Job-Lot.**

    Odd Lot Trdg., 33 W. 34 (5th-6th Avs.), 736-5243, B-D-F-N-QB-RR to 34; Queens, 19-40 37th St., Astoria, 932-3534, RR to Ditmars; Queens, 28-32 Steinway St., Astoria, 545-5604, RR to 30th Av., F-GG-N to Steinway St.; Queens, 103-54 94th St., Forest Hills, 263-5608, E-F to 75th Av.; Queens, 162-03 Jamaica Av., Jamaica, 657-4242, E-F to Parsons Blvd.; Queens, 103-54 94th St., Ozone Park, 738-2944, A-CC to Rockaway Blvd.; Brooklyn, 503 Fulton St., 625-7926, 2-3 to Hoyt; Brooklyn, 1166 E. 92nd St., 272-1482, LL to Rockaway Pkwy. All stores: MTWS 10-6, ThF 10-8, Sun 11-5, c.c., no ch., 7-day exch. or rfd. Other stores throughout the greater metropolitan area. Sells: **Non-Prescription, & Toiletries, Dinnerware & Cookware, Stationery & Art Supplies, Warehouse Salvage Job-Lot.**

    ✱✱ **Odds & Ends Job-Lots**, Queens, 88-09 Jamaica Av., Woodside, 441-6878, J to Woodhaven Blvd., M-S 9-6, Sun 9-3; Queens, 57-60 Woodside Av., Woodside, phoneless, 7 to 61st St., M-Th 10-7, F 10-9, S 9-6, Sun 9-5. Both stores: all cash, exch. or rfd. Sells: **Perfumes & Colognes, Non-Prescription, & Toiletries, Dinnerware & Cookware, Home-Improvement Items, Housewares, Jewelry & Gifts, Recordings & Tapes, Toys, Games & Hobbies, Warehouse Salvage Job-Lot.**

    ✱ **Park Av. Job Lot**, 270 Park Av. S. (21), 673-7536, 6 to 23, M-S 9-6, all cash, 7-day exch., no rfd. Many Slavic gift items. Sells: **Perfumes & Colognes, Clothing—Women's, Jewelry & Gifts, Warehouse Salvage Job-Lot.**

    ✱ **Pathmark Pharmacies**, 880 3rd Av. (53), 826-0670, E-F to Lex. Av.; 2039 Broadway (72), 787-2903, 1-2-3 to 72; 4910 Broadway (207), 569-2513, A to 207; 2551 Broadway at 96th, 222-2500, 1-2-3 to 96; Brooklyn, 376 Fulton St. (Smith), 624-4646, 2-3 to Hoyt, M-RR-2-3-4-5 to Borough Hall & Court St.; Brooklyn, 3823 Nostrand Av. (Z), 743-8933, no subway stop nearby; Queens, 57-13 Myrtle Av. (Seneca-Onderdonk), Ridgewood, 456-6067, M to Seneca; Queens, 1 Lefrack City Plaza (Junction Blvd. & L.I.E.), Elmhurst, 592-5525, F-GG-N to 63rd Dr. All stores: hours vary by location, ch., c.c., exch. or rfd. Other pharmacies in Pathmark supermarkets, Bkln., Qns., Bx., S.I. All stores recommended only for prescriptions, nothing

13: HEALTH & BEAUTY AIDS

else. Sells: **Prescription Drugs.**

Pay Less, 44 Water St. (Coenties Slip), 344-1084, N-RR-1 to South Ferry, M-F 7:30-6, all cash, exch., no rfd. Sells: **Non-Prescription, & Toiletries, Housewares.**

Pay Less Brooklyn, Brooklyn, 414 Av. U at E. 3rd St., 449-2678, no subway stop nearby, M-S 9-6, all cash, no exch. or rfd. Sells: **Non-Prescription, & Toiletries.**

Phil's, 9 E. 47 (5th Av.), 688-4144, B-D-F to 47, M-F 8:30-5:30, all cash, exch. or rfd. Sells: **Non-Prescription, & Toiletries.**

Prescription Headquarters, Queens, 40-06 Main St., Flushing, 886-4550, 7 to Main St., M-S 8-8; Queens, 106-24 71st Av., Forest Hills, 268-4066, E-F-GG-N to 71-Continental Avs., M-S 9-8. Both stores: all cash, exch. or rfd. Not good on toiletries and non-prescription items. Sells: **Prescription Drugs.**

Prism Optical, 10992 N.W. 7th Av., North Miami, FL 33168, ch., c.c., 30-day exch. or rfd. A mail-order operation. Send for catalog of frame-styles. Then send eyeglass-prescription. Sells: **Eyeglasses.**

Professional Contact Lens, 545 5th Av. (45), 14th floor, 883-0995, B-D-F to 47, 4-5-6-7 to Grand Central, by appt. (phone), ch., c.c., exch. or rfd. Sells: **Contact-Lenses.**

✳ **Pushcart**, 140 Church St. (Warren-Chambers), 962-4142, A-CC-1-2-3 to Chambers; 412 5th Av. (37-8), 398-9210, B-D-F to 42. Both stores: M-F 8-5:30, S 8-4:30, all cash, 15-day exch. or rfd. This is the same store as the Job Lot Trdg. Co., but the relative values in these merchandise-categories aren't as terrific; and most isn't even job-lot, but regular. Sells: **Perfumes & Colognes, Non-Prescription, & Toiletries, Vitamins, Cameras & Optical Eqt., Home-Improvement Items.**

✳ **Ray Variety**, 539 9th Av. at 40th, 736-2547, A-AA-CC-E to 42, M-S 9:30-6:30, all cash, exch. or rfd. Sells: **Non-Prescription, & Toiletries, Clothing—Men's, Linens.**

Robbins Men's Wear, 48 W. 14 (5th-6th), 691-2573, B-F-LL to 14th St. & 6th Av.; 146 E. 14 (3rd Av.), 260-0456, LL to 3rd Av.; 1265 Broadway (32), 684-5429, B-D-F-N-QB-RR to 34; 519 8th Av. (35), 564-3756, A-AA-CC-E to 34; 609 8th Av. (41), 564-1194, A-AA-CC-E to 42; 1717 Broadway (55), 581-7033, A-AA-B-CC-D-1 to 59; Queens, 38-17 Main St., Flushing, 445-7301, 7 to Main St.; Queens, 37-42 Junction Blvd., Corona, 424-0377, 7 to Junction Blvd.; Queens, 30-88 Steinway St., Astoria, 626-7180, F-GG-N to Steinway St.; Queens, 57-33 Myrtle Av. (Seneca), Ridgewood, 497-4489, M to Seneca; Brooklyn, 1213 Kings Hwy., 375-4133, D-M-QB to Kings Hwy.; Bronx, 279 E. Fordham Rd. (Kingsbridge Rd.), 367-2499, CC-D to Fordham Rd. All stores: M-S 9-7:30, all cash, exch. or rfd. No try-ons. Somewhat uneven values, but worth recommending for the things I'm recommending the chain for. Other stores in Long Island. Sells: **Non-Prescription, & Toiletries, Clothing—Men's, Sporting Goods.**

✳ **Roosevelt Drugs**, Queens, 74-19 Roosevelt Av., 424-1291, E-F-GG-N-7 to 74th-B'wy & Roosevelt-Jack.Hts., M-S 9-8, all cash, no exch. or rfd. Sells: **Prescription Drugs, Non-Prescription, & Toiletries.**

Royal Beauty Supply, Brooklyn, 1116 Av. U, 339-0700, D-M-QB to Av. U, M-F 9-6, S 9-5, c.c., no ch., exch. or rfd. Sells: **Beauty Supplies.**

✳✳ **RVP Vitamins**, 16 Nassau Av., Rockville Ctr., NY 11571, NY: 1-516-766-4140 call collect or outside the state: 1-800-645-2978. Write or phone for catalog. Sells: **Vitamins.**

S&J Stores, Brooklyn, 2029 86th St., 266-7837, B to 20th Av., MTThF 9-9, WS 9-8, Sun 10-5, all cash, exch. or rfd. Sells: **Non-Prescription, & Toiletries.**

Stur-Dee Vitamins, Austin Blvd., Island Park, NY 11558, for mail-order; and 222 Livingston St., Brooklyn, for retail (852-7600). Write for catalog. Sells: **Vitamins.**

SUNY Optometric Center, 100 E. 24 (Park Av. S.), 477-7900, 6 to 23, M-Th 9-7, F 9-5, ch., no c.c., exch. or rfd. Phone for appointment. Make sure optometrist indicates centers on the prescription he writes. See article above for details. Sells: **Optometrics.**

✳✳✳ **Sundown Vitamins**, P.O. Box 2247, Hollywood, FL 33022. Send for catalog. Sells: **Vitamins.**

Sweetheart Discount, 125 Church St. (Warren), 766-4537, A-CC-1-2-3 to Chambers, M-F 8:30-6, S 9:30-4, ch., no c.c., exch., no rfd. Sells: **Beauty Supplies, Perfumes & Colognes.**

The Bargain Lot, 333 7th Av. (28-9), 736-1346, 1 to 28, Sun-F 8-7:30, all

cash, no exch. or rfd. Sells: **Perfumes & Colognes, Warehouse Salvage Job-Lot.**
     Tight End, Brooklyn, 1309 Kings Hwy., 627-9765, D-M-QB to Kings Hwy., M-S 9-9, Sun 10-6, all cash, exch. or rfd. Sells: **Non-Prescription, & Toiletries.**
  ** **Townie Merchandise**, 212 W. 14 (7th Av), 929-8060 & 675-6662, 1-2-3 to 14, A-AA-CC-E-LL to 14 St. & 8 Av., M-S 10-6, all cash, exch., no rfd. Will special-order. Popular among seamen and Latin American tourists. Sells: **Perfumes & Colognes, Appliances, Clothing—Men's, Clothing—Women's.**
     Ultra Cosmetics, 135 W. 50 (6th-7th), 582-3510, B-D-F to 47, N-RR to 49th St., 7 days 8-8, c.c., no ch., exch. or rfd. Sells: **Beauty Supplies.**
     Unique Eyewear, 19 W. 34 (5th-6th), rm. 1218, 947-4977, B-D-F-N-QB-RR to 34, M-F 9-5, S 10-2, ch., no c.c., exch. or rfd. Sometimes very busy. Sells: **Eyeglasses.**
     United Beauty Supply, 49 W. 46 (5th-6th), 582-2324, B-D-F to 47, M-F 9-6, S 10-2:30, ch., no c.c., exch. or rfd. Sells: **Beauty Supplies.**
  ** **Vital Foods**, Redford Box 19340, Detroit, MI 48219, ch., c.c., exch. or rfd. Takes mail-orders. Catalog. Sells: **Vitamins.**
  ** **Weber's Job Lot**, 505 8th Av. at 35th, 564-7668, A-AA-CC-E to 34, M-F 10-6:30, S 10-6; 136 Church St. at Warren, 564-7668, A-CC-1-2-3 to Chambers, M-S 8-6; 2064 Broadway at 71st, 787-1644, 1-2-3 to 72, M-F 9-9, S 9-6, Sun 12-6. All stores: c.c., no ch., 7-day exch. or rfd. Some terrific values; others not good. Some prices wrongly marked on items each time I was at both stores; checkout counter said 'It's an error.' Sells: **Non-Prescription, & Toiletries, Dinnerware & Cookware, Home-Improvement Items, Jewelry & Gifts, Linens, Personal Accessories, Stationery & Art Supplies, Warehouse Salvage Job-Lot.**

14:
HIGH FIDELITY
Expect 25-60% discounts.

Here's a field where $100 spent knowledgeably and well can produce better results than $300 spent poorly. Not only are there tremendous variations in price between retail outlets on the same item, but there are equally wide variations in quality of components within a given price-range. In fact, an inexpensive component will occasionally be superior to one far more costly.

Most of the stores listed in this chapter will quote prices by phone. All you'll need to do is to tell the dealer the make and model-number of the item you want. But the big first decision is precisely that selection of components. This subject will be the focus of what follows.

Any wise choice of a hi-fi system has to be based on a clear conception of your own personal needs and priorities. For example, if you're heavy into tapes, a reel-to-reel machine may ultimately be lighter on your pocketbook than a cassette-model. But if you're only a light tape-user, you might as well go for the lighter deck. It'll cost you less, and you won't have to worry so much about the fact that the tapes will end up costing you more.

Once your specific needs have been determined, there are several publications which can greatly help narrow down the choice. Some of the high-fidelity testing and rating magazines publish annuals where you'll find charts comparing features and also manufacturers' technical specifications (which usually are quite reliable) for a vast range of competing components. *Audio* magazine's "Annual Equipment Directory" issue, published around October of each year, is the most thorough. Such charts ought to be the first stage in your search, but unfortunately the way they're presented—without exception—they tend to be just so much "So what?" One problem with them is that the definitions given of the technical specifications are either non-existent, or else comprehensible only to electrical engineers. None of the magazines provides definitions which tell the layman what kind of impact a particular spec will have on the sound he can expect to hear. Another major difficulty with these technical-comparison-charts is that they don't indicate which of the many quoted specs are the important ones; the average consumer isn't going to have the time or the patience to consider them all. Finally, the reader should have some way to know when an impressive spec is actually too impressive to hear. Herewith, then, are the chief things to look for in these charts, and definitions of these technical specs in terms of audible results:

AMPLIFIER CHARACTERISTICS:

Power per channel. For an average-sized room (about 2,000 cubic feet), and a speaker of average efficiency, you won't be able to use more than 25 watts RMS or 40 watts IHF, per channel, since this'll be sufficient to tear your ear drums out if played at full volume. If you use a highly efficient (or "sensitive") speaker, this wattage will be adequate even for a 9000-cubic-foot loft (say, 20' by 30' with 15'-high ceilings). A less efficient speaker will sock you with higher costs two ways: first, for the more powerful amplifier; and then for the higher electrical bills every month thereafter to run it. The only thing that's glamorous about a powerful amp is the corporate jet it helps buy for Con Ed's executives.

Distortion. This is given as a percentage-figure indicating how much of the output-signal is garbage that wasn't in the original (input-) signal. For hi-fi amplifiers, it shouldn't exceed 1%, and is usually well below that boundary, even at full power.

Frequency-Response. The audible frequency-range for the human ear, even for people with good hearing, is about 20-20,000 cycles per second (c.p.s.). No musical instrument goes below 25 c.p.s., and the ear has no reponse above 20,000 c.p.s. (Dogs can hear frequencies higher than that, but why should you pay $100 extra for an amplifier just to please your dog? Perhaps his musical tastes don't agree with yours.) If a hi-fi amp goes from 20-20,000 c.p.s. within a limit of 2, or at most 3, decibels (abbreviated "dB"), it'll reproduce sound indistinguishable from the original. The dB limit means that the response should not sink or rise more than the specified amount at any point throughout the 20-20,000 c.p.s. range. However, it's important to note—and little-recognized— that the deliverable frequency-response of an amplifier isn't given merely by the c.p.s.-range and associated dB-limits. It's totally dependent upon:

Power-Response. Also called "Power-Bandwidth." Like vibration for single-lens-reflex cameras, this is a technical specification which practically nobody talks about or pays any attention to, yet which determines whether other important specs are hogwash. If an amplifier is represented as going from 20-20,000 c.p.s., but delivers no power, say, below 50 or above 15,000 c.p.s., then those are the actual limits the amp will reproduce. Any frequency-response which is outside the range of the power-response is for all intents and purposes fictitious. It's not uncommon to find expensive amps specified flat all the way up to some absurd figure like 100,000 c.p.s., but whose power-response doesn't even go up to 30,000 c.p.s. If you're going to spend that kind of money, you might as well not disappoint Fido, who may be able to hear the difference.

TUNER CHARACTERISTICS:

Distortion. Same definition as given for amplifiers. Same standard: 1% or less.

Frequency-Response. Same definition as given for amplifiers. The applicable standard for FM tuners would be more tolerant, however. Few tuners are good to 20,000 c.p.s.; and even classical stations don't broadcast that high anyway, so what use would there be for that capacity? 40-15,000 c.p.s. within 2 dB would be a reasonable expectation.

Sensitivity. This is one—and generally the least important—of the three characteristics determining a tuner's capacity to receive weak signals. It's measured in micro-volts, or "uV." The lower the figure, the better. Expect less than 3 uV. Below 2 uV would be very good. But if the figure for a particular tuner is a bit too high, you can compensate by using a more powerful antenna. With the remaining two, you can't:

Capture-Ratio. This is another trait determining the number of stations the tuner will receive clearly. The unit of measurement is decibels. Again, the lower the figure, the better. Below 3 dB would be acceptable; less than 2 dB, very good. A poor capture-ratio will show up as a tendency for two stations on the same or nearby frequencies to be heard simultaneously. In a large metropolitan area like New York, with so many closely-spaced stations on the dial, this can be a more troublesome problem than sensitivity.

Selectivity. This is the third and last determinant of powerful reception. It's very similar to capture-ratio, only not as important; and otherwise virtually the same comments apply, except that here the measurement is given as a dB-figure within a specified number of kilohertz (kHz); and the higher the number of dB's and larger the number of kHz, the better. Plus or minus 400 kHz, the figure should be 60 dB; and 70 dB would be very good.

RECEIVERS:

These are simply amplifiers + tuners together.

RECORD-CHANGERS & TURNTABLES:

Tracking-Error. This is the major cause of distortion in the playing of records. The tone-arm changes its angle of orientation toward the direction of the record-groove as it plays from the outside to the inside of the disc. Ideally, the needle would always be held parallel to the groove, but the change in tone-arm-orientation prevents this. Tracking-error should be no more than 2 degrees, and on turntables it's usually within that limit, but on some makes of changers the figure runs higher. The longer the distance from the tone-arm pivot to the needle, the lower the tracking-error. Of course, error is always biggest at the innermost grooves of a record; and this is one reason why distortion there is also greater.

Wow & Flutter. These are irregularities in speed, and occur occasionally in machines whose printed specs don't show them. What's at issue, really, is the reliability of the mechanism. But still, if the figure for either wow (slow variation) or flutter (rapid variation) is half of a percent or more in the manufacturer's specifications, watch out. The mechanical-reliability factor is one reason why a consensus of opinions by the rating-magazines is especially important on turntables and changers, and so is the view hi-fi repair-specialists have of the various makes. (See the related comments about repairmen's opinions in Chapter One.) If your house-wiring isn't good, or if the current varies, you can expect serious problems here even with good equipment. A warning-sign in this regard is a slight dimming of light-bulbs or shrinking of the television-picture whenever the refrigerator-motor turns on. If this tends to happen in your apartment, one consequence might be some wow when playing records.

Rumble. You'll hear this as a thumping sound. This, too, is a mechanical problem which occurs more often with changers than with turntables which are simpler. In any case, the figure should be higher than 45 dB.

TAPES-DECKS & RECORDERS:

Reliability of the mechanism is a terribly important factor here; and the same comments apply that were just made under "Wow & Flutter" for record-changers and turntables. For reel-to-reel machines, there's one other immediate factor to consider: the slowest tape-speed. For example, the performance of Tandberg reel-to-reel decks is so outstanding at 7.5 and 3.75 inches-per-second, that these units also have a 1.88 i.p.s.-speed. That slow speed is a quick sign—and an accurate one—of the stellar performance of Tandberg reel-to-reel recorders. If a deck has a reputation for reliability, and also offers an especially slow operating-speed, you know that the unit is exceptional. Of course, a slow operating-speed has one more-direct advantage: It means that you can get a greater amount of music onto a reel of tape. A machine which matches at 3.75 i.p.s. the performance of other decks at 7.5 i.p.s. is going to cut your tape-costs in half. You'll be able to fit 3 stereo hours onto the normal 7" reel, rather than the usual 1.5 hours, without any sacrifice in sound-quality; and you won't have to turn the reel over as often.

Most of the important technical specifications applicable to decks have already been defined, and the standards are: not more than 1% distortion; a frequency-response from at least 40-15,000 c.p.s. within 2 dB, or 30-18,000 c.p.s. within 3 dB; less than .5% wow and flutter. (The slower the speed that meets these specs, the better the machine.) In addition, one should also consider:

Signal/Noise Ratio. This indicates how much tape-hiss you'll hear along with the music. 60 dB or higher is good on cassette-recorders and at the 7.5-i.p.s. speed on reel-to-reel machines.

SPEAKERS:

Here we have the weakest link in the hi-fi chain. Speakers are usually the greatest source of distortion—especially in the low-frequency or bass region—and the chief limiting factor for frequency-response. (For example, any speaker that can reproduce 40 c.p.s. within 3 dB, and with less than 5% distortion, is doing a Herculean job.) Two important factors in addition to those previously defined, which should be considered with regard to speakers, are:

Efficiency. The importance of this was earlier discussed in relation to amplifier-power. The measurement is usually expressed as sensitivity in dB for 1 watt at 1 meter, over the frequency-range of 100-10,000 c.p.s., with 80 dB being very inefficient, and 110 dB being super-efficient (and being many times louder than the inefficient speaker).

Transient Response. This is the speed with which a stopped sound stops. You don't want the speaker-diaphragm to bounce back and forth and make a suddenly stopped crash or "tone-burst" seem to the ear more like a thud. Poor transient response is actually a variety of distortion that's unique to loudspeakers, because it's caused by the momentum of the speaker-diaphragm.

Considering how expensive a hi-fi system can be, and how even a costly brand of component may be ill-suited to your particular needs, it's advisable to read as many test-reports on a component as you can before making your decision. Ruby's Book Sale, at 119 Chambers St. (732-8676), sells recent backissues of some audio magazines, and they're about half-price. Also, the public library has many of them. Ask the librarian to show you backissues of magazines that rate recordings and stereo equipment. The names of some of these publications: *Stereo Review, Musician, American Record Guide, Audiogram, Audio Alternatives, Audio, Consumers' Reports, Stereo & Tape Quarterly of Consumer Guide*. However, don't take these ratings as gospel. They can be especially misleading on tape decks and recorders, and on turntables and changers, where you'll want to know about the reputation for reliability of the mechanism, not just about electronic performance which is the chief thing that can be tested and rated by the numbers.

Many people think that they can simplify their choice of hi-fi components by basing their decisions on listening-room tests. But such a test can easily mislead. Through ineptitude or design on the salesman's part, you can get the wrong impression. For example, if you're shopping for speakers, the tone-controls of the ones being compared may not be in the same position. Or their efficiency may not be the same, so that one will sound much louder than the other. And if you're listening to two tape-decks, are you sure that each is set up with the kind of tape best suited to its particular characteristics? Finally, how do the showroom-acoustics compare with those in your home?

However, such a live demonstration can serve a useful function nonetheless. Some aspects of hi-fi performance are not reducible to technical specs—especially so with loudspeakers. Therefore, you might want first to select a few competing models of speakers by the specs, and then to go to a showroom which permits you to check that the tone-controls are set the same, and that the amplifiers etc. are the same. You'll be trying to find the most realistic-sounding speaker—the one which, for its price, sounds less like a speaker than the others do. But just keep in mind the limitations that such a demonstration can have. Otherwise, you may end up taking home the loudspeakers that the showroom wants to dump, rather than the best ones for you to buy.

In my product-recommendations below, I've taken into account equipment-reviews in many publications over the past decade, opinions of hi-fi repairmen I've spoken with, manufacturers' published technical specifications and explanatory literature, and my own personal impressions hearing equipment in apartments and in audio showrooms. The brands I've selected are those that seem most consistently to score highest against the price-competition from other makers. Most of the named manufacturers produce components in all price-ranges; and I've tried to exclude any makers—such as AR or KLH in speakers, for example—which offer uneven value throughout the particular line.

RECOMMENDED PRODUCTS:

Speakers: EPI (Epicure), Advent. **Receivers, Tuners, Amplifiers:** Toshiba, Technics, Sherwood. **Equalizers:** MXR (sold not at hi-fi outlets, but at musical-instrument dealers listed in Chapter 20). **Cassette Decks:** Toshiba, Onkyo. **Reel-to-Reel Decks:** Tandberg. (In the lower price-ranges, Akai has machines worth considering; but then I'd rather go cassette, because Tandberg is simply the only company that offers quality in reel-to-reel at anything less than stratospheric prices; they've got this field sewn up.) **Turntables, Changers:** Vector Research, Hitachi, JVC, Garrard, Dual, PE, Toshiba, Technics. **Phono Cartridges:** Grado. (This company is easily the standout in the entire audio field world-wide. Its factory and only offices are a modest storefront in Brooklyn. They never advertise, and don't even publish technical literature about their line. But their cartridges sell like hotcakes. Joe Grado used to be a watchmaker, and when he started applying this precision workmanship and engineering to cartridges 30 years ago, he just mowed down the competition, and he's been doing it ever since. His cartridges have always stunned equipment-reviewers with their value, getting consistent top ratings; yet they've always been priced about 80-90% below the competition. His latest, the model GTE+1, with his own patented high-output fluxbridging design, lists at $15, yet beats any $600 moving-coil cartridge. The Model G+, listing at $100, is a studio-cartridge used at many FM stations, and is superior to any other maker's units at any price. I discovered Grado about a decade ago when I noticed that reviewers were unanimously acclaiming the $10 Model FTR as the best-performing home-audio cartridge; and since then, I've bought only Grado and have found them consistently superb. The Grado company has announced that they should soon be coming out with their first speaker-system, which they claim in prototype outperforms anything that currently exists. Its size: 9x11x13 inches. The projected price: $500 each. Is Joe Grado now about to start knocking the speaker-industry, too, for a loop? Stay tuned.) Shure. (Recommended for cartridge-weights below 1.5 grams. Otherwise, stick with Grado, which is slightly better quality, and which of course is much cheaper.)

RECOMMENDED STORES:

hi-fi (ALSO SEE CH. 1, "SMALL APPL.")

(examples: amplifiers, cartridges, cassette recorders, changers, compact stereos, decks, headphones, loudspeakers, microphones, phonographs, receivers, recorders, speakers, stereos, tape recorders, tone arms, tuners, turntables)

Audio Audio (925-5868); ****L&J Audio (425-2530); ****Metro Electronics**

14: HIGH FIDELITY

(406-2760); ***Audiomatic Electronics** (686-5500); ***Bryce** (575-8600); ***Garment Hi-Fi** (944-2120); ***L&N Electroline** (924-8677); ***Morel Electronics** (964-4570); ***STL Electronics** (849-7627); ***Stereo & Video Wholesale** (939-8561); **+Eastern Odd Lot** (766-9151); **Audio Factory** (939-8561); **Classic Electronics** (732-5471); **EBA Associates** (Brooklyn, 252-3400); **E.Z. Stereo** (Brooklyn, 383-0150); **Park Av. Audio** (685-8101); **Ramco Electronics** (966-6056).

phono cartridges & needles
**Lyle Cartridges (Brooklyn, 871-3303).

records/tapes: CH. 25

hi-fi accessories
(examples: antennas, batteries, cords, plugs, tubes)
*+Court Radio (227-6456); ***Electronic Odd-Lots** (398-1759); ***Taft Electronics** (575-5194); **Ramco Electronics** (966-6056).

STORES-DIRECTORY

Phone a store before you go out of your way to visit it. Especially do this during July and August, when most establishments reduce or eliminate weekend-hours.

In the listings below, "*" means especially recommended, "+" means that the store offers a bonus discount to BF readers, "ch." and "c.c." mean respectively checks and credit cards, and "exch." and "rfd." mean respectively exchange and refund. Nearest subway-stops are shown. For example, "B-D-F to 47" means to take the B, D, or F train to 47th Street. Store-hours are also indicated, with days of the week abbreviated, like "M-S 8-6."

** Audio Audio, 42 Canal St. (Orchard), 925-5868, F to E. Broadway, 7 days 11-6, ch., c.c., +5% on c.c., exch., no rfd. Specializes in high-end (more expensive) audio brands. Has audio showroom. Sells: **Hi-Fi**.

Audio Factory, 939-8561, c.c., no ch. Sells strictly by phone. Sells: **Hi-Fi**.

* Audiomatic Electronics, 1263 Broadway (32), 2nd floor, 686-5500, B-D-F-N-QB-RR to 34, M-F 9:30-6:30, S 10-6, ch., c.c., exch., no rfd. Sells: **Hi-Fi, Recordings & Tapes**.

* Bryce, 115 W. 40 (6th-B'wy), 575-8600, B-D-F to 42, M-F 9-5:45, S 9-4, ch., c.c., exch., no rfd. Has audio showroom. Sells: **Hi-Fi, Appliances, Office Equipment**.

Classic Electronics, 91 Chambers St. (B'wy-Church), 732-5471, A-CC-1-2-3 to Chambers, N-RR to City Hall, M-S 9-5:30, c.c., no exch., no rfd. Sells: **Hi-Fi**.

*+ Court Radio, 143 Chambers St. (W. B'wy), 227-6456, A-CC-1-2-3 to Chambers, M-S 9:30-5:30, all cash, no exch. or rfd. Most is govt.-surplus, tubes and parts, no other accessories. Sells: **Hi-Fi Accessories, Home-Improvement Items**.

+ Eastern Odd Lot, 113 Chambers St. (Church-W.Bwy), 766-9151, A-CC-1-2-3 to Chambers, M-S 9:30-6, exch. no rfd. c.c., no ch. Radios and damaged speakers. Bonus discount to BF readers: 5% to 10%. Sells: **Hi-Fi**.

EBA Associates, Brooklyn, 2329 Nostrand Av. (I), 252-3400, 3-4 to Flatbush Av., MTTh 9-8:15, WFS 9-6, all cash, no exch. or rfd. Bonus discount to BF readers: 5% to 10%. Sells: **Hi-Fi, Appliances**.

* Electronic Odd-Lots, 60 W. 45 (6th Av.), 398-1759, B-D-F to 47, M-S 9-6, c.c., no ch., exch. or rfd. Sells: **Hi-Fi Accessories**.

E.Z. Stereo, Brooklyn, 892 Manhattan Av. (Greenpoint Av.), 383-0150&0168, GG to Greenpoint Av., MTFS 10-7, W 10-6, Th 10-8, c.c., no ch., exch., no rfd. Sells: **Hi-Fi, Appliances**.

* Garment Hi-Fi, 55 W. 39 (5th-6th), 944-2120, B-D-F to 42, M-F 9-7, S 10-4, c.c., no ch., 14-day exch., no rfd. Full audio showroom. Very nice people. Low-key atmosphere. Sells: **Hi-Fi, Appliances**.

14: HIGH FIDELITY

** **L&J Audio**, 3 Hanover Sq. (Wm.-Pearl), 425-2530, J-M-RR-2-3 to Wall & Broad Sts., M-F 8-6, Sun 10-3, c.c. +5%, no ch., no exch. or rfd. Will special-order. Takes mail-orders. Sells: **Hi-Fi, Appliances.**

* **L&N Electroline**, 42 W. 14 (5th-6th), 924-8677, B-F-LL to 14th St. & 6th Av., 7 days 10-7, ch., c.c. +6%, exch., no rfd. Sells: **Hi-Fi.**

** **Lyle Cartridges**, Brooklyn, 365 Dahill Rd. (Cortelyou), 871-3303 & 1-800-221-0906 outside NYS, F to Ditmas, M-F 9-4:30, exch., no rfd. Cash, money-order, or certified check. Mail-order. Catalog. Sells all makes. Sells: **Phono Cartridges & Needles.**

** **Metro Electronics**, 81 W.B'wy at Warren, 406-2760, A-CC-1-2-3 to Chambers, M-F 9-6, S 10-5, ch., c.c. +6%, exch., no rfd. Has audio showroom. Sells: **Hi-Fi.**

* **Morel Electronics**, 57 Park Place at W. B'wy, 964-4570, 2-3 to Park Place, M-F 9-6, S 10-5, ch., c.c., exch., no rfd. New and prime-condition used. Sells: **Hi-Fi.**

Park Av. Audio, 425 Park Av. S. at 29th St., 685-8101, 6 to 28, M-F 10-6, S 10-4, ch., c.c., exch., no rfd. Will special-order. Specializes in high-end audio only. Sells: **Hi-Fi.**

Ramco Electronics, 365 Canal St. (W. B'wy), 966-6056, A-AA-CC-E-1 to Canal, M-S 10-6, Sun 11-5, c.c., no ch., no exch. or rfd. Closeout speakers and accessories, and damaged speakers. Sells: **Hi-Fi, Hi-Fi Accessories.**

* **STL Electronics**, 849-7627&7571. For phone-quote, leave model number and your phone on their answering machine. Sells: **Hi-Fi, Appliances.**

* **Stereo & Video Wholesale**, 939-8561, c.c., no ch., no exch. or rfd. Sells by phone, ships. There's usually a busy-signal. Not easy to get through to them, so I'd skip this one. Sells: **Hi-Fi.**

* **Taft Electronics**, 68 W. 45 (6th Av.), 575-5194, B-D-F to 47; 27 Park Row, 964-8685, J-M-RR-4-5-6 to Chambers & Bkln. Bridge, A-CC-J-M-RR-2-3-4-5 to B'wy-Nassau & Fulton. Both stores: M-F 9-6, S 9-4, c.c., no ch., no exch. or rfd. Sells: **Hi-Fi Accessories, Recordings & Tapes.**

15:
HOME-IMPROVEMENT ITEMS
Expect 25-60% discounts.

Virtually all of the stores listed in this chapter will quote prices by phone. But be aware that in order for two prices to be able to be compared, you must first be quite specific about what you're seeking. For example, if one lumber-yard quotes on #1-grade shelving (free of knots), while another quotes on the far cheaper #3-grade (quite knotty), it's not fair to compare those two prices. You'd first have to visit your local lumber-yards to see samples, and to ask which shelving is which grade; then you'd learn what's suitable for your purposes. And then you'd be prepared to ask for phone-quotes.

BASIC HOUSEHOLD TOOL-KIT:

Everybody should have one—a kind of first-aid kit for the apartment—but what should it include? The following: 1) a screwdriver with a big tip for big screws; 2) a screwdriver with a small tip for small screws; 3) two pairs of slip-joint pliers, which may or may not be different from each other, but both of which will be needed because you've got two hands and you may need to use both to bend or twist or stretch something sometime; 4) a wire-cutter; 5) a steel file; 6) a power-drill, and a drill-set for same; 7) an electric hand-held jigsaw, and at least one blade for same, so that you can cut shelves and boards; 8) a hack-saw, with a blade for same, so that you can cut steel; 9) a heavy-duty springloaded or motorized stapler, with various-sized staple-sets for same; 10) an electrical extension-cord, and perhaps a 3-prong-to-2 adapter, so that you can use the power-tools at a distance from an outlet; 11) a claw-hammer with a 16-or 20-ounce head.

Now you can take on the world. Or at least your apartment.

BASIC BURGLAR-PROTECTION COURSE:

Your door probably has a bad lock on it, in this city where according to a poll in the *New York Times* 6 out of 10 residents either have been robbed in the past two years or know someone who has been. If your door-key can be copied in any hardware store, and for less than $2, then your door has a bad lock—one which can be picked in a few seconds by thousands of people who learn to do just that at crime-colleges called by names like "Rikers Island" or "Spofford Juvenile Detention Center." Maybe your lock will keep you out, or your friends, but not your enemies. Of course, there are individuals who want to let the burglars in, believing this to be their private contribution to the welfare of "the disadvantaged." These people, who equate the burglars with the poor—as if to be poor were to be criminal—do America's poor much injustice by this fallacious and classist sentiment; and they will prefer to use a bad lock. Others of us, however, will rather keep professional criminals out of our apartments, and so will seek out locks which can do what locks are supposedly constructed to do.

The thing that makes a bad lock bad is its cylinder. You don't need a locksmith to replace a cylinder; you can do it yourself, and cheaply—and that might well be the best and most sensible investment you can make in home-security. If you want to self-install, buy from one of the stores listed for "Hardware, Locks, Tools"; otherwise, check out the "Locksmiths."

The first step up from a bad lock-cylinder is the round-key type: about $10-15. Very few people can pick it. The next step up is the Medeco cylinder: about $20-30. Virtually no one—not even most skilled pros—can pick it; and anyone who could, would probably find easier ways to break in. The top step is the Fichet cylinder: about $60-80. It's pick-proof; and if you're willing to put in the rest of the huge investment needed to transform your apartment into a safe, this is the lock-cylinder for you.

But there's more to a good lock than a good lock-cylinder. The lock itself should be of a dead-bolt type, which means that slipping a card through the door-jamb won't force it open. Finally, there should be a guard-plate over the lock on the outside of the door, so that no one will be able to hack around the cylinder and rip it out. And you should consider a Fox police lock behind the door if the door-frame isn't strong. Burglars have been known to push many such doors in; the Fox lock prevents this.

Of course, if your apartment is accessible from the roof via the fire-escape, you're more vulnerable through the fire-escape window than by any door; and if in addition yours is one of the top two apartments nearest the roof, then statistics say you've probably been burgled many times already; and if you don't have gates over that window, then you're either very lucky or very much courting trouble. Many burglaries are from the roof, down the fire-escape, in through the window; and these are the apartments that are hit. Window-gates are closed and locked when you're gone, and they prevent burglaries of such apartments.

PAINTING & WALL-PAPERING:

The cheapest way to get wall-vinyls is to buy whole rolls from the two stores I recommend that are suppliers of coated fabrics—H&H, and M&R, both on Broadway near Grand. Then the price can be as low as about $1 per square yard. But these wall-coverings have no patterns. For Marimekko and the other design-stuff, check out the regular wall-coverings-stores I recommend.

One advantage of using wall-vinyls is that they can be a cheap and easy substitute for plastering and spackling.

The best brand of paint, both latex and oil-based, is Benjamin Moore. It has the best hiding-power, and is the most rugged against repeated washings. However, there have been problems with their yellow paints—only that color; the others are tops. Red Devil paints are cheaper, and are also good.

Two of the recommended paint-stores—Mercury and C.W. Keenan, both in Brooklyn (where most of the other discount paint-stores also are)—manufacture their own makes of commercial paints; and these offer even better value than do discounted Benjamin Moore or Red Devil. The two stores offer top-quality lines, as well as decent super-cheap budget lines, all of their own manufacture.

RECOMMENDED PRODUCTS:
See above.

RECOMMENDED STORES:

burglar & auto alarms

***+**C.O.M.B. Co.** (intermittent stock, outside NYC, 1-800-328-0609, catalog is free if you mention this book); ***Circle Auto Lock** (989-8650, only auto locks and alarms); ***Metro Lock** (564-2927); ***REM Security** (533-1555); **A.H. Burglar Alarms** (925-4415); **R.B.D. Lock & Alarm** (383-5888).

electrical parts

*+**Court Radio** (227-6456); **Trans-Am Electronics** (226-3893).

fences

****Boundary Wholesale Fence** (Queens, 847-3400).

fire-extinguishers

***Consumers Distributing** (Queens, 268-2091); +**Fire Extinguisher Sales** (924-2299); **Canal Surplus** (966-3275); **Fire Extinguisher Maintenance** (966-4830).

fireplace supplies

(includes: andirons, fireplaces, firewood)
*****Alexander's Hardware** (intermittent stock, 267-0336); ****Brass Loft Factory Outlet** (226-5467); **Quality Firewood** (260-7209).

garden/lawn eqt.

(examples: edge trimmers, lawn-mowers)
*****Job Lot Trdg.** (intermittent stock, 962-4142).

glass & mirrors

*****East Side Glass** (674-8355); ****Weiser & Teitel** (233-1441); ***Walton Mirror Works** (Brooklyn, 388-6710); **Alliance Art Glass** (410-3994); **Gramercy Window Systems** (777-5226); **Rainbow Mirror** (Brooklyn, 438-0332).

small tools

(includes: small locks, screwdrivers, tire-pumps)
*****Alexander's Hardware** (intermittent stock, 267-0336); *****Bag Man** (560 8952); *****Job Lot Trdg.** (intermittent stock, 962-4142); *****Odd Job Trdg.** (intermittent stock, 686-6825); ***+**Mills Sales** (477-1000); ****R&F Electronics** (679-5962); ****Weber's Job Lot** (intermittent stock, 564-7668); ***Eighty-Eight Cent Shops** (753-6969); ***Susan Trdg.** (431-8529); **First Cost** (intermittent stock, 697-0244).

hardware, locks, tools

(includes: adhesives, axes, brackets, buffers, drills, files, glues, hammers, hatchets, hinges, knife-sharpeners, lathes, levels, locks, nails, pliers, sandpapers, sanders, saws, screwdrivers, screws, sharpeners, shelving, towel-racks, vises, wrenches)

****+**C.O.M.B. Co.** (intermittent stock, outside NYC, 1-800-328-0609, catalog is free if you mention this book); ***Alexander's Hardware** (intermittent stock, 267-0336); ***Vercesi Hardware** (475-1883); **Leslie Schiffer Locks** (677-7530); **Odds & Ends Job-Lots** (intermittent stock, Queens, 441-6878); **Reliance Hardware** (473-3080); **Weilgus Bros. Hardware** (267-1512); *Black & Decker Service** (929-6450); *Hester St. Housewares** (260-6930); *Joann's Variety Store** (Brooklyn, 648-8517); *Pushcart** (962-4142); *Tinkers Paradise** (962-3826); **Long Island Janitor Supply** (Queens, 639-4131); **M. Kessler Hardware** (226-6722).

locksmiths (ALSO SEE PRECEDING)

*Metro Lock** (564-2927); *REM Security** (533-1555); +**A-Art Locksmiths** (674-7650); **R.B.D. Lock & Alarm** (383-5888).

light bulbs

***Alexander's Hardware** (intermittent stock, 267-0336); ***Job Lot Trdg.** (intermittent stock, 962-4142); **Odds & Ends Job-Lots** (intermittent stock, Queens, 441-6878); **Weber's Job Lot** (intermittent stock, 564-7668); *Eighty-Eight Cent Shops** (753-6969); **International Fluorescent** (966-1096).

lamp-parts

*Grand Brass Lamp Parts** (226-2567).

lumber

(includes: accoustical and ceiling tiles, cork, doors, plywood, shelving, windows, wood)

****+**Industro Bldg. Products** (Bronx, 294-8000); **Walter E. Umla Lumber** (Brooklyn, 624-3350); *Astoria Lumber** (Queens, 786-2770); *Fairway Lumber** (Queens, 392-4440); **Auction Outlet** (Queens, 641-5872); **Boro Park Lumber** (Brooklyn, 853-3100); **McDonald Home Ctr.** (Brooklyn, 338-5700).

masonry supplies

(examples: bricks, building-materials, cement, cinder-block, concrete, sand)

****+**Industro Bldg. Products** (Bronx, 294-8000); **Ferrara Bros.** (Queens, 848-8200); **Long Island Janitor Supply** (Queens, 639-4131); **McDonald Home Ctr.** (Brooklyn, 338-5700).

motors & fans (ALSO: CH.'S 1, 16)

****+**C.O.M.B. Co.** (intermittent stock, outside NYC, 1-800-328-0609, catalog is free if you mention this book); ***Alexander's Hardware** (intermittent stock, 267-0336); **Chandelier Warehouse** (Brooklyn, 388-800); **Lamp Warehouse** (Brooklyn, 436-2207); **NY Ceiling Fan Ctr.** (254-6720); **O.Q. Mktg.** (966-6735); **Canal Electric Motor** (966-1377); **Canal Surplus** (966-3275).

paints

(includes: air-brushes, brushes, compressors, drop-cloths, lacquers, plasters, rollers, sprayers, tarps, urethanes, varnishes)

*****Mercury Paint Factory** (Brooklyn, 469-8787); ****+**Harry Weinstein & Sons** (Brooklyn, 638-7207); ***Alexander's Hardware** (intermittent stock, 267-0336); ****C.W. Keenan Industrial Paints** (Brooklyn, 338-7800); ***Franklin & Lennon Paint** (864-2460); ***Vercesi Hardware** (475-1883); **Gemco Paint** (Brooklyn, 376-9001); **Midwood Paint/Wallpaper** (Brooklyn, 338-0595); **Weber's Job Lot** (intermittent stock,

15: HOME-IMPROVEMENT ITEMS

564-7668); ***Brooklyn Elton Paint** (Brooklyn, 743-0660); ***Pushcart** (962-4142); ***Schatz Steinway** (Queens, 721-0777); **Brooklyn Paint Fair** (Brooklyn, 434-8000); **D. Cohen Paints** (Brooklyn, 375-7042); **Long Island Janitor Supply** (Queens, 639-4131); **Nat Skop** (Brooklyn, 256-4913); **Resro Paint** (Brooklyn, 748-0338).

wallcoverings

(wallpapers and wallvinyls)

***+**Harry Weinstein & Sons** (Brooklyn, 638-7207); ****H&H Plastics** (226-7363); ****Irv-Dan-Ace Wallpaper** (Brooklyn, 338-6837); ****Midwood Paint/Wallpaper** (Brooklyn, 338-0595); *+**Sheila's Wallstyles** (966-1663); ***Brooklyn Elton Paint** (Brooklyn, 743-0660); ***Schatz Steinway** (Queens, 721-0777); ***Webster Wallpapers** (Bronx, 367-0055); **Art Brite Wallpaper** (354-6060); **Brooklyn Paint Fair** (Brooklyn, 434-8000); **M&R Plastic** (564-8824); **Wallpaper Mart** (889-4800).

plumbing supplies

(examples: bath tubs, bathroom vanities, faucets, pumps, shower stalls, sinks, toilets)

****Adco Distributing** (Brooklyn, 788-5916); ****Arnold Plumbing Supply** (Brooklyn, 629-1360); ***Pushcart** (962-4142); **Bruce Supply** (Brooklyn, 259-4900); **Hendel Plumbing Supply** (Queens, 845-3000); **L&A Plumbing Supply** (Brooklyn, 998-0130); **Long Island Janitor Supply** (Queens, 639-4131); **Majestic Plumbing Supply** (Queens, 843-6500).

hot tubs, jacuzzis, spas

***Baths International** (242-7158).

roofing supplies

(examples: sheet-metal, tar)
Standard Tinsmith (674-2240).

shades/blinds

***Bookbinder Modern Blinds** (966-1585); ***Kingsboro Venetain Blind** (Brooklyn, 238-5353); ***Mitsu** (947-7892).

radiator-enclosures

Kustom Radiator Enclosures (674-3213).

flags

Maybeck Flags (Queens, 297-4410).

gummed tapes

***Susan Trdg.** (431-8529); **C.K.&L. Surplus** (966-1745).

rubber & foam

Canal Rubber (226-7339).

STORES-DIRECTORY

Phone a store before you go out of your way to visit it. Especially do this during July and August, when most establishments reduce or eliminate weekend-hours.

In the listings below, "*" means especially recommended, "+" means that the store offers a bonus discount to BF readers, "ch." and "c.c." mean respectively checks and credit cards, and "exch." and "rfd." mean respectively exchange and refund. Nearest sub-

15: HOME-IMPROVEMENT ITEMS

way-stops are shown. For example, "B-D-F to 47" means to take the B, D, or F train to 47th Street. Store-hours are also indicated, with days of the week abbreviated, like "M-S 8-6."

+ **A-Art Locksmiths**, 187 2nd Av. (12), 674-7650, 6 to Astor, LL to 3rd Av., M-S 9-6, c.c., no ch., exch., no rfd. Very cooperative. Largest locks-selection in NYC. Makes keys for all. Extremely knowledgeable—and informative—about all brands. But discounts here are normally small. Bonus discount to BF readers: 5%. Sells: **Locksmiths.**

** **Adco Distributing**, Brooklyn, 571 3rd Av. (15), 788-5916, N-RR to Prospect Av., M-S 8:30-5, c.c., no ch., exch., no rfd. No TV sets, but good selection of large appliances; also some plumbing supplies. Sells: **Plumbing Supplies, Appliances.**

A.H. Burglar Alarms, 340 Canal St. (Church), 925-4415, A-AA-CC-E-1 to Canal, M-S 9:30-5:30, ch., (but not on Saturday) no c.c., exch., no rfd. Sells: **Burglar & Auto Alarms.**

*** **Alexander's Hardware**, 60 Reade St. (B'wy), 267-0336, N-RR to City Hall, A-CC-1-2-3 to Chambers, M-F 8:30-6, S 8:30-5, ch., c.c., exch. or rfd. Large selection. Merits a long time browsing. Has great bargains in some obscure corners. Often has top quality cutlery at incredibly low prices. Much furniture-hardware. Abrasives. Sells: **Fireplace Supplies, Small Tools, Hardware, Locks, Tools, Light Bulbs, Motors & Fans, Paints, Stationery & Art Supplies, Warehouse Salvage Job-Lot.**

Alliance Art Glass, 169 E. 88 (3rd Av.), 410-3994, 4-5-6 to 86, M-F 9-6, S 9-5, ch., no c.c., no exch. or rfd. Custom or do-it-yourself. Doesn't sell glass alone. Sells: **Glass & Mirrors, Stationery & Art Supplies.**

** **Arnold Plumbing Supply**, Brooklyn, 1254 Utica Av. (D), 629-1360, no subway stop nearby, M-F 7:30-4:30, S 8-2, ch., no c.c., no exch. or rfd. Sells: **Plumbing Supplies.**

* **Art Brite Wallpaper**, 46 W. 46 (6th Av.), 354-6060, B-D-F to 47, M-F 10-5, all cash, no exch. or rfd. Sells: **Wallcoverings.**

* **Astoria Lumber**, Queens, 29-70 Northern Blvd., L.I.C., 786-2770, E-F-GG-N-RR-7 to Queens(boro) Plaza, M-F 8-4:30, S 8-2, ch., c.c., no exch or rfd. Sells: **Lumber.**

Auction Outlet, Queens, 95-04 Liberty Av., Woodhaven, 641-5872, A-CC to Rockaway Blvd.; Brooklyn, 7305 New Utrecht Av., 259-3720, B to 71st St. Both stores: M-F 9-8, S 9-6, Sun 10-5, ch., c.c., exch., no rfd. No raw lumber; only paneling, louvered doors, shutters, shelving and room-dividers. Misnamed operation, no 'auction' or 'outlet.' Sells: **Lumber.**

*** **Bag Man**, 261 W. 34 (8th Av.), 560 8952, A-AA-CC-E to 34, M-S 10-7, all cash, exch., no rfd. One in the DAC Jewelry group. Sells: **Small Tools, Clothing—Women's, Jewelry & Gifts, Personal Accessories.**

* **Baths International**, 89 5th Av. (16-7), 10th floor, 242-7158, LL-N-QB-RR-4-5-6 to Union Sq., B-F-LL to 14th St. & 6th Av., M-F 10-5, S by appt., ch., c.c., no exch. or rfd. Sells: **Hot Tubs, Jacuzzis, Spas.**

* **Black & Decker Service**, 50 W. 23 (5th-6th), 929-6450, B-F to 23, M-F 8:30-5, S 9:30-3, ch., c.c., exch., no rfd. B&D power tools that've been returned under warranty as defective, then repaired and placed here for sale with the full new-tool warranty. Also lawn mowers. Sells: **Hardware, Locks, Tools.**

* **Bookbinder Modern Blinds**, 3 Lispenard St. at 6th Av., 966-1585, A-AA-CC-E-1 to Canal, M-F 9-4, ch., no c.c. Service, no refund. Sells: **Shades/Blinds.**

Boro Park Lumber, Brooklyn, 4601 New Utrecht Av., 853-3100, B to Ft. Ham. Pkwy.; Brooklyn, 470 Kent Av. (S. 8, facing waterfront), 387-1233, J-M to Marcy, then take free bus B24 back towards river. Both stores: M-Th 8-5, F 8-1:30, Sun 10-6, ch., c.c., exch. or rfd. Free delivery over $75. Sells: **Lumber.**

** **Boundary Wholesale Fence**, Queens, 131 02 Jamaica Av., Jamaica, 847-3400, J to Metropolitan, M-F 7-4:30, S by appt., all cash, no exch. or rfd. Sells: **Fences.**

** **Brass Loft Factory Outlet**, 20 Greene St. (Canal), 3rd floor, 226-5467, J-M-N-QB-RR-6 to Canal, A-AA-CC-E-1 to Canal, TWThSSun 10:30-5:30, ch., no c.c., 14-day exch., no rfd. If it's made of brass, they sell it, for 30-60% less than normal. Sells: **Fireplace Supplies, Furnishings, Jewelry & Gifts.**

* **Brooklyn Elton Paint**, Brooklyn, 2121 Av. U, 743-0660, D-M-QB to Av. U, M-F 7-6, S 7-5, c.c., no ch., no exch. or rfd. Sells: **Paints, Wallcoverings.**

Brooklyn Paint Fair, Brooklyn, 1010 Coney Island Av. (Foster),

15: HOME-IMPROVEMENT ITEMS

434-8000, D-M-QB to Newkirk, MTWF 7-5:30, Th 7-8, S 7-4:30, ch., c.c., no exch. or rfd. Sells: **Paints, Wallcoverings.**

    Bruce Supply, Brooklyn, 8805 18th Av., 259-4900, B to 18th Av.; Brooklyn, 6015 16th Av., 256-8890, B-N to 62nd St. & New Utrecht Av.; Brooklyn, 2004 Coney Island Av. (Kings Hwy.), 375-9528, D-M-QB to Kings Hwy. All stores: M-F 7:30-5, S 7:30-1, all cash, no exch. or rfd. Sells: **Plumbing Supplies.**

    Canal Electric Motor, 310 Canal St. (Mercer), 966-1377, J-M-N-QB-RR-6 to Canal, M-S 8-5, all cash, 90-day exch., no rfd. Sells: **Motors & Fans.**

    Canal Rubber, 329 Canal St. at Greene, 226-7339, A-AA-CC-E-1 to Canal, J-M-N-QB-RR-6 to Canal, M-F 9-5, S 9-4:30, c.c., no ch., no exch. or rfd. Sells: **Rubber & Foam.**

    Canal Surplus, 363 Canal St. (Wooster), 966-3275, A-AA-CC-E-1 to Canal, 7 days 9:30-7, all cash, exch., no rfd. Sells: **Fire-Extinguishers, Motors & Fans, Warehouse Salvage Job-Lot.**

※※   **Chandelier Warehouse**, Brooklyn, 40 Withers St. (Lorimer), 388-800, GG-LL to Lorimer & Metropolitan, 7 days 10-4, ch., c.c., exch., no rfd. Large selection. Their prices are low enough to qualify for two stars; then they'll bargain even 10% lower. Unusual. Their fans are Hunter ceiling, special-order. Sells: **Motors & Fans, Furnishings.**

※   **Circle Auto Lock**, 457 W. 18 (10th Av.), 989-8650, only auto locks and alarms, A-AA-CC-E-LL to 14 St. & 8 Av., M-F 8-5, S 8-2, ch., no c.c. They install what they sell. No home security-devices here. Sells: **Burglar & Auto Alarms.**

    C.K.&L. Surplus, 307 Canal St. (B'way/Mercer), 966-1745, J-M-N-QB-RR-6 to Canal, M-S 9-6, Sun 10-6, ch. $20+, no c.c., exch., no rfd. Carries a very good Italian make of scissor, cheaper but comparable to Wiss. Also metal parts and surplus, etc. Sells: **Gummed Tapes, Fabrics, Yarns & Notions, Furnishings.**

※※※+ **C.O.M.B. Co.**, 6850 Wayzata Blvd., Minneapolis, MN 55426, 1-800-328-0609, catalog is free if you mention this book, ch., c.c., exch., no rfd. Takes mail-orders. Catalog. Very cooperative. Catalog is free only if you mention Bargain Finder. Sells: **Burglar & Auto Alarms, Hardware, Locks, Tools, Motors & Fans, Cameras & Optical Eqt., Jewelry & Gifts, Personal Accessories, Warehouse Salvage Job-Lot.**

※   **Consumers Distributing**, Queens, 107-18 70th Rd., Forest Hills, 268-2091, E-F-GG-N to 71-Continental Avs.; Queens, 39-20 Bell Blvd., Bayside, 225-0253, no subway stop nearby; Queens, 156-16 Northern Blvd., Flushing, 961-5024, no subway stop nearby; Queens, 97-10 Queens Blvd., Rego Park, 896-7250, F-GG-N to 63rd Dr.; Brooklyn, Av. U at Mill Av. (nr. Kings Plaza), 241-7633, D-M-QB to Av. M; Queens, 54-30 Myrtle Av., Ridgewood, 386-2809, LL-M to Myrtle & Wyckoff. All stores: M-F 10-9 (Ridgewood 10-6), S 10-6, Sun 12-5, ch., c.c. during banking hours, 30-day exch. or rfd. Large selection. A catalog-showroom chain. Sells: **Fire-Extinguishers, Autos & Supplies, Bikes, Dinnerware & Cookware, Housewares, Jewelry & Gifts, Sporting Goods.**

※+ **Court Radio**, 143 Chambers St. (W. B'way), 227-6456, A-CC-1-2-3 to Chambers, M-S 9:30-5:30, all cash, no exch. or rfd. Most is govt.-surplus, tubes and parts, no other accessories. Sells: **Electrical Parts, High Fidelity.**

※※※+ **C.W. Keenan Industrial Paints**, Brooklyn, 1844 Flatbush Av. (K-L) 338-7800, 3-4 to Flatbush Av., M-F 9-5, S 10-3, all cash, exch. or rfd. House-brands only; budget to top quality; about 40% less than brand-name equivalents. Bonus BF discount: 10%. Sells: **Paints.**

    D. Cohen Paints, Brooklyn, 2415 Coney Island Av. (U), 375-7042, D-M-QB to Av. U, M-S 7-5, all cash, no exch. or rfd. Sells: **Paints.**

※※※ **East Side Glass**, 201 Chrystie St. (Rivington-Stanton), 674-8355, F to 2nd Av., M-F 8-5, S 8-2, all cash, no exch. or rfd. Sells: **Glass & Mirrors.**

※   **Eighty-Eight Cent Shops**, 591 Lexington Av. (52), 753-6969, E-F to Lex. Av., M-F 9:30-6; 1457 Broadway (41), 354-0111, N-QB-RR-1-2-3-7 to 42 & Times Square, M-F 7:15-6, Sun 12-6; 33 W. 8 (5th-6th), 475-6951, A-AA-B-CC-D-E-F to 6, Sun-F 11-10, S 11-12; 89 Chambers St. (B'way-Church), 267-6722, A-CC-1-2-3 to Chambers, N-RR to City Hall, M-F 7:30-6; 144 Fulton St. (B'way), 964-2142, A-CC-J-M-RR-2-3-4-5 to B'way-Nassau & Fulton, M-F 7:30-6. All stores: all cash, exch. or rfd. Everything in store is 88 cents; only the Fulton and Chambers stores have areas set aside for more expensive merchandise. Sells: **Small Tools, Light Bulbs, Dinnerware & Cookware, Foods, Health & Beauty Aids, Housewares, Stationery & Art Supplies, Toys, Games & Hobbies.**

※   **Fairway Lumber**, Queens, 34-35 Steinway St., Astoria, 392-4440, F-GG--

15: HOME-IMPROVEMENT ITEMS

N to Steinway St., M-F 8-5, S 8-12, ch., c.c. (only on large orders), no exch. or rfd. Sells: **Lumber.**

Ferrara Bros., Queens, 89-19 Liberty Av., Ozone Park, 848-8200, A-CC to 88th St., M-S 7-4:30, ch., no c.c., exch. or rfd. Sells: **Masonry Supplies.**

Fire Extinguisher Maintenance, 530 Broome St. (6th Av.), 966-4830, A-AA-CC-E to Spring, M-F 6-4:30, ch., no c.c., no exch. or rfd. Sells: **Fire-Extinguishers.**

+ **Fire Extinguisher Sales**, 29 W. 19 (5th Av.), 924-2299, N-RR to 23rd St., M-F 7-4:30, ch., no c.c., exch., no rfd. Bonus discount to BF readers: 5%. Sells: **Fire-Extinguishers.**

First Cost, 90 E. 42nd St. at Park Av., 697-0244, 4-5-6-7 to Grand Central, M-F 8-7, SSun 10-5; Queens, 46-20 108 St., Corona, 271-1121, 7 to 111, ThS 9-6, F 9-9. Both stores: all cash, 7-day exch. or rfd. Sells: **Small Tools, Clothing—Children's, Clothing—Men's, Clothing—Women's, Dinnerware & Cookware, Foods, Health & Beauty Aids, Jewelry & Gifts, Sporting Goods, Toys, Games & Hobbies, Warehouse Salvage Job-Lot.**

*** **Franklin & Lennon Paint**, 537 W. 125 (B'wy), 864-2460, 1 to 125, M-F 7-5, S 7-12, all cash, no exch. or rfd. Good selection. Sells: **Paints.**

** **Gemco Paint**, Brooklyn, 2001 Coney Island Av. (P), 376-9001&9191, D-M-QB to Kings Hwy., M-Th 7:30-6, F 7:30-3:30, Sun 8-4, ch., c.c., exch. or rfd. Sells: **Paints.**

Gramercy Window Systems, 777-5226. He comes to your home and installs windows. Sells: **Glass & Mirrors.**

* **Grand Brass Lamp Parts**, 221 Grand St. at Elizabeth, 226-2567, B-D to Grand, M-F 8-5, Sun 10-4, all cash, no exch. or rfd. Wide range of parts, plus glass shades. Sells: **Lamp-Parts.**

***+ **Harry Weinstein & Sons**, Brooklyn, 420 Tompkins Av. (Halsey), 638-7207, A-CC to Kingston-Throop, M-F 8-5, S 8-1, ch., c.c., exch., no rfd. Affiliated stores: Mineola and Oceanside (the latter carrying only wallcoverings). Bonus discount to BF readers: 5%. Sells: **Paints, Wallcoverings.**

Hendel Plumbing Supply, Queens, 98th St. at 95th Av., Ozone Park, 845-3000, A-CC to Rockaway Blvd., plus a long walk, M-F 8-5, all cash, no exch. or rfd. Sells: **Plumbing Supplies.**

* **Hester St. Housewares**, 59 Hester St. (Ludlow), 260-6930, F to E. Broadway, Sun-F 9-6, ch., no c.c., exch. or rfd. Sells: **Hardware, Locks, Tools, Housewares.**

** **H&H Plastics**, 508 Broadway (Broome-Spring), 226-7363, N-RR to Prince St., 6 to Spring, M-Th 9-5, F 9-2, Sun by appt., ch., no c.c., no exch. or rfd. Laminated vinyls not intended for wallcoverings, and with no design-patterns or prints, but superb quality for this use if you want plain wall-vinyl anyhow. Sells: **Wallcoverings.**

***+ **Industro Bldg. Products**, Bronx, 1870 Webster Av. (176-Tremont), 294-8000, CC-D to Tremont, M-Th 8-4, F 8-1, all cash, no exch. or rfd. City's biggest selection. City's smallest prices. Usually about 35-50% off normal prices. Bonus discount to BF readers: 5% to 10%. Sells: **Lumber, Masonry Supplies.**

International Fluorescent, 135 Bowery (Grand), 966-1096, B-D to Grand, J-M to Bowery, M-F 8-5, SSun 9:30-5, ch., c.c., exch. or rfd. Sells: **Light Bulbs, Furnishings.**

** **Irv-Dan-Ace Wallpaper**, Brooklyn, 1464 Coney Island Av. (K), 338-6837 & 377-9781, D-M-QB to Av. J, MTWFS 10-5, Th 10-8, ch., c.c., exch. or rfd. (But less 20% on returns.) Sells: **Wallcoverings.**

* **Joann's Variety Store**, Brooklyn, 2209 Av. X, 648-8517, D-M-QB to Neck Rd., M-S 9-6, ch., c.c., exch., no rfd. But no returns if package is opened. Sells: **Hardware, Locks, Tools, Appliances, Health & Beauty Aids, Housewares.**

*** **Job Lot Trdg.**, 140 Church St. (Warren-Chambers), 962-4142, A-CC-1-2-3 to Chambers; 412 5th Av. (37-8), 398-9210, B-D-F to 42. Both stores: M-F 8-5:30, S 8-4:30, all cash, 15-day exch. or rfd. Both are huge stores, with terrific selections. Sells: **Garden/Lawn Eqt., Small Tools, Light Bulbs, Clothing—Men's, Dinnerware & Cookware, Foods, Housewares, Jewelry & Gifts, Linens, Personal Accessories, Sporting Goods, Stationery & Art Supplies, Toys, Games & Hobbies, Warehouse Salvage Job-Lot.**

* **Kingsboro Venetain Blind**, Brooklyn, 8002 3rd Av., 238-5353, RR to 77th St., T-F 9-5:30, S 9-4, ch., no c.c., exch., no rfd. Sells: **Shades/Blinds.**

Kustom Radiator Enclosures, 674-3213. They deliver and install.

15: HOME-IMPROVEMENT ITEMS

Sells: **Radiator-Enclosures.**

L&A Plumbing Supply, Brooklyn, 519 Kings Hwy. (E. 3rd St.), 998-0130, F to Kings Hwy., M-F 8-5, S 8-4, ch., no c.c., no exch. or rfd. Sells: **Plumbing Supplies.**

** **Lamp Warehouse**, Brooklyn, 1073 39th St. at Ft. Ham. Pkwy., 436-2207, B to 9th Av., B to Ft. Ham. Pkwy., MTF 9-5:30, Th 9-9, SSun 10-5, ch., c.c., exch., no rfd. Large selection. Their fans are Casablanca and Hunter ceiling fans. Sells: **Motors & Fans, Furnishings.**

** **Leslie Schiffer Locks**, 34 Ludlow St. (Hester), 677-7530, F to E. Broadway, M-Th 9-5, SunF 9-1, all cash, exch., no rfd. Locks only—no other hardware. Their main business is supplying locks to locksmiths. They don't carry so wide a range of locks as do some of the recommended locksmiths. Sells: **Hardware, Locks, Tools.**

Long Island Janitor Supply, Queens, 75-15 Roosevelt Av., Jackson Hts., 639-4131, E-F-GG-N-7 to 74th-B'wy & Roosevelt-Jack.Hts., M-S 8:30-6, all cash, no exch. or rfd. Sells: **Hardware, Locks, Tools, Masonry Supplies, Paints, Plumbing Supplies.**

M. Kessler Hardware, 229 Grand St. (Bowery), 226-6722, B-D to Grand, M-F 8-4:30, ch., no c.c., no exch. or rfd. Sells: **Hardware, Locks, Tools.**

Majestic Plumbing Supply, Queens, 120-19 Rockaway Blvd., S. Ozone Park, 843-6500, no subway stop nearby, M-F 7:30-5, S 8-12, c.c., no ch., exch. or rfd. Sells: **Plumbing Supplies.**

Maybeck Flags, Queens, 134-16 Atlantic Av., Richmond Hill, 297-4410, J to Metropolitan, M-F 9-4:30, all cash, exch. or rfd. American only. Sells: **Flags.**

McDonald Home Ctr., Brooklyn, 1258 McDonald Av. (J), 338-5700 & 377-9574, F to Av. I, M-F 8-5:30, S 8-4:30, ch., no c.c., no exch. or rfd. Sells: **Lumber, Masonry Supplies.**

**** **Mercury Paint Factory**, Brooklyn, 4808 Farragut Rd. (Utica), 469-8787, no subway stop nearby, M-S 7-5:45, all cash, exch. or rfd. Takes mailorders. Makers of billboard-paints. Entirely suitable for home-use, and better quality than most for that application. Sells: **Paints.**

* **Metro Lock**, 4 W. 32 (5th Av.), 564-2927, B-D-F-N-QB-RR to 34, N-RR to 28th St., M-S 8-5:30, ch., no c.c., exch., no rfd. Sells: **Burglar & Auto Alarms, Locksmiths.**

** **Midwood Paint/Wallpaper**, Brooklyn, 1327 Coney Island Av. (J), 338-0595, D-M-QB to Av. J, M-Th 8-6, F 8-2, Sun 10-3, ch., c.c., no exch. or rfd. Sells: **Paints, Wallcoverings.**

***+ **Mills Sales**, 889 Broadway at 19th St., 477-1000, LL-N-QB-RR-4-5-6 to Union Sq., N-RR to 23rd St., M-F 9-5, S 9-2, all cash, no exch. or rfd. No retail sales (wholesale only) Labor Day through Xmas. A specialty here is steel ball-point pens super-cheap by the dozen. Bonus discount to BF readers: 5%. Sells: **Small Tools, Appliances, Dinnerware & Cookware, Jewelry & Gifts, Personal Accessories, Stationery & Art Supplies, Toys, Games & Hobbies.**

* **Mitsu**, 25 W. 35 (5th-6th), 947-7892, B-D-F-N-QB-RR to 34, M-S 10-6, all cash, exch., no rfd. Carries some of the same stuff as Azuma, but for about 20% less. Sells: **Shades/Blinds, Clothing—Men's, Jewelry & Gifts.**

M&R Plastic, 428 Broadway (Howard), 564-8824, J-M-N-QB-RR-6 to Canal, M-Th 9-5, F 9-1, all cash, no exch. or rfd. Laminated vinyls not intended as wall-vinyl, but good for such if you're not seeking decorative patterns but rather want solid colors. Similar to H&H. Sells: **Wallcoverings.**

Nat Skop, Brooklyn, 1942 86th St., 256-4913&6700, B to 20th Av., MTWS 7:30-6, ThF 7:30-9, c.c., no ch., no exch. or rfd. Limited housewares and lamps: only toilet seats and wall- and hanging-lamps. Sells: **Paints, Furnishings, Housewares.**

** **NY Ceiling Fan Ctr.**, 620-4 Broadway (Houston), 254-6720, B-D-F-6 to B'wy-Laf. & Bleecker, N-RR to Prince St., MTF 9:30-5:30, Th 9:30-9, SSun 10-5, ch., c.c., exch., no rfd. Affiliated with Lamp Warehouse, just smaller stock; but will special-order. Their fans are Casablanca and Hunter ceiling fans. Sells: **Motors & Fans, Furnishings.**

*** **Odd Job Trdg.**, 7 E. 40 (Mad.), 686-6825, B-D-F to 42, 7 to 5th Av.; 66 W. 48 (6th Av.), 575-0477, B-D-F to 47. Both stores: M-Th 8-5:30, F 8-3, Sun 10-5, ch., no c.c., 15-day exch. or rfd. Sells: **Small Tools, Clothing—Men's, Dinnerware & Cookware, Foods, Health & Beauty Aids, Housewares, Linens, Personal Accessories, Stationery & Art Supplies, Toys, Games & Hobbies, Warehouse Salvage Job-Lot.**

** **Odds & Ends Job-Lots**, Queens, 88-09 Jamaica Av., Woodside, 441-6878, J to Woodhaven Blvd., M-S 9-6, Sun 9-3; Queens, 57-60 Woodside Av.,

148 **15: HOME-IMPROVEMENT ITEMS**

Woodside, phoneless, 7 to 61st St., M-Th 10-7, F 10-9, S 9-6, Sun 9-5. Both stores: all cash, exch. or rfd. Sells: **Hardware, Locks, Tools, Light Bulbs, Dinnerware & Cookware, Health & Beauty Aids, Housewares, Jewelry & Gifts, Recordings & Tapes, Toys, Games & Hobbies, Warehouse Salvage Job-Lot.**

** **O.Q. Mktg.**, 300 Canal St. (B'wy), 1 flight up, 966-6735, J-M-N-QB-RR-6 to Canal, T-S 12-5, all cash, exch., no rfd. Motors and industrial-grade fans (not in housings), other surplus. Very knowledgable and informative on the merits and demerits (efficiency, durability, etc.) of various fans and motors. Sells: **Motors & Fans.**

* **Pushcart**, 140 Church St. (Warren-Chambers), 962-4142, A-CC-1-2-3 to Chambers; 412 5th Av. (37-8), 398-9210, B-D-F to 42. Both stores: M-F 8-5:30, S 8-4:30, all cash, 15-day exch. or rfd. This is the same store as the Job Lot Trdg. Co., but the relative values in these merchandise-categories aren't as terrific; and most isn't even job-lot, but regular. Sells: **Hardware, Locks, Tools, Paints, Cameras & Optical Eqt., Health & Beauty Aids.**

Quality Firewood, 260-7209, Sep.-Mar. 7 days 9-9, ch., no c.c., exch. or rfd. He delivers. Sells: **Fireplace Supplies.**

Rainbow Mirror, Brooklyn, 4805 New Utrecht Av., 438-0332&4416, B to 50th St., M-S 8-4, ch., no c.c. Free service. Sells: **Glass & Mirrors, Furnishings.**

R.B.D. Lock & Alarm, 653 Broadway (Bond-Bleecker), 383-5888, B-D-F-6 to B'wy-Laf. & Bleecker, M-F 8:30-7:30, S 8:30-4, ch., no c.c., exch., no rfd. Sells: **Burglar & Auto Alarms, Locksmiths.**

* **REM Security**, 27 E. 20 (B'wy), 533-1555, N-RR to 23rd St., M-F 9:30-6, S 9-4, ch., c.c., 14-day exch., no rfd. Sells: **Burglar & Auto Alarms, Locksmiths.**

** **Reliance Hardware**, 40 Ludlow St. (Hester), 473-3080, F to E. Broadway, Sun-F 9-5:30, all cash, exch., no rfd. Sells: **Hardware, Locks, Tools.**

Resro Paint, Brooklyn, 7315 3rd Av., 748-0338, RR to 77th St., M-S 8-6, all cash, exch., no rfd. Sells: **Paints.**

** **R&F Electronics**, 36 W. 29 (B'wy), 679-5962, N-RR to 28th St., M-Th 9-6, SunF 9-4:30, all cash, no exch. or rfd. Sells: **Small Tools, Appliances, Dinnerware & Cookware, Jewelry & Gifts.**

* **Schatz Steinway**, Queens, 28-31 Steinway St., Astoria, 721-0777&2011, F-GG-N to Steinway St., RR to 30th Av., MTW 6-6, ThF 6-8:30, S 6-7, ch., c.c., no exch. or rfd. Sells: **Paints, Wallcoverings.**

*+ **Sheila's Wallstyles**, 273 Grand St. (Forsyth-Eldridge), 966-1663, B-D to Grand, Sun-Th 9:30-5, F 9:30-2, ch., c.c., exch., no rfd. Bonus discount to BF readers: 5%. Sells: **Wallcoverings.**

Standard Tinsmith, 183 Chrystie St. (Rivington), 674-2240, F to 2nd Av., M-F 8-4, all cash, no exch. or rfd. Huge stock. Know what you want. Sells: **Plumbing Supplies.**

* **Susan Trdg.**, 300 Canal St. (B'wy), 431-8529, J-M-N-QB-RR-6 to Canal, 7 days 10-6, ch., c.c., exch., no rfd. Sells: **Small Tools, Gummed Tapes, Appliances, Furnishings, Personal Accessories.**

* **Tinkers Paradise**, 31 Park Row, 962-3826&2273, J-M-RR-4-5-6 to Chambers & Bkln. Bridge, A-CC-J-M-RR-2-3-4-5 to B'wy-Nassau & Fulton, M-F 7:15-5:45, S 8-2, ch., no c.c., exch., no rfd. Sells: **Hardware, Locks, Tools.**

Trans-Am Electronics, 383 Canal St. (6th Av.), 226-3893, A-AA-CC-E-1 to Canal, M-F 9-5, S 9-4, ch., no c.c., exch., no rfd. Sells: **Electrical Parts.**

*** **Vercesi Hardware**, 152 E. 23 (Lex.-3rd), 475-1883, 6 to 23, M-F 8-7:30, S 9-5:30, ch., no c.c., exch., no rfd. Only paint-brand stocked is Red Devil. Sells: **Hardware, Locks, Tools, Paints, Appliances.**

Wallpaper Mart, 187 Lexington Av. (31-2), 889-4800, 6 to 33, MTWF 10-6:30, Th 10-7, S 10-5, ch., no c.c., no exch. or rfd. Sells: **Wallcoverings.**

** **Walter E. Umla Lumber**, Brooklyn, 180 6th St. (2nd-3rd Av.), 624-3350, F-N-RR to 9th St. & 4th Av., M-F 8-3:30, ch., no c.c., no exch. or rfd. Sells: **Lumber.**

* **Walton Mirror Works**, Brooklyn, 61 Walton St. (Harrison), 388-6710 & 1-516-775-2323 & 1-201-432-1404, J-M to Lorimer, M-F 8-5, S 8-1, Sun 10-4, ch., c.c., exch. or rfd. They deliver, or you can pick it up there. Sells: **Glass & Mirrors.**

** **Weber's Job Lot**, 505 8th Av. at 35th, 564-7668, A-AA-CC-E to 34, M-F 10-6:30, S 10-6; 136 Church St. at Warren, 564-7668, A-CC-1-2-3 to Chambers, M-S 8-6; 2064 Broadway at 71st, 787-1644, 1-2-3 to 72, M-F 9-9, S 9-6, Sun 12-6. All stores: ch., no ch., 7-day exch. or rfd. Some terrific values; others not good. Some prices wrongly marked on items each time I was at both stores; checkout counter said 'It's an error.' Sells: **Small Tools, Light Bulbs, Paints, Dinnerware & Cookware, Health & Beauty Aids, Jewelry & Gifts, Linens, Personal Accessories, Stationery**

15: HOME-IMPROVEMENT ITEMS

& Art Supplies, Warehouse Salvage Job-Lot.

* **Webster Wallpapers**, Bronx, 2737 Webster Av. (197), 367-0055, CC-D to Kingsbridge, MF 9:30-9, TWTh 9:30-6, S 9:30-5, c.c., no ch., no exch. or rfd. Sells: **Wallcoverings.**

** **Weilgus Bros. Hardware**, 158 E. Broadway (Essex), 267-1512, F to E. Broadway, M-F 8:30-5:30, all cash, no exch. or rfd. No tools here. Sells: **Hardware, Locks, Tools.**

** **Weiser & Teitel**, 61 Reade St. (Church-B'wy), 233-1441, A-CC-1-2-3 to Chambers, N-RR to City Hall, M-F 7:30-5:30, S 7:30-4:30, c.c., no ch., exch. or rfd. Custom-made frames at the city's lowest prices. Also rather good on framed mirrors. Not a general glass place, but only framed products. Sells: **Glass & Mirrors, Stationery & Art Supplies.**

16:
HOUSEWARES
Expect 20-40% discounts.

I'll never understand why some people use spray-insecticides inside their homes (or restaurants, or offices). This is like doing volunteer-duty as a crop-picker just while planes are buzzing overhead spreading pesticides over the crops—and upon the farmworkers. Unfortunately, some people are so indigent that they've got to subject themselves to potent carcinogens or else lose their jobs. But most individuals who use spray-insecticides at home are not doing it out of extreme financial pressures. Perhaps they can't or don't read, and so don't know what's been discovered about these chemicals during the past forty years. But whatever the explanation, they're not poisoning only the roaches. They're poisoning people, too (themselves included), because they, too, breathe the stuff in. (Of course, the humans die slowly, from cancer; or else give birth to deformed children whose lives are thus cursed by their parents' carelessness. The insects, on the other hand, drop dead right away. To a pesticide, a human is just an insect in slow motion.)

People used to spray DDT at home. When I was a kid in the '50's, I told my mother about the dangers of spray-pesticides, and she stopped using them. Whenever I walked into a home where I smelled that distinctive odor in the air, I skedaddled pronto. Then, Rachel Carlson published *Silent Spring*, and finally the pesticide-makers switched over to peddling substitutes, equally lethal to people if not to insects. (In England, however, soap-makers long continued promoting their soaps "with DDT, for better personal hygiene.") The basic lesson was never learned: What kills insects, or even bacteria, usually kills people, too. We're organic beings, composed of single cells, each of which has remarkable similarities to the single cells known as bacteria, or to the single cells in roaches, or to any other single cells which are the basis of all life (not including viruses, which are molecular, sub-cellular, and thus not "life"-forms in anything like the same sense). So if you want to kill pests, try to do it in such a way that only the pests get the punch. The mechanical means—traps, as opposed to the use of chemical poisons—are the most obvious examples: Roach Motel is the best-advertised, the most overpriced, and one of the least efficient, of this type, which are based essentially on the fly-paper concept of catching the insect in a sticky glue. But there are also safe means which use poisonous chemicals that don't get into the air—or into you. These are applied locally to the places where the insects especially tend to congregate. Boric acid powder is an example. The insect walks over it, goes back into his crack, and dies if any of the boric has stuck to his body. Electrostatically charged boric acid is extremely effective, because it does stick. Just a little bit will de-roach a place for many months. The well-known brand of this is Roach Prufe, available only by mail-order. Sometimes much cheaper brands are available. Phone 581-2000 for availability and current prices of Roach Prufe and other brands of electrostatically charged boric acid roach-killers.

What's true of insecticides applies equally to bacteriacides. Dial soap used to have hexachloraphene in it, supposedly so that bacteria wouldn't live on the skin and form odors. PhisoHex (a "hospital-strength" anti-bacterial soap for washing and sterilizing babies) had even more of this chlorinated hydrocarbon. Then, it was finally realized that the hexachlorophene had been doing permanent nerve-damage to the infants. Dial and phisoHex no longer contain hexachlorophene. What has been substituted may, however, turn out to be even worse. The same applies to spray-Lysol, except that that gets directly into the body through the lungs. The TV ads try to make people think their homes to be infested with kooties. A sterilized, disinfected, anti-natural world, is the ideal that's being sold—and it does sell, just like designer-jeans or any other hollow puffery-scam. Only here, the public is in the process playing the role of guinea-pigs. This situation is a game which has umpires in the persons of commissioners at the federal regulatory agencies. Most of these umpires have been hired from the regulated industries. After doing their stints of "public service," they go back to serving the regulated industry as consultants or top executives at enormous salaries. If guinea-pigs were rational, they would be very suspicious of such umpires. Instead, guinea-pigs call the regulators "protectors and defenders of the public (i.e., of the guinea-pigs') interest."

The best rule to follow if one wants to avoid being a guinea-pig himself is this: To the extent reasonably possible, avoid exposure—through breathing, touching, or eating—to the family of chemicals known as halogenated hydrocarbons, which includes both chlorinated and fluorinated hydrocarbons. DDT (dichloro-diphenyl-trichloroethane), Agent Orange, and hexachlorophene are chlorinated hydrocarbons. Teflon is a fluorinated hydrocarbon, and the gases that rise from cooking on it are carcinogenic (and warnings to this effect are posted on such products in some countries, though not here). Such chemicals are produced by the blending of the intensely reactive elements fluorine or chlorine, with petroleum distillates. The latter can be recognized by the characteristic petrochemical prefixes and suffixes, some of the more common of which are: benz-(as in benzol, used for paint-thinner), meth-(as in methylene chloride, used to remove caffein from coffee), eth-(as in ethylene glycol solvent), prop-(as in propylene glycol solvent); -ene (exemplified just before), -yl (as in vinyl, propyl, ethyl, and methyl), -ane (as in methane gas), -ol (as in methanol). When you see a chemical with these in the name, along with either "chloro" or "fluoro," that substance should be considered as a probable carcinogen (cancer-causer) and mutagen (birth-defect-causer). Such materials tend to wreak havok with DNA, and so to warp genes, thus causing these health-problems. The fact that a chemical hasn't yet been restricted or banned in the U.S., or in some other country, doesn't necessarily mean that the evidence for such action is lacking or hasn't long existed. It could mean simply that a lot of money has somehow found its way to the proper officials in that particular government. The would-be guinea-pigs should be so-informed, and thus prepared to inquire and to decide themselves. The reality has always been "Caveat emptor"—Let the buyer beware. Unless you've got big cash, and know whom to pay off and how, Big Brother is usually on the other guy's side, in any country.

An analogous environmental-governmental abortion is reflected in the widespread use of radioactive smoke-detectors. In the summer of 1981, the aggressively inadequate members of NYC's City Council passed legislation requiring that by the end of that year smoke-detectors had to be installed in each apartment in the City. Now it just so happens that there are two kinds of these devices: ionizing (radioactive) and photoelectric (safe). But the local solons in their legislative wisdom made no distinction between the two. Instead of banning the radioactive ("ionizing") kind, as they should have done, they virtually guaranteed that millions of these dangerous devices would be installed all over the City within a period of only months—and that's exactly what happened.

The radioactive, ionization-type, smoke-detectors contain the element americium, a plutonium by-product with a half-life of 460 years. Usually, you can't tell anything about this radioactivity from the outside of the box, unless you just happen to have a Geiger-counter with you. But according to the small print inside, when the device becomes no longer serviceable (and how are you supposed to know that—when your apartment's burned down?), the owner (that's you or the landlord) is instructed that the thing must not be thrown into the trash, but should instead be shipped back to the manufacturer who will then dispose of this dangerous stuff into an authorized nuclear waste-dump. Most people, of course, never read this fine print; and the few who do will forget it by the time the smoke-detector becomes worn out. Or someone else may by then live in, or own, the apartment. So virtually every one of these dangerous smoke-detectors will end up in New York City's garbage—stuff, mind you, that's so dangerous it's supposed to be buried forever in an authorized nuclear dump. Too bad everybody doesn't just remove these things right now, bring them to City Hall, and dump them into the Council Chambers. But anyway, if you have occasion to buy a smoke-detector, make sure the box says that it's of the photoelectric type.

Finally, to speak of other less grisly matters, cleansers are another subject of this chapter; and from my own personal experience having tried probably all the dishwashing detergents available in this town, I recommend Ivory as unquestionably having the greatest grease-cutting effectiveness per unit-cost. This is one instance where an advertised brand-name product really does offer better value even than the off-brands. For example, I have found Octagon—a popular cheapy—to be more expensive than Ivory, though it's less expensive per unit of weight. *Consumer*

16: HOUSEWARES

Reports once top-rated Ivory; but more recently, they've preferred other brands. So I re-tried their current choices, and found them to be just as poor now as they were when *CR* previously rated them not preferred. I can't understand why *CR* changed its ratings on this, because so far as I can tell, the products themselves haven't changed; and from the descriptions of their tests given in the magazines, neither has Consumers' Union's testing-procedure. In any case, I find Ivory to be the best; and you, too, might find it worth a try.

RECOMMENDED PRODUCTS:
See above.

RECOMMENDED STORES:

major housewares

(examples: barbecues, bread-boxes, brooms, fans, ironing boards, lawn-furniture, medicine-chests, mirrors, scales, shopping-carts, smoke-detectors, thermos jugs, toilet seats, trash-cans, vaccuum jugs)

**Dollar Bills (867-0212); *Consumers Distributing (Queens, 268-2091); *Hester St. Housewares (260-6930); *Joann's Variety Store (Brooklyn, 648-8517); *Morris Discount (Brooklyn, 375-2529); *Variety Store (Brooklyn, 336-1100); +Abehill Discount II (Queens, 426-2644); Canal Self-Service (966-3069); City of Bargains (Brooklyn, 375-1000); El-Vee Outdoor Furniture (Brooklyn, 339-0788); G & Sons Dept. Store (Brooklyn, 438-2604); Lee-Or Discount (Brooklyn, 377-1010); M&G Bargains (227-3352); Nat Skop (Brooklyn, 256-4913); Rockwell Salvage (intermittent stock, Queens, 849-3696); Valco Discount (Queens, 274-1200).

small housewares

(examples: adhesive tapes, ash trays, batteries, bottle-openers, bottles, can-openers, canisters, cards, cleansers, detergents, flashlights, glues, insecticides, jugs, knives, masking tapes, mirrors, napkins, paper, paper plates, paper towels, playing cards, polishes, scissors, shades, spot-removers, sprinklers, tapes, thermometers, timers, tissues, waxes)

***Anything & Everything (Brooklyn, 332-1508); ***Job Lot Trdg. (intermittent stock, 962-4142); ***Odd Job Trdg. (intermittent stock, 686-6825); **Odds & Ends Job-Lots (intermittent stock, Queens, 441-6878); *Court Wholesale (Brooklyn, 625-2421); *Eighty-Eight Cent Shops (753-6969); *Joann's Variety Store (Brooklyn, 648-8517); *Milshap Pharmacy (674-7007); *Morris Discount (Brooklyn, 375-2529); Canal Self-Service (966-3069); First Cost (intermittent stock, 697-0244); Global Imports (intermittent stock, 741-0700); M&G Bargains (227-3352); Pay Less (344-1084).

party supplies & wedding favors

**Dixie Party Supplies (260-0514); *Broadway Supply (Brooklyn, 875-1707); Engelhard Bag & Paper (Brooklyn, 338-4680); Manhattan Wedding Ctr. (233-8250); Rubinstein's Party Favors (254-0162); Valco Discount (Queens, 274-1200); Y&T Soda and Paper (Brooklyn, 435-1313).

laundry-bags

***Hymie & Schelly's (962-9117).

garbage-bags

154　　　　　　　　　**16: HOUSEWARES**

Half-Price Trash Bag Co. (Brooklyn, 384-1900); **Upstate Plastics** (387-5071).

─────────────── **cardboard boxes** ───────────────

M&G Packaging (255-1441).

STORES-DIRECTORY

Phone a store before you go out of your way to visit it. Especially do this during July and August, when most establishments reduce or eliminate weekend-hours.

In the listings below, "*" means especially recommended, "+" means that the store offers a bonus discount to BF readers, "ch." and "c.c." mean respectively checks and credit cards, and "exch." and "rfd." mean respectively exchange and refund. Nearest subway-stops are shown. For example, "B-D-F to 47" means to take the B, D, or F train to 47th Street. Store-hours are also indicated, with days of the week abbreviated, like "M-S 8-6."

⁺　　**Abehill Discount II**, Queens, 37-46 74th St., Jackson Hts., 426-2644, E-F-GG-N-7 to 74th-B'wy & Roosevelt-Jack.Hts., M-S 9:30-7, Sun 11-5, c.c., no ch., 35-day exch. or rfd. Bonus BF discount is 10% off J.G. Durand glassware. Sells: **Major Housewares**.

***　　**Anything & Everything**, Brooklyn, 2930 Av. X (Nostrand), 332-1508, no subway stop nearby, MTWF 10-6, Th 10-9, S 10-6, Sun 12-5, all cash, exch. or rfd. Large selection. Practically a super-discount supermarket, but specializing in packaged non-perishable foods, etc., no fresh produce. Sells: **Small Housewares, Foods, Pets, Warehouse Salvage Job-Lot**.

*　　**Broadway Supply**, Brooklyn, 15 Cadams Plaza West (Front-Water Sts.), 875-1707, A-CC to High St., M-F 10-5:30, all cash, no exch. or rfd. Sells: **Party Supplies & Wedding Favors**.

　　Canal Self-Service, 270 Canal St. at Cortlandt Alley, 966-3069, J-M-N-QB-RR-6 to Canal, M-F 10-6, S 9-5:30, Sun 10-5, all cash, exch. or rfd. Large selection. Affiliated with M&G Bargains. Both have some occasional closeouts which are superb values. Sells: **Major Housewares, Small Housewares**.

　　City of Bargains, Brooklyn, 1111 Av. J (Coney Is. Av.), 375-1000, D-M-QB to Av. J, M-F 9:30-7, S 10-6, Sun 10-5, all cash, exch., no rfd. Sells: **Major Housewares, Toys, Games & Hobbies**.

*　　**Consumers Distributing**, Queens, 107-18 70th Rd., Forest Hills, 268-2091, E-F-GG-N to 71-Continental Avs.; Queens, 39-20 Bell Blvd., Bayside, 225-0253, no subway stop nearby; Queens, 156-16 Northern Blvd., Flushing, 961-5024, no subway stop nearby; Queens, 97-10 Queens Blvd., Rego Park, 896-7250, F-GG-N to 63rd Dr.; Brooklyn, Av. U at Mill Av. (nr. Kings Plaza), 241-7633, D-M-QB to Av. M; Queens, 54-30 Myrtle Av., Ridgewood, 386-2809, LL-M to Myrtle & Wyckoff. All stores: M-F 10-9 (Ridgewood 10-6), S 10-6, Sun 12-5, ch., c.c. during banking hours, 30-day exch. or rfd. Large selection. A catalog-showroom chain. Sells: **Major Housewares, Autos & Supplies, Bikes, Dinnerware & Cookware, Home-Improvement Items, Jewelry & Gifts, Sporting Goods**.

*　　**Court Wholesale**, Brooklyn, 244 Court St. (Baltic), 625-2421, F-GG to Bergen St., M-S 9-6:30, all cash, exch. or rfd. Small selection. Main business is supplying toiletries, brand-name candies, etc., to local housewares-stores. Sells: **Small Housewares, Foods**.

**　　**Dixie Party Supplies**, 1 Av. C (Houston), 260-0514, F to 2nd Av., plus a long walk, M-F 8-4, all cash, no exch. or rfd. Sells: **Party Supplies & Wedding Favors**.

**　　**Dollar Bills**, 99 E. 42 (Park Av.), 867-0212, 4-5-6-7 to Grand Central, M-W 8-6:30, ThF 8-7, S 10-6, ch., c.c., 7-day exch. or rfd. A small department store that's best on toiletries, housewares, and cigarettes, but good also on men's wear. Same owner: J. Chuckles, Strawberry, Sunshine, Zoom stores. Sells: **Major Housewares, Appliances, Clothing—Men's, Smoking Supplies**.

*　　**Eighty-Eight Cent Shops**, 591 Lexington Av. (52), 753-6969, E-F to Lex. Av., M-F 9:30-6; 1457 Broadway (41), 354-0111, N-QB-RR-1-2-3-7 to 42 & Times Square, M-F 7:15-6, Sun 12-6; 33 W. 8 (5th-6th), 475-6951, A-AA-B-CC-D-E-F to 4, Sun-F 11-10, S 11-12; 89 Chambers St. (B'wy-Church), 267-6722, A-CC-1-2-3 to

16: HOUSEWARES

Chambers, N-RR to City Hall, M-F 7:30-6; 144 Fulton St. (B'wy), 964-2142, A-CC-J-M-RR-2-3-4-5 to B'wy-Nassau & Fulton, M-F 7:30-6. All stores: all cash, exch. or rfd. Everything in store is 88 cents; only the Fulton and Chambers stores have areas set aside for more expensive merchandise. Sells: **Small Housewares, Dinnerware & Cookware, Foods, Health & Beauty Aids, Home-Improvement Items, Stationery & Art Supplies, Toys, Games & Hobbies.**

El-Vee Outdoor Furniture, Brooklyn, 2425 McDonald Av. (V-W), 339-0788, F to Av. X, MTh 10-9, TWF 10-6, S 11-3, Sun 11-3, c.c., no ch., exch., no rfd. Sells: **Major Housewares.**

Engelhard Bag & Paper, Brooklyn, 2358 Nostrand (J), 338-4680, 3-4 to Flatbush Av., M-F 9-5, all cash, exch., no rfd. Sells: **Party Supplies & Wedding Favors.**

First Cost, 90 E. 42nd St. at Park Av., 697-0244, 4-5-6-7 to Grand Central, M-F 8-7, SSun 10-5; Queens, 46-20 108 St., Corona, 271-1121, 7 to 111, ThS 9-6, F 9-9. Both stores: all cash, 7-day exch. or rfd. Sells: **Small Housewares, Clothing—Children's, Clothing—Men's, Clothing—Women's, Dinnerware & Cookware, Foods, Health & Beauty Aids, Home-Improvement Items, Jewelry & Gifts, Sporting Goods, Toys, Games & Hobbies, Warehouse Salvage Job-Lot.**

G & Sons Dept. Store, Brooklyn, 4806 New Utrecht Av., 438-2604, B to 50th St., MTTh 10-9, WSun 10-6, F 10-4, ch., c.c., exch. or rfd. Sells: **Major Housewares, Health & Beauty Aids, Sporting Goods, Stationery & Art Supplies, Toys, Games & Hobbies.**

Global Imports, 160 5th Av. at 21st St., 741-0700, N-RR to 23rd St., M-F 8-5, all cash, 7-day exch. or rfd. Sells: **Small Housewares, Recordings & Tapes, Smoking Supplies, Toys, Games & Hobbies.**

Half-Price Trash Bag Co., Brooklyn, 496 Wythe Av. at 9th St., 384-1900, J-M to Marcy, then take free bus B24 back towards river, Sun-Th 10-4, ch., no c.c., no exch. or rfd. Sells: **Garbage-Bags.**

* **Hester St. Housewares**, 59 Hester St. (Ludlow), 260-6930, F to E. Broadway, Sun-F 9-6, ch., no c.c., exch. or rfd. Sells: **Major Housewares, Home-Improvement Items.**

*** **Hymie & Schelly's**, 148 Church St. (Chambers-Warren) in front of Joe's Place, 962-9117 & 377-2118, A-CC-1-2-3 to Chambers, M-S 11-5, all cash, exch. or rfd. Nylon bags of every description, often at prices below the normal cost of the materials alone. Well-made, too. Sells: **Laundry-Bags.**

* **Joann's Variety Store**, Brooklyn, 2209 Av. X, 648-8517, D-M-QB to Neck Rd., M-S 9-6, ch., c.c., exch. or rfd. But no returns if package is opened. Sells: **Major Housewares, Small Housewares, Appliances, Health & Beauty Aids, Home-Improvement Items.**

*** **Job Lot Trdg.**, 140 Church St. (Warren-Chambers), 962-4142, A-CC-1-2-3 to Chambers; 412 5th Av. (37-8), 398-9210, B-D-F to 42. Both stores: M-F 8-5:30, S 8-4:30, all cash, 15-day exch. or rfd. Both are huge stores, with terrific selections. Sells: **Small Housewares, Clothing—Men's, Dinnerware & Cookware, Foods, Home-Improvement Items, Jewelry & Gifts, Linens, Personal Accessories, Sporting Goods, Stationery & Art Supplies, Toys, Games & Hobbies, Warehouse Salvage Job-Lot.**

Lee-Or Discount, Brooklyn, 1113 Av. J (Coney Is. Av.), 377-1010, D-M-QB to Av. J, Sun-Th 9:30-7, F 9:30-3, all cash, exch., no rfd. Sells: **Major Housewares, Appliances, Toys, Games & Hobbies.**

Manhattan Wedding Ctr., 181 Broadway (Dey), 4th floor, 233-8250, A-CC-J-M-RR-2-3-4-5 to B'wy-Nassau & Fulton, AA-E to World Trade Ctr., M-F 9-6:30, S 11-5, ch., no c.c., no exch. or rfd. Sells: **Party Supplies & Wedding Favors.**

M&G Bargains, 344 Broadway (Leonard), 227-3352, J-M-N-QB-RR-6 to Canal, M-F 8-5:30, all cash, exch. or rfd. Affiliated with Canal Self-Service. Sells: **Major Housewares, Small Housewares.**

M&G Packaging, 661 6th Av. (20-1), 255-1441, B-F to 23, M-F 8-5, all cash, no exch. or rfd. Sells: **Cardboard Boxes.**

* **Milshap Pharmacy**, 114 E. 16 (Irving Place), 674-7007, LL-N-QB-RR-4-5-6 to Union Sq., M-F 9-5:45, all cash, no exch. or rfd. Sells: **Small Housewares, Health & Beauty Aids.**

* **Morris Discount**, Brooklyn, 1620 Av. U, 375-2529, D-M-QB to Av. U, M-F 9-7:30, S 10-6, all cash, exch. or rfd. Sells: **Major Housewares, Small Housewares, Health & Beauty Aids.**

Nat Skop, Brooklyn, 1942 86th St., 256-4913&6700, B to 20th Av., MTWS

16: HOUSEWARES

7:30-6, ThF 7:30-9, c.c., no ch., no exch. or rfd. Limited housewares and lamps: only toilet seats and wall- and hanging-lamps. Sells: **Major Housewares, Furnishings, Home-Improvement Items.**

*** **Odd Job Trdg.**, 7 E. 40 (Mad.), 686-6825, B-D-F to 42, 7 to 5th Av.; 66 W. 48 (6th Av.), 575-0477, B-D-F to 47. Both stores: M-Th 8-5:30, F 8-3, Sun 10-5, ch., no c.c., 15-day exch. or rfd. Sells: **Small Housewares, Clothing—Men's, Dinnerware & Cookware, Foods, Health & Beauty Aids, Home-Improvement Items, Linens, Personal Accessories, Stationery & Art Supplies, Toys, Games & Hobbies, Warehouse Salvage Job-Lot.**

** **Odds & Ends Job-Lots**, Queens, 88-09 Jamaica Av., Woodside, 441-6878, J to Woodhaven Blvd., M-S 9-6, Sun 9-3; Queens, 57-60 Woodside Av., Woodside, phoneless, 7 to 61st St., M-Th 10-7, F 10-9, S 9-6, Sun 9-5. Both stores: all cash, exch. or rfd. Sells: **Small Housewares, Dinnerware & Cookware, Health & Beauty Aids, Home-Improvement Items, Jewelry & Gifts, Recordings & Tapes, Toys, Games & Hobbies, Warehouse Salvage Job-Lot.**

Pay Less, 44 Water St. (Coenties Slip), 344-1084, N-RR-1 to South Ferry, M-F 7:30-6, all cash, exch., no rfd. Sells: **Small Housewares, Health & Beauty Aids.**

Rockwell Salvage, Queens, 120-05 Atlantic Av., Richmond Hill, 849-3696, J to 121; Brooklyn, 1185 McDonald Av. (I-J), 253-3066, F to Av. I. Both stores: S-W 9-5, ThF 9-9, ch., c.c., no exch. or rfd. 30-40% off mostly damaged and closeout stuff. Their discounts on such-sourced goods really should be 60%. Barely worth recommending. Sells: **Major Housewares.**

Rubinstein's Party Favors, 876 Broadway (18), 254-0162&6992, N-RR to 23rd St., LL-N-QB-RR-4-5-6 to Union Sq., M-F 9-5, S 9-2, all cash, no exch. or rfd. Sells: **Party Supplies & Wedding Favors.**

Upstate Plastics, 387-5071, ch., no c.c. Takes mail-orders. Sells: **Garbage-Bags.**

Valco Discount, Queens, 32-40 & 32-62 Steinway St., Astoria, 274-1200 & 545-8443, F-GG-N to Steinway St., M-W 10-7, ThF 10-9, SSun 10:30-5:30, ch., no c.c., exch. or rfd. Large selection. Sells: **Major Housewares, Party Supplies & Wedding Favors, Bikes, Sporting Goods, Stationery & Art Supplies, Toys, Games & Hobbies.**

* **Variety Store**, Brooklyn, 1402 Av. U, 336-1100, D-M-QB to Av. U, M-S 10-6, all cash, no exch. or rfd. Large selection of kitchen cabinets and off-brand Chinese dishes, and that's practically the whole store. Sells: **Major Housewares, Dinnerware & Cookware.**

Y&T Soda and Paper, Brooklyn, 4813 New Utrecht Av., 435-1313 & 438-9525, B to 50th St., MTW 9-6, Th 9-8, F 8:30-5, Sun 10-5, all cash, no exch. or rfd. Sells: **Party Supplies & Wedding Favors.**

17:
JEWELRY & GIFTS
Discounts vary.

Here's a field where you can really get taken if you don't know where to shop. And considering that prices on some items run into the thousands of dollars, this can be a very serious matter.

Discounts generally run highest on semi-precious jewelry and on watches, where you can routinely save 40-80%, but even on the other items you'll always do 20% or better.

Once you've learned the basics of jewelry-quality (and the summary below should cover the ground on that pretty well), you'll be in a position to compare prices intelligently. You can then ring up the recommended stores for phone-quotes, and most of these places will give you prices this way, if only you'll specify precisely what it is that you want (e.g., how many pennyweights of how-many carat-gold in what design, or what grade of diamond, to cite the two cases discussed below).

The biggest problem for the consumer is recognizing quality in fine jewelry—especially in diamonds and other precious stones. But first, a word about gold:

If you're buying gold-jewelry, there are three questions you need answered before you can compare prices: 1) How many carats—or how pure—is the gold? (24-carats is 100%.) 2) How many pennyweights of that-carat gold are in the piece? 3) What's the design of the piece? (Certain designs mean more labor, and thus a higher cost per pennyweight. Usually, machine-made costs a little less than hand-made. Compare only same designs with same, and not machine-made with hand-made.)

A reputable dealer in precious stones—diamonds, etc.—will permit you to have a stone appraised before you buy it, and you should never purchase a stone without that appraisal. The cost is usually three-quarters of 1% of assessed valuation, and well worth it. If the price of the gem is $10,000 or more, it should be graded before it's appraised. The standard place to have this authoritatively done is the Gemological Institute of America (221-5858), which will charge about $100, depending on the number of carats. (Note that "carat" means something different here—not percentage of gold, but rather weight of a diamond.) When the GIA is done, they present you with a certificate definitively verifying the quality of the stone. The out-of-town diamond-dealers I recommend sell stones that already have the GIA certificate.

Diamond-grading runs on two parallel scales: clarity and color. The clarity-scale goes from F for Flawless (which is the top, and extremely rare and valuable), down through IF for Internally Flawless, VVS1 for Very Very Slightly (imperfect) 1, VVS2, VS1, VS2, SI1 (read "Slightly Imperfect 1"), SI2, and I for Imperfect. The color-scale extends from D, which is completely colorless and the most valuable, down through the letters of the alphabet. A color-grade as low as H is colorless to the untrained eye. Z is out-and-out yellow or gray. A one-step difference in color-grade affects price identically to a one-step difference in clarity-grade. Thus, for example, a 1-carat round stone will cost the same regardless whether it's VVS1, G; or VVS2, F.

There are three very different markets for diamonds: gemstones, which are at least 1 carat, VVS2, and H; jewelry diamonds; and finally the virtually worthless industrial diamonds, which are extremely small, flawed and colored. The prices of these three categories vary independently of each other. Which is a better investment: gemstones or jewelry-stones? There's no fixed answer which is valid at all times and in all markets. The question is like asking whether antiques are a better investment than blue-chip stocks.

If you want a diamond insured, an appraisal will be required. Your insurance-broker, or the underwriting department of the insurance-company, will recommend appraisers to you for this purpose. Appraisals may vary by as much as 25%, so most knowledgeable customers get several appraisals before buying, and then average the results. If you find that the appraisals are varying by more than 25%, contact the NYC Dept. of Consumer Affairs (577-0111), which has auhority in this area. Usually, the variation is less than that.

In any case, it's poor policy to buy a brand-name diamond, either via a catalog or through a jewelry-retailer. Brands don't make a bit of difference here, except in the price, which is invariably so inflated that even the discount-price in a catalog will be 20-40% higher than you need to pay.

What about precious stones other than diamonds? The major problem regarding colored stones is the lack of a reliable and universally accepted grading-system. The internationally respected GIA will not grade rubies or other colored stones, but will merely verify whether they are genuine or fake. Approximately 80% of such stones have been colored artificially by irradiation, heating, and other means. Even the GIA finds it impossible to determine if the color of one of these stones is natural. Someday, a method may be developed to distinguish natural from artificial color here. There will then be a great many greatly disillusioned "gem"-owners, and you shouldn't be one of them.

Art

This chapter also covers gift items, and in this category I include original art, that not fitting anywhere else quite so well as here (even if not so very well here, either).

Evaluating bargains in art can be a rather specialized skill if the objective of the buyer is investment. My standard here, however, is somewhat less precise and more personal: aesthetic enjoyment, based upon what I perceive to be the artist's technical skill in communicating a spiritually (or I might also say "metaphysically") significant emotional message. Though this is acknowledgedly a subjective criterion, I believe that ultimately the

17: JEWELRY & GIFTS

standard by which any art is judged must be subjective. On the other hand, since my friends have expressed considerable satisfaction at the art-discoveries they've made through my recommendations, I pass these recommendations along to you, for what they're worth (which, depending on whether your tastes happen to agree with mine, may be either something or nothing).

Most of the recommended artists show at outdoor art fairs—especially at the Washington Square Outdoor Art Exhibit, which starts each year on the Memorial-Day and Labor-Day weekends, and extends thereafter for a total of 3 weekends each time. The reason why I avoid gallery-artists is well-demonstrated by the following story I was told by one of these artists, John Russo. He had been approached by a gallery-owner to display his sculptures at the proprietor's posh Madison Avenue gallery, and the artist agreed to offer some pieces there on consignment. The gallery-owner then demanded that Mr. Russo stop showing at fairs, which the sculptor was not willing to do. The two were to meet at the gallery to discuss the matter, but when Russo arrived, he was dismayed to find his work being priced there at six times the rate he asks for the same pieces at fairs. The gallery-owner attempted to persuade Mr. Russo that displaying his creations at street-fairs is wrong for an artist's career, and told the sculptor, as an example to prove the point, that a representative of the Whitney Museum who had stopped by the gallery the day before, had inquired about showing some of Russo's pieces at the Museum. This artist, however, believes deeply in making his works affordable to all people, not merely to the rich. He's actually not interested in being famous; and it simply outraged him that the pieces he had been selling profitably on the street for $30 were tagged inside the gallery at $250. Thus he removed his art. This was the only time he ever showed inside a gallery; and he tells me it'll also be the last. That's consistent with his personality. Russo may be one of the greatest sculptors of this century; but he's also, quite authentically, a "man of the people," with no aspirations toward anything more than a comfortable income, which he already makes. Whether his art will turn out to be a good investment, I can't predict, though I doubt it—the man lacks the kind of ambition that would probably be needed to make it so. But from the standpoint of the incredibly high quality of the art that he produces and sells for an extremely modest price, his pieces are, in my opinion, an astounding bargain. And that's generally the basis on which I recommend the artists here that I do. These are individuals who, in my opinion, offer original work of the highest quality, but at a price that the man-in-the-street can afford.

RECOMMENDED PRODUCTS:
See above.

RECOMMENDED STORES:
gold jewelry
Expect 20-50% discounts.

17: JEWELRY & GIFTS

****+C.O.M.B. Co.** (intermittent stock, outside NYC, 1-800-328-0609, catalog is free if you mention this book); ****Florencia Collections** (696-1396); ****Gustavo Agudeo** (426-3382); ***+Ross Chains** (431-8822); **Davis Behar** (869-3991).

diamonds and colored gems
Expect 30-60% discounts.

***Aurico Gems (mainly colored stones, 953-9159); *****Rennie Ellen** (mainly diamonds, 869-5525); **Investment Rarities Inc.** (mainly colored stones, outside NYC, 1-800-328-1860); **Reliance** (only diamonds, outside NYC, 1-800-227-1590).

semi-precious jewelry
Expect 40-80% discounts.

***Tokar Import Jewelry (244-8293); ****American Pearl.** (221-3045); ****World of Bargains** (924-3588); ***David Su's 7-Art Jewelry** (777-3133); ***Hole-In-The-Wall** (533-1350); **Brooklyn Museum Gift Shop** (Brooklyn, 638-5000); **Christos Jewelry** (691-4034).

costume jewelry
Expect 25-40% discounts.

***Bag Man (560 8952); ****Kina Costume Jewelry** (685-3277); ****Terrific Costume Jewelry** (243-7110); ***David Su's 7-Art Jewelry** (777-3133); ***Park Av. Job Lot** (intermittent stock, 673-7536); **Estel Jewelry** (777-1750).

watches—cheap
Expect 30% discounts.

***Bag Man (560 8952); ****Ashreh Supply** (925-9507); ****Odds & Ends Job-Lots** (intermittent stock, Queens, 441-6878); ****The City Dump** (431-1670); ***Consumers Distributing** (Queens, 268-2091); **E. Nack Watch** (925-5012); **Global Mktg.** (924-3888); **Kris Watches** (691-3660); **New York Watches** (924-4516).

watches—brand-name
Expect 40-60% discounts.

+C.O.M.B. Co. (intermittent stock, outside NYC, 1-800-328-0609, catalog is free if you mention this book); ****D-M Sales** (254-8320); ****Romano Trdg.** (581-4248);-*Weinstock & Yaeger** (398-0780); ***Consumers Distributing** (Queens, 268-2091); ***Lou-Mark Trdg.** (242-9440); ***Michael C. Fina** (757-2530); **Lanas** (684-2760).

watches—prestige-name
Expect 30% discounts.

Tady-K (354-5118); ****Weinstock & Yaeger (398-0780).

watches—antique
Expect 55-70% discounts.

Leon (phoneless); *+Robert Kracauer** (874-7472); ***Ilana Fine Jewelry** (473-1057); ***Ipswich Clocks** (473-3597).

findings & beads
Expect 40-50% discounts.

17: JEWELRY & GIFTS

***Tokar Import Jewelry (244-8293); **Gampel Supply (398-9222); **World of Bargains (924-3588); *Hole-In-The-Wall (533-1350).

crystal glassware
Expect 50-60% discounts.

***Eastside China (Brooklyn, 633-8672); ***Half-Price Store (Brooklyn, 934-6938); ***Job Lot Trdg. (intermittent stock, 962-4142); **J.J.G. Warehouse (intermittent stock, 243-0632); **Odds & Ends Job-Lots (intermittent stock, Queens, 441-6878); *Crystal Factory Outlet (925-8783); *Glenwood Gift (Brooklyn, 649-3296); +Atlantic Export (Queens, 274-7900); A&R Novelty (Brooklyn, 856-8070); Co-op Sales (Brooklyn, 384-2443); East Side Gifts (982-7200); Greater NY Trdg. (226-2808); Jompole (594-0440); Lanac Sales (226-8925).

figurines
Expect 50-60% discounts.

***Galdi Industries (Brooklyn, 522-5395); ***Half-Price Store (Brooklyn, 934-6938); ***Job Lot Trdg. (intermittent stock, 962-4142); ***Sherrill Closeouts Warehouse (674-4430); **Weber's Job Lot (intermittent stock, 564-7668); *Glenwood Gift (Brooklyn, 649-3296); *Park Av. Job Lot (intermittent stock, 673-7536); +Atlantic Export (Queens, 274-7900); First Cost (intermittent stock, 697-0244); Gift Warehouse (intermittent stock, 675-4290); J. Finkelstein (475-1420).

art

****John Russo, Sculptor; **Geo. Forss, Photographer (467-2638, no store--sells only by mail-order); **Harry Pincus, Etchings (925-8871); *Claudette Haba, Painter.

gifts
Expect 30-60% discounts.

****Woodware (outside NYC, 1-802-388-6297); ***East Art Center (685-5370); ***Eastside China (Brooklyn, 633-8672); ***Galdi Industries (Brooklyn, 522-5395); ***Half-Price Store (Brooklyn, 934-6938); ***Job Lot Trdg. (intermittent stock, 962-4142); ***Sherrill Closeouts Warehouse (674-4430); ***Tokar Import Jewelry (244-8293); **Brass Loft Factory Outlet (226-5467); **J.J.G. Warehouse (intermittent stock, 243-0632); **Wildwood; *+Perplexity Lucite (688-3571); *Glenwood Gift (Brooklyn, 649-3296); *Hang Ups Wicker; *India Bazaar (732-0950); *Mitsu (947-7892); *Park Av. Job Lot (intermittent stock, 673-7536); +Atlantic Export (Queens, 274-7900); +Metro Interiors (Brooklyn, 252-4292); A. Benjamin (226-6013); A&R Novelty (Brooklyn, 856-8070); Brooklyn Museum Gift Shop (Brooklyn, 638-5000); Co-op Sales (Brooklyn, 384-2443); Decor Arts (691-8156); East Side Gifts (982-7200); First Cost (intermittent stock, 697-0244); Gift Warehouse (intermittent stock, 675-4290); Greater NY Trdg. (226-2808); J. Finkelstein (475-1420); Jompole (594-0440); Mandarin Products (691-0294); Murray's Pottery (Brooklyn, 376-6002); Sahadi Gift (Brooklyn, 624-4550); The Bowl Shop (962-1682).

commemorative gifts
Expect 45-60% discounts.

(examples: awards, medals, plaques, religious gifts, trophies)
Jompole (594-0440); Michael C. Fina (869-5050).

stones, semi-precious, rough

Expect 50-60% discounts.
(examples: agates, amethysts, dioptases, geodes, septarians, tourmalines)
***Inter-Ocean Trdg.; **Goddesses of The Earth (758-5555).

handcrafts
Expect 20-70% discounts.

****Woodware (outside NYC, 1-802-388-6297); **Charm Shop (242-6626); **Manos Del Uruguay (564-6115); **Wildwood; *+Buen Dia (673-1910); Brooklyn Museum Gift Shop (Brooklyn, 638-5000); Christos Jewelry (691-4034); Craft Caravan (966-1338).

memorabilia
Expect 20-40% discounts.

*Speakeasy (533-2440).

novelties
Expect 30-60% discounts.
(miscellaneous small or faddish gift items)
***+Mills Sales (477-1000); **R&F Electronics (679-5962); Estel Jewelry (777-1750); Mitchell Mogal (226-8378); Paramount Calendar & Specialty (686-6746).

greeting-cards
Expect 30-60% discounts.
(especially Xmas-cards)
***Job Lot Trdg. (intermittent stock, 962-4142); Charles Ree (685-9077).

STORES-DIRECTORY

Phone a store before you go out of your way to visit it. Especially do this during July and August, when most establishments reduce or eliminate weekend-hours.

In the listings below, "*" means especially recommended, "+" means that the store offers a bonus discount to BF readers, "ch." and "c.c." mean respectively checks and credit cards, and "exch." and "rfd." mean respectively exchange and refund. Nearest subway-stops are shown. For example, "B-D-F to 47" means to take the B, D, or F train to 47th Street. Store-hours are also indicated, with days of the week abbreviated, like "M-S 8-6."

    A. Benjamin, 80 Bowery (Canal) (in Manhattan Diamond Ctr.), 226-6013, J-M-N-QB-RR-6 to Canal, M-S 8:30-4, ch., c.c., exch. or rfd. (Except on special orders.) Sells: **Gifts, Dinnerware & Cookware.**

  **   **American Pearl**, 23 W. 47 (5th-6th), inside The Exchange 23, 221-3045, B-D-F to 47, M-F 9-5, ch., no c.c., exch., no rfd. Large selection. Necklaces. Sells: **Semi-Precious Jewelry.**

    A&R Novelty, Brooklyn, 1222 Flatbush Av. (Ditmas), 856-8070, D-M-QB to Beverly, 3-4 to Beverly, M-S 9:30-6, ch., no c.c., 24-day exch. or rfd. Small selection. Sells: **Crystal Glassware, Gifts, Stationery & Art Supplies, Toys, Games & Hobbies.**

  **   **Ashreh Supply**, 473 Broadway (Grand), 3rd floor, 925-9507, J-M-N-QB-RR-6 to Canal, Sun-Th 11-7, all cash, no exch. or rfd. Basically a wholesaler who accomodates retail-trade. Sells: **Watches—Cheap, Appliances, Cameras & Optical Eqt., Personal Accessories, Smoking Supplies, Stationery & Art Supplies.**

  +   **Atlantic Export**, Queens, 25-98 Steinway St., Astoria, 274-7900, RR to Astoria Blvd., M-W 11-7:30, ThF 11-9, Sun 12-6, c.c., no ch., exch., no rfd. Bonus discount to BF readers: 10% to 25%. Sells: **Crystal Glassware, Figurines, Gifts, Appliances, Dinnerware & Cookware.**

17: JEWELRY & GIFTS

*** Aurico Gems, 565 5th Av. (47), rm. 1212, 953-9159, B-D-F to 47, hours by appt., cert. ch., exch. or rfd. Sells: **Diamonds And Colored Gems.**

*** Bag Man, 261 W. 34 (8th Av.), 560 8952, A-AA-CC-E to 34, M-S 10-7, all cash, exch., no rfd. One in the DAC Jewelry group. Sells: **Costume Jewelry, Watches—Cheap, Clothing—Women's, Home-Improvement Items, Personal Accessories.**

** Brass Loft Factory Outlet, 20 Greene St. (Canal), 3rd floor, 226-5467, J-M-N-QB-RR-6 to Canal, A-AA-CC-E-1 to Canal, TWThSSun 10:30-5:30, ch., no c.c., 14-day exch., no rfd. If it's made of brass, they sell it, for 30-60% less than normal. Sells: **Gifts, Furnishings, Home-Improvement Items.**

Brooklyn Museum Gift Shop, Brooklyn, 200 Eastern Pkwy. at Washington Av. on N.E. corner of Prospect Park, 638-5000 x. 391, 2-3-4 to Brooklyn Museum, W-S 10-5, Sun 12-5, ch., c.c., exch. or rfd. Good values, hand-made items from around the world. Closeouts-displaycase has some terrific bargains. Sells: **Semi-Precious Jewelry, Gifts, Handcrafts.**

*+ Buen Dia, 108 W. Houston St. at Thompson, 673-1910, A-AA-B-CC-D-E-F to 4, M-S 12-7, Sun 2-6; 201 W. 11 at 7th Av., 673-1910, 1-2-3 to 14, M-S 12-7. Both stores: c.c., no ch., exch., no rfd. Very cooperative. Everything is knit in Latin America. Bonus discount to BF readers: 5% to 8%. Sells: **Handcrafts, Clothing—Women's, Personal Accessories.**

Charles Ree, 397 5th Av. (36-7), 685-9077, 6 to 33, B-D-F-N-QB-RR to 34, M-F 9-6:30, S 9-5, all cash, no exch. or rfd. Xmas cards and gift-wraps 20-50% off—but first check across the street (412 5th Av.) at Job Lot Trdg. for possibly bigger discounts. Sells: **Greeting-Cards.**

** Charm Shop, 143 W. 4 (6th-MacDougal), 1st floor upstairs, 242-6626, A-AA-B-CC-D-E-F to 4, TWThF 3-6 & 7:30-10, all cash, exch. or rfd. Small store. Small selection. Sells: **Handcrafts.**

Christos Jewelry, 57 7th Av. S. (Morton), 691-4034, 1 to Christopher St., WTh 4:30-7, F 4:30-9, SSun 1-8; 1260 Lexington Av. (85), 861-2675, 4-5-6 to 86, M-S 10-6. Both stores: all cash, exch., no rfd. Lex. Av. store is tiny. Sells: **Semi-Precious Jewelry, Handcrafts.**

* Claudette Haba, Painter, during Wash. Sq. Outdoor Art Exhibit (982-6255), on Univ. Pl. (12-3), near Amy's Restaurant. Or: 2 Wallingford Dr. Princeton, NJ 08540 (the artist's home), ch., no c.c., exch., no rfd. Good—sometimes magnificent—surrealist work, at a very reasonable price, but not cheap. Sells: **Art.**

***+ C.O.M.B. Co., 6850 Wayzata Blvd., Minneapolis, MN 55426, 1-800-328-0609, catalog is free if you mention this book, c.c., exch., no rfd. Takes mail-orders. Catalog. Very cooperative. Catalog is free only if you mention Bargain Finder. Sells: **Gold Jewelry, Watches—Brand-Name, Cameras & Optical Eqt., Home-Improvement Items, Personal Accessories, Warehouse Salvage Job-Lot.**

* Consumers Distributing, Queens, 107-18 70th Rd., Forest Hills, 268-2091, E-F-GG-N to 71-Continental Avs.; Queens, 39-20 Bell Blvd., Bayside, 225-0253, no subway stop nearby; Queens, 156-16 Northern Blvd., Flushing, 961-5024, no subway stop nearby; Queens, 97-10 Queens Blvd., Rego Park, 896-7250, F-GG-N to 63rd Dr.; Brooklyn, Av. U at Mill Av. (nr. Kings Plaza), 241-7633, D-M-QB to Av. M; Queens, 54-30 Myrtle Av., Ridgewood, 386-2809, LL-M to Myrtle & Wyckoff. All stores: M-F 10-9 (Ridgewood 10-6), S 10-6, Sun 12-5, ch., c.c. during banking hours, 30-day exch. or rfd. Large selection. A catalog-showroom chain. Sells: **Watches—Cheap, Watches—Brand-Name, Autos & Supplies, Bikes, Dinnerware & Cookware, Home-Improvement Items, Housewares, Sporting Goods.**

Co-op Sales, Brooklyn, 232 Broadway (Roebling-Havemeyer), 384-2443, J-M to Marcy, M-F 10-5:30, Sun 10-4, c.c., no ch., exch., no rfd. Will special-order. Sells: **Crystal Glassware, Gifts, Appliances, Furnishings.**

Craft Caravan, 127 Spring St. (Greene), 966-1338, A-AA-CC-E to Spring, Sun-F 10-6, ch., no c.c., exch. or rfd. African imports. Sells: **Handcrafts.**

* Crystal Factory Outlet, 53 Delancey St. (Eldridge), 925-8783, F-J-M to Delancey & Essex, J-M to Bowery, Sun-Th 10-5, all cash, exch., no rfd. All is half price. Sells: **Crystal Glassware.**

* David Su's 7-Art Jewelry, 872 Broadway (18), 777-3133, N-RR to 23rd St., LL-N-QB-RR-4-5-6 to Union Sq., M-S 9-6, ch., c.c., no exch. or rfd. Sells: **Semi-Precious Jewelry, Costume Jewelry.**

Davis Behar, 578 5th Av. at 47th St., inside Int'l. Jewelers Exch., 869-3991, B-D-F to 47, M-S 10-5, c.c., no ch., exch., no rfd. Sells: **Gold Jewelry.**

Decor Arts, 25 W. 14 (7th-8th), 691-8156, 1-2-3 to 14, A-AA-CC-E-LL to

17: JEWELRY & GIFTS

14 St. & 8 Av., M-F 10-6, S 10-5, ch., c.c., exch., no rfd. Directors chairs, Mexican chess sets, and other stuff, in an odd melange. Sells: **Gifts, Furnishings.**

** **D-M Sales**, 911 Broadway (20-1), 254-8320, N-RR to 23rd St., M-F 9-5:30, all cash, no exch. or rfd. Timex, Seiko, and others. Sells: **Watches—Brand-Name.**

E. Nack Watch, 226 Canal St. (Baxter), 925-5012, J-M-N-QB-RR-6 to Canal, M-S 10:30-6:30, all cash, no exch. or rfd. Top values in off-brand watches, but watch out! Salesman had patience to show me only one watch, and only for a few seconds. If a timepiece is a bummer, it's your risk. Sells: **Watches—Cheap.**

*** **East Art Center**, 455 3rd Av. (31), 685-5370, 6 to 33, M-S 11-6, ch., no c.c., no exch. or rfd. Sells: **Gifts, Furnishings.**

East Side Gifts, 351 Grand St. (Ludlow-Essex), 982-7200, F-J-M to Delancey & Essex, Sun-F 9:30-5:30, ch., c.c., no exch. or rfd. Sells: **Crystal Glassware, Gifts, Dinnerware & Cookware.**

*** **Eastside China**, Brooklyn, 5002 12th Av., 633-8672, B to 50th St., Sun-Th 10-6, F 10-2, ch., no c.c., exch., no rfd. Terrific discounts on current lines, and even more amazing closeout-specials. Huge selection of dishes. Phone for prices. Sells: **Crystal Glassware, Gifts, Dinnerware & Cookware.**

Estel Jewelry, 222 Park Av. S. at 18th St., 777-1750, LL-N-QB-RR-4-5-6 to Union Sq., M-F 9-5:30, S 9-3:30, all cash, no exch. or rfd. Sells: **Costume Jewelry, Novelties.**

First Cost, 90 E. 42nd St. at Park Av., 697-0244, 4-5-6-7 to Grand Central, M-F 8-7, SSun 10-5; Queens, 46-20 108 St., Corona, 271-1121, 7 to 111, ThS 9-6, F 9-9. Both stores: all cash, 7-day exch. or rfd. Sells: **Figurines, Gifts, Clothing—Children's, Clothing—Men's, Clothing—Women's, Dinnerware & Cookware, Foods, Health & Beauty Aids, Home-Improvement Items, Housewares, Sporting Goods, Toys, Games & Hobbies, Warehouse Salvage Job-Lot.**

** **Florencia Collections**, 267 5th Av. (29), rm. 910, 696-1396, N-RR to 28, M-F 9:30-6, ch., no c.c., exch. no rfd. Sells: **Gold Jewelry.**

*** **Galdi Industries**, Brooklyn, 290 Court St. at Douglass, 522-5395, F-GG to Bergen St., M-F 8-4:30, S 12-2, all cash, exch. or rfd. Only Capodimonte, a huge selection, which they import direct. Sells: **Figurines, Gifts, Furnishings.**

** **Gampel Supply**, 39 W. 37 (5th-6th), 398-9222, B-D-F-N-QB-RR to 34, B-D-F to 42, M-F 8:45-4:45, all cash, no exch. or rfd. Large selection of plastic beads, nothing else. Sells: **Findings & Beads.**

** **Geo. Forss, Photographer**, 729 E. New York Av., Brooklyn, NY 11203, 467-2638, no store—sells only by mail-order, 11' x 14' B/W matted photos of NYC and of animals, ch., (wait till clear) no c.c., exch., no rfd. Very cooperative. Phone or write for free catalog. I discovered Forss when he was selling on the street. Now he's been in Time Magazine, Today Show, and at I.C.P.; yet prices still good. Sells: **Art.**

Gift Warehouse, 28 W. 25 (B'wy), 2nd floor, 675-4290, N-RR to 23rd St., T-F 10-5, SSun 11-5, c.c., no ch., no exch. or rfd. Closeouts from a major distributor. Sells: **Figurines, Gifts.**

* **Glenwood Gift**, Brooklyn, 118 Conklin Av., 649-3296, LL to Rockaway Pkwy., TWFS 10:30-6:30, Th 10:30-8, ch., c.c., exch. or rfd. Takes phone-orders. Sells: **Crystal Glassware, Figurines, Gifts, Dinnerware & Cookware.**

Global Mktg., 49 W. 23 (5th-6th), 924-3888, B-F to 23, N-RR to 23rd St., M-Th 8-6, F 8-2, Sun 10-3, c.c., no ch., exch., no rfd. Sells: **Watches—Cheap, Appliances.**

** **Goddesses of The Earth**, 234 E. 58 (3rd-2nd), downstairs, 758-5555, N-RR-4-5-6 to 59th & Lex., hours by appt., ch., c.c., 7-day exch. or rfd. Sells: **Stones, Semi-Precious, Rough.**

Greater NY Trdg., 81 Canal St. (Eldridge-Allen), 226-2808&8850, F to E. Broadway, Sun-Th 10-5:30, F 10-3, ch., no c.c., 7-day exch. or rfd. Sells: **Crystal Glassware, Gifts, Appliances, Dinnerware & Cookware.**

** **Gustavo Agudeo**, 426-3382, exch. or rfd. Sells: **Gold Jewelry.**

*** **Half-Price Store**, Brooklyn, 2962 Av. U (Nostrand), 934-6938, D-M-QB to Av. U, plus a long walk, M-S 10-6, Sun 12-5, ch., no c.c., exch. or rfd. Large selection. Top name-brands. Stock changes often. Everything is discounted 50% or more. Sells: **Crystal Glassware, Figurines, Gifts, Warehouse Salvage Job-Lot.**

* **Hang Ups Wicker**, Canal at W. Broadway, A-AA-CC-E-1 to Canal, SSun 10-7; 39th St. at 9th Av., A-AA-CC-E to 42, WThF 10-7. Both stores: ch., no c.c. Sells: **Gifts, Furnishings.**

** **Harry Pincus, Etchings**, 210 Spring St. at 6th Av.; & Wash. Sq. Outdoor

17: JEWELRY & GIFTS

Art Exhibit (982-6255), 925-8871, hours by appt., ch., no c.c., exch., no rfd. His stuff often appears in places like the New York Times. He imbues his scenes and characters with atmosphere and soul. Sells: **Art**.

* **Hole-In-The-Wall**, 229 E. 14 (3rd-2nd), upstairs, 533-1350, LL to 3rd Av., M-S 2-6, ch., no c.c., exch., no rfd. Friendly. And the store's name is appropriate. Sells: **Semi-Precious Jewelry, Findings & Beads**.

* **Ilana Fine Jewelry**, 42 University Place (9-10), 473-1057, LL-N-QB-RR-4-5-6 to Union Sq., N-RR to 8th St., T-S 11-6, ch., c.c., no rfd. Sells: **Watches—Antique**.

* **India Bazaar**, 149 Church St. (Warren-Chambers), 732-0950, A-CC-1-2-3 to Chambers, M-S 8:30-6:30, c.c., no ch., 7-day exch., no rfd. Much Indian brassware. Sells: **Gifts**.

*** **Inter-Ocean Trdg.**, phone 752-5578, and speak to Paul F. Heubert, to inquire about colored, semi-precious stones, such as topazes, amethysts, tourmalines, aquamarines, and garnets, both rough and cut. For the craftsman, the collector, and the investor. Stones only. No finished jewelry. Sells: **Stones, Semi-Precious, Rough**.

Investment Rarities Inc., 1 Appletree Sq., Minneapolis, MN 55420, 1-800-328-1860. Diamonds only at auctions held in Minneapolis, but colored stones available here on the same basis that Reliance sells diamonds. So recommended especially for colored. Sells: **Diamonds And Colored Gems**.

* **Ipswich Clocks**, 175 2nd Av. (11), 473-3597, LL to 3rd Av., 6 to Astor, M-S 10-6:30, ch., no c.c., exch., no rfd. 6-month guarantee. Also carries antique clocks. Sells: **Watches—Antique**.

J. Finkelstein, 95 Delancey St. (Orchard-Ludlow), 475-1420, F-J-M to Delancey & Essex, Sun-F 10-5, ch., no c.c., no exch. or rfd. Sells: **Figurines, Gifts**.

** **J.J.G. Warehouse**, 36 W. 25 (B'wy), 243-0632, N-RR to 23rd St., M-F 10-5, SSun 10-4, c.c., no exch. or rfd. Constantly changing stock, always giftwares, but sometimes crystal, sometimes Limoges and Wedgewood closeouts, sometimes earthenware. Mostly 40-60% off. Up to 70%. Sells: **Crystal Glassware, Gifts, Dinnerware & Cookware**.

*** **Job Lot Trdg.**, 140 Church St. (Warren-Chambers), 962-4142, A-CC-1-2-3 to Chambers; 412 5th Av. (37-8), 398-9210, B-D-F to 42. Both stores: M-F 8-5:30, S 8-4:30, all cash, 15-day exch. or rfd. Both are huge stores, with terrific selections. Sells: **Crystal Glassware, Figurines, Gifts, Clothing—Men's, Dinnerware & Cookware, Foods, Home-Improvement Items, Housewares, Linens, Personal Accessories, Sporting Goods, Stationery & Art Supplies, Toys, Games & Hobbies, Warehouse Salvage Job-Lot**.

**** **John Russo, Sculptor**, during Wash. Sq. Outdoor Art Exhibit (982-6255), in front of 33 5th Av., showing his extremely dynamic nut-and-bolt figures, a form he created almost 30 yrs. ago; he's still the only master, ch., no c.c., exch. or rfd. Very cooperative. In my opinion, his best work is sublime—some of the best sculpture of the 20th Century, all from humble materials. This guy should be in the history books. Sells: **Art**.

Jompole, 330 7th Av. at 29th St., 3rd floor, 594-0440&2, 1 to 28, MTWF 10-4, Th 10-7, S 10-3, ch., no c.c., exch. or rfd. (But only if defective.) Sells: **Crystal Glassware, Gifts, Commemorative Gifts, Dinnerware & Cookware**.

** **Kina Costume Jewelry**, 1165 Broadway (27-8), 685-3277, N-RR to 28th St., M-F 8-6, SSun 9-4, all cash, no exch. or rfd. Sells: **Costume Jewelry**.

Kris Watches, 34 W. 14 (5th-6th Avs.), street stand, 691-3660, B-F-LL to 14th St. & 6th Av., M-S 11-6, all cash, exch., no rfd. Sells: **Watches—Cheap**.

Lanac Sales, 63 Canal St. at Allen, 226-8925 & 925-6422, F to E. Broadway, B-D to Grand, M-Th 10-6, F 10-2, Sun 9-5, ch., no c.c., exch. or rfd. Large selection of dishes. Sells: **Crystal Glassware, Dinnerware & Cookware**.

Lanas, 43 W. 30 (5th-6th), 684-2760&2482, B-D-F-N-QB-RR to 34, N-RR to 28th St., M-F 10-6, S 10-2, all cash, no exch. or rfd. Sells: **Watches—Brand-Name**.

** **Leon**, 252 Bleecker St. at Leroy, booth 25, phoneless, A-AA-B-CC-D-E-F to 4, Th-Sun 12-8, all cash, no exch. or rfd. Sells: **Watches—Antique**.

* **Lou-Mark Trdg.**, 13 E. 17 (5th Av.), 242-9440, LL-N-QB-RR-4-5-6 to Union Sq., M-F 9-6, Sun 9-12, all cash, exch., no rfd. Sells: **Watches—Brand-Name, Appliances, Health & Beauty Aids**.

Mandarin Products, 35 W. 23 (5th-6th), 691-0294, N-RR to 23rd St., B-F to 23, M-F 9-6, S 9-5, ch., c.c., exch., no rfd. The gift items are Indian brassware. Sells: **Gifts, Office Equipment**.

17: JEWELRY & GIFTS

** **Manos Del Uruguay**, 35 W. 36 (5th-6th), 12th floor, 564-6115, B-D-F-N-QB-RR to 34, open only 3rd Monday after Thanksgiving through Dec. 23, M-F 11-7, ch., c.c., no exch. or rfd. Beautiful multi-tonal sweaters, hats, scarves, ties, jackets, capes, and mittens. Wool is hand-spun and kettle-dyed. 50% off. No retail at other times than indicated. Sells: **Handcrafts, Clothing—Women's, Personal Accessories.**

+ **Metro Interiors**, Brooklyn, 3700 Nostrand Av. (X), 252-4292, no subway stop nearby, M-S 11-5, c.c., no ch., exch. or rfd. Only dinettes, home bars, room dividers, giftware. Bonus discount to BF readers: 2% to 5%. Sells: **Gifts, Furnishings.**

Michael C. Fina, 580 5th Av. at 47th, 2nd floor, 869-5050, B-D-F to 47, M-F 9-5:30, ch., c.c., exch. or rfd. Takes mail-orders. Catalog. Sells: **Watches—Brand-Name, Cameras & Optical Eqt., Dinnerware & Cookware, Personal Accessories.**

+ Mills Sales, 889 Broadway at 19th St., 477-1000, LL-N-QB-RR-4-5-6 to Union Sq., N-RR to 23rd St., M-F 9-5, S 9-2, all cash, no exch. or rfd. No retail sales (wholesale only) Labor Day through Xmas. A specialty here is steel ball-point pens super-cheap by the dozen. Bonus discount to BF readers: 5%. Sells: **Novelties, Appliances, Dinnerware & Cookware, Home-Improvement Items, Personal Accessories, Stationery & Art Supplies, Toys, Games & Hobbies.

Mitchell Mogal, 440 Broadway (Grand), 226-8378, J-M-N-QB-RR-6 to Canal, M-F 9-5, all cash, exch., no rfd. Terrific on Wiss scissors; also on miniature cap-guns. Sells: **Novelties, Fabrics, Yarns & Notions, Personal Accessories, Toys, Games & Hobbies.**

* **Mitsu**, 25 W. 35 (5th-6th), 947-7892, B-D-F-N-QB-RR to 34, M-S 10-6, all cash, exch., no rfd. Carries some of the same stuff as Azuma, but for about 20% less. Sells: **Gifts, Clothing—Men's, Home-Improvement Items.**

New York Watches, 18 W. 14 (5th-6th Avs.) street stand in front of N.Y. Jewelry, 924-4516, B-F-LL to 14th St. & 8 Av., 7 days, all cash, exch., no rfd. Sells: **Watches—Cheap.**

Murray's Pottery, Brooklyn, 802 Kings Hwy., 376-6002, D-M-QB to Kings Hwy., MWFS 11-6:30, TTh 11-9:30, ch., no c.c., exch., no rfd. Sells: **Gifts, Dinnerware & Cookware.**

** **Odds & Ends Job-Lots**, Queens, 88-09 Jamaica Av., Woodside, 441-6878, J to Woodhaven Blvd., M-S 9-6, Sun 9-3; Queens, 57-60 Woodside Av., Woodside, phoneless, 7 to 61st St., M-Th 10-7, F 10-9, S 9-6, Sun 9-5. Both stores: all cash, exch. or rfd. Sells: **Watches—Cheap, Crystal Glassware, Dinnerware & Cookware, Health & Beauty Aids, Home-Improvement Items, Housewares, Recordings & Tapes, Toys, Games & Hobbies, Warehouse Salvage Job-Lot.**

Paramount Calendar & Specialty, 52 W. 29 (6th Av.), 686-6746&5139, N-RR to 28th St., M-F 9-5:30, all cash, no exch. or rfd. Sells: **Novelties, Toys, Games & Hobbies.**

* **Park Av. Job Lot**, 270 Park Av. S. (21), 673-7536, 6 to 23, M-S 9-6, all cash, 7-day exch., no rfd. Many Slavic gift items. Sells: **Costume Jewelry, Figurines, Gifts, Clothing—Women's, Health & Beauty Aids, Warehouse Salvage Job-Lot.**

*+ **Perplexity Lucite**, 237 E. 53 (3rd-2nd Avs.), 688-3571, E-F to Lex. Av., M-S 10:30-6:30, Sun 12-5, ch., c.c. (only c.c. is AE), exch., no rfd. Another store in Carle Place, Long Island. Bonus discount to BF readers: 5%. Sells: **Gifts, Furnishings, Stationery & Art Supplies.**

Reliance, 1911 San Miguel Dr., Walnut Creek, CA 94596, 1-800-227-1590, only for diamonds, and they'll quote by phone if you'll tell them the diamond-specs, ch., c.c., but ch. must be cert., 10-day exch. or rfd. Catalog. Very cooperative. Large selection. Stones available both loose and set (but local jewelers will also set, if you prefer). Stones shipped direct to you from NYC cutters. Sells: **Diamonds And Colored Gems.**

*** **Rennie Ellen**, 15 W. 47, rm. 401, 869-5525, B-D-F to 47, hours by appt. teller's check, 5-day, exch. or rfd. Sells: **Diamonds And Colored Gems.**

* **R&F Electronics**, 36 W. 29 (B'wy), 679-5962, N-RR to 28th St., M-Th 9-6, SunF 9-4:30, no exch. or rfd. Sells: **Novelties, Appliances, Dinnerware & Cookware, Home-Improvement Items.**

Robert Kracauer, 252 Bleecker St. at Leroy, booth 44, 874-7472, A-AA-B-CC-D-E-F to 4, Th-Sun 12-8, all cash, exch. or rfd. Bonus discount to BF readers: 10% to 40%. Sells: **Watches—Antique.**

** **Romano Trdg.**, 628 W. 45th St. on 12th Av., 581-4248, A-AA-CC-E to 42, plus a long walk, M-F 8-5:30, S 8-5, all cash, exch. or rfd. Very cooperative. A little bit of everything, designer-name and major brand items. Sells: **Watches—Brand-Name,**

17: JEWELRY & GIFTS

Appliances, Clothing—Men's, Office Equipment, Personal Accessories, Stationery & Art Supplies, Toys, Games & Hobbies.

✩ + **Ross Chains**, 74 Bowery (Canal), 431-8822, J-M-N-QB-RR-6 to Canal, B-D to Grand, M-S 9:30-4, c.c., no ch., no exch. or rfd. Bonus discount to BF readers: 1% to 10%. Sells: **Gold Jewelry**.

Sahadi Gift, Brooklyn, 187 Atlantic Av. (Court-Clinton), 624-4550&5762, M-RR-2-3-4-5 to Borough Hall & Court St., M-S 9-7, all cash, exch. or rfd. Arabic items. Sells: **Gifts**.

✩✩✩ **Sherrill Closeouts Warehouse**, 12 E. 22 (B'wy), 674-4430, N-RR to 23rd St., 6 to 23, M-F 10-6, SSun 10-6, ch., c.c., no exch. or rfd. Oriental items, mostly hand-carved or hand-painted, 50-60% off. Sells: **Figurines, Gifts, Furnishings**.

✩ **Speakeasy**, 799 Broadway (11), 533-2440, LL-N-QB-RR-4-5-6 to Union Sq., N-RR to 8th St., phone for hours, ch., c.c., no exch. or rfd. Original posters, Beetles stuff, old postcards and magazines, games and toys, art deco, pin-on buttons, baseball cards, etc. Sells: **Memorabilia**.

✩✩ **Tady-K**, 36 W. 47th St., 354-5118&5579, B-D-F to 47, MTh 9-5:30, F 9-3, ch., c.c., exch. or rfd. Sells: **Watches—Prestige-Name**.

✩✩ **Terrific Costume Jewelry**, 861 Broadway (17), 243-7110, LL-N-QB-RR-4-5-6 to Union Sq., N-RR to 23rd St., M-F 8:30-6, S 8:30-4, Sun 10-2, all cash, no exch. or rfd. By the half-dozen, at 50-70% off. Sells: **Costume Jewelry**.

The Bowl Shop, 45 Mott St. (Bayard), 962-1682, J-M-N-QB-RR-6 to Canal, J-M-RR-4-5-6 to Chambers & Bkln. Bridge, B-D to Grand, W-M 12-11, T 12-9, all cash, exch., no rfd. Sells: **Gifts**.

✩✩ **The City Dump**, 334 Canal St. (Greene), 431-1670, A-AA-CC-E-1 to Canal, J-M-N-QB-RR-6 to Canal, 7 days 10-6, all cash, exch., no rfd. Outstanding values only on the items for which the store is here recommended. Otherwise uneven. Sells: **Watches—Cheap, Appliances, Sporting Goods**.

✩✩✩ **Tokar Import Jewelry**, 240 W. 37 (7th-8th), 244-8293, 1-2-3 to 34, A-AA-CC-E to 34, M-F 8:30-5, S 9-5, ch., no c.c., exch., no rfd. Large selection. Semi-precious jewelry sells here for the same price other places charge for costume jewelry. 80% discounts are routine. Friendly service, too. Sells: **Semi-Precious Jewelry, Findings & Beads, Gifts**.

✩✩ **Weber's Job Lot**, 505 8th Av. at 35th, 564-7668, A-AA-CC-E to 34, M-F 10-6:30, S 10-6; 136 Church St. at Warren, 564-7668, A-CC-1-2-3 to Chambers, M-S 8-6; 2064 Broadway at 71st, 787-1644, 1-2-3 to 72, M-F 9-9, S 9-6, Sun 12-6. All stores: c.c., no ch., 7-day exch. or rfd. Some terrific values; others not good. Some prices wrongly marked on items each time I was at both stores; checkout counter said 'It's an error.' Sells: **Figurines, Dinnerware & Cookware, Health & Beauty Aids, Home-Improvement Items, Linens, Personal Accessories, Stationery & Art Supplies, Warehouse Salvage Job-Lot**.

✩✩ **Weinstock & Yaeger**, 578 5th Av. at 47th St. inside Int'l. Jewelers Exch., 398-0780, ; 23 W. 47 (5th-6th) inside The Exchange 23, 581-0413&18, B-D-F to 47. Both stores: M-S 9-5, ch., c.c., exch. or rfd. Specialty here is the more expensive lines. Sells: **Watches—Brand-Name, Watches—Prestige-Name**.

✩✩ **Wildwood**, Levine, 10 Adams St., Port Washington, NY 11050, also during Wash. Sq. Outdoor Art Exh. (982-6255), on LaGuardia Place, ch., no c.c., exch., no rfd. Exquisite crafted clocks, and chess-sets & board-boxes, from wood, all worth the more expensive lines. Sells: **Handcrafts**.

✩✩✩✩ **Woodware**, Rt. 7 S., Middlebury, Vt., 1-802-388-6297. Such incredible value that I break the rules here. $20-25 for hand-carved wood lamps; other handmade wooden items, gifts, clocks. He even cuts down the trees himself. Sells: **Gifts, Handcrafts, Furnishings**.

✩✩ **World of Bargains**, 195 7th Av. (21), 924-3588, 1 to 23, T-S 12-5, all cash, no exch. or rfd. Sells: **Semi-Precious Jewelry, Findings & Beads**.

18:
LINENS
Expect 30-50% discounts.

RECOMMENDED STORES:

linens—basic

(examples: bathroom accessories, bed-sheets, blankets, comforters, curtains, draperies, mattress-pads, pillow-cases, pillows, place-mats, quilts, sheets, shower-curtains, towels)

***Job Lot Trdg.** (intermittent stock, 962-4142); ***Odd Job Trdg.** (intermittent stock, 686-6825); ***+Bedford/Bedmark Textile** (533-6717); ****Alee Discount** (intermittent stock, 619-2980); ****Cayne's 1** (695-8451); ****Cayne's 2** (244-8761); ****Cayne's 3** (564-3350); ****Kramer Textile** (226-4530); ****Meyer Ostrov's Sons** (226-3554); ****Penn Textile** (226-1250); ****Shelinsky** (226-1816); ****Weber's Job Lot** (intermittent stock, 564-7668); ***A&E Mosseri** (431-7443); ***Eldridge Jobbing** (226-5136); ***Jomark Textiles** (925-4100); ***L&S Textile** (925-7876); ***Ray Variety** (736-2547); ***Shorland Textile** (226-0228); **Ar-Tex Mfg.** (966-2162); **Canal Street Discount** (intermittent stock, 226-8796); **Ch. Dym** (925-8913); **L&K Merchandise** (475-9196); **Max Eilenberg** (925-4456); **Most's Dept. Store** (Queens, 225-3455); **Penchina Textile** (925-3880); **Sofsan** (989-7292); **Victoria Stores** (intermittent stock, 619-1338).

linens—designer

(larger selection of the above, especially from designers)

*Eldridge Jobbing (226-5136); ***L&S Textile** (925-7876); **Max Eilenberg** (925-4456); **Rubin & Green** (226-5015).

quilts & pillows (& SEE PRECEDING)

L. Schwartz & Sons (674-0326); ****Lucky Gift (233-0960); ****Rennert Mfg.** (925-1463); ***A&E Mosseri** (431-7443); ***I. Itzkowitz** (477-1788).

table linens

(examples: damasks, napkins, tablecloths)

Belcrest Linens (688-8118); ***Robin Imports (753-6475); ***Sam Hedaya** (868-0139).

STORES-DIRECTORY

Phone a store before you go out of your way to visit it. Especially do this during July and August, when most establishments reduce or eliminate weekend-hours.

In the listings below, "*" means especially recommended, "+" means that the store offers a bonus discount to BF readers, "ch." and "c.c." mean respectively checks and credit cards, and "exch." and "rfd." mean respectively exchange and refund. Nearest subway-stops are shown. For example, "B-D-F to 47" means to take the B, D, or F train to 47th Street. Store-hours are also indicated, with days of the week abbreviated, like "M-S 8-6."

*   **A&E Mosseri**, 86 Eldridge St. (Grand), 431-7443, B-D to Grand, Sun-F

18: LINENS

10-5, all cash, exch., no rfd. Ready-made and custom-made bedspreads and draperies; also polyester quilts. Sells: **Linens—Basic, Quilts & Pillows.**

** **Alee Discount**, 85 Chambers St. (B'wy-Church), 619-2980, A-CC-1-2-3 to Chambers, N-RR to City Hall, M-F 9-6, S 10-5, ch., c.c., 10-day exch. or rfd. Sells: **Linens—Basic, Clothing—Children's, Clothing—Men's, Clothing—Women's, Warehouse Salvage Job-Lot.**

Ar-Tex Mfg., 456 Broadway (Grand), up 1 flight, 966-2162, J-M-N-QB-RR-6 to Canal, Sun-F 9-5, ch., no c.c., exch. or rfd. Manufactures and sells bedspreads, curtains, and drapes. Sells: **Linens—Basic.**

+ **Bedford/Bedmark Textile, 611 Broadway at Houston, rm. 511, 533-6717, N-RR to Prince St., Sun-F 9-5:30, ch., no c.c., exch. or rfd. A very busy place. No down quilts or pillows. Bonus discount to BF readers: 2% to 5%. Sells: **Linens—Basic, Quilts & Pillows.**

** **Belcrest Linens**, 304 5th Av. (31), 688-8118, N-RR to 28th St., M-F 9-5, ch., no c.c., exch. or rfd. Sells: **Table Linens.**

Canal Street Discount, 255 Canal (Lafayette), 226-8796, J-M-N-QB-RR-6 to Canal, M-S 10-6, all cash, exch. or rfd. Sells: **Linens—Basic, Warehouse Salvage Job-Lot.**

** **Cayne's 1**, 1345 Broadway (36), 695-8451, B-D-F-N-QB-RR to 34, M-S 10-6:30, ch., no ch., 25-day exch. or rfd. One in the Cayne group. Sells: **Linens—Basic, Clothing—Men's, Clothing—Women's, Sporting Goods.**

** **Cayne's 2**, 225 W. 34 (7th-8th), basement downstairs, 244-8761, 1-2-3 to 34, A-AA-CC-E to 34, M-S 10-6:30, c.c., no ch., 25-day exch. or rfd. One in the Cayne group. Sells: **Linens—Basic, Clothing—Children's, Health & Beauty Aids.**

** **Cayne's 3**, 1333 Broadway (36), 564-3350, B-D-F-N-QB-RR to 34, M-S 10-6:30, c.c., no ch., 25-day exch. or rfd. One in the Cayne group. Sells: **Linens—Basic, Personal Accessories.**

Ch. Dym, 103 Eldridge St. (Grand), 925-8913, B-D to Grand, Sun-F 9-6, all cash, no exch. or rfd. Custom-makes slipcovers, draperies, and bedspreads. Sells: **Linens—Basic.**

* **Eldridge Jobbing**, 86 Eldridge St. (Grand), 226-5136&5481, B-D to Grand, Sun-F 9-5, c.c., no ch., exch., no rfd. Sells: **Linens—Basic, Linens—Designer.**

* **I. Itzkowitz**, 161 Allen St. (Stanton), 477-1788, F to 2nd Av., Sun-F 7-4, all cash, no exch. or rfd. Only down. Sells: **Quilts & Pillows.**

*** **Job Lot Trdg.**, 140 Church St. (Warren-Chambers), 962-4142, A-CC-1-2-3 to Chambers; 412 5th Av. (37-8), 398-9210, B-D-F to 42. Both stores: M-F 8-5:30, S 8-4:30, all cash, 15-day exch. or rfd. Both are huge stores, with terrific selections. Sells: **Linens—Basic, Clothing—Men's, Dinnerware & Cookware, Foods, Home-Improvement Items, Housewares, Jewelry & Gifts, Personal Accessories, Sporting Goods, Stationery & Art Supplies, Toys, Games & Hobbies, Warehouse Salvage Job-Lot.**

* **Jomark Textiles**, 515 Broadway (Spring-Prince), 925-4100, N-RR to Prince St., M-F 9-6, Sun 11-6, all cash, no exch. or rfd. Sells: **Linens—Basic.**

** **Kramer Textile**, 494 Broadway (Broome), 226-4530&5654, J-M-N-QB-RR-6 to Canal, M-F 9-5, Sun 9-4:30, all cash, exch., no rfd. No down quilts or pillows. Sells: **Linens—Basic, Quilts & Pillows.**

** **L. Schwartz & Sons**, 149 Allen St. (Rivington), 674-0326, F to 2nd Av., F-J-M to Delancey & Essex, B-D to Grand, Sun-F 9-6, all cash, no exch. or rfd. All kinds of quilts and pillows, ready-made and made-to-order, including goosedown and polyester fiberfill. Sells: **Quilts & Pillows.**

L&K Merchandise, 138 Ludlow St. (Rivington), 475-9196 & 533-8544, F-J-M to Delancey & Essex, T-W 9-5, all cash, exch. or rfd. Sells: **Linens—Basic.**

* **L&S Textile**, 276 Grand St. (Chrystie), 925-7876 & 226-9047, B-D to Grand, Sun-Th 9-6, F 9-2, ch., no c.c., exch., no rfd. Sells: **Linens—Basic, Linens—Designer.**

** **Lucky Gift**, 20 Bowery at Pell, 233-0960 & 962-9793, J-M-RR-4-5-6 to Chambers & Bkln. Bridge, F to E. Broadway, 7 days 10-8, all cash, no exch. or rfd. Small store. Chinese-made items. Sells: **Quilts & Pillows, Clothing—Men's.**

Max Eilenberg, 449 Broadway (Grand), 925-4456, J-M-N-QB-RR-6 to Canal, M-F 9-5, all cash, no exch. or rfd. Sells: **Linens—Basic, Linens—Designer.**

** **Meyer Ostrov's Sons**, 265 Broome St. at Allen, 226-3554&8553, B-D to Grand, Sun-Th 9-4, F 9-2, ch., no c.c., exch. or rfd. Sells: **Linens—Basic.**

Most's Dept. Store, Queens, 210-15 Horace Harding Blvd., Bayside,

18: LINENS

225-3455, no subway stop nearby, T-S 9:30-6, all cash, no exch. or rfd. Sells: **Linens—Basic, Clothing—Children's, Clothing—Men's, Clothing—Women's.**

***   **Odd Job Trdg.**, 7 E. 40 (Mad.), 686-6825, B-D-F to 42, 7 to 5th Av.; 66 W. 48 (6th Av.), 575-0477, B-D-F to 47. Both stores: M-Th 8-5:30, F 8-3, Sun 10-5, ch., no c.c., 15-day exch. or rfd. Sells: **Linens—Basic, Clothing—Men's, Dinnerware & Cookware, Foods, Health & Beauty Aids, Home-Improvement Items, Housewares, Personal Accessories, Stationery & Art Supplies, Toys, Games & Hobbies, Warehouse Salvage Job-Lot.**

Penchina Textile, 272 Grand St. (Forsyth), 925-3880 & 226-9355, B-D to Grand, Sun-F 9-5, ch., no c.c., exch., no rfd. Sells: **Linens—Basic.**

**   **Penn Textile**, 405 Broadway (Lispenard), 226-1250, J-M-N-QB-RR-6 to Canal, M-F 8:30-5:30, all cash, exch., no rfd. Sells: **Linens—Basic.**

*   **Ray Variety**, 539 9th Av. at 40th, 736-2547, A-AA-CC-E to 42, M-S 9:30-6:30, all cash, exch. or rfd. Sells: **Linens—Basic, Clothing—Men's, Health & Beauty Aids.**

**   **Rennert Mfg.**, 93 Greene St. (Spring), 925-1463, N-RR to Prince St., A-AA-CC-E to Spring, M-F 8:30-5, all cash, no exch. or rfd. Movers' quilts, made here, huge selection, extremely warm and attractive, great to keep warm in bed, or to use as bed-pads under bedsheets. Best-value are the cheapest. Sells: **Quilts & Pillows.**

Robin Imports, 510 Madison Av. (52-3), 753-6475, E-F to 5th Av., M-F 9-6, S 10-5, ch., c.c., exch., no rfd. Sells: **Table Linens, Dinnerware & Cookware.**

Rubin & Green, 290 Grand St. at Eldridge, 226-5015&0313, B-D to Grand, Sun-Th 9-5, F 9-4, ch., c.c., exch. or rfd. Large selection. Sells: **Linens—Designer.**

*   **Sam Hedaya**, 296 5th Av. (31), 868-0139, N-RR to 28th St., M-F 9-5, ch., no c.c., exch., no rfd. Sells: **Table Linens.**

**   **Shelinsky**, 448 Broadway (Grand), 226-1816, J-M-N-QB-RR-6 to Canal, M-F 9-5, Sun 10-3, all cash, exch., no rfd. (But only if unopened.) Sells: **Linens—Basic.**

*   **Shorland Textile**, 274 Grand St. (Chrystie), 226-0228, B-D to Grand, irregular hours, all cash, exch., no rfd. Sells: **Linens—Basic.**

Sofsan, 2 W. 14 (5th Av.), 989-7292 & 255-4367, B-F-LL to 14th St. & 6th Av.; Queens, 159-29 Jamaica Av., Jamaica, 526-0514, E-F to Parsons Blvd. Both stores: M-S 10:30-7, c.c., no ch., no exch. or rfd. Sells: **Linens—Basic, Dinnerware & Cookware.**

Victoria Stores, 114 Worth St. (B'wy), 619-1338, N-RR to City Hall, M-F 9:30-6, all cash, 14-day exch. or rfd. Sells: **Linens—Basic, Warehouse Salvage Job-Lot.**

**   **Weber's Job Lot**, 505 8th Av. at 35th, 564-7668, A-AA-CC-E to 34, M-F 10-6:30, S 10-6; 136 Church St. at Warren, 564-7668, A-CC-1-2-3 to Chambers, M-S 8-6; 2064 Broadway at 71st, 787-1644, 1-2-3 to 72, M-F 9-9, S 9-6, Sun 12-6. All stores: c.c., no ch., 7-day exch. or rfd. Some terrific values; others not good. Some prices wrongly marked on items each time I was at both stores; checkout counter said 'It's an error.' Sells: **Linens—Basic, Dinnerware & Cookware, Health & Beauty Aids, Home-Improvement Items, Jewelry & Gifts, Personal Accessories, Stationery & Art Supplies, Warehouse Salvage Job-Lot.**

19:
LIQUORS, WINES, BEERS, SODAS
Expect 15-35% discounts.

Virtually every dealer listed in this chapter will quote prices by phone.

In New York State, discounts on both wines and liquors are strictly limited by the State Liquor Authority; and liquor-discounts are especially restricted. Nonetheless, as will be seen, there are ways in which the wise wine-buyer especially can save substantially.

The sad fact is that the crooked hand of government regulation has thoroughly poisoned the wine-and-liquor industries; and as a consequence, the New York consumer is forced to pay a heavy tithe with each wine-or-liquor purchase. Not that the public gains anything from this regulation. As usually happens with such government-intervention, the public-benefits are more apparent than real; the corruption and other public-costs are more real than apparent. Yet the vast booboisie continues to believe in the essential goodness of a system which victimizes them. So the rotten system goes on, taking from the many to give to this or that well-positioned elite.

After all, why are there fully 2,000 wine-and-liquor dealers in just this one City? Because prices are kept up by the posting of legally mandated minimums, so that even if a store sells few bottles, the take is enough to make it profitable for the dealer at the expense of all his customers. Remove the fixed prices—the requirement that stores must sell at or above certain "minimum" prices or else loose their licenses—and most of these dealerships would simply fold. Of course, that would mean temporary hardship for the former owners of these overpriced stores—an unfortunate thing. But just because the government has created a mess, doesn't mean that the injustice should go on being perpetuated indefinitely. The public keeps paying for this mess, and if the government-protection of these overpricers stopped, then the overpriced shops would ultimately close, and their personnel would find more constructive work in non-governmentally controlled parts of the economy. These overpricers often style themselves as "mom-and-pop" liquor-stores. But the truth about such so-called "moms and pops" is that they have their hands in your wallet, and that some of the money such stores take from you ends up ultimately in the campaign-coffers of corrupt politicians who support the very same regulatory system that perpetuates this money-funnel from you to them. The overpriced dealers have a political organization with thousands of members statewide, and it has clout. So every time you purchase wine or liquor from a high-priced "mom and pop," just think of that fraction of the price that'll go to pay for you to be deceived by ads in the next political contest.

These ads work, which is why the system manages to perpetuate itself. That's just the way politics works for the benefit of the lucky and connected few, at the public's expense.

Fortunately, however, there's a small band of principled wine-and-liquor merchants who would like to abolish the governmentally-mandated minimum prices, and who have fought in Albany for this. They're called "The Retailers' Alliance," and although they discount as much as they legally can, they want to lower their prices still further. They want to make their livelihoods by offering you more value and so attracting more buyers (at the expense, of course, of the overpriced stores). They don't wish to have the government guarantee them a living. They'd rather earn their keep in the free market by giving you more and bigger bargains. Among the wine-and-liquor-store listings below, the NYC members of The Retailers' Alliance are given a star. If you buy from these discounters, then some of your money will go to fight against the system that robs all New York State wine-and-liquor consumers. One bonus-advantage: Most members of The Retailers' Alliance will offer a 10-20% bonus-discount off their regular low wine-prices if you show them this book. This is indicated by the store's name being preceded by both an "*" and a "+".

Two stars are given to the spirits-merchant that singlehandedly challenged the New York State Liquor Authority, and beat back their mandatory wine-price-fixing law in court: Domenick's Wines in Astoria, Queens. Because of Domenick's courageous (and to them costly) act, all New York Staters now enjoy the benefits of genuinely discounted wines (although some restrictions do continue to exist on wine-discounting). In fact, Domenick's itself now discounts all wines at least 20%, and they sell more than 100 different wines below $3. They're certainly one of the very top—if not the best—bargain stores for wines and liquors anywhere in the City.

The unstarred stores are also discounters. Some have even been active from time to time fighting alongside The Retailers' Alliance, but none has joined it.

Because of the governmentally fixed minimum prices, no dealer can discount very much on liquors. In fact, the liquor-price minimums are fixed so high that most "non-discount" stores sell most liquors at the legal minimums. Prices at different liquor-shops tend to be boringly the same as a result of government's usual intervention at the public's expense.

There's one other double-starred store, besides Domenick's in Queens: Frank Horan, at 33 7th Av., near 13th Street, in Manhattan (691-6246). This shop is unique in that it goes out of its way to offer you a large selection of the least expensive wines, where the profit is the smallest and the value to the consumer the greatest. As of the time of this writing (and for at least two years past), they've always had more than 30 different wines at $2, and another 30+ that are $2.50. Ask them to recommend ones to try. I have, and I've found some excellent cheap wines by following their advice. Among the wines they introduced to me (and before the distributor started advertising them, too) is the fine—and now widely

19: LIQUORS, WINES, BEERS, SODAS

available—Partager, both the (somewhat sweet) red, and the (somewhat dry) white—each of which is a true bargain, superior to others costing three times the low Partager price. Another recent, and even cheaper, winner that Horan's introduced me to, is the excellent Sommeliere; both the red and the white are magnificent bargains. You'll be surprised at how small this store is. But they really do pack in the wine-values.

You've no doubt seen all those TV ads for various brands of California wines, claiming that these domestic oenological products beat the finest of Europe. Well, although some California whites are OK, the sad fact is that California's red wines are abominable. I've never encountered a California red at any price that can even approach the quality of the best $3-5 reds from Spain or Portugal, or even France. All West-Coast reds, to a greater or lesser extent (with a few exceptions only among the more expensive bottles) have at least a tinge of a certain chemical-like stench to them, which evidently some professional wine-tasters, who are paid to do those ads, amazingly fail to notice. For example, the popular Gallo Hearty Burgundy, which many authorities claim to be a solidly excellent wine, tastes to me more like a waft of liquified bottled air from Elizabeth, New Jersey. The critically acclaimed Taylor California Cellars Burgundy, the same. California red wines are usually easy to recognize in a blindfold-test, because they quite literally stink. Furthermore, I find all California reds, without exception, and in all price-ranges, to be utterly lacking in those distinctive and exquisite elements of bouquet going down that marks any truly fine wine. There may be some exceptions to these generalities about California reds, but I've never encountered them if there are. (Another peculiarity: When I've tried to turn the most egregious California reds to vinegar so that I can get at least some use out of them, they mysteriously have failed to turn, even after many months. Bad—and good—wines from other countries turn quickly. Evidently, in California they sterilize the wines, or else add preservatives, probably in order to extend their shelf-life to cater to wine-tastes in a country which doesn't appreciate fine wines, but only wines that last long outside the refrigerator. In any case, I wouldn't call this stuff wine at all. I only wish I could call it vinegar.)

As I noted, California's whites are a different matter. But what white wine from California could approach, say, the supremely great (but not even vintage-marked!) Alexis Lichine Sauvignon Blanc that was available during 1980 for $3-$3.50 a bottle? Or practically any Meursault (also French, but this time rather expensive)? So far as I'm aware, California simply doesn't produce vinological grandeur at any price. Only that state's very cheapest jug-whites ever offer good value (sometimes excellent, in fact).

New York's vinyards are better. The reds here are bland rather than repulsive, and the whites are reliably as good as the German Rhine wines, even if hardly outstanding. The best jug-wine values tend to be the cheapest New York State whites.

The best-value importers of French wines are usually Alexis Lichine and Barton & Guestier, both of which often offer some

19: LIQUORS, WINES, BEERS, SODAS

superb and even great whites that are real steals. However, for reds, Spain and Portugal usually outperform the French competition while costing far less. Italian wines are rarely exceptionally good or bad, and tend to be blah-values. The German whites are usually better—but not terrific—values, though too sweet for some people's tastes.

As for liquors, the sharpest bargain-shopper will try out the off-brand, or a particular store's house-brand products, before he buys any of the advertised names (much of the price for which goes to pay for those ads rather than for the stuff inside the bottle). Even if you want an 8-year-old Scotch, there's a good selection of house-brands and off-brands for that; and when you find one you particularly enjoy, that information and that brand will save you money with each repeat-purchase, not just on the initial sale. So each time you purchase an advertised liquor, you're foregoing an opportunity to learn something (the identity of an equally good off-brand) of potentially substantial long-term future financial value to you.

The stores recommended for beers and sodas are an entirely different group than the wine-liquor dealers. Here, the deadly hand of government is not a factor (except for the high taxes applied to beers). But as with wines and liquors, the biggest savings come from choosing the best-value brands. In this case, that definitely means unadvertised off-brands. A typical 30-second beer-ad for TV costs a-quarter-to-a-half million dollars to produce, plus five-to-ten million dollars to telecast on the networks; and if you buy the advertised brand, then about half the price you pay goes for that ad, not for the beer or its container. But most people prefer to pay half their beer-expense for TV ads. The cheap unpromoted brands—even if slightly superior as they are in many instances—go begging at half the price. Ironically, what may well be the best beer-brand of them all—Old Bohemian—is a dirt-cheap unadvertised off-brand. Their bock is the richest, creamiest and best dark beer I've ever tasted, U.S. or foreign; and their Cream Ale and their Light Beer (the latter of which goes also under the name "Milwaukee") are both excellent. These beers, all produced by the Waukee Brewing Co. of Hammonton, N.J., are all made with pure artesian spring water.

RECOMMENDED PRODUCTS:
See above.

RECOMMENDED STORES:
——————————— liquors & wines ———————————

(examples: aperatifs, brandies, burgundies, chablis, champagnes, cognacs, cordials, gins, sauternes, scotches, sherrys, vodkas, whiskies)

**Dominick's Wines (Queens, 728-4666); **Frank J. Horan Liquors (691-6246); *+Acker, Merrall Liquors (787-1700); *+Arthur M. Ehrlich Liquors (877-6090); *+Astor Wines (674-7500); *+Bay Ridge Liquors (Brooklyn, 833-5700); *+Brill's Liquors (227-3390); *+Cork & Bottle (838-5300); *+Crossroads Wines (924-3060); *+Esposito Wines (567-5500); *+First Av. Wines (673-3600); *+Friedland Wines

19: LIQUORS, WINES, BEERS, SODAS

(368-3200); **+Giuliano's Liquor City** (Bronx, 597-5820); **+Gold Star Wines** (Queens, 459-0200); **+Golden Liquors** (428-1552); **+Gotham Liquors** (876-4120); **+Grand Wines & Liquors** (Queens, 728-2520); **+Great Eastern Liquors** (343-4145); **+Kings Liquor Plaza** (Brooklyn, 338-5900); **+Liquor City** (Staten Island, 273-5660); **+Liquor Giant** (Staten Island, 698-5900); **+Mar-Pat Liquors** (Queens, 762-8388); **+Morrell & Co. Wines** (688-9730); **+North End Liquors** (Bronx, 584-4100); **+Principe Wines** (Queens, 729-7559); **+Queens Wines** (Queens, 821-1500); **+Ritter Wines** (Brooklyn, 638-1234); **+Sutton Wines** (755-6626); *Tops Liquors (Brooklyn, 648-7300); +Bay Terrace Liquors (Queens, 428-4411); +Boro Hall Liquors (Brooklyn, 624-1666); +Stuyvesant Sq. Liquors (473-8061); +Troy-East Liquors (Brooklyn, 778-8000); +Warehouse Wines (982-7770); +Yorkville Liquors (288-6671); Ace Wines (Queens, 426-3980); Aida's Liquors (Staten Island, 987-0044); Allerton Liquors (Bronx, 798-4950); Ase Wines (Queens, 937-0909); Av. Z Discount Liquors (Brooklyn, 891-2242); Avrutis Liquors (Brooklyn, 833-8000); Bob's Discount Liquors (Brooklyn, 778-9094); Bolaf Wines (Brooklyn, 996-2300); Broadway Wines (865-1120); Buy Wise Liquors (Queens, 380-5300); Cash Wines (Brooklyn, 346-7271); Castelli Wines (Staten Island, 984-9347); City Line Wines (Bronx, 324-3431); Clearview Liquors (Queens, 224-7066); Commuter's Liquors (244-2470); D. Sokolin Wines (532-5893); Deegan's Discount Wines (Queens, 847-9154); D'Still Fine Wines (Brooklyn, 232-5039); Edenwald Liquors (Bronx, 652-5520); Egan Wines (Queens, 464-2141); Everybody's World Liquors (942-2100); Excelsior Liquors (247-7397); Fine Wines (865-7070); Five-L Discount Wines (Brooklyn, 332-3000); Forest Hills Liquors (Queens, 268-0800); Frank's Liquors (473-3231); Globe Liquors (Queens, 738-7878); H. Zimmerman Liquors (Bronx, 863-2379); Heights Liquors (568-6500); Hochberg Liquors (Brooklyn, 456-3700); Hudgins Discount Liquors (862-2900); Interboro Wines (Brooklyn, 389-4520); J&J Liquors (Queens, 793-3500); Lehigh Wines (Bronx, 863-2990); Leiser Liquors (Queens, 359-3106); L.G. Liquors (226-4594); Liquor Locker (Queens, 463-2727); Liquor World (Brooklyn, 332-2800); Lowery Discount Wines (Queens, 784-2334); Lumer's Liquors (535-6800); Mancini's Liquors (Queens, 658-0087); McAdam Liquors (679-1224); Mid-City Liquors (Queens, 641-4879); M&M Discount Liquors (Queens, 728-5542); Mosholu Wines (Bronx, 655-1119); Newkirk Station Liquors (Brooklyn, 434-4441); Old Broadway Wines (666-2200); Oz Liquors (234-9146); Palace Wines (Bronx, 379-8087); Pete Milano's Wines (Staten Island, 447-2888); Petzinger's Wines (Brooklyn, 836-0044); Quality House Wines (532-2944); R. Borrello Liquors (Brooklyn, 638-2387); Rego Drive Liquors (Queens, 459-2929); Riverdale Liquors (Bronx, 543-1110); Russo Wines (Bronx, 652-8296); Schacher Liquors (Brooklyn, 768-1232); Schumer's Wines (355-0940); Seventy-Fourth St. Wines (362-6627); Shelmar Wines (Brooklyn, 366-4033); Skyview Liquors (Bronx, 549-1229); Smart Shopper's Liquors (865-4391); Smith's Dongan Liquors (Staten Island, 351-2490); Somerman Discount Wines (Queens, 821-6565); Springfield Liquors (Queens, 276-1493); Starrett City Wines (Brooklyn, 642-8958); Tony's Wines (Queens, 845-6677); Tower's 57th St. Wines (355-3063); Towne Liquors (Brooklyn, 875-3667); Tozzi Discount Liquors (Brooklyn, 236-0151); Treg's Discount Wines (Brooklyn, 449-1368); Trepper's Liquors (Queens, 526-1771); Trylon Liquors (Queens, 459-6666); Twin Towers Wines (432-9220); Van Vleck Wines (Brooklyn, 625-5444); Vankeith Liquors (Bronx, 542-2820); Wakefield Wines (Bronx, 652-6113); Waldorf Liquors (Staten Island, 979-1910); Warren's Discount Liquors (Queens, 523-7328); Wine Hut (Staten Island, 761-3344); Wine Hut Bkln. (Brooklyn, 531-1861); World Liquors

19: LIQUORS, WINES, BEERS, SODAS

(Brooklyn, 462-8300); **Yorkshire Wines** (249-2300).

---
beers & sodas

(includes: ales, bocks, colas, seltzers, waters)

****Eliot Beer** (Queens, 497-0555); ****Flair Beverages** (569-8713); ****Pagano Beer** (Brooklyn, 373-2441); ****Wholesale Beer & Soda** (568-6010); ***Amendolara Beer** (Brooklyn, 443-0130); ***CAL Beer** (Bronx, 881-1144); ***C&R Beer Bronx** (Bronx, 597-7777); ***Myrtle Beer** (Queens, 347-5744); ***New Beer Wholesale** (473-8757); ***Serrano Beer** (243-6559); ***William Schmidt Beer** (Brooklyn, 386-4644); **Abelson Beer & Soda** (234-9331); **American Beverage** (Brooklyn, 875-0226); **Beer & Soda Discount** (Staten Island, 447-0281); **Boro Beverage** (Brooklyn, 331-7444); **Cobble Hts. Beer** (Brooklyn, 596-0871); **Community Beverage** (Queens, 458-5254); **C&R Beer** (Queens, 358-3211); **Cross Bay Cold Beer** (Queens, 641-5049); **East Side Beer** (Brooklyn, 345-4003); **Family Beer** (Queens, 849-5003); **Forest Beverage** (Staten Island, 442-8433); **Grill Beverage** (475-7171); **Gun Hill Beer** (Bronx, 379-3332); **Houston St. Beer** (677-1460); **Lawrence Beverage** (Staten Island, 351-1023); **Miranda Beer** (Brooklyn, 385-3636); **Neptune Beer** (Brooklyn, 769-4933); **Oldtown Beer** (247-1652); **Sieb Beer** (Queens, 386-1480); **Sixty-Ninth St. Beer** (Queens, 478-5493); **Vito Santoro Beer** (Queens, 821-6539); **Wakefield Beer** (Bronx, 324-5270); **White House Beer** (Staten Island, 698-4055).

STORES-DIRECTORY

Phone a store before you go out of your way to visit it. Especially do this during July and August, when most establishments reduce or eliminate weekend-hours.

In the listings below, "*" means especially recommended, "+" means that the store offers a bonus discount to BF readers, "ch." and "c.c." mean respectively checks and credit cards, and "exch." and "rfd." mean respectively exchange and refund. Nearest subway-stops are shown. For example, "B-D-F to 47" means to take the B, D, or F train to 47th Street. Store-hours are also indicated, with days of the week abbreviated, like "M-S 8-6."

Abelson Beer & Soda, 552A Lenox Av. (138), 234-9331, 2-3 to 135. Sells: **Beers & Sodas.**

Ace Wines, Queens, 85-10 Grand Av., Elmhurst, 426-3980, F-GG-N to Grand Av. Sells: **Liquors & Wines.**

*+ **Acker, Merrall Liquors**, 2373 Broadway (86-7), 787-1700, 1 to 86. Bonus BF discount: 10-20% off wines, if you show this book. Might not apply to special-sale items. Sells: **Liquors & Wines.**

Aida's Liquors, Staten Island, 2626 Hylan Blvd., 987-0044, no subway stop nearby. Sells: **Liquors & Wines.**

Allerton Liquors, Bronx, 693 Allerton Av., 798-4950, 2-5 to Allerton. Sells: **Liquors & Wines.**

* **Amendolara Beer**, Brooklyn, 1377 DeKalb Av. (Wilson Av.), 443-0130, M to Knickerbocker, M to Central. Sells: **Beers & Sodas.**

American Beverage, Brooklyn, 252 Court St. (Kane), 875-0226, F-GG to Bergen St. Sells: **Beers & Sodas.**

*+ **Arthur M. Ehrlich Liquors**, 222 Amsterdam Av. (70), 877-6090, 1-2-3 to 72. Bonus BF discount: 10-20% off wines, if you show this book. Might not apply to special-sale items. Sells: **Liquors & Wines.**

Ase Wines, Queens, 28-18 Jackson Av., L.I.C., 937-0909, E-F-GG-N-RR-7 to Queens(boro) Plaza. Sells: **Liquors & Wines.**

*+ **Astor Wines**, 12 Astor Place, 674-7500, N-RR to 8th St., 6 to Astor. Bonus BF discount: 10-20% off wines, if you show this book. Might not apply to special-sale items. Sells: **Liquors & Wines.**

Av. Z Discount Liquors, Brooklyn, 1315 Av. Z, 891-2242, D-M-QB to

19: LIQUORS, WINES, BEERS, SODAS 177

Sheepshead Bay. Sells: **Liquors & Wines.**
    Avrutis Liquors, Brooklyn, 8702 5th Av., 833-8000, RR to 86th St. Sells: **Liquors & Wines.**
⁕⁺   **Bay Ridge Liquors**, Brooklyn, 425 86th St., 833-5700, RR to 86th St. Bonus BF discount: 10-20% off wines, if you show this book. Might not apply to special-sale items. Sells: **Liquors & Wines.**
⁺   **Bay Terrace Liquors**, Queens, 212-37 26th Av., Bayside, 428-4411, no subway stop nearby. Bonus BF discount: 5% off wines, if you show this book. Might not apply to special-sale items. Sells: **Liquors & Wines.**
    Beer & Soda Discount, Staten Island, 1134 Hylan Blvd. (Clove Rd.), 447-0281, no subway stop nearby. Sells: **Beers & Sodas.**
    Bob's Discount Liquors, Brooklyn, 627 Nostrand Av. (Bergen), 778-9094, A-CC to Nostrand, plus a long walk. Sells: **Liquors & Wines.**
    Bolaf Wines, Brooklyn, 2997 Cropsey Av., 996-2300, B to Bay 50th, plus a long walk. Sells: **Liquors & Wines.**
    Boro Beverage, Brooklyn, 1675 63rd St., 331-7444, B-N to 62nd St. & New Utrecht Av. Sells: **Beers & Sodas.**
⁺   **Boro Hall Liquors**, Brooklyn, 105 Court St. (State), 624-1666, M-RR-2-3-4-5 to Borough Hall & Court St. Bonus BF discount: 5-10% off wine-cases, if you show this book. Might not apply to special-sale items. Sells: **Liquors & Wines.**
⁕⁺   **Brill's Liquors**, 150 Chambers St. (W. B'wy), 227-3390, A-CC-1-2-3 to Chambers. Bonus BF discount: 10-20% off wines, if you show this book. Might not apply to special-sale items. Sells: **Liquors & Wines.**
    Broadway Wines, 2780 Broadway (107), 865-1120, 1 to 110. Sells: **Liquors & Wines.**
    Buy Wise Liquors, Queens, 79-05 Main St., Flushing, 380-5300, no subway stop nearby. Sells: **Liquors & Wines.**
⁕   **CAL Beer**, Bronx, 740 E. 233 (Wt. Plns. Rd.), 881-1144, 2-5 to 233. Sells: **Beers & Sodas.**
    Cash Wines, Brooklyn, 767 Rockaway Av. (Riverdale), 346-7271, 2 to Rockaway Av. Sells: **Liquors & Wines.**
    Castelli Wines, Staten Island, 4334 Amboy Rd., 984-9347, no subway stop nearby. Sells: **Liquors & Wines.**
    City Line Wines, Bronx, 4727 Wt. Plns. Rd. (242), 324-3431, 2-5 to 241. Sells: **Liquors & Wines.**
    Clearview Liquors, Queens, 205-17 35th Av., Bayside, 224-7066, no subway stop nearby. Sells: **Liquors & Wines.**
    Cobble Hts. Beer, Brooklyn, 185 Atlantic Av. (Court), 596-0871, M-RR-2-3-4-5 to Borough Hall & Court St. Sells: **Beers & Sodas.**
    Community Beverage, Queens, 80-04 Grand Av., Elmhurst, 458-5254, F-GG-N to Grand Av., plus a long walk. Sells: **Beers & Sodas.**
    Commuter's Liquors, 211 W. 34 (7th Av.), 244-2470, 1-2-3 to 34, A-AA-CC-E to 34. Sells: **Liquors & Wines.**
⁕⁺   **Cork & Bottle**, 1158 1st Av. (63-4), 838-5300, N-RR-4-5-6 to 59th & Lex. Bonus BF discount: 10-20% off wines, if you show this book. Might not apply to special-sale items. Sells: **Liquors & Wines.**
    C&R Beer, Queens, 133-31 32nd Av., Flushing, 358-3211, 7 to Main St., plus a long walk. Sells: **Beers & Sodas.**
⁕   **C&R Beer Bronx**, Bronx, 1263 Wt. Plns. Rd. (Westch. Av.), 597-7777, 6 to E. 177. Sells: **Beers & Sodas.**
    Cross Bay Cold Beer, Queens, 164-44 Cross Bay Blvd., Howard Beach, 641-5049, no subway stop nearby. Sells: **Beers & Sodas.**
⁕⁺   **Crossroads Wines**, 55 W. 14 (6th Av.), 924-3060, B-F-LL to 14th St. & 6th Av. Bonus BF discount: 10-20% off wines, if you show this book. Might not apply to special-sale items. Sells: **Liquors & Wines.**
    D. Sokolin Wines, 178 Madison Av. (34), 532-5893, 6 to 33. Sells: **Liquors & Wines.**
    Deegan's Discount Wines, Queens, 95-19 Jamaica Av., Woodhaven, 847-9154, J to Woodhaven Blvd. Sells: **Liquors & Wines.**
⁕⁕   **Dominick's Wines**, Queens, 28-22 Astoria Blvd., Astoria, 728-4666, RR to Astoria Blvd. This is the outfit that beat back New York State's law that demanded wine price-fixing (i.e., the law had demanded that no store discount much). Sells: **Liquors & Wines.**

19: LIQUORS, WINES, BEERS, SODAS

D'Still Fine Wines, Brooklyn, 6908 New Utrecht Av., 232-5039, B to 71st St. Sells: **Liquors & Wines.**

East Side Beer, Brooklyn, 431 Stone Av. (Belmont), 345-4003, LL to Sutter. Sells: **Beers & Sodas.**

Edenwald Liquors, Bronx, 930 E. 233 (Bronxwood), 652-5520, 2-5 to 233. Sells: **Liquors & Wines.**

Egan Wines, Queens, 218-46 Hillside Av., Queens Village, 464-2141, no subway stop nearby. Sells: **Liquors & Wines.**

** **Eliot Beer**, Queens, 60-03 Eliot Av. (Metropolitan), 497-0555, no subway stop nearby. Sells: **Beers & Sodas.**

*+ **Esposito Wines**, 608 W. 207 (B'way), 567-5500, A to 207. Bonus BF discount: 10-20% off wines, if you show this book. Might not apply to special-sale items. Sells: **Liquors & Wines.**

Everybody's World Liquors, 148 Dyckman St., 942-2100, A to 200-Dyckman, 1 to Dyckman-200. Sells: **Liquors & Wines.**

Excelsior Liquors, 332 W. 57 (B'way), 247-7397, A-AA-B-CC-D-1 to 59. Sells: **Liquors & Wines.**

Family Beer, Queens, 93-25 Jamaica Av., Woodhaven, 849-5003, J to Woodhaven Blvd. Sells: **Beers & Sodas.**

Fine Wines, 700 Columbus Av. (94), 865-7070, A to 190. Sells: **Liquors & Wines.**

*+ **First Av. Wines**, 383 1st Av. (22-3), 673-3600, 6 to 23. Bonus BF discount: 10-20% off wines, if you show this book. Might not apply to special-sale items. Sells: **Liquors & Wines.**

Five-L Discount Wines, Brooklyn, 2312 Knapp St. (W), 332-3000, no subway stop nearby. Sells: **Liquors & Wines.**

** **Flair Beverages**, 3857 9th Av. (207), 569-8713, 1 to 207. Sells: **Beers & Sodas.**

Forest Beverage, Staten Island, 2079 Forest Av. (Union), 442-8433, no subway stop nearby. Sells: **Beers & Sodas.**

Forest Hills Liquors, Queens, 108-09 Queens Blvd., Forest Hills, 268-0800, E-F-GG-N to 71-Continental Avs. Sells: **Liquors & Wines.**

** **Frank J. Horan Liquors**, 33 7th Av. (12-3), 691-6246, 1-2-3 to 14. The emphasis here is on the least expensive wines, of which they offer an extraordinary selection, especially for such a small store. Sells: **Liquors & Wines.**

Frank's Liquors, 46 Union Sq. E. (17), 473-3231, LL-N-QB-RR-4-5-6 to Union Sq. Sells: **Liquors & Wines.**

*+ **Friedland Wines**, 605 Lenox Av. (140), 368-3200, 2-3 to 135. Bonus BF discount: 10-20% off wines, if you show this book. Might not apply to special-sale items. Sells: **Liquors & Wines.**

*+ **Giuliano's Liquor City**, Bronx, Bruckner Blvd. at Wt. Plns. Rd., 597-5820, 6 to E. 177, plus a long walk. Bonus BF discount: 10-20% off wines, if you show this book. Might not apply to special-sale items. Sells: **Liquors & Wines.**

Globe Liquors, Queens, 74-10 101st Av., Ozone Park, 738-7878, A-CC to Grant. Sells: **Liquors & Wines.**

*+ **Gold Star Wines**, Queens, 103-05 Queens Blvd., Forest Hills, 459-0200, E-F-GG-N to 71-Continental Avs. Bonus BF discount: 10-20% off wines, if you show this book. Might not apply to special-sale items. Sells: **Liquors & Wines.**

*+ **Golden Liquors**, Queens, 41-07 Bell Blvd., Bayside, 428-1552, no subway stop nearby. Bonus BF discount: 10-20% off wines, if you show this book. Might not apply to special-sale items. Sells: **Liquors & Wines.**

*+ **Gotham Liquors**, 1543 3rd Av. (87), 876-4120, 4-5-6 to 86. Bonus BF discount: 10-20% off wines, if you show this book. Might not apply to special-sale items. Sells: **Liquors & Wines.**

*+ **Grand Wines & Liquors**, Queens, 30-05 31st St., Astoria, 728-2520, RR to 30th Av. Bonus BF discount: 10-20% off wines, if you show this book. Might not apply to special-sale items. Sells: **Liquors & Wines.**

*+ **Great Eastern Liquors**, 600 Hempstead Tnpk., Elmont, 343-4145. Bonus BF discount: 10-20% off wines, if you show this book. Might not apply to special-sale items. Sells: **Liquors & Wines.**

Grill Beverage, 261 Delancey St. (Columbia), 475-7171, F-J-M to Delancey & Essex. Sells: **Beers & Sodas.**

Gun Hill Beer, Bronx, 2850 Mickle Av. (Gun Hill Rd.), 379-3332, 5 to Gun

19: LIQUORS, WINES, BEERS, SODAS

Hill Rd. Sells: **Beers & Sodas.**

H. Zimmerman Liquors, Bronx, 39 Hugh Grant Circle, 863-2379, 6 to E. 177. Sells: **Liquors & Wines.**

Heights Liquors, 547 W. 181 (Audubon), 568-6500, 1 to 181. Sells: **Liquors & Wines.**

Hochberg Liquors, Brooklyn, 325 Knickerbocker Av., 456-3700, M to Knickerbocker. Sells: **Liquors & Wines.**

Houston St. Beer, 298 E. 2 (Houston St. betw. Avs. C & D), 677-1460, F to 2nd Av., plus a long walk. Sells: **Beers & Sodas.**

Hudgins Discount Liquors, 1720 Amsterdam Av. at 145th, 862-2900, 1 to 145, A-AA-B-CC-D to 145. Sells: **Liquors & Wines.**

Interboro Wines, Brooklyn, 907 Manhattan Av. (Greenpoint Av.), 389-4520, GG to Greenpoint Av. Sells: **Liquors & Wines.**

J&J Liquors, Queens, 71-06 Kissena Blvd., Flushing, 793-3500, no subway stop nearby. Sells: **Liquors & Wines.**

*+ **Kings Liquor Plaza**, Brooklyn, 2481 Flatbush Av. at U, 338-5900, no subway stop nearby. Bonus BF discount: 10-20% off wines, if you show this book. Might not apply to special-sale items. Sells: **Liquors & Wines.**

Lawrence Beverage, Staten Island, 1589 Hylan Blvd. (Atlantic), 351-1023, no subway stop nearby. Sells: **Beers & Sodas.**

Lehigh Wines, Bronx, 2929 Westchester Av. (Buhre), 863-2990, 6 to Buhre Av. Sells: **Liquors & Wines.**

Leiser Liquors, Queens, 41-30 162nd St., Flushing, 359-3106, no subway stop nearby. Sells: **Liquors & Wines.**

L.G. Liquors, 133 Bowery at Grand, 226-4594, B-D to Grand, J-M to Bowery. Sells: **Liquors & Wines.**

*+ **Liquor City**, Staten Island, 2239 Forest Av. (South Av.), 273-5660, no subway stop nearby. Bonus BF discount: 10-20% off wines, if you show this book. Might not apply to special-sale items. Sells: **Liquors & Wines.**

*+ **Liquor Giant**, Staten Island, S.I. Convenience Mall, 698-5900, no subway stop nearby. Bonus BF discount: 10-20% off wines, if you show this book. Might not apply to special-sale items. Sells: **Liquors & Wines.**

Liquor Locker, Queens, 172-10 46th Av., Flushing, 463-2727, no subway stop nearby. Sells: **Liquors & Wines.**

Liquor World, Brooklyn, 3080 Ocean Av. (Voorhies), 332-2800, D-M-QB to Sheepshead Bay. Sells: **Liquors & Wines.**

Lowery Discount Wines, Queens, 40-14 Queens Blvd., Sunnyside, 784-2334, 7 to 40th St. Sells: **Liquors & Wines.**

Lumer's Liquors, 1479 3rd Av. (83-4), 535-6800, 4-5-6 to 86. Sells: **Liquors & Wines.**

Mancini's Liquors, Queens, 106-31 150th St., Jamaica, 658-0087, no subway stop nearby. Sells: **Liquors & Wines.**

*+ **Mar-Pat Liquors**, Queens, 31-12 Farrington St., Whitestone, 762-8388, no subway stop nearby. Bonus BF discount: 10-20% off wines, if you show this book. Might not apply to special-sale items. Sells: **Liquors & Wines.**

McAdam Liquors, 398 3rd Av. (28), 679-1224, 6 to 28. Sells: **Liquors & Wines.**

Mid-City Liquors, Queens, 155-12 Cross Bay Blvd., Howard Beach, 641-4879, A-CC to Howard Beach. Sells: **Liquors & Wines.**

Miranda Beer, Brooklyn, 2451 Dean St. (E. NY Av.), 385-3636, LL to Atlantic. Sells: **Beers & Sodas.**

M&M Discount Liquors, Queens, 38-09 Broadway, Astoria, 728-5542, F-GG-N to Steinway St. Sells: **Liquors & Wines.**

*+ **Morrell & Co. Wines**, 307 E. 53 (2nd Av.), 688-9730, E-F to Lex. Av. Bonus BF discount: 10-20% off wines, if you show this book. Might not apply to special-sale items. Sells: **Liquors & Wines.**

Mosholu Wines, Bronx, 288 E. 204, 655-1119, D to 205. Sells: **Liquors & Wines.**

* **Myrtle Beer**, Queens, 255-47 Jamaica Av., Floral Park, 347-5744, no subway stop nearby. Sells: **Beers & Sodas.**

Neptune Beer, Brooklyn, 257 Neptune Av. (Brighton 6th), 769-4933, D-M-QB to Brighton Beach. Sells: **Beers & Sodas.**

19: LIQUORS, WINES, BEERS, SODAS

* **New Beer Wholesale**, 167 Chrystie St. (Delancey), 473-8757 & 260-4360, J-M to Bowery. Sells: **Beers & Sodas.**

Newkirk Station Liquors, Brooklyn, 11 Newkirk Plaza, 434-4441, D-M-QB to Newkirk. Sells: **Liquors & Wines.**

*+ **North End Liquors**, Bronx, 2509 Webster Av. (Fordham Rd.), 584-4100, CC-D to Fordham Rd. Bonus BF discount: 10-20% off wines, if you show this book. Might not apply to special-sale items. Sells: **Liquors & Wines.**

Old Broadway Wines, 574 W. 125 (B'wy), 666-2200, 1 to 125. Sells: **Liquors & Wines.**

Oldtown Beer, 738 10th Av. (50), 247-1652, A-AA-CC-E to 50. Sells: **Beers & Sodas.**

Oz Liquors, 2610 8th Av. at 139th St., 234-9146, A-AA-B-CC to 135. Sells: **Liquors & Wines.**

** **Pagano Beer**, Brooklyn, 2078 Stillwell (86th St.), 373-2441, B to 25th Av. Sells: **Beers & Sodas.**

Palace Wines, Bronx, 117 Dreiser Loop (Co-op City), 379-8087, 5 to Baychester, plus a long walk. Sells: **Liquors & Wines.**

Pete Milano's Wines, Staten Island, 1531 Forest Av., 447-2888, no subway stop nearby. Sells: **Liquors & Wines.**

Petzinger's Wines, Brooklyn, 123 Bay Ridge Av. (69th), 836-0044, RR to Bay Ridge Av. Sells: **Liquors & Wines.**

*+ **Principe Wines**, Queens, 45-22 46th St., L.I.C., 729-7559, 7 to 46th St. Bonus BF discount: 10-20% off wines, if you show this book. Might not apply to special-sale items. Sells: **Liquors & Wines.**

Quality House Wines, 2 Park Av. (33), 532-2944, 6 to 33. Sells: **Liquors & Wines.**

*+ **Queens Wines**, Queens, 59-03 71st Av., Ridgewood, 821-1500, M to Forest Av. Bonus BF discount: 10-20% off wines, if you show this book. Might not apply to special-sale items. Sells: **Liquors & Wines.**

R. Borrello Liquors, Brooklyn, 751 Bergen St. (Washington), 638-2387, D-M-QB to 7th Av., plus a long walk. Sells: **Liquors & Wines.**

Rego Drive Liquors, Queens, 94-20 63rd Dr., Rego Park, 459-2929, F-GG-N to 63rd Dr. Sells: **Liquors & Wines.**

*+ **Ritter Wines**, Brooklyn, 549 Classon Av. (Fulton), 638-1234, A-CC to Franklin. Bonus BF discount: 10-20% off wines, if you show this book. Might not apply to special-sale items. Sells: **Liquors & Wines.**

Riverdale Liquors, Bronx, 207 W. 231, 543-1110, 1 to 231. Sells: **Liquors & Wines.**

Russo Wines, Bronx, 4176 Wt. Plns. Rd. (232), 652-8296, 2-5 to 233. Sells: **Liquors & Wines.**

Schacher Liquors, Brooklyn, 322 7th Av. (8-9), 768-1232, F to 7th Av. Sells: **Liquors & Wines.**

Schumer's Wines, 59 E. 54 (Park Av.), 355-0940, E-F to Lex. Av. Sells: **Liquors & Wines.**

* **Serrano Beer**, 351 W. 14 (9th Av.), 243-6559, A-AA-CC-E-LL to 14 St. & 8 Av. Sells: **Beers & Sodas.**

Seventy-Fourth St. Wines, 291 Amsterdam Av. (73-4), 362-6627, 1-2-3 to 72. Sells: **Liquors & Wines.**

Shelmar Wines, Brooklyn, 1445 Myrtle Av. (Knickerbocker), 366-4033, M to Knickerbocker. Sells: **Liquors & Wines.**

Sieb Beer, Queens, 418 Seneca Av. at Himrod, Ridgewood, 386-1480, LL to DeKalb. Sells: **Beers & Sodas.**

Sixty-Ninth St. Beer, Queens, 55-13 69th St., Maspeth, 478-5493, no subway stop nearby. Sells: **Beers & Sodas.**

Skyview Liquors, Bronx, 5681 Riverdale Av. (259), 549-1229, no subway stop nearby. Sells: **Liquors & Wines.**

Smart Shopper's Liquors, 268 W. 125 (7th-8th), 865-4391, A-AA-B-CC-D to 125. Sells: **Liquors & Wines.**

Smith's Dongan Liquors, Staten Island, 1662 Richmond Rd., 351-2490, no subway stop nearby. Sells: **Liquors & Wines.**

Somerman Discount Wines, Queens, 78-17 Myrtle Av., Glendale, 821-6565, no subway stop nearby. Sells: **Liquors & Wines.**

19: LIQUORS, WINES, BEERS, SODAS

Springfield Liquors, Queens, 134-42 NY Blvd., 276-1493, no subway stop nearby. Sells: **Liquors & Wines**.

Starrett City Wines, Brooklyn, 1370 Pennsylvania Av., 642-8958, no subway stop nearby. Sells: **Liquors & Wines**.

+ **Stuyvesant Sq. Liquors**, 333 2nd Av. (19-20), 473-8061, LL to 3rd Av. Bonus BF discount: 5% off wines, if you show this book. Might not apply to special-sale items. Sells: **Liquors & Wines**.

*+ **Sutton Wines**, 403 E. 57 at 1st Av., 755-6626, N-RR-4-5-6 to 59th & Lex. Bonus BF discount: 10-20% off wines, if you show this book. Might not apply to special-sale items. Sells: **Liquors & Wines**.

Tony's Wines, Queens, 93-08 Liberty Av., Ozone Park, 845-6677, A-CC to Rockaway Blvd. Sells: **Liquors & Wines**.

* **Tops Liquors**, Brooklyn, 2816 Av. U, 648-7300, no subway stop nearby. Sells: **Liquors & Wines**.

Tower's 57th St. Wines, 157 E. 57 at 3rd Av., 355-3063, N-RR-4-5-6 to 59th & Lex. Sells: **Liquors & Wines**.

Towne Liquors, Brooklyn, 73 Clark St. (Henry), 875-3667, 2-3 to Clark. Sells: **Liquors & Wines**.

Tozzi Discount Liquors, Brooklyn, 8615 18th Av., 236-0151, B to 18th Av. Sells: **Liquors & Wines**.

Treg's Discount Wines, Brooklyn, 8774 Bay Pkwy., 449-1368, B to Bay Pkwy. Sells: **Liquors & Wines**.

Trepper's Liquors, Queens, NY & Farmer's Blvds., Springfield Gardens, 526-1771, no subway stop nearby. Sells: **Liquors & Wines**.

+ **Troy-East Liquors**, Brooklyn, 300 Troy Av. (Eastern Pkwy.), 778-8000, 2 to Kingston. Bonus BF discount: 10% off wines, if you show this book. Might not apply to special-sale items. Sells: **Liquors & Wines**.

Trylon Liquors, Queens, 98-85 Queens Blvd., Forest Hills, 459-6666, F-GG-N to 67th Av. Sells: **Liquors & Wines**.

Twin Towers Wines, 305 World Trade Ctr. Concourse (nr. IND subway), 432-9220, AA-E to World Trade Ctr. Sells: **Liquors & Wines**.

Van Vleck Wines, Brooklyn, 116 Montague St. (Henry), 625-5444, M-RR-2-3-4-5 to Borough Hall & Court St. Sells: **Liquors & Wines**.

Vankeith Liquors, Bronx, 1438 Boston Rd., 542-2820, 2-5 to Freeman. Sells: **Liquors & Wines**.

Vito Santoro Beer, Queens, 1820 Bleecker (Seneca), Ridgewood, 821-6539, M to Seneca. Sells: **Beers & Sodas**.

Wakefield Beer, Bronx, 857 E. 241 (Baych. Av.), 324-5270, 2-5 to 241. Sells: **Beers & Sodas**.

Wakefield Wines, Bronx, 3965 Wt. Plns. Rd. at 225th St., 652-6113, 2-5 to 225. Sells: **Liquors & Wines**.

Waldorf Liquors, Staten Island, 2750 Hylan Blvd., 979-1910, no subway stop nearby. Sells: **Liquors & Wines**.

+ **Warehouse Wines**, 735 Broadway (8), 982-7770, N-RR to 8th St. Bonus BF discount: 5-10% off wine-cases, if you show this book. Might not apply to special-sale items. Sells: **Liquors & Wines**.

Warren's Discount Liquors, Queens, 175-25 Jamaica Av., Jamaica, 523-7328, E-F to 179th St., plus a long walk. Sells: **Liquors & Wines**.

White House Beer, Staten Island, 953 Manor Rd. (Ocean Ter.), 698-4055, no subway stop nearby. Sells: **Beers & Sodas**.

** **Wholesale Beer & Soda**, 2201 Amsterdam Av. (169), 568-6010, A-AA-B-1 to 168-B'wy. Sells: **Beers & Sodas**.

* **William Schmidt Beer**, Brooklyn, 367 Johnson Av. (Morgan), 386-4644, LL to Morgan. Sells: **Beers & Sodas**.

Wine Hut, Staten Island, 2353 Richmond Av., 761-3344, no subway stop nearby. Sells: **Liquors & Wines**.

Wine Hut Bkln., Brooklyn, 2139 Ralph Av., 531-1861, no subway stop nearby. Sells: **Liquors & Wines**.

World Liquors, Brooklyn, 1711 Church Av., 462-8300, D-M-QB to Church. Sells: **Liquors & Wines**.

Yorkshire Wines, 324 E. 86 (1st-2nd), 249-2300, 4-5-6 to 86. Sells: **Liquors & Wines**.

19: LIQUORS, WINES, BEERS, SODAS

+ **Yorkville Liquors**, 1392 3rd Av. at 79th St., 288-6671, 6 to 77. Bonus BF discount: 5-10% off wines, if you show this book. Might not apply to special-sale items. Sells: **Liquors & Wines.**

20:
MUSICAL INSTRUMENTS
Expect 30-50% discounts.

RECOMMENDED STORES:

pianos & organs

+Renard Piano (Bronx, 292-3485); ****American Conservatory Pianos (228-3055); ****Larry's Pianos** (Brooklyn, 469-9378); ***Stello's Pianos** (695-4523); **Weser Piano** (564-4960).

band/orchestra instruments

(examples: accordions, banjos, bassoons, bugles, castanets, cellos, clarinets, concertinas, cornets, drums, flutes, guitars, harmonicas, horns, kazoos, marimbas, metronomes, oboes, piccolos, recorders, trombones, trumpets, violins, xylophones, zithers)

Alex Musical Instruments (765-7738); **Fred Olivero Used Bow Instr.** (757-4943); **Gardinelli Band Instruments** (575-5959); **Manny's** (757-0577); **Paul Ash's Musikatalog** (Brooklyn, 645-3886); **Sam Ash** (245-4778); **Silver & Horland** (869-3870); **We Buy Guitars** (869-3985).

STORES-DIRECTORY

Phone a store before you go out of your way to visit it. Especially do this during July and August, when most establishments reduce or eliminate weekend-hours.

In the listings below, "*" means especially recommended, "+" means that the store offers a bonus discount to BF readers, "ch." and "c.c." mean respectively checks and credit cards, and "exch." and "rfd." mean respectively exchange and refund. Nearest subway-stops are shown. For example, "B-D-F to 47" means to take the B, D, or F train to 47th Street. Store-hours are also indicated, with days of the week abbreviated, like "M-S 8-6."

Alex Musical Instruments, 164 W. 48 (7th Av.), 765-7738, N-RR to 49th St., M-S 9-6, c.c., no ch., 1-day exch., no rfd. Sells: **Band/Orchestra Instruments.**

** **American Conservatory Pianos**, 188 1st Av. (12), 228-3055, LL to 1st Av., 7 days 8:30-7 but phone first, ch., no c.c., no exch. or rfd. 1 free tuning. Sells: **Pianos & Organs.**

Fred Olivero Used Bow Instr., 200 W. 57 at 7th Av., rm. 610, 757-4943, N-QB-RR to 57th St., usually M-S 9-5, ch., no c.c., exch. or rfd. Only used bow instruments. Sells: **Band/Orchestra Instruments.**

Gardinelli Band Instruments, 151 W. 46 (6th-7th), 3rd floor, 575-5959, B-D-F to 47, N-RR to 49th St., M-F 8:30-5:30, S 9-2, c.c., no ch., 10-day exch. or rfd. Only woodwinds and brass. Sells: **Band/Orchestra Instruments.**

** **Larry's Pianos**, Brooklyn, 1787 Nostrand (D), 469-9378, 3-4 to Newkirk, M-S 9-4:45, ch., c.c. 10-yr. guarantee. Carries new and used. Sells: **Pianos & Organs.**

Manny's, 156 W. 48 (6th-7th), 757-0577, N-RR to 49th St., B-D-F to 47, M-S 9-6, ch., c.c., exch., no rfd. Sells: **Band/Orchestra Instruments.**

Paul Ash's Musikatalog, Brooklyn, 1669 E. 13 (Kings Hwy.), 645-3886, D-M-QB to Kings Hwy., TWFS 9-6, MTh 9-9, ch., c.c., exch., no rfd. Sells: **Band/Orchestra Instruments.**

+ **Renard Piano, Bronx, 3rd Av. at 159th St., 292-3485, 2-5 to 3rd Av., then transfer to free bus BX-55 up 3rd Av., M-S 10-6; Queens, 112-04 Queens Blvd., Forest Hills, 544-2111, E-F to 75th Av., M-S 10-5:30. Both stores: ch., c.c., no exch. or rfd. Free service. Huge selection of makes. Don't look just at the Baldwins and Steinways. Often the lesser brands at half the price sound better. Carries new and used. Bonus discount to BF readers: 5%. Sells: **Pianos & Organs.**

Sam Ash, 160 W. 48 (6th-7th), 245-4778, N-RR to 49th St., B-D-F to 47, M-S 9-6, ch., c.c., exch., no rfd. Sells: **Band/Orchestra Instruments.**

Silver & Horland, 170 W. 48 (7th Av.), 869-3870, N-RR to 49th St., M-S 9:30-6, ch., c.c., exch., no rfd. Sells: **Band/Orchestra Instruments.**

* **Stello's Pianos**, 400 W. 34 at 9th Av., 695-4523, A-AA-CC-E to 34, M-Th 10-6, FS 10-5, all cash, 30-day exch., no rfd. Carries new and used. Sells: **Pianos & Organs.**

We Buy Guitars, 159 W. 48 (6th-7th), 869-3985, N-RR to 49th St., B-D-F to 47, M-S 10-6, c.c., no ch., no exch. or rfd. Used, but most are in very good condition. Sells: **Band/Orchestra Instruments.**

Weser Piano, 524 W. 43 (10th-11th), 6th floor, 564-4960, A-AA-CC-E to 42, M-S 10-6, all cash, 5-yr. guarantee. Carries new and used, mostly used. Sells: **Pianos & Organs.**

21:
OFFICE EQUIPMENT
Expect 20-40% discounts.

Practically every store recommended in this chapter will be glad to quote you prices over the phone.

Typewriters

Even if you're buying only for personal use, an office-typewriter is well worth considering. You can get a reconditioned like-new IBM typewriter for about the same price as a new machine made for home-use, but in terms of quality there's no comparison—or if there is, then I'd call the latter a shoddy toy, not a typewriter.

The reconditioned IBM Executive and Standard models are especially good values. They cost less (usually far less) than the Selectric (ball-typing-element) units, and all three have about the same frequencies-and-costs-of-repair. (Machines made for home-use, incidentally, are more expensive to maintain, because they've got higher frequencies-of-repair than do office-machines.) The Selectrics offer the advantage of exchangeable typefaces, since the typing-ball is removable; but for most people there's virtually no practical use for that, since one beautiful typeface is normally more functional than ten ugly ones. The IBM Executives and Standards come with single-use carbon-ribbons which produce a far superior appearance to the back-and-forth cloth-variety found on home-machines; but because these are much longer ribbons than the repeat-use cloth-equivalents, they manage to achieve as much as half (or more) the life-expectancy of the latter. Since they're also priced about half, the per-word typing-cost comes out approximately the same with both types of ribbon. Therefore, a carbon-ribbon offers much better value than does the cloth-type.

The difference between the Standard and Executive models is simply that the latter has proportional spacing—like professional typesetting. In fact, the "Boldface" typestyles available on the Executive machines look rather like book-print. However, proportional spacing also means that typing corrections doesn't require merely a single back-space per character. Some characters take up two spaces; some as many as five. Thus, the first thing to do with your new (or rather like-new reconditioned) IBM Executive typewriter is to write out and memorize a list of the number of spaces-per-each-character on the keyboard. The total procedure won't require more than 30-60 minutes; and after you've done it, corrections will be virtually as easy as with a standard typewriter or with a Selectric.

In addition to the local recommended sources for typewriters, you might find it worth checking out the following out-of-town mail-order discounters:

American International Typewriter Co., 745 Alexander Rd.,

Princeton, NJ 08540. Write for their free catalog, which however, does not contain IBM's, only new machines from makers like Brother, Smith Corona, etc. (However, for those, you'll usually do better buying from the small-appliance stores listed in Chapter 1.)

Word Processing Exchange, 1-800-521-3085, 209A N. Main, Ann Arbor, MI 48107. They specialize in IBM intelligent typewriters, which are actually midway between typewriters and real word-processors. They, too, have a free catalog, and the prices are very good, but still in the very low thousands.

Personal Computers

I'm typesetting this on a leased Apple. For the first month, this leased new machine was out on repair about ten times: The repairman told me that I should throw this bitter Apple—more appropriately called Lemon—out the window. Usually, however, computers aren't quite so bad. But still, I wouldn't advise anyone to buy a personal computer just yet, unless there's a specific business-need for one (in which case, it might save you money, even with all the problems). The field is in enormous flux. There are major questions yet to be resolved concerning compatibility and standardization of both hardware and software. Small computers are still experimental, and will probably remain so until about 1985. Furthermore, there are dozens of manufacturers now in the small-computer field; and in order to get good product-value, you'll have to acquaint yourself with the models put out by the lesser-known makers, not just by the famous ones such as Apple, Radio Shack, and Atari. Commodore, Osborne, and NEC, are currently reputed to be the best values, but that could change anytime. Software also is in flux. For example, in writing this, I'm using the most popular word-processing program that exists—Wordstar—but among its many egregious stupidities is the blatant one that although it has the capacity to erase forward either a letter or a whole word (neither of which, of course, has yet been written), it can erase backward—which is what the writer really needs far more often—only a single letter at a time. So, for example, if the last three words are in error, I've got to punch a key the same number of times as the number of letters and spaces in those three words. But if I want to erase the next word that I haven't written, well the system will do that in just a single keystroke. That's only one of the many frustrating and moronic flaws in this program—and most software that's available today is even more in need of revision. The other program I've used—DBASE—is still more outrageously poorly designed. No doubt, in years to come, these software-bugs will be weeded out. But right now, if you're buying software, then you'll probably be paying hundreds of dollars for a program which will quickly be outdated by one that's cheaper and far better. And soon after, another that's even less stupidly designed will come along, until ultimately good ones will be available. Then, too, the training manuals seem to have been written by monkeys who were working under a one-week deadline. You'll probably need a friend to tell you how to use any program you buy. The only major exceptions are computer-games.

21: OFFICE EQUIPMENT

If you do buy a computer, it's advisable that you keep it on nonstop for the first week that you have it, in order to "burn out" the defective chips that you can expect will be in there. It's best to do this as early as possible during the warranty-period. Don't worry about the cost in terms of electricity; it'll be negligible, because a computer consumes only a very small fraction of the juice that a light-bulb does. (But keep the TV monitor turned off when you're away—the chips aren't in there, and that does use a far more substantial amount of electricity.) With most computers, just one week of continuous running will result in every defective chip being zapped, and this means that after these initial problems are corrected, your hardware will function the way it's supposed to, and will give you years of trouble-free service.

The best single up-to-date source of useful information on personal and small-business computers is *Byte* magazine, and you might do well to look at backissues of it at the library, and perhaps also to get the current one on newsstands. Also, Ruby's Book Sale, downtown on Chambers St. (732-8676), which is listed in Chapter 24 ("Publications"), occasionally has last month's issue of *Byte* at 40% discount.

One of the advantages of *Byte* is that it has ads from most of the nation's discount-computer dealers. Also, in the back of this fat 500-pages-per-issue magazine are free "unclassified ads" from readers who want to sell their used equipment—and this can be another potential source of computer-bargains.

Although I cannot vouch for the reliability of the following places (since they're not in NYC), they all advertise in *Byte* very good discounts on computers and associated supplies; and so you may find it worthwhile to check them for comparison-prices. Generally, the NYC computer-dealers I recommend in the stores-listing are a shade more expensive than some of these non-NYC sources; and since you won't have to pay any sales-tax if you buy from out-of-state, you might be able to save (including shipping-costs) perhaps 5% off the lowest NYC price if you purchase from one of these. But if you'll need after-purchase service or attention, you'd best buy locally. After the phone number, I'll list only the computers, but not the supplies—software, terminals, printers, etc.—that the outlet sells: **1-800-423-5886** (Apple, Altos, Sharp, NEC, HP); **1-800-421-8045** (Apple, TI, HP, Ohio Scientific, Atari); **1-800-854-6654** (Apple, NEC, Atari, VIC); **1-800-526-5313** (Atari, Radio Shack, Apple); **1-800-841-0860** (Radio Shack); **1-800-343-6522** (Altos, Zenith, Atari); **1-800-528-1054** (Altos, Northstar, Zenith, Atari); **1-800-343-5691** (Atari); **1-800-854-7635** (Televideo, Northstar, Morrow, Zenith, Systems); **1-800-547-2492** (Apple, Atari); **1-800-528-8960** (Altos, Apple, Atari, Zenith); **1-800-322-1873** (Atari, Commodore, Superbrain); **1-800-531-7466** (Radio Shack, HP); **1-800-233-8950** (Atari, VIC, Commodore); **1-800-433-5184** (Radio Shack); **call collect 1-303-945-2864** (Radio Shack); **1-800-227-2288** (Alpha Micro, Altos, Apple, Archives, CCS, Cromemco, Dynabyte, Ithaca, NEC, Northstar, Televideo, Vector); **1-800-854-1941** (Apple, Atari); **call collect 1-516-887-1500** (Northstar). In addition, the following specializes in an incredible range of software: **1-800-854-2003** ext. 823.

Safes

There are two basic types of safes: fire-resistant, and burglar-resistant. The first—also called "record safes"—usually protects legal documents, such as deeds, wills, insurance policies, etc. The second is for holding gold, jewelry and other valuables.

A skilled burglar has no difficulty breaking into a fire-safe. And a fire can quickly destroy the contents of a burglary-safe.

Statistically, burglary has a higher likelihood than fire.

Safes that are designed for both fires and burglaries do exist, but they're very expensive.

Intelligent safe-shopping entails comparing prices of equally-rated safes. (Look for the Underwriters' Laboratory test-rating metal label that's affixed only to tested safes.) Two identically test-rated safes that hold the same number of cubic feet inside are equally good, and whichever is cheaper will offer the better value.

However, the best values are normally the most recent-model second-hand safes, some of which are not UL-rated. If you're shopping for one of these non-test-rated bargains, you've got to be especially careful that the unit you're buying will do what you want it to, and not what some burglar would prefer.

Here are the things to look for in a used safe:

If it's a fire-safe, does white powder show on the door-saddle? If so, then the insulation may be deteriorating.

If it's a burglary-safe, you don't want a painted-over or reconstituted fire-safe, which means that generally speaking you'll want to avoid: one whose original factory color was black, one with wheels, one that's light enough to be portable, one with double doors, one with full-length doors inside, one with a primitive outdated lock.

RECOMMENDED PRODUCTS:
See above.

RECOMMENDED STORES:

answering machines (ALSO: CH. 1)

A-Mark Communications (734-7700); ****Romano Trdg. (581-4248).

computers

(includes: accessories, discs, printers, terminals, word-processors)
+Village Computers (254-9191); **+Washington Electric** (226-2121); ***Bryce** (575-8600); ***Computer Factory** (687-5000); ***Cromemco Computer** (Queens, 937-2900); ***Live Wire Electronics** (Queens, 544-6145); **Compuco** (619-3360); **Computer Center**.

copiers

****Lease Liquidators (410-0100); **G&F Copy**; **Precision Photocopy** (242-8970); **United Photocopy** (929-4826).

office furniture—new

(examples: book cases, credenzas, chairs, desks, stools, tables)

21: OFFICE EQUIPMENT

**Rocket Desk (Brooklyn, 875-7525); *Allen Office Furniture (929-8228); *Reliable Office Furniture (929-2890); A.C. Desk (226-3920); Adirondack Direct (687-8555); Arenson Warehouse (675-6378); Crown Discount (Queens, 937-171); Frank Eastern (677-9100); Mandarin Products (691-0294).

─────────── office furniture—used ───────────

***Kahan National Furniture (intermittent stock, Brooklyn, 782-2760); *Allen Office Furniture (929-8228); *Merit Office Supplies (925-8750); *Reliable Office Furniture (929-2890); AA Best Used Office Furniture (581-8420); Aallee (989-2343); Mandarin Products (691-0294).

─────────── safes & vaults ───────────

Aaron Safe (226-1380); Empire Safe (226-1969); Murray Safe (Brooklyn, 768-1041); Standard Safe (966-5030).

─────────── steel shelving—new ───────────

**Pyramid Steel Shelving (Queens, 784-4110); **+Jack Luckner Shelving (Brooklyn, 453-4100).

─────────── steel shelving—used ───────────

*AA Steel Shelving (254-0445); AAAA Metropolitan Shelving (741-3385).

─────────── typewriters (ALSO: CH. 1, "SMALL") ───────────

(These places also do repairs.)

****+Brian Leasing (964-1190); ***Francis Typewriter (242-1037); ***+Central Typewriter (686-0930); **+Lincoln Typewriters (787-9397); *Pearl Bros. Typewriters (Brooklyn, 875-3024); Ace Typewriter (869-0988); Classon Typewriter (Brooklyn, 338-6000); IOA Data (673-9300); Typex Inc. (243-8086).

STORES-DIRECTORY

Phone a store before you go out of your way to visit it. Especially do this during July and August, when most establishments reduce or eliminate weekend-hours.

In the listings below, "*" means especially recommended, "+" means that the store offers a bonus discount to BF readers, "ch." and "c.c." mean respectively checks and credit cards, and "exch." and "rfd." mean respectively exchange and refund. Nearest subway-stops are shown. For example, "B-D-F to 47" means to take the B, D, or F train to 47th Street. Store-hours are also indicated, with days of the week abbreviated, like "M-S 8-6."

AA Best Used Office Furniture, 721 11th Av. at 51st St., 581-8420, A-AA-CC-E to 50, plus a long walk, M-F 9-5, ch., no c.c., no exch. or rfd. Sells: **Office Furniture—Used.**

* **AA Steel Shelving**, 158 Franklin St. (Hudson), 254-0445 & 966-6388, 1 to Franklin, M-F 8-5, ch., no c.c., no exch. or rfd. Sells: **Steel Shelving—Used.**

AAAA Metropolitan Shelving, 165 W. 23 (7th Av.), 741-3385, 1 to 23, M-F 9-5, S 9-4, ch., no c.c., no exch. or rfd. Sells: **Steel Shelving—Used.**

Aallee, 134 W. 23 (6th-7th), 989-2343, 1 to 23, B-F to 23, M-F 9:30-5, S 11-3:30, ch., no c.c., exch., no rfd. Only files. Sells: **Office Furniture—Used.**

Aaron Safe, 11 Howard St. at Lafayette, 226-1380, J-M-N-QB-RR-6 to Canal, M-F 9-5, ch., no c.c. 1-yr. warranty. Sells: **Safes & Vaults.**

A.C. Desk, 86 Walker St. (B'wy-Lafayette), 226-3920, J-M-N-QB-RR-6 to Canal, M-F 8:15-4:45, ch., no c.c., no exch. or rfd. Sells: **Office Furniture—New.**

Ace Typewriter, 131 W. 45 (6th-7th), 869-0988, B-D-F to 47, N-QB-

21: OFFICE EQUIPMENT

RR-1-2-3-7 to 42 & Times Square, M-F 8:30-5:30, all cash, exch., no rfd. 90 days free service. Sells: **Typewriters**.

Adirondack Direct, 219 E. 42 (3rd Av.), 5th floor, 687-8555 & 1-800-221-2444, 4-5-6-7 to Grand Central, M-F 9-5, ch., c.c., exch., no rfd. Mail-orders. Catalog. Sells: **Office Furniture—New**.

* **Allen Office Furniture**, 165 W. 23 (7th Av.), 929-8228, 1 to 23, M-F 9-5, S 10-4, ch., held till cleared no c.c., no exch. or rfd. Sells: **Office Furniture—New, Office Furniture—Used**.

** **A-Mark Communications**, 218 E. 82 (2nd-3rd), 734-7700, 4-5-6 to 86, M-F 11:30-7, S 10-5, all cash, no exch. or rfd. Large selection. Sells: **Answering Machines**.

Arenson Warehouse, 447 W. 18 (9th-10th), 675-6378, A-AA-CC-E-LL to 14 St. & 8 Av., plus a long walk, T-S 9-4, ch., c.c., no exch. or rfd. Sells: **Office Furniture—New**.

***+ **Brian Leasing**, 66 W. B'wy (Warren), rm. 405, 964-1190, N-RR to City Hall, A-CC-1-2-3 to Chambers, M-S 8:30-5 but phone first for appt., ch., no c.c., exch., no rfd. 90 days free service. They also occasionally hold auctions, where machines can be picked up shockingly cheaply (but with no warranty or service). Bonus discount to BF readers: 10% to 35%. Sells: **Typewriters**.

* **Bryce**, 115 W. 40 (6th-B'wy), 575-8600, B-D-F to 42, M-F 9-5:45, S 9-4, ch., c.c., exch., no rfd. Has audio showroom. Sells: **Computers, Appliances, High Fidelity**.

***+ **Central Typewriter**, 40 E. 33 (Mad.), 686-0930, 6 to 33, M-F 8:30-7, S 10-4, all cash, 90 days free service. Bonus discount to BF readers: 5% to 10%. Sells: **Typewriters**.

Classon Typewriter, Brooklyn, 1344 Coney Island Av. (J), 338-6000, D-M-QB to Av. J, M-F 9-6, S 9-4, Sun 11-3, ch., c.c., 90-days free service. Sells: **Typewriters**.

Compuco, 170 Broadway at Maiden Ln., rm. 1201, 619-3360, A-CC-J-M-RR-2-3-4-5 to B'wy-Nassau & Fulton, M-F 9-5, weekends by appt., ch., c.c., no exch. or rfd. Outstanding if you're looking to rent or lease a computer or a word-processor. Sells: **Computers**.

Computer Center, 31 E. 31 (Mad.), N-RR to 28th St., 6 to 33; 480 Lexington Av. (46-7), 4-5-6-7 to Grand Central; 21 West St. (Rector), N-RR-1 to Rector. All stores: 889-8130 & 1-800-221-3144, M-F 9-7, S 10-6, ch., c.c., no exch. or rfd. Apple-Atari-Cromemco. Sells: **Computers**.

* **Computer Factory**, 485 Lexington Av. at 46th St., 687-5000, 4-5-6-7 to Grand Central, M-F 10-6, S 11-5; Queens, 100-17 Queens Blvd., Forest Hills, 896-0700, F-GG-N to 67th Av., T-F 11-7, S 11-4. Both stores: ch., c.c., no exch. or rfd. Apple-Commodore-Xerox-Atari-TI. Other stores: Garden City, Yonkers. Sells: **Computers**.

* **Cromemco Computer**, Queens, 21-55 44th Rd., L.I.C., 937-2900, 7 to 45th Rd., E-F to Ely Av. & 23rd, M-F 9-6, weekends by appt., all cash, no exch. or rfd. Sells: **Computers**.

Crown Discount, Queens, 31-28 Queens Blvd., L.I.C., 937-171 & 1-516-352-8844, 7 to 33rd St., M-F 9-8, S 9-6, ch., c.c., exch., no rfd. Sells: **Office Furniture—New, Stationery & Art Supplies**.

Empire Safe, 103 Grand (Mercer), 226-1969, J-M-N-QB-RR-6 to Canal, M-F -5, ch., no c.c., no exch. or rfd. 1 yr. free service. Sells: **Safes & Vaults**.

*** **Francis Typewriter**, 141 W. 10 (7th Av.), basement, 242-1037, 1 to Christopher St., M-S 9a.m.-12mdnt., Sun 12-12, ch., c.c., exch., no rfd. 90 days free service. Extremely cooperative. They'll even tell you where to go for a bargain if they don't have what you want. An extraordinary place. Sells: **Typewriters**.

Frank Eastern, 625 Broadway (Houston), 2nd floor, 677-9100 & 1-800-677-9100, B-D-F-6 to B'wy-Laf. & Bleecker, N-RR to Prince St., M-F 9-5, S 10-2, ch., c.c., no exch. or rfd. Takes mail-orders. Catalog. Sells: **Office Furniture—New**.

G&F Copy, 895-0494 & 1-516-822-8121 & 1-201-343-7331 & 1-914-682-1450, & 1-203-357-0101, M-F 9-5, ch., no c.c., no exch. or rfd. Sells: **Copiers**.

IOA Data, 383 Lafayette at 4th St., 673-9300, B-D-F-6 to B'wy-Laf. & Bleecker, M-F 9-4, ch., no c.c. 90 days free service. Sells: **Typewriters**.

*+ **Jack Luckner Shelving**, Brooklyn, 323 Herkimer St. (Kingston), 453-4100, A-CC to Kingston-Throop, M-F 9-5, ch., no c.c., no exch. or rfd. Takes mail-

21: OFFICE EQUIPMENT

orders. Bonus discount to BF readers: 8%. Sells: **Steel Shelving—New.**

*** **Kahan National Furniture**, Brooklyn, 60 Broadway (Wythe), 782-2760, J-M to Marcy, then take free bus B24 back towards river, phone first, but hours usually M-Th 10-5 and Sun by appt., ch., no c.c., no exch. or rfd. Large selection. Hotel-furniture liquidators. When major hotels change the furniture (including office-) every 3 yrs. or so, it ends up here, selling at 70-80% discount, good condition. Sells: **Office Furniture—Used, Furnishings.**

**** **Lease Liquidators**, 1763 2nd Av. (92), 410-0100, 6 to 96, M-F 10-4, ch., no c.c., exch., no rfd. 30-day warranty. Reconditioned, with new photo-receptor drum. About 90%+ discount off new price. All are Saxon plain-paper models that were formerly out on lease. Sells: **Copiers.**

*+ **Lincoln Typewriters**, 100 W. 67 at Columbus, basement, 787-9397, 1 to 66, M-F 9-6, S 11-4, ch., no c.c. 90 days free service. Also rentals credited to purchases. Very cooperative. Bonus discount to BF readers: 3% to 5%. Sells: **Typewriters.**

* **Live Wire Electronics**, Queens, 107-21 Continental Av., Forest Hills, 544-6145, E-F-GG-N to 71-Continental Avs., M-F 9:30-6:30, Sun 10:30-4, c.c., no ch., no exch. or rfd. Video, TV, and Commodore computers. Sells: **Computers, Appliances, Recordings & Tapes.**

Mandarin Products, 35 W. 23 (5th-6th), 691-0294, N-RR to 23rd St., B-F to 23, M-F 9-6, S 9-5, ch., c.c., exch., no rfd. The gift items are Indian brassware. Sells: **Office Furniture—New, Office Furniture—Used, Jewelry & Gifts.**

* **Merit Office Supplies**, 104 Grand St. at Mercer, 925-8750, J-M-N-QB-RR-6 to Canal, M-F 9-5, S 10-4, all cash, exch. or rfd. Sells: **Office Furniture—Used, Stationery & Art Supplies.**

Murray Safe, Brooklyn, 92 19th St. (3rd Av.), 768-1041, N-RR to Prospect Av., M-F 9-5, ch., c.c., no exch. or rfd. 1 yr. free service. Sells: **Safes & Vaults.**

* **Pearl Bros. Typewriters**, Brooklyn, 476 Smith St. at 9th St., 875-3024, F-GG to Smith & 9th Sts., M-F 7:30-4, S 8-2, ch., no c.c. 90 days free service. Mainly wholesalers. Cooperative. Trucks and services throughout the City, especially Manhattan. Sells: **Typewriters.**

Precision Photocopy, 150 5th Av. at 20th, rm. 318, 242-8970, N-RR to 23rd St., M-F 9-5 (but most sales are special-orders by phone), ch., no c.c., no exch. or rfd. Will special-order. 180 days free service. Sells: **Copiers.**

** **Pyramid Steel Shelving**, Queens, 8-11 43rd Rd., L.I.C., 784-4110, 7 to 45th Rd., plus a long walk, M-Th 8-5:30, F 8-4, S 8-12, ch., no c.c., no exch. or rfd. Sells: **Steel Shelving—New.**

* **Reliable Office Furniture**, 118 W. 23 (6th Av.), 929-2890 & 7299, B-F to 23, M-F 9-5, all cash, no exch. or rfd. Sells: **Office Furniture—New, Office Furniture—Used.**

** **Rocket Desk**, Brooklyn, 177 Tillary St. at Gold, immediately over Bkln. Bridge, 875-7525, A-CC-F to Jay St. & Boro Hall, M-F 9-4, all cash, exch., no rfd. Sells: **Office Furniture—New.**

** **Romano Trdg.**, 628 W. 45th St. on 12th Av., 581-4248, A-AA-CC-E to 42, plus a long walk, M-F 8-5:30, S 8-5, all cash, exch. or rfd. Very cooperative. A little bit of everything, designer-name and major brand items. Sells: **Answering Machines, Appliances, Clothing—Men's, Jewelry & Gifts, Personal Accessories, Stationery & Art Supplies, Toys, Games & Hobbies.**

Standard Safe, 138 Lafayette St. at Howard, 966-5030, J-M-N-QB-RR-6 to Canal, M-F 9-5, ch., no c.c., no exch. or rfd. 1 yr. free service. Sells: **Safes & Vaults.**

Typex Inc., 119 W. 23 (6th Av.), 243-8086 & 1-800-221-9332, B-F to 23, M-Th 9:30-5:30, F 9-3, Sun by appt., ch., c.c., exch., no rfd. 90 days free service. Very cooperative. Sells: **Typewriters.**

United Photocopy, 915 Broadway (21), 20th floor, 929-4826, M-F 9-5:30, Not recommended if you'll need after-purchase service or attention. Sells: **Copiers.**

*** **Village Computers**, 687 Broadway (3-4), 254-9191, B-D-F-6 to B'wy-Laf. & Bleecker, M-S 11-6, ch., c.c., no exch. or rfd. Apple-Xerox-IBM-Atari. Takes pride in not selling what customers don't need. Extremely honest about advantages/disadvantages even of what they don't carry. Bonus discount to BF readers: 1% to 2%. Sells: **Computers.**

+ **Washington Electric, 97 Spring St. (B'wy), 226-2121 & 1-800-221-5416, 6 to Spring, N-RR to Prince St., M-F 9-5, c.c., no ch., no exch. or rfd. Almost every make but Apple, Atari, Commodore, and Radio Shack. Offer good advice on what's currently best value, but no help on decision whether to get a computer. Bonus discount to BF readers: 2% to 5%. Sells: **Computers.**

22:
PERSONAL ACCESSORIES
Expect 35-70% discounts.

These are items peripheral to clothing. Generally, they're carried rather than worn.

Knowledgeable shopping offers the biggest payoffs when buying umbrellas. As is the case with so many other product-categories, the well-known umbrella-brands (Knirps, Totes, and the various designer-names) cost twice the price, without offering any advantage whatsoever. In the previous editions of this book, I wrote that the cheaper Asian imported umbrellas were actually superior to the famous-name variety, because while the latter had thin sheet-metal spokes with a u-shaped cross-section, and while such u-shaped spokes tended to snap and break on very windy days—virtually littering New York's streets and trashcans with the remains of thousands of dead and useless umbrellas after each heavy rain—the much cheaper Asian makes outlasted such weather, because they were constructed with round wire spokes which bent (rather than broke) with the wind. Well, now the more expensive makers have almost totally ceased to produce such garbage, and are instead importing their umbrellas from—you guessed it—Asia. The Hong Kong umbrellas have taken over the world. But the famous-name umbrella "manufacturers" (actually importers) still charge sucker-exploiting rates for their wares, even though they're now selling virtually the same stuff made in the same factories that produce the least expensive competition. As usual, for those who want to buy such overpriced top brand-name stuff, the low-value well-advertised umbrellas are all available at discount at the stores I recommend for that. But I expect that most people will be more interested in checking out the places I list for the off-brand makes. In the recommended-store listings below, a shop that's recommended for designer-name umbrellas is indicated by a "2" before the store's name, while a place recommended for Totes or Knirps would be shown by a "3" before its name; and the shops recommended for off-brand umbrellas—many of which umbrellas are as good in actual quality as the best of the preceding—would be recognized by a "4" before the retailer's name. So the "quality"-ratings in this chapter don't in every instance have a direct correlation with real quality, but sometimes indicate merely price.

Good advice to follow with any umbrella if you want it to last, is to apply a drop or two of Duco Cement glue (available from housewares stores and hardware stores) at the tip of each spoke, right over the threads which attach the fabric to the end of the spoke. This will help assure that the fabric won't come loose from the spokes—the main reason umbrellas give up the ghost.

RECOMMENDED PRODUCTS:
See above.

RECOMMENDED STORES:

Numbers which precede store-names indicate
the quality and fashionableness of offerings:

"1" refers to extravagantly high quality merchandise.
"2" is designer-name, or else nearly supreme quality.
"3" shows that the retailer offers major-brand items.
"4" is off-brands or unbranded, but quality = 2&3 above.
"5" shows that the place carries medium quality stuff.
"6" refers to merchandise that's truly poor quality.

handbags & attaches

5 ***Bag Man (560-8952); **5 ***Cayne's DAC Jewelry** (244-8933); **4&5 ***Giselle Handbag** (684-7800); **3&4 ***Odd Job Trdg.** (intermittent stock, 686-6825); **4&5 **Bag It** (242-8750); **5 **Cayne's 3** (564-3350); **4 **Fashion By Helou** (679-1739); **2 **Ito Leather** (832-3765); **2&3 **Jet Handbag** (Brooklyn, 438-1181); **2&3&4 **Romano Trdg.** (581-4248); **5 **Weber's Job Lot** (intermittent stock, 564-7668); **3&6 **Young Jin Trdg.** (684-4320); **3&5 *+Ranna Handbags** (244-8048); **5&6 *Bag City** (391-2544); **5 *Bags By Zeno** (686-2869); **4&5 *J. Chuckles** (867-3771); **5 *Kingdom of Gifts** (989-9763); **3 *La Gigi Handbags** (254-3670); **5 *Man-Dee Bag** (840-2233); **3&4&5 *New Fashion** (227-1880); **4&5 *New York, NY** (679-3370); **4&5 *Strawberry** (986-7030); **2&3 +Lynn Richards Handbags** (Brooklyn, 891-2914); **3 Abe's Handbags & Luggage** (Queens, 526-9887); **2&3 Ace Leather** (Brooklyn, 891-9713); **3&4 Bags 'N Things** (Queens, 520-8755); **4 East Village Variety** (674-8300); **2&3 Fine & Klein** (674-6720); **2&3&4&5 Gold Style Bags** (226-2320); **4 Joli Madame Boutique** (477-2471); **5 Kasbar's Bags** (786-1308); **5 Leon's Hand Bags** (Brooklyn, 469-0575); **4&5 Martha's Leather** (255-1971); **4 Naem Bros.** (254-0120); **1 Phil Piniaz** (245-3616); **4&5 The Cow's Outside** (260-8299).

luggage (ALSO: CH. 1, "SMALL APPL.")

(includes: briefcases, garment-bags, luggage-carriers, suitcases, tote-bags)

****+C.O.M.B. Co. (intermittent stock, outside NYC, 1-800-328-0609, catalog is free if you mention this book); **5 ***Bag Man** (560-8952); **5 ***Cayne's DAC Jewelry** (244-8933); **3&4 ***Odd Job Trdg.** (intermittent stock, 686-6825); **3&4 **Bob's Discount** (intermittent stock, 674-4296); **5 **Cayne's 3** (564-3350); **2&3&4 **Romano Trdg.** (581-4248); **3 **Urico** (685-7962); **3&6 **Young Jin Trdg.** (684-4320); **3 *Altman Luggage** (254-7275); **3 *Deepak** (227-4088); **3 *Michael C. Fina** (869-5050); **3 *Mitu Enterprises** (685-7946); **3 Abe's Handbags & Luggage** (Queens, 526-9887); **3 Bettinger's Luggage** (475-1690); **2&3&4&5 Gold Style Bags** (226-2320); **2&3 Luggage King** (732-2562); **3 Odds & Ends Sundries** (Brooklyn, 854-1453); **3&4 Pennsylvania Luggage** (736-1523).

purses & wallets

3&4 ***Carter Leather (475-3537); **4&5 ***Giselle Handbag** (684-7800); **5 ***+Mills Sales** (477-1000); **2&3&4 **Romano Trdg.** (581-4248); **4&5 **Urico** (685-7962); **5&6 *Abbie's General Store** (349-3394).

sunglasses

4&5 ***Bag Man (560 8952); **4&5 ***Cayne's DAC Jewelry** (244-8933); **4**

22: PERSONAL ACCESSORIES

***Job Lot Trdg.** (intermittent stock, 962-4142); **4 **+Mills Sales** (477-1000); **4 **Ashreh Supply** (925-9507); **4&5 **Cayne's 3** (564-3350); **2&3&4 **Romano Trdg.** (581-4248); **4&5 *Han's Oriental** (243-3443); **4&5 *Sang's Bargain** (242-5049); **4 Mimex Sunglasses** (686-0106); **Mitchell Mogal** (226-8378).

umbrellas

4&5 ***Bag Man (560 8952); **4&5 ***Cayne's DAC Jewelry** (244-8933); **4 ***Mills Sales** (477-1000); **4&5 **Cayne's 3** (564-3350); **4 **Cho's Variety** (349-7544); **2&3&4 **Romano Trdg.** (581-4248); **4 **S.F. Fruits** (431-1588); **3 **Triest Export** (246-1548.); **3&5 **+Ranna Handbags** (244-8048); **4&5 *Han's Oriental** (243-3443); **4&5 *Sang's Bargain** (242-5049); **4&5 *Susan Trdg.** (431-8529); **3 Essex Umbrella** (674-3394); **3 Gloria Umbrella** (475-7388); **3&4 Pennsylvania Luggage** (736-1523).

handkerchiefs & scarves

4 ***Job Lot Trdg. (intermittent stock, 962-4142); **3&4 **Joe's Bargain Center** (phoneless); **2&3&4 **Romano Trdg.** (581-4248); **3&4 Bernard Krieger** (226-1929).

hand-knit scarves, bags, etc.

2 **Manos Del Uruguay (564-6115); **4 **+Buen Dia** (673-1910).

STORES-DIRECTORY

Phone a store before you go out of your way to visit it. Especially do this during July and August, when most establishments reduce or eliminate weekend-hours.

In the listings below, "*" means especially recommended, "+" means that the store offers a bonus discount to BF readers, "ch." and "c.c." mean respectively checks and credit cards, and "exch." and "rfd." mean respectively exchange and refund. Nearest subway-stops are shown. For example, "B-D-F to 47" means to take the B, D, or F train to 47th Street. Store-hours are also indicated, with days of the week abbreviated, like "M-S 8-6."

*   **Abbie's General Store**, 306 8th Av. (25-6), 349-3394, A-AA-CC-E to 23, 7 days 9-6, all cash, exch., no rfd. Small store. Specializes in new broken radios and calculators sold cheap as-is. Sells: **Purses & Wallets, Recordings & Tapes, Warehouse Salvage Job-Lot.**

   Abe's Handbags & Luggage, Queens, 176-39 Union Tnpk., Flushing, 526-9887, no subway stop nearby, M-S 10-6, ch., c.c., 7-day exch., no rfd. Sells: **Handbags & Attaches, Luggage.**

   Ace Leather, Brooklyn, 2211 Av. U, 891-9713, D-M-QB to Av. U, MTWFS 10-6, Th 10-8, ch., c.c., exch. or rfd. Sells: **Handbags & Attaches.**

   Altman Luggage, 135 Orchard St. (Delancey-Rivington), 254-7275, F-J-M to Delancey & Essex, 7 days 9:30-6, ch., c.c., exch. or rfd. Large selection. They offer practically every brand. Sells: **Luggage.**

*   **Ashreh Supply**, 473 Broadway (Grand), 3rd floor, 925-9507, J-M-N-QB-RR-6 to Canal, Sun-Th 11-7, all cash, no exch. or rfd. Basically a wholesaler who accomodates retail-trade. Sells: **Sunglasses, Appliances, Cameras & Optical Eqt., Jewelry & Gifts, Smoking Supplies, Stationery & Art Supplies.**

*   **Bag City**, 63 W. 37 (6th Av.), 391-2544, B-D-F-N-QB-RR to 34, M-F 10-6, ch., c.c., no exch. or rfd. Sells: **Handbags & Attaches.**

**   **Bag It**, 160 5th Av. (21), lobby right, 242-8750&8723 (ask for 'Bag It'), N-RR to 23rd St., T-F 10-5, all cash, no exch. or rfd. Small store. Small selection. Casual sporty styles. Sells: **Handbags & Attaches.**

*** **Bag Man**, 261 W. 34 (8th Av.), 560 8952, A-AA-CC-E to 34, M-S 10-7, all cash, exch., no rfd. One in the DAC Jewelry group. Sells: **Handbags & Attaches, Luggage, Sunglasses, Umbrellas, Clothing—Women's, Home-Improvement**

22: PERSONAL ACCESSORIES

Items, Jewelry & Gifts.

* **Bags By Zeno**, 1211 Broadway (29-30), 686-2869, N-RR to 28th St., M-F 9-7, S 9-3, all cash, exch., no rfd. Sells: **Handbags & Attaches.**

** **Bags 'N Things**, Queens, 71-07 Austin St., Forest Hills, 520-8755, E-F-GG-N to 71-Continental Avs., M-S 9:30-6, ch., c.c., exch., no rfd. Sells: **Handbags & Attaches.**

Bernard Krieger, 316 Grand St. (Orchard), 226-1929&4927, B-D to Grand, F-J-M to Delancey & Essex, Sun-Th 9-4:30, F 9-3, ch., no c.c., exch., no rfd. Sells: **Handkerchiefs & Scarves, Clothing—Men's, Clothing—Women's.**

Bettinger's Luggage, 80 Rivington St. (Allen), 475-1690, F-J-M to Delancey & Essex, Sun-F 9-7, ch., c.c., exch., no rfd. Large selection. Sells: **Luggage.**

** **Bob's Discount**, 109 Ludlow St. (Delancey), 674-4296, F-J-M to Delancey & Essex, W-M 10-5, all cash, exch., no rfd. Sells: **Luggage, Clothing—Men's, Sporting Goods, Warehouse Salvage Job-Lot.**

*+ **Buen Dia**, 108 W. Houston St. at Thompson, 673-1910, A-AA-B-CC-D-E-F to 4, M-S 12-7, Sun 2-6; 201 W. 11 at 7th Av., 673-1910, 1-2-3 to 14, M-S 12-7. Both stores: c.c., no ch., exch., no rfd. Very cooperative. Everything is knit in Latin America. Bonus discount to BF readers: 5% to 8%. Sells: **Hand-Knit Scarves, Bags, Etc., Clothing—Women's, Jewelry & Gifts.**

*** **Carter Leather**, 41 E. 11 (University), 5th floor, 475-3537, LL-N-QB-RR-4-5-6 to Union Sq., N-RR to 8th St., M-F 9-5 (for other hours, phone first), all cash, exch., no rfd. Very-good-quality leather wallets; medium-quality belts for women. An authentic factory-outlet. Sells: **Purses & Wallets, Clothing—Women's.**

** **Cayne's 3**, 1333 Broadway (36), 564-3350, B-D-F-N-QB-RR to 34, M-S 10-6:30, c.c., no ch., 25-day exch. or rfd. One in the Cayne group. Sells: **Handbags & Attaches, Luggage, Sunglasses, Umbrellas, Linens.**

*** **Cayne's DAC Jewelry**, 205 W. 34 (7th Av.), 244-8933, 1-2-3 to 34, M-S 10-7, all cash, exch., no rfd. One in the DAC Jewelry group. Sells: **Handbags & Attaches, Luggage, Sunglasses, Umbrellas.**

** **Cho's Variety**, 121 Chambers St. (Church-W. B'wy), 349-7544, A-CC-1-2-3 to Chambers, M-S 11-6, all cash, exch. or rfd. Small store. Street-stand. Sells: **Umbrellas, Clothing—Men's, Clothing—Women's, Toys, Games & Hobbies.**

***+ **C.O.M.B. Co.**, 6850 Wayzata Blvd., Minneapolis, MN 55426, 1-800-328-0609, catalog is free if you mention this book, ch., c.c., exch., no rfd. Takes mail-orders. Catalog. Very cooperative. Catalog is free only if you mention Bargain Finder. Sells: **Luggage, Cameras & Optical Eqt., Home-Improvement Items, Jewelry & Gifts, Warehouse Salvage Job-Lot.**

* **Deepak**, 28 Canal St. at Essex, 227-4088, F to E. Broadway, 7 days 10-6, all cash, no exch. or rfd. Samsonite half price; also good luggage-carriers. Almost all the appliance-stores in this neighborhood (see Ch. 1) carry these same items at about the same prices. Sells: **Luggage.**

East Village Variety, 186 1st Av. (11-12), 674-8300, LL to 1st Av., 7 days 9-8, all cash, exch., no rfd. Sells: **Handbags & Attaches, Clothing—Men's.**

Essex Umbrella, 101 Essex St. (Delancey), 674-3394, F-J-M to Delancey & Essex, Sun-F 9-6, ch., c.c., exch. or rfd. Sells: **Umbrellas.**

** **Fashion By Helou**, 32 W. 28 (B'wy), 679-1739, N-RR to 28th St., M-F 8-6, S 10-4, ch., no c.c., exch., no rfd. All is leather. Sells: **Handbags & Attaches.**

Fine & Klein, 119 Orchard St. (Delancey), 674-6720, F-J-M to Delancey & Essex, Sun-F 9-5:45, ch., c.c., exch., no rfd. Huge selection. Very crowded and busy. Sells: **Handbags & Attaches.**

*** **Giselle Handbag**, 309 5th Av. (31-2), 684-7800, N-RR to 28th St., 6 to 33, M-Th 9-6, F 9-4, Sun 10-3, all cash, exch., no rfd. All is leather. Sells: **Handbags & Attaches, Luggage, Purses & Wallets.**

Gloria Umbrella, 39 Essex St. (Grand), 475-7388, F to E. Broadway, Sun-Th 10-5, F 10-3, ch., no c.c., exch., no rfd. Sells: **Umbrellas.**

Gold Style Bags, 13 Orchard St. on Canal, 226-2320, F to E. Broadway, Sun-Th 9-5, F 9-3, ch., no c.c., exch., no rfd. Handbags are medium-quality; luggage includes designer and brand-name. Sells: **Handbags & Attaches, Luggage.**

* **Han's Oriental**, 100 W. 14 at 6th Av., 243-3443 & 255-8113, B-F-LL to 14th St. & 6th Av., M-S 10-7, all cash, exch., no rfd. Sells: **Sunglasses, Umbrellas, Clothing—Children's, Sporting Goods.**

** **Ito Leather**, 662 Lexington Av. (55-6), 832-3765, N-RR-4-5-6 to 59th & Lex., E-F to Lex. Av., MTS 11-7, WThF 11-8, ch., c.c., exch., no rfd. Designer-style

22: PERSONAL ACCESSORIES

bags. Low 'list' prices; permanent 'sale.' Sells: **Handbags & Attaches.**

    *   **J. Chuckles**, 321 Madison Av. at 42nd St., 867-3771, 4-5-6-7 to Grand Central, M-F 10-7, S 10-6; 1290 6th Av. (52), 757-6240, B-D-F to 47, M-F 10-7, S 10-6, Sun 12-6. Both stores: ch., c.c., exch., no rfd. Large selection. Boutique styles. Listed 'regular' prices are about 15% below competition on most items; 80% of stock is discounted 25-50% off that. Zoom is clearance-store for chain. Sells: **Handbags & Attaches, Clothing—Women's.**

   **   **Jet Handbag**, Brooklyn, 102 Cortelyou at McDonald, 438-1181, F to Ditmas, M-F 9-5, Sun 9-3, ch., no c.c., exch., no rfd. Sells: **Handbags & Attaches.**

  ***   **Job Lot Trdg.**, 140 Church St. (Warren-Chambers), 962-4142, A-CC-1-2-3 to Chambers; 412 5th Av. (37-8), 398-9210, B-D-F to 42. Both stores: M-F 8-5:30, S 8-4:30, all cash, 15-day exch. or rfd. Both are huge stores, with terrific selections. Sells: **Sunglasses, Handkerchiefs & Scarves, Clothing—Men's, Dinnerware & Cookware, Foods, Home-Improvement Items, Housewares, Jewelry & Gifts, Linens, Sporting Goods, Stationery & Art Supplies, Toys, Games & Hobbies, Warehouse Salvage Job-Lot.**

  **   **Joe's Bargain Center**, 123 1st Av. (7-8), phoneless, LL to 1st Av., F to 2nd Av., M-F 10-6, all cash, no exch. or rfd. Irregulars. Sells: **Handkerchiefs & Scarves, Clothing—Men's.**

      Joli Madame Boutique, 145 Orchard St. (Rivington), 477-2471, F-J-M to Delancey & Essex, F to 2nd Av., 7 days 10-6, c.c., no ch., exch., no rfd. Sells: **Handbags & Attaches, Clothing—Women's.**

      Kasbar's Bags, 129 Chambers St. (W. B'wy), 786-1308, A-CC-1-2-3 to Chambers, M-S 11-6, ch., no c.c., exch., no rfd. Sells: **Handbags & Attaches.**

    *   **Kingdom of Gifts**, 184 5th Av. (23), 989-9763, N-RR to 23rd St., M-F 7:30-6:30, S 12-6, all cash, exch., no rfd. Sells: **Handbags & Attaches.**

    *   **La Gigi Handbags**, 92 Rivington St. (Orchard-Ludlow), 254-3670, F-J-M to Delancey & Essex, M-Th 10-5, F 10-3, Sun 9-6, ch., c.c. $25+, 14-day exch., no rfd. Sells: **Handbags & Attaches.**

      Leon's Hand Bags, Brooklyn, 920 Cortelyou Rd. (Con. Is. Av.), 469-0575, D-M-QB to Cortelyou, M-S 8:30-12 & 2-6, all cash, exch., no rfd. Sells: **Handbags & Attaches.**

      Luggage King, 261 Broadway (Warren), 732-2562, N-RR to City Hall, M-F 9-5:45, S 9-3, ch., c.c., exch. or rfd. Sells: **Luggage.**

    +   **Lynn Richards Handbags**, Brooklyn, 1664 Sheepshead Bay Rd. (Jerome-Voorhies), 891-2914, D-M-QB to Sheepshead Bay, MTWS 10-6, ThF 10-7, ch., c.c., exch., no rfd. Bonus discount to BF readers: 10% to 15%. Sells: **Handbags & Attaches.**

    *   **Man-Dee Bag**, 39 W. 37 (5th-6th), 840-2233, B-D-F-N-QB-RR to 34, M-F 8-4:30, all cash, no exch. or rfd. No attaches. Sells: **Handbags & Attaches.**

   **   **Manos Del Uruguay**, 35 W. 36 (5th-6th), 12th floor, 564-6115, B-D-F-N-QB-RR to 34, open only 3rd Monday after Thanksgiving through Dec. 23, M-F 11-7, ch., c.c., no exch. or rfd. Beautiful multi-tonal sweaters, hats, scarves, ties, jackets, capes, and mittens. Wool is hand-spun and kettle-dyed. 50% off. No retail at other times than indicated. Sells: **Hand-Knit Scarves, Bags, Etc., Clothing—Women's, Jewelry & Gifts.**

      Martha's Leather, 45 Christopher St. at Waverly, 255-1971, 1 to Christopher St., M-S 12-9, Sun 12-6, ch., c.c., exch., no rfd. Sells: **Handbags & Attaches.**

    *   **Michael C. Fina**, 580 5th Av. at 47th, 2nd floor, 869-5050, B-D-F to 47, F 9-5:30, ch., c.c., exch. or rfd. Takes mail-orders. Catalog. Sells: **Luggage, Cameras & Optical Eqt., Dinnerware & Cookware, Jewelry & Gifts.**

  +   **Mills Sales, 889 Broadway at 19th St., 477-1000, LL-N-QB-RR-4-5-6 to Union Sq., N-RR to 23rd St., M-F 9-5, S 9-2, all cash, no exch. or rfd. No retail sales (wholesale only) Labor Day through Xmas. A specialty here is steel ball-point pens super-cheap by the dozen. Bonus discount to BF readers: 5%. Sells: **Purses & Wallets, Sunglasses, Umbrellas, Appliances, Dinnerware & Cookware, Home-Improvement Items, Jewelry & Gifts, Stationery & Art Supplies, Toys, Games & Hobbies.**

      Mimex Sunglasses, 33 W. 29 (B'wy), 686-0106, N-RR to 28th St., M-F 8-6, S 8-12, 1st Sun each month 10-2, all cash, no exch. or rfd. Sells: **Sunglasses.**

      Mitchell Mogal, 440 Broadway (Grand), 226-8378, J-M-N-QB-RR-6 to Canal, M-F 9-5, all cash, exch., no rfd. Terrific on Wiss scissors; also on miniature cap-guns. Sells: **Sunglasses, Fabrics, Yarns & Notions, Jewelry & Gifts, Toys, Games & Hobbies.**

22: PERSONAL ACCESSORIES

* **Mitu Enterprises**, 128 Madison Av. (30-31), 685-7946, 6 to 33, M-S 106, Sun 11-5, c.c., no ch., exch., no rfd. American Tourister and Samsonite, like the stores listed under 'Small Appliances' in Chapter 1. Sells: **Luggage**.

* **Naem Bros.**, 128 MacDougal St. (3), 254-0120, A-AA-B-CC-D-E-F to 4, 7 days 12-9, ch., c.c., exch., no rfd. All is leather. Sells: **Handbags & Attaches**.

* **New Fashion**, 158 Church St. (Chambers-Reade), 227-1880, A-CC-1-2-3 to Chambers, M-F 8-6, S 10-5, ch., c.c., 7-day exch., no rfd. Sells: **Handbags & Attaches**.

* **New York, NY**, 1235 Broadway (30), 679-3370, N-RR to 28th St., 7 days 9-7, all cash, exch. or rfd. Sells: **Handbags & Attaches**.

*** **Odd Job Trdg.**, 7 E. 40 (Mad.), 686-6825, B-D-F to 42, 7 to 5th Av.; 66 W. 48 (6th Av.), 575-0477, B-D-F to 47. Both stores: M-Th 8-5:30, F 8-3, Sun 10-5, ch., no c.c., 15-day exch. or rfd. Sells: **Handbags & Attaches, Luggage, Clothing—Men's, Dinnerware & Cookware, Foods, Health & Beauty Aids, Home-Improvement Items, Housewares, Linens, Stationery & Art Supplies, Toys, Games & Hobbies, Warehouse Salvage Job-Lot**.

Odds & Ends Sundries, Brooklyn, 4809 New Utrecht Av., 854-1453, B to 50th St., Sun-Th 10-6, F 10-1, ch., no c.c., exch. or rfd. Sells: **Luggage, Clothing—Men's, Clothing—Women's, Toys, Games & Hobbies**.

Pennsylvania Luggage, 7th Av. & 33rd St., N.E. corner, downstairs to subway, 736-1523, 1-2-3 to 34, M-S 10-7, c.c., no ch., exch. or rfd. Sells: **Luggage, Umbrellas**.

Phil Piniaz, 129 W. 46 (6th-7th), 245-3616, B-D-F to 47, M-S 11-6, all cash, exch., no rfd. If Bloomingdales carried the bags he makes and charges $100 and up for, the prices would be $200 and up; but they don't. His quality is unmatched. Sells: **Handbags & Attaches**.

*+ **Ranna Handbags**, 10 W. 32 (5th Av.), 244-8048, B-D-F-N-QB-RR to 34, M-F 9:30-5, ch., no c.c., exch., no rfd. Totes are the '3' in the quality-rating, and the value here on them is superb. Handbags are the '5' in the quality-rating, and the value here on these is good. Bonus discount to BF readers: 10%. Sells: **Handbags & Attaches, Umbrellas**.

** **Romano Trdg.**, 628 W. 45th St. on 12th Av., 581-4248, A-AA-CC-E to 42, plus a long walk, M-F 8-5:30, S 8-5, all cash, exch. or rfd. Very cooperative. A little bit of everything, designer-name and major brand items. Sells: **Handbags & Attaches, Luggage, Purses & Wallets, Sunglasses, Umbrellas, Handkerchiefs & Scarves, Appliances, Clothing—Men's, Jewelry & Gifts, Office Equipment, Stationery & Art Supplies, Toys, Games & Hobbies**.

* **Sang's Bargain**, 148 W. 14 (6th-7th), 242-5049, B-F-LL to 14th St. & 6th Av., 1-2-3 to 14, M-S 9-6:30, Sun 9-5, all cash, no exch. or rfd. Sells: **Sunglasses, Umbrellas**.

** **S.F. Fruits**, 125 Canal St. at Chrystie, 431-1588, B-D to Grand, 7 days 9-7, all cash, exch., no rfd. Sells: **Umbrellas**.

Strawberry, 129 E. 42 at Lex., 986-7030, 4-5-6-7 to Grand Central, M-F 10-7, S 10-6, Sun 12-6; 80 Broad St. (Stone-Beaver), 425-6627, 4-5 to Bowling Green, J-M-RR-2-3 to Wall & Broad Sts., M-F 9:30-6:30; 501 Madison Av. (51), 753-5008, 6 to 51, E-F to 5th Av., M-F 8:30-7, S 10-6; 120 W. 49 (6th Av.), 391-8718, B-D-F to 47, N-RR to 49th St., M-F 9:30-6:45, S 10-6; 14 W. 34 (Empire State Bldg.), 279-8664, B-D-F-N-QB-RR to 34, MTWS 10-7, ThF 10-8:30, Sun 12-6; 147 E. 86 (Lex.), 427-1318, 4-5-6 to 86, M-F 10-9, S 10-7, Sun 12-6; 880 3rd Av. (53-4), 888-6666, E-F to Lex. Av., M-F 10-7, S 10-6; Brooklyn, 490 Fulton St. (Hoyt-Bond), 858-8984, 2-3 to Hoyt, M-S 10-7, Sun 12-6. All stores: ch., c.c., exch., no rfd. Large selection. Boutique styles. Listed 'regular' prices are about 15% below competition o most items; 80% of stock is discounted 25-50% off that. Zoom is clearance-store for chain. Sells: **Handbags & Attaches, Clothing—Women's**.

* **Susan Trdg.**, 300 Canal St. (B'wy), 431-8529, J-M-N-QB-RR-6 to Canal, 7 days 10-6, ch., c.c., exch., no rfd. Sells: **Umbrellas, Appliances, Furnishings, Home-Improvement Items**.

The Cow's Outside, 1 W. 8 (5th Av.), 260-8299, A-AA-B-CC-D-E-F to 4, N-RR to 8th St.; 33 Greenwich Av. (10), 691-0903, A-AA-B-CC-D-E-F to 4, 1-2-3 to 14. Both stores: M-S 11-7, Sun 1-6, ch., c.c., 15-day exch., no rfd. Buy only the sale items (of which there always are many). The other things are not discounted, and are not good values. Sells: **Handbags & Attaches**.

** **Triest Export**, 560 12th Av. (44), 246-1548., A-AA-CC-E to 42, plus a long walk, Sun-F 7-6, all cash, no exch. or rfd. Very busy. Expect long wait on line. Popular

22: PERSONAL ACCESSORIES

with seamen and foreign tourists. Sells: **Umbrellas, Appliances, Cameras & Optical Eqt., Clothing—Men's, Toys, Games & Hobbies.**

** **Urico**, 842 6th Av. (29-30), 685-7962, B-D-F-N-QB-RR to 34, N-RR to 28th St., MWF 8-6, TTh 8-8, S 8-4, all cash, no exch. or rfd. Terrific bargain on the best-quality luggage-carrier made, and also on Moroccan leather wallets. That explains the '3&5' quality-rating. No actual luggage here. Sells: **Luggage, Purses & Wallets.**

** **Weber's Job Lot**, 505 8th Av. at 35th, 564-7668, A-AA-CC-E to 34, M-F 10-6:30, S 10-6; 136 Church St. at Warren, 564-7668, A-CC-1-2-3 to Chambers, M-S 8-6; 2064 Broadway at 71st, 787-1644, 1-2-3 to 72, M-F 9-9, S 9-6, Sun 12-6. All stores: c.c., no ch., 7-day exch. or rfd. Some terrific values; others not good. Some prices wrongly marked on items each time I was at both stores; checkout counter said 'It's an error.' Sells: **Handbags & Attaches, Dinnerware & Cookware, Health & Beauty Aids, Home-Improvement Items, Jewelry & Gifts, Linens, Stationery & Art Supplies, Warehouse Salvage Job-Lot.**

** **Young Jin Trdg.**, 47 W. 29 (B'wy), 684-4320, N-RR to 28th St., M-F 8-7, S 9-3, all cash, exch., no rfd. Terrific bargain on the best-quality luggage-carrier made; also very good values on cheap-quality for both handbags and luggage. That explains the '3&6' quality-rating. Sells: **Handbags & Attaches, Luggage.**

23:
PETS
Expect 20-40% discounts.

The most humane way to acquire a pet is also the least expensive—through an animal-shelter. In most instances, animals not picked up within a certain amount of time—often only a week—are killed, because of space-limitations at shelters. So you'll probably be saving your pet's life by picking him up in this manner. Frank Inn, the owner of the million-dollar television-star dog Benji, is proud that he acquired Benji at the pound. "I saved his life," he said on the *Today* show, beaming. But there's another, and very practical, advantage, of getting an animal this way: You won't have to worry about exchange-policies at an animal-shelter, as you usually will at a pet-store (since the latter will generally not take an animal back once he's been sold).

If you do decide to purchase an animal at a pet-shop, you'll be at the receiving-end of a huge industry which trades in prettified tragedy. About two-thirds of the nation's pet-sales are via puppy-mills where pups are "often treated worse than cabbages (and are actually shipped two-to-a-cabbage-crate for long distances)" according to an investigation by the Humane Society of the United States, reported in Jack Anderson's column. This investigation "found dogs starving in transit, freezing in airplane holds, sold with hideous diseases and shuddering with trauma." Many dogs die before they get to the store; you'll be getting one of the survivors. To acquire an animal in this manner is to finance a continuation of this trade.

The Better Business Bureau has established the following minimum standards for pet-shop guarantees, but few pet-shops will offer a guarantee meeting these guidelines:

"The pet retailer or breeder should give a five-day health guarantee. The guarantee requires that the pet be examined by a veterinarian. On written request from the vet, the guarantee-period should be extended an additional five days. If during this period, the vet deems the animal unsuitable for reasons of health, it should be exchangeable for a second animal. In addition, a retailer or breeder should grant a 30-day extended exchange guarantee from date of purchase, covering distemper, hepatitis and congenital defects. If it's necessary to provide a replacement, the seller shall do so within 45 days of return.

"Furthermore, if a puppy is represented as AKC registerable, the seller shall, at the time of sale, furnish the AKC standard blue registration application properly filled out, or if unable to do so, seller shall provide written identification, to include breed, the names of sire, dam, breeder, and date of birth of the puppy. Also, a statement that papers will be forwarded as soon as possible, but in no event should it be later than 90 days."

23: PETS

On a long-term basis, the area of biggest savings is pet-foods, since this constitutes a recurring expense. Therefore, I list below not only animal-shelters and pet-stores, but also places that offer New York City's best discounts on pet-foods.

RECOMMENDED STORES:

pets from shelters
****Your Nearest Animal Shelter.

pets from shops
*JBJ Discount Pets (982-5310); Exotic Aquatics (675-6355); Fish & Cheeps (475-6450).

tropical fish
(includes: aquariums, aquatic plants, fish, tanks)
*JBJ Discount Pets (982-5310); Age of Aquarium (Queens, 544-9696); Exotic Aquatics (675-6355); Tropical Fish Supermarket (Brooklyn, 338-5069).

pet foods
***Anything & Everything (Brooklyn, 332-1508); *+The Pet Nosh (Queens, 229-8976); *Dog Delight (Brooklyn, 837-7441); American Cat & Dog Food (673-1031); Animal Pantry (Brooklyn, 680-2220); Beastly Bite (Brooklyn, 237-1883); Discount Pet Foods (Staten Island, 979-1657); K-9 Caterers & C&K (Queens, 275-5614); Vita Chow (Brooklyn, 499-9565).

dog-diet supplements
***American Lecithin Co. (Queens, 274-4350).

STORES-DIRECTORY

Phone a store before you go out of your way to visit it. Especially do this during July and August, when most establishments reduce or eliminate weekend-hours.

In the listings below, "*" means especially recommended, "+" means that the store offers a bonus discount to BF readers, "ch." and "c.c." mean respectively checks and credit cards, and "exch." and "rfd." mean respectively exchange and refund. Nearest subway-stops are shown. For example, "B-D-F to 47" means to take the B, D, or F train to 47th Street. Store-hours are also indicated, with days of the week abbreviated, like "M-S 8-6."

Age of Aquarium, Queens, 116-06 Queens Blvd., Forest Hills, 544-9696, E-F to Union Tnpk., M-F 11:30-8:30, SSun 11:30-5, c.c., no ch., no exch. or rfd. Sells: **Tropical Fish**.

American Cat & Dog Food, 147 Av. A (9-10), 673-1031, 6 to Astor, LL to 1st Av., M-S 10-6, all cash, exch. or rfd. Sells: **Pet-Foods**.

*** **American Lecithin Co.**, Queens, 32-34 61st St. (Northern Blvd.), Woodside, 274-4350, F-GG-N to Northern Blvd., M-F 9-5. Very cooperative. Takes mail-orders. Phone; specify liquid (8-lb. tin) or granulated (4-lb. bag), or dog-diet supplement, UPS-shipped; send M.O. (or a check on subsequent orders); they ship pronto. Nice! Sells: **Dog-Diet Supplements, Health & Beauty Aids**.

Animal Pantry, Brooklyn, 699 86th St., 680-2220, RR to 86th St., M-S 10-6:30, all cash, exch. or rfd. Sells: **Pet-Foods**.

*** **Anything & Everything**, Brooklyn, 2930 Av. X (Nostrand), 332-1508, no subway stop nearby, MTWF 10-6, Th 10-9, S 10-6, Sun 12-5, all cash, exch. or rfd. Large selection. Practically a super-discount supermarket, but specializing in packaged non-perishable foods, etc., no fresh produce. Sells: **Pet-Foods, Foods, House-**

23: PETS

wares, Warehouse Salvage Job-Lot.

    Beastly Bite, Brooklyn, 78 Henry (Pineapple), 237-1883, 2-3 to Clark, M-S 11-2 & 3-7:30; Brooklyn, 140 Court St. (Pacific), 522-5133, F-GG to Bergen St., M-RR-2-3-4-5 to Borough Hall & Court St., M-S 10-7, Sun 12:30-7. Both stores: all cash, exch. or rfd. Sells: **Pet-Foods**.

    Discount Pet Foods, Staten Island, 1814 Hylan Blvd. (Buel Av.), 979-1657, no subway stop nearby, M-ThS 10-6, F 10-8, Sun 12-4, all cash, exch. or rfd. Sells: **Pet-Foods**.

✻   **Dog Delight**, Brooklyn, 6215 18th Av., 837-7441, N to 18th Av., M-S 10-7, all cash, exch. or rfd. Sells: **Pet-Foods**.

    Exotic Aquatics, 8 Cornelia (Bleeker), 675-6355, A-AA-B-CC-D-E-F to 4; 271 Amsterdam (73), 873-8655, 1-2-3 to 72. Both stores: ch., c.c., no exch. or rfd. Sells: **Pets From Shops, Tropical Fish**.

    Fish & Cheeps, 104 2nd Av. (6-7), 475-6450, F to 2nd Av., 6 to Astor, M-F 11-7, S 11-6, all cash, 7-day exch., no rfd. Sells: **Pets From Shops**.

✻   **JBJ Discount Pets**, 151 E. Houston St. at Eldridge, 982-5310, F to 2nd Av., M-S 11-6, Sun 11-3, all cash, no exch. or rfd. Only 1 bike; many pets. Sells: **Pets From Shops, Tropical Fish, Bikes**.

    K-9 Caterers & C&K, Queens, 89-50 Metropolitan Av. at Woodhaven Blvd., Rego Park, 275-5614&5719, no subway stop nearby, M-S 9-6:30, all cash, exch. or rfd. Sells: **Pet-Foods**.

✻⁺   **The Pet Nosh**, Queens, 254-11 Northern Blvd., Little Neck, 229-8976, no subway stop nearby, M-F 10-6, S 9-5, all cash, exch. or rfd. Bonus BF discount: 10% off accessories, if you show this book. Might not apply to special-sale accessories. Sells: **Pet-Foods**.

    Tropical Fish Supermarket, Brooklyn, 2890 Nostrand Av. (Kings Hwy & P), 338-5069, no subway stop nearby, MTThF 10-8, WSun 10-4, S 10-6, ch., c.c., exch. or rfd. Sells: **Tropical Fish**.

    Vita Chow, Brooklyn, 284A 9th St. (4th-5th), 499-9565, F-N-RR to 9th St. & 4th Av., M-S 9:30-6:30, all cash, exch. or rfd. Sells: **Pet-Foods**.

✻✻✻✻ **Your Nearest Animal Shelter**, address and phone shown under 'Animal Shelters,' in the Yellow Pages, Sells: **Pets From Shelters**.

24:
PUBLICATIONS
Discounts vary.

RECOMMENDED PRODUCTS:

Magazines: *The Nation.* I've often asked myself what periodical publication I'd subscribe to if I could never read any other—in other words, which one gives the best-rounded and most intelligently skeptical and critical coverage of politics and the state of the world. *The Nation* would be my choice (even over any newspaper), because its extremely pithy articles cover a broad range of subjects in depth and with reliable accuracy. The articles are, indeed, quite short. Yet they pack in an incredible amount of facts; all in a meaningful, significant, context, though not reeking of ideology. The magazine is thus especially attractive to a reader who has a busy schedule and who consequently demands the maximum amount of important news and objective analysis in the fewest words. The ideological content, such as it is (and that's populist leftist) is about as strong as is, say, that of *Time* (which by contrast is big-corporate conservative), or *Newsweek* (which is actually similar to its competitor, though with just a touch of big-corporate liberalism). It is not obtrusive, such as one finds, for example, in *National Review, Reason, American Spectator, Human Events, The Progressive,* or *Mother Jones,* all of which are often more propagandistic than reportorial. Occasionally—but only rarely—*The Nation* does waste some of its precious few pages ideologising, and each issue of the magazine does also have small sections devoted to books, theater, and films (cogently and literately written ones, too); but basically the focus of this magazine is power, especially political power, and here is where it really digs in, reporting the kind of news that one often can't find even in the big bulky pages of the *New York Times.* Nor does the magazine pull punches to play it safe with a broad, colorless mash of readership, maximizing universal inoffensiveness for the sake of circulation-gains. For example, a recent issue of *The Nation* had an article, "Why The Big Banks Love Martial Law," explaining in far greater detail than I've seen in any newspaper or magazine, the relationship between the Polish military crackdown, the huge Polish debt, and the large European and American banks. (The leading capitalists in bed with the communists? Now, that's ideology-transcendant news-digging!) In this same brief issue, another article, "A Classic Cartel in Action," reported on the International Electrical Association, an obscure global organization which for 50 years has had an almost iron grip on the world's heavy electrical equipment trade, setting prices, and—according to leaked internal documents—rigging bids. Previous issues of *The Nation* had articles predicting the fall of the Shah (well before the C.I.A. claims it had any intimation of that), chronicling Henry Kissinger's early hstory as a snoop and informant for the F.B.I, and laying bare the role of the large petroleum companies in intentionally precipitating the oil-shortages and the consequent rises in oil-prices. But despite the magazine's strong no-holds-barred issue-orientation—and in striking contrast to other, ideologically narrower, "think"-magazines, such as *The Progressive* (socialist) at one end, and *National Review* (nationalist right-wing) at the other—there is no obsessive ideological hatchet-wielding which narrows the range of subjects critically probed. (*The Progressive* reports in depth only on a few subjects like nuclear arms and nuclear energy; it even went so far as virtually to ignore the Iranian-hostages problem and its background. *National Review*, on the other hand, has no coverage to speak of concerning the subjects that its leftist counterpart relishes: nothing on the dangers of nuclear energy, the scandals of Pentagon-industrial corruption.) And unlike *Harper's* and *The Atlantic*, which are intentionally edited for intellectuals with a stronger bent for literature than for either politics or investigative reporting (indeed, an editor at *Harper's* once told me that they outright shun investigative-reporting articles because the magazine's readers "do not respond to that"), the strong suit of *The Nation* is precisely the latter—and that's the kind of magazine I'd like to have on a desert island. **Bonus discount to BF readers: Half off the regular subscription-price to new subscribers only, if you mention that you found them recommended in this book.** Phone them at 242-8400, and ask for the subscription-manager, or write to him at 72 5th Av., NYC 10011.

RECOMMENDED STORES:

current bestsellers

Expect 10-50% discounts.

(50% for reviewers' copies at Strand Bookshop.)

****Barnes & Noble Sale Annex** (675-5500); ****Strand** (473-1452); ***Barnes & Noble** (765-0592); ***Metropolitan Books** (254-8609); +**Jackson Hts. Discount Books** (Queens, 426-0202); **Discount Bookshop** (628-7341).

remainders, clearance-books

Expect 50-80% discounts.

****Barnes & Noble Sale Annex** (675-5500); ****Strand** (473-1452); *+**Discount Book Store** (Brooklyn, 232-7233); ***Barnes & Noble** (765-0592); ***Metropolitan Books** (254-8609); ***Ruby's Book Annex** (732-8676); ***Ruby's Book Sale** (732-8676); ***The Book Store** (425-6095).

used books

Expect about 50% discount.

****Barnes & Noble Sale Annex** (675-5500); ****Strand** (473-1452); ***Ruby's Book Annex** (732-8676); ***Ruby's Book Sale** (732-8676); ***The Book Store** (425-6095); +**Jackson Hts. Discount Books** (Queens, 426-0202); **Forest Hills Discount Books** (Queens, 897-6100); **Paperback Exchanges** (982-8825).

24: PUBLICATIONS

---
textbooks

Expect 60-90% off non-current.

Barnes & Noble Sale Annex (675-5500); ***Ruby's Book Annex (732-8676).

---
encyclopedias & dictionaries

Expect 20-40% discounts.

Barnes & Noble Sale Annex (675-5500); ***Barnes & Noble (765-0592); **Literary Mart** (684-0588); **Reference Book Center** (677-2160).

---
magazine backissues

Expect 40% discount.

*Back-Date Magazines (695-4897); ***Ruby's Book Sale** (732-8676); ***The Book Store** (425-6095).

---
magazine subscriptions

Expect 20-50% discounts.

College Store Service Bureau; Macy's Magazine Service; Magazine Buyers' Service; Publishers Clearing House; Select Information Exchange (874-6408); **United Subscription Svc.**

---
posters

Expect 50-70% discounts.

**Barnes & Noble Sale Annex (675-5500).

---
greeting-cards: CH.17

STORES-DIRECTORY

Phone a store before you go out of your way to visit it. Especially do this during July and August, when most establishments reduce or eliminate weekend-hours.

In the listings below, "*" means especially recommended, "+" means that the store offers a bonus discount to BF readers, "ch." and "c.c." mean respectively checks and credit cards, and "exch." and "rfd." mean respectively exchange and refund. Nearest subway-stops are shown. For example, "B-D-F to 47" means to take the B, D, or F train to 47th Street. Store-hours are also indicated, with days of the week abbreviated, like "M-S 8-6."

*   **Back-Date Magazines**, 274 W. 43 (8th Av.), 695-4897, A-AA-CC-E to 42, M-F 10-6, S 10-5, all cash, no exch. or rfd. Huge selection, especially strong on old—not recent—backissues. (For the latter, Ruby's Book Sale offers a bigger choice.) Sells: **Magazine Backissues**.

*   **Barnes & Noble**, 600 5th Av. (48), 765-0592, B-D-F to 47, MTWF 9:45-6:45, Th 9:45-8, S 9:45-6, Sun 12-6; 248 World Trade Center Concourse 5, 466-9206, AA-E to World Trade Ctr., M-F 8-7, S 10-6; 175 W. 57 at 7th Av., 586-8460, N-QB-RR to 57th St., M-F 10-9, S 10-10, Sun 12-8; 999 3rd Av. (59), 753-1694, N-RR-4-5-6 to 59th & Lex., M-Th 11-10, FS 11-11, Sun 1-5; 750 3rd Av. at 47th St., 697-2251, 6 to 51, M-F 8:30-8, S 11-6, Sun 12-6; 33rd St. at 7th Av., 695-1677, 1-2-3 to 34, M-F 7:30-8, S 10-6; 2105 Broadway (73), 873-0819, 1-2-3 to 72, M-S 10-9, Sun 12-5; 120 E. 86 (Lex.), 427-0686, 4-5-6 to 86, M-Th 9:45-10, FS 9:45-11, Sun 12-8; 1521 Broadway (45), 944-2604, N-QB-RR-1-2-3-7 to 42 & Times Square, M-F 9:45-11, S 10-12, Sun 12-6; 56 W. 8 (6th Av.), 254-0562, A-AA-B-CC-D-E-F to 4, M-F 10-9, S 10-11, Sun 12-6; Brooklyn, Albee Sq. Mall, DeKalb at Fulton, 858-8330, 2-3 to Hoyt, B-D-M-N-QB-RR to DeKalb, MTWFS 10-8, Th 10-9, Sun 11-5; Brooklyn, Kings

24: PUBLICATIONS

Plaza, Av. U at Flatbush, 253-5283, no subway stop nearby, M-S 10-9:30, Sun 12-5; Queens, 107-21 Continental Av., Forest Hills, 793-0496, E-F-GG-N to 71-Continental Avs., M-F 10-9, S 10-11, Sun 12-6. All stores: ch., c.c., 7-day exch., 3-day rfd. Although the Sale Annex (separately recommended here) has a larger selection of books at discount, these other stores are also good. Sells: **Current Bestsellers, Remainders, Clearance-Books, Encyclopedias & Dictionaries.**

** **Barnes & Noble Sale Annex**, 128 5th Av. at 18th St. (across street from the main store), 675-5500, N-RR to 23rd St., LL-N-QB-RR-4-5-6 to Union Sq., B-F-LL to 14th St. & 6th Av., M-F 9:45-6:15, S 9:45-6, Sun 10-5, ch., c.c., 7-day exch., 3-day rfd. The used books include a whole huge section devoted to second-hand paperbacks--mostly quality, not pulp, from both obscure and known publishers. Sells: **Current Bestsellers, Remainders, Clearance-Books, Used Books, Textbooks, Encyclopedias & Dictionaries, Posters.**

College Store Service Bureau, National Assn. of College Stores, Oberlin, OH 44074. Price-list and subscription-blank distributed free at your nearest college bookstore. Sells: **Magazine Subscriptions.**

*+ **Discount Book Store**, Brooklyn, 1908 86th St., 232-7233, B to 20th Av., MTThF 10-5:45, WS 10-4:45, all cash, no exch. or rfd. Very strong on Harlequins, super on Mills & Boons. Bonus discount to BF readers: 10% to 20%. Sells: **Remainders, Clearance-Books.**

Discount Bookshop, 1448 1st Av. (75), 628-7341, 6 to 77; 897 1st Av. (50), 751-3839, 6 to 51. Both stores: M-S 1-10, Sun 1-8, ch., c.c., no exch. or rfd. Sells: **Current Bestsellers.**

Forest Hills Discount Books, Queens, 63-56 108th St., Forest Hills, 897-6100, F-GG-N to 67th Av., plus a long walk, M-F 10:30-7, S 10-6, Sun 10:30-5:30, all cash, exch., no rfd. 25% credit for returns. Basically a paperback exchange, like the others. Sells: **Used Books.**

+ **Jackson Hts. Discount Books**, Queens, 77-15 37th Av., Jackson Hts., 426-0202, E-F-GG-N-7 to 74th-B'wy & Roosevelt-Jack.Hts., M-S 9-9, Sun 11:30-6:30, all cash, exch., no rfd. Special-orders current hard and soft at 20% off, and stocks softcovers used. Bonus BF discount applies only to the latter—10% more off used paperbacks if you show BF. Sells: **Current Bestsellers, Used Books.**

Literary Mart, 1261 Broadway (32), rm. 701, 684-0588, B-D-F-N-QB-RR to 34, M-F 9:30-6:30, S 10:30-4:30, ch., no c.c., exch., no rfd. Children's encyclopedias exchangeable when outgrown, price credited—less $1 per month—toward purchase of high school or adult set. Sells: **Encyclopedias & Dictionaries.**

Macy's Magazine Service, 151 W. 34, NY, NY 10001. Write for current price-list. Sells: **Magazine Subscriptions.**

Magazine Buyers' Service, 809 P. St., P.O. Box 8115, Lincoln, NE 68544. Send for price-list. Sells: **Magazine Subscriptions.**

* **Metropolitan Books**, 38 E. 23 (Madison), 254-8609, 6 to 23, N-RR to 23rd St., M-F 7:45-6, S 9-5, ch., no c.c., exch., no rfd. Will special-order. Sells: **Current Bestsellers, Remainders, Clearance-Books.**

Paperback Exchanges, 270 3rd Av. (21-2), 982-8825, 6 to 23, M-S 10-10, Sun 11-7; 489 3rd Av. (33-4), 686-8202, 6 to 33, Sun-Th 10-11, F 10-4; 1437 1st Av. (74-5), 535-4372, 6 to 77, Sun-Th 10-11, F 10-4; 2145 Broadway (75-6), 595-2283, 1-2-3 to 72, M-S 10-10, Sun 11-7; 355 E. 86 (1st Av.), 369-5023, 4-5-6 to 86, Sun-Th 9:30-11, F 9:30-4. All stores: all cash, exch., no rfd. 25% credit for returns. Half off current pulp. Many also have a few used LP records about $2—phone first to ask. Most of these stores aren't affiliated w. each other. Sells: **Used Books.**

Publishers Clearing House, Port Washington, NY 11050. Ask for price-list. Sells: **Magazine Subscriptions.**

Reference Book Center, 175 5th Av. (23), 7th floor, 677-2160, N-RR to 23rd St., M-F 10-4:30, S 10-1, ch., no c.c., exch., no rfd. Sells: **Encyclopedias & Dictionaries.**

* **Ruby's Book Annex**, 74 Reade St. (Church), 732-8676, A-CC-1-2-3 to Chambers, M-S 10-6:15, ch., no c.c., no exch. or rfd. The used ones are hardcover, and also there are some comics. Sells: **Remainders, Clearance-Books, Used Books, Textbooks.**

* **Ruby's Book Sale**, 119 Chambers St. (Church-W.B'wy), 732-8676, A-CC-1-2-3 to Chambers, M-S 10-6:15, ch., no c.c., no exch. or rfd. The used ones are half-price paperbacks. The selection of recent magazine backissues is especially good, though some older copies are also available here. Sells: **Remainders, Clearance-Books, Used Books, Magazine Backissues.**

24: PUBLICATIONS

Select Information Exchange, 2095 Broadway (72-3), NY, NY 10023, 874-6408. A subscription-service for investment-advisory publications only. Request catalog. Sells: **Magazine Subscriptions.**

** **Strand**, 828 Broadway at 12th St., 473-1452, LL-N-QB-RR-4-5-6 to Union Sq., N-RR to 8th St., M-S 9:30-6:30, Sun 11-5, ch., no c.c., exch. or rfd. Newly published books (reviewers' copies) half cover-price. Huge stock out-of-print hardcovers author-alphabetized. Large selection art books. Sells: **Current Bestsellers, Remainders, Clearance-Books, Used Books.**

* **The Book Store**, 83 Maiden Lane (William-Pearl), 425-6095, J-M-RR-2-3 to Wall & Broad Sts., M-F 8:15-5:30, ch., no c.c., no exch. or rfd. Small store. Small selection. Sells: **Remainders, Clearance-Books, Used Books, Magazine Back-issues.**

United Subscription Svc., 515 Abbott Drive, Broomall, PA 19008. Write for price-list. Sells: **Magazine Subscriptions.**

25:
RECORDINGS & TAPES
Expect 30-80% discounts.

The biggest savings come from buying top-brand blank tapes without the brand-name (or any) label. I'm not talking about junky cheap cassettes which jam up your machine. These tapes—cassettes and reel-to-reels—are good quality, identical to the stuff that's marketed with the labels, but lacking only those labels and the high prices that go with the brand names. To be specific, I'm recommending the following, sold by a store that doesn't discount sufficiently on an across-the-board basis to warrant being recommended in this book as a store, but these are astoundingly good values nonetheless:

SF&T Collector Series Tapes, available only at Studio Film and Tape, 630 9th Av. (44-45), 8th floor, 977-9330, M-F 9-5:30, credit cards, no checks, 30-day exch., no rfd. They sell by mail-order as well. Their unmarked blank cassettes are actually BASF, and are very good in all respects. Their unmarked reel-to-reel tapes are made by a manufacturer which doesn't want its name disclosed, but which is identified only as "one of the largest audio tape firms in the United States"; and the quality of this is also good—in fact, I use the tape myself, and I find it to be better than some of the major-name tape-brands I've tried. SF&T Collector Series cassettes come in the following lengths: C-10, C-30, C-45, C-60, and C-90. SF&T Collector Series reel-to-reel tapes come in 1200' and 1800' lengths, on 7" plastic reels, and packaged in unmarked white boxes. These tapes are guaranteed to be defect-free, to have no splices, and not to be seconds or irregulars in any way. They are not to be compared with Shamrock or other spliced end-runs. (It's a pity that Shamrock, which used to supply good quality spliced tapes, no longer does. But for uncritical uses, Shamrock is still a good value at the stores I recommend in this chapter for off-brand stuff.) Both the cassettes and the reel-to-reels of the SF&T Collector Series, are sold at about 40% of the brand-name prices for the same tapes. **Bonus discount to BF readers: If you bring this book in with you to Studio Film & Tape, they'll give you these tapes I've mentioned at 10% off their already low prices if you buy tape-quantities of 1-50 open-reel, or 1-143 cassette; and 5% off their super-discounted bulk-purchase prices, if you buy larger quantities.**

Whatever tape you buy, especially if you're paying a brand-name price for it, you ought to look at the manufacturer's technical spec-sheet on it. If you do this for Maxell, Scotch, or any of the major-name tapes, you'll find that the technical specifications are virtually identical for a given maker's medium-priced lines as they are for its most expensive "premium" tapes. Most often, what one pays extra for at the high end is simply the snob-appeal that the

25: RECORDINGS & TAPES

word "premium" (or its equivalents) has for people who are incapable of evaluating quality on their own. Spec-sheets commonly show differences like one decibel in the signal/noise ratio, $^{2}/_{10}$ths of one-percent in distortion, and equally inaudible differences in frequency-response, for the high-end and medium-priced lines of a given manufacturer. There will usually be much greater variations in quality between two equally-positioned and priced tapes of different makers than there will be between the high-end and medium-priced lines of any given manufacturer. Studio Film and Tape will show you a copy of the spec-sheet for any major brand of tape they carry (that's several of the famous ones). Also, you can get spec-sheets by writing directly to the manufacturers.

RECOMMENDED PRODUCTS:
See above.

RECOMMENDED STORES:

discs—used pop

Second Coming Seconds (228-1313); ***Second Coming on Christopher (924-5858); ***Second Coming** (228-1313); ***Vinyl Mania** (691-1720); **Free Being Records** (260-1774); **Hall Place Records** (982-1604); **Titus Oaks Record Exchange** (Brooklyn, 646-7400).

discs—used classical

Second Coming Seconds (228-1313); ***Academy Book Store (242-4848); ***Second Coming on Christopher** (924-5858); **Dayton's Records** (254-5084); **Free Being Records** (260-1774); **Hall Place Records** (982-1604).

discs—used jazz

Second Coming Seconds (228-1313); ***Audiomatic Electronics (686-5500); ***Second Coming on Christopher** (924-5858); ***Vinyl Mania** (691-1720); **Free Being Records** (260-1774); **Soho Music Gallery** (966-1637).

discs/tapes—new pop

Odds & Ends Job-Lots (intermittent stock, Queens, 441-6878); ***Audiomatic Electronics (686-5500); ***Disc O Rama** (243-3610); ***International Record & Tape** (594-1690); ***Record King** (outside NYC, 1-800-446-7964); **Bondy's Records** (964-5886); **Disc-O-Mat** (575-0686); **J&R Pop Records** (732-8600); **Listen Records** (921-0136); **Record Explosion** (233-3890); **Record Factory** (228-4800); **St. Marks Sounds** (677-3444).

discs/tapes—new classical

Berkshire Record Outlet (outside NYC, 1-413-637-2415); ***International Record & Tape (594-1690); ***Superior Merchandising** (intermittent stock, 233-4615); **Barnes & Noble Classical** (675-5500); **Blue Angel Records** (outside NYC, 1-800-446-7964); **Canal St. Merch. Exch.** (226-0540); **Chesterfield Music** (964-3380); **Eighth Av. Records** (675-1311); **J&R Classical & Jazz** (349-8400); **Listen Records** (921-0136).

discs/tapes—new jazz

*Disc O Rama (243-3610); ***International Record & Tape** (594-1690); ***Taft Electronics** (outside NYC, 1-800-446-7964); **Chesterfield Music** (964-3380); **J&R Classical & Jazz** (349-8400); **Listen Records** (921-0136); **Soho Music Gallery** (966-1637); **St. Marks Sounds** (677-3444).

blank tapes—off-brands

Annex Outlet (964-8661); ****Odds & Ends Job-Lots (intermittent stock, Queens, 441-6878); ***Abbie's General Store** (349-3394); ***International Record & Tape** (594-1690); **Global Imports** (intermittent stock, 741-0700).

blank tapes—brand-name (ALSO: CH. 1)

Annex Outlet (964-8661); ***Mecca (679-9336); ***Newport of Japan** (686-1320); **Canal St. Merch. Exch.** (226-0540); **Cohen's Electronics** (571-1392); **Warren St. Merchandise** (227-8330).

video tapes—blank

***Spectrum (338-4111); ****Annex Outlet** (964-8661); ***Harmony Video** (Brooklyn, 627-8960); ***Live Wire Electronics** (Queens, 544-6145); ***Tape City** (679-1606).

video tapes—recorded

Dynamite (689-8908); ***Tape City (679-1606); ***Disc O Rama** (243-3610).

STORES-DIRECTORY

Phone a store before you go out of your way to visit it. Especially do this during July and August, when most establishments reduce or eliminate weekend-hours.

In the listings below, "*" means especially recommended, "+" means that the store offers a bonus discount to BF readers, "ch." and "c.c." mean respectively checks and credit cards, and "exch." and "rfd." mean respectively exchange and refund. Nearest subway-stops are shown. For example, "B-D-F to 47" means to take the B, D, or F train to 47th Street. Store-hours are also indicated, with days of the week abbreviated, like "M-S 8-6."

* **Abbie's General Store**, 306 8th Av. (25-6), 349-3394, A-AA-CC-E to 23, 7 days 9-6, all cash, exch., no rfd. Small store. Specializes in new broken radios and calculators sold cheap as-is. Sells: **Blank Tapes—Off-Brands, Personal Accessories, Warehouse Salvage Job-Lot.**

* **Academy Book Store**, 10 W. 18 (5th), 242-4848, B-F-LL to 14th St. & 6th Av., N-RR to 23rd St., M-F 10:30-7, S 10:30-6, Sun 11-5, all cash, no exch. or rfd. More top-condition used classical than any other store; the clearance-bins are super. Definitely not recommended for books, though. Sells: **Discs—Used Classical.**

** **Annex Outlet**, 43 Warren St. (Church), 964-8661, A-CC-1-2-3 to Chambers, MTTh 8-6, W 8-9, F 8-3:30, Sun 9-5, all cash, 7-day exch., no rfd. Sells: **Blank Tapes—Off-Brands, Blank Tapes—Brand-Name, Video Tapes—Blank, Appliances.**

* **Audiomatic Electronics**, 1263 Broadway (32), 2nd floor, 686-5500, B-D-F-N-QB-RR to 34, M-F 9:30-6:30, S 10-6, ch., c.c., exch., no rfd. Sells: **Discs—Used Jazz, Discs/Tapes—New Pop, High Fidelity.**

Barnes & Noble Classical, 128 5th Av. at 18th St., 675-5500, N-RR to 23rd St., B-F-LL to 14th St. & 6th Av., M-S 10-9, Sun 10-5; 600 5th Av. at 48th St., 765-0592, B-D-F to 47, MTWF 10-6:45, Th 10-8, S 10-6, Sun 12-6, ch., c.c.; Both stores: 7-day exch., 3-day rfd. Especially strong on imports. Sells: **Discs/Tapes—New Jazz.**

** **Berkshire Record Outlet**, 428 Pittsfield-Lenox Rd., Lenox, MA 01240, 1-413-637-2415, M-S 11:30-5:30, ch., no c.c., exch. no rfd. Mail-order. Catalog. Specializes in classical cut-outs, including imports. Huge selection. Sells: **Discs/Tapes—New Classical.**

25: RECORDINGS & TAPES

Blue Angel Records, 1738 Allied St., Charlottesville, VA 22901, 1-800-446-7964, ch., c.c., exch., no rfd. Will phone-quote. Takes mail-orders. Catalog. Very cooperative. Ask for their catalog. Sells: **Discs/Tapes—New Pop, Discs/Tapes—New Classical, Discs/Tapes—New Jazz**.

Bondy's Records, 38 Park Row (Beekman), 964-5886, J-M-RR-4-5-6 to Chambers & Bkln. Bridge, A-CC-J-M-RR-2-3-4-5 to B'wy-Nassau & Fulton, M-S 10-6:30, ch., c.c. $20+, exch., no rfd. Sells: **Discs/Tapes—New Pop**.

Canal St. Merch. Exch., 253 Canal (Lafayette), 226-0550, J-M-N-QB-RR-6 to Canal, M-S 9-6, c.c., no ch., exch. or rfd. Sells: **Discs/Tapes—New Classical, Blank Tapes—Brand-Name**.

Chesterfield Music, 12 Warren St. (B'wy), 5th floor, 964-3380, A-CC-1-2-3 to Chambers, N-RR to City Hall, M-F 9-5, ch., c.c., exch. no rfd. Mail-order. Catalog. Sells: **Discs/Tapes—New Classical, Discs/Tapes—New Jazz**.

Cohen's Electronics, 182 Church St. (Reade-Duane), 571-1392, A-CC-1-2-3 to Chambers, 1 to Franklin, 7 days 9-6, all cash, exch., no rfd. Sells: **Blank Tapes—Brand-Name, Appliances**.

Dayton's Records, Broadway at 12th St., 254-5084, N-RR to 8th St., M-F 10-6, S 10-5, all cash, exch. or rfd. Sells: **Discs—Used Classical**.

* **Disc O Rama**, 247 Bleecker St. (Cornelia), 243-3610, A-AA-B-CC-D-E-F to 4, 7 days 10-10; 40 Union Sq. E. (16-7), 260-8616, LL-N-QB-RR-4-5-6 to Union Sq., M-S 8-6. Both stores: c.c., no ch., exch., no rfd. Sells: **Discs/Tapes—New Pop, Discs/Tapes—New Jazz**.

Disc-O-Mat, 1518 Broadway (44-5), 575-0686, N-QB-RR-1-2-3-7 to 42 & Times Square; 101 E. 42 (Park Av.), 682-2151, 4-5-6-7 to Grand Central; 716 Lexington Av. (57-8), 759-3777, N-RR-4-5-6 to 59th & Lex.; 474 7th Av. (35-6), 736-1150, A-AA-CC-E to 34. All stores: M-F 9-7, S 10-7 (B'wy open till midnight and Sun 10-6), all cash, 7-day exch., no rfd. Also a store in River Edge, NJ. Sells: **Discs/Tapes—New Pop**.

** **Dynamite**, 1165 Broadway at 27th St., 689-8908, N-RR to 28th St., 7-days 9-6, c.c., no ch., exch., no rfd. Usually carries the best off-brands. Also cheap movie-rentals. Sells: **Video Tapes—Recorded, Appliances**.

Eighth Av. Records, 153 8th Av. (17-18), 675-1311, A-AA-CC-E-LL to 14 St. & 8 Av., M-S 10-6, ch., no c.c., exch. or rfd. Closeouts and cut-outs. Sells: **Discs/Tapes—New Classical**.

Free Being Records, 129 2nd Av. (8), 260-1774, 6 to Astor, M-S 12-9, Sun 12-8, all cash, exch., no rfd. Sells: **Discs—Used Pop, Discs—Used Classical, Discs—Used Jazz**.

Global Imports, 160 5th Av. at 21st St., 741-0700, N-RR to 23rd St., M-F 8-5, all cash, 7-day exch. or rfd. Sells: **Blank Tapes—Off-Brands, Housewares, Smoking Supplies, Toys, Games & Hobbies**.

Hall Place Records, 41 E. 7th (2nd-3rd), 982-1604, 6 to Astor, MTThFS 12:30-7:30, all cash, no exch. or rfd. Sells: **Discs—Used Pop, Discs—Used Classical**.

* **Harmony Video**, Brooklyn, 2357 Con. Is. Av. (T-U), 627-8960 & 1-800-221-8927, D-M-QB to Av. U, M-Th 9-6, F 9-2, Sun 10-4, c.c., no ch., no exch. or rfd. Only VTR's, video tapes, and answering machines. Sells: **Video Tapes—Blank, Appliances**.

* **International Record & Tape**, 315 W. 36 (8th Av.), 11th floor, 594-1690, A-AA-CC-E to 34, M-Th 8:30-4:30, F 8:30-3:30, ch., c.c., exch. or rfd. Will special-order. Takes mail-orders. Catalog. Always good, but occasionally excellent sales, 40% off all current Schwann. City's best prices on Shamrock tape. Also the lowest regular prices on new discs. Sells: **Discs/Tapes—New Pop, Discs/Tapes—New Classical, Discs/Tapes—New Jazz, Blank Tapes—Off-Brands**.

J&R Classical & Jazz, 33 Park Row (Ann-Beekman), 349-8400, J-M-RR-4-5-6 to Chambers & Bkln. Bridge, A-CC-J-M-RR-2-3-4-5 to B'wy-Nassau & Fulton, M-S 9:25-6:15, ch., c.c. $25+, 10-day exch., no rfd. Sells: **Discs/Tapes—New Classical, Discs/Tapes—New Jazz**.

J&R Pop Records, 23 Park Row (Ann-Beekman), 732-8600, J-M-RR-4-5-6 to Chambers & Bkln. Bridge, A-CC-J-M-RR-2-3-4-5 to B'wy-Nassau & Fulton, M-S 9:15-6:15, ch., c.c. $25+, 10-day exch., no rfd. Sells: **Discs/Tapes—New Pop**.

Listen Records, 18 W. 45 (5th Av.), 921-0136, B-D-F to 47, M-S 10-6, ch., no c.c., 7-day exch. or rfd. Sells: **Discs/Tapes—New Pop, Discs/Tapes—New Classical, Discs/Tapes—New Jazz**.

25: RECORDINGS & TAPES

✻ **Live Wire Electronics**, Queens, 107-21 Continental Av., Forest Hills, 544-6145, E-F-GG-N to 71-Continental Avs., M-F 9:30-6:30, Sun 10:30-4, c.c., no ch., no exch. or rfd. Video, TV, and Commodore computers. Sells: **Video Tapes—Blank, Appliances, Office Equipment.**

✻ **Mecca**, 1167 Broadway (27), 679-9336, N-RR to 28th St., M-F 10-5, all cash, no exch. or rfd. Sells: **Blank Tapes—Brand-Name, Appliances.**

✻ **Newport of Japan**, 1201 Broadway (28-9), 686-1320, N-RR to 28th St., M-F 9-6, S 10-2, all cash, no exch. or rfd. Sells: **Blank Tapes—Brand-Name, Appliances.**

✻✻ **Odds & Ends Job-Lots**, Queens, 88-09 Jamaica Av., Woodside, 441-6878, J to Woodhaven Blvd., M-S 9-6, Sun 9-3; Queens, 57-60 Woodside Av., Woodside, phoneless, 7 to 61st St., M-Th 10-7, F 10-9, S 9-6, Sun 9-5. Both stores: all cash, exch. or rfd. Sells: **Discs/Tapes—New Pop, Blank Tapes—Off-Brands, Dinnerware & Cookware, Health & Beauty Aids, Home-Improvement Items, Housewares, Jewelry & Gifts, Toys, Games & Hobbies, Warehouse Salvage Job-Lot.**

Record Explosion, 53 Nassau St. (Maiden Ln.), 233-3890, A-CC-J-M-RR-2-3-4-5 to B'wy-Nassau & Fulton; 400 5th Av. (37), 736-5624, B-D-F to 42, 7 to 5th Av.; Queens, 166-39 Jamaica Av., Jamaica, 658-5555, E-F to Parsons Blvd., plus a long walk. All stores: hours vary by location, all cash, exch., no rfd. Sells: **Discs/Tapes—New Pop.**

Record Factory, 17 W. 8 (5th-MacDougal), 228-4800, A-AA-B-CC-D-E-F to 4, N-RR to 8th St., 7 days 10:30-9; Brooklyn, 453 86th St., 748-6753, RR to 86th St., M-S 10:30-9. Both stores: c.c. $20+, no ch., exch., no rfd. Sells: **Discs/Tapes—New Pop.**

✻ **Record King**, 314 W. 125 (St. Nicholas), 866-3211, A-AA-B-CC-D to 125, 7 days 10-10, all cash, exch., no rfd. Sells: **Discs/Tapes—New Pop.**

✻ **Second Coming**, 235 Sullvan St. (3), 228-1313, A-AA-B-CC-D-E-F to 4, M-Th 12-10, FS noon-1a.m., all cash, 7-day exch., no rfd. Sells: **Discs—Used Pop.**

✻ **Second Coming on Christopher**, 82 Christopher St. (Bleecker-7th), 924-5858, 1 to Christopher St., 7 days 12-10, all cash, 7-day exch., no rfd. Especially good stock on showtunes, soundtracks, and vocalists. Sells: **Discs—Used Pop, Discs—Used Classical, Discs—Used Jazz.**

✻✻ **Second Coming Seconds**, 240 Sullivan St. (3), 228-1313, A-AA-B-CC-D-E-F to 4, M-Th 12-10, FS noon-1a.m., all cash, no exch. or rfd. Clearance outlet for the other two Second Coming stores. Sells: **Discs—Used Pop, Discs—Used Classical, Discs—Used Jazz.**

Soho Music Gallery, 26 Wooster St. at Grand, 966-1637, J-M-N-QB-RR-6 to Canal, A-AA-CC-E-1 to Canal, M-F 11-10, S 11-11, Sun 1-8, ch., c.c., exch. or rfd. Sells: **Discs—Used Jazz, Discs/Tapes—New Jazz.**

St. Marks Sounds, 20 St. Marks Place (2nd-3rd), 677-3444, 6 to Astor, M-Th 12-9:30, FS 12-10:30, Sun 12-7:30, all cash, 7-day exch., no rfd. Sells: **Discs/Tapes—New Pop, Discs/Tapes—New Jazz.**

✻ **Superior Merchandising**, 12 Warren St. (B'wy-Church), 233-4615, A-CC-1-2-3 to Chambers, N-RR to City Hall, M-S 7-6, all cash, no exch. or rfd. Very uneven. Some sensational bargains. Some not good. Sells: **Dog-Diet Supplements, Clothing—Men's.**

✻ **Taft Electronics**, 68 W. 45 (6th Av.), 575-5194, B-D-F to 47; 27 Park Row, 964-8685, J-M-RR-4-5-6 to Chambers & Bkln. Bridge, A-CC-J-M-RR-2-3-4-5 to B'wy-Nassau & Fulton. Both stores: M-F 9-6, S 9-4, c.c., no ch., no exch. or rfd. Sells: **Discs/Tapes—New Jazz, High Fidelity.**

✻ **Tape City**, 404 Park Av. S. (28-9), 679-1606 & (mail-order) 1-800-223-1586, 6 to 28, M-F 9-5:30, ch., c.c., exch. or rfd. Takes mail-orders. Catalog. Large selection. Extremely busy. Sells: **Video Tapes—Blank, Video Tapes—Recorded.**

Titus Oaks Record Exchange, Brooklyn, 1928 Av. U, 646-7400, D-M-QB to Av. U, M-F 11:30-8, S 11-8, Sun 12-6, all cash, exch. or rfd. Sells: **Discs—Used Pop.**

✻ **Vinyl Mania**, 30 Carmine St. (Bleecker), 691-1720, A-AA-B-CC-D-E-F to 4, M-S 11-7, all cash, 5-day exch. or rfd. Sells: **Discs—Used Pop, Discs—Used Jazz.**

Warren St. Merchandise, 32 Warren St. (Church), 227-8330, A-CC-1-2-3 to Chambers, N-RR to City Hall, M-S 9-6, ch., no c.c., exch. or rfd. Only ball-point pens, small off-brand walkman-type radios etc., car-radios, and brand-name blank cassettes. Street-stand, extends indoors. Sells: **Blank Tapes—Brand-Name, Appliances, Stationery & Art Supplies.**

26:
SMOKING SUPPLIES
Expect 20-50% discounts.

Is smoking worth the health-risks? For the typical cigarette-smoker, to whom puffing is as automatic a behavior as sleepwalking—and just as compulsive—the only rational answer would have to be "No." Such a person isn't even aware of the taste and aroma of his smoke, so how can he possibly enjoy the act? But there are others who do derive pleasure from tobacco, and for them the answer isn't so simple. If you're in this latter group, you'll probably want to weigh the pleasure-benefits against the health-risks. Here, then, are those dangers in a nutshell, as reported by the U.S. Surgeon General, based on his review of the hundreds of studies that have appeared in the medical literature pertaining to the health-effects of smoking:

• Cigarette-smoking increases the death-rate from 44-83% among all the studies.

• Pipe-and-cigar-smoking have negligible effects on the overall death-rate, though 3 studies showed a 5-10% increase for both types of smokers; and one report indicated that the kidney-cancer rate was hiked 13-fold for cigar-smokers, and 10-fold for pipe-smokers, versus "only" a 5-fold increase for cigarette-smokers.

• Periodontal disease and the loss of teeth—even of all teeth—occurs twice as frequently among smokers than among non-smokers; and this problem is more severe for women than for men, simply because women in any case lose their teeth due to gum-disease more often than do men.

• Cancer-deaths are 32% higher for smokers of pipes and cigars, and 156% higher for cigarette-smokers.

• For cigarette-smokers, the hike in deaths from heart-attacks and other coronary diseases is even greater than the rise in the cancer-death rate, considerable though the latter is.

• Regardless whether you smoke cigars, pipes, or cigarettes, you're greatly increasing your probability of developing cancers of the lip and tongue, and also multiplying almost 3-fold your chances of developing peptic ulcer.

• For cigarette-smokers, the chances of getting bronchitis or emphysema are more than 600% higher than for the non-smoking population.

Decisions, Decisions....

The question, then: What to do about this?

One option for the smoker is to become a non-smoker. Studies have shown that clinics for this purpose are useless; people stop if and when they as individuals develop the motivation and determination to do so. There is no magic, and no "system." But if you nonetheless want to try a stop-smoking clinic, it might as well be the one run by the American Cancer Society (phone 586-8700), since theirs costs only a fraction as much as the commercial ones.

Another possibility is to switch from cigarettes to cigars or pipes—but only if you don't carry with you the habit of inhaling, which many cigar-and-pipe converts continue to do, and which ruins any benefit that might be had from this approach.

Finally, you can switch to low tar-and-nicotine brands. But there are severe problems here. If the tar is low and the nicotine isn't, the nicotine itself—even without the tar—is a potent carcinogen; and the medical mechanisms for its carcinogenic action are by now well-established and understood. If the nicotine is low and the tar isn't, you've not only got the problem of the tar's carcinogenicity, but you'll probably end up consuming even more tar than before, because you'll need to smoke more cigarettes to get the nicotine-fix that your body craves. And what if both the tar and nicotine are low? Then you still won't satisfy your nicotine-addiction, unless you increase your cigarette-intake. You might as well just go cold-turkey. So these "safer" cigarettes are just an empty gimmick which fails to address the basic addictive problem.

The above-mentioned options are invalid also because they're based on a fallacy: the idea that tobacco is safe if only you get rid of its tar and nicotine. In fact, however, dozens of very potent poisons have already been isolated in tobacco leaves, and others are suspected. The latest finding along these lines appeared in *The New England Journal of Medicine* in late winter of 1982. It was a study which showed that smoking half a pack of cigarettes daily results in a cumulative 100-fold increase in radioactivity in the lungs over that which occurs naturally from background-radiation. This tobacco-induced radioactivity is in the form of particles—the form most inclined to causing lung-cancer. It seems that the tobacco-plant draws radioactive elements from its environment—the soil, etc.—and deposits the stuff into the lungs as small particles when smoked. Tobacco-smoke is especially rich in radioactive polonium. So all of the tobacco-leaf should be considered to be poisonous or possibly poisonous. (Have you ever stopped to wonder why this plant is not eaten? If you smoke any poisonous plant or thing, you'll get poisonous smoke; and tobacco is not a vegetable; it's a poison.) In other words, the object should be for you to let as little of the tobacco into your body as possible. Forget about tar and nicotine—they're only two of the many tobacco-poisons.

This means that the real options are total tobacco-withdrawal on the one hand, and—for those whose smoking is not merely an addictive act, but also a genuinely pleasurable one—switching to cigars or pipes, but without inhaling the smoke. Practically speaking, both should amount to nicotine-cold-turkey. In other words, both will mean a withdrawal from the smoker's addicted state. Since the first option is so straightforward, I'll concentrate on the second. Here, then, is the safest way to smoke pipes and cigars:

Before lighting up, swallow a vitamin-C tablet with a glass of water. 100 milligrams of ascorbic acid neutralizes the poisons from smoking 5 cigarettes or 1 cigar or pipeful. Draw the fumes only into

26: SMOKING SUPPLIES

the mouth; don't circulate them out through the nose. Most important: Don't swallow saliva while you smoke, since the nicotine that immediately permeates the saliva is what causes the ulcers in the stomach and the cancers in the kidneys. After you're done smoking, wash your mouth out with water, wine, or whatever it takes to get rid of the "smoker's breath" and the dissolved smoke and nicotine that causes it. Then, if possible, brush your teeth and gums to clean away any remaining dissolved smoke. (This tobacco-residue rots gums the way sugar rots teeth. It causes gingivitis which destroys the gum-tissue that holds the teeth in place.)

Choose the mildest possible tobaccos; i.e., those which least irritate the mouth, tongue and gums. It would seem reasonable to assume that any smoke which mottles and pits the tongue and makes the mouth raw, does so because of poisons which would be equally destructive of other parts of your body; and it's best to select the least poisonous tobaccos possible. If you're a pipe-smoker, this need not be such a terrific sacrifice, since the 6 least irritating ones are also extremely tasty: Barking Dog, which has the flavor of roasted nuts, and of which copies are available at some exclusive custom-tobacco stores at several times the price; Bond Street, which costs even less than Barking Dog, and which has a distinctive flavor that can't be described (somewhat like charbroiled steak); Barney's Value Blend Natural (available only from Barney's Cut-Rate Tobaccos, 25 W. 42, 354-1366), surely one of the least expensive tobaccos in the world, a middle-of-the-road smoke—somewhat sweet, somewhat nutty, somewhat meaty; Barney's Value Blend Tropical (same source and price) with a sweet taste, like cake, a little fruity; Barney's Balkan Blend (same source), which is a copy of the also nut-like Balkan Sobranie (in the white-and-black tin), and which is slightly superior to the original, in both mildness (being considerably less irritating than Sobranie) and taste (having extraordinary balance), though it costs half as much as the original—still expensive, nearly twice the price of Barking Dog, but a tobacco-masterpiece that's worth trying nonetheless; Trinity Smoke Shop Blend 326 (available only from that shop at 160 Pearl St., 425-0070), a vanila-sweet smoke, similar to the popular Captain Black, but better, and much less irritating; and Demark's Value Blend Whiskey (available at Barney's abovementioned), like Barney's Value Blend Natural, but less sweet and with a touch of whiskey. The next-mildest tobaccos also have attractive tastes: Barney's Value Blend Vanila, Barney's All Black Cavendish, Argosy Black, Hickory, Walnut, Borkum Riff Whiskey, Tobacco Center Continental Blend (from the Tobacco Center), Barclay Rex Blend 6, Barclay Rex Coffee (both from Barclay Rex), and Trinity Smoke Shop Sir Vincent's Blend.

For all the brand-name tobaccos just mentioned, the best prices can be found at Wolf's Smoke Shop, in Brooklyn, at the corner of Atlantic and Court, 522-5651. Arthur's Smoke Shop in Manhattan is the second-best source. (Argosy Black, incidentally, isn't carried at many stores; but you'll find it at the Barney's on Canal St.) Of all the custom-blends, those at Barney's on 42nd St.

26: SMOKING SUPPLIES

are the best value. (They're made by Century Tobacco, in Saddle River, N.J.)

This is acknowledgedly a Spartan regimen. But one can get into it by stages. And though being rigorous, it's far from being unenjoyable; indeed, it may introduce the smoker to far better taste-experiences than he's been accustomed to. Cigarettes, after all, are well-known to contain the lowest-grade tobaccos.

The regular way of smoking is simply not enjoyable at all—it's merely addictive. To keep a cigarette, pipe or cigar dangling incessantly from one's mouth is so automatic and unconscious an act that it obliterates pleasure. Enjoyment must be conscious in order to exist at all; but most smokers are merely machines controlled by tobacco—specifically by nicotine. Every aspect of the smoking-act should be both conscious and consciously enjoyed; and only then can it be controlled and made less dangerous. The addictive smoker gets the worst of both worlds: more disease, and less smoking-pleasure.

This brings us to the farthest extension of the search for the mildest "tobacco": no tobacco at all. Specifically: tea. That's right, regular drinking tea. It can be purchased loose, by the pound, and costs less than any tobacco (especially when you consider that it burns twice as long). It's milder than any tobacco. There's one problem, however: It burns hotter in the pipe-bowl than does tobacco, and this can threaten a poor-quality pipe if you draw too frequently on it. But smoking tea produces no tar, no nicotine, and not even any caffein (since the high-temperature burning breaks that down). As a result, there's no tarry goo at the bottom of the pipe, and no drugging effect of any kind—neither the nicotine-grog, nor the caffein-jolt. The taste of the smoke is lighter than that of any tobacco, and quite a nice change-of-pace, if nothing else.

I've tried smoking practically everything that can fit into a pipe-bowl, from dried tree-leaves to a wide range of spices and herbs; and tea is by far the mildest—the least irritating—its only observable effects being its taste and aroma. The fragrance is very much like that of burning autumn leaves. Some people find this aroma objectionable, but others like it. My favorite smoking-teas are A&P Our Own, and Lipton's, both loose. But all teas smoke about the same, so the choice of brands here doesn't make much difference.

When buying a pipe, the key things to look for are, first of all, that the hole at the bottom of the bowl leading to the stem be as near as possible to the center of the bowl, so that the tobacco will burn evenly and you won't have to re-light the pipe as often; secondly, that the bowl be shallow, so that air will get to the embers and you won't have to puff continually to keep the pipe lit; and finally, that the pipe be briar (preferably unlacquered) rather than wood or corn-cob which burn out soon and must be thrown away. The best-value pipes are usually the cheapest briar pipes at Barney's, or for a fancier grade, the ones at Wolf's in Brooklyn and the seconds at Barclay Rex.

One of the pipe-smoker's major difficulties tends to be keeping the pipe lit. If you dry out the tobacco before smoking, this problem will be greatly reduced; and contrary to the popular myth among smokers, dry tobacco is not more irritating to the mouth. The tobacco-humidor is counter-productive and a waste. One more thing that will help keep the pipe from going out: tamping down the tobacco with the head of a 2-inch roofers' nail available at any hardware-store. (It's the best—and cheapest—pipe-tool.)

As for the cigar-option, I don't find it attractive, and so have no constructive suggestions, except this negative one: Even the most expensive pipe-tobacco costs about one tenth as much to smoke (per minute of puffing) as does an average cigar. The cheapest is about a fortieth as costly. So pipe-smoking has at least the advantage of being overwhelmingly less expensive than any other form of tobacco-smoking. It also produces fumes which are the least objectionable—even pleasant—to non-smokers.

But I must repeat, unless you love the taste of smoking, quit! This is a poisonous entertainment, however you cut it.

RECOMMENDED PRODUCTS:
See text above.

RECOMMENDED STORES:

cigarettes

****Barney's Cut-Rate Brooklyn** (Brooklyn, 643-0643); ****Dollar Bills** (867-0212); ***Barney's** (732-3799); ***Barney's Canal Cut-Rate** (226-3796); **King's Pharmacy** (Brooklyn, 253-0200).

cigars

***+**Famous Smoke Shop** (221-1408); ****Barney's Cut-Rate Brooklyn** (Brooklyn, 643-0643); ****J&R Tobacco** (869-8777); **+**5th Av. & 22nd St. Tobacco** (243-1943); ***Barney's Canal Cut-Rate** (226-3796).

pipe tobaccos

*****Barney's Cut-Rate Tobaccos** (354-1366); *****Wolf's Wholesale** (Brooklyn, 522-5651); ***+**Famous Smoke Shop** (221-1408); ****Barney's Cut-Rate Brooklyn** (Brooklyn, 643-0643); ****The Tobacco Center** (674-2208); *+**5th Av. & 22nd St. Tobacco** (243-1943); ***Barney's Canal Cut-Rate** (226-3796); ***Barney's** (732-3799); **Barclay Rex Pipe** (962-3355); **Trinity Pipe Shop** (425-0070).

pipes

*****Wolf's Wholesale** (Brooklyn, 522-5651); ***+**Famous Smoke Shop** (221-1408); ****Barney's Cut-Rate Brooklyn** (Brooklyn, 643-0643); *+**5th Av. & 22nd St. Tobacco** (243-1943); ***Barney's Canal Cut-Rate** (226-3796); **Barclay Rex Pipe** (962-3355).

lighters

***+**Famous Smoke Shop** (221-1408); ****Ashreh Supply** (925-9507); ****Barney's Cut-Rate Brooklyn** (Brooklyn, 643-0643); **+**5th Av. & 22nd St. Tobacco** (243-1943); ***Barney's Canal Cut-Rate** (226-3796); ***Barney's Cut-Rate Pharmacy** (719-1940); **Global Imports** (intermittent stock, 741-0700).

head-shop goods

+Discount Head Shop (989-6933).

STORES-DIRECTORY

Phone a store before you go out of your way to visit it. Especially do this during July and August, when most establishments reduce or eliminate weekend-hours.

In the listings below, "*" means especially recommended, "+" means that the store offers a bonus discount to BF readers, "ch." and "c.c." mean respectively checks and credit cards, and "exch." and "rfd." mean respectively exchange and refund. Nearest subway-stops are shown. For example, "B-D-F to 47" means to take the B, D, or F train to 47th Street. Store-hours are also indicated, with days of the week abbreviated, like "M-S 8-6."

*+ **5th Av. & 22nd St. Tobacco**, 172 5th Av., 243-1943, B-F to 23, M-F 6:30-5:45, all cash, exch. or rfd. Bonus discount to BF readers: 5% to 10%. Sells: **Cigars, Pipe Tobaccos, Pipes, Lighters.**

** **Ashreh Supply**, 473 Broadway (Grand), 3rd floor, 925-9507, J-M-N-QB-RR-6 to Canal, Sun-Th 11-7, all cash, no exch. or rfd. Basically a wholesaler who accomodates retail-trade. Sells: **Lighters, Appliances, Cameras & Optical Eqt., Jewelry & Gifts, Personal Accessories, Stationery & Art Supplies.**

Barclay Rex Pipe, 7 Maiden Ln. (B'wy), 962-3355, A-CC-J-M-RR-2-3-4-5 to B'wy-Nassau & Fulton, M-F 8-6, c.c., no ch., no exch. or rfd. Takes mail-orders. Very cooperative. Blend 6, and coffee blend, are good values, as are the seconds on their classy pipes (about 60% discount). Sells: **Pipe Tobaccos, Pipes.**

* **Barney's**, 41 John St. (Nassau), 732-3799 (pharmacy), 372-7271 (tobaccos), A-CC-J-M-RR-2-3-4-5 to B'wy-Nassau & Fulton, M-F 9-5, ch., no c.c., exch. or rfd. Not affiliated with the other Barney's stores. Sells: **Cigarettes, Pipe Tobaccos, Health & Beauty Aids.**

* **Barney's Canal Cut-Rate**, 259 Canal St. (Lafayette), 226-3796, J-M-N-QB-RR-6 to Canal, M-F 7:15-5:45, S 9-4, all cash, exch., no rfd. Sells: **Cigarettes, Cigars, Pipe Tobaccos, Pipes, Lighters.**

** **Barney's Cut-Rate Brooklyn**, Brooklyn, 76 Court St. at Livingston, 643-0643 (pharmacy), 875-8355 (tobacco), M-RR-2-3-4-5 to Borough Hall & Court St., M-S 8-6, ch., no c.c., exch. or rfd. Sells: **Cigarettes, Cigars, Pipe Tobaccos, Pipes, Lighters, Health & Beauty Aids.**

* **Barney's Cut-Rate Pharmacy**, 25 W. 42 (5th-6th), 719-1940, 7 to 5th Av., B-D-F to 42, M-F 8-6, ch., no c.c., exch. or rfd. Sells: **Lighters, Health & Beauty Aids.**

*** **Barney's Cut-Rate Tobaccos**, 25 W. 42 (5th-6th), 354-1366, 7 to 5th Av., B-D-F to 42, M-F 8-6:30, S 9-5, ch., c.c., exch. or rfd. House-blends are sensational bargains; branded tobaccos not as good values as at Wolf's Wholesale or even Famous Smoke. Good also on pipes, cigars, and cigarettes. Sells: **Pipe Tobaccos.**

\+ **Discount Head Shop**, 183 7th Av. (21), 989-6933, 1 to 23, 7 days 11-7, all cash, no exch. or rfd. Bonus discount to BF readers: 5% to 8%. Sells: **Head-Shop Goods.**

** **Dollar Bills**, 99 E. 42 (Park Av.), 867-0212, 4-5-6-7 to Grand Central, M-W 8-6:30, ThF 8-7, S 10-6, ch., c.c., 7-day exch. or rfd. A small department store that's best on toiletries, housewares, and cigarettes, but good also on men's wear. Same owner: J. Chuckles, Strawberry, Sunshine, Zoom stores. Sells: **Cigarettes, Appliances, Clothing —Men's, Housewares.**

+ **Famous Smoke Shop, 1450 Broadway (40-1), 221-1408 & 1-800-847-4062, N-QB-RR-1-2-3-7 to 42 & Times Square, M-F 7-6, S 8-2, ch., no c.c., exch. or rfd. Takes mail-orders. Catalog. Pipes & lighters all Dunhill on special-order. Bonus BF discount: free 3 Te Amo cigars (one time only) with purchase of any cigar-box, if you show this book. Sells: **Cigars, Pipe Tobaccos, Pipes, Lighters.**

Global Imports, 160 5th Av. at 21st St., 741-0700, N-RR to 23rd St., M-F 8-5, all cash, 7-day exch. or rfd. Sells: **Lighters, Housewares, Recordings & Tapes, Toys, Games & Hobbies.**

** **J&R Tobacco**, 11 E. 45 (5th Av.), 869-8777 & 1-914-351-4716 & 1-800-431-2380, 4-5-6-7 to Grand Central, B-D-F to 47, M-F 8-6, S 9-4; 219 Broadway

26: SMOKING SUPPLIES

(Vesey), 233-6620, 2-3 to Park Place, AA-E to World Trade Ctr., M-F 8-5. Both stores: ch., no c.c., exch. or rfd. Takes mail-orders. Catalog. 45th St. store stocks huge selection. Sells: **Cigars.**

King's Pharmacy, Brooklyn, 2474 Flatbush Av. (U), 253-0200, no subway stop nearby; Brooklyn, 1928 Kings Hwy., 339-3500, D-M-QB to Kings Hwy.; Brooklyn, 1110 Kings Hwy., 375-5700, D-M-QB to Kings Hwy.; Brooklyn, 472 Kings Hwy., 336-5400, F to Kings Hwy.; Brooklyn, 3082 Ocean Av. (Voorhies), 891-8201, D-M-QB to Sheepshead Bay; Queens, 93-17 63rd Dr., Rego Park, 459-3564, F-GG-N to 63rd Dr. All stores: M-S 9-10:45, Sun 10-9, ch., c.c., exch. or rfd. Sells: **Cigarettes, Health & Beauty Aids.**

** **The Tobacco Center**, 130 St. Marks Place (Av. A), 674-2208, LL to 1st Av., 6 to Astor, M-F 9-6, all cash, exch., no rfd. Primarily a wholesaler. Unintended but nice turn-of-the-century ambiance. Same location since 1902. All house-blends; no brands. Best blend is 'Continental.' Sells: **Pipe Tobaccos.**

Trinity Pipe Shop, 160 Pearl St. (Pine-Wall), 425-0070, J-M-RR-2-3 to Wall & Broad Sts., M-F 7-6, all cash, exch. or rfd. Takes mail-orders. Small store. Best is Blend 326. Sir Vincent's is also good. Place not recommended except for its custom blends. Sells: **Pipe Tobaccos.**

*** **Wolf's Wholesale**, Brooklyn, 126 Court St. at Atlantic, 522-5651, M-RR-2-3-4-5 to Borough Hall & Court St., M-F 6:30-6, S 7-6, all cash, exch. or rfd. Regular brand-name items only. (For pipes and lighters, though, also check out the values at the Barney's at 76 Court St.) Sells: **Pipe Tobaccos, Pipes, Foods.**

27:
SPORTING GOODS
Expect 20-40% discounts.

One of the biggest commercial rip-offs is top-brand jogging shoes. If you look inside a Puma or Adidas, for example, you might find a label saying "macht mit qualitat"—to impress you that the shoe is made with quality, supposedly in Europe. Then, look further inside the shoe, and you'll find a snippet of a label saying in small print "made in Korea" or "made in Taiwan". Well, these same Oriental factories that produce the overpriced stuff also produce their own off-brands, often of the same quality, and these are only 20% as expensive. The rest (80%) of what you pay for the advertised name goes to finance the very slick sales promotion—ads and reviews in the runners' magazines, sponsorship of athletic events, endorsements from pros and experts, etc. Your feet could care less; they'll hardly benefit from the ads, so why pay the huge tab?

The simplest way to recognize a *quality* off-brand is that: 1) the leather parts are real, not phony; 2) the thing atop the tongue through which the shoe-lace is to be drawn, is a sewn-on strip of suede or other material, not just a slit made into the tongue (or as in some shoes absent altogether); 3) the arch is firm and fully covered, and; 4) the heel and sole have foam padding, rather than being hollow. Most of the off-brands—and most (not all) of the jogging shoes made for the overpriced names—fulfill all these requirements. Ones that do are good quality also in the more subtle more important ways.

To get the best selection and value on off-brands, first check out the stores along the north side of 34th Street on the block between 7th-8th Avs.; then, perhaps also, explore a bit those on the south side of 14th St. between 5th-8th Avs. In both districts the shoes will be out on the pavement, so the comparison-shopping will be zippy-quick. Both strips are open 7 days a week.

If you insist on famous-brand jogging shoes, probably the best place is Carlsen Imports at 524 Broadway. However, you might also want to stop by G&S Sporting Goods at 43 Essex St.

RECOMMENDED STORES:
category-one sports

(includes: baseball, basketball, football, tennis, badminton, volleyball, ping pong, soccer, boxing, basic gym eqt., barbells, duffle bags, skates)

Bill Allan's Sports (Queens, 545-8233); *Consumers Distributing (Queens, 268-2091); **Byhoff's** (Brooklyn, 645-1780); **G & Sons Dept. Store** (Brooklyn, 438-2604); **G&S Sporting Goods** (777-7590); **Herman's** (233-0733); **Spiegel's** (227-8400); **Valco Discount** (Queens, 274-1200).

category-two sports

27: SPORTING GOODS

(examples: archery, bowling, croquet, diving, goggles, golf, shuffleboard, skiing)

Haber's (473-7007); **Herman's** (233-0733); **Sam Sharrow Golf** (921-5678); **Spiegel's** (227-8400).

camping eqt.

(examples: air mattresses, army surplus, back-packing, canopies, compasses, hammocks, insect-repellants, knives, lanterns, parkas, sleeping bags, surplus, tents)

The City Dump (431-1670); *+Down In The Village** (260-2330); ***United Chambers Trdg.** (267-0488); **Kol-Bo Discount** (473-7829); **Robbins Men's Wear** (691-2573); **Shoes, Boots, Etc.** (285-9750).

fishing eqt.

(includes: reels, rods, tackle)

***Job Lot Trdg. (intermittent stock, 962-4142); **Capitol Fishing Tackle** (929-6132).

marine eqt. & boats

(includes: canoes, rafts, yachts, barometers, compasses, depth-finders, hygrometers, life jackets, pumps, ropes, outboard motors)

*Revere Supply (736-5400); **Goldberg's Marine Eqt.** (840-8280); **Ripley Marine Eqt.** (Queens, 457-7075); **Yacht Exchange**.

jogging shoes

***Frankel's Discount Clothing (intermittent stock, Brooklyn, 768-9788); ****Bill Allan's Sports** (Queens, 545-8233); ****Bob's Discount** (intermittent stock, 674-4296); ****Carlsen Import** (431-5940); ****Cayne's 1** (695-8451); ****Cayne's 4** (560-9212); ***Han's Oriental** (243-3443); **Brown's Army-Navy** (Queens, 429-8508); **G&S Sporting Goods** (777-7590); **First Cost** (intermittent stock, 697-0244); **Sasson** (929-7070).

jogging suits.

**The Finals (431-1414).

exercize eqt.

Abbott Exercize Eqt. (Bronx, 671-9800).

STORES-DIRECTORY

Phone a store before you go out of your way to visit it. Especially do this during July and August, when most establishments reduce or eliminate weekend-hours.

In the listings below, "*" means especially recommended, "+" means that the store offers a bonus discount to BF readers, "ch." and "c.c." mean respectively checks and credit cards, and "exch." and "rfd." mean respectively exchange and refund. Nearest subway-stops are shown. For example, "B-D-F to 47" means to take the B, D, or F train to 47th Street. Store-hours are also indicated, with days of the week abbreviated, like "M-S 8-6."

    Abbott Exercize Eqt., Bronx, 263 E. 204 (Grand Conc.), 671-9800, CC-D to Bedford Pk. Blvd., 4 to Bedford Pk. Blvd., hours by appt., ch., no c.c. Free repair. They'll install & set up eqt. in your home. Sells: **Exercize Eqt**.

  ** **Bill Allan's Sports**, Queens, 25-77 Steinway St., Astoria, 545-8233, RR to Astoria Blvd., MTTh 10-7, WS 10-6, F 10-8, c.c., no ch., exch., no rfd. Sells: **Category-One Sports, Jogging Shoes.**

  ** **Bob's Discount**, 109 Ludlow St. (Delancey), 674-4296, F-J-M to Delancey & Essex, W-M 10-5, all cash, exch., no rfd. Sells: **Jogging Shoes, Clothing—**

27: SPORTING GOODS

Men's, Personal Accessories, Warehouse Salvage Job-Lot.

Brown's Army-Navy, Queens, 83-18 37th Av., Jackson Hts., 429-8508, 7 to 82nd St.; Queens, 74-17 Roosevelt Av., Jackson Hts., 476-8447, E-F-GG-N-7 to 74th-B'wy & Roosevelt-Jack.Hts. Both stores: M-S 9-8, ch., c.c., exch. or rfd. Sells: **Jogging Shoes, Clothing—Men's.**

Byhoff's, Brooklyn, 1322 Kings Hwy., 645-1780, D-M-QB to Kings Hwy., MTThF 9:30-6:45, WS 9:30-5:30, ch., c.c., exch., no rfd. Sells: **Category-One Sports.**

Capitol Fishing Tackle, 218 W. 23 (7th Av.), 929-6132, 1-2-3 to 14, M-F 8-5:30, S 9-4, all cash, exch., no rfd. Sells: **Fishing Eqt..**

** **Carlsen Import**, 524 Broadway at Spring, 3rd floor, 431-5940, 6 to Spring, N-RR to Prince St., M-F 9-5, S 9-12:30, all cash, exch. or rfd. (But only if unworn.) Large selection. Also sneakers. Sells: **Jogging Shoes.**

** **Cayne's 1**, 1345 Broadway (36), 695-8451, B-D-F-N-QB-RR to 34, M-S 10-6:30, c.c., no ch., 25-day exch. or rfd. One in the Cayne group. Sells: **Jogging Shoes, Clothing—Men's, Clothing—Women's, Linens.**

** **Cayne's 4**, 247 W. 34 (7th-8th), 560-9212, A-AA-CC-E to 34, 1-2-3 to 34, M-S 10-6:30, c.c., no ch., 25-day exch. or rfd. One in the Cayne group. Sells: **Jogging Shoes, Clothing—Children's, Clothing—Men's.**

* **Consumers Distributing**, Queens, 107-18 70th Rd., Forest Hills, 268-2091, E-F-GG-N to 71-Continental Avs.; Queens, 39-20 Bell Blvd., Bayside, 225-0253, no subway stop nearby; Queens, 156-16 Northern Blvd., Flushing, 961-5024, no subway stop nearby; Queens, 97-10 Queens Blvd., Rego Park, 896-7250, F-GG-N to 63rd Dr.; Brooklyn, Av. U at Mill Av. (nr. Kings Plaza), 241-7633, D-M-QB to Av. M; Queens, 54-30 Myrtle Av., Ridgewood, 386-2809, LL-M to Myrtle & Wyckoff. All stores: M-F 10-9 (Ridgewood 10-6), S 10-6, Sun 12-5, ch., c.c., during banking hours, 30-day exch. or rfd. Large selection. A catalog-showroom chain. Sells: **Category-One Sports, Autos & Supplies, Bikes, Dinnerware & Cookware, Home-Improvement Items, Housewares, Jewelry & Gifts.**

*+ **Down In The Village**, 652 Broadway (Bleecker), 260-2330, B-D-F-6 to B'wy-Laf. & Bleecker, M-S 10-6, Sun 12-5, ch., c.c., exch., no rfd. Specializes in carrying practically every name in down clothing. Bonus discount to BF readers: 10%. Sells: **Camping Eqt., Clothing—Men's.**

First Cost, 90 E. 42nd St. at Park Av., 697-0244, 4-5-6-7 to Grand Central, M-F 8-7, SSun 10-5; Queens, 46-20 108 St., Corona, 271-1121, 7 to 111, ThS 9-6, F 9-9. Both stores: all cash, 7-day exch. or rfd. Sells: **Jogging Shoes, Clothing—Children's, Clothing—Men's, Clothing—Women's, Dinnerware & Cookware, Foods, Health & Beauty Aids, Home-Improvement Items, Housewares, Jewelry & Gifts, Toys, Games & Hobbies, Warehouse Salvage Job-Lot.**

*** **Frankel's Discount Clothing**, Brooklyn, 3924 3rd Av. at 40th St., 768-9788 & 788-9402, B-N-RR to 36th St., W-S 10-7, Sun 10-5, c.c., no ch., exch. or rfd. Large selection. Especially good on Frye boots. This place is basically an army-navy type store with casual-clothing job lots. Sells: **Jogging Shoes, Clothing—Children's, Clothing—Men's, Clothing—Women's, Warehouse Salvage Job-Lot.**

G & Sons Dept. Store, Brooklyn, 4806 New Utrecht Av., 438-2604, B to 50th St., MTTh 10-9, WSun 10-6, F 10-4, ch., c.c., exch. or rfd. Sells: **Category-One Sports, Health & Beauty Aids, Housewares, Stationery & Art Supplies, Toys, Games & Hobbies.**

Goldberg's Marine Eqt., 12 W. 46 (5th Av.), 840-8280, B-D-F to 47, MTWF 9:30-6, Th 9:30-7, ch., c.c., exch., no rfd. Takes mail-orders. Catalog. Large selection. Sells: **Marine Eqt. & Boats.**

G&S Sporting Goods, 43 Essex St. (Grand), 777-7590, F-J-M to Delancey & Essex, Sun-F 9:30-6, c.c., no ch., exch., no rfd. Sells: **Category-One Sports, Jogging Shoes.**

Haber's, 33 Essex St. (Grand), 473-7007, F-J-M to Delancey & Essex, Sun-F 9-6, ch., c.c., exch. or rfd. Large selection top brand pens at excellent discounts. Sells: **Category-Two Sports,, Stationery & Art Supplies.**

* **Han's Oriental**, 100 W. 14 at 6th Av., 243-3443 & 255-8113, B-F-LL to 14th St. & 6th Av., M-S 10-7, all cash, exch., no rfd. Sells: **Jogging Shoes, Personal Accessories.**

Herman's, 110 Nassau St. at Ann, 233-0733, A-CC-J-M-RR-2-3-4-5 to B'wy-Nassau & Fulton; 135 W. 42 (6th-7th), 730-7400, B-D-F to 42, N-QB-RR-1-2-3-7 to 42 & Times Square; 845 3rd Av. (52), 688-4603, E-F to Lex. Av.; 39 W. 34 (5th-6th), 279-8900, B-D-F-N-QB-RR to 34; Brooklyn, Kings Plaza, Flatbush at U, 258-3100, no

27: SPORTING GOODS

subway stop nearby; Queens, 90-15 Queens Blvd., Elmhurst, 592-7400, F-GG-N to Woodhaven Blvd.; Staten Island, Staten Island Mall, 698-7800. All stores: hours vary by location (phone first), ch., c.c., 7-day exch. or rfd. (But only if unused.) Other stores nationwide. Sells: **Category-One Sports, Category-Two Sports.**

*** **Job Lot Trdg.**, 140 Church St. (Warren-Chambers), 962-4142, A-CC-1-2-3 to Chambers; 412 5th Av. (37-8), 398-9210, B-D-F to 42. Both stores: M-F 8-5:30, S 8-4:30, all cash, 15-day exch. or rfd. Both are huge stores, with terrific selections. Sells: **Fishing Eqt., Clothing—Men's, Dinnerware & Cookware, Foods, Home-Improvement Items, Housewares, Jewelry & Gifts, Linens, Personal Accessories, Stationery & Art Supplies, Toys, Games & Hobbies, Warehouse Salvage Job-Lot.**

Kol-Bo Discount, 611 Broadway at Houston, 473-7829, N-RR to 8th St., B-D-F-6 to B'way-Laf. & Bleecker, M-F 7:30-6, SSun 10-4, all cash, exch., no rfd. In the recommended categories, carries: earmuffs, cheap small backpacks, berets, Chinese bedroom-shoes. Sells: **Camping Eqt., Clothing—Men's.**

* **Revere Supply**, 607 W. 29 (11th Av.), 2nd floor, 736-5400, A-AA-CC-E to 34, 1 to 28, plus a long walk, M-F 8-4, ch., no c.c., exch. or rfd. Will special-order. Takes mail-orders. Catalog. Small store. Small selection. Specialty is safety-at-sea eqt. Sells: **Marine Eqt. & Boats.**

Ripley Marine Eqt., Queens, 66-00 Long Island Expwy., Maspeth, 457-7075, no subway stop nearby, MWTh 9-5:30, F 9-7:30, S 9-2, ch., no c.c., exch., no rfd. Sells: **Marine Eqt. & Boats.**

Robbins Men's Wear, 48 W. 14 (5th-6th), 691-2573, B-F-LL to 14th St. & 6th Av.; 146 E. 14 (3rd Av.), 260-0456, LL to 3rd Av.; 1265 Broadway (32), 684-5429, B-D-F-N-QB-RR to 34; 519 8th Av. (35), 564-3756, A-AA-CC-E to 34; 609 8th Av. (41), 564-1194, A-AA-CC-E to 42; 1717 Broadway (55), 581-7033, A-AA-B-CC-D-1 to 59; Queens, 38-17 Main St., Flushing, 445-7301, 7 to Main St.; Queens, 37-42 Junction Blvd., Corona, 424-0377, 7 to Junction Blvd.; Queens, 30-88 Steinway St., Astoria, 626-7180, F-GG-N to Steinway St.; Queens, 57-33 Myrtle Av. (Seneca), Ridgewood, 497-4489, M to Seneca; Brooklyn, 1213 Kings Hwy., 375-4133, D-M-QB to Kings Hwy.; Bronx, 279 E. Fordham Rd. (Kingsbridge Rd.), 367-2499, CC-D to Fordham Rd. All stores: M-S 9-7:30, all cash, exch. or rfd. No try-ons. Somewhat uneven values, but worth recommending the chain for the things I'm recommending the chain for. Other stores in Long Island. Sells: **Camping Eqt., Clothing—Men's, Health & Beauty Aids.**

Sam Sharrow Golf, 147 W. 42 at B'wy, rm. 410, 921-5678, N-QB-RR-1-2-3-7 to 42 & Times Square, M-F 10-6, S 9-1, ch., c.c., exch. or rfd. Sells: **Category-Two Sports.**

Sasson, 154 W. 14 (7th Av.), 929-7070, 1-2-3 to 14, 7 days 9-8, all cash, no exch. or rfd. Sells: **Jogging Shoes, Dinnerware & Cookware.**

Shoes, Boots, Etc., 63 Warren St. at W. B'wy, 285-9750, A-CC-1-2-3 to Chambers, M-S 10-6, all cash, exch., no rfd. Small store. Many irregulars of military-surplus-type clothing and camping gear. Sells: **Camping Eqt., Clothing—Men's, Warehouse Salvage Job-Lot.**

Spiegel's, 105 Nassau St. at Ann, 227-8400, A-CC-J-M-RR-2-3-4-5 to B'wy-Nassau & Fulton, M-F 9-6, S 9-5, ch., c.c., exch., no rfd. Sells: **Category-One Sports, Category-Two Sports.**

** **The City Dump**, 334 Canal St. (Greene), 431-1670, A-AA-CC-E-1 to Canal, J-M-N-QB-RR-6 to Canal, 7 days 10-6, all cash, exch., no rfd. Outstanding values only on the items for which the store is here recommended. Otherwise uneven. Sells: **Camping Eqt., Appliances, Jewelry & Gifts.**

** **The Finals**, 149 Mercer St. (Prince), 431-1414 & 1-800-431-9111, N-RR to Prince St., T-S 10-6, Sun 11-6, ch., c.c. $25+, exch., no rfd. Takes mail-orders. Catalog. Sells own brand competitive with Adidas & Speedo, but half the price. Sells: **Jogging suits, Clothing—Men's, Clothing—Women's.**

* **United Chambers Trdg.**, 83 Chambers St. (B'wy-Church), 267-0488, A-CC-1-2-3 to Chambers, N-RR to City Hall, M-F 9-6, S 9-5, c.c. $15+, no ch., 10-day exch. or rfd. Often has some sensational values in slight irregulars and in closeouts. Sells: **Camping Eqt., Clothing—Men's.**

Valco Discount, Queens, 32-40 & 32-62 Steinway St., Astoria, 274-1200 & 545-8443, F-GG-N to Steinway St., M-W 10-7, ThF 10-8, SSun 10:30-5:30, ch., no c.c., exch. or rfd. Large selection. Sells: **Category-One Sports, Bikes, Housewares, Stationery & Art Supplies, Toys, Games & Hobbies.**

Yacht Exchange, 1-800-327-2515. About 5,000 boats listed. Owner's price +10%. A national listing-service. Sells: **Marine Eqt. & Boats.**

28:
STATIONERY & ART SUPPLIES
Expect 20-60% discounts

On art-supplies it's especially important to phone and check prices at all the recommended stores, because it's entirely up to chance which place will have the best buys on which items, in which week. The stores play a continual game of musical chairs on their rotating numerous "specials." And they do phone-quote.

RECOMMENDED STORES:

pens (&: CH. 1 "SMALL," & BELOW)

***Job Lot Trdg.** (intermittent stock, 962-4142); ***Odd Job Trdg.** (intermittent stock, 686-6825); ***+Mills Sales** (477-1000); ****Ashreh Supply** (925-9507); ****Romano Trdg.** (581-4248); ****Weber's Job Lot** (intermittent stock, 564-7668); ***Eighty-Eight Cent Shops** (753-6969); **A&R Novelty** (Brooklyn, 856-8070); **G & Sons Dept. Store** (Brooklyn, 438-2604); **Goodwear** (475-5430); **Haber's** (473-7007); **Odd Lot Trdg.** (intermittent stock, 736-5243); **Valco Discount** (Queens, 274-1200); **Warren St. Merchandise** (227-8330).

stationery—office

(examples: adhesive-tape, envelopes, globes, inks, labels, letter-openers, markers, paper, pencil-sharpeners, pencils, pens, punches, rubber stamps, scissors, stencils, staplers)

Crazy Ciro (406-1323); ***Merit Office Supplies (925-8750); **Crown Discount** (Queens, 937-7171); **Haber's** (473-7007); **Holland Stationery** (226-0118).

art-supplies

(examples: blackboards, air-brushes, brushes, canvases, easels, frames, gessos, letterings, markers, pads, paints, pens, portfolios, scissors)

Greenwich Art Supply (677-6038); **New York Central Art Supply** (473-7705); **Pearl Art Supplies** (431-7932); **Tay Art Supply** (475-7365); **Tribecca Art Materials** (349-2223); **Utrecht Art Supplies** (777-5353).

frames (ALSO SEE PRECEDING)

Weiser & Teitel (233-1441); *+Perplexity Lucite** (688-3571); **Alliance Art Glass** (410-3994).

envelopes (IN QUANTITY)

(at least 500, printed or not)
Embassy Envelopes (675-4220); ****Gem Envelopes (255-8093); **Star Envelope** (691-9230).

business-&-calling cards

***+Cooper Enterprises (Queens, 268-5353); ****Sunset Process Prtg.** (473-2273); ***Paramount Process Prtg.** (691-3700); **Sun Press** (255-0733).

28: STATIONERY & ART SUPPLIES

return-address labels

**Brewster Sales; **Imprint Products; Walter Drake & Sons.

copies—xerox-type

**+Cooper Enterprises (Queens, 268-5353); **Crazy Ciro (406-1323); **Flushing Duplicating (Queens, 762-8336); **Gallery Printing (475-2074); **John St. Reproductions (374-1212); *Philipson Press (966-3617); +Fast Copy (732-4418); Big Apple Copy (962-4282); Longacre Copy (944-0410).

copies—quality xerox-type

*George's Copy (254-7465); *Heuston Copy (222-2149); *MacDougal Copy (460-8591); *Unique Copies Plus (777-9690); Copyquick (749-7650); Quick Quality Copies (246-5528); The Word Center (787-8610); Unsloppy Copy (254-7336).

copies—offset printed

**Brewster Sales; **Crazy Ciro (406-1323); **Flushing Duplicating (Queens, 762-8336); **Gallery Printing (475-2074); **Henry Harris Photographer (227-4297); **John St. Reproductions (374-1212); Big Apple Copy (962-4282).

copies—quality offset

**Henry Harris Photographer (227-4297); Johnson Copy (564-5120); Mainline Offset (243-1432); Raymar Printing (255-1500).

blank paper

***Alexander's Hardware (intermittent stock, 267-0336); ***Job Lot Trdg. (intermittent stock, 962-4142); **Crazy Ciro (406-1323); *Eighty-Eight Cent Shops (753-6969).

copies of photos: CH.4

STORES-DIRECTORY

Phone a store before you go out of your way to visit it. Especially do this during July and August, when most establishments reduce or eliminate weekend-hours.

In the listings below, "*" means especially recommended, "+" means that the store offers a bonus discount to BF readers, "ch." and "c.c." mean respectively checks and credit cards, and "exch." and "rfd." mean respectively exchange and refund. Nearest subway-stops are shown. For example, "B-D-F to 47" means to take the B, D, or F train to 47th Street. Store-hours are also indicated, with days of the week abbreviated, like "M-S 8-6."

*** **Alexander's Hardware**, 60 Reade St. (B'way), 267-0336, N-RR to City Hall, A-CC-1-2-3 to Chambers, M-F 8:30-6, S 8:30-5, ch., c.c., exch. or rfd. Large selection. Merits a long time browsing. Has great bargains in some obscure corners. Often has top quality cutlery at incredibly low prices. Much furniture-hardware. Abrasives. Sells: **Pens, Blank Paper, Home-Improvement Items, Warehouse Salvage Job-Lot.**

    Alliance Art Glass, 169 E. 88 (3rd Av.), 410-3994, 4-5-6 to 86, M-F 9-6, S 9-5, ch., no c.c., no exch. or rfd. Custom or do-it-yourself. Doesn't sell glass alone. Sells: **Frames, Home-Improvement Items.**

    A&R Novelty, Brooklyn, 1222 Flatbush Av. (Ditmas), 856-8070, D-M-QB to Beverly, 3-4 to Beverly, M-S 9:30-6, ch., no c.c., 24-day exch. or rfd. Small Selection. Sells: **Pens, Jewelry & Gifts, Toys, Games & Hobbies.**

28: STATIONERY & ART SUPPLIES

** Ashreh Supply, 473 Broadway (Grand), 3rd floor, 925-9507, J-M-N-QB-RR-6 to Canal, Sun-Th 11-7, all cash, no exch. or rfd. Basically a wholesaler who accomodates retail-trade. Sells: **Pens, Appliances, Cameras & Optical Eqt., Jewelry & Gifts, Personal Accessories, Smoking Supplies.**

Big Apple Copy, 87 Nassau St. at Fulton, rm. 205, 962-4282, A-CC-J-M-RR-2-3-4-5 to B'wy-Nassau & Fulton, M-Th 8:30-5:30, F 8:30-3, ch., no c.c., exch., no rfd. Sells: **Copies—Xerox-Type, Copies—Offset Printing.**

** Brewster Sales, 808 Washington St., St. Louis, MO 63101. Takes mail-order. Catalog. Very cooperative. Large selection. Sells: **Return-Address Labels, Copies—Offset Printing.**

+ Cooper Enterprises, Queens, 114-41 Queens Blvd., Forest Hills, 268-5353, E-F to Van Wyck Blvd., M-F 10-7:30, S 10-2:30, ch., no c.c., exch., no rfd. Bonus discount to BF readers: 5% to 50%. Sells: **Business-&-Calling Cards, Copies—Xerox-Type.

Copyquick, 1211 Amsterdam Av. (119-20), 749-7650, 1 to 116, M-F 9-6, S 10-5, ch., no c.c., exch., no rfd. Sells: **Copies—Quality Xerox-Type.**

** Crazy Ciro, 23 Warren St. (Church-B'wy), 406-1323, A-CC-1-2-3 to Chambers, M-S 8-6:30, ch., no c.c., exch., no rfd. An utterly unique operation. Sells: **Stationery—Office, Copies—Xerox-Type, Copies—Offset Printing, Blank Paper.**

Crown Discount, Queens, 31-28 Queens Blvd., L.I.C., 937-7171 & 1-516-352-8844, 7 to 33rd St., M-F 9-8, S 9-6, ch., c.c., exch., no rfd. Sells: **Stationery—Office, Office Equipment.**

* Eighty-Eight Cent Shops, 591 Lexington Av. (52), 753-6969, E-F to Lex. Av., M-F 9:30-6; 1457 Broadway (41), 354-0111, N-QB-RR-1-2-3-7 to 42 & Times Square, M-F 7:15-6, Sun 12-6; 33 W. 8 (5th-6th), 475-6951, A-AA-B-CC-D-E-F to 4, Sun-F 11-10, S 11-12; 89 Chambers (B'wy-Church), 267-6722, A-CC-1-2-3 to Chambers, N-RR to City Hall, M-F 7:30-6; 144 Fulton St. (B'wy), 964-2142, A-CC-J-M-RR-2-3-4-5 to B'wy-Nassau & Fulton, M-F 7:30-6. All stores: all cash, exch. or rfd. Everything in store is 88 cents; only the Fulton and Chambers stores have areas set aside for more expensive merchandise. Sells: **Pens, Blank Paper, Dinnerware & Cookware, Foods, Health & Beauty Aids, Home-Improvement Items, Housewares, Toys, Games & Hobbies.**

** Embassy Envelopes, 655 6th Av. at 20th St., 675-4220, B-F to 23, M-Th 4-3:30, F 4-2, all cash, exch., no rfd. Takes mail-orders. Mr. Wien, the owner and only person, is somewhat curt, so it's best if you understand what he says the first time he says it. Sells: **Envelopes.**

+ Fast Copy, 79 Chambers St. (B'wy-Church), upstairs, 732-4418, A-CC-1-2-3 to Chambers, N-RR to City Hall, M-F 9-5, ch., no c.c., exch., no rfd. Bonus discount to BF readers: 5% to 10%. Sells: **Copies—Xerox-Type.**

** Flushing Duplicating, Queens, 150-34 Northern Blvd., Flushing, 762-8336, no subway stop nearby, M-F 9-5, S 9-1, ch., no c.c., exch., no rfd. Sells: **Copies—Xerox-Type, Copies—Offset Printed.**

G & Sons Dept. Store, Brooklyn, 4806 New Utrecht Av., 438-2604, B to 50th St., MTTh 10-9, WSun 10-6, F 10-4, ch., c.c., exch. or rfd. Sells: **Pens, Health & Beauty Aids, Housewares, Sporting Goods, Toys, Games & Hobbies.**

** Gallery Printing, 68 W. 3 (LaGuardia), 475-2074, A-AA-B-CC-D-E-F to 4, M-F 9-7, S 11-4, ch., no c.c., exch., no rfd. Their 3-day Xerox-rates are super-bargains. Sells: **Copeis—Xerox-Type, Copies—Offset Printed.**

** Gem Envelopes, 10 W. 19 (5th Av.), 255-8093 & 243-8380&8655, N-RR to 23rd St., M-F 8-5:30, ch., until cleared no c.c., exch., no rfd. Takes mail-orders. Sells: **Envelopes.**

* George's Copy, 146 W. 4 (6th Av.), 254-7465, A-AA-B-CC-D-E-F to 4, M-F 8-8, S 9:30-7, ch., no c.c., exch., no rfd. Sells: **Copies—Quality Offset-Type.**

Goodwear, 793 Broadway (11), 475-5430, 6 to Astor, LL-N-QB-RR-4-5-6 to Union Sq., M-F 8-5:30, S 9-2, all cash, exch. or rfd. Off-brand ball-points, good selection; but Mills Sales' values are even better. Sells: **Pens.**

Greenwich Art Supply, 32 3rd Av. (9), 677-6038, LL to 3rd Av., 6 to Astor, M-S 10-6, c.c., exch., no rfd. Sells: **Art-Supplies.**

Haber's, 33 Essex St. (Grand), 473-7007, F-J-M to Delancey & Essex, Sun-F 9-6, ch., c.c., exch. or rfd. Large selection top brand pens at excellent discounts. Sells: **Pens, Stationery—Office, Sporting Goods.**

** Henry Harris Photographer, 21 Barclay St. (B'wy-Church), 2nd floor, 227-4297, AA-E to World Trade Ctr., 2-3 to Park Place, M-F 8:30-4:30, ch., no c.c., exch., no rfd. Also does commercial photography. Sells: **Copies—Offset Printed,**

28: STATIONERY & ART SUPPLIES

Copies—Quality Offset.

* **Heuston Copy**, 2879 Broadway (112), 222-2149, 1 to 110, M-Th 8a.m.-11p.m., F 8-9, S 9-9, Sun 12-11; 11 Waverly Place (B'wy), 228-8668, N-RR to 8th St., M-F 8a.m.-9p.m., S 9-9, Sun 12-9. Both stores: ch. $10+, no c.c., exch., no rfd. Especially recommended for copying half-tones and screens. Sells: **Copies—Quality Xerox-Type.**

Holland Stationery, 325 Canal St. (Greene), 226-0118, J-M-N-QB-RR-6 to Canal, M-F 8-4:30, all cash, no exch. or rfd. Sells: **Stationery—Office.**

** **Imprint Products**, 482 Sunrise Hwy., Rockville Ctr., NY 11570. Mail-orders. Sells: **Return-Address Labels.**

*** **Job Lot Trdg.**, 140 Church St. (Warren-Chambers), 962-4142, A-CC-1-2-3 to Chambers; 412 5th Av. (37-8), 398-9210, B-D-F to 42. Both stores: M-F 8-5:30, S 8-4:30, all cash, 15-day exch. or rfd. Both are huge stores, with terrific selections. Sells: **Pens, Blank Paper, Clothing—Men's, Dinnerware & Cookware, Foods, Home-Improvement Items, Housewares, Jewelry & Gifts, Linens, Personal Accessories, Sporting Goods, Toys, Games & Hobbies, Warehouse Salvage Job-Lot.**

** **John St. Reproductions**, 11 John St. (B'wy), 374-1212, A-CC-J-M-RR-2-3-4-5 to B'wy-Nassau & Fulton, M-F 8-5:30, ch., no c.c., exch., no rfd. Sells: **Copies—Xerox-Type, Copies—Offset Printed.**

Johnson Copy, 100 W. 31 at 6th Av., 564-5120, B-D-F-N-QB-RR to 34, M-F 8:30-5:30, ch., no c.c., exch., no rfd. Sells: **Copies—Quality Offset.**

Longacre Copy, 32 W. 40 (5th-6th), 944-0410, B-D-F to 42, M-F 9-6, ch., no c.c., exch., no rfd. Sells: **Copies—Xerox-Type.**

* **MacDougal Copy**, 127 MacDougal St. (3-4), 460-8591, A-AA-B-CC-D-E-F to 4, M-Th 8:30-7:30, F 8:30-7, S 10-7, Sun 12-6, ch., no c.c., exch., no rfd. Sells: **Copies—Quality Xerox-Type.**

Mainline Offset, 32 W. 22 (5th-6th), 243-1432, N-RR to 23rd St., B-F to 23, M-F 9-6, S 9-1, ch., c.c., exch., no rfd. Sells: **Copies—Quality Offset.**

* **Merit Office Supplies**, 104 Grand St. at Mercer, 925-8750, J-M-N-QB-RR-6 to Canal, M-F 9-5, S 10-4, all cash, exch. or rfd. Sells: **Stationery—Office, Office Equipment.**

***+ **Mills Sales**, 889 Broadway at 19th St., 477-1000, LL-N-QB-RR-4-5-6 to Union Sq., N-RR to 23rd St., M-F 9-5, S 9-2, all cash, no exch. or rfd. No retail sales (wholesale only) Labor Day through Xmas. A specialty here is steel ball-point pens super-cheap by the dozen. Bonus discount to BF readers: 5%. Sells: **Pens, Appliances, Dinnerware & Cookware, Home-Improvement Items, Jewelry & Gifts, Personal Accessories, Toys, Games & Hobbies.**

New York Central Art Supply, 63 3rd Av. (11), 473-7705, LL to 3rd Av., 6 to Astor, M-S 8:30-6:30, ch., c.c., exch., no rfd. Large selection. Especially for press-on lettering. Sells: **Art-Supplies.**

*** **Odd Job Trdg.**, 7 E. 40 (Mad.), 686-6825, B-D-F to 42, 7 to 5th Av.; 66 W. 48 (6th Av.), 575-0477, B-D-F to 47. Both stores: M-Th 8-5:30, F 8-3, Sun 10-5, ch., no c.c., 15-day exch. or rfd. Sells: **Pens, Clothing—Men's, Dinnerware & Cookware, Foods, Health & Beauty Aids, Home-Improvement Items, Housewares, Linens, Personal Accessories, Toys, Games & Hobbies, Warehouse Salvage Job-Lot.**

Odd Lot Trdg., 33 W. 34 (5th-6th Avs.), 736-5243, B-D-F-N-QB-RR to 34; Queens, 19-40 37th St., Astoria, 932-3534, RR to Ditmars; Queens, 28-32 Steinway St., Astoria, 545-5604, RR to 30th Av., F-GG-N to Steinway St.; Queens, 103-54 94th St., Forest Hills, 263-5608, E-F to 75th Av.; Queens, 162-03 Jamaica Av., Jamaica, 657-4242, E-F to Parsons Blvd.; Queens, 103-54 94th St., Ozone Park, 738-2944, A-CC to Rockaway Blvd.; Brooklyn, 503 Fulton St., 625-7926, 2-3 to Hoyt; Brooklyn, 1166 E. 92nd St., 272-1482, LL to Rockaway Pkwy. All stores: MTWS 10-6, ThF 10-9, Sun 11-5, c.c., no ch., 7-day exch. or rfd. Other stores throughout the greater metropolitan area. Sells: **Pens, Dinnerware & Cookware, Health & Beauty Aids, Warehouse Salvage Job-Lot.**

* **Paramount Process Prtg.**, 20 W. 22 (5th-6th), 691-3700, N-RR to 23rd St., M-F 9-4:30, ch., no c.c., exch., no rfd. Sells: **Business-&-Calling Cards.**

Pearl Art Supplies, 308 Canal St. (B'wy), upstairs, 431-7932, J-M-N-QB-RR-6 to Canal, M-F 8-5:30, S 8-4:30, ch., no c.c., 14-day exch. or rfd. Huge selection—even larger than Utrecht or NY Central in most categories of art supplies. Sells: **Art-Supplies.**

*+ **Perplexity Lucite**, 237 E. 53 (3rd-2nd Avs.), 688-3571, E-F to Lex. Av., M-S 10:30-6:30, Sun 12-5, ch., c.c., (only c.c. is AE), exch., no rfd. Another store in

28: STATIONERY & ART SUPPLIES

Carle Place, Long Island. Bonus discount to BF readers: 5%. Sells: **Frames, Furnishings, Jewelry & Gifts.**

* **Philipson Press**, 52 Warren St. (Church), 966-3617, A-CC-1-2-3 to Chambers, N-RR to City Hall, M-F 9-5:45, S 10-4; 12 John St. (B'wy), 962-4321, A-CC-J-M-RR-2-3-4-5 to B'wy-Nassau & Fulton, M-F 9-5:45. Both stores: ch., no c.c., exch., no rfd. Sells: **Copies—Xerox-Type.**

Quick Quality Copies, 945 8th Av. (56), 246-5528, A-AA-B-CC-D-1 to 59; 370 7th Av. (31), 1 to 28. Both stores: M-F 9-6, ch., no c.c., exch. or rfd. Competes with Gallery for 3-day-wait service. Sells: **Copies—Quality Xerox-Type.**

Raymar Printing, 333 Hudson at Charlton, 5th floor, 255-1500, 1 to Houston, M-F 7:30-4:30, ch., no c.c., exch., no rfd. Sells: **Copies—Quality Offset.**

* **Romano Trdg.**, 628 W. 45th St. on 12th Av., 581-4248, A-AA-CC-E to 42, plus a long walk, M-F 8-5:30, S 8-5, all cash, exch. or rfd. Very cooperative. A little bit of everything, designer-name and major brand items. Sells: **Pens, Appliances, Clothing—Men's, Jewelry & Gifts, Office Equipment, Personal Accessories, Toys, Games & Hobbies.**

Star Envelope, 151 W. 19, 4th floor, 691-9230, 1 to 18, M-F 9-5, ch., no c.c., exch., no rfd. Takes mail-orders. Sells: **Envelopes.**

Sun Press, 88 University Place (11-12), 7th floor, 255-0733, LL-N-QB-RR-4-5-6 to Union Sq., N-RR to 8th St., M-F 9-5, ch., no c.c., exch., no rfd. Sells: **Buisiness-&-Calling Cards.**

** **Sunset Process Prtg.**, 95 University Place (11-12), 9th floor, 473-2273, LL-N-QB-RR-4-5-6 to Union Sq., N-RR to 8th St., M-F 8:30-4:30, ch., no c.c., exch., no rfd. Sells: **Buisiness-&-Calling Cards.**

Tay Art Supply, 27 3rd Av. (8), 475-7365, 6 to Astor, M-F 9-6:15, S 10-5:30, ch., c.c., exch., no rfd. Small store. Sells: **Art-Supplies.**

The Word Center, 150 W. 72 (Columbus-Amsterdam), 787-8610, 1-2-3 to 72, A-AA-B-CC to 72, M-S 9-7, ch., no c.c. Sells: **Copies—Quality Xerox-Type.**

Tribecca Art Materials, 142 Chambers St. (W.B'wy-Greenwich), 349-2223, A-CC-1-2-3 to Chambers, M-S 9-7, ch., c.c., exch. or rfd. Sells: **Art-Supplies.**

* **Unique Copies Plus**, 252A Greene St. (Waverly-8th), 777-9690,; 29 Waverly Place (Greene), 228-8640, N-RR to 8th St. Both stores: M-Th 8:30-8:30, F 8:30-7, S 10-6, ch., no c.c., exch., no rfd. Sells: **Copies—Quality Xerox-Type, Art-Supplies.**

Unsloppy Copy, 5 W. 8 (5th Av.), 254-7336, A-AA-B-CC-D-E-F to 4, N-RR to 8th St., M-Th 8:30a.m.-10p.m., F 8:30-8, S 10-7; 97 Worth St. (B'wy-Church), 226-4058, 1 to Franklin, M-F 9-6. Both stores: c.c., no ch., exch., no rfd. Specializes in copying half-tones and screens. Sells: **Copies—Quality Xerox-Type.**

Utrecht Art Supplies, 111 4th Av. (11), 777-5353, LL-N-QB-RR-4-5-6 to Union Sq., M-S 9:30-6, ch., no c.c., exch. or rfd. Large selection. Sells: **Art-Supplies.**

Valco Discount, Queens, 32-40 & 32-62 Steinway St., Astoria, 274-1200 & 545-8443, F-GG-N to Steinway St., M-W 10-7, ThF 10-8, SSun 10:30-5:30, ch., no c.c., exch. or rfd. Large selection. Sells: **Pens, Bikes, Housewares, Sporting Goods, Toys, Games & Hobbies.**

Walter Drake & Sons, Drake Bldg., Colorado Springs, CO 80940. Takes mail-orders. Catalog. Very cooperative. Large selection. Sells: **Return-Address Labels.**

Warren St. Merchandise, 32 Warren St. (Church), 227-8330, A-CC-1-2-3 to Chambers, N-RR to City Hall, M-S 9-6, ch., no c.c., exch. or rfd. Only ballpoint pens, small off-brand walkman-type radios etc., car-radios, and brand-name blank cassettes. Street-stand, extends indoors. Sells: **Pens, Appliances, Recordings & Tapes.**

** **Weber's Job Lot**, 505 8th Av. at 35th, 564-7668, A-AA-CC-E to 34, M-F 10-6:30, S 10-6; 136 Church St. at Warren, 564-7668, A-CC-1-2-3 to Chambers, M-S 8-6; 2064 Broadway at 71st, 787-1644, 1-2-3 to 72, M-F 9-9, S 9-6, Sun 12-6. All stores: c.c., no ch., 7-day exch. or rfd. Some terrific values; others not good. Some prices wrongly marked on items each time I was at both stores; checkout counter said 'It's an error. Sells: **Pens, Dinnerware & Cookware, Health & Beauty Aids, Home-Improvement Items, Jewelry & Gifts, Linens, Personal Accessories, Warehouse Salvage Job-Lot.**

** **Weiser & Teitel**, 61 Reade St. (Church-B'wy), 233-1441, A-CC-1-2-3 to Chambers, N-RR to City Hall, M-F 7:30-5:30, S 7:30-4:30, c.c., no ch. or rfd. Custom-made frames at the city's lowest prices. Also rather good on framed mirrors.

28: STATIONERY & ART SUPPLIES

Not a general glass place, but only framed products. Sells: **Frames, Home-Improvement Items.**

29:
TOYS, GAMES & HOBBIES
Expect 20-40% discounts.

This is one of the mushrooming consumer-products fields, thanks to computer-chips. Some of the inexpensive self-contained video games are as sophisticated and challenging as the far more expensive TV-hookup units.

RECOMMENDED PRODUCTS:

Video Games, Self-Contained: Entex Galaxian 2 (competes with Atari's Space Invaders TV-hookup cartridge), Entex 3-D Grand Prix (player is at the controls of a race-car), Matel World Championship Baseball (competes with Intellivision's Major League Baseball TV-hookup cartridge), Parker Brothers Split-Second (eight maze-, chase-, and target-games), Milton Bradley Microvision (a bargain handheld unit with a choice of more than ten inexpensive cartridges, including the challenging "Mindbuster" and "Alien Raiders").

RECOMMENDED STORES:

hobbies

(examples: model-kits, planes, trains)

⁺**Doll Hs. & Miniature Factory** (Brooklyn, 338-8411); **Habild of New Dorp** (Staten Island, 987-4335); **Red Caboose** (575-0155); **Roundhouse** (575-1753).

some toys & games

*****Job Lot Trdg.** (intermittent stock, 962-4142); *****Odd Job Trdg.** (intermittent stock, 686-6825); *****Mills Sales** (477-1000); ****Cho's Variety** (349-7544); ****Fun Creators** (685-4280); ****G.M.E. Stuffed Toy Animals** (328-7345); ****Odds & Ends Job-Lots** (intermittent stock, Queens, 441-6878); ***Eighty-Eight Cent Shops** (753-6969); **A&R Novelty** (Brooklyn, 856-8070); **First Cost** (intermittent stock, 697-0244); **Global Imports** (intermittent stock, 741-0700); **Mitchell Mogal** (226-8378); **Odds & Ends Sundries** (Brooklyn, 854-1453).

many toys & games

(including the Fisher-Price line)

*****Twenty-Third St. Toy Distr.** (675-6930); ****Romano Trdg.** (581-4248); ****Toys 'R' Us** (Brooklyn, 258-2061); ****Triest Export** (246-1548.); **City of Bargains** (Brooklyn, 375-1000); **G & Sons Dept. Store** (Brooklyn, 438-2604); **Lee-Or Discount** (Brooklyn, 377-1010); **Rite** (477-0280); **Valco Discount** (Queens, 274-1200).

computer-games (& SEE: CH. 1, "SMALL")

****Toys 'R' Us** (Brooklyn, 258-2061).

tricks & jokes

29: TOYS, GAMES & HOBBIES

Paramount Calendar & Specialty (686-6746).

STORES-DIRECTORY

Phone a store before you go out of your way to visit it. Especially do this during July and August, when most establishments reduce or eliminate weekend-hours.

In the listings below, "*" means especially recommended, "+" means that the store offers a bonus discount to BF readers, "ch." and "c.c." mean respectively checks and credit cards, and "exch." and "rfd." mean respectively exchange and refund. Nearest subway-stops are shown. For example, "B-D-F to 47" means to take the B, D, or F train to 47th Street. Store-hours are also indicated, with days of the week abbreviated, like "M-S 8-6."

A&R Novelty, Brooklyn, 1222 Flatbush Av. (Ditmas), 856-8070, D-M-QB to Beverly, 3-4 to Beverly, M-S 9:30-6, ch., no c.c., 24-day exch. or rfd. Small selection. Sells: **Some Toys & Games, Jewelry & Gifts, Stationery & Art Supplies.**

** **Cho's Variety**, 121 Chambers St. (Church-W. B'wy), 349-7544, A-CC-1-2-3 to Chambers, M-S 11-6, all cash, exch. or rfd. Small store. Street-stand. Sells: **Some Toys & Games, Clothing—Men's, Clothing—Women's, Personal Accessories.**

City of Bargains, Brooklyn, 1111 Av. J (Coney Is. Av.), 375-1000, D-M-QB to Av. J, M-F 9:30-7, S 10-6, Sun 10-5, all cash, exch., no rfd. Sells: **Many Toys & Games, Housewares.**

+ **Doll Hs. & Miniature Factory**, Brooklyn, 1871 Albany Av. (= E. 41st St.) (J), 338-8411, 3-4 to Flatbush Av., plus a long walk, hours by appt., all cash, no exch. or rfd. Everything for the doll-house. Bonus discount to BF readers: 5% to 10%. Sells: **Hobbies.**

* **Eighty-Eight Cent Shops**, 591 Lexington Av. (52), 753-6969, E-F to Lex. Av., M-F 9:30-6; 1457 Broadway (41), 354-0111, N-QB-RR-1-2-3-7 to 42 & Times Square, M-F 7:15-6, Sun 12-6; 33 W. 8 (5th-6th), 475-6951, A-AA-B-CC-D-E-F to 4, Sun-F 11-10, S 11-12; 89 Chambers St. (B'wy-Church), 267-6722, A-CC-1-2-3 to Chambers, N-RR to City Hall, M-F 7:30-6; 144 Fulton St. (B'wy), 964-2142, A-CC-J-M-RR-2-3-4-5 to B'wy-Nassau & Fulton, M-F 7:30-6. All stores: all cash, exch. or rfd. Everything in store is 88 cents; only the Fulton and Chambers stores have areas set aside for more expensive merchandise. Sells: **Some Toys & Games, Dinnerware & Cookware, Foods, Health & Beauty Aids, Home-Improvement Items, Housewares, Stationery & Art Supplies.**

First Cost, 90 E. 42nd St. at Park Av., 697-0244, 4-5-6-7 to Grand Central, M-F 8-7, SSun 10-5; Queens, 46-20 108 St., Corona, 271-1121, 7 to 111, ThS 9-6, F 9-9. Both stores: all cash, 7-day exch. or rfd. Sells: **Some Toys & Games, Clothing—Children's, Clothing—Men's, Clothing—Women's, Dinnerware & Cookware, Foods, Health & Beauty Aids, Home-Improvement Items, Housewares, Jewelry & Gifts, Sporting Goods, Warehouse Salvage Job-Lot.**

** **Fun Creators**, 15 E. 30 (Mad.), 3rd floor, 685-4280, 6 to 28, M-F 9-5, all cash, exch., no rfd. Stuffed animals, stocking stuffers, dolls, music boxes, chess sets. Sells: **Some Toys & Games.**

G & Sons Dept. Store, Brooklyn, 4806 New Utrecht Av., 438-2604, B to 50th St., MTTh 10-9, WSun 10-6, F 10-6, ch., c.c., exch. or rfd. Sells: **Many Toys & Games, Health & Beauty Aids, Housewares, Sporting Goods, Stationery & Art Supplies.**

Global Imports, 160 5th Av. at 21st St., 741-0700, N-RR to 23rd St., M-F 8-5, all cash, 7-day exch. or rfd. Sells: **Some Toys & Games, Housewares, Recordings & Tapes, Smoking Supplies.**

** **G.M.E. Stuffed Toy Animals**, pier 40 at Clarkson St. off the Hudson River, 328-7345, 1 to Houston, T-Sun 11-6, ch., no c.c., exch., no rfd. Only stuffed toy animals, some of which are very large. Sells: **Some Toys & Games.**

Habild of New Dorp, Staten Island, 60 Winham Av. (New Dorp Ln.), 987-4335, no subway stop nearby, M-S 10-8, Sun 12-6, ch., c.c., exch. or rfd. Kits, planes, trains. Sells: **Hobbies.**

*** **Job Lot Trdg.**, 140 Church St. (Warren-Chambers), 962-4142, A-CC-1-2-3 to Chambers; 412 5th Av. (37-8), 398-9210, B-D-F to 42. Both stores: M-F

29: TOYS, GAMES & HOBBIES

8-5:30, S 8-4:30, all cash, 15-day exch. or rfd. Both are huge stores, with terrific selections. Sells: **Some Toys & Games, Clothing—Men's, Dinnerware & Cookware, Foods, Home-Improvement Items, Housewares, Jewelry & Gifts, Linens, Personal Accessories, Sporting Goods, Stationery & Art Supplies, Warehouse Salvage Job-Lot.**

Lee-Or Discount, Brooklyn, 1113 Av. J (Coney Is. Av.), 377-1010, D-M-QB to Av. J, Sun-Th 9:30-7, F 9:30-3, all cash, exch., no rfd. Sells: **Many Toys & Games, Appliances, Housewares.**

+ **Mills Sales, 889 Broadway at 19th St., 477-1000, LL-N-QB-RR-4-5-6 to Union Sq., N-RR to 23rd St., M-F 9-5, S 9-2, all cash, no exch. or rfd. No retail sales (wholesale only) Labor Day through Xmas. A specialty here is steel ball-point pens super-cheap by the dozen. Bonus discount to BF readers: 5%. Sells: **Some Toys & Games, Appliances, Dinnerware & Cookware, Home-Improvement Items, Jewelry & Gifts, Personal Accessories, Stationery & Art Supplies.**

Mitchell Mogal, 440 Broadway (Grand), 226-8378, J-M-N-QB-RR-6 to Canal, M-F 9-5, all cash, exch., no rfd. Terrific on Wiss scissors; also on miniature capguns. Sells: **Some Toys & Games, Fabrics, Yarns & Notions, Jewelry & Gifts, Personal Accessories.**

*** **Odd Job Trdg.**, 7 E. 40 (Mad.), 686-6825, B-D-F to 42, 7 to 5th Av.; 66 W. 48 (6th Av.), 575-0477, B-D-F to 47. Both stores: M-Th 8-5:30, F 8-3, Sun 10-5, ch., no c.c., 15-day exch. or rfd. Sells: **Some Toys & Games, Clothing—Men's, Dinnerware & Cookware, Foods, Health & Beauty Aids, Home-Improvement Items, Housewares, Linens, Personal Accessories, Stationery & Art Supplies, Warehouse Salvage Job-Lot.**

** **Odds & Ends Job-Lots**, Queens, 88-09 Jamaica Av., Woodside, 441-6878, J to Woodhaven Blvd., M-S 9-6, Sun 9-3; Queens, 57-60 Woodside Av., Woodside, phoneless, 7 to 61st St., M-Th 10-7, F 10-9, S 9-6, Sun 9-5. Both stores: all cash, exch. or rfd. Sells: **Some Toys & Games, Dinnerware & Cookware, Health & Beauty Aids, Home-Improvement Items, Housewares, Jewelry & Gifts, Recordings & Tapes, Warehouse Salvage Job-Lot.**

Odds & Ends Sundries, Brooklyn, 4809 New Utrecht Av., 854-1453, B to 50th St., Sun-Th 10-6, F 10-1, ch., no c.c., exch. or rfd. Sells: **Some Toys & Games, Clothing—Men's, Clothing—Women's, Personal Accessories.**

Paramount Calendar & Specialty, 52 W. 29 (6th Av.), 686-6746&5139, N-RR to 28th St., M-F 9-5:30, all cash, no exch. or rfd. Sells: **Tricks & Jokes, Jewelry & Gifts.**

Red Caboose, 16 W. 45 (5th-6th), 4th floor (fire there, temporarily closed), 575-0155 & 244-2102, B-D-F to 47, irregular hours (usually M-S 11:30-7), ch., c.c. +5%, no exch. or rfd. Trains. Sells: **Hobbies.**

Rite, 113 Ludlow St. (Delancey), 477-0280, F-J-M to Delancey & Essex, 7 days 9-6, all cash, exch., no rfd. Fisher-Price. Sells: **Many Toys & Games.**

** **Romano Trdg.**, 628 W. 45th St. on 12th Av., 581-4248, A-AA-CC-E to 42, plus a long walk, M-F 8-5:30, S 8-5, all cash, exch. or rfd. Very cooperative. A little bit of everything, designer-name and major brand items. Sells: **Many Toys & Games, Appliances, Clothing—Men's, Jewelry & Gifts, Office Equipment, Personal Accessories, Stationery & Art Supplies.**

Roundhouse, 14 W. 45 (5th Av.), up 1 flight, 575-1753, B-D-F to 47, M-F 10-6, S 10-5, ch., c.c., exch., no rfd. Trains, kits. Sells: **Hobbies.**

** **Toys 'R' Us**, Brooklyn, 2875 Flatbush Av. (Belt Pkwy.), 258-2061, no subway stop nearby, M-S 10-9, Sun 11-5, ch., c.c., 90-day exch. or rfd. Large selection. Other stores nationwide. Sells: **Many Toys & Games, Computer-Games, Bikes.**

** **Triest Export**, 560 12th Av. (44), 246-1548., A-AA-CC-E to 42, plus a long walk, Sun-F 7-6, all cash, no exch. or rfd. Very busy. Expect long wait on line. Popular with seamen and foreign tourists. Sells: **Many Toys & Games, Appliances, Cameras & Optical Eqt., Clothing—Men's, Personal Accessories.**

*** **Twenty-Third St. Toy Distr.**, 23 W. 23 (5th Av.), 675-6930, N-RR to 23rd St., B-F to 23, M-Th 8:30-6, F 8:30-2, Oct.-Dec. Sun 10-4, ch., no c.c., exch., no rfd. Fisher-Price, Milton Bradley, etc. Sells: **Many Toys & Games.**

Valco Discount, Queens, 32-40 & 32-62 Steinway St., Astoria, 274-1200 & 545-8443, F-GG-N to Steinway St., M-W 10-7, ThF 10-8, SSun 10:30-5:30, ch., no c.c., exch. or rfd. Large selection. Sells: **Many Toys & Games, Bikes, Housewares, Sporting Goods, Stationery & Art Supplies.**

30:
WAREHOUSE SALVAGE JOB-LOT
Expect 40-80% discounts.

These are orphanages for stranded and lonely merchandise. If the parents (the manufacturer, distributor, or retailer) have died (gone bankrupt) or have simply abandoned their children (gone into a different line of business, or decided that they need instant cash for their entire inventory so that they can pay some pressing bills, or etc.), a job-lot salvage operation will take the merchandise in and put it up for adoption—and you may end up being the "foster-parent," at 50 cents on the dollar. The children at these "merchandise-orphanages" change constantly, so you won't know what to expect to find there from one month to the next.

The world's greatest store of this type may well be the **Job Lot Trading Co.**, which until recently had only one location, at 140 Church St., near Chambers. I've been told that this outlet does a larger dollar-volume of sales per square foot of floor-space than any other store in the world, and I believe it. At lunch-time on weekdays, or any time on Saturdays, the place is so packed with customers jammed elbow-to-elbow throughout both of the large selling-floors, that you'd think the merchandise were being given away. However, the enormous success of this place isn't due merely to the consistently low prices; some other job-lot dealers are as cheap, but none is quite as successful. The key is rather that you'll find here the world's most attractive bunch of orphans, so everybody wants to adopt them. I've never once seen here the kind of thing I've encountered at least occasionally at all other job-lot dealers: merchandise that *looks* like leftovers. The buyers for this operation resist the temptation to take in battered or junky items.

Incidentally, if you don't happen to enjoy elbow-to-elbow shopping, you'll prefer the Job Lot Trading Co.'s midtown store on 5th Av. between 37th and 38th Streets. It has twice the floor-space, with the same merchandise and the same number of shoppers, so you'll have more room to breathe.

The closest thing to Job Lot Trading Co. is **Odd Job Trading Co.**, on 40th St. just east of 5th Av.; and 48th St. just east of 6th Av. (The latter is the larger of the two stores.) They're almost as selective with their merchandise as is the Job Lot. (I should point out, however, that this place ought not to be confused with the well-advertised chain, Odd Lot Trading Co., which is far inferior, and which just barely made the ratings in this book.)

Weber's Job Lot, with three stores—8th Av. at 35th St., Church St. at Warren, and Broadway at 71st—has less-consistent bargains, but sometimes even more sensational ones than at the previous two mentioned operations. Some of the stuff is schlock; some is very good. Often, the displays don't do justice to the offerings. There's a good deal of damaged merchandise here, but even some of this is actually better than it looks.

First Cost, 42nd St. at Park Av. in Manhattan, and with another branch in Corona Queens, is another place with poor displays and some schlocky-looking stuff mixed in with the handsome.

First Cost is affiliated with the Commodities Assistance Corporation, the world's largest transportation salvage company, which is a wholesaler but not retailer of job-lot merchandise. The literature C.A.C. sends out to prospective clients, seeking lots of distressed or abandoned merchandise for wholesale distribution, is informative for the general consumer, because it explains how the job-lot business works. So I'll quote from it:

"We will purchase virtually any commodity. . . . Lost, unidentified, abandoned and damaged goods are our business. From chemicals to foodstuffs, clothing to industrial hardware, housewares, automotive parts, etc., no lot is too small or too unusual. . . . Even small lots or single items can be disposed of quickly through our own retail store (First Cost). Our research department can identify and appraise your most unusual items. Our multi-lingual field representatives will travel anywhere, on behalf of you or your clients, in order to dispose of problem merchandise, thereby reducing both your dock accumulation and financial losses. . . . We pay you cash. . . . You reduce your losses."

Along the same lines, the Job Lot Trading Co., which is strictly a retail-operation, rather than wholesale-retail, ran its own ad in the *New York Times*, saying: "Our company, with $35 million in annual sales, is prepared to purchase your supplies or obsolete inventories. Your invoices will be paid within 7 days from receipt of goods. We do not advertise your merchandise and will not disturb your normal distribution channels."

Specialized Job-Lot Stores

Some job-lot dealers specialize in specific categories of merchandise. The following are the best of these:

Alexander's Hardware, downtown on Reade St., between Broadway and Church, carries mostly industrial leftovers that have usefulness to the average consumer. It's the kind of treasure-trove that warrants a good hour for browsing, because some of this store's best bargains will be found in obscure crevices: for example, Sabatier-quality knives that the store itself occasionally makes and sells for $2-$3 (worth five times that).

Frankel's Discount Clothing, in Brooklyn at 3rd Av. and 40th St. This is certainly the City's best outlet for work-and-outdoor clothing, including top-name Western boots at half price.

Anything & Everything, in Brooklyn at Av. X near Nostrand. This is like a 30-50%-off supermarket but without fresh produce. The lowest-priced general foodstore in the City.

In addition, for those looking to buy clothing, on Warren St. and also along its neighbor Chambers St., will be found several stores specializing in job-lots of clothing for both men and women. These are the streets bordering the downtown store of the Job Lot Trading Co., and a block south of Alexander's Hardware. Warren, Chambers, and Reade Streets, from Broadway to West Broadway,

30: WAREHOUSE SALVAGE JOB-LOT

is New York's job-lot shopping paradise. The neighborhood is open for business generally 9-6 weekdays, 9-4 Saturdays (except July and August, when it's weekdays only). See map entitled "Chambers St. & Financial District," in Chapter 45.

Now, for the ratings, and the "hard facts," about these and the other job-lot dealers:

RECOMMENDED STORES:
STORES-DIRECTORY

Phone a store before you go out of your way to visit it. Especially do this during July and August, when most establishments reduce or eliminate weekend-hours.

In the listings below, "*" means especially recommended, "+" means that the store offers a bonus discount to BF readers, "ch." and "c.c." mean respectively checks and credit cards, and "exch." and "rfd." mean respectively exchange and refund. Nearest subway-stops are shown. For example, "B-D-F to 47" means to take the B, D, or F train to 47th Street. Store-hours are also indicated, with days of the week abbreviated, like "M-S 8-6."

* **Abbie's General Store**, 306 8th Av. (25-6), 349-3394, A-AA-CC-E to 23, 7 days 9-6, all cash, exch., no rfd. Small store. Specializes in new broken radios and calculators sold cheap as-is. Sells: **Job Lots, Personal Accessories, Recordings & Tapes.**

** **Alee Discount**, 85 Chambers St. (B'wy-Church), 619-2980, A-CC-1-2-3 to Chambers, N-RR to City Hall, M-F 9-6, S 10-5, ch., c.c., 10-day exch. or rfd. Sells: **Job Lots, Clothing—Children's, Clothing—Men's, Clothing—Women's, Linens.**

*** **Alexander's Hardware**, 60 Reade St. (B'wy), 267-0336, N-RR to City Hall, A-CC-1-2-3 to Chambers, M-F 8:30-6, S 8:30-5, ch., c.c., exch. or rfd. Large selection. Merits a long time browsing. Has great bargains in some obscure corners. Often has top quality cutlery at incredibly low prices. Much furniture-hardware. Abrasives. Sells: **Job Lots, Home-Improvement Items, Stationery & Art Supplies.**

*** **Anything & Everything**, Brooklyn, 2930 Av. X (Nostrand), 332-1508, no subway stop nearby, MTWF 10-6, Th 10-9, S 10-6, Sun 12-5, all cash, exch. or rfd. Large selection. Practically a super-discount supermarket, but specializing in packaged non-perishable foods, etc., no fresh produce. Sells: **Job Lots, Foods, Housewares, Pets.**

** **Bob's Discount**, 109 Ludlow St. (Delancey), 674-4296, F-J-M to Delancey & Essex, W-M 10-5, all cash, exch., no rfd. Sells: **Job Lots, Clothing—Men's, Personal Accessories, Sporting Goods.**

Canal Street Discount, 255 Canal (Lafayette), 226-8796, J-M-N-QB-RR-6 to Canal, M-S 10-6, all cash, exch. or rfd. Sells: **Job Lots, Linens.**

Canal Surplus, 363 Canal St. (Wooster), 966-3275, A-AA-CC-E-1 to Canal, 7 days 9:30-7, all cash, exch., no rfd. Sells: **Job Lots, Home-Improvement Items.**

***+ **C.O.M.B. Co.**, 6850 Wayzata Blvd., Minneapolis, MN 55426, 1-800-328-0609, catalog is free if you mention this book, c.c., exch., no rfd. Takes mailorders. Catalog. Very cooperative. Catalog is free only if you mention Bargain Finder. Sells: **Job Lots, Cameras & Optical Eqt., Home-Improvement Items, Jewelry & Gifts, Personal Accessories.**

Dr. Schlock's, 19 Warren St. (B'wy-Church), 766-8627, A-CC-1-2-3 to Chambers, N-RR to City Hall, M-F 8-6, S 8:30-5, all cash, exch. or rfd. Small store. Sells: **Job Lots, Dinnerware & Cookware, Fabrics, Yarns & Notions, Foods.**

First Cost, 90 E. 42nd St. at Park Av., 697-0244, 4-5-6-7 to Grand Central, M-F 8-7, SSun 10-5; Queens, 46-20 108 St., Corona, 271-1121, 7 to 111, ThS 9-6, F 9-9. Both stores: all cash, 7-day exch. or rfd. Sells: **Job Lots, Clothing—Children's, Clothing—Men's, Clothing—Women's, Dinnerware & Cookware, Foods, Health & Beauty Aids, Home-Improvement Items, Housewares, Jewelry & Gifts, Sporting Goods, Toys, Games & Hobbies.**

*** **Frankel's Discount Clothing**, Brooklyn, 3924 3rd Av. at 40th St.,

30: WAREHOUSE SALVAGE JOB-LOT

768-9788 & 788-9402, B-N-RR to 36th St., W-S 10-7, Sun 10-5, c.c., no ch., exch. or rfd. Large selection. Especially good on Frye boots. This place is basically an army-navy type store with casual-clothing job lots. Sells: **Job Lots, Clothing—Children's, Clothing—Men's, Clothing—Women's, Sporting Goods.**

*** **Fredwin**, 130 E. 44 (Lex), 661-2766, 4-5-6-7 to Grand Central; 77 New St. (Wall), 269-9130, J-M-RR-2-3 to Wall & Broad Sts., 4-5 to Wall St., N-RR-1 to Rector. Both stores: M-F 8-6, all cash, 5-day exch. or rfd. Affiliated with Winfred, Scott's Dress, and Stuart's. All merchandise sells for below its original wholesale—at least two-thirds discount. Sells: **Job Lots, Clothing—Women's.**

*** **Half-Price Store**, Brooklyn, 2962 Av. U (Nostrand), 934-6938, D-M-QB to Av. U, plus a long walk, M-S 10-6, Sun 12-5, ch., no c.c., exch. or rfd. Large selection. Top name-brands. Stock changes often. Everything is discounted 50% or more. Sells: **Job Lots, Jewelry & Gifts.**

*** **Job Lot Trdg.**, 140 Church St. (Warren-Chambers), 962-4142, A-CC-1-2-3 to Chambers; 412 5th Av. (37-8), 398-9210, B-D-F to 42. Both stores: M-F 8-5:30, S 8-4:30, all cash, 15-day exch. or rfd. Both are huge stores, with terrific selections. Sells: **Job Lots, Clothing—Men's, Dinnerware & Cookware, Foods, Home-Improvement Items, Housewares, Jewelry & Gifts, Linens, Personal Accessories, Sporting Goods, Stationery & Art Supplies, Toys, Games & Hobbies.**

* **Leon**, 1 Essex (Canal), 254-1880, F to E. Broadway, Sun-F 11:30-6, ch., no c.c., 5-day exch. or rfd. Sportswear closeouts. Sells: **Job Lots, Clothing—Women's.**

*+ **Mr. Excitement**, Queens, 81-53 Lefferts Blvd. at Cuthbert, 847-3600, E-F to Union Tnpk., TThFS 11-6, ch., c.c., exch. or rfd. Small store. Bonus discount to BF readers: 10% to 20%. Sells: **Job Lots, Clothing—Men's.**

* **No Name**, 28 and 30 Warren St. (Church), 766-9766, A-CC-1-2-3 to Chambers, N-RR to City Hall, M-S 8-6, all cash, exch., no rfd. Arrow shirts, thirds and damaged. Other closeouts and odd lots. Sells: **Job Lots, Clothing—Men's.**

*** **Odd Job Trdg.**, 7 E. 40 (Mad.), 686-6825, B-D-F to 42, 7 to 5th Av.; 66 W. 48 (6th Av.), 575-0477, B-D-F to 47. Both stores: M-Th 8-5:30, F 8-3, Sun 10-5, ch., no c.c., 15-day exch. or rfd. Sells: **Job Lots, Clothing—Men's, Dinnerware & Cookware, Foods, Health & Beauty Aids, Home-Improvement Items, Housewares, Linens, Personal Accessories, Stationery & Art Supplies, Toys, Games & Hobbies.**

** **Odd Lot Trdg.**, 33 W. 34 (5th-6th Avs.), 736-5243, B-D-F-N-QB-RR to 34; Queens, 19-40 37th St., Astoria, 932-3534, RR to Ditmars; Queens, 28-32 Steinway St., Astoria, 545-5604, RR to 30th Av., F-GG-N to Steinway St.; Queens, 103-54 94th St., Forest Hills, 263-5608, E-F to 75th Av.; Queens, 162-03 Jamaica Av., Jamaica, 657-4242, E-F to Parsons Blvd.; Queens, 103-54 94th St., Ozone Park, 738-2944, A-CC to Rockaway Blvd.; Brooklyn, 503 Fulton St., 625-7926, 2-3 to Hoyt; Brooklyn, 1166 E. 92nd St., 272-1482, LL to Rockaway Pkwy. All stores: MTWS 10-6, ThF 10-8, Sun 11-5, c.c., no ch., 7-day exch. or rfd. Other stores throughout the greater metropolitan area. Sells: **Job Lots, Dinnerware & Cookware, Health & Beauty Aids, Stationery & Art Supplies.**

** **Odds & Ends Job-Lots**, Queens, 88-09 Jamaica Av., Woodside, 441-6878, J to Woodhaven Blvd., M-S 9-6, Sun 9-3; Queens, 57-60 Woodside Av., Woodside, phoneless, 7 to 61st St., M-Th 10-7, F 10-9, S 9-6, Sun 9-5. Both stores: all cash, exch. or rfd. Sells: **Job Lots, Dinnerware & Cookware, Health & Beauty Aids, Home-Improvement Items, Housewares, Jewelry & Gifts, Recordings & Tapes, Toys, Games & Hobbies.**

* **Park Av. Job Lot**, 270 Park Av. S. (21), 673-7536, 6 to 23, M-S 9-6, all cash, 7-day exch., no rfd. Many Slavic gift items. Sells: **Job Lots, Clothing—Women's, Health & Beauty Aids, Jewelry & Gifts.**

*** **Scott's Dress**, 30 E. 23 (Mad.), 982-2131, N-RR to 23rd St., 6 to 23; 179 Broadway (Dey), 962-9926, N-RR-1 to Cortlandt. Both stores: M-F 8-6, all cash, 5-day exch. or rfd. Affiliated with Winfred, Fredwin's and Stuart's. All merchandise sells for below its original wholesale price—at least two-thirds discount. Sells: **Job Lots, Clothing—Women's.**

Shoes, Boots, Etc., 63 Warren St. at W. B'wy, 285-9750, A-CC-1-2-3 to Chambers, M-S 10-6, all cash, exch., no rfd. Small store. Many irregulars of military-surplus-type clothing and camping gear. Sells: **Job Lots, Clothing—Men's, Sporting Goods.**

So Cheap, 704 Broadway (4), 982-7918, B-D-F-6 to B'wy-Laf. & Bleecker, M-F 11-6:30, S 10:30-6, all cash, no exch. or rfd. Uneven values, occasionally terrific. Many damaged items. Sells: **Job Lots, Clothing—Men's, Clothing—Women's.**

*** **Stuart's**, 1420 St. Nicholas Av. (181), 928-9691, 1 to 181, M-S 10-6, all

30: WAREHOUSE SALVAGE JOB-LOT

cash, 5-day exch. or rfd. Affiliated with Winfred, Fredwin, and Scott's Dress. All merchandise sells for below its original wholesale price—at least two-thirds discount. Sells: **Job Lots, Clothing—Women's.**

The Bargain Lot, 333 7th Av. (28-9), 736-1346, 1 to 28, Sun-F 8-7:30, all cash, no exch. or rfd. Sells: **Job Lots, Health & Beauty Aids.**

Tri-Surplus, 63 Reade St. (B'wy-Church), 964-9237, A-CC-1-2-3 to Chambers, M-F 9-5:30, S 9-4:30, ch., no c.c., exch. or rfd. Small store. Small selection. Sells: **Job Lots, Furnishings.**

** **United Salvage Alka Seltzer**, 7 E. Broadway (Catherine), 962-5567, J-M-N-QB-RR-6 to Canal, J-M-RR-4-5-6 to Chambers & Bkln. Bridge, M-Th 10-5:30, Sun 9:30-3:30, all cash, no exch. or rfd. Small store. Small selection. Sells: **Job Lots, Clothing—Men's.**

Victoria Stores, 114 Worth St. (B'wy), 619-1338, N-RR to City Hall, M-F 9:30-6, all cash, 14-day exch. or rfd. Sells: **Job Lots, Linens.**

** **Weber's Job Lot**, 505 8th Av. at 35th, 564-7668, A-AA-CC-E to 34, M-F 10-6:30, S 10-6; 136 Church St. at Warren, 564-7668, A-CC-1-2-3 to Chambers, M-S 8-6; 2064 Broadway at 71st, 787-1644, 1-2-3 to 72, M-F 9-9, S 9-6, Sun 12-6. All stores: c.c., no ch., 7-day exch. or rfd. Some terrific values; others not good. Some prices wrongly marked on items each time I was at both stores; checkout counter said 'It's an error.' Sells: **Job Lots, Dinnerware & Cookware, Health & Beauty Aids, Home-Improvement Items, Jewelry & Gifts, Linens, Personal Accessories, Stationery & Art Supplies.**

*** **Winfred**, 2183 Broadway (77-8), 874-8465, 1 to 79, M-S 10-6, all cash, 5-day exch. or rfd. Affiliated with Fredwin, Scott's Dress, and Stuart's. All merchandise sells for below its original wholesale price—at least two-thirds discount. Sells: **Job Lots, Clothing—Women's.**

31: SERVICES

You're probably aware of all the caveats that must apply to any recommendation of a service. Not only are such cautions a matter of basic good sense, but if you're acquainted with the previous editions of this book, you may remember that I was extremely reluctant to endorse any services at all. One reason for this is that I was afraid that by recommending a place I'd cause it to become overbooked. That concern turned out to have little foundation: A few of the businesses expanded, yet there were no significant difficulties either with added pressure on prices, or with quality-control. One other—and more real—problem, however, has to do with the inevitable fact that occasionally there are going to be performance-snags even with the most conscientious and reliable service-provider. Finally, I can't personally check out each place the same way I check prices at a store. Here, there are no brands, no standard items—we're dealing basically with handwork, not mass-production; no two "items" are exactly the same. Therefore, these endorsements can't be recommendations in the same sense that a listing of a store is, and I don't intend them to be interpreted as if they were.

My basis for the following selections is usually two-fold: the price is definitely low, and I've heard (from sources I respect) that the service is good. In some instances, however, I've actually employed the particular service myself, and then it's with some degree of personal conviction—and not by mere heresay—that I make the recommendation as to quality. Wherever this is the case, I indicate so.

Hairstylists

First will be listed inexpensive professional hairstylists. Then will come a group of hairstyling schools which have "clinics" for the public, where prices on a wash, cut, and dry or set, run about a half to a third of the rates at the least expensive professional salons. At these schools, senior students do your hair under the supervision of their teachers. The overall quality that can be expected—so I hear from people who've used them—is about the same as you'll find at the average professional salon, but there's this disadvantage: If you like what's been done on your first visit, and want the same person to style your hair next time, he probably won't be there—he'll more likely have graduated. Regular haircuts also are very inexpensive at the four-star-rated beauty-schools, but at the others are not.

PROFESSIONALS:

****Tony's**, 2 E. 32 (right off 5th Av.), 684-4864. This is where I go. A highly particular lady-friend of mine also has used him for years.

31: SERVICES

When you tell him what you want, he understands—and he does it just as you had imagined. The place looks like a barber-shop, but does top quality work. Ask for Tony.

**Mr. Edward, 1400A 2nd Av. (72-3), 650-9200.

*Arista, 2511 Broadway (93-4), 678-9805. A barber-shop that does hairstyling. Ask for Tony.

*Geometric Haircut, 807 Lex. Av. (62), 2nd floor rear, 832-0683.

Top Men, 35 7th Av. (12-3), 691-0672.

On Stage, 127 E. 60 (Park Av.), 2nd floor, 753-7722.

HAIRSTYLING SCHOOLS:

****Jingles, Empire State Bldg., basement, facing elevators, 695-9365. Graduate hairstylists from all over the world come here to learn the newest styles and techniques.

****Ultissima Beauty Institute, 22 W. 34, 2nd floor, 564-5777; Brooklyn, 2384 86th St., 373-2400; Ridgewood, 54-40 Myrtle Av., 456-5558; Flushing, 136-12 Roosevelt Av., 886-2300; and 6 locations on Long Island.

****Hair Design Institute, Brooklyn, 169 Livingston St. (Smith), 2nd floor, 857-9060.

****Atlas Barber School, 44 3rd Av. (10), 475-1360.

****School of Hair Design, 161 W. 66 (B'way), 496-8650.

***+Wilfred Academy, 1657 Broadway (51-52), 265-1122; Brooklyn, 81 Willoughby St. (Bridge), 855-2750; Jamaica, 91-14 Merrick Blvd., 658-6240; Bronx, 210 E. 188 (at Grand Conc.), 365-5555; Staten Island, 2600 Hylan Blvd., 979-5800. Bonus discount to BF readers: **FREE first wash, cut, and blowdry or hairset, if you show this book.** ( )

***Flexer Beauty School, Flushing, 38-15 Main St., 939-4222.

*Concord Beauty School, Astoria, 38-15 Broadway, 726-8383.

*Fiance Hair Design Inst., 404 5th Av. (37), 2nd floor, 947-4731; Flushing, 39-02 Main St., 939-7733; Bronx, 2435 Grand Concourse (188), 584-8040.

*Bo-Mar Beauty School, Brooklyn, 5605 5th Av., 439-6466.

Telephone-Answering & Mail-Pickup

****+Benson, 307-1510, 1697 B'wy (53), rm. 906A. I've heard good things about their service, but I had to wait several times on the phone in order to get information from them. **Bonus discount to BF readers: One month free if you mention this book.**

****+Echo, 724-7554, 2067 B'wy (72), Rm. 41. I've heard good things about their service. **Bonus BF discount: One free month.**

***+Standby, 541-7600, 250 W. 54 (B'wy), rm. 811. A friend who's used them for years says that their service is excellent. But I've had to wait on the phone to get information from them. **Bonus discount to BF readers: One month of free service.**

***+On Call, 541-9400, 250 W. 54. **Bonus BF discount: One free month.**

**Ansa-Ring, 5-31 50th Av., L.I.C., 361-2078. (Located a half block from the first Queens stop on the #7 subway.) Offers many unique services, and charges on an equally unique basis, per call (or letter) handled, with a one-time up-front fee. Provides the least expensive way to set up with a full "office" and "secretary."

*+**Action**, 279-3870, 134 W. 32 (B'wy), rm. 602. **Bonus discount to BF readers: 10%.**

***Response**, 868-3793&3330, 316 5th Av. (at 32), rm. 301.

***Abbey**, 490-1888 & 799-9190, 51 E. 42 (Mad.), rm. 517, and 2067 Broadway (72), Rm 27.

***Pamela's**, 242-3900, 249 W. 18 (8th Av.).

***Budget**, 719-5322, 32 W. 38, rm. 4.

+**Actor's**, 753-2310 & 757-3995, 701 7th Av. (at 47), rm. 900. **Bonus discount to BF readers: 10%.**

AAA, 677-2200, 175 5th Av. (at E. 23), rm. 1101.

Exec. & Prof. Svcs., 233-1626, 170 Broad St., Red Bank, NJ.

Long-Distance Telephone

**Metrophone, 1-800-631-7144. (Western Union.)

**ITT, 1-800-438-9428.

MCI, 1-800-234-2140.

Sprint, 1-800-521-4949.

Telex

**Telegraphic Word Processing, 947-2722, 500 8th Av. (35-6), rm. 910. For small-volume users.

***Action Telex**, 944-1080, 230 W. 41 (7th-8th), rm. 1603. For larger-volume users. Numeric answerback. No extra charge for telexgrams.

Auto-Typed Letters

Whether it's to invite people to your big party, or to send out urgent announcements for the next meeting of your social club, or simply for business, this one's a real winner:

***Great Neck Letter Service, 300 Northern Blvd., Great Neck, NY 11021, 1-516-487-5676. I've used them, and found their service to be extraordinarily inexpensive, conscientious, and competent. They beat out all their competition in the City.

Medical & Dental

If it weren't for **Workmen's Circle**, this would be a hornet's nest. I can't, for example, simply recommend the physicians that I go to, because then they'd become even more jammed up than they already are. Here the Bargain-Finding solution will certainly have to be an institutionalized, rather than an individual, service-provider. Workmen's Circle has the following advantages: Membership is cheap and is open to all; the performance of physicians who participate in their medical program is monitored by both a physicians' panel and a lay committee; all specialists are board-certified; all the doctors agree to a pre-set reduced fee for service; and there are a variety of group health-insurance plans available (for which see Chapter 32, "Personal Finance"). For information about joining, phone 889-6800.

Cleaners

**Super, 94 Hester (Allen), 966-2226

**CLL, 127 E. Broadway (Allen), 267-8534.

*Sunshine, 506 E. 82 (York), 288-2340.
*Michel's, 2957 Broadway (116), 662-7710.
Barbara, 126 9th Av. (18), 989-5470.
Bakalian Dikran, 186 9th Av. (21), 243-4592.
Tina, 2702 Broadway (103), 864-3700.

Carpet & Upholstery Cleaners

*Bernard Roth, 265 Cherry St. (Grand), 243-3310.

Others

Appraisals, Auctions & Tag Sales: See Chapter 32.
Auto Insurance & Repair: See Chapter 2.
Copying & Printing: See Chapter 28.
Film-Developing & Photo-Reproduction: See Chapter 4.
Finance & Insurance: See Chapter 32.
Limousines: See Chapter 38.
Locksmiths: See Chapter 15.
Optometrists & Opticians: See Chapter 13.
Patent Agents: See Chapter 32.
Tailors—Custom: See Chapters 6 & 7.
Travel Agents: See Chapter 38.
Typewriter Repair: See Chapter 21.

32:
PERSONAL FINANCE

Though there are many top-selling books on this subject, the following few pages pack in more information that's useful to you than you'll usually find in many a full volume. The following are the "creme de la creme" of personal-finance services (but keep in mind the same caveats that opened the previous chapter—they apply here, too):

Savings Accounts

See **NOTE** concluding "Money Funds" below.

Checking Accounts

See "NOW Checking Accounts" below.

Money Funds

For the past three years, I've tracked the performance of all funds of $100 million or more in size, and have examined the portfolios of all the high-yielding ones. The following two are outstanding in that they alone have had consistently above-average yields combined with extremeley safe, conservative, investments (meaning: exclusively federal-government obligations; or else Moody's P-1 and S&P's A-1 commercial paper, no Eurodollar CD's, only FDIC-members' bankers' acceptances, and repurchase-agreements only with Federal Reserve member banks and with nationally listed brokerage houses):

******Fairfax Asset Growth Fund**, 17 Light St., Baltimore, MD 21202, 1-800-368-2552. Very high-yielding (in fact, the highest), conservatively invested, soundly state-insured—a real winner. Nominally not a money-fund, but rather a very special kind of savings-and-checking account, well worth anyone's serious consideration.

*****Government Investors Trust**, 1800 N. Kent St., Arlington, VA 22209, 1-800-336-3063. Since it was founded in February 1979, this has consistently been the top-yielding money-market fund investing strictly in federally insured U.S. Government securities. It outperforms the money-fund average, yet is invested far more conservatively than practically all the others—and as conservatively as any. Also, I've not found their phone-line to be clogged up; calls get put through fast. Unquestionably the best money-fund. I put a friend onto it, and he tells me that he's been delighted with the results.

****First Investors Cash Management Fund**, 120 Wall St. (near the East River), 742-9620 & 1-800-221-3790. I use this one. Except for the government-obligations funds such as GIT, it's at the very top of the heap safety-wise; and the yield has been the same as GIT's—which is to say, consistently above average. Their service is simply phenomenal: I've never once gotten a busy-signal; everyone there has always been totally courteous and efficient; and from the moment I phone them, they never take more than a day to wire funds to the designated other account.

NOTE: If you have more than $2,000 in a traditional savings account, you're loosing a substantial amount of interest, for no reason or advantage, and would get a much higher yield, with virtually the same degree of safety, and with more convenience (because of the free check-writing and money-wiring features, which savings accounts don't have), if you were to use one of these money funds instead. Also worth exploring are the Insured Money Market Plus Account at Citytrust (1-800-526-5368). Traditional low-interest savings accounts are outdated. NOW (interest-bearing) checking accounts (see below), combined with money funds, have replaced them. Even the new high-yield savings accounts usually don't match the yields on money funds.

Money-Fund Alternatives

*****Donald Sheldon Government Securities**, 1 Wall St. (at B'wy), 747-9215. Their super-safe government-insured GNMA's are the highest-yielding around. Minimum required investment varies, but is usually around $5,000 to $7,500. This is the best way to lock in current high yields if you expect interest rates to start falling. These GNMA's usually yield a shade higher even than the top money funds, and also higher than CD's. But if you buy them and then interest rates soar, you'll be locked into a lower old yield, and looking yearningly after those new higher money-fund rates. On the other hand, your yield on these government-insured GNMA's is often taxed at a much lower (capital-gains) rate than is the return on a CD or money fund.

Bank of New York, 1-800-942-1784, 9 Manhattan branches, 2 in Queens, others statewide in phone book. Their government-insured money-market CD's pay the top permissible interest, and are available for much lower minimum investment than other banks require (ask for their "loophole CD's"). Again, you're locking in an interest-rate.

Amalgamated Bank, 11 Union Sq., 255-6200; 54th at Broadway, 245-3200; Bronx, Co-op City, 671-1800. Their 1-year fixed-yield USave certificates have very low minimums, with fairly high interest, which is free of state and city tax.

Individual Retirement Accounts

These supply interest which is tax-free until you retire, when you'll presumably be in a lower tax-bracket. You can stash away up to $2,000 a year into an IRA, and lots of people who don't believe any longer in the Social Security system are doing precisely that. For fixed-rate IRA's, Bankers Federal Savings and Amalgamated Bank and Bank of New York usually have the edge; but Israel Discount Bank and Independence Savings Bank are normally preferable on variable-rate ones. Details on these banks are given elsewhere in this chapter. However, far better IRA's can usually be obtained through:

*****Donald Sheldon Govt. Securities**, 1 Wall St. (B'wy), 747-9215.

NOW Checking Accounts

These are interest-bearing. They're actually savings accounts with free checks (no service-charge if you meet the bank's minimum-balance requirements) replacing the old-fashioned passbook. They're superior to all other checking accounts, which they antiquate. The best NOW-account deals are found at:

Amalgamated Bank, 11 Union Sq., 255-6200; 54th at Broadway, 245-3200; Bronx, Co-op City, 671-1800.

Bankers Federal Savings, 24 John St. (Nassau), 227-4040; 340 6th Av. (4), 473-4870; 130 2nd Av. (8), 674-3350; Flushing, 187-15 Union Tnpk., 454-0700; Flushing, 156-10 N. Blvd., 961-5500; Brooklyn, 1764 Rockaway Pkwy. (L), 251-0100.

Israel Discount Bank, 511 5th (43), 551-8500; 1350 Broadway (35), 551-8750.

Independence Savings Bank, 250 Lex. Av. (34), 685-2206; Brooklyn, Atlantic & Court, 624-6620; Brooklyn, 6424 18th Av., 259-5100; Brooklyn, 23 Newkirk Plaza, 859-8888; Brooklyn, 1769 86th St., 236-4400; Bayside, 23-56 Bell Blvd., 631-4700; Bronx, 1416 East Av., 931-5000.

Travelers' Checks

They're free of that usual 1% fee at:

Barclays Bank, 19 Nassau St. (Pine), 233-4200; 3 Park Av. (33), 689-9009; 300 Park Av. (57), 421-1400; 15 W. 50, 265-1105; 9 W. 57, 644-0850.

Credit Cards

European American Bank, 437-4300. Free Visa and MasterCard—without any annual service charges—but only if you meet rigid salary-requirements.

First Nationwide Savings, 399-2200. Free Visa if you have $1,000 in an account there.

Stockbrokers

Academic studies so numerous they'd fill this book, have repeatedly and consistently shown that "dart-board" funds—chosen entirely at random—perform as well as managed brokerage accounts. So when stockbrokers tell you that their high trading charges are necessary to pay for their research departments to select "the right" stocks for you, just hang up the phone, go out and get a set of darts, and start pummeling the pages of the *Wall Street Journal*. You'll "select" your investments equally as well that way. The only thing you're getting from a "full-service house" is somebody to throw the darts for you—and why let them? It's more fun to do it yourself. If you're going to lose money (and especially if you're not, but are going to make a killing), then you at least might as well have a ball doing it!

There's one notable exception to what I've just said: a discount stockbroker recommended below, Kenneth Kass, which unlike just about every other discount-operation, does do stock-picks, and which moreover was recently cited in a national market letter for being one of the very few whose selections have outperformed

32: PERSONAL FINANCE

the stock-market averages. In other words, if you're looking for a "full-service house," you might as well go for the one that's both better **and** cheaper.

These are the least expensive of all the discount-stockbrokers:

*****Tradex**, 425-7800 & 1-800-221-7874, 82 Beaver St. Does stocks, options, commodities. Tops on trading penny-stocks.

****Stock Cross**, 1-800-225-6196, 1 Washington Mall, Boston, Mass. 02108.

****Ovest**, 76 Beaver St. (Pearl), 23rd floor, 425-3003 & 1-800-221-5713.

****Bevill, Bresler & Schulman**, 1-800-631-1159 & call collect 1-201-994-1802, 301 S. Livingston Av., Livingston NJ 07039. The least expensive for trades of 280 shares or less.

***Odd Lots Securities**, 60 E. 42 (Park Av.), rm. 2227, 661-6755 & 1-800-221-2095.

***Kenneth Kass**, 11 Broadway (Beaver), 344-5112 & 1-800-526-4472 & 1-201-966-1595. Head office: 147 Columbia Tnpk., Florham Park, NJ 07932. Offers free research. Also on a discount basis: manages portfolios as an investment-adviser; sells tax-shelters; sells commodities-futures.

***Wall St. Discount**, 100 Wall St. (at Water St.), 28th floor, 747-5011 & 1-800-221-7990.

***Spencer-Winston**, 46 W. 47, 4th floor, 840-2444 & 398-1470.

***Pace**, 225 Park Av. (45), 490-6363 & 1-800-221-1660.

***Compusec**, 120 Broadway (Pine), 21st floor, 233-1700 & 1-800-221-7918.

Discount Brokerage, 67 Wall St. (William), 9th floor, 943-7800 & 1-800-221-8210. Sometimes slow to answer phone.

Liss, Tenner, Goldberg, 39 Broadway (Wall), rm. 1910, 483-0722 & 1-800-221-5092.

Investment Advice

****SIE Performance Review**, 2095 Broadway (73), 874-6408. This is a service which objectively rates and numerically ranks the best-performing investment publications in accord with sophisticated analytical criteria, using near-term and cumulative long-term historical data as the data-base; and lists the ten stocks most recommended for purchase, and those most recommended for sale, by the highest-performing market letters. It's the first such service that's worth its salt, and the price is not high—in fact, the best bargain of any market letter going.

***Select Information Exchange**, 2095 Broadway (73), 874-6408. This is really a discount subscription service specializing in market-letters. They have the most extensive catalog of these publications to be found anywhere. They're also the publishers of the previously-mentioned advisory service.

Mutual Funds

If you'd prefer to have your investment-decisions made for you rather than to make them yourself, then you're looking for a mutual fund. But which one? Annually at the end of August, *Forbes* magazine publishes an honor-roll of top-performing funds which have exhibited year-in and year-out excellent yields in both up and down markets. You could hardly do better than to select one of these. Here's the honors-list from the August 31, 1981, issue of *Forbes* (no asterisks here, because the ratings aren't my own, but for the detailed ratings on these and all other mutual funds, see the above-referenced source):

AMCAP Fund, Capital Research & Management, 333 S. Hope St., Los Angeles, CA 90071. 1-213-624-2780.

American General Comstock Fund, American General Capital Management, 2777 Allen Pkwy., Houston TX 77019. 1-800-231-3638.

ASA Limited, U.S. & Foreign Securities, P.O. Box 1724, FDR Station, NY, NY 10150. 754-9374.

Charter Fund, Fund Management, 2100 Republic Bank TWR, Dallas, TX 75201. 1-214-742-6567.

Founders Special Fund, Founders Mutual Depositor, 1300 First of Denver Plaza, Denver, CO 80202. 1-303-292-1820.

General American Investors, G.A.I. Corp., 330 Madison Av., NY, NY 10017. 949-2800.

International Investors, I.I. Corp., 122 E. 42, NY, NY 10017. 687-5200.

Kemper Total Return Fund, Kemper Financial, 120 S. LaSalle St., Chicago, IL 60603. 1-312-781-1121.

Madison Fund, 919 Market St., Wilmington, DE 19801. 1-302-428-3500.

Mathers Fund, 125 S. Wacker Drive, Chicago, IL 60606. 1-312-236-8215.

Mutual Shares, Heine Securities, 170 Broadway, NY, NY 10038. 267-4200 & 344-4200.

Petroleum & Resources Fund, Adams Express, 201 N. Clark St., Baltimore, MD 21201. 1-301-752-5900.

Templeton Growth Fund, Securities Fund Investors, 41 Beach Drive, St. Petersburg, FL 33701. 1-813-823-8712.

20th Century Select Investors, Investors Research, 605 W. 47 St., Kansas City, MO 64112. 1-816-531-5575.

Vance, Sanders, Special Fund, Eaton Howard, 24 Federal St., Boston, MA 02110. 1-617-482-8260 & NYC (212) 943-7570.

Weingarten Equity Fund, Prescott, Ball & Turben, 331 Madison Av., NY, NY 10017. 557-8787.

Commodities

The following recommendation should be of great interest to millionaires, but unfortunately it's not very helpful to others.

*****Advocom Corp.**, 120 Broadway (Pine), rm. 2114, 732-0871 & 1-914-631-7050, is in my opinion the most advanced, state-of-the-art, money-management firm around. They track by computer the portfolio-performance of a large and growing number of commodities-account managers, select the best, and then create "diversified portfolios of top portfolios" by pairing off outstanding commodities-managers whose records and approaches demonstrate not merely quality but also mutual complementarity. The result is a very impressive reduction in volatility and increase in predictability of high performance of each client's diversified "portfolio" of managed high-growth portfolios. With this extremely advanced technique, Advocom realistically can project for its clients far greater asset-appreciation with much better safety than has formerly been possible. In fact, they guarantee to the investor an annual after-tax net yield of 35%, at a bare minimum. The hitch is that this firm does not handle small or medium-sized accounts.

Venture-Capital Deals

There are three that I strongly recommend that seek backing. I happen to be the entrepreneur for each. Phone 242-0041 if you wish to participate, and we'll talk:

Patent pending super-insulative fill for cold-weather outergarments, boots, and gloves. Field-tests show it to be 7 times as insulative as goose down. (One-quarter inch thickness of this provides as much warmth as does nearly two inches of goose down.) Material costs no more than polyester fiberfill, and is lighter even than down. Can be laundered and dry cleaned. Seeking: venturesome clothing-manufacturer interested in royalty arrangement or outright buy; or else financial backers (minimum participation $10,000, 100% risk-capital) subsequent to presentation of prospectus.

Patented Alpha Sleeper provides comfortable sleep to passengers seated on long overnight rides. Prevents sleepless night in transit, and "crick neck" in the morning, but doesn't require increased seat-space or reduced passenger load-factors. Especially suitable for long airplane-flights, like N.Y.-Tokyo. Seeking: Consumer-products manufacturer; or else bus or airline co. backer.

Predictors' Performance, a financial data-service which would rate the performance of hundreds of securities analysts and investment advisors, based on tracking all their buy-and-sell recommendations for the past five years, showing trend-graphs of performance, for both appreciation and safety of recommended portfolios, separately for short-term, medium-term, and long-term investment-calls. Aimed primarily at bank trust departments and other fiduciaries, to help them select, hire, and fire analysts and advisors. Seeks: seed capital of $750,000. Minimum individual investment: $75,000.

Gold, Platinum, Silver

Includes precious-metal coins. All of the cheapest places are out-of-state, mainly because they save you the sales-tax:

**United Precious Metals, 1-800-327-3753, 950 N. Federal Hwy., Pompano Beach, FL 33062. A subsidiary of Investment Rarities Inc., listed below under "Diamonds."

**International Gold Bullion, 1-800-327-2811, 1 Corporate Plaza, 110 E. Broward Blvd., Ft. Lauderdale, FL 33301.

Tri-State Refining, 1-800-843-9854, 1600 A Av., Sioux Falls, SD 57104.

Fiscal & Monetary Svcs., 1-800-258-7322, 104 Congress St., Portsmouth, NH 03801.

First National Monetary, 1-800-327-0207 (ask to speak to a

salesman), 400 Town Ctr., Southfield, MI 48075.

Diamonds

For information about this volatile area of investment—and comparing diamonds versus other gemstones—See Chapter 17. However, strictly from an investment standpoint, diamonds are a very speculative play, with poor long-term potential. In fact, the entry of Australia into the market as a diamond-producer may well destroy the stabilizing force of the dying DeBeers monopoly, with consequent tumbling diamond-prices.

For recommended dealers, see page 160. For free subscription to the "Diamond Report Newsletter," which discusses the current state of the market, phone 1-800-227-1590.

Appraisals, Tag-Sales, Auctions

*Richard Schlessinger, 847-3600. Handles antiques, fine arts, and estates, for personal, business, insurance, and tax purposes. To have diamonds appraised, see Chapter 17.

Patent Agents

****Nathaniel Altman, 271 Mad. Av. (40), rm. 208, 685-2493. I've used him many times, and he certainly merits one of the most unqualified and strongest endorsements in this book. I once asked him why he charges such a tiny fraction of what everybody else does, for work that's of unsurpassed quality, and he told me, "I sleep well at night. I know I've earned my keep." Then he added, not really as an afterthought, "And besides, I love what I do." I've spoken with around 20 patent attorneys—many of whom charge 5 times what Altman does—and none of them is more competent at the patent-business. Few are *as* competent.

*Richard Miller, 233 Broadway (Murray), rm. 3612, 267-5252. He drew up one of my patents. His work is generally good.

Loans, General

The accumulated cash-value of a whole-life life-insurance policy is usually the cheapest loan-source for the insured person. If that's you, take advantage of it; contact your insurance-agent or sales rep. Then, after you've borrowed, you might consider switching to term-insurance, which is usually a better value than whole-life. (See "Insurance" below.)

Other cheap loan-sources are:

Workmen's Circle, a fraternal organization, open to all, and with a credit union that loans to the credit-worthy, at very low rates. Phone 889-6800 for information about joining. While the maximum that they will lend is only $1,500, there are other fraternal organizations where the limit is higher. For a list of other fraternals, see below, under "Insurance, Health." Ask whether they have credit unions, and if so then what the conditions and maximums are.

Provident Loan Society, non-profit pawnbrokers, with several locations in all boros but Staten Island. They offer lower rates and longer terms than other pawnbrokers. Phone 685-0380.

Loans, Bank

These include car loans, home improvement loans, and others. According to a U.S. Government study, the following nearby non-NYC banks offer lower-than-average rates: Midlantic, National Community, and United Jersey, all of N.J.; and National of Westchester, and Nanuet National, of N.Y. From my own research, the Bank of New York has the lowest rates of the major New York State banks, but the following institutions have the lowest loan-rates of all banks I've checked in New York City:

Amalgamated Bank, 11 Union Sq., 255-6200; 54th at Broadway, 245-3200; Bronx, Co-op City, 671-1800.

Merchants Bank of N.Y., 434 Broadway (Canal), 669-6600; 93 Canal St. (Eldridge), 669-6678; 757 3rd Av. (47), 669-6706; 295 5th Av. (31), 669-6666; 62 W. 47, 669-6688.

Dime Savings Bank, 643-7104&4200. 8 offices, Manhattan and Brooklyn.

Insurance

This is not really an investment. It's an expense. What you're buying is security, as opposed to future return or yield. Only Blue Cross, group health, and group life insurance even come close (90%) to repaying the moneys put in. Other forms return to premium-payers as little as ten cents on the dollar. As an insured, you're paying for security, not making an investment. But if you buy it right, it can almost become an investment. The subject here is how to buy it right.

AUTO INSURANCE: See Chapter 2.

HEALTH INSURANCE: Here the only way to save substantially is by being a member of a group; and if you aren't already in some group-plan, you'll recoup many times the dues by joining a fraternal organization. Furthermore, some fraternals also offer excellent deals on life insurance, and various other benefits such as credit unions, death and orphans' benefits, etc.

Workmen's Circle, 45 E. 33 (Mad.), 889-6800 & 686-5954. Membership is open to all. They offer Blue Cross, Blue Shield, and an excess major medical plan, all at group-rates. Also, they have a very wide range of other benefits, including homes for the aged, group travel, discounts on eyeglasses and automobiles, summer resort and children's camp, etc.

Knights of Columbus, 387-3909. Membership with coverage open only to male baptized Catholics, single or married, and to their wives (or widows), children, and grandchildren, but not to unmarried Catholic women.

Labor Zionist Alliance, 114 5th Av. (16), 989-0300.

B'nai Brith, 823 U.N. Plaza, 557-1164.

Lutheran Brotherhood, 894-1032. Open only to Lutherans. Only life insurance.

Independent Order of Foresters, 869-9100. Open to any individual of good character. Excellent life insurance, death benefits, orphans' benefits, retirement villages, and credit union; but no health insurance.

Association for Humanistic Psychology, 674-8785. Not a fraternal organization, but very good, open to anyone, and offering many excellent benefits, especially their new group health and life insurance plans. Annual membership dues are very modest.

Others for which you might qualify can be found in the Yellow Pages, under "Fraternal Organizations." Of the sources listed above, I'd first try Workmen's Circle, Assn. for Humanistic Psychology, and the Independent Order of Foresters.

LIFE INSURANCE: To compare costs, you should know the types of life insurance that are available. There are two basic kinds. First, term-insurance, which is pure insurance and nothing else. Then, whole-life (or "straight life" or "ordinary life"), which is both insurance plus a usually low-interest-bearing savings account. Each of these can be either participating (dividend-paying) or non-participating (without dividends). More recently, there have been added whole-life variants called "universal life" and "variable life," which offer a higher yield on the invested portion of the premiums, and also greater flexibility than regular whole-life; these variants, however, are not yet generally available. As a rule, you'll do best by taking out term-insurance, and by using the above-recommended money funds for the invested portion. One reason for this is that there is then no "load" or salesman's commission on the invested portion. If you're interested in the generally preferable term-insurance, you'll usually do best with the variant of that known as "revertible." Here, your premiums generally start out much lower, and they will subsequently be either raised or reduced at the end of the pre-specified term, depending on whether you have or haven't acquired some dreaded illness or otherwise become a worse insurance-risk during the interim. If things remain as they were when you initially signed on, you're considered to have proven yourself to have been a good insurance-risk, and your premiums are then lowered. Basically, you're assuming part of the risk yourself, against the possibility that your likely viability might decrease during the term, in which case your premiums will rise at the end of it.

The New York State Insurance Dept., at 2 World Trade Center, 25th floor, 488-5642, publishes and gives out free of charge a 70-page booklet, *Consumers Shopping Guide for Life Insurance*, which lists comparative cost-figures (what are called "interest-adjusted cost" indexes) for life insurance from many companies. This guide, and also a similarly titled 40-page one which explains life-insurance terms and which is also helpful, can be obtained by mail from: State of New York, Insurance Dept., Empire State Plaza, Albany, NY 12257. A more exhaustive guidebook dealing with comparative costs of all companies' life-insurance policies, and which you can find at the library, is *Interest-Adjusted Index*, by National Underwriter, Chicago. Insurance agents whom I've found to be helpful sources of information on these matters, are John Demuro at 687-0522, Alfred Braun at 679-3310, Jacob Marrus at 685-4676, Al Suzan at 688-0615, and Campbell at 227-3320.

Generally speaking, these are the best-value life-insurance suppliers (having the lowest interest-adjusted indexes):

SBLI, Savings Bank Life Insurance, available at any NY savings bank. Only participating. Maximum coverage: $30,000.

32: PERSONAL FINANCE

TIAA, Teachers Insurance & Annuity Assn., 730 3rd Av., 490-9000. Open only to college-employees and a few others. Only participating.

Home Life Non-Smokers, Al Suzan at Welger-Siegel Group, 770 Lex. Av. (60), 688-0615. Open, of course, only to non-smokers.

Fraternal organizations, for which see the list under "Health Insurance," immediately above. Especially good life-insurance deals are offered by the Independent Order of Foresters, Knights of Columbus, Assn. for Humanistic Psychology, and Lutheran Brotherhood. However, if you're joining a fraternal primarily for the low-cost life insurance, get its rates before you join. Some fraternals aren't as much of a bargain on some forms of life insurance as they are on health-insurance. Always ask what the interest-adjusted cost is for a particular kind of policy that you're considering.

Professional associations, in case you happen to belong to one that offers this. The deals here, too, are usually very good.

OTHER FORMS OF INSURANCE: Better to put the erstewhile premiums into a money-fund, relying on that growing kitty to take care of all contingencies—a form of universal coverage for all emergencies. Other forms of insurance are simply far too expensive for the meager benefits paid out; and with your own "universal coverage," you're playing the role of the "insurance company" yourself, and so making all the "profits" from your own "premiums."

There are two rules of insurance: 1) Coverage that you don't have to buy you shouldn't buy. 2) Any discretionary insurance should be self-insurance. (And then you'll not really be buying coverage at all. You'll be investing money.)

Tax-Dodges

***Donald Sheldon & Co.**, 1 Wall St., NY, NY 10005, 747-9215 & 1-800-528-6050 x. 1516. A triple-tax-exempt municipal bond fund, the N.Y. Muny Fund, with free checking.

***Kenneth Kass**, 11 Broadway (Beaver), 344-5112 & 1-800-526-4472 & 1-201-635-9494. Tax-shelter specialist.

***Universal Life Church**, 601 3rd St., Modesto, CA 95351, 1-209-527-8111 & 1-209-537-0553. The good Reverend Hensley has been ordaining so many ministers that heaven—heaven forbid—seems doomed to end up looking like the subway stations at rush hour. The attraction: His price is dirt-cheap, and the investment returns manyfold just on the initiate's first year's taxes. (So that's what's been bringing so many people to the Lord? For shame!) What he sells for $50, some enterprising cherubs then resell for $900. Like everything else, holiness costs more at retail; so why not buy it wholesale, direct from the source? The vast majority of his "ministers" are never audited; and most of those who are, come through with their tax-savings unscathed. It used to be said that death and taxes had this in commom: They were the only sure things. Now that's no longer true, and the modern version should read instead: Death and taxes have this in common: They're bringing lots of people to God.

32: PERSONAL FINANCE

Ask the church to send you its price-list and literature.

33:
N.Y.C. NEIGHBORHOODS

This City has twice as many residents as does the average state in the United States; and the New York Metropolian Area has four times as many. So it's perhaps natural that diversity is one of Gotham's great prides. That's why almost any generalization you might hear describing this town is bound to be accurate for some of its neighborhoods, and dead wrong for others.

Nonetheless, we do all have the same mayor, watch the same local TV newscasts, read the same daily newspapers, and cheer the same sports-teams. So despite the diversity, there actually is such a thing as "New York City." And what a crazy place it is!

It's a metropolis whose contrasts are so great they're incomprehensible even to the most seasoned native. The sophisticates trotting around the galleries along Madison Avenue have just about as much in common with the row-house residents of Bayside, or with the Haitians of Crown Heights, as they do with the Afghan rebels. In fact, sometimes the physical distance of just one block in NYC means a sociological distance of light-years.

New York used to be called "the melting-pot." Now, it's merely millions of people living on top of, and next-door to, each other; in some cases, loving each other; in others—increasingly often—scared of each other; but most often, just too hectically busy to notice or think of each other.

And through it all, there are the neighborhoods, from Soho to Chinatown to Little Italy to Bensonhurst to Forest Hills to the Upper East Side Gold Coast to nearby East Harlem.

The international core of New York, which makes it "New York," is New York County, otherwise called Manhattan. In recent years, there's been a boom on this island. Even though the whole City's subways are plunging from chaos into catastrophe; and though City-services are going from terrible to worse; and though the "outer boroughs"—the 80% of the City that's not Manhattan—are going from recession into depression, with the plague of gutted buildings and spreading ghettos creeping into areas which only ten years ago were decently middle-class; and though crime throughout New York like elsewhere in the United States is high and soaring out of sight—despite all these things, Manhattan Island south of around 96th Street is experiencing an unprecendented boom in both office- and residential-construction, and tens of thousands of young professional people are pouring into Manhattan every year from other parts of the country. Nearly 60% of all residential building permits issued in the City last year were on this little island. From 1977-80, more than 90% of the City's private-employment growth was also in Manhattan; and there's no sign that the high proportion is diminishing, or that it will do so within the forseeable future.

Manhattan is unquestionably where the money is. Per capita personal income here exceeds $14,000, while in Queens—the second-most-prosperous borough—it's 30% lower.

But despite the island's prosperity (or should I rather say because of it), this is also the borough with the highest crime-rate. In fact, the number of crimes divided by the number of residents is 50% higher here than it is in Brooklyn—the second-crimeiest borough. This, however, is a deceptive statistic. Most of the people in Manhattan are not residents; they're workers and shoppers. Therefore, it's grossly unfair to divide the crime-numbers by the resident population—though that's the way crime-rates are calculated. That's probably why cities have high crime-rates. The fewer the residents, and the more there are of workers and shoppers, the higher the crime-rate will be. So official crime-rates say little or nothing about the relative safety of cities, suburbs, and rural areas, but a lot about the stupidity of the way government calculates crime-rates.

However, I should point out that this doesn't mean that our town hasn't got a big crime-problem. To the contrary: On an average day in New York City, the following numbers of crimes are committed: 582 burglaries, 232 robberies (mostly muggings), 274 car-thefts (these vehicles being subsequently dismembered by an estimated 1,000 secret chop-shops operating in this city), and 5 murders. That's a lot of action. But in that same 24-hour period, only 3 people are convicted and sent to prison. Obviously, our legal authorities don't exist in order to punish crime. They may, however, serve some function—who knows? Oddly, the United States imprisons a higher percentage of its people than does any other country except the Soviet Union and South Africa. We Americans just commit a lot of crimes—about 30 times more than do Europeans, for example. But crime is not a New York problem. It's an American problem. In fact, according to just about every important indicator, this city doesn't even rank among the top ten crimiest cities in this country.

There are three neighborhoods in the outer boroughs that in terms of income, atmosphere, and cosmopolitan character, rival Manhattan's: Riverdale in the Bronx, Forest Hills in Queens, and Brooklyn Heights. You'll find all of them marked in blue-ink type on the subway map that's given out free at token-booths.

But in my opinion, the most attractive neighborhoods in New York are all—except for Brooklyn Heights—in Manhattan. You'll find them marked on the subway-map. These are:

West Village. This is a middle and upper-middle class area, with a touch of the offbeat. It extends generally westward from Broadway, between Houston (which would be Zero St. if it were numbered) and 14th Street. It's especially beautiful along Hudson St., Bank St., Christopher St., the side-streets off lower 5th Avenue, Washington Square, and MacDougal Street.

East Village. Here the old Ukrainians mix with (or to be more accurate, ignore) the young punkers, who used to be the hippies, who before that were called the beatniks, who had formerly been known as the bohemians, who decades ago lived also in West

33: N.Y.C. NEIGHBORHOODS

Village when "The Village" meant a low-rent area where the artists congregated. Now, in East Village, the artists are mostly gone, and the low rents are going fast. (In West Village, both left long ago.) The hub is St. Marks Place (a part of E. 8th St.), where the punkers hob-nob. From 6th St. up to about 10th, between 3rd and 1st Avenues—and even extending one block further eastward, to Av. A—the area is being "gentrified," and already is quite attractive. Further east than this, the neighborhood is primarily Puerto Rican, and mostly unattractive. Av. D is primarily heroin, and very scary.

Soho. This used to be a light-industry district. Then the artists moved in and made it beautiful. Then the speculators moved in and made it expensive. Now it's just like one big artsy-craftsy Madison Avenue South, loaded with galleries (mostly avant garde) and with the young rich whose parents live uptown. The main drag is West Broadway, from Canal St. to Houston. Side-streets are glutted with still more galleries, singles bars, and boutiques.

Little Italy. Popular legend has it that Mafiosi get shot dead on the streets here. Actually, this kind of thing happens more often in Brooklyn and Queens. Little Italy is a much safer place than most out-of-town farmers might think. It's just a very lively ethnic neighborhood surrounding Grand St. near Mulberry, jammed full of Italian restaurants and coffee houses.

Chinatown. This is North America's most beautiful and vibrant Chinatown. Mott St., south of Canal, is the core. The small streets are crowded with Chinamen, tourists, and Chinese restaurants and stores.

Tribeca and Financial District. The first is to the west of lower Broadway; the second, to the east. The whole area is beautiful, and becoming increasingly residential. Adding greatly to the atmosphere of each, is the fact that originally neither was residential. Tribeca started out primarily as light industry and shipping. The financial district is the oldest part of the City, with narrow streets and tall buildings, and still retains its antique quality.

Gramercy Park. This peaceful private oasis at the very southernmost tip of Lexington Av. at 22nd St. resembles some of the better parts of London. The beauty continues eastward and westward along the neighboring blocks from 17th to 21st St., excluding the numbered avenues.

Brooklyn Heights. The area around Willow St. looks like Boston's Beacon Hill. The Promenade above the Brooklyn-Queens Expressway, facing the Manhattan skyline across the river, is dramatic. The antique-shops, and Middle Eastern restaurants and food-stores, directly to the south along Atlantic Av. from Henry to Court Sts., give this neighborhood a distinctive cosmopolitan character which transcends its merely residential beauty. Added assets are the immediate access to Brooklyn's downtown business district and to all subway lines.

I've not mentioned several of Manhattan's main residential areas, such as Chelsea, the Upper East Side, and the Upper West Side. That's because I don't consider them beautiful. Most of uptown Manhattan is composed of tall and impersonal buildings without the intimate ambiance that I feel makes Manhattan something more than an ugly, impersonal, city.

34: APARTMENT BARGAINS

The chief determinant of rent is neighborhood. And there is such a thing as bargain neighborhoods. These are naturally the places where you'll find bargain apartments.

The first thing that comes to the average New Yorker's mind when he thinks of a "low-rent neighborhood" is crime. He envisions an ugly part of town that's not safe to walk in or to live in. He thinks of a slum. (Isn't that a quaint term? "Slum." One can still "go slumming," but no longer in "slums." In "ghettos," perhaps, but "slums" no longer officially exist. Newspeak has ruled that the word isn't sufficiently *ethnic* to be employed any longer.)

There once used to be a time when crime really was higher in the slums. But that's not true any longer. Take, for example, the dreaded South Bronx: Morrisania, Melrose, and Hunts Point. These areas now have far fewer robberies than the "safe" neighborhoods to the east and west. Or consider East Harlem. For about the last decade-and-a-half, it's had no higher crime-rates than the famous bastion of the white middle-class, the Upper West Side; and now both of these areas have the same figures as the long-turbulent Central Harlem district. East Village also has had the reputation of being "dangerous." Now West Village shows the same incidence of serious crimes. Bedford-Stuyvesant was once thought of as an urban jungle. But if you look at the current crime-figures, the region directly to the south of it, in central Brooklyn, is worse.

The "nice" neighborhoods now only cost more. No longer are they safer. But real-estate values continue to reflect the old outdated prejudices. That's why anyone considering to rent or buy an apartment or house would do well to look into slum neighborhoods. From the standpoint of crime, virtually all of New York has become slummy, and the suburbs are racing to catch up. When considering where to live, there's no longer a link between a neighborhood's status and its safety.

So I suggest that you settle into a comfortable slum, where you'll be able to thumb your nose at the snobs while you install your pick-resistant Medeco lock, and perhaps sympathetically hold the hands of your Upper-East-Side acquaintances who've just had their fur-closets unexpectedly cleaned out.

Ultimately, the realities are going to have an impact upon real-estate values. If you want to live in New York, slums are increasingly the places to be, and they'll someday even be the places to invest, as the trendy masses exodus from the prestige neighborhoods to find greater safety in the urban pits.

The process, in fact, has already begun. For example, rentals and building-prices have started to rise rapidly in East Village. So if you intend to move in there, look for the best-value accomodations, and then try to lock in the deal with the longest possible lease. But even if you take only a short lease, there's really no need to worry especially much. Under New York's rent-stabilization law, there are legally-set maximums for increasing rent when old leases expire. The way these maximums are set, it can always be expected that the longest lease is going to be the best value. (For current percentages, phone the Rent Stabilization Association's Dial Tape Library at 944-4700.)

But whatever may be the *investment*-prospects, it's at least clear that from the *renter's* standpoint, slums now merit a very serious look. And that's where the real problem with them is—they often don't look too nice. However, some slums are coming up fast. These ones are the "pioneering" neighborhoods. Any good real-estate dealer or rental agent will identify for you the locations of these. They're the places most knowledgeable people now want to be (if they want to be in New York, that is).

One thing about rental agents: It's a notorious fact that many if not most of the ones who demand an up-front fee are crooks who make their incomes from those fees, not from renting apartments. Often, the alleged apartments they have for rent don't even exist. Sometimes the apartments do, but are occupied. Never pay an up-front fee to a rental agent, no matter how appealing his claimed apartment-availabilities may seem to be. You shouldn't pay any fee until you've signed the lease.

In Manhattan, the cheapest rentals in areas that are accessible to subways and to main business-districts, are found in East Village and in the far-west fourties (Clinton). The former is already a pioneering neighborhood, with increasing numbers of very good-looking blocks (and with the unfortunate real-estate speculation that usually goes along with that). Another good neighborhood which hasn't yet reached the level of stratospheric rentals is the area surrounding Lafayette and Centre Streets—very attractive, and likely to be the next Soho (which means that it may not remain affordable for very long). This area also has the advantage of an unusually low crime-rate. (So, too, generally, does the entire Lower East Side, the area of Manhattan south of Houston St., north of the Brooklyn Bridge, and east of Broadway.)

If you're new to New York, East Village may well be the first place you'll want to check out. East of 4th Avenue, above 4th Street, and below 11th, you're likely to find something suitable and reasonable. Especially the area I mentioned in the previous chapter, from 6th to 10th Streets, and from 3rd Av. (Bowery) to 1st Av. or even Av. A, has many attractive and relatively safe blocks.

The Clinton area (also known as "Hell's Kitchen") isn't yet so far along toward rehabilitation, but it's starting. Brooklyn has many neighborhoods at various stages on the road toward gentrification. In any such area, you'll end up spending perhaps 50-70% of the rent you'd be charged in the most expensive parts of town (which are the Upper East Side, Midtown East Side, and West Village). The following neighborhoods might warrant a look: Boerum Hill, Park Slope, Carroll Gardens, and Cobble Hill.

Before you finally settle on an area, however, it's a good idea to phone the local police precinct in the neighborhood you're consid-

34: APARTMENT BARGAINS

ering, and to ask to speak with the crime-statistics officer, who's the person most knowledgeable about the relative safety of the various blocks in his jurisdiction. Sometimes, the difference of just one or two blocks can mean a difference of as much as 100% in the amount of crime. As a potential resident, you'll be most concerned with the burglary-figures, the robbery-statistics, and (if you're a woman) rape. ("Burglary" officially means something different from "robbery." The first is breaking and entering an apartment; the second is a mugging or holdup, which is a crime not only against property, but also against the person who's threatened.)

The most important thing in choosing an apartment, however, may well be not its neighborhood, but rather the location of the apartment in its building. By all means, avoid any apartment on or near the top floor and accessible by the fire-escape from the roof, because these are overwhelmingly the apartments that are burgled. These residences generally face the rear, not the front of the building, since that tends to be where the fire-escape has access from the roof. The most common way that burglaries are carried out is this: The thief gets onto your roof (having entered there via your building's lobby or from the roof next door), comes down the fire-escape that has access to the roof, opens or breaks the window and then enters. For further information on this and related matters, see the "Basic Burglar-Protection Course" section in Chapter 15, Home Improvement.

One other problem with top-floor apartments is leaking of snow and rain. Also, on our scorching New York summer days, you've got the heat sizzling the black roof, which is the other side of your ceiling. Finally, if there's a fire, you're in the worst possible position, the least safe. A real-estate agent won't tell you these things, and upper-floor rents aren't discounted on their account.

Of course, ground-floor and basement locations are also vulnerable—especially those to a building's rear, since break-ins of rear-apartments can't be observed from the street. The safest apartments in a building are generally those above the ground-floor, but not on the upper two floors, and those whose fire-escapes can't be accessed from the roof.

35:
WHERE TO GO WHEN THINGS GO WRONG

First, the bad news: It's going to be a hard road to hoe. Getting your complaint heard by an agency that can do something about it, may turn out to be like searching for the proverbial needle-in-a-haystack. However, the list given below should at least ease that chore considerably. And here comes the good news: In New York City, there are so many consumer agencies, public and private, that there'll probably be at least one that'll ultimately come through for you if only you keep at it.

Persistence is indeed the name of this game. Putting up with those telephone busy-signals, assembling all that documentation, and mailing out all those letters, is going to take a lot of time and hard work. But if you're up to it, and if your cause is just, then you may well have your way eventually. So where should you start? With the phone-numbers below.

Usually, the governmental agencies are about as efficient in their processing of consumer-complaints as they are with everything else—which of course means not very. Go and visit their offices, and wait for them to finish their two-hour lunch breaks. Enjoy the peace and serenity that's inconceivable at all private-industry bureaucratic offices except those perched high among some large corporations' executive suites. Breathe deep of this calm air. For you, the placid scene will be a brief respite from your woes—a time to relax—unless you get angry thinking of how long it took these people to answer the phone when you dialed, or of how it took them three months to acknowledge receiving your first letter.

Therefore, best start with the private agencies, which would fire executives and office-workers who ran their places like this. First and foremost, there's the industrious Better Business Bureau, at 533-6200, from 10-3 weekdays. Although unthinkingly knocked by some of the more rigidly cliche-ridden consumer-activists who take it on faith that only a governmental agency can be a fair and effective do-gooder, the BBB usually far outperforms such agencies in achieving fast and satisfactory resolutions of complaints. Also, in hard-to-resolve cases, where mediation has failed, the BBB, upon mutual consent of both parties, provides a free arbitration-service, using unpaid volunteers, and adhering to rules of procedure established by the American Arbitration Association. This is a fast, cheap, easy, efficient, and fair, alternative to small claims court. Then, there's WMCA Radio's public-spirited "Call for Action," at 586-6666, from 11-1 noontime weekdays, which serves as a general consumer-complaint ombudsman. Both WMCA and the BBB will also be helpful in directing you to the other appropriate private and governmental agencies to phone and write to with your complaints. Finally, there are the consumer-aid panels of the various trade associations. Addresses of these are given in the list

35: WHERE TO GO WHEN THINGS GO WRONG

below.

Most problems can be resolved this way. But for those that can't, where your complaint concerns a truly crooked firm which doesn't give a hoot about consumer-goodwill or professional standing, you'll need the muscle of legal coercion, and then the only effective route is going to have to be one of the governmental agencies, including ultimately possibly the courts. Your first line of attack, when available, should be to address the city or state agency responsible for licensure of the kind of business you're complaining about. Whenever this approach is applicable, I include the phone number and name of the licensing bureau that handles that given field of business. A caveat, here, however: These governmental licensing offices are normally extremely reluctant to de-certify unless you're the ten-thousandth complainant about that particular firm, or unless that offending company has not been paying its expected political dues. So don't get your hopes up too high, or else you might become disappointed and rather unpleasantly angry.

Where this approach fails, the next and final stage is to file suit in the civil courts. For information about this, phone 374-8174. If the suit is to be for less than $1,500, the matter can be handled in the small claims court of the civil courts, and you won't need a lawyer. The number for this is 374-8402. (In boros other than Manhattan, it's different. Look in the blue-pages section of the phone book, under: New York City Government, Courts, Civil Court, Small Claims Court.)

Finally, a note about the phone numbers below: Governmental agencies are constantly playing musical chairs with their offices and phones, and so those numbers change at a breathtaking clip. Therefore, I'm giving not only the phone-contacts, but also the divisions of federal, state, or city government, as shown in the blue pages at the end of the Manhattan phone book, so that if the number has since changed, you can more easily find the current one if it's shown in the phone book. You'll also find useful the "Easy Reference List" at the beginning of that section of the telephone directory. If the place I'm listing is private, I give its name as shown in the phone book's white pages.

Of course, don't complain to any agencies until you've already first contacted—and failed to get satisfaction from—the firm itself. Otherwise, your complaint won't be taken seriously by anybody.

Advertising, False: 577-0111 (New York City, Dept. of Consumer Affairs), 488-7530 (New York State, Dept. of Law, Attorney General, Consumer Fraud Bureau), 264-1949 (United States, Federal Trade Commission), 533-6200 from 10 a.m. to 3 p.m. (Better Business Bureau, 257 P.A.S., NY, NY 10017. Phone is often busy. You'll have to write with documentation anyway, so you might as well just do that to start with.)

Air Freight: Consumer Affairs Dept., Civil Aeronautics Board, 1825 Connecticut Av. N.W., Washington, D.C. 20428.

Airline & Air Freight: 486-0700 (American Society of Travel

35: WHERE TO GO WHEN THINGS GO WRONG

Agents).

Air Pollution: 966-7500 24-hours (NYC, Environmental Protection Dept.), 943-2400 (Citizens for Clean Air), 349-7255 (Clean Air Campaign).

Apartment: 598-4900 from 2-6 p.m. (Metropolitan Council on Housing); also see "Housing" below.

Apartment-Finding Service: 587-5740&7 (NYS, Dept. of State, Div. of Licensing), 577-0111 (NYC, DCA), 533-6200 (BBB).

Appliance: Major Appliance Consumer Action Panel, 20 N. Wacker Dr., Chicago, Il. 60606. Call collect: (312) 984-5858.

Appliance Repairman: 577-0111 (NYC, DCA), 533-6200 (BBB).

Auctioneer: 577-0111 (NYC, DCA).

Auto, Unsafe: 1-800-424-9393 (US, Dept. of Transportation, National Highway Traffic Safety Administration, Wash. D.C.).

Auto Dealer: 1-800-342-3823 (NYS, Dept. of Motor Vehicles, Bur. of Consumer Facilities, Empire State Plaza 12228), 577-0111 (NYC, DCA), 533-6200 (BBB).

Auto Recall: 1-800-424-9393 (US, DT, NHTSA).

Auto Rental: 577-0111 (NYC, DCA), 533-6200 (BBB).

Auto Repair: 587-4277 (NYS, DMV, Dealers Unit), 1-800-342-3823 (NYS, DMV, BCF), 533-6200 (BBB).

Bank: For NYS-registered: 488-2353 (NYS, Banking Dept.). For US-registered: 944-3495 (US, Treasury Dept., Comptroller of the Currency, Regional Administrator). For a Savings & Loan: 432-2000 (Federal Home Loan Bank).

Barber or Beauty Parlor: 587-5740&7 (NYS, DS, DL).

Cabaret: 577-0111 (NYC, DCA).

Camera Shop: 488-7530 (NYS, DL, AG), 577-0111 (NYC, DCA), 533-6200 (BBB).

Carpet & Rug Dealer: Consumer Action Panel, Carpet & Rug Institute, Holiday Av., Dalton, Ga. 30720. 488-7530 (NYS, DL, AG), 577-0111 (NYC, DCA), 533-6200 (BBB).

Caterer: 577-0111 (NYC, DCA).

Commodities Trader: 1-800-424-9838 (US, Commodities Futures Trading Commission).

Cosmetics: See "Drugs."

Crime: 488-5080 (NYS, Crime Victims Compensation Board), 577-7777 (Victim Services Agency).

Dangerous Products (not autos or foods & drugs): 264-1125 & 1-800-638-8326 (US, Consumer Product Safety Commission).

Dentist: 986-3937 (Dental Society), 557-2104 (NYS, Dept. of Education, Professional Conduct Division). In NYS, but outside NYC: 1-800-442-8106 (NYS, DE, PCD, Albany).

Doctor: 696-2619 (NYS, Dept. of Health, Medical Conduct Unit), 557-2104 (NYS, DE, PCD), 1-516-488-6100 (Medical Society). In NYS, but outside NYC: 1-800-442-8106 (NYS, DE, PCD, Albany).

Drugs, Cosmetics, Toiletries: 965-5725 (US, Food & Drug Administration).

Dry Cleaner or Laundry: 684-0945 (Neighborhood Cleaners Assn.), 533-6200 (BBB), 577-0111 (NYC, DCA).

Employment Agency: 577-0111 (NYC, DCA).

Foods: 965-5725 (US, FDA), 577-0111 (NYC, DCA), 285-9503 &

35: WHERE TO GO WHEN THINGS GO WRONG

334-7737 & 566-7726 (NYC, Dept. of Health, Bureau of Sanitary Inspection), 488-4820 (NYS, Dept. of Agriculture).

Foods on Street-Stands: 577-0111 (NYC, DCA).

Furniture: Furniture Industry Consumer Advisory Panel, Box 591, High Point, NC 27261. 587-5740&7 (NYS, DS, DL), 577-0111 (NYC, DCA), 533-6200 (BBB).

Garage: 577-0111 (NYC, DCA).

Home-Improvement Contractor: 577-0111 (NYC, DCA), 533-6200 (BBB).

Hotel: 265-4506 (American Hotel Assn.)

Housing: 960-4800 24-hours. Also: 598-4900 (MCH), 960-4800 & 566-6222 & 566-6205 (NYC, Dept. of Housing Preservation & Development, Rent & Housing Maintenance Office).

Who is the landlord?: 248-6359 (NYC, DHPD, RHMO, Code Enforcement). If there are fewer than 3 apartments in the building: 566-3734 (NYC, County Clerk).

Electrical wiring: 566-3150 (NYC, General Services Dept.)

Elevators: 566-2380&4 (NYC, Dept. of Buildings).

Heat: 248-8819 (NYC, DB).

Plumbing: 566-2491 (NYC, DB).

Other: 566-2384. (NYC, DB).

Public subsidized housing: For information: 566-4440 (NYC, DHPD, Public Affairs), 433-2525 (NYC, Housing Authority). For applications: 233-8878 & 433-5117 (NYC, HA).

Rent control: 566-5054&6906 (NYC, DHPD, RHMO, Rent Control).

Rent deposits: 488-4479&7530 (NYS, DL, AG).

Rent stabilized: 265-5105 (Conciliation & Appeals Board). What is the law?: 944-4700 (Rent Stabilization Assn.).

Residential hotels: 737-2511 (Metropolitan Hotel Industry Stabilization Assn.).

Insurance: Life & health: 488-5642 (NYS, Insurance Dept.). Auto: 488-5630 & 775-1011 (NYS, ID). Other: 488-4760 & 488-5642 (NYS, ID). General: 533-6200 (BBB).

Investments: See "Commodities," "Real Estate," and "Securities."

Jeweler: 577-0111 (NYC, DCA), 753-1304 (Jewelers Vigilance Committee).

Land Sales: 587-5776&5787 (NYS, DS, Subdivided Land Unit), 488-7530 (NYS, DL, AG, CFB), 533-6200 (BBB).

Landlord: 532-3100 (Real Estate Board). Also see "Housing."

Laundromat: See "Dry Cleaner."

Lawyer: 840-3550 (Assn. of The Bar, Grievance Com.).

Legal Help Free: 431-7200 (Community Action for Legal Serviceing), 577-3300 & 227-2755 (Legal Aid Society).

Locksmith: 577-0111 (NYC, DCA).

Magazines: 752-0055 (Magazine Publishers Assn.), and:

Mail Order: 577-0111 (NYC, DCA), 533-6200 (BBB), 689-4977 (Direct Mail Marketing Assn.), 264-1949 (US, FTC).

Motion Picture Theatre: 577-0111 (NYC, DCA).

Mover or Trucker: 264-1072 & 1-800-424-9312 (US, Interstate Commerce Commission), 488-5618&4396 (NYS, Dept. of Transpor-

tation), 533-6200 (BBB).
 Parking Lot: 577-0111 (NYC, DCA).
 Pawnbroker: 577-0111 (NYC, DCA).
 Pharmacist: 557-2136 (NYS, DE, Board of Pharmacy).
 Plumber: 248-8828 (NYC, DB, Licensing Div.).
 Product-Recalls: 1-800-638-8326 (US, CPSC).
 Real Estate Purchases: Regarding NYC properties: 566-7530 (NYC, General Services, Real Property). Regarding brokers: 587-5740&7 (NYS, DS, DL). Regarding condos and co-ops: 488-7530&4141 (NYS, DL, AG).
 Restaurant: 285-9503 (NYC, Dept. of Health, Complaints).
 Second-Hand Shop: 577-0111 (NYC, DCA).
 Securities, Investment: 264-1620 (US, Securities & Exchange Commission).
 Sidewalk Cafe or Vendor: 577-0111 (NYC, DCA).
 Sightseeing Bus or Tour: 577-0111 (NYC, DCA).
 Skating Rink: 577-0111 (NYC, DCA).
 Small Claims Courts: 374-8174&8402 (NYC, Courts, Civil Court, Small Claims Court).
 Subscriptions: See "Mail Order."
 Thrift Shop: See "Second-Hand Shop."
 Toiletries: See "Drugs."
 Toys: 488-7530 (NYS, DL, AG), 264-1125 & 1-800-638-8326 (US, CPSC).
 Travel Agent: 486-0700 (American Society of Travel Agents, Dir. of Consumer Affairs), 264-1700 (US, Civil Aeronautics Board), 577-0111 (NYC, DCA), 488-7530 (NYS, DL, AG), 533-6200 (BBB).
 Warehouse: 577-0111 (NYC, DCA).
 Warranty Violations: 264-1237 (US, FTC), 488-7530 (NYS, DL, AG), 533-6200 (BBB).

36:
AM-FM-TV STATIONS

This is New York's home-entertainment menu:

RADIO

Stations are FM unless indicated otherwise:

Rock:

WPLJ—95.5: Moderately hard rock. Announcers are "personalities." Some sound-distortion.

WYNY—97.1: Upbeat rock. Mostly hits from the '60's and '70's. Good sonics.

WPIX—101.9: Hard rock. Some sound-distortion.

WNEW—102.7: Progressive rock. Announcers are rock-aficionados.

WAPP—103.5: Upbeat rock.

Disco:

WKTU—92.3: Pounding, thumping rhythms.

WKSS—98.7: Relentless, pounding beat.

WBLS—107.5: Upbeat soul-sound.

Jazz:

WBGO—88.3: A good share of oldies.

WVNJ—100.3 Nighttime only: Mellow jazz.

Background Easy Listening:

WPAT—93.1: Upbeat melodies. Smooth arrangements. Outstanding hi-fi sonics.

WVNJ—100.3 Daytime only: A touch jazzy.

WRFM—105.1: Downbeat sound.

Country Western:

WKHK—106.7: Slick and noisy.

Nostalgia, 1940's Music:

WNEW-AM—1130: Big-band sound. Upbeat.

Classical:

WNYC—93.9: Routinely ignores scheduled programming. No commercials, but frequent beg-a-thons. This town's only venturesome classical fare; emphasis on the contemporary.

WQXR—96.3: Engineers routinely sharply boost volume on quiet passages, and compress climaxes. Station often can't be reached by phone except 9-5 weekdays.

WNCN—104.3: Big on chamber music, baroque and other small-group pieces. Aims to appeal to socially elite audience. Good sonics.

Talk-Shows:

WMCA-AM—570: Phone-in format.

36:: AM-FM-TV STATIONS

WOR-AM—710: Phone-in format. Many show-hosts specialize in specific subjects.

WABC-AM—770: Phone-in format.

WBAI—99.5: Sometimes phone-in format. Primarily leftist social issues and agitprop. Very independent, fiercely progressive, often amateurish. Also odd music. No commercials, but frequent beg-a-thons.

Non-Stop News:

WCBS-AM—880: Announcers with just a touch of "personality."

WINS-AM—1010: Hard-core reporting. Fast-moving, but sometimes in-depth on major breaking stories.

TELEVISION

WCBS—Channel 2: CBS flagship station.

WNBC—Channel 4: NBC flagship station.

WNEW—Channel 5: Mostly network re-runs.

WABC—Channel 7: ABC flagship station.

WOR—Channel 9: Some network re-runs; some good old Hollywood movies.

WPIX—Channel 11: Some network re-runs. Excellent Independent Network News at 12:30 noon and 10 at night.

WNET—Channel 13: PBS public television. Movies on the local station are mostly tastelessly-selected Hollywood and British fare, plus some Japanese; virtually no French, Italian, Spanish, or Latin American, which is what a non-profit station ought to be strongest in, since that includes most of the greatest art-films.

What's Best

National News: "All Things Considered," on WNYC-FM at 5 p.m.
Local News: WINS-AM 24 hours.
Music & Other: See above listings.
TV Dramas: WNET, mostly evenings.

What's Missing

This City needs, and the New York market will support: a psychedelic and new-wave rock FM station, a Reggae and folk-rock FM station, a good classical-music FM station, and a good full-time jazz and jazz-rock FM station with practically nothing pre-1960 except some mellow sounds like Billie Holiday. Also, a city this size deserves a Qube system on cable-TV. I hope that in the next edition I'll be able to report that some of these exist.

37:
NYC'S 40 BARGAIN-HOTELS

If you think that because this is New York—America's most extravagant city—you're going to have to pay an arm and a leg in order to get suitable hotel-accomodations, you'll be very pleasantly surprised to find out that you were wrong—dead wrong. Room-rates here for comparable facilities can be gotten for half of what you'd pay, for example, in Boston, Niagara Falls, or most other major tourist-centers. The only hitch is that some hotels in NYC really are overpriced. Some are terribly overpriced. But others—the ones I list below—are bargains that would be bargains in any other touristed part of the country. The thing that makes this town so unique, is that those other cities generally don't have such hotel-bargains. For some reason, in New York, you don't always get what you pay for—sometimes you get a great deal more.

The hotels below are grouped in order of increasing expensiveness. The cheapest place—Category-2—is what you'd expect from a very, very inexpensive hotel, only it costs half as much. It's marginally tolerable, at best. At the other end, the very top—Category-18 and even several of those all the way down to Category-13—will be found some hotels that are luxury-class, and others that are super-luxury in the company of this city's (or indeed of the world's) most exclusive places, but only half to a third as expensive. At Category-6 (inexpensive), you'll again find some of these very same luxury and super-luxury hotels, appearing this time on the merits of their weekend-rates, which are astoundingly good values: less than 20% of the price at comparable hotels.

The Category-System

Category-numbers indicate relative expensiveness. The single Category-2 hotel is approximately 2/18th's—or one ninth—as expensive as the only Category-18 hotel; and the latter is approximately 18/6th's—or three times—as expensive as any of the Category-6 hotels (amongst which, by coincidence, is that very same Category-18 hotel on its weekend-special rates). In other words, these hotels' room-charges are approximately proportionate to their respective category-numbers. Thus, if you phone for rates at one of these places, you'll have a basis for estimating the prices at all the others. I felt that this was a better system than indicating specific dollar-prices, because this way, even rapid economic inflation won't outdate the list, and also because you need make only one phone-call in order to get an idea of the rates at all the places.

I assigned category-numbers based on each hotel's across-the-board prices. Some places are much better values for certain types of rooms or lengths of stays than they are for others. Thus, for example, there will be a few instances where a double room with bath for a one-night stay will not cost twice as much at a Category-6 hotel as it does at a Category-3, but perhaps only 1.5 times more, or 2.5 times more. However, when a hotel is particularly strong or weak, say, for single-night stays, or for weekly rates, or for suites, I try to indicate that in my description of the place. This helps compensate for some of the unavoidable approximateness of this—or indeed of any—price-ranking system.

You'll notice that there are no hotels recommended between Categories 6 and 10. That's because the ones I saw priced there are actually nothing more than overpriced Category-6's. This list includes hotels in every quality-range from marginally tolerable all the way up to the very top.

Of course, as always, the number of stars I give a hotel reflects my estimate of its value. Although all of the recommended places are bargains, the hotels with the greater numbers of stars are the better bargains.

So sleep well!

Category 2
(near rockbottom)

*****Bond Hotel**, 125 Chambers St. (at W. B'wy), 962-4390. Somewhat dilapidated. Lumpy beds. Bath in hall. Nice location not far from financial district, in major bargain-shopping area which is very quiet at night. Near all major subway lines. Not recommended for weekly rates.

Category 3
(super-cheap)

******Franklin Hotel**, 164 E. 87 (Lexington-3rd Avs.), 289-5958&9873. Unquestionably the best-value hotel in NYC for daily rates; also good on a weekly basis. Very nice rooms. Located on a side-block in the pleasant Yorkville area, near the Lex.-Av.-and-86th-St. stop on the Lex.-Av. subway (trains numbers 4, 5, and 6). Also easily accessible via any of the 3rd-Avenue buses.

****Vanderbilt YMCA**, 224 E. 47 (3rd Av.), 755-2410, telex 237581YVUTUR. Has swimming pool. Located in east-side business-district near U.N. Take #6 subway train to 51st St.

****McBurney YMCA**, 215 W. 23 (7th Av.), 741-9226. Swimming pool and sauna. Residential neighborhood. Take AA, CC, E, or 6, subway to 23rd St.

***Lexington Residence Hotel**, 120 E. 31 (Lexington Av.), 685-3060. No nightly rates—weekly only. Somewhat dilapidated, but decent. #6 subway to 33rd Street. OK location. No rooms with private bath. Unusually low weekly rates.

***Hotel Ashland**, 429 Park Av. S. (29-30), 683-0977. Somewhat rundown, but fairly homey. Lumpy mattresses. #6 subway to 28th Street. Fairly good location. Especially low weekly rates.

***Hotel Rio**, 132 W. 47 (6th Av.), 757-3870. Sparce, but clean. Rather unattractive and busy block near Times Square. B, D, and F subways to 47th St.

***Sloane YMCA**, 356 W. 34 (at 9th Av.), 760-5860. A tolerable location. A, AA, CC, and E, subways to 34th St.

Category 4
(extremely cheap)

**Washington Jefferson Hotel, 320 W. 51 (8th Av.), 246-7550. Nice ambiance. A nice block off the Times-Square area. AA, CC, and E subways to 50th Street. Good weekly rates.

*West Side YMCA, 5 W. 63 (directly west of Central Park), 787-4400. Swimming pool. A, AA, B, CC, D, and 1 subways to 59th St.

*Hotel Le Marquis, 12 E. 31 (5th Av.), 684-7480. Sparce. Nice quiet block, 5-minute walk from midtown. Often booked up. Make reservations by mail if possible. Especially low weekly rates. #6 subway to 33rd St.

*The Deauville, 103 E. 29 (Park Av. S.), 683-0990. #6 subway to 28th St. Fairly nice block.

*Hotel Seventeen, 225 E. 17 (3rd Av.), 475-2845. Homey but somewhat dilapidated. Rather lumpy beds. Nice quiet residential block adjoining attractive Stuyvesant Square. No rooms with private bath. Ask to see other rooms if first shown you is inadequate. Especially low weekly rates. Any subway to Union Sq.

*Hotel Kenmore, 145 E. 23 (Lexington Av.), 475-3840. Decent. Small rooms. #6 subway to 23rd Street. Free use of swimming pool, steam room, and sun terrace. Best values are bath-in-hall. Especially low weekly rates.

Hotel Arlington, 18 W. 25 (Broadway), 929-8960. Sparce. RR subway to 28th Street. Good weekly rates.

Category 5
(very cheap)

***Aberdeen Hotel, 17 W. 32 (5th Av.), 736-1600. B, D, F, QB, N, RR subways to 34th Street. Good central location. Sometimes excellent weekly rates can be arranged.

***Hotel Remington, 129 W. 46 (6th Av.), 221-2600. Busy block near Times Square. B, D, F subways to 47th Street.

**Hotel Lenox, 149 W. 44 (Broadway), 221-3722. On Times Square's theatre-row. Any subway to Times Square.

*Pickwick Arms, 230 E. 51 (3rd Av.), 355-0300. Very nice. Homey, and on an attractive block. #6 subway to 51st St.

Seton Hotel, 144 E. 40 (Lexington Av.), 889-5301. Tolerable. No foyer downstairs. Buried amongst tall office buildings. Take any subway to Grand Central Station. Especially low weekly rates.

Gracie Square Hotel, 451 E. 86 (York), 534-9297. Clean, sparce rooms, in a very quiet neighborhood off the fringe of Yorkville. Somewhat lumpy beds. Shower in hall; sink in room.

American Hotel, 331 E. 86 (2nd Av.), 534-9713. Identical to Gracie Square Hotel above, but closer to the busy part of Yorkville. 3rd Av. bus to 86th St.

Category 6
(cheap)

****Hotel Latham, 4 E. 28 (5th Av.), 685-8300. Tasteful, homey, unpretentious. Rooms and suites. Room-service. Attractive, quiet block, 7-minute walk from midtown. 5th-Av. bus or RR subway to

28th Street. A modest luxury hotel. Especially low 2-week rates—certainly the city's best value for such stays.

******Luxury-New-York-weekend special** for the 4 affiliated luxury and super-luxury hotels that are listed at the end of this paragraph, and that you'll find described in detail under categories 13 through 17 following. Phone 689-5227, or in NY State 1-800-522-5680, or outside NY State 1-800-223-6663, for weekend-special rates and reservations either for the (huge) 2-person bedroom with kitchen and bath; or for the (yet-larger) 3-room 4-person suite (the most sensational value of all, only marginally more expensive than the 2-person bedroom—and some of these suites even throw in an extra 2nd bathroom); or else for the still slightly larger 4-room 6-person suite (2 bedrooms, 2 baths, living room, and kitchen). These 4 hotels are among the 8 luxury and super-luxury establishments owned by the evidently perfectionistic Denihan family; and even without the special, all 8 hotels in this group charge bargain-rates and are recommended. Participating hotels in this weekend-special, which offers perhaps New York's greatest hotel-bargains, are: **Southgate Tower, Shelburne, Eastgate Tower, Beekman Tower.**

****Roger Williams Hotel**, Madison Av. at 31st St., 684-7500. Attractive hotel. Nice location 7-minute walk from midtown. Rooms available only on a nightly basis; kitchenettes on a weekly basis.

***Murray Hill Hotel**, 42 W. 35 (6th Av.), 947-0200. A very friendly place, centrally located. Good weekly rates.

Category 10
(reasonable)

Hotel Tudor, 304 E. 42 (2nd Av.), 986-8800. Semi-luxury hotel with mostly small rooms. On a rather sterile east-side block near the United Nations. Decor is neo-ornate—pretentious but not offensive. Room-service.

Category 11
(rather reasonable)

***Prince George Hotel**, 14 E. 28 (5th Av.), 532-7800. Semi-luxury hotel on quiet block, 7-minute walk from midtown. Impressive lobby. Halls decorated in blue and gold—not tasteful. Best values are rooms, not suites. Room-service.

Madison Towers, 22 E. 38 (at Mad. Av.), 685-3700. Semi-luxury hotel without room-service, located in good midtown area.

Category 12
(high reasonable)

New York Statler, 401 7th Av. (at 33rd, across the street from Penn Station and Madison Square Garden), 736-5000 & 1-800-228-2121, telex NYSTAT 12-7583. Has 50 conference-rooms, many trade-shows. Central location, in the fashion-district. Room-service. Offers special weekend-package deals. Recommended especially for business-travelers.

Category 13
(very low moderate)

***Southgate Tower, 371 7th Av. (at 31st, across from Penn Station and Madison Square Garden), 533-1800; in NY State: 1-800-522-5680; outside NY State: 1-800-223-6663; abroad, telex: 225 666 SHEL. Super-luxury hotel in excellent taste, with quiet—though somewhat cavernous—lobby, and with huge and elegantly appointed rooms, all of which are equipped with kitchenettes. Exceptionally courteous attendants. Centrally located in the fashion-district. Has meeting rooms, room-service. Super-low weekend-rates. Suites are especially strongly recommended.

**Algonquin Hotel, 59 W. 44 (5th Av.), 840-6800; outside NY State: 1-800-223-5077&5352; cable: Algonquin, New York; international telex: 66532. A joyously homey, thoroughly tasteful, luxury hotel, with a gorgeous oak-paneled lobby, and with well-furnished—though sometimes small—rooms, decorated with art. An elegant country inn on a relatively quiet street in the middle of bustling midtown; a true home-away-from-home. Especially beloved by artists, writers, and Europeans. Very popular and hard-to-book. Lobby, restaurants, and bar, often jampacked. Room-service.

**Gramercy Park Hotel, 2 Lexington Av. (at 21), 475-4320 & 1-800-221-4083. A luxury hotel that's homey and tasteful in a friendly, informal, almost rustic way, like an intimate country inn. Overlooks New York's most beautiful one-block park, surrounding which is one of the city's finest residential areas. Room-service. Very good rates for groups. Especially strongly recommended for suites.

Category 14
(low moderate)

***Lyden House, 320 E. 53 (2nd Av.), 888-6070; in NY State: 1-800-522-5680; outside NY State: 1-800-223-6663; abroad, telex: 225 666 SHEL. Super-luxury hotel, but without room-service. Nice eastside-midtown location. Sedate, quiet, lobby. Huge and elegantly appointed rooms, all of which are equipped with kitchenettes. Excellent taste throughout. Exceptionally courteous attendants. Suites are especially strongly recommended.

Category 15
(moderate)

***Shelburne, 303 Lexington Av. (at 37), 689-5200; in NY State: 1-800-522-5680; outside NY State: 1-800-223-6663; abroad, telex: 225 666 SHEL. Super-luxury hotel, nicely located, 5-minute walk from midtown. Sedate, quiet, lobby. Huge and elegantly appointed rooms, all of which are equipped with kitchenettes. Excellent taste throughout. Exceptionally courteous attendants. Room-service. Ballroom. Meeting rooms. Super-low weekend-rates. Suites are especially strongly recommended.

**Lyden Gardens, 215 E. 64 (3rd Av.), 355-1230; in NY State: 1-800-522-5680; outside NY State: 1-800-223-6663; abroad, telex: 225 666 SHEL. Super-luxury hotel, but without room-service. Located in sterile area of rich upper east side. Sedate, quiet, lobby. Huge and elegantly appointed rooms, all of which are equipped with kitchenettes. Excellent taste throughout. Exceptionally courteous attendants. Suites are especially strongly recommended.

Category 16
(high moderate)

**Eastgate Tower, 222 E. 39 (2nd Av.), 687-8000; in NY State: 1-800-522-5680; outside NY State: 1-800-223-6663; abroad, telex: 225 666 SHEL. Super-luxury motor-hotel, nicely located 5-minute walk from midtown. Sedate, quiet, lobby. Huge and elegantly appointed rooms, all of which are equipped with kitchenettes. Excellent taste throughout. Exceptionally courteous attendants. Room-service. Super-low weekend-rates. Suites are especially strongly recommended.

*Plaza 50, 155 E. 50 (at 3rd Av.), 751-5710; in NY State: 1-800-522-5680; outside NY State: 1-800-223-6663; abroad, telex: 225 666 SHEL. Super-luxury hotel, but without room-service. Nice eastside-midtown location. Sedate, quiet, lobby. Huge and elegantly appointed rooms, all of which are equipped with kitchenettes. Excellent taste throughout. Exceptionally courteous attendants. Suites are especially strongly recommended.

Category 17
(very low expensive)

*Beekman Tower, 1st Av. at 49th St., 355-7300; in NY State: 1-800-522-5680; outside NY State: 1-800-223-6663; abroad, telex: 225 666 SHEL. Super-luxury hotel, but without room-service. Sterile-posh neighborhood across from United Nations. Sedate, quiet, lobby. Huge and elegantly appointed rooms, all of which are equipped with kitchenettes. Excellent taste throughout. Exceptionally courteous attendants. Super-low weekend-rates. Suites are especially strongly recommended.

Category 18
(low expensive)

**Surrey, 20 E. 76 (Madison Av.), 288-3700; in NY State: 1-800-522-5680; outside NY State: 1-800-223-6663; abroad, telex: 225 666 SHEL. Super-luxury hotel, located in the heart of posh-ville, near the galleries. Sedate, quiet lobby. Huge and elegantly appointed rooms, all of which are equipped with kitchenettes. Excellent taste throughout. Exceptionally courteous attendants. Room-service. Suites are especially strongly recommended.

Category 40
(the top—way overpriced)

These are the prestige-hotels, which in quality do not surpass the top ones I've just listed. If you're interested, just ask your travel agent which hotels are NYC's most expensive. For some reason, the places are well-booked.

38: TRAVEL SERVICES

How do you get free drive-away cars? Which are the cheapest auto-rental agencies? The cheapest limousine services? Where do you get good free maps of New York and of other cities and states? Why is Newark Airport not only the pleasantest to get to from Manhattan, but also the safest to fly from (or to)? Which are the safest airlines? What travel agencies specialize in doing the comparison-shopping for you, and in keeping on top of the least expensive travel-alternatives, domestic and foreign? This chapter is a hodge-podge, but it can save you big bucks, and more.

Free Maps

Exxon Travel Information Center, 1251 6th Av. (49-50), Exxon Building lobby, 398-2690. 8:30-5 M-F. Free Exxon road and street maps, covering the entire U.S. Courteous and helpful auto-travel counselors are there to help you plan your vacation.

Free Travelers' Checks

Barclay's Bank, locations and phones listed in Chapter 32, "Personal Finance." They don't charge any fee, whereas other travelers' checks, like the well-advertised but not at all superior American Express, assess a 1% fee, as do others.

Best Exchange-Rates

Usually, on most foreign currencies, on most days, the following companies are 0-2% cheaper than Perera, and 0-5% cheaper than Manfra, Tordella & Brookes:

Harold Reuter, 200 Park Av. at 45th St., rm. 367, 661-0826. Open only M-F 8:30-4.

Bank Leumi, 382-4000. Almost 20 branches in NYC, many centrally located.

Travel Agencies

Since you pay nothing extra for the assistance of travel agents, you might as well take advantage of their help. It's free to you because they make their incomes as sales commissions from airlines, etc.; and if you buy direct, you pay those same sales commissions, only directly to the supplier, not to the travel agency. So let an agent do the comparison-shopping for you. That's how he earns his keep. The following are the ones I've found who really do earn their keeps.

FOR FOREIGN TRAVEL ONLY:
*****Vikings of New York**, 501 5th Av. (42), rm. 2215, 490-3907 & 1-800-223-6130. Ask for Robbin. Mention *BARGAIN FINDER*.

FOR DOMESTIC TRAVEL ONLY:
***The Travel Co.**, 501 5th Av. (42), rm. 2214, 953-9050.

BOTH FOREIGN & DOMESTIC:

Sunbeam, 8 W. 40 (5th Av.), rm. 1203, 354-2830.
Global, 521 5th Av. (43), 17th floor, 379-3532.
Feti, 1440 Broadway (40), lobby, 221-4555.

Cheapest & Safest Airlines

For the cheapest, the above travel agents should be on top of that. However, just to be sure, it might do well for you to ask them whether the following inexpensive airline companies have anything to offer you—or else you can check with the airlines themselves in the phone book: Capitol Air (domestic & overseas), World Airways (domestic & overseas); the following are only domestic: New York Air, Empire Airlines, People Express, Air Florida, Piedmont Airlines.

For the safest, first keep this in mind: A U.S. airline-pilot has a 1% chance of a job-related death; coal miners, 2%, and construction workers 5%. Now, here are the safest airlines on which long historical data exist: American, British Caledonian, Continental, Delta, Eastern, Lufthansa, Pan Am, Qantas, SAS, Swissair, TAP, TWA, and United. Among the unsafest: CSA of Czechoslovakia, Egyptair, Tarom of Romania, PAL of the Philippines, Garuda of Indonesia. By far the unsafest country to fly to or from is Colombia. India is definitely the least safe major country. From top to bottom, here's the safety-order among the leading air-traffic nations: Holland, Australia, Scandanavia, U.S., West Germany, Britain, Canada, Japan, Italy, Belgium, France, Brazil, and (far less safe than Brazil) India.

A poll of frequent airline passengers by the Airline Passengers Association showed that the only major carrier singled out to avoid for poor service is Eastern. However, one recent study showed Pan American to be overwhelmingly the most complained-about airline. The air carriers with the lowest complaint-rates were Delta, Aloha, and Hawaiian. The top-rated airports in the A.P.A. poll were Tampa, Dallas-Ft.Worth, Washington Dulles, and Newark. The bottom-rated airports: Atlanta, Los Angeles, Washington National, and New York's Kennedy.

Getting to Airports

As just mentioned, Kennedy is far less good an airport than Newark. One reason for this is that when people talk of flying to or from NYC, they usually don't even give a second thought to a nearby New Jersey destination—it's not "New York." Consequently, Kennedy is far more crowded; Newark much more pleasant. Because of the under-utilization of Newark, it's also generally considered a safer airport. (Unlike JFK, which is red-starred as "unsafe" by the International Federation of Airline Pilots, this New Jersey airport, equally near to Manhattan, is rated "safe." Incidentally, among the airports which the pilots give a black star, indicating outright "dangerous," are St. Thomas Virgin Islands, and Nassau Bahamas; as well as Los Angeles Airport, and Boston's Logan.) Newark also happens to be easier to get to from Manhattan, via the PATH trains (far cheaper, and also more pleasant, than the NYC subways) to Newark, and the $2 airport-bus direct from there 15 minutes to the airport. The whole ride is far less grungy than taxi, cab, bus, or subway, to Kennedy or to La Guardia. Furthermore, it usually doesn't take any more time, and occasionally turns out to be faster. You can pick up the PATH at four stations along 6th Av. from 9th to 33rd Sts., and at Christopher St., and at the World Trade Center. For information on using this approach to get to Newark International Airport, phone 466-7649, M-F 9-5; and 1-201-963-2558, at other hours.

If you've got any valuables with you, don't leave them in baggage that you check with the airline. Baggage-theft is routine, but the extent of it is widely covered up by the airlines and even by the FBI, according to Queens District Attorney John Santucci, who called JFK particularly "a playground for the underworld," and then complained, "Nobody cooperates in those investigations." The U.S. Postal Service now sends armed guards to accompany every shipment of mail to and from JFK, but your luggage is fair game once it's out of your sight. The organized rings that control the freight-sheds are skilled at instantaneously recognizing the richest luggage to open and rifle. Most other airports are as bad as JFK. Airlines shown secretly filmed thefts from Boston's Logan Airport took no action. London's Heathrow has been nicknamed "Thiefrow."

It's generally best to avoid using cabs to get to or from the area's airports. Especially Kennedy has quite a few cabbies who have developed sophisticated ways to charge customers as much as three times the proper fare; and the local legal authorities just say "Isn't that terrible," and then blink. The *New York Times* had an article on this. A Swiss friend of mine coming from JFK was recently charged more than twice the proper fare into the City. Returning to the airport, she took the subway.

To get to or from Kennedy or LaGuardia via subway and bus (very cheap, and there's no aberrant cabbie who can rob you), do as follows:

To Kennedy: Take the A train to Lefferts Blvd., and then get on the Q-10 bus to the airport.

To LaGuardia: Take the E or F trains to Roosevelt Av., or the 7 train to 74th St.-Broadway (which is the same stop actually), and then get on the Q-33 bus to LaGuardia.

Both of these approaches are shown on the subway-map that's given out free at token-booths. On average, it'll take you about 20% longer to get to either airport this way than if you'd taken either a cab or the special subway train called the JFK Express (nicknamed "the train to the plane"); and this approach is by far cheaper—only 2 tokens. However, the JFK Express (which also is a subway and a bus, not a direct subway) is the reasonable alternative instead of a cab or airport-bus. For any of these subway-approaches to the airports, phone 330-1234, or as I'd mentioned, look at the subway-map.

Free Travel-Insurance

The Bank of New York, which offers both Visa and Mastercard at rather low annual fees, also gives all its credit-cardholders

38: TRAVEL SERVICES

$100,000 of free travel accident insurance.

Free Cars to Drive

Many cars are left stranded when the owner drives to his destination and then flys back home. He's glad when someone drives it back home for him. That someone could be you; and it's the cheapest way to see the U.S.A.! But you can't dawdle. If you want to visit Chicago, and then San Francisco, for example, you'll probably have to do it by arranging a second drive-away once you've finished exploring Chicago. Here's how it's done:

See "Automobile Transporters & Drive-Away Companies" in the Yellow Pages. Usually, you'll leave the company a $100 deposit, which is returned to you at the other end by the car-owner. You'll get one free tank of gas; supply the rest yourself. **TO QUALIFY:** Must be over 19 years old—usually over 21. Company photographs, usually fingerprints—and sometimes bonds—you, for owner's security getting his car back. You can go like this from city to city, repeating the entire process in each major town. Phone numbers of a few of the leading drive-away firms in Manhattan: 354-7777, 244-5240, 736-6697, 934-2414, 840-6262.

Ride-Shares

Before I mention discount car-rental agencies, there's one other alternative that's worth considering: sharing a car. The student unions at New York University and Columbia University both have "ride boards" on which people post where they are driving to or where they want to go. NYU's is downstairs at Loeb Student Center, on Washington Square South, at the corner of LaGuardia Place. However, there usually are very few rides posted at any time other than right before school-breaks.

Also, the New York Ride Center, at 134 W. 32, 279-3870, which charges $10 a year for membership, keeps a large number of rides posted, and these are not dependent upon university schedules.

Car-Rentals

When inquiring about rates, ask how many free miles, how much for each additional mile, and how much deductible on the insurance. (A lot of people don't ask about the latter, but suppose you scratch the fender—who pays?)

*****Ryan Chrysler-Plymouth**, 3588 Sunrise Hwy., Wantaugh, L.I. 1-516-785-0095. If it's for more than a week, these people are usually the best, even though they're out of town.

+Aegina Rent/Car**, 4779 Broadway (200-Dyckman), 942-9500. **Bonus discount to BF readers: 5-8%.**

****Goldie Leasing**, 47-11 11th St., L.I.C., 392-5435. Old cars, like Rent-A-Wreck below.

***Rent-A-Wreck**, Branches all over town, 580-6861. These aren't really wrecks, but they're not new, either. Best for short trips where fuel-guzzling cars are no great disadvantage.

***Hertz Airport Rates**, are lower than if car is picked up in town. Car can be dropped off at any Hertz location. 1-800-654-3131.

***Luby Car Rental**, 105-20 Queens Blvd., Forest Hills, 263-7700.

***East Coast Rent-A-Car**, 79-00 Queens Blvd., Elmhurst,

651-4900.

Gateway Ford, 104th St. at Rockaway Blvd., Ozone Park, 738-9500.

Rental Limousines

When asking for rates, inquire whether it's a regular limo or rather a stretch one, what make and year, whether it has a bar, if so then whether drinks are supplied at the bar, whether there's a TV, and if so then whether it's color or B/W; also whether the hourly rate is charged from the time the car leaves their garage to the time it returns.

+ **Rizique**, 84-04 256 St., Hillside, 347-8152. Rate is free of travel-time to and from customer, but there's a 3-hour minimum. **Bonus discount for BF Readers: 5%.**

Gotham, 242 E. 85, 772-1610.

Midtown, 101 Park Av., 724-2455.

McKee Cadillac, 155 W. 81, 362-3495.

Rand's, 443 W. 50, 977-3155.

Fugazy, 618 W. 49, 247-5800. Also offers blue Chrysler New Yorkers as taxis at rates competitive with those charged by radio-equipped taxis.

39:
THE 146 BARGAIN-RESTAURANTS

This was by far the most expensive part of the book for me to research. Unlike other restaurant-reviewers, I paid for every meal myself. The restaurants were unaware that I was dining there in order to evaluate them. The food that I ate is therefore presumably the same that will be made for you. It was not prepared with special care, and served free to a critic, so as to obtain a favorable review—the normal situation. My own feeling is that when a critic visits a dining-establishment, identifies himself and his purpose, and gets a freebie as a result, that meal may well be different—and probably better—than what you're going to eat and pay for. To me, it was worth paying the extra few thousand dollars in order to produce a restaurant-list that has some credibility.

New York City is, of course, widely considered to be one of the great culinary centers of the world. And there are about a dozen guidebooks available to help lead you through the maze of local dining-establishments. Nonetheless, in my opinion, none of these books is at all good from the standpoint of the restaurant-goer who wants to experience the best food for a given price. Perhaps the customary free meals for critics help explain that.

A few guides to cheap eateries do exist, but some of the food I've experienced at places that are recommended in each of these books has been so poor it's left me shocked. Of course, virtually any restaurant will have occasional off-days, or weaker dishes. But a good establishment should never sink to the level of the downright terrible. And it isn't only the allegedly "bargain" places that have surprised me with their bad food. Many of the expensive chow-houses I've tried that are listed as outstanding in regular non-bargain-oriented restaurant-guides have also left me wondering whether the reviewer ever actually sampled the food, or whether perhaps the food that was especially prepared for the critic was far superior to that which is served to the regular anonymous patron.

To be fair to restaurant-critics, however, perhaps part of the reason for the unreliability of their selections, is that the most important person in a restaurant is the chef—and there's no assurance that this single key individual will stay on at the same place from one year to the next. Indeed, as the present chapter was being prepared, two of the city's more competent French chefs, Leslie Revsin the culinary genius who had owned Restaurant Leslie and had made it the most consistently magnificent French dining-spot in town, and Robert Voorhees who had been responsible for turning the lunches at Mitchell's into something more than merely good, were both in the process of moving to different establishments. (Ms. Revsin is now at Fifth Avenue Restaurant.) But when the chef leaves while the restaurant itself survives—as hap-

39: THE 146 BARGAIN-RESTAURANTS

pened with Mitchell's—a certain standard should nonetheless be expected to be maintained by virtue of the owner's selectivity in finding a replacement, and it's not always easy to tell for certain from just a few visits to a place, whether indeed mere luck—a fluke in an owner's having stumbled upon a magnificent chef—is the real reason for a particular dining-establishment's grandeur. This is the biggest caveat that must apply to the recommendations in any restaurant-guide.

One thing, however, for which I can find not even a hypothetical excuse justifying the observed poor performance of restaurant-critics, is their general tendency to visit, and rate, the same well-worn eateries. Perhaps the culinary oracles fear that their opinions won't be taken seriously unless the best-known and highest-priced dining-spots receive the ritual praise—or at least mention—that seems to be expected. This is unfortunate, because often the finest meals are served at establishments which are never even visited, much less reviewed, by the critics. For example, pub-restaurants—even exceptionally fine ones—are almost universally ignored by those whose job it supposedly is to review such things. The same snobbery also results in the infrequent or non-existent press-coverage given to all French dining-places except the dozen or so that are outrageously overpriced. Rest assured, there actually do exist some very moderately priced French restaurants which offer food as good as, or better than, you'll find at some of the famous and much-reviewed prestige-ones that charge four times as much. In fact, this city's most consistently great French dining-establishment isn't one of those stratospherically-priced places at all, but rather one only half as expensive. However, for a real Bargain Finder, that's only the beginning. You can pay still half again less at some of the other French restaurants I recommend, where the food is usually better than it is at some of those terribly overpriced establishments. And if you're looking for truly magnificent world-class Chinese or Indian food, there are places I recommend where that can often be had for still half again less.

The restaurant-list below is intended to provide what currently does not exist (nor to my knowledge has it ever): a guide to top-value dining in New York City. However, I must state here one important restriction. It would frankly have been impossible for me even to begin to do justice to the dining-scene throughout all the five boroughs. Thus, this part of *BARGAIN FINDER* is primarily a guide to Manhattan. The only coverage given to restaurants in the outer boroughs is some Arabic dining-spots in or near Brooklyn's Atlantic-Avenue Arabic quarter, which is an attractive and easily-accessible part of the City that warrants visiting for other reasons than just its bargain-dining.

This was the only chapter which required that I actually had to buy the product or service myself in order to evaluate it. Along the way, I filled my belly with many mediocre meals, a few terrible ones, and also a satisfyingly substantial number of good-to-great ones. In most instances, I've dined at least twice at the places I recommend; this has especially been the case with the restaurants I've rated tops for food, because an excellent or great meal is more likely to be a fluke than is one that's merely good, or even fair. Often, an excellent dish turns out to be simply an unusually good offering at a fairly good restaurant. So wherever I found the cuisine to be exceptionally good, I was naturally a bit skeptical, and I tended to explore such places in greater depth than usual. As I mentioned at the beginning, I never identified myself as a restaurant-reviewer, and I got no free meals. I have every reason to believe that what I was served is what you'll get.

One thing I discovered in the process of researching this chapter, is that not only is there no predictable relationship between a restaurant's price and its quality; and not only is there no predictable relationship between what the majority of reviewers say about it (if anything) and its quality; but there also—and even more surprisingly—is no predictable relationship between a restaurant's popularity and its quality. One of the most overpriced and critically-acclaimed dining-establishments in New York is so popular that it's booked up for reservations months in advance, with willing victims for merely good-to-great food at around $100 per person. At the opposite end, there's the most popular dining-spot in Little Italy, which is recommended in two restaurant-"bargain" guidebooks, but where the food is so bad that I turned it away. (And the prices there aren't the lowest, either.) Many friends whose opinions on such matters I respect, and who've dined at this place several times over the past decade, tell me they've had the same disastrous experience. It's good to know that I'm not the only person who wonders how such an establishment manages to be listed in restaurant-guides, and to pack in the customers even at off-hours. And in between, there's a chain of moderate-priced Northern Italian restaurants in West Village, which offer only fair undistinguished food, but which often have lines waiting outside. I've decided that there's such a thing as a human-lemming phenomenon. Others might call it the crowd-mentality. As a certain dumbfounded acquaintance commented to me about her own experience at one of the restaurants I've just referred to: "People seem to have lost their shit-detectors." In the following restaurant-recommendations, I've taken care to be more discriminating than is evidently customary. You'll be the final judge as to whether I've succeeded.

The Category-System

Category-numbers indicate relative expensiveness. An entre at one of the Category-5 restaurants will cost you roughly $5/20$th's—or one fourth—as much as it will at one of the Category-20 establishments. As a general rule, you'll find that prices at the various places are approximately proportionate to their respective category-numbers. Thus, if you dine at one of the recommended restaurants, you can easily calculate by extension from the prices you find there, what the approximate costs will be at any one of the other recommended restaurants. Another chief advantage of this system is that, unlike listing specific menu-prices, even rapid economic inflation won't cause the restaurant-guide to become outdated.

39: THE 146 BARGAIN-RESTAURANTS

I assigned a category-number to each restaurant based on the average price of its frequently-ordered dinner-entres—in other words, based on the actual price that the average person there pays for a full-sized filling entre at dinner. In cases where the establishment charges less for lunch than for dinner, this is reflected in the category-number only if the restaurant was perched on the fence between two category-numbers, in which event I then assigned it to the lower one—otherwise to the higher. These category-numbers basically reflect prices at dinner, because that's when most people do their discretionary—and non-business-credit-card—dining out. I should also mention that any restaurant which charges unusually high for non-entre items, compared to the prices for its entres, would be listed in a slightly higher category-number as a result. This, however, didn't happen at any of the recommended places. Such things as a general rule are not encountered except at the city's most expensive dining-establishments, such as Lutece, and it need hardly be pointed out that such places wouldn't be listed in a book like this, because there are other places—which are recommended instead—which offer food that's as good or better, but that charge far less. One final point about the category-numbers: Some of the recommended restaurants offer primarily or exclusively complete dinners; and in such cases I estimated what share of the total cost went for the entre.

Just to give you an idea of what the prices were like when this chapter was being put together: An average entre at a Category-5 restaurant was going for about $2.50; at a Category-10, about $5; and at a Category-20, about $10. The city's top price-category (where of course I have no recommended restaurants, because the value is terrible) was upwards of a Category-80—or above $40. So those were the entre-prices. The cost of a full-course dinner was generally approximately the same as each place's respective category-number.

The Rating-System

There are four ratings: First, of course, there's the number of stars, which indicates how good the value is—how much quality you're getting for the money. This rating primarily reflects how good the food is for the money—and how much of it. (Unusually small portions reduce the rating). But it also reflects the quality of the ambiance for the money; and to a still lesser extent, the service for the money. So the stars, as always, are the value-rating system.

Then, separately, I rate food, ambiance, and service, each on a 1-to-10 scale (independent of price), where 10 represents the top quality-range, and 1 the bottom. At no restaurant was the food worse than fair (a 5), or the service worse than fair-to-poor (a 4); but one place had ambiance rated as low as very poor (a 2, at a hole-in-the-wall falafel-shop on MacDougal St.). Here are the ratings that are used for each of the three, and their meanings:

FOOD:	AMBIANCE:	SERVICE:
10—gourmet, world-class	10—excellent, elegant	10—excellent, attentive
9—excellent,	9—excellent,	9—excellent,

near-gourmet	informal	informal
8—very good	8—very good	8—very good
7—good	7—good	7—good
6—fair-to-good	6—fair-to-good	6—fair-to-good
5—fair	5—fair	5—fair
4—fair-to-poor	4—fair-to-poor	
3—poor		
2—very poor		

Before each restaurant is rated in these three categories, I state the nationality or nationalities of foods, or the kinds of foods, that are served. Also, if a restaurant is a cafeteria or other self-service establishment, I indicate that—in which case the place is not given a rating for service. The object of this system, and of the resulting listings below, is to give you as complete a picture of the place as possible, and to use the minimum of space and of words in which to do it, so that you can tell at a glance whether a particular dining-spot will suit your desires.

After all of the restaurants have been listed in order of increasing price-categories, you'll find them separately grouped by the top-rated places for quality of food, the top-rated ones from the standpoint of ambiance, the best dining-spots for vegetarians, and finally, groupings by the kind or nationality of cuisines, and by the restaurants' locations. This way, you'll be able to tell even faster which ones will best fulfill your particular needs, for location, price, value, kind of food, quality of food, and ambiance. For example, if you're looking for a very impressive-looking formal dining-spot for a dress-up occasion, and where the food should be good, but doesn't need to be great, you'll want a place rated 10 ("excellent, elegant") on ambiance, and at least 7 ("good") on cuisine; and you'll find all such restaurants (mixed in with other good-looking but not elegant ones) listed—with their ambiances verbally described—on the "Ambiance Honor Roll" which comes at the end of the category-numbers listing. Similarly, if you're looking for places which at least occasionally come up with uncompromisingly great food, you'll find all the best gourmet eateries listed on the "Gourmet Honor Roll." And vegetarians will find a separate honor roll listing the best dining-establishments to serve them.

Category 5
(rockbottom)

*****Leshko's**, 111 Av. A (at 7th St.), 473-9208. American & Slavic. Food: 6-7. Ambiance: 6. Service: 6.

***Garden Sandwich Shop**, 139 W. 33 (6th-7th Avs.), 564-3151. Cafeteria. American & Italian. Food: 5-7. Ambiance: 3. Self-service.

***Exchange Bar**, 634 8th Av. (40-1), 221-9513. Cafeteria. American. Food: 5-6. Ambiance: 4. Self-service.

***Jin Seafood**, 136 W. Broadway (Duane), 349-5375. Fast-food. Fried seafood. Food: 6. Ambiance: 4. Self-service. Closes at 6.

Victorian Cafeteria, 52 W. 45 (5th-6th Avs.), 840-1064. Cafeteria. American & Italian. Food: 5. Ambiance: 3. Self-service.

Mamoun's Falafel, 119 MacDougal St. (3), 674-9246. Fast-food.

39: THE 146 BARGAIN-RESTAURANTS

Mid-Eastern Falafels. Food: 5-7. Ambiance: 2. Self-service. Their falafel sandwich has skillful spicing.

Category 6
(near rockbottom)

******Dojo**, 24 St. Marks Place (= E. 8 St, 2-3 Avs.), 674-9821. Eclectic American & Japanese. Food: 7-10. Ambiance: 8. Service: 7-9. Unique whole-grain recipies. Especially popular are chicken yakisoba, and soyburger dinner. Best is the soyburger dinner, especially with swiss cheese. Make sure you tell waitress you want plenty of the sauce on the soyburger dinner—that's what makes it a real culinary hit. Terrific breakfasts. Extremely imaginative cuisine, as intelligently nutritious as it is delicious. Deservedly has a large and devoted following of sophisticated young people. One of NYC's great restaurants.

******Panna**, 330 E. 6 (1st-2nd Avs.), 475-9274. Indian. Food: 7-8. Ambiance: 7. Service: 8. Brown rice upon request; no extra charge. Sometimes a trifle bit too oily.

******Milon**, 93 1st Av. (5-6), up 1 flight, 228-4896. Indian. Food: 7-8. Ambiance: 6. Service: 8. Brown rice upon request; no extra charge. Both entres and complete dinners are good values here. A magnificent spiced tea served free at no extra charge.

******Good Karma**, 328 E. 6 (1st-2nd Avs.), 533-9332. Indian. Food: 7-9. Ambiance: 7. Service: 7. Brown rice upon request; no extra charge. Fairly wide selection of entres.

*****Royal Indian**, 93 1st Av. (6), 473-9673. Indian. Food: 6-7. Ambiance: 7. Service: 8. Same comments as Panna above.

****Anar Bagh**, 338 E. 6 (1st-2nd Avs.), 533-2177. Indian. Food: 5-9. Ambiance: 7. Service: 6. Brown rice upon request; no extra charge. Fairly wide selection of entres. Identical menu, prices, and ownership to Good Karma.

****Odessa**, 117 Av. A (7-8), 473-8916. American. Food: 6. Ambiance: 6. Service: 7.

****McCoy's**, 51 Nassau St. (at Maiden Ln.), 267-8312; 20 E. 42 (Mad. Av.), 697-7362. Pub-cafeterias. American. Food: 6. Ambiance: 7. Self-service.

****Martin's**, 11 Broadway (Beaver), 269-1294; 1847 Broadway (60-61), 247-6640. Pub-cafeterias. American. Food: 5. Ambiance: 6. Self-service.

****Samaria**, 129 Spring St. (at Greene), 966-3459. Cafeteria. American & Italian. Food: 6. Ambiance: 6. Self-service. Closes at 5.

***Blarney Rock**, 137 W. 33 (6th-7th Avs.), 947-0826. Pub-cafeteria. American. Food: 5. Ambiance: 5. Self-service.

***Treaty Stone**, 139 W. 33 (6th-7th Avs.), 560-9223. Pub-cafeteria. American. Food: 5. Ambiance: 5. Self-service.

Mauro, 39 E. 31 (Mad. Av.), 686-8066. Cafeteria. American & Italian. Food: 5. Ambiance: 4. Self-service. Closes at 5.

Category 7
(super-cheap)

*****Shah Bagh**, 320 E. 6 (1st-2nd Avs.), 677-8876. Indian. Food: 7. Ambiance: 5. Service: 7-8. Brown rice upon request; no extra charge. A la carte is better value than table d'hote.

*****Kismoth**, 326 E. 6 (1st-2nd Avs.), 473-9416. Indian. Food: 7. Ambiance: 4. Service: 5. Same comments as Shah Bagh immediately above.

****Wo On**, 16 Mott St. (Chatham Sq.), 962-8266. Chinese & Szechuan. Food: 6-7. Ambiance: 4. Service: 5. Quite possibly NYC's best-value Chinese restaurant. Most are so much alike, and this one is far cheaper. Too bad that this town lacks great Chinese restaurants; especially since China possesses perhaps the world's greatest cuisines. Anyway, this dining-spot gives its subject a fair run, and you can't beat the price anywhere.

****Nishan**, 330 E. 6 (2nd-3rd Avs.), 473-9612. Indian & Seafood. Food: 6-7. Ambiance: 7. Service: 7-8. Large seafood selection. Brown rice upon request; no extra charge.

***Shamoly**, 328 E. 6 (2nd-3rd Avs.), 982-6790. Indian & Seafood. Food: 5-7. Ambiance: 6. Service: 7-8. Brown rice upon request; no extra charge.

***Wo Hop**, 17 Mott St. downstairs (Chatham Sq.), 962-8617. Chinese without Szechuan. Food: 5-6. Ambiance: 4. Service: 5.

***Taco Rico**, 121 MacDougal St. (3), 777-9250; 176 W. 72 (B'wy), 874-9891. Fast-food. Mexican. Food: 6. Ambiance: 4. Self-service. The only reasonably good Mexican fast-food I've encountered anywhere in this country. Enormous portions. The burrito is practically a full meal.

***Jolanta**, 119 1st Av. (7-8), 254-9109. American & Slavic. Food: 5. Ambiance: 4. Service: 6.

***Lantern**, 160 W. 46 (6th-7th Avs.), 221-3796. Japanese. Food: 5-7. Ambiance: 4. Service: 5.

James Self-Service, 24 W. 56 (5th Av.), 586-6175. Cafeteria. American & Italian. Food: 5. Ambiance: 5.

Chick-Teri, 123 W. 45 (6th-7th Avs.), 765-6370. Japanese. Food: 5. Ambiance: 6. Service: 6 nighttimes; cafeteria daytimes.

Blarney Castle, 110 Chambers St. (Church), 962-8638. Pub-cafeteria. American. Food: 5. Ambiance: 6. Self-service.

P.S. Restaurant, 32 W. 38 (5th-6th Avs.), 221-3334. American. Food: 5. Ambiance: 5. Service: 6. Closes at 6.

Category 8
(extremely cheap)

******Curry & Tandoor**, 324 E. 6 (1st-2nd Avs.), 982-8127. Indian. Food: 7-10. Ambiance: 8 cozy. Service: 8-9. Brown rice upon request; no extra charge. Especially strongly recommended are the magnificent chicken rasmikebab and chana bhaji, though also superb are the tandoori chicken, tandoori shrimp, lamb masala, beef masala, and chana ponir. Wide selection of entres. As with all the recommended Indian restaurants, it's best to order an entre plus the assorted appetizers, rather than the dinner. When the owner, Lal Khan, is serving as the chef, as he often does, the food here is stratospheric. One of NYC's great restaurants.

*****West End**, 2911 Broadway (114), 666-8750. Pub-restaurant. American. Food: 6. Ambiance: 7 without the free live jazz, 9 with it (after 9 p.m. each night). Service: 7. (Also offers cafeteria self-service, except in the jazz-room.) Some of the top jazz musicians play here. Never a cover or admission charge, only a small minimum. This is the chief off-campus hangout for students from Columbia University 2 blocks away.

**Moroccan Star, Brooklyn, 205 Atlantic Av. (Court St.), 596-1919. Arabic. Food: 7-8. Ambiance: 6. Service: 7-8.

*Tad's Steaks, 119 W. 42, 354-0730; 707 7th Av. (47), 575-8787; 18 E. 42, 867-6832; 200 W. 50, 247-1752; 104 E. 14, 228-8383; 154 W. 34, 244-4085; 228 W. 42, 354-5530; 607 Lex. Av. (53), 832-2294. Cafeterias. American, steaks and burgers. Food: 5. Ambiance: 5-6. Self-service.

*Eva's, 11 W. 8 (5th-MacDougal), 677-3496; 1074 2nd Av. (57), 935-4882. Cafeterias. Mid-Eastern. Food: 6. Ambiance: 6. Self-service.

*Shamiana, 119 Lex. Av. at 28th St., 689-5150. Indian. Food: 8. Ambiance: 7 light, modern. Service: 7. Highly and skillfully spiced food, though purists might object to these pre-fab meals.

Punjab India, 175 Bleecker St. (Sullivan), 677-4510. Indian. Food: 6. Ambiance: 5. Service: 7.

Caldron, 306 E. 6 (2nd Av.), 473-9543. Macrobiotic Japanese. Food: 5. Ambiance: 5. Service: 6.

Lucky Garden, 224 W. 50 (7th-8th Avs.), 541-5236. Chinese & Szechuan. Food: 5. Ambiance: 4. Service: 5.

Category 9
(very cheap)

****Rathbone's, 1702 2nd Av. (88), 369-7361. Pub-restaurant. American. Food: 7-8. Ambiance: 8. Service: 7. Competes with Drake's Drum as best-value steak-house.

***Hobeau's, 963 1st Av. (53), 421-2888;

***Nodelini's, 1311 Madison Av. (92-3), 369-5677;

***Butterfish Hole, 1394 3rd Av. (at 79), 879-0991;

***Squid Roe, 1468 2nd Av. (at 77), 249-4666;

***Cockeyed Clams, 1678 3rd Av. (at 94), 831-4121; All 5 of the preceding: Seafood (huge selection). Food: 6-8. Ambiance: 8. Service: 5-9 (during rushed hours, they sometimes mistakenly serve wrong dish; in which case, ask them to change it).

*Eastern Garden, 2628 Broadway (100), 866-0160 & 864-9631. Chinese & Szechuan. Food: 6. Ambiance: 5. Service: 5.

*Atlas, 171 W. 29 (at 7th Av.), 2nd floor, 695-6998. Greek. Food: 6. Ambiance: 6. Service: 6. Lunch only.

+McAnn's, 133 W. 33 (6th-7th Avs.), 695-8429; 687 Lexington Av. (57), 421-8730; 130 E. 40 (Lex. Av.), 689-0934. American. Food: 6. Ambiance: 7. Service: 7. **Bonus-discount to BF readers: 10% off if you show this book.**

+Alpine Tavern, 50 W. 34 (in McAlpin Hotel), 695-3264; 871 7th Av. (56th St.), 245-0295. American. Food: 6. Ambiance: 6. Service: 7. **Bonus-discount to BF readers: 10% off if you show this book.**

Madras Woodlands, 310 E. 44 (1st-2nd), 986-0620. Indian vegetarian. Food: 8-9. Ambiance: 8. Service: 2-4 (perfunctory, and twice I waited more than 20 minutes for service, while many others seated after me—mostly Indians—were nonetheless served before

I was). Many unusual dishes.

Ideal Lunch, 238 E. 86 (2nd-3rd Av.), 650-1632. German. Food: 5. Ambiance: 3. Service: 6.

Category 10
(cheap)

**** + **Drake's Drum**, 1629 2nd Av. (85), 988-2826. Pub-restaurant. American. Food: 7-9. Ambiance: 9. Service: 7-9. One of the most beautiful pubs in the city. Homey, informal, cozy. Often their charbroiled prime burgers are unsurpassable. Their daytime-specials are stunning super-bargains. **Bonus-discount to BF readers: 5-10% off (except on the daytime-specials) if you show this book. (See inside-back cover for details.)**

******Fedora**, 239 W. 4th St. (Charles St.), 242-9691. Southern Italian. Food: 7-8. Ambiance: 7 small, cozy, well-worn. Service: 7. Dinner only. An extraordinary place. Come at 5:30-6 p.m. before the crowd (mostly locals), and experience the Village regulars greeting each other and chatting with Fedora, who manages the kitchen, and her husband, Henry, who tends bar. This is an authentic local haunt, which gives meaning to the "Village" in "Greenwich Village." NYC's lowest prices for bottles of wine, which are better values here than are the tiny carafes.

*****Sung Ho Lo**, 211 7th Av. (22), 924-8580. Chinese & Szechuan. Food: 8-9. Ambiance: 7. Service: 8. This is probably the best-value Chinese-Szechuan restaurant in NYC.

*****Donegal Inn**, 103 W. 72 (Columbus), 874-4268. Pub-restaurant. American. Food: 7-8. Ambiance: 6. Service: 8-9. The menu is small, but for prime steaks and burgers this place beats out most restaurants that charge twice the price.

****Finnegan's Wake** 1361 1st Av. (73), 737-3664. Pub-restaurant. American. Food: 6. Ambiance: 7. Service: 7-8.

***Delphi**, 109 W. Broadway (at Reade), 227-6322. Mid-Eastern & Greek. Food: 6. Ambiance: 7. Service: 7-8.

***Greek Village**, 1016 Lexington Av. (72-73), 288-7378. Mid-Eastern & Greek. Food: 6. Ambiance: 6. Service: 8.

***Hang Zhou Lou**, 68 E. Broadway (Market St.), 925-5144. Chinese & Szechuan. Food: 7. Ambiance: 6. Service: 8-9.

***Ho Me Dor**, 27 Division St. (Chatham Sq.), 966-7663. Chinese & Szechuan. Food: 6-7. Ambiance: 6. Service: 7-8.

***Dragon Garden**, 47 Division St. (Market St.), 966-6180. Chinese & Szechuan. Food: 6-7. Ambiance: 6. Service: 8.

***Wu Fang**, 36 E. Broadway (Catherine), 925-7498. Chinese & Szechuan. Food: 6-8. Ambiance: 5. Service: 8.

***Beansprout**, 37 Barrow St. (at 7th Av.), 255-3066. Chinese & Szechuan. Food: 6-7. Ambiance: 8. Service: 7.

***Son of the Sheik**, Brooklyn, 165 Atlantic Av. (Clinton), 625-4023. Arabic. Food: 6-7. Ambiance: 5. Service: 7.

Chuan Hong, 2748 Broadway (105-6), 866-5920 & 678-9479. Chinese & Szechuan. Food: 5-6. Ambiance: 4. Service: 7. Has 3 main menus, + lunch-menu, + specials-menu—vast range of offerings.

Captain Mike's, 126 Chambers St. (Church), 349-0059 & 962-8124. Seafood. Food: 5. Ambiance: 5. Service: 7. Closed weekends.

Souen Uptown, 2444 Broadway (90), 787-1110. Macrobiotic Japanese. Food: 5-7. Ambiance: 6. Service: 7. The pies here are especially good.

Category 11
(moderately cheap)

***Singles**, 951 1st Av. (52-53), 486-9832 & 355-8817. Pub-restaurant. American. Food: 7-8. Ambiance: 8. Service: 7. Superb specials all day long. Drinks half price at the bar until 7. A very friendly place. Chicken parmigian and prime ribs are especially popular.

**Empire Szechuan Gourmet*, 2574 Broadway (at 97), 663-6980&7063. Chinese & Szechuan. Food: 6-9. Ambiance: 7. Service: 9. If you're ordering Szechuan, best to tell them you want it highly flavored, not bland.

**Peppers Sichuan*, 2536 Broadway (at 95), 865-3440. Chinese & Szechuan. Food: 7-8. Ambiance: 7. Service: 9. Unusually hotly spiced Szechuan dishes. I'm told that this is the authentic way it's done in Sichuan (Szechuan) Province.

**Szechuan Omei Too*, 1485 1st Av. (78), 249-5700. Chinese & Szechuan. Food: 7. Ambiance: 8. Service: 8.

Szechuan Taste West, 2332 Broadway (84-85), 873-6665. Chinese & Szechuan. Food: 7. Ambiance: 7. Service: 7. Not affiliated with the other "Szechuan Taste" restaurants.

*Z, 117 E. 15 (Irving), 254-0960. Greek. Food: 7. Ambiance: 8. Service: 7-8. Very inexpensive wine-list. The best retsina I've ever tasted.

*Brass 'N Wood Inn, 124 Chambers St. (Church), 227-7074. Seafood. Food: 6. Ambiance: 7. Service: 7.

*Taiz Yemen, Brooklyn, 172 Court St. (Amity), 625-3907&8397. Arabic & French. Food: 7-8. Ambiance: 8. Service: 8.

*Green Tree, 1034 Amsterdam Av. (at 111), 864-9106. Hungarian. Food: 7. Ambiance: 7. Service: 7.

Pig 'N Whistle, 36 W. 48 (5th-6th Avs.), 247-3070. American. Food: 6. Ambiance: 7. Service: 8.

Hunan Inn, 61 2nd Av. (4), 777-6868. Chinese & Szechuan. Food: 5-7. Ambiance: 6. Service: 8.

Long River, 10 W. 45, 840-1831. Chinese & Szechuan. Food: 6. Ambiance: 7. Service: 7. Small menu.

Szechuan Palace, 2602 Broadway (98-99), 662-2683&8290. Chinese & Szechuan. Food: 6. Ambiance: 7. Service: 7.

Hot Wok, 2188 Broadway (77-78), 595-8053 & 799-8760. Chinese & Szechuan. Food: 6. Ambiance: 6. Service: 6.

Category 12
(high cheap)

**Hunan Pan*, 550 Hudson St. (at Perry), 242-5566. Chinese & Szechuan. Food: 8-9. Ambiance: 8 somewhat rustic. Service: 7.

**Empire Szechuan Balcony*, 381 3rd Av. (27-28), 685-6215. Chinese & Szechuan. Food: 7-9. Ambiance: 7. Service: 8. If you're ordering Szechuan, best to tell them you want it highly flavored, not bland.

****Hunan Balcony**, 2596 Broadway (at 98), 865-0400. Chinese & Szechuan. Food: 7-9. Ambiance: 7. Service: 7.

****Hunan Park**, 235 Columbus Av. (70-71), 724-4411. Chinese & Szechuan. Food: 7-9. Ambiance: 8 (small, nice). Service: 8-9.

****Tang Tang**, 1470 1st Av. (77), 744-9320. Chinese & Szechuan. Food: 7-9. Ambiance: 8. Service: 7.

****Serendipity**, 225 E. 60 (2nd-3rd Avs.), 838-3531. Unique American, huge sandwiches, salads, desserts. Food: 7-8. Ambiance: 9. Service: 8-9. Desserts are the real specialty here—elaborate, extremely rich, and enormous. Entres also are good values. Everything is extravagant, including even the expensive fixtures and furnishings. Jammed with the Bloomingdale's crowd. Expect long lines and waits, unless you've made reservations for an off-hour. A phenomenon.

****Broome St. Bar (Ken & Bob's)**, 363 W. Broadway (at Broome), 925-2086. Bar and restaurant. Imaginative American cuisine. Great salads. Food: 7-8. Ambiance: 9. Service: 9. An artsy neighborhood singles bar.

****Acapulco**, 1555 2nd Av. (81), 650-1718&9077. Mexican & Spanish. Food: 7-8. Ambiance: 8. Service: 8-9.

***Tijuana**, 217 E. 86 (2nd-3rd Avs.), 289-9627. Mexican & Spanish. Food: 7-8. Ambiance: 7. Service: 8-9.

***Mexico Lindo**, 459 2nd Av. (at 26), 679-3665. Mexican & Spanish. Food: 7-8. Ambiance: 7. Service: 8-9.

***Sevilla**, 62 Charles St. (at W. 4), 929-3189 & 243-9513. Spanish. Food: 6. Ambiance: 9 cozy, usually crowded. Service: 9. If only Spanish food were capable of the same heights that, say, Mexican is, this could have been a great restaurant.

***Magic Carpet**, 52 Carmine St. (Bleecker), 929-9329. Mid-Eastern. Food: 9. Ambiance: 7. Service: 5-8 very slow. This is the place to open the mind of the person who is under the misconception that Mid-Eastern food can't be of gourmet calibre. Try the spinach pie deluxe platter, the vegetarian combination platter #2, or the ouzi.

***Empire Szechuan Bleecker**, 160A Bleecker St. (at Sullivan), 260-0206. Chinese & Szechuan. Food: 5-10. Ambiance: 9 (tastefully cheery). Service: 9. Incredibly uneven food, from bland to heavenly (and it seems that the heavenly may only have been for the first few weeks that the place was open). If you're having Szechuan, best to tell them you want it hignly flavored.

***Olde New York**, 1567 2nd Av. (81-82), 650-1869. American. Food: 6-7. Ambiance: 7. Service: 8. Excellent lunch specials.

***Bavarian Inn**, 232 E. 86 (2nd-3rd Avs.), 650-1056. German. Food: 6. Ambiance: 8 friendly. Service: 8. For the less expensive items on the menu, prices are only slightly higher than at the Ideal Restaurant nearby, and the value here is thus much better. But Ideal charges a third less for the dearer dishes, so the two match values on those.

***Almontaser**, Brooklyn, 218 Court St. (Warren), 624-9267. Arabic & French. Food: 7-8. Ambiance: 7. Service: 8.

+**Near East**, Brooklyn, 136 Court St. (at Atlantic), 625-9559. Arabic. Food: 7. Ambiance: 7. Service: 8. **Bonus discount to BF**

39: THE 146 BARGAIN-RESTAURANTS

readers: 10% if you show this book.

Adnan, Brooklyn, 129 Atlantic Av. (Henry), 625-8697. Arabic. Food: 7. Ambiance: 7. Service: 7.

Hunan Fortune, 302 E. 72 (2nd Av.), 861-8761. Chinese & Szechuan. Food: 7-8. Ambiance: 6. Service: 7.

Souen Downtown, 210 6th Av. (at Prince), 255-4890. Japanese Macrobiotic. Food: 5-7. Ambiance: 9 calm. Service: 7. The pies here are especially good, but rather expensive.

Category 13
(very low reasonable)

***+**MTC**, 731 Broadway (Astor), 475-6814. Thai. Food: 8-10. Ambiance: 8. Service: 8-9. One of the world's greatest national cuisines, done "to a T." Try Kaeng Hung Ray chicken curry, which is stellar. Also good: Yum Nuer, and Pla Ladd Preeg. Thai is a spicey cuisine, comparable to Szechuan. One of NYC's great restaurants. Free live music some nights. **Bonus BF discount: 10% off if you show this book.**

*****Bangcock Cuisine**, 1470 1st Av. (77), 772-2492. Thai. Food: 9. Ambiance: 9. Service: 9. Dark and romantic with food to match. One of NYC's great restaurants.

*+**Manhattan Bridge Club**, 27 W. 72 (Columbus), penthouse, Olcott Hotel, 799-4242. American. Food: 7. Ambiance: 7. Self-service at lunch. 12-1:30 7 days, smorgasbord lunch free with modest bridge-game fee. 6:30-7:30 Sunday nights, $2 dinner with bridge-game fee. **Bonus BF discount: 10% off any series of bridge lessons.**

***La Fondue**, 43 W. 55 (5th-6th Avs.), 581-0820. Swiss. Food: 7. Ambiance: 8. Service: 9. "In" among the young chic set.

***Thomas St. Inn**, 8 Thomas St. (B'wy), 349-6350. American & Italian. Food: 7-8. Ambiance: 9. Service: 8-9.

O'Melia's, 1559 2nd Av. (at 81), 988-9330 & 650-9076. American. Food: 7. Ambiance: 8. Service: 8.

K.C. Place Uptown, 807 9th Av. (53-54), 246-4258. Seafood. Food: 7. Ambiance: 7. Service: 8.

Emilio's, 307 6th Av. (3), 929-9861. Italian. Food: 6-7. Ambiance: 9. Service: 8.

Category 14
(low reasonable)

****Monte's**, 97 MacDougal St. (Bleecker), 674-9456. Italian. Food: 7-9. Ambiance: 7. Service: 6-9.

****The Right Bank**, 822 Madison Av. (69), 737-2811. American & French. Food: 7-8. Ambiance: 7. Service: 8.

****Trattoria Pino**, 981 3rd Av. (58), 688-3817. Italian. Food: 7. Ambiance: 8. Service: 8. Small portions.

***Steak Pommes Frites**, 22 W. 56 (5th-6th Avs.), 974-9431. French & American. Food: 7. Ambiance: 8 homey. Service: 8.

Reidy's, 22 E. 54 (Mad. Av.), 753-2419. American & Seafood. Food: 6-7. Ambiance: 7. Service: 8-9.

Uncle Lulu's, 16 W. 56 (5th Av.), 541-9291. American. Food: 6. Ambiance: 7. Service: 8.

Category 15

(reasonable)

***Il Ponte Vecchio**, 206 Thompson St. (Bleecker), 473-9382. Northern Italian. Food: 9. Ambiance: 9 very European, yet modest and unpretentious; in its own very quiet way, one of the City's most beautiful dining-environments. Service: 10. One of NYC's great restaurants. Dinner only.

Mitchell's, 122 E. 27 (Park-Lex.), 689-2058. American & French. Food: 7-9. Ambiance: 7-8. Service: 8-9. Very friendly. Popular among the local office-workers.

Catetgory 16
(rather reasonable)

Benito, 163 Mulberry St. (Grand), 226-9012. Southern Italian. Food: 8-9. Ambiance: 8 small, casual, somewhat homey. Service: 8. Generally the best restaurant in Little Italy. One of NYC's great restaurants.

Mont St. Michel, 327 W. 57 (8th-9th Avs.), 581-1032. French. Food: 7-9. Ambiance: 8 rear-room—cheery, homey, inviting; 5 front-room—should be re-done. Service: 7-8. The chocolate mousse here has chocolate chunks which radiate aroma.

La Maison Japonaise, 334 Lexington Av. (at 39), 682-7375. French & Japanese. Food: 7. Ambiance: 9 elegant but a little cramped. Service: 9.

Villa Pensa, 198 Grand St. (Mulberry), 226-8830. Italian. Food: 7. Ambiance: 6. Service: 9. Closed Wednesdays.

Category 17
(high reasonable)

K.C. Place Downtown, 46 Lexington Av. (24), 532-6402. Seafood. Food: 6-7. Ambiance: 8. Service: 8-9.

Category 18
(very low moderate)

Chez Cardinale, 347 W. 46 (8th-9th Avs.), 245-9732 & 247-4284. French. Food: 7-9. Ambiance: 8 subdued. Service: 8-9.

Chez Jacqueline, 213 6th Av. (at King), 255-6885. French, from Nice. Food: 7. Ambiance: 7. Service: 9.

Category 19
(low moderate)

***Fiorella**, 1081 3rd Av. (64), 838-7570. Northern Italian with French influence. Food: 10. Ambiance: 9. Service: 10. Sensational. One of NYC's great restaurants. Free chamber music concerts in the front room at Sunday brunch.

Category 20
(moderate)

Vivolo, 140 E. 74 (Lex.), 737-3533. Italian. Food: 8. Ambiance: 10 cozy and romantically elegant, in a fireplaced townhouse. Service: 10.

Anche Vivolo, 222 E. 58 (2nd-3rd Avs.), 308-0112. Italian. Food: 8. Ambiance: 10 small and formal. Service: 10.

The Sumptuary, 400 3rd Av. (28-29), upstairs, 889-6056. North-

39: THE 146 BARGAIN-RESTAURANTS

ern Italian and Southern French. Food: 7-8. Ambiance: 9. Service: 9-10.

*L'Escargot, 47 W. 55 (5th-6th Avs.), 245-4266. French. Food: 7. Ambiance: 9. Service: 8.

*Le Champignon, 35 W. 56 (5th-6th Avs.), 245-6335. French. Food: 6. Ambiance: 10 possibly the most beautiful restaurant in NYC, elegant downstairs, cozy upstairs. Service: 7.

*Cafe des Sports, 329 W. 51 (8th-9th Avs.), 581-1283. French. Food: 7. Ambiance: 8 cozy. Service: 8-9.

*Cafe 58, 232 E. 58 (2nd-3rd Avs.), 757-5665. French. Food: 7 small portions. Ambiance: 9. Service: 8.

*Du Midi, 311 W. 48 (8th-9th Avs.), 974-9097. French. Food: 7. Ambiance: 6. Service: 7-9.

Cafe de France, 330 W. 46 (8th-9th Avs.), 586-0088. French. Food: 5-6. Ambiance: 7. Service: 8.

Le Grand Saloon, 1644 3rd Av. (at 92), 289-1112. Mostly French. Food: 6. Ambiance: 7. Service: 8.

Category 22
(rather moderate)

*Il Cortile, 125 Mulberry St. (Hester), 226-6060. Italian, large menu. Food: 8. Ambiance: 8 neo-ornate. Service: 9-10.

Category 24
(high moderate)

S.P.Q.R., 133 Mulberry St. (Grand), 925-3120. Italian, very large menu. Food: 8. Ambiance: 9 elegant but somewhat impersonal. Service: 5.

Category 26
(very low expensive)

**Fifth Avenue, 24 5th Av. (at 9th St.), 475-0880. French. Food: 10. Ambiance: 10. Service: 10. French nouvelle cuisine the way it started but unfortunately no longer is. Chef is Leslie Revsin, formerly of Restaurant Leslie. This is now what that was: the finest French dining-establishment in NYC. Setting is elegant, but not at all stiff. One of NYC's great restaurants.

40:
THE 3 CULINARY HONOR-ROLLS

This is for quick reference, so that you can immediately identify which places will satisfy which needs.

GOURMET HONOR-ROLL

These are the dining-establishments that at least occasionally serve unsurpassable dishes (up to 10-rated for food). For all the ones that occasionally come close—and there are a much larger number of those—see the top-starred restaurants in price-categories 6, 8, 10, 11, 12, and 15 on up.

Before each establishment's name, is shown its price-category number. Address, phone, and specific ratings, for each establishment, will be found under its listing within that category-number. All that's shown here, in addition to category-number, will be the nature of the cuisine, since this honor-roll is for quick reference about food.

6 ******Dojo.** Unique American & Japanese.
8 ******Curry & Tandoor.** Indian.
10 *****Sung Ho Lo.** Chinese & Szechuan.
12 ***Magic Carpet.** Mid-Eastern.
12 ****Hunan Pan.** Chinese & Szechuan.
12 ****Hunan Park.** Chinese & Szechuan.
13 *****MTC.** Thai.
13 *****Bangcock Cuisine.** Thai.
15 *****Il Ponte Vecchio.** Northern Italian.
19 *****Fiorella.** Italian.
26 ****Fifth Avenue.** French.

AMBIANCE HONOR-ROLL

The same as before, only here are selected the most attractive-looking places—those rated 8, 9, or 10, for ambiance.

6 ******Dojo.** Casual, hip, young, artsy, crowded.
8 ******Curry & Tandoor.** Small, subdued, cozy.
8 *****West End.** College hangout, free jazz at night.
9 *****Hobeau's.** Casual, pub-atmosphere.
9 *****Nodelini's.** Casual, pub-atmosphere.
9 *****Butterfish Hole.** Casual, pub-atmosphere.
9 *****Cockeyed Clams.** Casual, pub-atmosphere.
10 ****+ **Drake's Drum.** Homey, cozy, singles-pub.
10 ***Beansprout.** Slightly homey.
11 ***** Singles.** Friendly singles bar-restaurant.
11 *** Z.** Somewhat dressy. Open-air dining in rear.
12 ****Hunan Pan.** Rustic, airy, but somewhat small.
12 ****Broome St. Bar.** Artsy neighborhood singles-bar.
12 ****Hunan Park.** Somewhat dressy; small.

40: THE 3 CULINARY HONOR-ROLLS

12 **Serendipity. "In," informal, extravagant.
12 **Acapulco. Casual. A bit of Mexico.
12 *Sevilla. Cozy, crowded, romantic.
12 *Empire Szechuan Bleeker. Cheery.
12 *Bavarian Inn. Homey, friendly.
12 Souen Downtown. Calm, woody, geometric.
13 ***MTC. Subdued.
13 ***Bangcock Cuisine. Dark, romantic.
13 *La Fondue. Casual. "In." Sophisticated young.
13 *Thomas St. Inn. Calming. Casually elegant.
13 O'Melia's. Homey, informal.
13 Emilio's. Easygoing, friendly.
14 **Trattoria Pino. Bare brick, but slightly dressy.
14 *Steak Pommes Frites. Informal, homey.
15 ***Il Ponte Vecchio. Unpretentiously continental.
16 **Benito. Small, casual, somewhat homey.
16 **Mont St. Michel rear room. Homey, cheerful.
16 *La Maison Japonaise. Small, elegant.
17 K.C. Place Downtown. Inviting, somewhat casual.
18 **Chez Cardinale. Subdued, almost romantic.
19 ***Fiorella. Dressy, yet easygoing.
20 *Vivolo. Elegant, cozy, fireplaced townhouse.
20 *Anche Vivolo. Formal, small.
20 *The Sumptuary. Cozy, intimate.
20 *L'Escargot. Somewhat cozy, dressy.
20 *Cafe 58. A bit subdued, inviting.
20 *Le Champignon. Supreme: elegant, cozy. Dressy.
22 *Il Cortile. Neo-ornate, but still nice.
24 S.P.Q.R. Formal. Huge.
26 **Fifth Avenue. Elegant, with warmth.

VEGETARIAN HONOR-ROLL

The same as before, only this time the focus is on those recommended restaurants which have the widest selection (at least 3) of good, filling, wholesome, substantial, vegetarian entres.

6 ****Dojo. ****Good Karma. ****Panna. ****Milon. ***Royal Indian. **Anar Bagh.

7 **Wo On. ***Shah Bagh. ***Kismoth. **Nishan. *Shamoly. *Wo Hop. *Taco Rico.

8 ****Curry & Tandoor. *Eva's. *Shamiana. Punjab India. Caldron. Lucky Garden.

9 Madras Woodlands (largest vegetarian selection in NYC). *Eastern Garden.

10 ***Sung Ho Lo. *Delphi. *Greek Village. *Hang Zhou Lou. *Ho Me Dor. *Dragon Garden. *Wu Fang. *Beansprout. Chuan Hong.

11 **Empire Szechuan Gourmet. **Peppers Sichuan. *Szechuan Taste West. Szechuan Palace. Human Inn. Hot Wok.

12 **Hunan Pan. **Empire Szechuan Balcony. **Hunan Balcony. **Hunan Park. **Broome St. Bar. **Acapulco. *Tijuana. *Mexico Lindo. *Empire Szechuan Bleeker. Hunan Fortune.

41:
THE 17 TYPES OF CUISINES SERVED

As before, but this time, it's a question of "Shall we dine Italian or Szechuan tonight? Or perhaps go to a seafood place?"

American: 5: ***Leshko's, *Garden Sandwich Shop, *Exchange Bar, Victorian Cafeteria. **6:** ****Dojo, **Odessa, **McCoy's, **Martin's, **Samaria, *Blarney Rock, *Treaty Stone, Mauro. **7:** *Jolanta, James Self-Service, P.S., Blarney Castle. **8:** ***West End, *Tad's Steaks. **9:** ****Rathbone's, +McAnn's, +Alpine Tavern. **10:** ****+Drake's Drum, ***Donegal Inn, **Finnegan's Wake. **11:** ***Singles, Pig 'N Whistle. **12:** **Serendipity, **Broome St. Bar, *Olde New York. **13:** *+Manhattan Bridge Club, *Thomas St. Inn, O'Melia's. **14:** **The Right Bank, *Steak Pommes Frites, Reidy's, Uncle Lulu's. **15:** **Mitchell's. **18:**

Arabic (also see "Mid-Eastern" & "Greek"): **8:** **Moroccan Star. **10:** *Son of the Sheik. **11:** *Taiz Yemen. **12:** *Almontaser, +Near East, Adnan.

Chinese & Szechuan: 7: **Wo On, * Wo Hop (but no Szechuan). **8:** Lucky Garden. **9:** *Eastern Garden. **10:** *Hang Zhou Lou, *Ho Me Dor, *Dragon Garden, *Wu Fang, *Beansprout, Chuan Hong. **10:** ***Sung Ho Lo. **11:** **Empire Szechuan Gourmet, **Peppers Sichuan, **Szechuan Omei Too, *Szechuan Taste West, Long River, Szechuan Palace, Human Inn, Hot Wok. **12:** **Hunan Pan, **Tang Tang, **Empire Szechuan Balcony, **Hunan Balcony, **Hunan Park, *Empire Szechuan Bleecker, Hunan Fortune.

French: 11: *Taiz Yemen (& Arabic—only Arabic at lunch). **12:** *Almontaser (& Arabic—only Arabic at lunch). **14:** **The Right Bank (& American), *Steak Pommes Frites (& American). **15:** **Mitchell's (& American), **Mont St. Michel, *La Maison Japonaise (& Japanese). **18:** **Chez Cardinale, Chez Jacqueline. **20:** *The Sumptuary (& Italian), *L'Escargot, *Le Champignon, *Cafe des Sports, *Cafe 58, *Du Midi, Cafe de France, Le Grand Saloon. **26:** **Fifth Avenue.

German: 9: Ideal Lunch. **12:** *Bavarian Inn.

Greek (also see "Arabic" & "Mid-Eastern"): **9:** *Atlas (lunch only). **10:** *Delphi, *Greek Village. **11:** *Z.

Hungarian: 11: *Green Tree.

Indian: 6 ****Good Karma, ****Panna, ****Milon, ***Royal Indian, **Anar Bagh. **7:** ***Shah Bagh, ***Kismoth, ***Nishan (& Seafood), *Shamoly (& Seafood). **8:** ****Curry & Tandoor. *Shamiana. **9:** Madras Woodlands.

Italian: 5: *Garden Sandwich Shop, Victorian Cafeteria. **6:** **Samaria, Mauro. **7:** James Self-Service. **10:** ****Fedora. **13:** *Thomas St. Inn (only dinner), Emilio's. **14:** **Monte's, **Trattoria Pino. **15:** ***Il Ponte Vecchio. **16:** **Benito, Villa Pensa. **19:** ***Fiorella. **20:** *Vivolo, *Anche Vivolo, *The Sumptuary (& French). **22:** *Il Cortile. **24:** S.P.Q.R.

41: THE 17 TYPES OF CUISINES SERVED

Japanese: 6: ****Dojo (& American). **7:** *Lantern, Chick-Teri. **8:** Caldron (Macrobiotic). **10:** Souen Uptown (Macrobiotic). **12:** Souen Downtown. **16:** *La Maison Japonaise (& French).

Mexican: 7: *Taco Rico. **12:** **Acapulco, *Tijuana, *Mexico Lindo.

Mid-Eastern (also see "Arabic" & "Greek"): **5:** Mamoun's Falafel. **8:** *Eva's. **10:** *Delphi (& Greek), *Greek Village (& Greek). **12:** *Magic Carpet.

Seafood: 5: **Jin Seafood. **7:** **Nishan, *Shamoly. **9:** ***Hobeau's, ***Nodelini's, ***Butterfish Hole, ***Cockeyed Clams. **10:** Captain Mike's. **11:** *Brass 'N Wood Inn. **And also see restaurants listed under their national cuisines.**

Slavic (Czech, Polish, Russian, Ukrainian): **5:** ***Leshko's. **7:** *Jolanta.

Spanish: 12: **Acapulco, *Sevilla, *Tijuana, *Mexico Lindo.

Swiss: 13: *La Fondue.

Thai: 13: ***MTC, ***Bangcock Cuisine.

42:
THE RESTAURANTS BY LOCATION

The list starts at the southern tip of Manhattan, then goes northward, and closes with the Arabic places in Brooklyn near Atlantic & Court.

Below 14th Street in Manhattan, where the streets often aren't numbered but rather named, I group restaurants by neighborhood for easy reference, and within each neighborhood they're in order according to rising expensiveness.

Above 14th Steet, establishments are listed first on the East Side, then on the West Side, strictly in geographical order from south to north.

For example, let's say that you're looking for as good as possible a restaurant in price-category 15 ("reasonable") or cheaper, located in the East 50's. You go down the listing, "East Side Above 14th St.," until you get to restaurants in the 50's; there you'll notice "11 ***Singles," and "9 ***Hobeau's." The fact that both these places are highly starred for value, and that they're reasonably close to price-category 15, suggests that these might be what you're seeking. Then, too, there's "14 Reidy's," not starred, but closer to price-category 15. To choose between these places, you'll find the detailed information about them under their listings in their respective price-categories, Category 14 (low reasonable), Category 11 (moderately cheap), and Category 9 (very cheap). There, you'll find that while all three places are good, and have fine ambiance, the cheaper two actually have the edge on food. You'll also find that Singles has expecially cheap specials, and that Hobeau's is basically a seafood restaurant.

WALL ST.—FINANCIAL DISTRICT
6: **Martin's, 11 Broadway (Beaver), 269-1294.
6: **McCoy's, 51 Nassau at Maiden, 267-8312.

CHAMBERS ST.—JOB-LOT DISTRICT, TRIBECCA
5: **Jin Seafood, 136 W. B'wy (Duane), 349-5375.
7: Blarney Castle, 110 Chambers (Church), 962-8638.
10: *Delphi, 109 W. B'wy at Reade, 227-6322.
10: Capt. Mike's, 126 Chambers (Church), 349-0059.
11: *Brass 'N Wood, 124 Chambers (Church), 227-7074.
13: *Thomas St. Inn, 8 Thomas (B'wy), 349-6350.

CHINATOWN—NR. L.E.SIDE & CANAL ST.
7: **Wo On, 16 Mott (Chatham Sq.), 962-6475.
7: *Wo Hop, 17 Mott (Chatham), 962-8617.
10: *Hang Zhou Lou, 68 E. B'wy (Market St.), 925-5144.
10: *Ho Me Dor, 27 Division (Mkt. St.), 966-7663.
10: *Dragon Garden, 47 Division (Mkt.), 966-6180.
10: *Wu Fang, 36 E. B'wy (Mkt.), 925-7498.

LITTLE ITALY—NR. L.E.SIDE & CANAL ST.
16: **Benito, 163 Mulberry (Grand), 226-9012.

42: THE RESTAURANTS BY LOCATION

16: Villa Pensa, 198 Grand (Mulberry), 226-8830.
22: *Il Cortile, 125 Mulberry (Grand), 226-6060.
24: S.P.Q.R., 133 Mulberry (Grand), 925-3120.

SOHO—NR. BROADWAY & CANAL ST.
6: **Samaria, 129 Spring at Grand, 966-3459.
12: **Broome St. Bar, 363 W. B'wy at Broome, 925-2086.
18: Chez Jacqueline, 213 6th Av. at King, 255-6885.

WEST VILLAGE—NR. WASHINGTON SQ.
5: Mamoun's Falafel, 119 MacDougal St. (3), 674-9246.
7: *Taco Rico, 121 MacDougal (3), 777-9250.
8: Punjab India, 175 Bleecker (McD.), 677-4510.
10: ****Fedora, 239 W. 4 (Charles), 242-9691.
10: *Beansprout, 37 Barrow at 7th Av., 255-3066.
12: **Hunan Pan, 550 Hudson at Perry, 242-5566.
12: *Magic Carpet, 52 Carmine (Blkr.), 929-9329.
12: *Empire Szechuan Bleecker, 160 Blkr. 260-0206.
12: *Sevilla, 62 Charles at 4th St., 929-3189.
12: Souen Downtown, 210 6th Av. at Prince, 255-4890.
13: Emilio's, 307 6th Av. (3), 929-9861.
14: **Monte's, 97 MacDougal (Blkr.), 674-9456.
15: ***Il Ponte Vecchio, 206 Thompson (3), 473-9382.
26: **Fifth Avenue, 24 5th Av. (9), 673-0750.

EAST VILLAGE—BROADWAY TO AV. A
5: ***Leshko's, 111 Av. A (7), 473-9208.
6: ****Dojo, 24 St. Marks (=8 St., 3 Av.), 674-9821.
6: ****Panna, 330 E. 6 (1-2 Avs.), 475-9274.
6: ****Milon, 93 1st Av. (6), 228-4896.
6: ****Royal Indian, 93 1st Av. (6), 473-9673.
6: **Anar Bagh, 338 E. 6 (1-2 Avs.), 533-2177.
6: **Odessa, 117 Av. A (7), 473-8916.
7: ***Shah Bagh, 320 E. 6 (1-2 Avs.), 677-8876.
7: ***Kismoth, 326 E. 6 (1-2 Avs.), 473-9416.
7: ***Nishan, 330 E. 6 (1-2 Avs.), 473-9612.
7: *Shamoly, 328 E. 6 (1-2 Avs.), 982-6790.
7: *Jolanta, 119 1st Av. (7), 254-9109.
8: ****Curry & Tandoor, 324 E. 6 (1-2), 982-8127.
8: Caldron, 306 E. 6 (2nd Av.), 473-9543.
11: *Hunan Inn, 61 2nd Av. (4), 777-6868.
13: ***MTC, 731 Broadway (8), 475-6814.

EAST SIDE ABOVE 14TH ST.—ST. #'s GETTING HIGHER
8: *Tad's, 104 E. 14 (4th Av.), 228-8383.
11: *Z, 117 E. 15 (Irving), 254-0960.
17: K.C. Place, 45 Lex. Av. (24), 532-6402.
12: *Mexico Lindo, 459 2nd Av. at 26, 679-3665.
15: **Mitchell's, 122 E. 27 (Lex.), 689-2058.
12: **Empire Szech. Balc., 381 3 Av. (27), 685-6215.
20: **The Sumptuary, 400 3rd Av. (28), 889-6056.
8: *Shamiana, Lex. at 28th St., 689-5150.
6: Mauro, 39 E. 31 (Mad.), 686-8066.
16: *La Maison Japonaise, 334 Lex. at 39, 682-7375.
9: *+McAnn's, 130 E. 40 (Lex.), 689-0934.
6: **McCoy's, 20 E. 42 (Mad.), 697-7362.

42: THE RESTAURANTS BY LOCATION

- **8:** *Tad's, 18 E. 42 (Mad.), 867-6832.
- **8:** *Tad's, 607 Lex. (52), 832-2294.
- **11:** ***Singles, 951 1st Av. (52), 486-9832.
- **9:** ***Hobeau's, 963 1st Av. (53), 421-2888.
- **14:** Reidy's, 22 E. 54 (Mad.), 753-2419.
- **9:** +McAnn's, 687 Lex. (57), 421-8730.
- **8:** *Eva's, 1074 2nd Av. (57), 935-4882.
- **20:** *Anche Vivolo, 222 E. 58 (2nd-3rd), 308-0112.
- **20:** *Cafe 58, 232 E. 58 (2nd-3rd Avs.), 758-5665.
- **14:** **Trattoria Pino, 981 3rd Av. (59), 688-3817.
- **12:** **Serendipity, 225 E. 60 (2nd-3rd Avs.), 838-3531.
- **19:** ***Fiorella, 1081 3rd Av. (64), 838-7570.
- **14:** **The Right Bank, 822 Mad. (69), 737-2811.
- **12:** Hunan Fortune, 302 E. 72 (2nd Av.), 861-8761.
- **10:** *Greek Village, 1016 Lex. (72), 288-7378.
- **10:** **Finnegan's Wake, 1361 1st Av. (73), 737-3664.
- **20:** *Vivolo, 140 E. 74 (Lex.), 737-3533.
- **12:** **Tang Tang, 1470 1st Av. (77), 744-9320.
- **13:** ***Bangcock Cuisine, 1470 1st Av. (77), 772-2492.
- **11:** **Szechuan Omei Too, 1485 1st Av. (78), 369-7361.
- **9:** *Squid Roe, 77th & 2nd, 249-4666.
- **9:** ***Butterfish Hole, 1394 3rd Av at 79, 879-0991.
- **12:** **Acapulco, 1555 2nd Av. (81), 650-9077.
- **13:** O'Melia's, 1559 2nd Av. at 81, 988-9330.
- **12:** *Olde New York, 1567 2nd Av. (81),
- **10:** ****+Drake's Drum, 1629 2nd Av. (85), 988-2826.
- **13:** October, 1617 York at 85, 535-4480.
- **12:** *Bavarian Inn, 232 E. 86 (2nd-3rd Avs.), 650-1056.
- **9:** Ideal Lunch, 238 E. 86 (2nd-3rd Avs.), 650-1632.
- **12:** *Tijuana, 217 E. 86 (3rd Av.), 289-9627.
- **9:** ****Rathbone's, 1702 2nd Av. (88), 369-7361.
- **20:** Le Grand Saloon, 1644 3rd Av. at 92, 289-1112.
- **9:** ***Nodelini's, 1311 Mad. Av. (93), 369-5677.
- **9:** ***Cockeyed Clams, 1678 3rd Av. at 94, 831-4121.

WEST SIDE ABOVE 14TH ST.—ST. #'s GETTING HIGHER

- **10:** ***Sung Ho Lo, 211 7th Av. (22), 924-8580.
- **9:** *Atlas, 171 W. 29 (7th Av.), 695-6998. Closes 3pm.
- **9:** +McAnn's, 133 W. 33 (6th-7th Avs.), 695-8429.
- **6:** *Blarney Rock, 137 W. 33 (6th-7th), 947-0826.
- **5:** *Garden Sandwich, 139 W. 33 (6th-7th), 564-3151.
- **6:** *Treaty Stone, 139 W. 33 (6th-7th), 560-9223.
- **9:** +Alpine Tavern, 50 W. 34 (5th-6th), 695-3264.
- **8:** *Tad's, 154 W. 34 (7th), 244-4085.
- **7:** P.S., 32 W. 38 (5th-6th), 221-3334.
- **5:** *Exchange Bar, 634 8th Av. (40), 221-9513.
- **8:** *Tad's, 119 W. 42 (6th), 354-0730.
- **8:** *Tad's, 228 W. 42 (7th-8th), 354-5530.
- **11:** Long River Chinese, 10 W. 45 (5th), 840-1831.
- **5:** Victorian Cafeteria, 52 W. 45 (6th), 840-1064.
- **7:** Chick-Teri, 123 W. 45 (6th), 765-6370.
- **7:** *Lantern, 160 W. 46 (7th), 221-3796.
- **20:** Cafe de France, 330 W. 46 (8th), 586-0088.

42: THE RESTAURANTS BY LOCATION

- **18:** **Chez Cardinale, 347 W. 46 (8th-9th), 245-9732.
- **8:** *Tad's, 707 7th (47), 575-8787.
- **11:** Pig 'N Whistle, 36 W. 48 (5th), 247-3070.
- **20:** *Du Midi, 311 W. 48 (8th), 974-9097.
- **8:** *Tad's, 200 W. 50 (7th), 247-1752.
- **8:** Lucky Garden, 224 W. 50 (B'wy), 541-5236.
- **20:** *Cafe des Sports, 329 W. 51 (8th), 581-1283.
- **13:** K.C. Place, 807 9th Av. (54), 246-4258.
- **7:** James Self-Svc., 24 W. 56 (5th), 586-6175.
- **11:** *La Fondue, 43 W. 55 (5th-6th), 581-0820.
- **20:** *L'Escargot, 47 W. 55 (5th-6th), 755-0968.
- **14:** *Steak Pommes Frites, 22 W. 56 (5th), 974-9431.
- **14:** Uncle Lulu's, 16 W. 56 (5th), 541-9291.
- **20:** *Le Champignon, 35 W. 56 (5th-6th), 245-6335.
- **9:** +Alpine Tavern, 871 7th Av. (56), 245-0295.
- **16:** **Mont St. Michel, 327 W. 57 (8th-9th), 581-1032.
- **6:** **Martin's, 1847 Broadway (60), 247-6640.
- **12:** **Hunan Park, 235 Columbus (70), 724-4411.
- **13:** *+Manhattan Bridge Club, 27 W. 72, 799-4242.
- **10:** ***Donegal Inn, 103 W. 72 (Columbus), 874-4268.
- **7:** *Taco Rico, 176 W. 72 (B'wy), 874-9891.
- **11:** Hot Wok, 2188 Broadway (77), 595-8053.
- **11:** *Szechuan Taste West, 2332 B'wy (84), 873-6665.
- **11:** **Peppers Sichuan, 2536 Broadway (95), 865-3440.
- **11:** **Empire Szechuan, 2574 B'wy (97), 663-6980.
- **12:** **Hunan Balcony, 2596 Broadway (98), 865-0400.
- **11:** Szechuan Palace, 2602 Broadway (99), 662-2683.
- **9:** *Eastern Garden, 2628 Broadway (100), 866-0160.
- **10:** Chuan Hong, 2748 Broadway (105), 866-5920.
- **11:** *Green Tree, 1034 Amsterdam (111), 864-9106.
- **8:** ***West End, 2911 Broadway (114), 666-8750.

BROOKLYN, NEAR ATLANTIC & COURT.

- **8:** **Moroccan Star, 205 Atlantic (Court), 596-1919.
- **10:** *Son of The Sheik, 165 Atlntc. (Clntn.), 625-4023.
- **11:** *Taiz Yemen, 172 Court (Amity), 625-3907.
- **12:** *Almontaser, 218 Court (Warren), 624-9267.
- **12:** +Near East, 136 Court at Atlantic, 624-9251.
- **12:** Adnan, 129 Atlantic (Henry), 625-8697.

43:
THE 40 FREE-OR-CHEAP ENTERTAINMENTS

Unquestionably the best bet for anyone seeking free or inexpensive entertainments in New York City is the free nightly jazz concerts at the West End Bar, a Columbia University hangout at 2911 Broadway (114), 666-8750. Not only is this place a bargain restaurant, but the jazz there is usually very good; and sometimes major-name performers are featured.

Two listings of free and dirt-cheap entertainments will follow. First will come those that don't have any fixed locations. Included in this first list will be some terrific resources like the Theatre Development Fund (TDF) and Brooklyn's Downtown Cultural Center (DCC), both of which are associated with hundreds of arts and neighborhood organizations which are continually putting on plays, concerts, lectures, and so forth—all very reasonably priced or (as in the case of DCC) occasionally even free. Then will come a geographical listing of fixed-location organizations, so that you can phone the outfits closest to you (or perhaps to the restaurant you're visiting tonight—for which see the geographical directory of restaurants at the end of the restaurants-chapter), to make as easy as possible your planning a Bargain Finder's night on the town.

Also, for the most extensive current daily listings of inexpensive and free events—and especially of things (including dating services) of interest to singles—see the weekly newspaper *Metropolitan Almanac*, available at many newsstands. It's slender and overpriced; cross-streets are not indicated; sometimes phone numbers are not listed for events; and often the prices of events are not shown—but it unfortunately has no competition.

The only movie-house listing that shows which theatres have the lowest admission-charges is the one which appears every day in the *New York Post* in the middle of the newspaper as the "Neighborhood Movie Guide" page. Often, the same hit motion-pictures which are being screened at full price at some movie-houses in the City are showing elsewhere, and listed here, with an admission charge half that (or even less). In addition, if you're interested in film classics (or "art films"), the Bleecker Street Cinema and Carnegie Hall Cinema (under the same management) have a yearly membership deal which is good for heavy movie-goers, because it offers half-price admissions, and even free admissions to some films, plus a free subscription to their monthly newspaper which has interesting articles on great film-directors, and of course, the monthly screening-schedule of both movie-houses. Phone 533-9270 for details.

General Resources

New York Public Library, 340-0849 & 930-0717. Free plays, concerts, lectures, films, children's events, and exhibitions, in 86 li-

43: THE 40 FREE-OR-CHEAP ENTERTAINMENTS

braries. Also, you can find a current listing of these events just by stopping by your nearest branch library and picking up the Events Calendar.

Brooklyn Arts & Cultural Association (BACA), and Downtown Cultural Center (DCC). BACA publishes a (presently 32-page) monthly booklet called the *Monthly Calendar*, in which virtually all of Brooklyn's many cultural events are listed—and many of these are free. A copy can be picked up free of charge at BACA, 209 Joralemon (at Court); DCC, 111 Willoughby (near Fulton St. Mall); A&S; and Brooklyn Museum.

NY Convention & Visitors Bureau, 397-8222. A potpourri of events.

NYC Parks Dept., 755-4100. Another potpourri.

Theatre Development Fund (TDF), 1501 Broadway (42), 221-0013. This is a non-profit organization which provides subsidized vouchers for low-cost admissions to plays (Broadway, off, and off off) and to dance and musical concerts, for people who qualify: students, professional educators, members of an employee organization or youth group, clergy, and retirees. If you're unemployed, on welfare, or just plain poor, they may, at their own whim, fudge the regressive regulations under which they were established. However, to be safe, you might just tell them that you belong to one of the abovementioned priviledged qualifying groups. A lot of people do that.

Assn. for Humanistic Psychology, 2 Washington Square Village, Suite 1-U, 674-8785. This is an organization which doesn't fit any easily-categorizable mold. But it's an outstanding, inexpensive, educational, and enjoyable, way for singles to meet singles. This academic organization arose as a reaction against the mechanistic emphasis in the American psychological professions. It has always been open to the public, and there is no scholarly snobbishness of any kind. Membership is very inexpensive, and their annual conferences, in which thousands of people attend workshops in every imaginable form of social interaction, are great fun.

Geographical Listing
(south to north)

Brooklyn Museum and Botanical Garden, Eastern Parkway & Washington Av., Brooklyn, 638-5000. Easily accessible by subways 2, 3, 4, and 5, to Brooklyn Museum. The museum is the least crowded, one of the most attractive, and one of the very top ones in NYC. A truly great collection of 18th & 19th Century American art; other major exhibits as well. A terrific museum-shop with low prices on global handcrafts. On Sundays, October through May, free 12:30 concerts, and 3:30 poetry-readings. Museum-admission is by voluntary contribution. Botanic garden is gorgeous in spring. Free admission.

DCC, 111 Willoughby St. (near Fulton St. Mall), Brooklyn, 596-2222. M, RR, to Lawrence; 2, 3, to Hoyt; A, CC, to Jay. Puts on free events of all kinds, including concerts, plays, exhibits, performing-arts training workshops, and others. Phone them to receive free by mail a current listing of upcoming events.

43: THE 40 FREE-OR-CHEAP ENTERTAINMENTS

B.G. Cantor Sculpture Center, 1 World Trade Center, 105th floor, 938-5136. The world's largest private Rodin-collection. By appoiontment only, weekdays. Free.

White Columns, 325 Spring St. (at Greenwich St.), 924-4212. Free lectures, films, exhibits. Open every day. No mornings.

New York University, the Washington Square area. (Various precise locations.) Free. (Ask for their free and open-to-the-public productions.) After you've spoken with one of the following, request the University operator to transfer the call to the next number: 598-2401 (plays); 598-3459 (dance concerts); 598-3491 (musical concerts); 598-2091 (undergraduate plays); 598-3395 (Latin American feature films, including a few cinema-masterpieces); 598-2874 spring & fall (lectures by famous artists, musicians, writers); 598-2027 (general—the Loeb Program Board).

Cooper Union, The Great Hall, 7th Street & 3rd Av., 254-6300 ext. 205. Free: lectures by famous people, concerts, poetry and literary readings.

St. Marks Church, 10th St. at 2nd Av., 674-0910. Free poetry readings. Sometimes famous avant-garde poets.

H.B. Theatre, 124 Bank St. (Greenwich-Washington), 989-6540. Free, fully professional, productions of mostly poor (and never innovative or experimental) plays.

Lee Strassberg Theatre, 115 E. 15 (Irving), 533-5500. Free plays.

Peoples Symphony Concerts, Washington Irving H.S., 40 Irving Place (15), 586-4680. World-famous soloists. Dirt-cheap.

Amer. Acad. of Dramatic Arts, 120 Mad. Av. (30), 686-9244. Join Friends of The Academy, $15 a year, about 30 free plays.

CUNY Graduate Center, 33 W. 42, 790-4395. Free movies and concerts.

New Dramatists, 424 W. 44 (9th Av.), 757-6960. Free plays. Ask for their "staged readings." Very good.

Ensemble Studio Theatre, 549 W. 52 (11th Av.), 2nd floor, 247-2982. Free plays. Ask for their "workshops."

Citicorp Center, 53rd & Lex., 559-4259. Free concerts and kids' productions.

Charlotte Bergen Concerts, Carnegie Hall, 57th St. & 7th Avenue. Full symphony conducted by Ms. Bergen, once a year. Free. To get on her mailing list for announcement and invitation, write to them at: Box 522, Bernardsville, NJ 07924.

UPPER EAST SIDE:

Institute for Rational Living, 45 E. 65 (Mad.), 535-0822. Inexpensive Friday night psychological workshops run by Albert Ellis. Fun, and a great place for singles to meet.

ACA Galleries, 21 E. 67 (Mad.),28-2440. A beautiful place showing—and selling—20th Century and late 19th Century American art. Free admission.

Bosendorfer Concerts, Center for Inter-American Relations, 680 Park Av. (at 68), 753-5200. Free Saturday night classical concerts featuring fast-rising—and sometimes already world-famous—pianists.

Peoples Symphony Concerts, Hunter College Assembly Hall,

43: THE 40 FREE-OR-CHEAP ENTERTAINMENTS

69th St. between Park & Lex. Avs., 586-4680. Chamber orchestras and chamber music, famous groups, rather inexpensive.

Frick Museum, 1 E. 70 (at 5th), 288-0700. Admission price is not especially low, but this is the most beautiful museum in NYC. The collection, though small, is of very high quality traditional European masterpieces; and they schedule classical music concerts by world-famous artists, free with admission to the museum, but by advance ticket only—and the demand for tickets is great, so these concerts are only for the lucky.

Mannes College of Music, 157 E. 74 (Lex.), 737-0700. Many free classical concerts.

Whitney Museum, 945 Madison Av. (75), 570-3676. A truly magnificent collection of American art—probably the greatest such display anywhere. Free admission Tuesday evenings after 5.

Noortman & Brod Galleries, 1020 Madison Av. (77), 772-3370. A beautiful place showing—and selling—17th Century European art. Free admission.

Graham Gallery, 1041 Madison Av. (78), 535-5767. A beautiful place showing—and selling—19th & 20th Century American art. Free admission.

Acquavella Contemporary Art, 18 E. 79 (Mad.), 734-6300. A beautiful place showing—and selling—current American art. Free admission.

Metropolitan Museum, 5th Av. at 84th St., 570-3711. Huge. Terribly popular. Ceaseless mobs of people trying to crowd around mostly tastelessly selected million-dollar paintings that are poorly displayed. Only major saving grace is an outstanding collection of 19th Century European and British art beautifully hung in the Andre Meyer wing. Admission is by voluntary contribution.

UPPER WEST SIDE:

Gene Frankel Theatre, 36 W. 62 (B'wy), 581-2775. Plays. "Works-in-progress" productions are free. "Showcase" productions are cheap. Generally both are good.

Juillard Concerts, Alice Tully Hall, Lincoln Center, 799-5000 ext. 235. Free symphonic and recital concerts—often excellent. Advance tickets required, and usually available.

NYC Ballet, State Theatre, Lincoln Center, 870-5570. The quality is high, and the cheapest seats are very cheap indeed.

International Folk Dancing, Central Park off Belvedere Lake at 81st St., April-October, Sundays 2 p.m.-dusk. Free. 673-3930 & 243-2182.

The Dialogue Center, 257 W. 88 (B'wy), 787-7600. Free lectures by famous people, October-December.

Bloomingdale House of Music, 323 W. 108 (B'wy), 663-6021. Occasional free classical Friday night concerts by faculty. Other concerts inexpensive.

Cathedral of St. John The Divine, Amsterdam Av. at 112th St., 678-6888. The largest cathedral in the world, the second-largest church building in the world, and the largest church building in the Western Hemisphere. Anyway, it's beautiful.

West End Bar, 2911 Broadway (114), 666-8750. Like I said at the beginning of the chapter, this one's tops for its good day-in-and-day-out freebie: the nightly live jazz. There's a minimum in the jazz-room, but it's so low that it's practically nothing—and the food's very good value.

Manhattan School of Music, Broadway at 122nd St., 749-2802. Free classical music concerts.

44:
BARGAIN-FINDER WALKING TOURS

Whether you're a tourist or a New York native, I think you'll find that the day-long walk I describe in this chapter is going to be the culmination of this book—not only enormously entertaining, but also a veritable orgasm of money-saving.

Walking tours are usually found in tourist guidebooks. However, there's a problem with a lot of these travel-guides: they're written by tourists. Now, I've been a tourist myself, and I have nothing against them. In fact, some of my best friends are tourists, from time to time. Still, I wouldn't want to follow the suggestions of a travel-book that was written by one. I speak from experience on this. There used to be a time when I travelled with guidebooks, and I always ended up throwing them away after the second or third city. I invariably found out that I could discover on my own as much that's good in a place—the best hotels, restaurants, etc.—as did the tourist who wrote the book that I was following. The local residents simply know their own cities a lot better than does some character who comes riding into town on a publisher's advance, holds up in a hotel for a few days or weeks, and then packs his bags and goes onto the next place he's supposed to write about. I aim for this book to be the best tourist-guide that's ever been written for New York City, and I have one advantage over many of my competitors: I actually live here. In fact, I've lived in this town for 15 years, and before that I dreamt of living here. New York City has been an obsession of mine ever since I was 5 years old when my family started coming to the Big Apple for vacations, and that was a full third of a century ago. And my love-affair with this crazy place still hasn't stopped.

The high point of New York's local color is its terrific ethnic and other specialized neighborhoods, each of which is actually a city—and even a world—unto itself. I describe my favorite ones in Chapter 33, "NYC Neighborhoods." Below, you'll find a rather long one-day's continuous walking tour of 7 of these 9 neighborhoods—the ones with special appeal because of their cornucopia of bargains, both stores and restaurants: East Village, West Village, Soho, Little Italy, Chinatown, Tribeca, and the Financial District. On the way, you'll pass through the Lower East Side, with its superabundance of bargain-shopping, and the Chambers-Street-job-lot-stores district, where they practically throw the merchandise into your shopping bag, they're so eager to get rid of their closeouts. And you'll also pass by some very nice and marvelously inexpensive places to dine, so that you can refresh yourself from your exhausting bargain-shopping orgy.

This can either be taken as a full day's 7-hour tour; or else be broken down into two or three shorter mini-trips. Except for the very northern portion of the walk, which is to say East and West

Greenwich Village (the part where the bargains don't come showering down on you so thick and fast, and which are included more for their character and the restaurants), you'll find that virtually the entire walk is covered in maps 2, 3, and 4, at the back of this book.

It's best if you can do this on a weekday, because some of the best bargain-shopping is shut down on Saturdays (the Lower East Side), while another portion of the route is closed on Sundays (the Chambers Street area and the Financial District). Furthermore, during the two months of July and August, the part that I just mentioned to be closed on Sundays is dead on Saturdays as well, and is open only on weekdays. If you're doing the tour on a weekday, start at the beginning, where the headline says, "WEEKDAY TOUR STARTS." If you're doing it on a Saturday, you come in where the headline says, "SATURDAY TOUR STARTS." If you're doing it on a Sunday, you begin where the headline says, "SUNDAY TOUR STARTS."

Along these routes, I'll indicate the Bargain Finder recommended restaurants, and the best of the Bargain Finder recommended stores, concentrating especially on those which sell things that you can conveniently carry. I wouldn't want you to get overloaded before you finish your trip! (If you've got a big back-pack, you'll do well to bring it along. Also carry plenty of travelers' checks, and your credit cards; and personal checks, too, if you're a local resident. Even if you think that you'll resist the temptation to shop, at these prices you might be surprised how quickly your bags will fill up!)

NOTE: Skip stores or restaurants you're not interested in. My descriptions of the various stopping-points are intended to let you know whether the place will be of interest to you; and if it's not, then you'll save valuable time by skipping it and just going on to the next thing on the itinerary. However, you'll be missing some of the most characterful parts of NYC if you also skip some streets or blocks and jump forward on the itinerary. After all, this walk is drawn up not merely for having the best stops, but also for having the best scenery. Some places are so optional that I label them as such, or mention them only in briefest passing, because they appeal only to very narrow needs or tastes; and when a place that's of such specialized interest is off the main track, I mention this, so that you won't go onto wild goose chases for no purpose. Also, please keep in mind that some of these stores and restaurants close down or move. That's why the main track of this Bargain-Finder's tour is selected for the scenery. The bargains actually are just a bonus. But come prepared for them. There'll be plenty of them!

WEEKDAY TOUR STARTS

A-CC-2-3-4-5-J-M-RR SUBWAYS TO BROADWAY-NASSAU & FULTON.

144 Fulton St. (Nassau-Broadway), 88-Cent Shop. Little dodads, still-littler prices. Turn right when leaving. Take:

Fulton eastward to Nassau Street (address-numbers are getting smaller) only to the corner. Turn right. Take:

Nassau St. southward to 79 Nassau, Zoom. (Address-numbers

44: BARGAIN-FINDER WALKING TOURS

are getting smaller.) Zoom sells medium-quality women's wear at terrific discounts. It's the outlet-store for several affiliated discount-chains: Strawberry, J. Chuckles, and Sunshine. Turn right when leaving. Take:

Nassau St. southward to 51 Nassau at Maiden Lane, McCoy's. Opens at 10. A very nice pub-cafeteria, in case you're now ready for lunch. If you're skipping the following optional interlude, leave your southward trek along Nassau St. here, and turn right onto Maiden Lane towards Broadway. Across Broadway, Maiden Lane becomes Cortlandt St. Cross Broadway onto Cortlandt.

Optional 30-60-minute interlude: Visiting the financial district. Walk farther (southward) along Nassau St., which becomes Broad St. At Broad and Wall Streets is the Stock Exchange—a very beautiful intersection, with handsome Trinity Church one short block to your right at the end of Wall St., facing you from Broadway. (If the time happens to be around noon, there might be a free concert or other entertainment at Trinity.) Turn right onto Wall, toward the Church, to Broadway, and then right again, northward (address-numbers increasing) up Broadway; and then turn left onto Cortlandt St., at the intersection where Broadway meets Maiden Lane to the right and Cortlandt St. to the left.

Cortlandt St. westward to 12 Cortlandt, Century 21. Upstairs you'll find better quality women's wear at very good discounts. The other floors also have many bargains. Men's shirts are good here. Appliances are not. Turn left when leaving. Take:

Cortlandt St. eastward back to Broadway. Turn left (northward). Address-numbers are increasing. Take:

Broadway northward to 219 Broadway, J&R Cigars. Bargain-cigars, if you're interested. Turn left when leaving, continuing northward up Broadway. Take:

Broadway northward to Park Place, on your left, at the southern tip of City Hall Park, which is ahead of you on your right across Broadway. Turn left onto Park Place, crossing Church St.

SATURDAY TOUR STARTS
WEEKDAY TOUR CONTINUES
(but no Saturdays in July & August)

TO START SATURDAY TOUR, TAKE SUBWAYS AA-E TO CHAMBERS STREET, 2-3 TO PARK PLACE.

Park Place westward from Church St. to 45 Park Place, Sym's. This is perhaps the best store in NYC for current and almost-current top-designer men's wear. Some irregulars. The higher floors are women's wear, generally not as well-selected. Turn left when leaving. Take:

Park Place eastward back to Church St., which is just to the corner. Turn left. Take:

Church St. northward to 136 Church St. at Warren St., Weber's Job Lot. Some great bargains mixed in with schlock. When leaving, turn left. Take:

Warren St. westward to 43 Warren, Annex Outlet, a few paces in. Top-brand appliances, hi-fi components, and recording tapes, are here priced among the lowest in the City. Turn right when

44: BARGAIN-FINDER WALKING TOURS

leaving. Take:

Warren St. eastward. Cross Church. Staying on the south side of Warren, you'll find mostly rather schlocky job-lot stores. But if you're looking for a terrific value on stationery supplies, **Ciro at 23 Warren**, will be worth your checking out. Coming back westward on the north side of Warren, are several interesting job-lot stores. Some have irregular Arrow men's shirts at extremely low prices, and other similar goodies, which you should check thoroughly before buying. When done: Take:

Warren St. westward back to Church St. Cross Church. Turn right. Take:

Church St. northward to 140 Church St., Job Lot Trading Co., a few paces from the corner. You're here at last! I hope that your back-pack isn't full yet, because here you're likely to need it most. Stuff on the selling-floors is close-out super-bargains; what's against the walls is primarily just reasonably priced regular housewares and hardware-items. Turn left when leaving. Take:

Church St. northward to Chambers St., which is only the next corner. Cross Chambers, turn left. Take:

Chambers St. westward to 119 Chambers, Ruby's Book Sale, which is only a half-block in. Here you'll find recent backissues of magazines, 40% off, and paperbacks in the rear, half off. The following is highly optional, depending on whether you're a cheese-freak, and if so then on what your time-frame happens to be right now:

Further westward to 153 Chambers, Cheese of All Nations. Cheese-addicts will have another stab at satiating their cravings at the end of the trip, at East Village Cheese, which closes at 7 p.m. Virtually the same low prices at both places, but if you're looking to find cheeses you've never even heard of, this is the heaven you've been dreaming of.

LUNCH BREAK: Here are the recommended options, if you happen to be a bit hungry by now (otherwise, skip this, and go on to "To Resume:"):

Unless it's Saturday, you can wait about 30 minutes later in the trip, to have a very nice and reasonably priced meal in a highly attractive environment, at the Thomas Street Inn, which you'll soon be passing, and which serves American food weekdays at lunch; otherwise, you can take advantage of the following immediately nearby places, also good, but not as classy (but starting with the classiest, then the cheapest, then the nearest):

Delphi, 109 W. Broadway, around the corner. As you leave Ruby's, turn right, and turn right again at the corner; as you leave the cheese store, to your left, then left again; it's one block up, at the intersection of W. B'wy & Reade. Greek food of good quality, attractive ambiance, and rather low prices, make this place very popular. This is the nearest restaurant to the optional good-to-top-quality-shoes store for women (Anbar—mostly narrow sizes stocked) that's coming up ahead.

Jin Seafood, 136 W. Broadway, a half-block farther up W. B'wy. Very inexpensive, quite a decent fish-and-chips place, mostly a take-out business. This is the nearest restaurant to the optional medium-to-good-quality-shoes store for men (Interstate Foot-

44: BARGAIN-FINDER WALKING TOURS

wear) that's coming up ahead.

Blarney Castle, 110 Chambers, across the street from Ruby's. Pub-cafeteria, decent food and ambiance, low prices.

Capt. Mike's, 126 Chambers, across the street from Ruby's. Decent seafood and ambiance, rather low prices.

Brass 'N Wood, 124 Chambers,, across the street from Ruby's. Decent seafood, rather good ambiance, reasonable prices.

TO RESUME:

If you're interested in medium-to-good-quality shoes for men:

Interstate Footwear, 152 Duane St. at W. B'wy. This street is two blocks up (north) from Chambers. The store gives a 10% bonus-Bargain-Finder-discount off their low regular (not special-sale) prices if you show them this book.

If you're interested in good-to-top-quality shoes for women:

Anbar, 97 Reade St., one block up from Chambers, between Church and W. B'wy. Mostly narrow sizes, mostly last season's goods, terrific prices.

Our trip continues:

Chambers St. eastward to Broadway. The following stores along the north (left) side of Chambers are often of interest: **85 Chambers, Alee Discount,** dirt-cheap women's and children's shoes, also bargains on linen-items; **83 Chambers, United Chambers Trdg.**, which specializes in irregulars of parkas (Woolrich and others), and generally in camping and backpacking gear which is discounted at least slightly; **77 Chambers, Parezio II**, which has good prices on designer jeans. Turn left at Broadway. Take:

Broadway northward to Reade St., one block. Turn left across the street. Take:

Reade westward to 60 Reade, Alexander's Hardware, a few paces in from Broadway. A treasure-trove both on the main floor and downstairs, with weird bargains stashed away in obscure corners. Often, they have Sabatier-quality stainless steel chefs' knives of their own manufacture, 80% below the Sabatier price. They also have some small backpacks that are sold at many other stores in the City, but here at by-far the lowest prices, 20-40% below those charged elsewhere. Turn left when leaving. Take:

Reade eastward back to Broadway. Turn left.

If you're not interested in medium-to-good quality shoes for women, skip this paragraph, and go on to the next. Otherwise, take Broadway northward one block to Duane, and turn left to **116 Duane, Shoe Steal.** Excellent value. Then return to Broadway and continue northward. Then:

If you've dined already, or if it's Saturday, skip this and the next paragraph, and go on to the one after the next. Otherwise, if you're in the mood for a meal, and if it's a weekday, take Broadway northward to Thomas St., which is two blocks beyond Reade, one block beyond Duane. Turn left (westward) to:

Thomas St. Inn, 8 Thomas St., a few paces off Broadway. This place is owned by a local artist, and the ambiance is very calming; the food, good, and good value. When you're done, return to Broadway. Turn left. Take:

Broadway northward to Canal St. Turn left.

44: BARGAIN-FINDER WALKING TOURS

SUNDAY TOUR STARTS
WEEKDAY TOUR CONTINUES
SATURDAY TOUR CONTINUES

TO START SUNDAY TOUR, TAKE SUBWAYS 6-N-RR-J-M-QB TO CANAL STREET.

Canal St. westward from B'wy to 304 Canal, Canal Jean Co. All kinds of army-surplus and cheap-chic clothing, often including excellent values on men's dress-shirts. Sometimes incredible values on top quality blue jeans. If you show them this book, they'll give you a bonus-Bargain-Finder discount of 5-20% off their low regular (not special-sale) prices. When leaving, turn left. Take:

Canal St. westward a few paces to 308 Canal, upstairs, Pearl Art Supply. Here, you'll find everything from Glu-stick to exotic fountain pens, drafting pens, art paper, gesso, all at good discounts. When leaving:

Cross Canal St. to 307 Canal, C.K.&L. Surplus. This place has various kinds of gummed tape, and other utilitarian oddities, at very good discounts. But the power-tools aren't discounted at all. When leaving, turn left. Take:

Canal St. eastward to 271 Canal, Lever & Greenberg. They've got some good values on mostly medium-quality men's dress-wear, especially raincoats and several-seasons-old-styles of suits. If you show this book, they'll give you a bonus-Bargain-Finder discount of 10% off their low regular (not special-sale) prices.

Cross Canal to 270 Canal, Canal Self Service. All kinds of housewares, at very reasonable cost. When leaving, turn right. Take:

Canal St. eastward to 234 Canal, China Mall. Excellent discounts on many top names in designer jeans, also Chinese quilted vests, kung-fu slippers ideal as bedroom slippers, and (in wintertime) down coats. When leaving, turn right. Take:

Canal St. eastward to Mulberry St. Turn right. Take:

Mulberry St. southward to 91 Mulberry, C.A.T. Trdg., which isn't far from the corner. All kinds of non-perishable Chinese foods, at very good prices. Here's the place for gift-teas in attractive tins, and for the fixings to make Chinese cuisine at home. For recommended teas, see China Rose Tea, and the gold-yellow The Au Jasmin, which I describe under the sub-head "Stimulant Teas" in Chapter 11, Foods. When leaving, turn left. Take:

Mulberry St. northward back to Canal. Turn right one block. Take:

Canal eastward to Mott St. Turn right. Take:

Mott St. southward to Chatham Square. This leads through the heart of Chinatown. Highlights are **Fong Inn, at 46 Mott;** and **Wo On, at 16 Mott.** The first is a retail-supplier of beansprouts and bean curd (soybean tofu) at incredibly low prices, about half what's charged elsewhere. The second is a restaurant, serving both regular and Szechuan Chinese cuisine, fairly good food, fairly poor ambiance, incredibly inexpensive, Chinatown's best restaurant-value, and quite possibly the best-value Chinese restaurant in the City. (But note that another and somewhat fancier Chinese restau-

44: BARGAIN-FINDER WALKING TOURS

rant—the Empire Szechuan Bleecker—will be coming up in a few hours, in Greenwich Village.) At the bottom of Mott, at Chatham Sq., turn left. Take:

Chatham Sq. (becomes Bowery) northward to Canal. On the way, at the corner of Bowery and Pell, is **Lucky Gift**, with terrific prices on Chinese-made down quilts and parkas.

LOWER EAST SIDE
WEEKDAY TOUR CONTINUES
SUNDAY TOUR CONTINUES
SATURDAY TOUR SKIPS AHEAD
TO LITTLE ITALY
(via Bowery up to Grand, left on Grand)
Look below for headline: "Little Italy."

When you get to Canal, turn right. Take:

Canal St. eastward to Essex St. You're heading into the area that's closed on Saturdays, and also on late Friday afternoons, but open all other days. Highlights en-route are:

95 Canal, S&A Clothing, across from the bridge. This small store has terrific values on men's suits, jackets, parkas, and coats, good quality. On top of that, if you show them this book, they'll knock their low regular (not special-sale) prices still lower by 10-20%, for us Bargain Finders only.

63 Canal, Lanac Sales. All the top names in dinnerware and flatware, at good but not great discounts of about 30% off the department-store prices.

51 Canal, Benny's Import. Top-name appliances, watches, and hi-fi, at excellent discounts.

50 Canal, S&W Appliances. Just the same as Benny's.

45 Canal, Kunst Sales. Similar to Benny's.

27 Canal, Kurtz Textiles. Superb discounts on Wrangler jeans, Kayser hosiery, Hanes underwear, Danskins, various housedresses.

Canal at Essex, Essex Fruiterers. good prices on fresh fruits and vegetables. This is the end of Canal St. Turn left onto Essex St.

Essex northward to Hester St. At the corner is:

51 Hester at Essex, Kadouri Import. Terrific prices on spices. Good costs on other things. Sometimes different charges on same item in different parts of the store. When leaving: **Return to Essex Street,** turn left. At **27 Essex St., The Pickleman** is worth checking out. All kinds of pickles. Excellent prices. Take **Essex Street farther northward to Grand St. Turn left one block to Ludlow St. Turn right. Take:**

Ludlow St. northward to 87 Ludlow, J. Wolsk. Candies, dried fruits, and nuts, at very low cost. Take:

Ludlow St. back southward to Grand St. Turn right on Grand, headed westward. If you've got plenty of time, you might want to check out Orchard Street as you're passing it on Grand. Whether you head southward on Orchard, back to Canal, and then come up the other side of Orchard back to Grand, or do the same circuit in the other direction, it's all the same. But don't feel sorry if you've not got time to explore Orchard. It's basically a clothing-street; and if this is a weekday, then what you've already covered so far on this trip beats Orchard on practically everything. You can leave Orchard Street for those who don't know better, and who "oooh" and "aaah" mere 20% discounts. Although I recommend a goodly number of Orchard Street stores, I generally endorse more highly the clothing-places you've already passed. Take:

Grand St. farther westward. You're headed through to Little Italy, then Soho. First, however, the real specialties, in case you happen to be interested in them, are linens-stores on Grand, and fabrics-houses on Eldridge St., which crosses Grand. The only other shop that's of more-than-usual interest is a designer-wall-coverings place at **273 Grand, Sheila's Wallstyles.** (If you're not looking for any of these things, skip the rest of this paragraph.) You'll find more great stores for both linens and fabrics coming up soon on Broadway, but Sheila's Wallstyles is unique on this trip. Here's the information on all of these places. The wallcoverings-shop not only has Manhattan's lowest prices on current patterns of major-name wallvinyls and wallpapers, but if you show them this book then they'll give you an added discount of 5-10% off their normal low prices. Now, here are the steepest-discount linens-places in order as you come upon them along Grand: **290 Grand at Eldridge, Rubin & Green** (specializes in designers' stuff); **88 Eldridge near Grand, Eldridge Jobbing; 274 Grand, Shorland Textile; 272 Grand, Penchina Textile.** As for fabrics, here are the ones on Eldridge, (they're to the right off Grand St., and going two blocks up): **110 Eldridge, Leratex; 113 Eldridge, Dana; 118 Eldridge, Grunberg, and also Recht.** Now, here's Little Italy, where the specialty is food (which I assume everyone's interested in).

LITTLE ITALY
SATURDAY TOUR CONTINUES
SUNDAY TOUR CONTINUES
WEEKDAY TOUR CONTINUES

Grand St. to 190 Grand St., Piemonte Ravioli. Here are Perugina candies and other Italian yummies, at the city's lowest prices. When leaving, turn right, to Mulberry St. If you happen to need a bite to eat, one of the City's fine Italian restaurants is a half-block to your right across the street, **Benito, at 163 Mulberry.** The food here is well-spiced, and extremely tasty. But within about an hour, you'll find yourself passing another even better—and slightly cheaper—Italian restaurant, in West Village, Il Ponte Vecchio, which starts serving at 5 p.m. Monday through Saturday, and 2 p.m. Sunday. When done, or if you're not in the mood to dine right now, continue westward along Grand, to Broadway, and then:

448 Broadway near Grand, Shelinsky. Superb low prices on basic linens.

449 Broadway near Grand, Max Eilenberg. Another good linens-place.

If you've got plenty of time, and especially if it's Sunday, you might want to explore a bit up and down Broadway between Canal

44: BARGAIN-FINDER WALKING TOURS

linens-place.

If you've got plenty of time, and especially if it's Sunday, you might want to explore a bit up and down Broadway between Canal St. to the south, and Bleecker St. to the north. The major specialties here are fabrics and lower quality women's wear. Some of the recommended fabrics-stores are **Jacob Weisenfeld, 450 Broadway; Budlee Fabrics, 458 Broadway; Monezel Textiles, 470 Broadway; K Trimmings, 519 Broadway**. Then back to Grand.

Grand St. farther westward to W. B'wy. En route, is **Soho Music Gallery at 26 Wooster at Grand,** where the discounts are good on used, closeout, rare and out-of-print jazz, and rock and blues closeouts, but not outstanding in other areas. (Some superb record-discount stores will come up in West Village and East Village ahead.) You've now entered Soho, where the avant-garde art galleries are, along with many singles hoping not to stay that way. When you get to W. B'wy, turn right. Take:

West Broadway northward to Broome St. Bar, "Ken & Bob's," at the corner of Broome. Pub-restaurant. Wide variety of very good and filling salads; also burgers, etc.; all reasonably priced. A beautiful, casual, cozy place, very busy at night. Continue straight on. Take:

West Broadway northward to Prince St. En-route are many galleries. Take your pick, or skip them all. Turn left. Take:

Prince St. westward to Sullivan St., two blocks. Turn right.

If you're interested in terrific values on earthy Latin American hand-made knit clothing (scarves, hats, gloves, sweaters, handbags, etc.), then read the next paragraph. Otherwise, skip to the one after.

When you cross Houston St., turn right, eastward, one block to the corner, **108 W. Houston, Buen Dia,** at the corner. Not only do they beat all the competition on these things, which they directly import, but on top of that, if you show them this book, they'll discount their already-low regular store-prices 5-8% lower. When you're done, return to Sullivan St. Turn right. Take:

Sullivan St. northward to Bleecker St. You're now in West Greenwich Village. At this corner is:

160A Bleecker St., Empire Szechuan Bleecker, an extremely uneven restaurant—sometimes divine, at other times bland. However, the ambiance is good, and the service is always incredibly fast and very good. When it's in top form this place is among the finest dining-spots of any sort in NYC, and a real bargain at its moderate prices. However, you're soon to pass one of New York's finest (and also reasonable) Italian restaurants, Il Ponte Vecchio. And within the hour, you'll be at the greatest bargain-restaurant of them all so far on this trip, at around where the walk ends—Dojo, in East Greenwich Village, a place which can boast food both terrific and dirt-cheap. Also at the end of the trip comes an equally magnificent Indian restaurant, Curry & Tandoor. So dining-wise, you're entering the Bargain Finder's heaven. Turn Left. Take:

Bleecker St. westward to 201 Bleecker, Porto Rico, a coffee-tea importer, with tea-prices about half those charged at most other coffee-tea specialty stores which carry the same loose teas. They'll

Orange. (Sniff the stuff; isn't it terrific? Well, the taste of the tea is even better!) Other shops charge two to three times the price for this sweet-toothed gourmet's delight. Another superb flavored tea here is Apple. But most of the other spiced and flavored teas at this place—and elsewhere—don't taste as good as they smell. As for the loose coffees here, they're not comparatively such great bargains, since there are a few other stores that undersell this shop by a shade on some of these. On the other hand, none of those other coffee-suppliers has such a wide selection. And here's a coffee that I cerainly do consider a bargain: my favorite blend from Porto Rico (it's inexpensive, rich, well-balanced, and free of bitterness): one-third French Mocha, one-third Venezuelan, one-third Colombian. When leaving, turn left. Take:

Bleecker St. back eastward to MacDougal, at the corner. You'll now explore one of the most attractive and intimate little corners of West Village. Turn left. Take:

MacDougal St. northward to 3rd St., one block up. Turn right. Take:

3rd St. eastward to Sullivan St., one block. Turn right. Take:

Sullivan St. southward to 240 Sullivan St., Second Coming 2nds. Used records, at very low prices. Some super-bargains. Across the street is:

235 Sullivan, Second Coming. The main store of the 3 in the Second Coming group. You were just now at the clearance-store for the other two, but prices are good at all 3. When leaving, turn left. Take:

Sullivan St. southward to Bleecker. Turn left. Take:

Bleecker St. eastward one block to Thompson St. Turn left. Take:

Thompson St. northward to 206 Thompson, Il Ponte Vecchio, near the corner. Reasonably priced Italian food that's really excellent. Ambiance is very continental, calm, relaxed. One of NYC's great restaurants. When leaving, turn right. Take:

Thompson St. northward to Washington Square. You're on the campus of New York University. At the northwest corner of the Square, farther northward to the right in front of you, turn right onto Waverly Place. Take:

Waverly Place eastward to Broadway. En-route, at the corner of Mercer St., is the Waverly Coffee Shop, where I often stop by to pick up one of my favorite take-out desserts on the way to what may well be New York's greatest bargain-restaurant, the Dojo, which is five minutes ahead. I'm talking about the yummiest, moistest, most aromatically flavorful muffin I've encountered anywhere, the peach-bran muffin, which is up front here, at the muffin-counter for take-out orders. Their blueberry muffin is also very good. However, I often find that the attendants here stuff the wrong muffin into the bag (sometimes it's a regular peach muffin, for example, instead of the peach-bran one); and they normally use a stingily and very inconveniently small paper sack. The solution is to verify what they put into your bag, and also to check that the bag itself is tall enough to hold the muffins so that you won't have to squeeze them to a crummy mass while you're carrying your goodies out. At

Broadway, turn left. Take:

Broadway northward to 731 Broadway, MTC, the city's greatest Thai restaurant, and even its finest Oriental restaurant of any type. Very spicey food. The chicken curry with peanuts and ginger is especially outstanding. We're soon about to encounter great Japanese and Indian restaurants as well (much cheaper than this). A few paces farther, after MTC, and you're passing Warehouse Wines on your left, and coming upon Astor Wines just ahead to your right on Astor Place. Both are good, and both give bonus-Bargain-Finder discounts on wines, Astor's bonus-discounts being the larger, and being applicable to single bottles and not just to cases. The first of these two places, **735 Broadway, Warehouse Wines,** will give you 5-10% off their low regular (not special-sale) case-prices on wines, if you show them this book. They have a good selection of the usually very-fine-value Alexis Lichine wines. When leaving, Astor Place is ahead on your right. Take:

Astor Place one block to 12 Astor Place, Astor Wines, at the corner of Lafayette Street. This huge store will give you 10-20% off their low regular (not special-sale) prices on wines, if you show them *BARGAIN FINDER*. They deliver free of charge in Manhattan on orders of $35 and more. The bonus-discount applies to single-bottle wine-purchases, as well as to cases; and this can be particularly fortunate for you right now if you'd like to have wine with your dinner at one of the Bargain Finder restaurants this evening. Some of the greatest bargain-restaurants in Manhattan, other than the Dojo coming up (which serves its own wines, so you have to pay the restaurant-price for the booze there), are the Indian places a 12-minute walk from here, and they don't serve wine—you bring your own.

If you're looking to attend a play this evening, you might first want to check with the box-office at the NY Shakespeare Festival building at 425 Lafayette St., a bit to your right and across the street as you're leaving Astor Wines. It's the big structure with the flag. Ask at the box-office whether they've got any free plays coming up, and generally what's doing. Also, when you get back to the continuation of Astor Place, crossing Cooper Square to the right, you might want to check inside the big red-stone building on your right, which is the main building of Cooper Union. The "Great Hall" there often has excellent free concerts and other events.

Further along in the same direction as Astor Place. Now you're crossing Cooper Square, with the big abstract cubic sculpture to your left, and probably many impropmtu street-vendors selling their own belongings on the pavement where you're walking. The big building to your right is the main one for Cooper Union, a highly regarded college which provides free education for gifted architectural and visual-arts students. When you've crossed 3rd Avenue, you're on St. Marks Place, which is really just an extension of E. 8th St.

20 St. Marks Place, St. Marks Sounds. Upstairs. Good prices on new and used records.

24 St. Marks Place, Dojo Restaurant. Their soyburger dinner is the best possible introduction to good vegetarian dining. Their

Chicken Yakisoba also is marvelous. The place serves breakfasts throughout the day, and these are the tastiest anywhere in the City. The owner is a culinary genius who has designed unique dishes that are hard to categorize, but simple, and nutritionally better balanced than I know of from any other restaurant. Combine these virtues with the fine casual ambiance, and with the low prices, and you've got one of New York's top restaurants. Another is the Curry & Tandoor, coming up.

Here are the options now:

East Village Cheese, 239 E. 9th St., around the corner to the left, and to the left again, near 2nd Av. and 9th Street. Very low prices.

Curry & Tandoor, 324 E. 6th St., around the corner to the right from the Dojo, down 2nd Av. to 6th St., left onto 6th. This is a block chock-a-bloc with super-cheap Indian restaurants, the best bargains of which I recommend in the restaurants-chapter, amongst which is this one, which generally has the best cuisine of the bunch. Others I recommend, which are even cheaper, and good but not (as the Curry & Tandoor fairly often is) magnificent and great, are: Good Karma, 328 E. 6th (probably the 2nd-best after the Curry and Tandoor), Panna, 330 E. 6th; Shah Bagh, 320 E. 6th; Milon, 93 1st Av. (6th), 2nd floor; Royal Indian, 93 1st Av. (6th); and Kismoth, 326 E. 6th. They're all excellent bargains. You can bring your own wine to any of them.

St. Marks Cinema, 2nd Av. right north of St. Marks Pl. Here movies cost less than elsewhere, but some bums sleep in the seats, and the floors are dirty.

Well, now you're loaded up with food, inside both your belly and your backpack. And you must be tired, carrying all the stuff that's in there. It probably gave your wallet quite a workout, too, but hopefully less than your would have thought.

Whoever said that New York's an expensive city? Probably some character who read too many tourguides written by tourists.

I hope that you've enjoyed your day!

45:
MAPS

CHAMBERS STREET & FINANCIAL DISTRICT

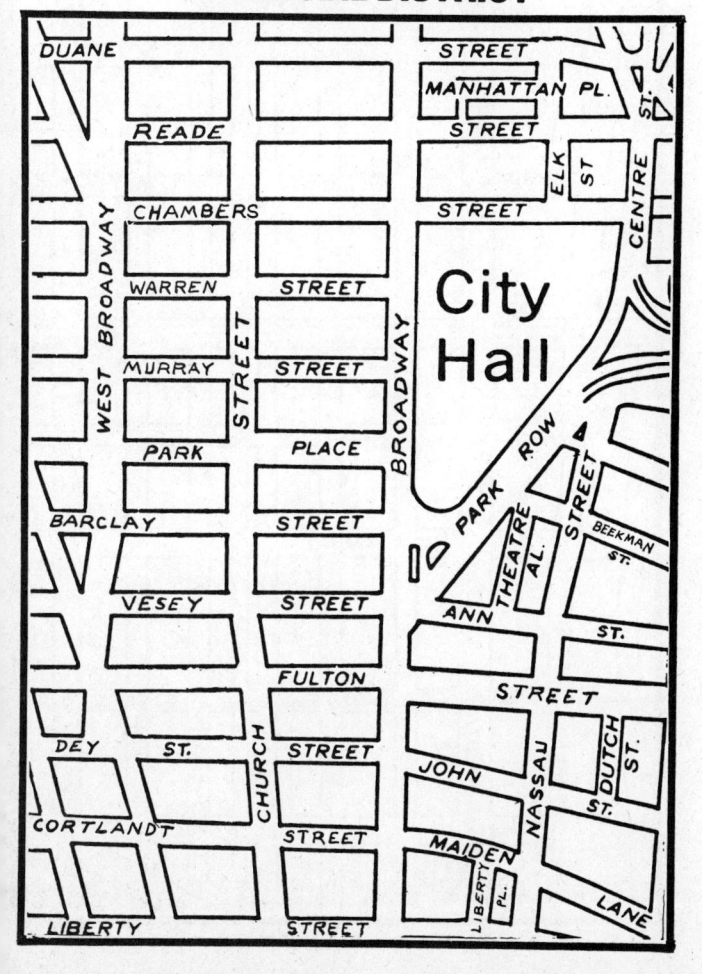

LOWER EAST SIDE

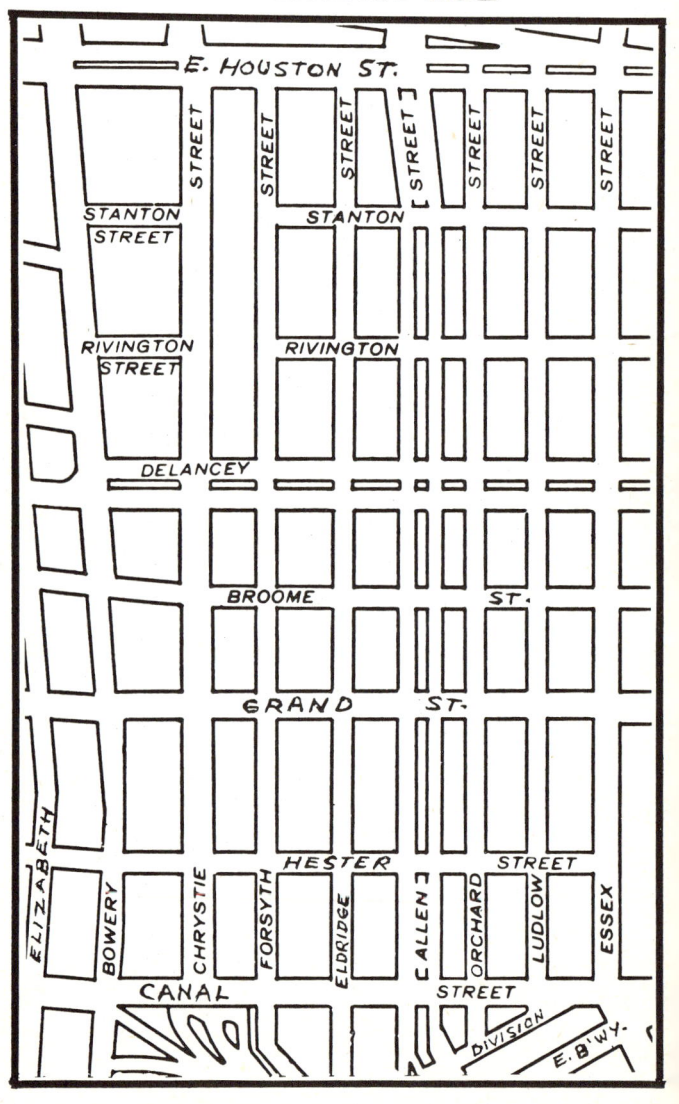

SOHO & CANAL STREET

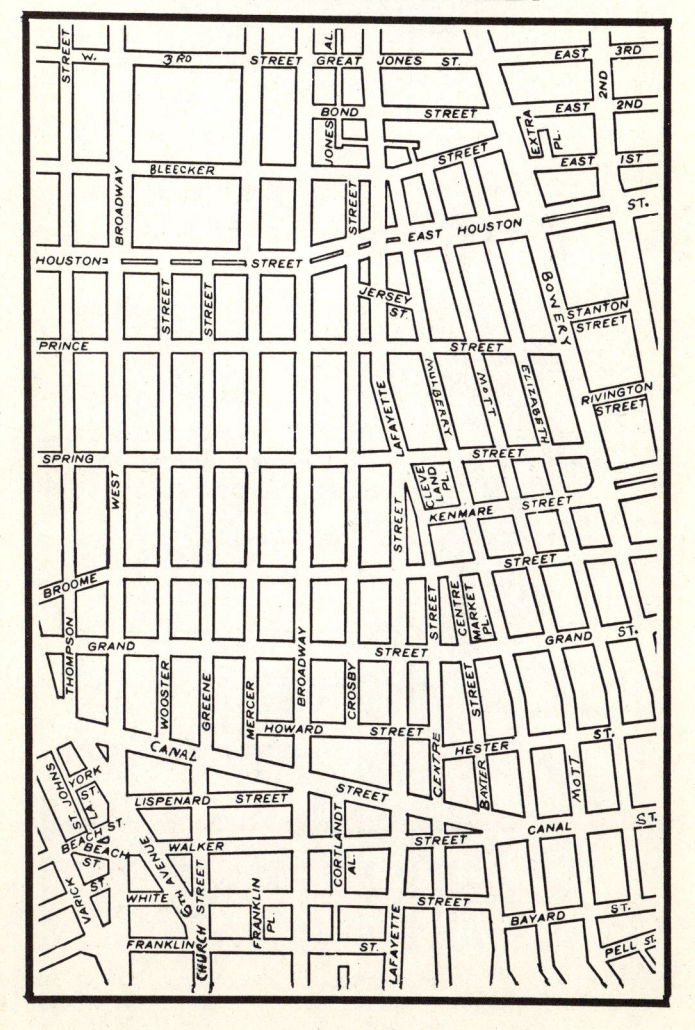

45: MAPS

N.Y.C. SUBWAYS

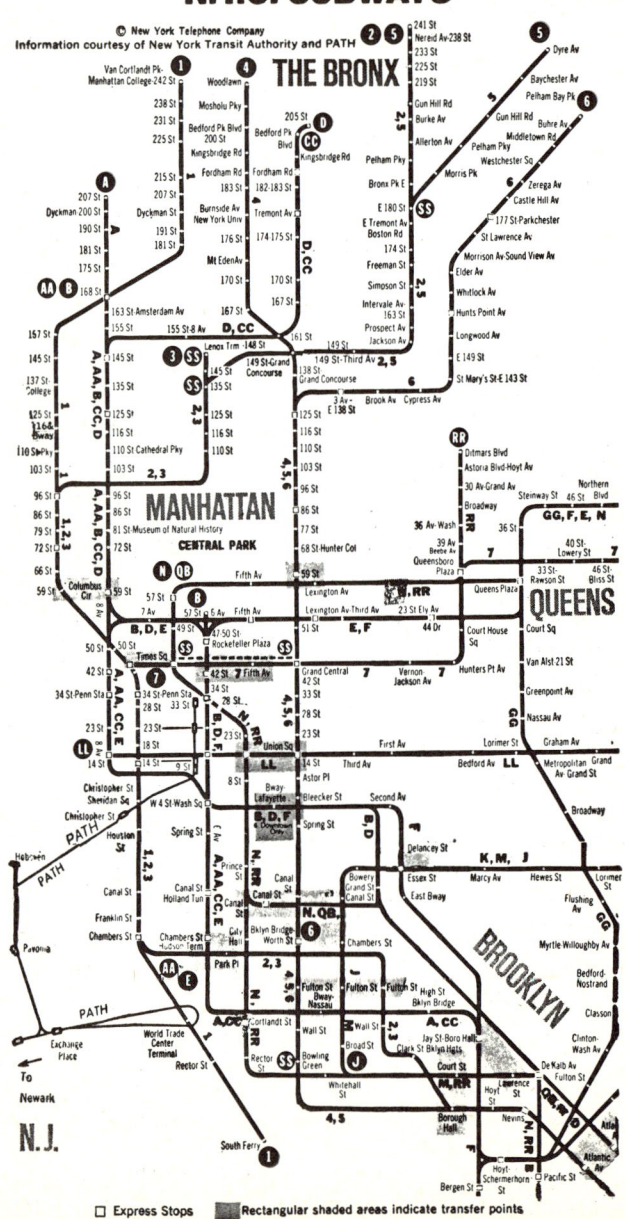

GUIDE TO NEW YORK STREETS

First Ave.
100 at 6 St.
200 at 12 St.
500 at 29 St.
800 at 45 St.
1000 at 55 St.
1200 at 65 St.
1400 at 74 St.
1600 at 83 St.
1800 at 94 St.
2000 at 103 St.
2200 at 113 St.
2400 at 124 St.

Second Ave.
100 at 6 St.
200 at 12 St.
500 at 28 St.
800 at 43 St.
1000 at 53 St.
1200 at 63 St.
1400 at 73 St.
1600 at 83 St.
1800 at 94 St.
2000 at 103 St.
2200 at 114 St.
2400 at 123 St.
2500 at 128 St.

Third Ave.
100 at 12 St.
200 at 18 St.

300 at 23 St.
400 at 28 St.
500 at 34 St.
800 at 49 St.
1000 at 59 St.
1200 at 70 St.
1400 at 79 St.
1600 at 90 St.
1800 at 100 St.
2000 at 110 St.
2200 at 120 St.
2400 at 128 St.

Fourth Ave.
100 at 11 St.
200 at 17 St.
300 at 23 St.
400 at 28 St.
500 at 32 St.

Fifth Ave.
100 at 16 St.
200 at 23 St.
300 at 31 St.
400 at 37 St.
500 at 42 St.
600 at 49 St.
700 at 55 St.
800 at 61 St.
900 at 72 St.
1000 at 81 St.
1200 at 100 St.

Sixth Ave.
74 at Canal St.
400 at 8 St.
600 at 18 St.
800 at 28 St.
1000 at 37 St.
1100 at 42 St.
1200 at 47 St.
1300 at 52 St.
1500 at 59 St.

1400 at 115 St.
2000 at 124 St.
2200 at 135 St.

Seventh Ave.
100 at 16 St.
200 at 22 St.
300 at 27 St.
400 at 32 St.
500 at 37 St.
800 at 52 St.
1800 at 110 St.
1900 at 115 St.
2000 at 120 St.
2100 at 125 St.
2200 at 131 St.

Eighth Ave.
100 at 15 St.
200 at 20 St.
300 at 25 St.

500 at 35 St.
800 at 49 St.
1000 at 114 St.
2100 at 119 St.
2300 at 124 St.
2400 at 129 St.

Ninth Ave.
100 at 17 St.
200 at 23 St.
400 at 33 St.
500 at 38 St.
700 at 48 St.
900 at 59 St.

Tenth Ave.
100 at 17 St.
200 at 22 St.
300 at 27 St.
400 at 33 St.
500 at 38 St.
600 at 43 St.
700 at 48 St.
800 at 54 St.
900 at 59 St.

Amsterdam Ave.
1 at 59 St.
100 at 64 St.
200 at 70 St.

300 at 74 St.
500 at 84 St.
800 at 99 St.
1000 at 110 St.
1200 at 119 St.
1400 at 129 St.

Broadway
100 at Wall St.
200 at Fulton St.
300 at Duane St.
400 at Canal St.
500 at Spring St.
600 at Houston St.
700 at 4 St.
800 at 11 St.
900 at 20 St.
1000 at 23 St.
1100 at 24 St.
1200 at 29 St.
1300 at 34 St.
1400 at 39 St.
1500 at 44 St.
1600 at 49 St.
1700 at 54 St.
1800 at 59 St.
1900 at 64 St.
2000 at 68 St.
2100 at 73 St.
2200 at 78 St.
2300 at 84 St.
2400 at 89 St.
2500 at 94 St.

2600 at 98 St.
3000 at 119 St.
3500 at 143 St.
4000 at 168 St.

Central Pk. W.
50 at 65 St.
100 at 70 St.
200 at 81 St.
300 at 90 St.
400 at 100 St.
500 at 110 St.

Columbus Ave.
1 at 59 St.
100 at 64 St.
200 at 69 St.
300 at 75 St.
500 at 85 St.
800 at 100 St.
1000 at 110 St.

East End Ave.
50 at 81 St.
100 at 84 St.
200 at 89 St.

Lexington Ave.
100 at 27 St.
200 at 32 St.
300 at 37 St.
400 at 42 St.

500 at 47 St.
700 at 57 St.
1000 at 72 St.
1200 at 82 St.
1400 at 92 St.
1600 at 102 St.
1800 at 112 St.
2000 at 122 St.
2200 at 130 St.

Madison Ave.
1 at 23 St.
100 at 29 St.
200 at 35 St.
300 at 42 St.
400 at 47 St.
500 at 52 St.
700 at 63 St.
800 at 68 St.
900 at 78 St.
1000 at 84 St.
1200 at 87 St.
1500 at 103 St.
1800 at 117 St.
2000 at 127 St.

Park Ave.
1 at 34 St.
200 at 45 St.
300 at 49 St.
500 at 59 St.
700 at 69 St.
900 at 79 St.
1100 at 89 St.

1300 at 99 St.
1500 at 109 St.
1700 at 119 St.
1900 at 129 St.

Riverside Dr.
1 at 72 St.
100 at 83 St.
200 at 93 St.
300 at 103 St.
400 at 113 St.
500 at 123 St.
600 at 137 St.

West End Ave.
100 at 64 St.
200 at 70 St.
300 at 74 St.
400 at 79 St.
500 at 84 St.
600 at 89 St.
700 at 94 St.
800 at 99 St.
900 at 104 St.

York Ave.
1113 at 60 St.
1200 at 65 St.
1300 at 70 St.
1400 at 75 St.
1500 at 80 St.
1600 at 85 St.
1700 at 89 St.

KEY TO NEW YORK CITY STREET AND AVENUE NUMBER LOCATIONS

1. Select the avenue in question—such as Fifth Avenue.
2. To locate a number—such as 500—run finger down to number or number nearest to it.
3. Read across to left—this is nearest street—in this case 42nd Street.

Street No.	York Ave.	1st Ave.	2nd Ave.	3rd Ave.	Lex. Ave.	Park Ave. South	Mad. Ave.	5th Ave.	6th Ave.	7th Ave.	8th Ave.	B'way	9th Ave.	10th Ave.	11th Ave.
1		1	1									603			
5		84	85									698			
10		164	160	46				30				778			19
15		256		142		75		96			97	843			120
20		342	350	240				148	240	79	195	902	76	160	215
25		428	440	340	63	251	31		343	171	299	1122	164	260	315
30		514	542	430	161	345	119	276	443	262	401	1216	254	350	411
35		616	638	522	263	443	199	368	547	363	493	1332	352	450	507
40		702	748	620	357	Park Ave. 101	279	452	653	453	617	1430	450	536	
									753	561			544		
45		802	846	718	461	230	357	544	853	Longacre Sq.	719	1538	642	634	603
50		886	946	816	559	300	435	621		761	829	1636	742	734	698
55		1006	1044	936	659	418	519	700	1063	865	929	1730	842	828	796
									1155		C.P. West		Col. Ave.	Amsterdam	West End
60	1116	1102	1140	1010	767	520	653	786	1257		15	1830	28	21	72
65	1221	1200	1242	1110	869	610	753	837	1357		50	1936	216	117	114
70	1308	1306	1330	1210	963	718	843	883			101	2040	216	221	213
75	1414	1420	1442	1308	1057	812	955	936			161	2139	318	321	317
80	1510	1528	1540	1406	1173	910	1055	988				2236	416	417	409

CROSSTOWN GUIDE

All crosstown street numbers begin at Fifth Avenue, East or West.

46:
BEST FREE MAPS

FOR RESIDENTS:
"Aerobic Exercise Map," printed separately for each borough, showing every street, and highlighting all free and cheap facilities for exercising: Y's, city-run swimming pools, etc. It even shows street-addresses. However, there's no street name index. Available at: NY Heart Assn., 205 E. 42, 4th fl., 661-5335

FOR TOURISTS:
"New York City & Long Island," showing every Manhattan street from Central Park southward, highlighting major hotels, theatres, parks, and tourist-sights; further showing all the chief roads and highways throughout the five boroughs and the greater metropolitan area. Available at Exxon Travel Info. Ctr., Exxon Bldg., street level lobby, 1251 6th Av. (49-50), 398-2690. (You can also obtain there free travel-maps for all parts of the U.S.A.)

FOR EVERYONE:
The subway map available at subway token booths. (If one booth is temporarily out, go to the next.)

47:
GEOGRAPHICAL DIRECTORY

This is a directory only of stores, since restaurants and some other long recommended-facilities lists in this book have their separate geographical directories.

Organization is by subway-stop. This list runs generally from southern Manhattan to northern Bronx; then from southern Brooklyn to northern Queens; stores in areas such as all of Staten Island, where there are no subways within walking distance, will then be listed.

The numbers that follow after each store's address are the numbers of each of the chapters in which the store is recommended. In the store-directory at the end of any one of those chapters, you'll find the complete information about that particular store. So the numbers tell you both what the shop sells, and where you can find the full information on it.

MANHATTAN

N-RR-1 to South Ferry
PAY LESS, 44 Water St. Ch.'s: **13, 16**.
STEP 'N STYLE SHOES, 1 New York Plaza. Ch.: **7**.

4-5 to Bowling Green
BEAVER ELECTRONIC, 20 Beaver St. Ch.: **1**.
DUANE READE DRUGS, 37 Broadway. Ch.: **13**.
STRAWBERRY, 80 Broad St. Ch.'s: **7, 22**.

N-RR-1 to Rector
COMPUTER CENTER, 21 West St. Ch.: **21**.
FREDWIN, 77 New St. Ch.'s: **7, 30**.
SHOE MART, 69 New St. Ch.: **7**.

4-5 to Wall St.
CENTURY 21, 12 Cortlandt St. Ch.'s: **5, 6, 7, 13**.
FREDWIN, 77 New St. Ch.'s: **7, 30**.
SHOE MART, 69 New St. Ch.: **7**.
TRI-STATE CAMERA, 179 Broadway. Ch.: **4**.

J-M-RR-2-3 to Wall & Broad Sts.
DUANE READE DRUGS, 40 Beaver St. Ch.: **13**.
DUANE READE DRUGS, 50 Pine St. Ch.: **13**.
ESSENTIAL PRODUCTS, 90 Water St. Ch.: **13**.
FREDWIN, 77 New St. Ch.'s: **7, 30**.
L&J AUDIO, 3 Hanover Sq. Ch.'s: **1, 14**.
SHOE MART, 69 New St. Ch.: **7**.
STRAWBERRY, 80 Broad St. Ch.'s: **7, 22**.
THE BOOK STORE, 83 Maiden Lane. Ch.: **24**.
TRINITY PIPE SHOP, 160 Pearl St. Ch.: **26**.

N-RR-1 to Cortlandt
ELM DRUGS, 114 Liberty St. Ch.: **13**.
SCOTT'S DRESS, 179 Broadway. Ch.'s: **7, 30**.

AA-E to World Trade Ctr.
ALEXANDER'S AT WORLD TRADE CTR., 4 WTC. Ch.'s: **6, 7**.
BARNES & NOBLE, 248 World Trade Center Concourse 5. Ch.: **24**.
DUANE READE DRUGS, 1 World Trade Ctr. Ch.: **13**.
HENRY HARRIS PHOTOGRAPHER, 21 Barclay St. Ch.: **28**.
J&R TOBACCO, 219 Broadway. Ch.: **26**.
MANHATTAN WEDDING CTR., 181 Broadway. Ch.: **16**.
MERN'S, 75 Church St. at Vesey. Ch.'s: **6, 7**.
TWIN TOWERS WINES, 305 World Trade Ctr. Concourse. Ch.: **19**.

2-3 to Park Place
DUANE READE DRUGS, 19 Park Place. Ch.: **13**.
FITZPATRICK'S FOR COATS, 51 Murray St. Ch.: **7**.
HENRY HARRIS PHOTOGRAPHER, 21 Barclay St. Ch.: **28**.
J&R TOBACCO, 219 Broadway. Ch.: **26**.
MOREL ELECTRONICS, 57 Park Place at W. B'wy. Ch.: **14**.
SYM'S, 45 Park Place. Ch.: **6**.

A-CC-1-2-3 to Chambers
ALEE DISCOUNT, 85 Chambers St. Ch.'s: **5, 6, 7, 18, 30**.
ALEXANDER'S HARDWARE, 60 Reade St. Ch.'s: **15, 28, 30**.
AMERICAN ARION, 149 Church St. Ch.: **6**.
ANBAR SHOES, 97 Reade St. Ch.: **7**.
ANNEX OUTLET, 43 Warren St. Ch.'s: **1, 25**.
BRIAN LEASING, 66 W. B'wy. Ch.: **21**.
BRILL'S LIQUORS, 150 Chambers St. Ch.: **19**.
CAMERA DISCOUNT CTR., 89A Worth St. Ch.: **4**.
CANAL BARGAIN, 121 Chambers St. Ch.: **6**.
CHEESE OF ALL NATIONS, 153 Chambers St. Ch.: **11**.
CHO'S VARIETY, 121 Chambers St. Ch.'s: **6, 7, 22, 29**.
CLASSIC ELECTRONICS, 91 Chambers St. Ch.: **14**.
COHEN'S ELECTRONICS, 182 Church St. Ch.'s: **1, 25**.
COURT RADIO, 143 Chambers St. Ch.'s: **14, 15**.
CRAZY CIRO, 23 Warren St. Ch.: **28**.
DESIGNERS CHOICE, 46 Warren St. Ch.: **7**.
DR. SCHLOCK'S, 19 Warren St. Ch.'s: **8, 9, 11, 30**.
DUANE READE DRUGS, 299 Broadway. Ch.: **13**.
EASTERN ODD LOT, 113 Chambers St. Ch.: **6**.
EASY LOOK PILLOW FURN., 62 Thomas St. Ch.: **12**.
EIGHTY-EIGHT CENT SHOPS, 89 Chambers St. Ch.'s: **8, 11, 13, 15, 16, 28, 29**.
FAST COPY, 79 Chambers St. Ch.: **28**.
FLEETWOOD MARKET, 28 & 30 Warren St. Ch.'s: **6, 7**.
HYMIE & SCHELLY'S, 148 Church St. Ch.: **16**.
INDIA BAZAAR, 149 Church St. Ch.: **17**.
INTERSTATE FOOTWEAR, 152 Duane St. at W. B'wy. Ch.: **6**.
JOB LOT TRDG., 140 Church St. Ch.'s: **6, 8, 11, 15, 16, 17, 18, 22, 27, 28, 29, 30**.
KASBAR'S BAGS, 129 Chambers St. Ch.: **22**.
METRO ELECTRONICS, 81 W.B'wy at Warren. Ch.: **14**.
NEW FASHION, 158 Church St. Ch.: **22**.
NO NAME, 28 and 30 Warren St. Ch.'s: **6, 30**.
PAREZIO II, 77 Chambers St. Ch.'s: **6, 7**.
PHANTOM, 185 Church St. Ch.: **6**.
PHILIPSON PRESS, 52 Warren St. Ch.: **28**.
PUSHCART, 140 Church St. Ch.'s: **4, 13, 15**.
RUBY'S BOOK ANNEX, 74 Reade St. Ch.: **24**.
RUBY'S BOOK SALE, 119 Chambers St. Ch.: **24**.
SHOE STEAL, 116 Duane St. Ch.: **7**.
SHOES, BOOTS, ETC., 63 Warren St. at W. B'wy. Ch.'s: **6, 27, 30**.
STEP 'N STYLE SHOES, 84 Chambers St. Ch.: **7**.
SUPERIOR MERCHANDISING, 12 Warren St. Ch.'s: **6, 25**.

47: GEOGRAPHICAL DIRECTORY 325

SWEETHEART DISCOUNT, 125 Church St. Ch.: **13.**
TRIBECCA ART MATERIALS, 142 Chambers St. Ch.: **28.**
TRI-SURPLUS, 63 Reade St. Ch.'s.: **12, 30.**
UNITED CHAMBERS TRDG., 83 Chambers St. Ch.'s.: **6, 27.**
WARREN ST. MERCHANDISE, 32 Warren St. Ch.'s.: **1, 25, 28.**
WEBER'S JOB LOT, 136 Church St. at Warren. Ch.'s.: **8, 13, 15, 17, 18, 22, 28, 30.**
WEISER & TEITEL, 61 Reade St. Ch.'s.: **15, 28.**

N-RR to City Hall

ALEE DISCOUNT, 85 Chambers St. Ch.'s.: **5, 6, 7, 18, 30.**
ALEXANDER'S HARDWARE, 60 Reade St. Ch.'s.: **15, 28, 30.**
BRIAN LEASING, 66 W. B'way. Ch.: **21.**
CLASSIC ELECTRONICS, 91 Chambers St. Ch.: **14.**
DR. SCHLOCK'S, 19 Warren St. Ch.'s.: **8, 9, 11, 30.**
DUANE READE DRUGS, 299 Broadway. Ch.: **13.**
EIGHTY-EIGHT CENT SHOPS, 89 Chambers St. Ch.'s.: **8, 11, 13, 15, 16, 28, 29.**
FAST COPY, 79 Chambers St. Ch.: **28.**
FLEETWOOD MARKET, 28 & 30 Warren St. Ch.'s.: **6, 7.**
LUGGAGE KING, 261 Broadway. Ch.: **22.**
NO NAME, 28 and 30 Warren St. Ch.'s.: **6, 30.**
PAREZIO II, 7 Chambers St. Ch.'s.: **6, 7.**
PHILIPSON PRESS, 52 Warren St. Ch.: **28.**
STEP 'N STYLE SHOES, 84 Chambers St. Ch.: **7.**
SUPERIOR MERCHANDISING, 12 Chambers St. Ch.'s.: **6, 25.**
UNITED CHAMBERS TRDG., 83 Chambers St. Ch.'s.: **6, 27.**
VICTORIA STORES, 114 Worth St. Ch.'s.: **18, 30.**
WARREN ST. MERCHANDISE, 32 Warren St. Ch.'s.: **1, 25, 28.**
WEISER & TEITEL, 61 Reade St. Ch.'s.: **15, 28.**

A-CC-J-M-RR-2-3-4-5 to B'way-Nassau & Fulton

AMERICAN VISION CENTERS, 93 Nassau St. Ch.: **13.**
BARCLAY REX PIPE, 7 Maiden Ln. Ch.: **26.**
BARNEY'S, 41 Ann St. Ch.'s.: **13, 26.**
BEE HIVE, 75 Nassau St. Ch.: **7.**
BIG APPLE COPY, 87 Nassau St. at Fulton. Ch.: **28.**
BONDY'S RECORDS, 38 Park Row. Ch.: **25.**
CENTURY 21, 12 Cortlandt St. Ch.'s.: **5, 6, 7, 13.**
COMPUCO, 170 Broadway at Maiden Ln. Ch.: **21.**
DESIGNERS BELOW, 150 Fulton St. Ch.: **6.**
DRAKE BROS., 114 Fulton St. Ch.: **1.**
DUANE READE DRUGS, 90 John St. Ch.: **13.**
EIGHTY-EIGHT CENT SHOPS, 144 Fulton St. Ch.'s.: **8, 11, 13, 15, 16, 28, 29.**
HERMAN'S, 110 Nassau St. at Ann. Ch.: **27.**
JOHN ST. REPRODUCTIONS, 11 John St. Ch.: **28.**
J&J CLASSICAL & JAZZ, 33 Park Row. Ch.: **25.**
J&R POP RECORDS, 23 Park Row. Ch.: **25.**
KAZOOTIE, 59 Nassau St. Ch.: **7.**
MANHATTAN WEDDING CTR., 181 Broadway. Ch.: **16.**
MODAK APPAREL, 29 John St. Ch.: **6.**
PARKWAY, 52 Fulton St. at Cliff. Ch.: **6.**
PHILIPSON PRESS, 12 John St. Ch.: **28.**
RAINBARREL FACTORY OUTLET, 116 John St. at Pearl. Ch.: **6.**
RECORD EXPLOSION, 53 Nassau St. Ch.: **25.**
SABRA SHOES, 1 John St. Ch.: **7.**
SPIEGEL'S, 105 Nassau St. at Ann. Ch.: **27.**
SUNSHINE, 10 Maiden Lane. Ch.: **7.**
TAFT ELECTRONICS, 27 Park Row. Ch.'s.: **14, 25.**
THE FOOT LOT, 70 Fulton St. at Ryders Alley. Ch.: **7.**
TINKERS PARADISE, 31 Park Row. Ch.: **15.**
TRI-STATE CAMERA, 179 Broadway. Ch.: **4.**
WENDY'S FOOTWEAR, 123 Nassau St. Ch.: **7.**
YOUNG'S HATS, 139 Nassau St. at Beekman. Ch.: **6, 7.**
ZOOM, 79 Nassau St. Ch.: **7.**

J-M-RR-4-5-6 to Chambers & Bkln. Bridge

BCA DEPT. STORE, 49 E. Broadway. Ch.: **1.**
BOK LEI BO, 78 Bayard St. Ch.'s.: **6, 7.**
BONDY'S RECORDS, 38 Park Row. Ch.: **25.**
DAVID FABRICS, 168 William St. at Beekman. Ch.: **9.**
FONG INN, 46 Mott St. Ch.: **11.**
G.H. TAILOR, 18B Doyers. Ch.: **7.**
J&R CLASSICAL & JAZZ, 33 Park Row. Ch.: **25.**
J&R POP RECORDS, 23 Park Row. Ch.: **25.**
LEUNG TRDG., 44 E. Broadway. Ch.: **7.**
LUCKY GIFT, 20 Bowery at Pell. Ch.'s.: **6, 18.**
PEARL RIVER, 13 Elizabeth St. Ch.'s.: **7, 8.**
S. REDISCH FURNITURE, 27 E. Broadway. Ch.: **12.**

TAFT ELECTRONICS, 27 Park Row. Ch.'s.: **14, 25.**
THE BOWL SHOP, 45 Mott St. Ch.: **17.**
TINKERS PARADISE, 31 Park Row. Ch.: **15.**
UNITED SALVAGE ALKA SELTZER, 7 E. Broadway. Ch.'s.: **6, 30.**
WAH FUN, 43A Mott St. Ch.: **7.**
WENDY'S FOOTWEAR, 123 Nassau St. Ch.: **7.**
WING LEE LUNG FOOD FAIR, 50 E. Broadway. Ch.: **11.**

1 to Franklin

AA STEEL SHELVING, 158 Franklin St. Ch.: **21.**
CAMERA DISCOUNT CTR., 89A Worth St. Ch.: **4.**
COHEN'S ELECTRONICS, 182 Church St. Ch.'s.: **1, 25.**
EASY LOOK PILLOW FURN., 62 Thomas St. Ch.: **12.**
FRONTIER FABRICS, 251 Church St. Ch.: **9.**
INTERSTATE FOOTWEAR, 152 Duane St. at W. B'wy. Ch.: **6.**
LEONARD ST. CARPET WAREHOUSE, 14 Leonard St. Ch.: **12.**
PEERLESS FABRICS, 88 Franklin St. Ch.: **9.**
RELATEX FABRICS, 360 Broadway. Ch.: **9.**
SHOE STEAL, 116 Duane St. Ch.: **7.**
UNSLOPPY COPY, 97 Worth St. Ch.: **28.**
WORTH AUTO PARTS, 232 W. Broadway. Ch.: **2.**

A-AA-CC-E-1 to Canal

A.H. BURGLAR ALARMS, 340 Canal St. Ch.: **15.**
ALL-BRANDS AUTO PARTS, 15 Laight St. at Canal. Ch.: **2.**
ART PLASTICS, 359 Canal St. Ch.: **12.**
BOOKBINDER MODERN BLINDS, 3 Lispenard St. at 6th Av. Ch.: **15.**
BRASS LOFT FACTORY OUTLET, 20 Greene St. Ch.'s.: **12, 15, 17.**
CANAL RUBBER, 329 Canal St. at Greene. Ch.: **15.**
CANAL SURPLUS, 363 Canal St. Ch.'s.: **15, 30.**
HANG UPS WICKER, Canal at W. Broadway. Ch.'s.: **12, 17.**
MINTZER MERCANTILE, 313 Church St. Ch.: **7.**
RAMCO ELECTRONICS, 314 Canal St. Ch.: **14.**
SOHO MUSIC GALLERY, 26 Wooster St. at Grand. Ch.: **25.**
THE CITY DUMP, 334 Canal St. Ch.'s.: **1, 17, 27.**
TRANS-AM ELECTRONICS, 383 Canal St. Ch.: **15.**

J-M-N-QB-RR-6 to Canal

A. BENJAMIN, 80 Bowery. Ch.'s.: **6, 17.**
AARON SAFE, 11 Howard St. at Lafayette. Ch.: **21.**
A.C. DESK, 86 Walker St. Ch.: **21.**
ALMA LANERA, 482 Broadway. Ch.: **7.**
AR-TEX MFG., 456 Broadway. Ch.: **18.**
ASHREH SUPPLY, 473 Broadway. Ch.'s.: **1, 4, 17, 22, 26, 28.**
B&A TEXTILE, 430 Broadway. Ch.: **9.**
BARNEY'S CANAL CUT-RATE, 259 Canal St. Ch.: **26.**
BOK LEI BO, 78 Bayard St. Ch.'s.: **6, 7.**
BRASS LOFT FACTORY OUTLET, 20 Greene St. Ch.'s.: **12, 15, 17.**
BUDLEE FABRICS, 458 Broadway. Ch.: **9.**
CANAL ELECTRIC MOTOR, 310 Canal St. Ch.: **15.**
CANAL JEAN CO., 504 Broadway. Ch.: **6, 7.**
CANAL RUBBER, 329 Canal St. at Greene. Ch.: **15.**
CANAL SELF-SERVICE, 270 Canal St. at Cortlandt Alley. Ch.: **16.**
CANAL ST. MARKET, 234 Canal St. Ch.: **7.**
CANAL ST. MERCH. EXCH., 253 Canal. Ch.: **25.**
CANAL STREET DISCOUNT, 255 Canal. Ch.'s.: **18, 30.**
CHINA BRILLIANCE, 32 E. Broadway. Ch.: **11.**
CHINA MALL, 234 Canal St. Ch.'s.: **6, 7.**
CHINESE AMERICAN TRDG., 91 Mulberry St. Ch.: **11.**
C.K.&L. SURPLUS, 307 Canal St. Ch.'s.: **9, 12, 15.**
E. NACK WATCH, 226 Canal St. Ch.: **17.**
EMPIRE SAFE, 103 Grand. Ch.: **21.**
FONG INN, 46 Mott St. Ch.: **11.**
GALLERIA INTERNATIONAL, 542 Croadway. Ch.: **7.**
G.H. TAILOR, 18B Doyers. Ch.: **7.**
HOLLAND STATIONERY, 325 Canal St. Ch.: **28.**
INTER COASTAL TEXTILE, 480 Broadway. Ch.: **9.**
JACOB WIESENFELD, 450 Broadway. Ch.: **9.**
KRAMER TEXTILE, 494 Broadway. Ch.: **18.**
LEVER & GREENBERG, 271 Canal St. Ch.: **6.**
LOUIS BARALL & SON, 58 Lispenard St. Ch.: **6.**
MARGARET'S FABRICS, 430 Broadway. Ch.: **9.**
MAX EILENBERG, 449 Broadway. Ch.: **18.**
MERIT OFFICE SUPPLIES, 104 Grand St. at Mercer. Ch.'s.: **21, 28.**
M&G BARGAINS, 344 Broadway. Ch.: **16.**
MING HING, 82 Walker St. Ch.: **11.**
MITCHELL MOGAL, 440 Broadway. Ch.'s.: **9, 17, 22,**

47: GEOGRAPHICAL DIRECTORY

29.
M&J SPORTSWEAR, 486 Broadway at Broome. Ch.: **7.**
MONEZEL TEXTILES, 470 Broadway. Ch.: **9.**
M&R PLASTIC, 428 Broadway. Ch.: **15.**
O.Q. MKTG., 300 Canal St. Ch.: **15.**
PEARL ART SUPPLIES, 308 Canal St. Ch.: **28.**
PEARL RIVER, 131 Elizabeth St. Ch.'s.: **7, 8.**
PENN TEXTILE, 405 Broadway. Ch.: **18.**
PIEMONTE RAVIOLI, 190 Grand St. Ch.: **11.**
RAINBOW TEXTILES, 414 Broadway. Ch.: **9.**
ROSS CHAINS, 74 Bowery. Ch.: **17.**
S&A CLOTHING, 95 Canal St. Ch.: **6.**
SHELINSKY, 448 Broadway. Ch.: **18.**
SOHO MUSIC GALLERY, 26 Wooster St. at Grand. Ch.: **25.**
STANDARD SAFE, 138 Lafayette St. at Howard. Ch.: **21.**
STEP INN SHOES, 257 Canal St. Ch.: **7.**
SUSAN TRDG., 300 Canal St. Ch.'s.: **1, 12, 15, 22.**
THE BOWL SHOP, 45 Mott St. Ch.: **17.**
THE CITY DUMP, 334 Canal St. Ch.'s.: **1, 17, 27.**
UNITED SALVAGE ALKA SELTZER, 7 E. Broadway. Ch.'s.: **6, 30.**
WAH FUN, 43A Mott St. Ch.: **7.**
WING LEE LUNG FOOD FAIR, 50 E. Broadway. Ch.: **11.**

F to E. Broadway

ABC TRDG., 31 Canal St. Ch.: **1.**
ATLANTIC CLOTHING, 1 Allen St. at Division. Ch.: **6.**
AUDIO AUDIO, 42 Canal St. Ch.: **14.**
A&Z APPLIANCES, 34 Canal St. Ch.: **1.**
B. KAMINSKY, 18 Canal St. Ch.: **5.**
BCA DEPT. STORE, 49 E. Broadway. Ch.: **1.**
BENNY'S IMPEX, 1 Canal St. Ch.: **1.**
BONDY EXPORT, 40 Canal St. Ch.: **1.**
BRIDGE MERCHANDISE, 74 Orchard St. Ch.'s.: **6, 7.**
CHINA BRILLIANCE, 32 E. Broadway. Ch.: **11.**
DEEPAK, 28 Canal St. at Essex. Ch.: **22.**
EASTERN SILVER, 54 Canal St. Ch.: **8.**
EICHLER BROS., 70 Canal at Allen. Ch.: **1.**
ESSEX CAMERA/ELECTRONICS, 17 Essex St. Ch.'s.: **1.**
ESSEX FRUITERERS, Essex at Canal. Ch.: **11.**
FORMAN'S BASEMENT, 82 Orchard St. Ch.: **7.**
FRANK'S BIKE SHOP, 553 Grand St. Ch.: **3.**
FRED KRUPNIK, 29 Orchard St. Ch.: **6.**
GLORIA UMBRELLA, 39 Essex St. Ch.: **22.**
GOLD STYLE BAGS, 13 Orchard St. on Canal. Ch.: **22.**
GOLDMAN & COHEN, 54 Orchard St. Ch.: **7.**
GREATER NY TRDG., 81 Canal St. Ch.'s.: **1, 8, 17.**
GUILD SEWING MACHINES, 139 E. Broadway. Ch.: **1.**
HESTER ST. HOUSEWARES, 59 Hester St. Ch.'s: **15, 16.**
I. GUS PICKLES, 42 Hester St. Ch.: **11.**
I. TUSCHMAN & SONS, 61 Orchard St. Ch.'s.: **6, 7.**
J. SHERMAN SHOES, 121 Division St. Ch.: **7.**
JEANS & THINGS, 197 Madison Street. Ch.: **7.**
KADOURI IMPORT, 51 Hester St. at Essex. Ch.: **11.**
KAM FOOK, 101 E. Broadway. Ch.: **11.**
KUNST SALES, 45 Canal St. Ch.: **1.**
LANAC SALES, 63 Canal St. at Allen. Ch.'s.: **8, 17.**
LEON, 1 Essex. Ch.: **7, 30.**
LESLIE SCHIFFER LOCKS, 34 Ludlow St. Ch.: **15.**
LEUNG TRDG., 44 E. Broadway. Ch.: **7.**
LEWI SUPPLY, 15 Essex St. Ch.: **1.**
LUCKY GIFT, 20 Bowery at Pell. Ch.'s.: **6, 18.**
M. FRIEDMAN HOSIERY, 326 Grand St. Ch.'s.: **6, 7.**
MILTON SIEGEL, 14 Orchard St. Ch.: **6.**
MITCHELL'S LEATHER WEAR, 33 Canal St. Ch.: **6.**
NATHAN KURTZ, 27 Canal St. Ch.'s.: **6, 7.**
PAULA KNITWEAR, 37 Orchard St. Ch.: **7.**
REGENT'S WEAR, 34 Orchard St. Ch.: **6.**
RELIANCE HARDWARE, 40 Ludlow St. Ch.: **15.**
ROSALIE FASHIONS, 32 Orchard St. Ch.: **7.**
ROUND HOUSE FASHIONS, 41 Orchard St. Ch.: **7.**
S. REDISCH FURNITURE, 27 E. Broadway. Ch.: **12.**
S&A CLOTHING, 95 Canal St. Ch.: **6.**
SAVERITE PHOTO ELEC., 46 Canal St. Ch.'s.: **1, 4.**
SONA ELECTRICAL, 135 Division St. at Canal. Ch.: **1.**
S&W ELECTRONICS, 50 Canal St. Ch.'s.: **1, 4.**
THE PICKLEMAN, 27 Essex St. Ch.: **11.**
WEILGUS BROS. HARDWARE, 158 E. Broadway. Ch.: **15.**
WING LEE LUNG FOOD FAIR, 50 E. Broadway. Ch.: **11.**
WORLD WIDE DISCOUNT, 37 Canal St. at Ludlow. Ch.: **1.**

F-J-M to Delancey & Essex

A. ROSENTHAL, 92 Orchard St. Ch.: **7.**
A&G CHILDREN'S WEAR, 261 Broome St. Ch.: **5.**
ALLEN RUHALTER MEAT, 104 Essex St. Ch.: **11.**
ALTMAN LUGGAGE, 135 Orchard St. Ch.: **22.**
ANTONY, 106 Orchard St. Ch.: **6.**
BELL YARN, 75 Essex St. Ch.: **9.**
BEN FREEDMAN, 137 Orchard St. Ch.: **6.**
BEN'S BABYLAND, 87 Av. A. Ch.: **12.**
BERNARD KRIEGER, 316 Grand St. Ch.: **6, 7, 22.**
BETTINGER'S LUGGAGE, 80 Rivington St. Ch.: **22.**
B&M YARN, 151 Essex St. Ch.: **9.**
BOB'S DISCOUNT, 109 Ludlow St. Ch.'s.: **6, 22, 27, 30.**
BONI KNITWARE, 93 Allen St. Ch.: **7.**
BRIDGE MERCHANDISE, 74 Orchard St. Ch.'s.: **6, 7.**
CENTRAL HAT, 144 Orchard St. Ch.: **6.**
CRYSTAL FACTORY OUTLET, 53 Delancey St. Ch.: **7.**
D&S DRESSES, 80 Essex St. Ch.: **7.**
EAST SIDE GIFTS, 351 Grand St. Ch.'s.: **8, 17.**
EMPRESS GIFT SHOP, 332 Grand St. Ch.: **12.**
ESSEX UMBRELLA, 101 Essex St. Ch.: **22.**
FIEDLER'S, 140 Orchard St. Ch.: **6.**
FINE & KLEIN, 119 Orchard St. Ch.: **22.**
F.M. HANDBAGS & SHOES, 126 Ludlow St. Ch.: **7.**
FORMAN'S BASEMENT, 82 Orchard St. Ch.: **7.**
GENAO'S SHOES, 95 Rivington St. Ch.: **6, 7.**
GOLDMAN & COHEN, 54 Orchard St. Ch.: **7.**
GRILL BEVERAGE, 261 Delancey St. Ch.: **19.**
G&S SPORTING GOODS, 43 Essex St. Ch.: **27.**
HABER'S, 33 Essex St. Ch.'s.: **27, 28.**
HARRY JULIUS (S&G STANLEY), 120 Essex St. Ch.: **11.**
HIGH FASHION, 149 Orchard St. Ch.: **7.**
IDEAL HOSIERY, 339 Grand St. Ch.'s.: **6, 7.**
I&Z LEATHER, 191 Orchard St. Ch.: **6.**
J. FINKELSTEIN, 95 Delancey St. Ch.: **17.**
J. WOLSK, 87 Ludlow. Ch.: **11.**
JACOB YOUNG & SON, 329 Grand St. Ch.: **7.**
J.B.Z. UNLIMITED, 121 Orchard St. Ch.: **7.**
JEFF'S BOUTIQUE, 122 Orchard St. Ch.: **7.**
JOHN CIPRIANO SHOES, 148 Orchard St. Ch.: **6.**
JOLI MADAME BOUTIQUE, 145 Orchard St. Ch.'s.: **7, 22.**
JULIUS THE CANDY KING, Essex St. Market immediately north of Delancey. Ch.: **11.**
KAUFMAN ELECTRIC, 365 Grand St. Ch.'s.: **1, 8, 17.**
KAYMORE, 92 Orchard St. Ch.: **7.**
L. SCHWARTZ & SONS, 149 Allen St. Ch.: **18.**
LA GIGI HANDBAGS, 92 Rivington St. Ch.: **22.**
LACE UP, 119 Orchard St. Ch.: **7.**
L.B.C. CLOTHING, 337 Grand St. Ch.: **6.**
LEA'S, 81 Rivington St. Ch.: **7.**
LISMORE HOSIERY, 334 Grand St. Ch.'s.: **6, 7.**
LITTLE RASCALS, 101 Orchard St. Ch.: **5.**
L&K MERCHANDISE, 138 Ludlow St. Ch.: **18.**
LYNN'S SHOES, 163 Orchard St. Ch.: **7.**
M. FRIEDMAN HOSIERY, 326 Grand St. Ch.'s.: **6, 7.**
MAX EAGLE FABRICS, 61 Delancey St. Ch.: **9.**
MUTUAL DRIED FRUIT, 127 Ludlow St. Ch.: **11.**
PECK & CHASE SHOES, 161 Orchard St. Ch.: **6.**
RITE, 115 Ludlow St. Ch.: **29.**
S. SOSINSKY & SON, 143 Orchard St. Ch.: **7.**
SAM POPPER, 87 Orchard St. at Broome. Ch.: **6.**
SAM'S KNITWEAR, 93 Orchard St. Ch.: **7.**
SCHNEIDER'S, 20 Av. A. at 2nd St. Ch.: **12.**
S&G HOSIERY, 263 Broome St. Ch.'s.: **6, 7.**
SHOES-N-THINGS, 131 Allen St. Ch.: **6.**
SLEP, 132 Orchard St. Ch.: **6, 7.**
SPITZER'S CORNER STORE, 101 Rivington St. at Ludlow. Ch.: **7.**
SUNRAY YARN, 349 Grand St. Ch.: **9.**
SUPERIOR FLOOR COVERING, 155 Essex St. Ch.: **12.**
THE PICKLEMAN, 27 Essex St. Ch.: **11.**
TWO-MORROW, 111 Rivington. Ch.: **12.**
WILLIAM ROSENGARTEN, 326 Grand St. Ch.: **6.**
W.M. MEN'S WEAR, 145 Orchard St. Ch.: **6.**
WYSE WEAR, 266 Broome St. at Allen. Ch.: **7.**
YOUNG'S, 319 Grand St. at Orchard. Ch.: **6.**

B-D to Grand

ABC FOAM, 77 Allen St. at Grand. Ch.: **12.**
A&E MOSSERI, 86 Eldridge St. Ch.: **18.**
A&G CHILDREN'S WEAR, 261 Broome St. Ch.: **5.**
BERNARD KRIEGER, 316 Grand St. Ch.: **6, 7, 22.**
BOK LEI BO, 78 Bayard St. Ch.: **6, 7.**
BOWERY LIGHTING CLEARANCE, 240 Grand St. Ch.: **12.**
CH. DYM, 103 Eldridge St. Ch.: **18.**
CHINA BRILLIANCE, 32 E. Broadway. Ch.: **11.**
DAC LIGHTING, 164 Bowery. Ch.: **12.**
DANA FABRICS, 113 Eldridge St. Ch.: **9.**
EICHLER BROS., 70 Canal at Allen. Ch.: **1.**

47: GEOGRAPHICAL DIRECTORY

ELDRIDGE JOBBING, 86 Eldridge St. Ch.: **18**.
EMPIRE FOOD SERVICE, 114 Bowery. Ch.: **8**.
FONG INN, 46 Mott St. Ch.: **1**.
G.H. TAILOR, 18B Doyers. Ch.: **7**.
GRAND BRASS LAMP PARTS, 221 Grand St. at Elizabeth. Ch.: **15**.
HARRY GRUNBERG, 118 Eldridge. Ch.: **9**.
I. TUSCHMAN & SONS, 61 Orchard St. Ch.'s: **6, 7**.
INTERNATIONAL FLUORESCENT, 135 Bowery. Ch.'s: **12, 15**.
KING GLASSWARE, 112 Bowery. Ch.: **8**.
KIRSCH DRAPERY HARDWARE, 105 Eldridge St. Ch.: **9**.
K-O RESTAURANT EQT., 99 Bowery. Ch.: **8**.
L. SCHWARTZ & SONS, 149 Allen St. Ch.: **18**.
LANAC SALES, 63 Canal St. at Allen. Ch.'s: **8, 17**.
LERATEX FABRICS, 110 Eldridge St. Ch.: **8**.
LEUNG TRDG., 44 E. Broadway. Ch.: **7**.
L.G. LIQUORS, 133 Bowery at Grand. Ch.: **19**.
L&S TEXTILE, 276 Grand St. Ch.: **8**.
M. FRIEDMAN HOSIERY, 326 Grand St. Ch.'s: **6, 7**.
M. KESSLER HARDWARE, 229 Grand St. Ch.: **15**.
MEYER OSTROV'S SONS, 265 Broome St. at Allen. Ch.: **18**.
M.RECHT TEXTILE, 118 Eldridge St. Ch.: **8**.
PEARL RIVER, 13 Elizabeth St. Ch.'s: **7, 8**.
PENCHINA TEXTILE, 272 Grand St. Ch.: **18**.
PIEMONTE RAVIOLI, 190 Grand St. Ch.: **11**.
ROSS CHAINS, 74 Bowery. Ch.: **17**.
RUBIN & GREEN, 290 Grand St. at Eldridge. Ch.: **18**.
SANG KUNG KITCHEN SUPPLIES, 108 Bowery. Ch.: **8**.
S.F. FRUITS, 125 Canal St. at Chrystie. Ch.: **22**.
S&G HOSIERY, 263 Broome St. Ch.'s: **6, 7**.
SHEILA'S WALLSTYLES, 273 Grand St. Ch.: **15**.
SHORLAND TEXTILE, 274 Grand St. Ch.: **18**.
THE BOWL SHOP, 45 Mott St. Ch.: **17**.
W.M. TEXTILE, 108 Eldridge St. Ch.: **8**.
WYSE WEAR, 266 Broome St. at Allen. Ch.: **7**.

J-M to Bowery
CRYSTAL FACTORY OUTLET, 53 Delancey St. Ch.: **17**.
DAC LIGHTING, 164 Bowery. Ch.: **12**.
EMPIRE FOOD SERVICE, 114 Bowery. Ch.: **8**.
INTERNATIONAL FLUORESCENT, 135 Bowery. Ch.'s: **12, 15**.
KALAT & JENMAR AUTO PARTS, 141 Chrystie St. Ch.: **2**.
KING GLASSWARE, 112 Bowery. Ch.: **8**.
K-O RESTAURANT EQT., 99 Bowery. Ch.: **8**.
L.G. LIQUORS, 133 Bowery at Grand. Ch.: **19**.
MAX EAGLE FABRICS, 61 Delancey St. Ch.: **9**.
NEW BEER WHOLESALE, 167 Chrystie St. Ch.: **19**.
PENNYWISE SALES, 99 Allen St. Ch.'s: **6, 7**.
SANG KUNG KITCHEN SUPPLIES, 108 Bowery. Ch.: **8**.
SHOES-N-THINGS, 131 Allen St. Ch.: **6**.
WYSE WEAR, 266 Broome St. at Allen. Ch.: **7**.

F to 2nd Av.
A. ALTMAN, 182 Orchard St. Ch.: **7**.
A&M TEXTILE, 185 E. Houston St. at Orchard. Ch.: **7**.
BEST HOUSEKEEPING, 17 A. Av. Ch.: **12**.
DISHES & AUCTION GOODS, 280 Bowery. Ch.: **8**.
DIXIE PARTY SUPPLIES, 1 Av. C. Ch.: **16**.
EAST SIDE GLASS, 201 Chrystie St. Ch.: **15**.
ECONOMY FOAM, 173 E. Houston St. at Allen. Ch.: **12**.
ESSEX AUTO PARTS, 5 Av. A at Houston. Ch.: **2**.
FISH & CHEEPS, 104 2nd Av. Ch.: **23**.
H. TENZER, 49 1st Av. at 3rd St. Ch.: **8**.
HIGH FASHION, 149 Orchard St. Ch.: **7**.
HOUSTON ST. BEER, 298 E. 2. Ch.: **19**.
I. ITZKOWITZ, 161 Allen St. Ch.: **18**.
I&Z LEATHER, 191 Orchard St. Ch.: **6**.
JBJ DISCOUNT PETS, 151 E. Houston St. at Eldridge. Ch.'s: **3, 23**.
JOE'S BARGAIN CENTER, 123 1st Av. Ch.'s: **6, 22**.
JOLI MADAME BOUTIQUE, 145 Orchard St. Ch.'s: **7, 22**.
KINGS HOUSTON DRUGS, 201 E. Houston St. Ch.: **13**.
KLEIN'S, 199 Orchard St. Ch.: **6**.
L. SCHWARTZ & SONS, 149 Allen St. Ch.: **18**.
LYNN'S SHOES, 163 Orchard St. Ch.: **7**.
M. FRANKEL ('MOE'S'), 39 1st Av. Ch.: **6**.
M.E., 177 E. Houston St. Ch.: **9**.
M&M MENSWEAR, 167 Orchard St. Ch.: **7**.
N&L CORP., 163 Orchard St. Ch.: **6**.
RUSS & DAUGHTERS, 175 E. Houston St. Ch.: **11**.
SCHNEIDER'S, 20 Av. A. at 2nd St. Ch.: **12**.
SLEP, 132 Orchard St. Ch.'s: **6, 7**.
SOFIA SAM MILICH, 177 E. Houston St. Ch.: **6**.
STANDARD CHINA, 231 Bowery. Ch.: **8**.
STANDARD TINSMITH, 183 Chrystie St. Ch.: **15**.
W.M. MEN'S WEAR, 145 Orchard St. Ch.: **6**.
Z&L IMPORT, 159 Orchard St. Ch.: **6**.

6 to Spring
ADVANCE SEWING MACHINE, 521 Broadway. Ch.'s: **1, 9**.
BETTER WEAR MFG., 500 Broadway. Ch.: **6**.
CARLSEN IMPORT, 524 Broadway at Spring. Ch.: **7**.
GOLDSTONE SPORTSWEAR, 533 Broadway. Ch.: **7**.
H&H PLASTICS, 508 Broadway. Ch.: **15**.
K TRIMMING, 519 Broadway. Ch.: **9**.
PREMIER TEXTILE, 512 Broadway. Ch.'s: **6, 7**.
SHALOM EXPORT, 513 Broadway. Ch.: **9**.
SILT SPORTUAR, 487 Broadway at Broome. Ch.: **6**.
SOL'S, 535 Broadway. Ch.: **7**.
WASHINGTON ELECTRIC, 97 Spring St. Ch.: **21**.

N-RR to Prince St.
ADVANCE SEWING MACHINE, 521 Broadway. Ch.'s: **1, 9**.
BEDFORD/BEDMARK TEXTILE, 611 Broadway at Houston. Ch.'s: **13**.
BETTER WEAR MFG., 500 Broadway. Ch.: **6**.
BROADWAY FASHION, 581 Broadway. Ch.'s: **5, 6, 7**.
CARLSEN IMPORT, 524 Broadway at Spring. Ch.: **27**.
CASA INTERNATIONAL, 595 Broadway. Ch.: **7**.
CROWN MERCANDISE, 543 Broadway. Ch.: **7**.
EVER READY LINGERIE, 568 Broadway. Ch.: **7**.
FRANK EASTERN, 625 Broadway. Ch.: **21**.
GOLDSTONE SPORTSWEAR, 533 Broadway. Ch.: **7**.
H&H PLASTICS, 508 Broadway. Ch.: **15**.
JOMARK TEXTILES, 515 Broadway. Ch.: **18**.
K TRIMMING, 519 Broadway. Ch.: **9**.
MANUFACTURER'S SHOE OUTLET, 537 Broadway. Ch.'s: **5, 6, 7**.
M.C.W. APPAREL, 546 Broadway. Ch.: **7**.
M&R FASHIONS, 596 Broadway. Ch.: **7**.
NY CEILING FAN CTR., 620-4 Broadway. Ch.'s: **12, 15**.
QUE LINDA, 594 Broadway. Ch.: **7**.
RENNERT MFG., 93 Greene St. Ch.: **18**.
SHALOM EXPORT, 513 Broadway. Ch.: **9**.
SOL'S, 535 Broadway. Ch.: **7**.
THE FINALS, 149 Mercer St. Ch.'s: **6, 7, 27**.
THREE STAR TAILORING, 561 Broadway. Ch.'s: **6, 7**.
WASHINGTON ELECTRIC, 97 Spring St. Ch.: **21**.
WHOLEFOODS, 117 Prince St. Ch.: **11**.

A-AA-CC-E to Spring
CRAFT CARAVAN, 127 Spring St. Ch.: **17**.
FIRE EXTINGUISHER MAINTENANCE, 530 Broome St. Ch.: **15**.
RENNERT MFG., 93 Greene St. Ch.: **18**.
WHOLEFOODS, 117 Prince St. Ch.: **11**.

1 to Houston
BELUGA CAVIAR CORP., 180 Varick St. Ch.: **11**.
G.M.E. STUFFED TOY ANIMALS, pier 40 at Clarkson St. off the Hudson River. Ch.: **29**.
PHANTOM, 180 Varick St. Ch.: **6**.
RAYMAR PRINTING, 333 Hudson at Charlton. Ch.: **28**.

B-D-F-6 to B'way-Laf. & Bleecker
DOWN IN THE VILLAGE, 652 Broadway. Ch.'s: **6, 27**.
FRANK EASTERN, 625 Broadway. Ch.: **21**.
IOA DATA, 383 Lafayette at 4th St. Ch.: **21**.
KOL-BO DISCOUNT, 611 Broadway at Houston. Ch.'s: **6, 27**.
NY CEILING FAN CTR., 620-4 Broadway. Ch.'s: **12, 15**.
PLUMBLINE DESIGN, 654 Broadway. Ch.: **12**.
R.B.D. LOCK & ALARM, 653 Broadway. Ch.: **15**.
SO CHEAP, 704 Broadway. Ch.'s: **6, 7, 30**.
VILLAGE COMPUTERS, 687 Broadway. Ch.: **21**.
WEARHOUSE, 687A Broadway. Ch.: **7**.
WORTH AUTO PARTS, 27 Cooper Sq. at 5th St. & Bowery. Ch.: **2**.

A-AA-B-CC-D-E-F to 4
BARNES & NOBLE, 56 W. 8. Ch.: **24**.
BLEECKER ST. PASTRY, 245 Bleecker St. Ch.: **11**.
BUEN DIA, 108 W. Houston St. at Thompson. Ch.'s: **7, 17, 22**.

47: GEOGRAPHICAL DIRECTORY

CHARM SHOP, 143 W. 4. Ch.: **17**.
DISC O RAMA, 247 Bleecker St. Ch.: **25**.
EIGHTY-EIGHT CENT SHOPS, 33 W. 8. Ch.'s.: **8, 11, 13, 15, 16, 28, 29**.
EXOTIC AQUATICS, 272 Bleeker St. at Morton. Ch.: **23**.
GALLERY PRINTING, 68 W. 3. Ch.: **28**.
GEORGE'S COPY, 146 W. 4. Ch.: **28**.
JEANS 'N THINGS, 140 W. 4. Ch.'s.: **6, 7**.
LAFAYETTE FRENCH PASTRY, 298 Bleecker St. Ch.: **11**.
LEON, 252 Bleecker St. at Leroy. Ch.: **17**.
MACDOUGAL COPY, 127 MacDougal St. Ch.: **28**.
MURRAY'S CHEESE, 42 Cornelia St. Ch.: **11**.
NAEM BROS., 128 MacDougal St. Ch.: **22**.
PORTO RICO IMPORTING, 201 Bleecker St. Ch.: **11**.
RECORD FACTORY, 17 W. 8. Ch.: **25**.
REPRISE, 14 5th Av. Ch.: **7**.
ROBERT KRACAUER, 252 Bleecker St. at Leroy. Ch.: **17**.
ROCCO'S PASTRY SHOP, 243 Bleecker St. Ch.: **11**.
SCHAPIRA COFFEE, 117 W. 10. Ch.: **11**.
SECOND COMING, 235 Sullvan St. Ch.: **25**.
SECOND COMING SECONDS, 240 Sullivan St. Ch.: **25**.
SIXTH AV. GREENERY, 355 6th Av. Ch.: **10**.
THE COW'S OUTSIDE, 1 W. 8. Ch.: **22**.
THE COW'S OUTSIDE, 33 Greenwich Av. Ch.: **22**.
UNSLOPPY COPY, 5 W. 8. Ch.: **28**.
VINYL MANIA, 30 Carmine St. Ch.: **25**.

1 to Christopher St.
CHRISTOS CLOTHIER, 57 7th Av. S. Ch.: **17**.
FRANCIS TYPEWRITER, 141 W. 10. Ch.: **21**.
LAFAYETTE FRENCH PASTRY, 298 Bleecker St. Ch.: **11**.
MARTHA'S LEATHER, 45 Christopher St. at Waverly. Ch.: **22**.
SECOND COMING ON CHRISTOPHER, 82 Christopher St. Ch.: **25**.
SECOND COUSIN, 142 7th Av. S. Ch.: **5**.

N-RR to 8th St.
ASTOR WINES, 12 Astor Place. Ch.: **19**.
CARTER LEATHER, 41 E. 11. Ch.'s.: **7, 22**.
DAYTON'S RECORDS, Broadway at 12th St. Ch.: **25**.
DRESS SHOPPE, 70 E. 9. Ch.: **7**.
HEUSTON COPY, 11 Waverly Place. Ch.: **28**.
ILANA FINE JEWELRY, 42 University Place. Ch.: **17**.
KOL-BO DISCOUNT, 611 Broadway at Houston. Ch.'s.: **6, 7**.
PACIFIC TRADERS, 742 Broadway. Ch.: **7**.
RECORD FACTORY, 17 W. 8. Ch.: **25**.
REPRISE, 14 5th Av. Ch.: **7**.
S.K. FRIEDMAN, 740 Broadway at Astor Place. Ch.: **7**.
SPEAKEASY, 799 Broadway. Ch.: **17**.
STRAND, 828 Broadway at 12th St. Ch.: **24**.
SUN PRESS, 88 University Place. Ch.: **28**.
SUNSET PROCESS PRTG., 95 University Place. Ch.: **28**.
THE COW'S OUTSIDE, 1 W. 8. Ch.: **22**.
TRAFFICO, 722 Broadway. Ch.: **7**.
UNIQUE COPIES PLUS, 29 Waverly Place. Ch.: **28**.
UNSLOPPY COPY, 5 W. 8. Ch.: **28**.
WAREHOUSE WINES, 735 Broadway. Ch.: **19**.

6 to Astor
A-ART LOCKSMITHS, 187 2nd Av. Ch.: **15**.
AMERICAN CAT & DOG FOOD, 147 Av. A. Ch.: **23**.
ASTOR WINES, 12 Astor Place. Ch.: **19**.
BEN'S BABYLAND, 87 Av. A. Ch.: **12**.
BLACK FOREST BAKERY, 177 1st Av. at 11th St. Ch.: **11**.
BOHRER'S CHILDREN'S WEAR, 139 1st Av. Ch.: **5**.
DIAMOND DISCOUNT FABRIC, 165 1st Av. Ch.: **9**.
DRESS SHOPPE, 70 E. 9. Ch.: **7**.
EAST VILLAGE CHEESE, 239 E. 9. Ch.: **11**.
FISH & CHEEPS, 104 2nd Av. Ch.: **23**.
FREE BEING RECORDS, 129 2nd Av. Ch.: **25**.
GOODWEAR, 793 Broadway. Ch.: **28**.
GREENWICH ART SUPPLY, 32 3rd Av. Ch.: **28**.
HALL PLACE RECORDS, 41 E. 7th. Ch.: **25**.
IPSWICH CLOCKS, 175 2nd Av. Ch.: **17**.
M&M TAILORS, 105 Av. A. Ch.'s.: **6, 7**.
NEW YORK CENTRAL ART SUPPLY, 63 3rd Av. Ch.: **28**.
PRANA FOODS, 145A 1st Av. at 9th Ch.: **11**.
ST. MARKS SOUNDS, 20 St. Marks Place. Ch.: **25**.
TAY ART SUPPLY, 27 3rd Av. Ch.: **28**.
THE TOBACCO CENTER, 130 St. Marks Place. Ch.: **26**.
WORTH AUTO PARTS, 27 Cooper Sq. at 5th St. & Bowery. Ch.: **2**.

LL-N-QB-RR-4-5-6 to Union Sq.
ABE BLOOM & SONS, 6 W. 19. Ch.: **9**.
ARTHUR RICHARDS, 91 5th Av. at 17th St. Ch.: **6**.
BARNES & NOBLE SALE ANNEX, 128 5th Av. at 18th St. Ch.: **24**.
BATHS INTERNATIONAL, 89 5th Av. Ch.: **15**.
BORISLAW CLOTHIER, 2 E. 17 at 5th Av. Ch.: **6**.
CARTER LEATHER, 41 E. 11. Ch.'s.: **7, 22**.
CATANIA CLOTHING, 85 5th Av. at 16th St. Ch.: **6**.
CENTRAL PRESCRIPTION PHARMACY, 145A 4th Av. Ch.: **13**.
DAVID SU'S 7-ART JEWELRY, 872 Broadway. Ch.: **17**.
DISC O RAMA, 40 Union Sq. E. Ch.: **25**.
DORSON CLOTHES, 87 5th Av. Ch.: **6**.
ESTEL JEWELRY, 222 Park Av. S. at 18th St. Ch.: **17**.
FABULOUS FIND, 25 E. 17. Ch.: **6**.
FRANK'S LIQUORS, 46 Union Sq. E. Ch.: **19**.
GOODWEAR, 793 Broadway. Ch.: **28**.
HAMPSHIRE CLOTHES, 85 5th Av. at 16th. Ch.: **6**.
ILANA FINE JEWELRY, 42 University Place. Ch.: **17**.
LESH CLOTHING, 100 5th Av. at 15th St. Ch.: **6**.
LOU-MARK TRDG., 13 E. 17. Ch.'s.: **1, 13, 17**.
MILLS SALES, 889 Broadway at 19th St. Ch.'s.: **1, 8, 15, 17, 22, 28, 29**.
MILSHAP PHARMACY, 114 E. 16. Ch.'s.: **13, 16**.
MR. TONY, 134 5th Av. Ch.'s.: **6, 7**.
PADAWER CARPETS & REMNANTS, 112 4th Av. Ch.: **12**.
PINA COLADA, 145 4th Av. Ch.: **7**.
ROTHMAN, 111 5th Av. at 17th St. Ch.: **6**.
RUBINSTEIN'S PARTY FAVORS, 876 Broadway. Ch.: **16**.
SIMON KLINGER, 144 5th Av. Ch.'s.: **6, 7**.
SPEAKEASY, 799 Broadway. Ch.: **17**.
STANLEY GONCHER, 12 W. 19. Ch.: **6**.
STRAND, 828 Broadway at 12th St. Ch.: **24**.
SUN PRESS, 88 University Place. Ch.: **28**.
SUNSET PROCESS PRTG., 95 University Place. Ch.: **28**.
SUNSHINE, 110 5th Av. Ch.: **7**.
TERRIFIC COSTUME JEWELRY, 861 Broadway. Ch.: **17**.
THE INDIVIDUAL MAN, 85 5th Av. at 16th St. Ch.: **6**.
UTRECHT ART SUPPLIES, 111 4th Av. Ch.: **28**.
UNITED PHOTOCOPY, 915 Broadway. Ch.: **21**.

B-F-LL to 14th St. & 6th Av.
ABE BLOOM & SONS, 6 W. 19. Ch.: **9**.
ACADEMY BOOK STORE, 10 W. 18. Ch.: **25**.
ARTHUR RICHARDS, 91 5th Av. at 17th St. Ch.: **6**.
BARNES & NOBLE SALE ANNEX, 128 5th Av. at 18th St. Ch.: **24**.
BARNES & NOBLES CLASSICAL, 128 5th Av. at 18th St. Ch.: **25**.
BATHS INTERNATIONAL, 89 5th Av. Ch.: **15**.
BOMZE-JAYBEE, 7 E. 19. Ch.: **4**.
CAROL-ANN SHOPPES, 142 W. 14. Ch.: **7**.
CAROL-ANN SHOPPES, 30 W. 14. Ch.: **7**.
CATANIA CLOTHING, 85 5th Av. at 16th St. Ch.: **6**.
CROSSROADS WINES, 55 W. 14. Ch.: **19**.
DEE & DEE STORES, 22 W. 14. Ch.'s.: **6, 7**.
DEMS BARGAIN STORES, 146 W. 14. Ch.'s.: **6, 8**.
DESIGN COLLECTIVE, 13 W. 18. Ch.: **12**.
DORSON CLOTHES, 87 5th Av. Ch.: **6**.
ED-EL ELECTRONICS, 62 W. 14. Ch.: **1**.
F&A TRDG., 14 W. 14. Ch.: **8**.
FABULOUS FIND, 25 E. 17. Ch.: **6**.
FOURTEENTH ST. AUDIO, 40 W. 14. Ch.: **1**.
HAMPSHIRE CLOTHES, 85 5th Av. at 16th. Ch.: **6**.
HAN'S ORIENTAL, 100 W. 14 at 6th Av. Ch.'s.: **5, 22**.
H.M. DISCOUNT, 112 W. 14. Ch.: **8**.
JACK'S BARGAIN STORES, 2 W. 14 at 5th Av. Ch.'s.: **3, 5, 7, 12**.
JAY'S BARGAIN STORE, 40 W. 14. Ch.: **5**.
KRIS WATCHES, 34 W. 14. Ch.: **17**.
LESH CLOTHING, 100 5th Av. at 15th St. Ch.: **6**.
L&N ELECTROLINE, 42 W. 14. Ch.: **14**.
LYNN'S, 103 W. 14. Ch.: **7**.
MR. TONY, 134 5th Av. Ch.'s.: **6, 7**.
NEW YORK WATCHES, 18 W. 14. Ch.: **6**.
OLAF DAUGHTERS OUTLET, 34 W. 17. Ch.: **7**.
ROBBINS MEN'S WEAR, 48 W. 14. Ch.'s.: **6, 13, 27**.
ROTHMAN, 111 5th Av. at 17th St. Ch.: **6**.
S&A FUTURE, 108 W. 14. Ch.'s.: **6, 8**.
SANG'S BARGAIN, 148 W. 14. Ch.: **22**.
SIMON KLINGER, 144 5th Av. Ch.'s.: **6, 7**.
SOFSAN, 2 W. 14. Ch.'s.: **8, 18**.
STANLEY GONCHER, 12 W. 19. Ch.: **6**.
SUNSHINE, 110 5th Av. Ch.: **7**.
THE INDIVIDUAL MAN, 85 5th Av. at 16th St. Ch.: **6**.
THE YARDSTICK FABRICS, 54 W. 14. Ch.: **9**.

47: GEOGRAPHICAL DIRECTORY

1-2-3 to 14

ADAMICI OUTLET, 88 7th Av. Ch.: **6**.
BUEN DIA, 201 W. 11 at 7th Av. Ch.'s: **7, 17, 22**.
CAPITOL FISHING TACKLE, 218 W. 23. Ch.: **27**.
CAROL-ANN SHOPPES, 142 W. 14. Ch.: **7**.
COLONY, 56 7th Av. Ch.'s: **6, 7**.
DECOR ARTS, 25 W. 14. Ch.'s: **12, 17**.
DEMS BARGAIN STORES, 146 W. 14. Ch.'s: **6, 8**.
FRANK J. HORAN LIQUORS, 33 7th Av. Ch.: **19**.
JBJ CARPET REMNANTS, 233 W. 14. Ch.: **12**.
JOHN'S SHOE OUTLET, 204 W. 14. Ch.: **6**.
SANG'S BARGAIN, 148 W. 14. Ch.: **22**.
SASSON, 154 W. 14. Ch.'s: **8, 27**.
THE COW'S OUTSIDE, 33 Greenwich Av. Ch.: **22**.
TOWNIE MERCHANDISE, 212 W. 14. Ch.'s: **1, 6, 7, 13**.

A-AA-CC-E-LL to 14 St. & 8 Av.

ADOLF KUSY MEATS, 861 Washington St. Ch.: **11**.
ARENSON WAREHOUSE, 447 W. 18. Ch.: **21**.
BASIOR-SCHWARTZ, 421 W. 14. Ch.: **11**.
CIRCLE AUTO LOCK, 457 W. 18. Ch.: **15**.
CUT-WELL BEEF, 426 W. 13. Ch.: **11**.
DECOR ARTS, 25 W. 14. Ch.'s: **12, 17**.
EIGHTH AV. RECORDS, 153 8th Av. Ch.: **25**.
INTEGRAL YOGA FOODS, 250 W. 14. Ch.: **11**.
JBJ CARPET REMNANTS, 233 W. 14. Ch.: **12**.
MEAT-N-FOODS WAREHOUSE, 403A W. 14. Ch.: **11**.
OLD BOHEMIAN MEAT, 425 W. 13. Ch.: **11**.
SERRANO BEER, 351 W. 14. Ch.: **19**.
STUYVESANT BICYCLE, 349 W. 14. Ch.: **3**.
TOWNIE MERCHANDISE, 212 W. 14. Ch.'s: **1, 6, 7, 13**.
UNIVERSAL FOODS, 408 W. 14. Ch.: **11**.

LL to 3rd Av.

A-ART LOCKSMITHS, 187 2nd Av. Ch.: **15**.
EAST VILLAGE CHEESE, 239 E. 9. Ch.: **11**.
FASHION DELIGHT, 131 3rd Av. Ch.: **7**.
GREENWICH ART SUPPLY, 32 3rd Av. Ch.: **28**.
HOLE-IN-THE-WALL, 229 E. 14. Ch.: **17**.
IPSWICH CLOCKS, 175 2nd Av. Ch.: **17**.
NEW YORK CENTRAL ART SUPPLY, 63 3rd Av. Ch.: **28**.
ROBBINS MEN'S WEAR, 146 E. 14. Ch.'s: **6, 13, 27**.
STUYVESANT SQ. LIQUORS, 333 2nd Av. Ch.: **19**.

LL to 1st Av.

AMERICAN CAT & DOG FOOD, 147 A. A. Ch.: **23**.
AMERICAN CONSERVATORY PIANOS, 188 1st Av. Ch.: **20**.
BIKES BY GEORGE, 351 E. 12. Ch.: **3**.
BLACK FOREST BAKERY, 177 1st Av. at 11th St. Ch.: **11**.
BOHRER'S CHILDREN'S WEAR, 139 1st Av. Ch.: **5**.
CHEAP JACK'S CLEARANCE STORE, 151 1st Av. Ch.'s: **6, 7**.
DIAMOND DISCOUNT FABRIC, 165 1st Av. Ch.: **9**.
EAST VILLAGE VARIETY, 186 1st Av. Ch.'s: **6, 22**.
GABAY'S OUTLET, 225 1st Av. Ch.'s: **6, 7**.
JOE'S BARGAIN CENTER, 123 1st Av. Ch.'s: **6, 22**.
MARY BAKERY, 224 Av. B. Ch.: **11**.
PRANA FOODS, 145A 1st Av. at 9th St. Ch.: **11**.
RICHIE'S SHOES, 183 Av. A. Ch.: **5**.
THE TOBACCO CENTER, 130 St. Marks Place. Ch.: **26**.

1 to 18

STAR ENVELOPE, 151 W. 19. Ch.: **28**.
VIAVENTI, 171 7th Av. at 20th St. Ch.: **12**.

A-AA-CC-E to 23

ABBIE'S GENERAL STORE, 306 8th Av. Ch.'s: **22, 25, 30**.
D&M FILM & PAPER, 508 W. 26. Ch.: **4**.
SAVANNAH WAREHOUSE, 229 10th Av. Ch.: **7**.
VALUE HOSIERY, 255 W. 23. Ch.: **7**.

1 to 23

AAAA METROPOLITAN SHELVING, 165 W. 23. Ch.: **21**.
AALLEE, 134 W. 23. Ch.: **21**.
ALLEN OFFICE FURNITURE, 165 W. 23. Ch.: **21**.
DISCOUNT HEAD SHOP, 183 7th Av. Ch.: **26**.
LEWIS & CLARK, 228 7th Av. Ch.: **6**.
WORLD OF BARGAINS, 195 7th Av. Ch.: **17**.

B-F to 23

5TH AV. & 22ND ST. TOBACCO, 172 5th Av. Ch.: **26**.
AALLEE, 134 W. 23. Ch.: **21**.
BLACK & DECKER SERVICE, 50 W. 23. Ch.: **15**.
BONSAI PLANTS, 777 6th Av. Ch.: **10**.
BREITMAN'S, 671 6th Av. Ch.: **9**.
CHATEAU CREATIONS, 114 W. 26. Ch.: **7**.
CONVERTIBLE CONNECTION, 666 6th Av. Ch.: **12**.
DAVE'S ARMY/NAVY, 779 6th Av. Ch.: **6**.
DAVID JACKENDOFF, 763 6th Av. Ch.: **6**.
EMBASSY ENVELOPES, 655 6th Av. at 20th St. Ch.: **28**.
GLOBAL MKTG., 49 W. 23. Ch.'s: **1, 17**.
HOPKINS PHOTO, 56 W. 22. Ch.: **4**.
INTERNATIONAL SOLGO, 77 W. 23. Ch.: **1**.
MAINLINE OFFSET, 32 W. 22. Ch.: **28**.
MANDARIN PRODUCTS, 35 W. 23. Ch.'s: **17, 21**.
MCB TRDG., 25 W. 23. Ch.'s: **1, 4**.
M&G PACKAGING, 661 6th Av. Ch.: **16**.
RELIABLE OFFICE FURNITURE, 118 W. 23. Ch.: **21**.
SHELGO FACTORY OUTLET, 641 6th Av. Ch.: **7**.
SIXTH AV. WHOLESALE GREENERY, 771 6th Av. Ch.: **10**.
TWENTY-THIRD ST. TOY DISTR., 23 W. 23. Ch.: **29**.
TYPEX INC., 119 W. 23. Ch.: **21**.
VENDOME TRDG., 69 W. 23. Ch.: **1**.

N-RR to 23rd St.

ABE BLOOM & SONS, 6 W. 19. Ch.: **9**.
ACADEMY BOOK STORE, 10 W. 18. Ch.: **25**.
A-ONE FURNITURE, 45 E. 20. Ch.: **12**.
AZRIEL ALTMAN, 204 5th Av. Ch.: **7**.
BAG IT, 160 5th Av. Ch.: **22**.
BARNES & NOBLE SALE ANNEX, 128 5th Av. at 18th St. Ch.: **24**.
BARNES & NOBLES CLASSICAL, 128 5th Av. at 18th St. Ch.: **25**.
BFO PLUS, 149 5th Av. at 21st St. Ch.: **6**.
BFO SUITS, 149 5th Av. at 21st St. Ch.: **6**.
BOMZE-JAYBEE, 7 E. 19. Ch.: **4**.
CAROL-ANN SHOPPES, 44 E. 23. Ch.: **7**.
CONSUMERS FURNITURE, 45 E. 20. Ch.: **12**.
DAVID SU'S 7-ART JEWELRY, 872 Broadway. Ch.: **17**.
DESIGN COLLECTIVE, 13 W. 18. Ch.: **12**.
DESIGN WORLD, 55 W. 21. Ch.: **12**.
DIXIE FOAM, 20 E. 20. Ch.: **12**.
D-M SALES, 911 Broadway. Ch.: **17**.
FIRE EXTINGUISHER SALES, 29 W. 19. Ch.: **15**.
GEM ENVELOPES, 10 W. 19. Ch.: **28**.
GIFT WAREHOUSE, 28 W. 25. Ch.: **17**.
GINO NAPOLI, 141 5th Av. at 21st St. Ch.: **6**.
GLOBAL IMPORTS, 160 5th Av. at 21st St. Ch.'s: **16, 25, 26, 29**.
GLOBAL MKTG., 49 W. 23. Ch.'s: **1, 17**.
HOPKINS PHOTO, 56 W. 22. Ch.: **4**.
JDS FURNITURE, 45 E. 20. Ch.: **12**.
J.J.G. WAREHOUSE, 36 W. 25. Ch.'s: **8, 17**.
KINGDOM OF GIFTS, 184 5th Av. Ch.: **22**.
MAINLINE OFFSET, 32 W. 22. Ch.: **28**.
MANDARIN PRODUCTS, 35 W. 23. Ch.'s: **17, 21**.
MANSFIELD CLOTHES, 141 5th Av. at 21st St. Ch.: **6**.
MCB TRDG., 25 W. 23. Ch.'s: **1, 4**.
METROPOLITAN BOOKS, 38 E. 23. Ch.: **24**.
MILLS SALES, 889 Broadway at 19th St. Ch.'s: **1, 8, 15, 17, 22, 28, 29**.
MOE GINSBURG, 162 5th Av. at 21st St. Ch.: **6**.
MR. TONY, 134 5th Av. Ch.'s: **6, 7**.
PARAMOUNT PROCESS PRTG., 20 W. 22. Ch.: **28**.
PARK KENNY CLOTHES, 141 5th Av. at 21st St. Ch.'s: **6, 7**.
PILLOW FURNITURE, 144 5th Av. Ch.: **21**.
PRECISION PHOTOCOPY, 150 5th Av. at 20th. Ch.: **21**.
REM SECURITY, 27 E. 20. Ch.: **15**.
REFERENCE BOOK CENTER, 175 5th Av. Ch.: **24**.
ROYAL FASHION, 915 Broadway. Ch.: **6**.
RUBINSTEIN'S PARTY FAVORS, 876 Broadway. Ch.: **16**.
SAMUEL ZIMBLER, 176 5th Av. Ch.: **6**.
SCOTT'S DRESS, 30 E. 23. Ch.'s: **7, 30**.
SHERRILL CLOSEOUTS WAREHOUSE, 12 E. 22. Ch.'s: **12, 17**.
SIMON KLINGER, 144 5th Av. Ch.'s: **6, 7**.
STANLEY GONCHER, 12 W. 19. Ch.: **6**.
TERRIFIC COSTUME JEWELRY, 861 Broadway. Ch.: **17**.
TWENTY-THIRD ST. TOY DISTR., 23 W. 23. Ch.: **29**.

6 to 23

ARISTA SURGICAL, 67 Lexington Av. Ch.: **13**.
CAROL-ANN SHOPPES, 44 E. 23. Ch.: **7**.
DUANE READE DRUGS, 300 Park Av. S. at 22nd St. Ch.: **13**.
FIRST AV. WINES, 383 1st Av. Ch.: **19**.
FRSG QUALITY KNITWEAR, 333 Park Av. S. Ch.: **7**.
HARRON DISTRIBUTORS, 352 3rd Av. Ch.: **1**.
KAZOOTIE, 303 Park Av. S. at 23rd Ch.: **7**.

47: GEOGRAPHICAL DIRECTORY

METRO SHOE MART, 339 Park Av. S. Ch.: **7**.
METROPOLITAN BOOKS, 38 E. 23. Ch.: **24**.
M&M FURNITURE DISCOUNT, 303 Park Av. S. at 23rd St. Ch.: **12**.
NAM NAM BOUTIQUE, 303 Park Av. S. Ch.: **7**.
PAPERBACK EXCHANGES, 270 3rd Av. Ch.: **24**.
PARK AV. JOB LOT, 270 Park Av. S. Ch.'s.: **7, 13, 17, 30**.
PHANTOM, 323 Park Av. S. Ch.: **6**.
SCOTT'S DRESS, 30 E. 23. Ch.'s.: **7, 30**.
SECOND TIME AROUND, 220 E. 23. Ch.'s.: **6, 7**.
SHERRILL CLOSEOUTS WAREHOUSE, 12 E. 22. Ch.s.: **12, 17**.
SUNY OPTOMETRIC CENTER, 100 E. 24. Ch.: **13**.
VERCESI HARDWARE, 152 E. 23. Ch.s.: **1, 15**.

▬▬▬▬ N-RR to 28th St.

AHDOUT ORIENTAL RUGS, 220 5th Av. at 26th St. Ch.: **12**.
ATLAS PHOTO, 45 W. 27. Ch.: **4**.
BAGS BY ZENO, 1211 Broadway. Ch.: **22**.
BELCREST LINENS, 304 5th Av. Ch.: **18**.
BELLA ORIENTAL RUGS & ANTIQUES, 281 5th Av. on E. 30th St. Ch.: **12**.
BI-RITE PHOTO & ELECTRONICS, 15 E. 30. Ch.: **4**.
BONSAI PLANTS, 777 6th Av. Ch.: **10**.
CLASSIQUE PERFUMES, 220 5th Av. at 26th St. Ch.: **13**.
COMPUTER CENTER, 31 E. 31. Ch.: **21**.
CRESCENT CARPET, 29 W. 26. Ch.: **12**.
DAVE'S ARMY/NAVY, 779 6th Av. Ch.: **9**.
DAVID JACKENDOFF, 763 6th Av. Ch.: **9**.
DRAGON GATE IMPORT, 784 6th Av. Ch.: **12**.
DYNAMITE, 1165 Broadway at 27th St. Ch.'s.: **1, 25**.
FARSH INTERNATIONAL, 245 5th Av. Ch.: **12**.
FASHION BY HELOU, 32 W. 28. Ch.: **22**.
FISHLER FLOORS, 34 E. 29. Ch.: **12**.
FLORENCIA COLLECTION, 267 5th Av. Ch.: **17**.
FOREMOST FURNITURE, 8 W. 30. Ch.: **12**.
GISELLE HANDBAG, 309 5th Av. Ch.: **22**.
GRAND STEREO, 1175 Broadway. Ch.: **1**.
GURIAN FABRICS, 6 W. 30. Ch.: **9**.
JAMES ROY FURNITURE, 15 E. 32. Ch.: **12**.
KINA COSTUME JEWELRY, 1165 Broadway. Ch.: **17**.
LANAS, 43 W. 30. Ch.: **17**.
LEBANON FASHIONS, 1179 Broadway. Ch.: **7**.
MECCA, 1167 Broadway. Ch.'s.: **1, 25**.
METRO LOCK, 4 W. 32. Ch.: **15**.
MICHELLE IMPORTS, 1187 Broadway. Ch.: **7**.
MIMEX SUNGLASSES, 33 W. 29. Ch.: **22**.
NEW YORK FURNITURE CTR., 41 E. 31. Ch.: **12**.
NEW YORK, NY, 1235 Broadway. Ch.: **22**.
NEWPORT OF JAPAN, 1201 Broadway. Ch.'s.: **1, 25**.
NORMAN'S HOUSE OF DEALS, 1164 Broadway. Ch.: .
PALISADES INTERNATIONAL, 245 5th Av. Ch.: **12**.
PARAMOUNT CALENDAR & SPECIALTY, 52 W. 29. Ch.'s.: **17, 29**.
PARKAY DESIGNS, 14 W. 29. Ch.: **7**.
PARVIZ SHENASSA, 220 5th Av. at 26. Ch.: **12**.
PLANT CONNECTION, 823 6th Av. Ch.: **10**.
PRIMA IMPEX, 1185 Broadway. Ch.: **7**.
PUBLIC FLOWER MKT., 796 6th Av. at 27th St. Ch.: **10**.
R&F ELECTRONICS, 36 W. 29. Ch.'s.: **1, 8, 15, 17**.
SAAB INTERNATIONAL, 34 W. 28. Ch.: **7**.
SAM HEDAYA, 296 5th Av. Ch.: **18**.
SASSON IMPORTS, 244 5th Av. Ch.: **12**.
SHARP PHOTO, 1225 Broadway. Ch.: **4**.
SIXTH AV. WHOLESALE GREENERY, 771 6th Av. Ch.: **10**.
STULBAUM'S FLORIST, 810 6th Av. Ch.: **10**.
SUNBRIGHT, 1153 Broadway. Ch.: **1**.
SUPERIOR FLORISTS, 828 6th Av. Ch.: **10**.
SUPERIOR RIBBON, 48 W. 27. Ch.: **9**.
TAJ INTERNATIONAL, 255 5th Av. Ch.: **12**.
TORANGE RUGS, 220 5th Av. at 26th St. Ch.: **12**.
T.H. COLOR, 5 W. 30. Ch.: **4**.
ULTRA SMART HOSIERY, 15 E. 30. Ch.: **7**.
URICO, 842 6th Av. Ch.: **22**.
WINGDALE HOSIERY, 34 W. 30. Ch.'s.: **6, 7**.
YORK FLORAL, 804 6th Av. Ch.: **10**.
YOUNG JIN TRDG., 47 W. 29. Ch.: **22**.

▬▬▬▬ 6 to 28

ANNAPURNA, 127 E. 28. Ch.: **11**.
DUANE READE DRUGS, 360 Park Av. S. at 26th St. Ch.: **13**.
EMPIRE, 469 2nd Av. Ch.: **7**.
FISHLER FLOORS, 34 E. 29. Ch.: **12**.
FUN CREATORS, 15 E. 30. Ch.: **29**.
GEREMIA CARPETING, 418 Park Av. S. Ch.: **12**.
GOODFRIEND'S, 381 Park Av. S. at 27th St. Ch.: **7**.
INDIA SPICE, 110 Lexington Av. Ch.: **11**.

INTERNATIONAL HOME, 440 Park Av. S. Ch.: **12**.
JENNIFER HOUSE CONVERTIBLES, 404 Park Av. S. at 28th St. Ch.: **12**.
K. KALUSTYAN, 123 Lexington Av. Ch.: **11**.
LITTLE INDIA, 128 E. 28. Ch.: **11**.
MCADAM LIQUORS, 398 3rd Av. Ch.: **19**.
M.S. DISTRIBUTION, 76 Madison Av. at 28th. Ch.: **1**.
NOURY & SONS, 440 Park Av. S. at 30th St. Ch.: **12**.
PARK AV. AUDIO, 425 Park Av. S. at 29th St. Ch.: **14**.
RUNWAY FASHIONS, 418 Park Av. at 29th St. Ch.: **7**.
SINHA TRDG., 120 Lexington Av. at 28th St. Ch.: **11**.
TAPE CITY, 404 Park Av. S. Ch.: **25**.
ULTRA SMART HOSIERY, 15 E. 30. Ch.: **7**.
YASSIN INTERNATIONAL, 132 E. 26. Ch.: **11**.

▬▬▬▬ 6 to 33

CENTRAL TYPEWRITER, 40 E. 33. Ch.: **21**.
CHARLES REE, 397 5th Av. Ch.: **17**.
COMPUTER CENTER, 31 E. 31. Ch.: **21**.
D. SOKOLIN WINES, 178 Madison Av. Ch.: **19**.
DOOR STORE CLEARANCE, 191 Lexington Av. at 32nd St. Ch.: **12**.
EAST ART CENTER, 455 3rd Av. Ch.'s.: **12, 17**.
FURNITURE TREE, 192 Lexington Av. at 32nd St. Ch.: **12**.
GISELLE HANDBAG, 309 5th Av. Ch.: **22**.
GUTIERREZ TRDG., 149 Madison Av. at 32. Ch.: **1**.
JAMES ROY FURNITURE, 15 E. 32. Ch.: **12**.
MITU ENTERPRISES, 128 Madison Av. Ch.: **22**.
NEW YORK FURNITURE CTR., 41 E. 31. Ch.: **12**.
PALAZZETTI, 461 Park Av. S. Ch.: **12**.
PAPERBACK EXCHANGES, 489 3rd Av. Ch.: **24**.
QUALITY HOUSE WINES, 2 Park Av. Ch.: **19**.
THIRD AV. GREENERY, 557 3rd Av. at 37th. Ch.: **10**.
WALLPAPER MART, 187 Lexington Av. Ch.: **15**.
WHAT'S NEW DISCOUNT, 166 Madison Av. Ch.: **7**.

▬▬▬▬ B-D-F-N-QB-RR to 34

ADDING MACHINE SERVICE, 59 W. 30. Ch.: **7**.
ADORAMA CAMERA, 138 W. 34. Ch.: **4**.
ALBERT FURNITURE, 22 W. 34. Ch.: **12**.
ARDEN, 1014 6th Av. Ch.: **7**.
ARIEL FASHIONS, 30 W. 32. Ch.: **7**.
AUDIOMATIC ELECTRONICS, 1263 Broadway. Ch.'s.: **14, 25**.
BAG CITY, 63 W. 37. Ch.: **22**.
BAYARD INTERNATIONAL, 35 W. 32. Ch.'s.: **6, 7**.
BERNIE'S DISCOUNT, 821 6th Av. Ch.: **1**.
BLOOMING, 23 W. 34. Ch.: **7**.
BRASS BED FACTORY, 15 W. 36. Ch.: **12**.
CAMERA WORLD CLEARANCE, 100 W. 32. Ch.: **1**.
CARPET DISPLAY, 129 W. 35. Ch.: **12**.
CAYNE'S 1, 1345 Broadway. Ch.'s.: **6, 7, 18, 27**.
CAYNE'S 3, 1333 Broadway. Ch.s.: **18, 22**.
CHARLES REE, 397 5th Av. Ch.: **17**.
ELEVEN WEST, 11 W. 34. Ch.'s.: **5, 6, 7**.
EXPECTATIONS, 1027 6th Av. Ch.: **7**.
GAMPEL SUPPLY, 39 W. 37. Ch.: **17**.
GOLF TRADING, 21 W. 35. Ch.: **26**.
GURIAN FABRICS, 6 W. 30. Ch.: **9**.
HAPPY BUYING CENTER, 22 W. 32. Ch.'s.: **1, 12**.
HERMAN'S, 39 W. 34. Ch.: **27**.
HOLIDAY BRIDAL, 120 W. 37. Ch.: **7**.
JACK'S BARGAIN STORES, 142 W. 34. Ch.'s.: **3, 5, 7, 12**.
JOHN HARLEY, 54 W. 33. Ch.: **12**.
JOHNSON COPY, 100 W.-31 at 6th Av. Ch.: **28**.
LANAS, 43 W. 30. Ch.: **17**.
LITERARY MART, 1261 Broadway. Ch.: **24**.
LORD'S EX-IMP., 73 W. 38. Ch.: **7**.
LUSO SALES, 63 W. 36. Ch.: **6**.
M. STEUER HOSIERY, 31 W. 32. Ch.: **7**.
MAN-DEE BAG, 39 W. 37. Ch.: **22**.
MANOS DEL URUGUAY, 35 W. 36. Ch.'s.: **7, 17, 22**.
METRO LOCK, 4 W. 32. Ch.: **15**.
MITSU, 35 W. 35. Ch.'s.: **6, 15, 17**.
MR. TONY, 120 W. 37. Ch.: **6, 7**.
ODD LOT TRDG., 33 W. 34. Ch.'s.: **8, 13, 28, 30**.
OLDEN CAMERA, 1265 Broadway. Ch.: **4**.
OLYMPIC ELECTRONICS, 123 W. 30. Ch.: **1**.
ONE BLOCK OVER, 131 W. 35. Ch.: **7**.
PRESTIGE PHOTO, 373 5th Av. at 35th. Ch.: **4**.
RANNA HANDBAGE, 10 W. 32. Ch.: **22**.
RELIABLE BUTTON WORKS, 65 W. 37 at 6th Av. Ch.: **9**.
ROBBINS MEN'S WEAR, 1265 Broadway. Ch.'s.: **6, 13, 27**.
SEAMAR, 25 W. 32. Ch.: **7**.
SPIRATONE LENSES/ACCESSORIES, 130 W. 31. Ch.: **4**.
STRAWBERRY, 14 W. 34. Ch.'s.: **7, 22**.
TINSEL TRDG., 47 W. 38. Ch.: **9**.
T.R. COLOR, 5 W. 30. Ch.: **4**.
UNIQUE EYEWEAR, 19 W. 34. Ch.: **13**.

47: GEOGRAPHICAL DIRECTORY

URICO. 842 6th Av. Ch.: **22.**
WAI LEE. 1026 6th Av. Ch.: **7.**
WINGDALE HOSIERY. 34 W. 30. Ch.'s: **6, 7.**

1-2-3 to 34

ADORAMA CAMERA. 138 W. 34. Ch.: **4.**
ALEX LEATHER CITY. 526 7th Av. Ch.: **6.**
BARNES & NOBLE. 33rd St. at 5th Av. Ch.: **24.**
CARPET DISPLAY. 129 W. 35. Ch.: **12.**
CAYNE'S 2. 225 W. 34. Ch.'s: **5, 13, 18.**
CAYNE'S 4. 247 W. 34. Ch.'s: **5, 6, 27.**
CAYNE'S DAC JEWELRY. 205 W. 34. Ch.: **22.**
COMMUTER'S LIQUORS. 211 W. 34. Ch.: **19.**
FUN FOX LTD. 512 7th Av. Ch.: **7.**
HOLIDAY BRIDAL. 120 W. 37. Ch.: **7.**
JACK'S BARGAIN STORES. 142 W. 34. Ch.'s: **3, 5, 7, 12.**
ONE BLOCK OVER. 131 W. 35. Ch.: **7.**
PENNSYLVANIA LUGGAGE. 7th Av. & 33rd St., Ch.: **22.**
TOKAR IMPORT JEWELRY. 240 W. 37. Ch.: **17.**

1 to 28

BERKSHIRE HOUSE CONVERTIBLES. 242 W. 27. Ch.: **12.**
CHATEAU CREATIONS. 114 W. 26. Ch.: **7.**
GATRIMONE SHOES. 371 7th Av. Ch.: **6.**
HARRIS'S WOMEN'S APPAREL. 275 7th Av. Ch.: **7.**
HAZY ELECTRONICS. 358 7th Av. Ch.: **1.**
JOMPOLE. 330 7th Av. at 29th St. Ch.'s: **8, 17.**
KALGA LEATHER SPORTSWEAR. 245 W. 29. Ch.: **6.**
NEW STORE. 289 7th Av. Ch.: **7.**
OLYMPIC ELECTRONICS. 123 W. 30. Ch.: **1.**
PHANTOM. 315 7th Av. Ch.: **6.**
QUICK QUALITY COPIES. 370 7th Av. Ch.: **28.**
REVERE SUPPLY. 607 W. 29. Ch.: **27.**
SHEEPSKIN MARKET. 218 W. 29. Ch.: **6.**
S&W FASHIONS. 283. Ch.: **7.**
THE BARGAIN LOT. 333 7th Av. Ch.'s: **13, 30.**
THE SHOE RACK. 150 W. 28. Ch.: **7.**

A-AA-CC-E to 34

ABE J. GELLER. 491 7th Av. Ch.: **7.**
AMERICAN BOUTIQUE. 470 7th Av. Ch.: **7.**
AMERICAN VISION CENTERS. Penn Sta. Ch.: **13.**
ARZEE FABRICS. 270 W. 38. Ch.: **9.**
BABY SITE ELECTRONICS. 269 W. 34. Ch.: **1.**
BAG MAN. 261 W. 34. Ch.'s: **7, 15, 17, 22.**
BASKIN FLOORS. 320 W. 37. Ch.: **12.**
CAYNE'S 2. 225 W. 34. Ch.'s: **5, 13, 18.**
CAYNE'S 4. 247 W. 34. Ch.'s: **5, 6, 27.**
CHARMING BRIDAL. 254 W. 35. Ch.: **7.**
COMMUTER'S LIQUORS. 211 W. 34. Ch.: **19.**
DISC-O-MAT. 474 7th Av. Ch.: **25.**
EIGHTH AV. BARGAIN KING. 306 W. 36 at 8th Av. Ch.'s: **6, 7.**
EIGHTH AV. ELECTRONICS. 520 8th Av. Ch.: **1.**
FARMER GREY'S. 327 10th Av. at 29th St. Ch.: **10.**
FELIPITO'S PLACE. 314 W. 36. Ch.'s: **6, 7.**
FRAN'S FABRICS BARGAINS. 369 W. 34. Ch.: **9.**
H.E.R. MATERNITY. 319 W. 35. Ch.: **7.**
INTERNATIONAL RECORD & TAPE. 315 W. 36. Ch.: **25.**
JAY'S ADVANCE. 491 7th Av. at 37th St. Ch.: **7.**
MS. MISS or MRS.. 462 7th Av. Ch.: **7.**
PHANTOM. 207 W.38. Ch.: **6.**
REVERE SUPPLY. 607 W. 29. Ch.: **27.**
ROBBINS MEN'S WEAR. 519 8th Av. Ch.'s: **6, 13, 27.**
STELLO'S PIANOS. 400 W. 34 at 9th Av. Ch.: **20.**
STEREO KING. 550 8th Av. Ch.: **1.**
THE LOFT. 491 7th Av. Ch.: **7.**
TOKAR IMPORT JEWELRY. 240 W. 37. Ch.: **17.**
WEBER'S JOB LOT. 505 8th Av. at 35th. Ch.'s: **8, 13, 15, 17, 18, 22, 28, 30.**
WORTHMORE. 245 W. 34. Ch.: **7.**

A-AA-CC-E to 42

ABERDEEN FABRICS. 250 W. 39. Ch.: **9.**
ARZEE FABRICS. 270 W. 38. Ch.: **9.**
BACK-DATE MAGAZINES. 274 W. 43. Ch.: **24.**
BARETTA FASHIONS 2. 642 8th Av. Ch.: **6.**
BASKIN FLOORS. 320 W. 37. Ch.: **12.**
CENTRAL FISH. 527 9th Av. Ch.: **11.**
CHURCHILL INT'L GROCERY. 519 9th Av. Ch.: **11.**
CUZINS MEAT. 515 9th Av. Ch.: **11.**
FLO-ANN TEXTILES. 300 W. 39. Ch.: **9.**
HANG UPS WICKER. 39th St. at 8th Av. Ch.'s: **12, 17.**
HARRY KANTROWITZ. 555 8th Av. Ch.: **9.**
INTERNATIONAL GROCERY. 529 9th Av. Ch.: **11.**
J.&A. STELZER FABRICS. 239 W. 39. Ch.: **9.**
MODLIN FABRICS. 240 W. 40. Ch.: **9.**
PHANTOM. 207 W.38. Ch.: **6.**
RAY VARIETY. 539 9th Av. at 40th. Ch.'s: **6, 13, 18.**
REDI-CUT CARPETS. 471 W. 42. Ch.: **12.**
ROBBINS MEN'S WEAR. 609 8th Av. Ch.'s: **6, 13, 27.**
ROMANO TRDG.. 628 W. 45th St. on 12th Av. Ch.'s: **1, 6, 17, 21, 22, 28, 29.**
SEA BREEZE FISH. 541 9th Av. at 40th Ch.: **11.**
STEREO KING. 550 8th Av. Ch.: **1.**
SUTTER TEXTILE. 257 W. 39. Ch.: **9.**
TRIEST EXPORT. 560 12th Av. Ch.'s: **1, 4, 6, 22, 29.**
WASHINGTON BEEF. 575 9th Av. Ch.: **11.**
WESER PIANO. 524 W. 43. Ch.: **20.**
YOAV SHOES. 252 W. 40. Ch.: **7.**

N-QB-RR-1-2-3-7 to 42 & Times Square

ABERDEEN FABRICS. 250 W. 39. Ch.: **9.**
ACE TYPEWRITER. 131 W. 45. Ch.: **21.**
ALEX LEATHER CITY. 526 7th Av. Ch.: **6.**
BARNES & NOBLE. 1521 Broadway. Ch.: **24.**
DISC-O-MAT. 1518 Broadway. Ch.: **25.**
DUANE READE DRUGS. 1412 Broadway. Ch.: **13.**
EIGHTY-EIGHT CENT SHOPS. 1457 Broadway. Ch.'s: **8, 11, 13, 15, 16, 28, 29.**
FAMOUS SMOKE SHOP. 1450 Broadway. Ch.: **26.**
GORDON BUTTON. 142 W. 38. Ch.: **9.**
HERMAN'S. 135 W. 42. Ch.: **27.**
J.&A. STELZER FABRICS. 239 W. 39. Ch.: **9.**
MODLIN FABRICS. 240 W. 40. Ch.: **9.**
SAM SHARROW GOLF. 147 W. 42 at B'wy. Ch.: **27.**
SUTTER TEXTILE. 257 W. 39. Ch.: **9.**

B-D-F to 42

ARDEN. 1014 6th Av. Ch.: **7.**
BARNEY'S CUT-RATE PHARMACY. 25 W. 42. Ch.'s: **13, 26.**
BARNEY'S CUT-RATE TOBACCOS. 25 W. 42. Ch.: **26.**
BEE HIVE. 55 W. 42. Ch.: **7.**
BRYCE. 115 W. 40. Ch.'s: **1, 14, 21.**
BUDGET BOUTIQUE. 1 W. 42. Ch.: **7.**
CAROL-ANN SHOPPES. 55 W. 42. Ch.: **7.**
ETI-QUETTE. 20 W. 38. Ch.: **7.**
EXPECTATIONS. 1027 6th Av. Ch.: **7.**
GAMPEL SUPPLY. 39 W. 37. Ch.: **17.**
GARMENT HI-FI. 55 W. 39. Ch.'s: **1, 14.**
GORDON BUTTON. 142 W. 38. Ch.: **9.**
GREAT NORTH WOODS. 425 5th Av. Ch.: **12.**
HERMAN'S. 135 W. 42. Ch.: **27.**
HUNTER AUDIO. 507 5th Av. Ch.: **1.**
JOB LOT TRDG.. 412 5th Av. Ch.'s: **6, 8, 11, 15, 16, 17, 18, 22, 27, 28, 29, 30.**
JUDY BETTER DRESSES. 20 W. 43. Ch.: **7.**
LAWRENCE FASHIONS. 1000 6th Av. Ch.: **13.**
LONGACRE COPY. 32 W. 40. Ch.: **28.**
LORD'S EX-IMP.. 73 W. 38. Ch.: **7.**
ODD JOB TRDG.. 7 E. 40. Ch.'s: **6, 8, 11, 13, 15, 16, 18, 22, 28, 29, 30.**
PUSHCART. 412 5th Av. Ch.'s: **4, 13, 15.**
RECORD EXPLOSION. 400 5th Av. Ch.: **25.**
TINSEL TRDG.. 47 W. 38. Ch.: **9.**
WAI LEE. 1026 6th Av. Ch.: **7.**
WILLIAM TANNENBAUM. 39 W. 38. Ch.: **7.**

7 to 5th Av.

BARETTA FASHIONS MIDTOWN. 22 E. 43. Ch.: **6.**
BARNEY'S CUT-RATE PHARMACY. 25 W. 42. Ch.'s: **13, 26.**
BARNEY'S CUT-RATE TOBACCOS. 25 W. 42. Ch.: **26.**
BEE HIVE. 55 W. 42. Ch.: **7.**
BUDGET BOUTIQUE. 1 W. 42. Ch.: **7.**
CAROL-ANN SHOPPES. 55 W. 42. Ch.: **7.**
GREAT NORTH WOODS. 425 5th Av. Ch.: **12.**
HUNTER AUDIO. 507 5th Av. Ch.: **1.**
JUDY BETTER DRESSES. 20 W. 43. Ch.: **7.**
ODD JOB TRDG.. 7 E. 40. Ch.'s: **6, 8, 11, 13, 15, 16, 18, 22, 28, 29, 30.**
RECORD EXPLOSION. 400 5th Av. Ch.: **25.**
TREND QUALITY JOB LOT. 408 E. 41. Ch.: **6.**
YAIR IMPORT. 17 E. 45. Ch.: **1.**

4-5-6-7 to Grand Central

ADIRONDACK DIRECT. 219 E. 42. Ch.: **21.**
AURORA DESIGN TAILOR. 104 E. 40. Ch.'s: **6, 7.**
BARETTA FASHIONS MIDTOWN. 22 E. 43. Ch.: **6.**
CAROL-ANN SHOPPES. 129 E. 45. Ch.: **7.**
CAROL-ANN SHOPPES. 429 Lexington Av. Ch.: **7.**
CAROL-ANN SHOPPES. 712 3rd Av. Ch.: **7.**
COMPUTER CENTER. 480 Lexington Av. Ch.: **21.**
COMPUTER FACTORY. 485 Lexington Av. at 46th St. Ch.: **21.**
DISC-O-MAT. 101 E. 42. Ch.: **25.**
DOLLAR BILLS. 99 E. 42. Ch.'s: **1, 6, 16, 26.**
DUANE READE DRUGS. 144 E. 44. Ch.: **13.**

47: GEOGRAPHICAL DIRECTORY

DUANE READE DRUGS, 20 E. 46. Ch.: **13.**
DUANE READE DRUGS, 304 Madison Av. Ch.: **13.**
DUANE READE DRUGS, 370 Lexington Av. Ch.: **13.**
FREDWIN, 130 E. 44. Ch.: **13.**
FREEDA VITAMINS, 36 E. 41. Ch.: **13.**
J. CHUCKLES, 321 Madison Av. at 42nd St. Ch.'s: **7, 22.**
J&R TOBACCO, 11 E. 45. Ch.: **26.**
LINEA GARBO, 109 E. 42. Ch.: **7.**
MIDTOWN EAST PHARMACY, 725 3rd Av. Ch.: **13.**
MOHAN'S CUSTOM TAILOR, 60 E. 42. Ch.: **6.**
PROFESSIONAL CONTACT LENS, 545 5th Av. Ch.: **13.**
STRAWBERRY, 129 E. 42 at Lex. Ch.'s.: **7, 22.**
SUNSHINE, 396 Madison Av. Ch.: **7.**
THIRD AV. GREENERY, 557 3rd Av. at 37th. Ch.: **10.**
TREND QUALITY JOB LOT, 40 E. 41. Ch.: **6.**
WHAT'S NEW DISCOUNT, 122 E. 42. Ch.: **7.**
WHAT'S NEW DISCOUNT, 405 Lexington Av. Ch.: **7.**
YAIR IMPORT, 17 E. 45. Ch.: **1.**

6 to 51
BARNES & NOBLE, 750 3rd Av. at 47th St. Ch.: **24.**
DISCOUNT BOOKSHOP, 897 1st Av. Ch.: **24.**
DUANE READE DRUGS, 485 Lexington Av. at 47th St. Ch.: **13.**
LE BAKLAVA, 325 E. 48. Ch.: **11.**
PIER 333, 511 Lexington Av. at 48th St. Ch.: **7.**
RUKICO TAILORS, 511 Lex. Av. at 48th St. Ch.'s.: **6, 7.**
STRAWBERRY, 501 Madison Av. Ch.'s.: **7, 22.**

B-D-F to 47
ACE TYPEWRITER, 131 W. 45. Ch.: **21.**
AMERICAN PEARL, 23 W. 47. Ch.: **17.**
ART BRITE WALLPAPER, 46 W. 46. Ch.: **15.**
AURICO GEMS., 565 5th Av. Ch.: **17.**
BARNES & NOBLE, 600 5th Av. Ch.: **24.**
BARNES & NOBLES CLASSICAL, 600 5th Av. at 48th St. Ch.: **25.**
DAVIS BEHAR, 578 5th Av. at 47th St. Ch.: **17.**
DE SILVA LTD., 32 W. 46. Ch.: **6.**
DUANE READE DRUGS, 1150 6th Av. Ch.: **13.**
DUANE READE DRUGS, 50 W. 51. Ch.: **13.**
ELECTRONIC ODD-LOTS, 60 W. 46. Ch.: **14.**
GARDINELLI BAND INSTRUMENTS, 151 W. 46. Ch.: **20.**
GOLDBERG'S MARINE EQT., 12 W. 46. Ch.: **27.**
INDIA MALAYSIA IMPORTS, 28 W. 46. Ch.: **7.**
J. CHUCKLES, 1290 6th Av. Ch.'s.: **7, 22.**
JERRY SAMUELS, 48 W. 47. Ch.: **8.**
J&R TOBACCO, 11 E. 45. Ch.: **26.**
LINEA GARBO, 620 5th Av. Ch.: **7.**
LISTEN RECORDS, 18 W. 45. Ch.: **25.**
L.S. MEN'S CLOTHING, 23 W. 45. Ch.: **6.**
MANNY'S, 156 W. 48. Ch.: **20.**
MASTER PHOTO, 165 W. 46. Ch.: **4.**
MICHAEL C. FINA, 580 5th Av. at 47th. Ch.'s.: **4, 8, 17, 22.**
MIDTOWN FOTO, 21 W. 47. Ch.: **4.**
ODD JOB TRDG., 66 W. 48. Ch.'s.: **6, 8, 11, 13, 15, 16, 18, 22, 28, 29, 30.**
ODD LOT SHOPS, 5 E. 46. Ch.: **6.**
PHIL PINIAZ, 129 W. 46. Ch.: **22.**
PHIL'S, 9 E. 47. Ch.: **13.**
PROFESSIONAL CONTACT LENS, 545 5th Av. Ch.: **13.**
RED CABOOSE, 16 W. 45. Ch.: **29.**
RENNIE ELLEN, 15 W. 47. Ch.: **17.**
ROUNDHOUSE, 14 W. 45. Ch.: **29.**
SAM ASH, 160 W. 48. Ch.: **20.**
STEP 'N STYLE SHOES, 30 Rockefeller Plaza. Ch.: **7.**
STRAWBERRY, 120 W. 49. Ch.'s.: **7, 22.**
TADY-K, 36 W. 47th St. Ch.: **17.**
TAFT ELECTRONICS, 68 W. 45. Ch.'s.: **14, 25.**
ULTRA COSMETICS, 135 W. 50. Ch.: **13.**
UNITED BEAUTY SUPPLY, 49 W. 46. Ch.: **13.**
U.S.A. ELECTRONICS, 125 W. 45. Ch.: **1.**
WE BUY GUITARS, 159 W. 48. Ch.: **20.**
WEINSTEIN & YAEGER, 23 W. 47. Ch.: **17.**
YAIR IMPORT, 17 E. 45. Ch.: **1.**

N-RR to 49th St.
ALEX MUSICAL INSTRUMENTS, 164 W. 48. Ch.: **20.**
GARDINELLI BAND INSTRUMENTS, 151 W. 46. Ch.: **20.**
MANNY'S, 156 W. 48. Ch.: **20.**
MASTER PHOTO, 165 W. 46. Ch.: **4.**
SAM ASH, 160 W. 48. Ch.: **20.**
SILVER & HORLAND, 170 W. 48. Ch.: **20.**
STRAWBERRY, 120 W. 49. Ch.'s.: **7, 22.**
ULTRA COSMETICS, 135 W. 50. Ch.: **13.**
WE BUY GUITARS, 159 W. 48. Ch.: **20.**

1 to 50
ROSE DISTRIBUTORS, 247 W. 46. Ch.: **1.**

A-AA-CC-E to 50
AA BEST USED OFFICE FURNITURE, 721 11th Av. at 51st St. Ch.: **21.**
DECORATORS' WAREHOUSE, 665 11th Av. Ch.: **12.**
FAIRSTRYK FILM & PAPER, 445 W. 50. Ch.: **4.**
FRANKLIN PHOTO, 353 W. 48. Ch.: **4.**
IRVING'S SHOES, 752 9th Av. Ch.: **6.**
OLDTOWN BEER, 738 10th Av. Ch.: **19.**
ROSE DISTRIBUTORS, 247 W. 46. Ch.: **1.**

B-D-E to 7th Av.
DUANE READE DRUGS, 224 W. 57 at Broadway. Ch.: **13.**

A-AA-B-CC-D-1 to 59
CAMROD CYCLE, 610 W. 57. Ch.: **3.**
COUNCIL THRIFT SHOP, 842 9th Av. at 55th St. Ch.'s.: **6, 7.**
DEL PINO SHOES, 1871 Broadway. Ch.: **6.**
DUANE READE DRUGS, 224 W. 57 at Broadway. Ch.: **13.**
EXCELSIOR LIQUORS, 332 W. 57. Ch.: **19.**
FEET, 1841 Broadway. Ch.: **7.**
JENNIFER HOUSE CONVERTIBLES, 1770 Broadway. Ch.: **12.**
M.C. CORNER, 240 Central Park South at Broadway on Columbus Circle. Ch.: **6.**
PHANTOM, 954 8th Av. Ch.: **6.**
QUICK QUALITY COPIES, 945 8th Av. Ch.: **28.**
ROBBINS MEN'S WEAR, 1717 Broadway. Ch.'s.: **6, 13, 27.**

N-OB-RR to 57th St.
BARNES & NOBLE, 175 W. 57 at 7th Av. Ch.: **24.**
FRED OLIVERO USED BOW INSTR., 200 W. 57 at 7th Av. Ch.: **20.**
PARON FABRICS, 140 W. 57. Ch.: **9.**
POLI FABRICS, 130 W. 57. Ch.: **9.**

B to 57
PARON FABRICS, 140 W. 57. Ch.: **9.**
POLI FABRICS, 130 W. 57. Ch.: **9.**

E-F to 5th Av.
GUCCI ON 7, 699 5th Av. Ch.'s.: **6, 7.**
MAX'S BETTER DRESS, 510 Madison Av. Ch.: **7.**
MERN'S, 525 Madison Av. Ch.'s.: **6, 7.**
ROBIN IMPORTS, 510 Madison Av. Ch.'s.: **8, 18.**
STRAWBERRY, 501 Madison Av. Ch.'s.: **7, 22.**

E-F to Lex. Av.
CITI COSMETICS, 643 Lexington Av. Ch.: **13.**
EIGHTY-EIGHT CENT SHOPS, 591 Lexington Av. Ch.'s.: **8, 11, 13, 15, 16, 28, 29.**
GREAT NORTH WOODS, 683 Lexington Av. Ch.: **12.**
HERMAN'S, 845 3rd Av. Ch.: **27.**
HONG KONG IMPORT, 252A E. 51. Ch.'s.: **6, 7.**
ITO LEATHER, 662 Lexington Av. Ch.: **22.**
JENNIFER HOUSE CONVERTIBLES, 1014 2nd Av. Ch.: **12.**
MORRELL & CO. WINES, 307 E. 53. Ch.: **19.**
PATHMARK PHARMACIES, 880 3rd Av. Ch.: **13.**
PERPLEXITY LUCITE, 237 E. 53. Ch.s.: **12, 17, 28.**
SCHUMER'S WINES, 59 E. 54. Ch.: **19.**
STRAWBERRY, 880 3rd Av. Ch.'s.: **7, 22.**
SUE'S DISCOUNT DRESS, 638 Lexington Av. Ch.: **7.**
THE TOWNSMAN, 666 Lexington Av. Ch.: **6.**

N-RR-4-5-6 to 59th & Lex.
BARNES & NOBLE, 999 3rd Av. Ch.: **24.**
CAVIARTERIA, 29 E. 60. Ch.: **11.**
CORK & BOTTLE, 1158 1st Av. Ch.: **19.**
DESIGNER LIQUIDATORS, 127 E. 57. Ch.: **7.**
DISC-O-MAT, 716 Lexington Av. Ch.: **25.**
EMPIRE, 1206 2nd Av. Ch.: **7.**
ETI-QUETTE, 860 Lexington Av. Ch.: **7.**
GALLERY DRUGS, 131 E. 60. Ch.: **13.**
GODDESSES OF THE EARTH, 234 E. 58. Ch.: **17.**
GREAT NORTH WOODS, 683 Lexington Av. Ch.: **12.**
HELEN PERL SHOES, 692 Lexington Av. Ch.: **6.**
ITO LEATHER, 662 Lexington Av. Ch.: **22.**
KAZOOTIE, 136 E. 57 at Lex. Ch.: **7.**
SILK SURPLUS SCALAMANDRE, 223 E. 58. Ch.: **9.**
SILK SURPLUS SCALAMANDRE, 843 Lexington Av. Ch.: **9.**
SUTTON WINES, 403 E. 57 at 1st Av. Ch.: **19.**
TOWER'S 57TH ST. WINES, 157 E. 57 at 3rd Av. Ch.: **19.**

6 to 68
ENCORE RESALE DRESS, 1132 Madison Av. Ch.: **7.**
ETI-QUETTE, 860 Lexington Av. Ch.: **7.**
EUROPEAN LIQUIDATORS, 1404 2nd Av. Ch.'s.: **6,**

47: GEOGRAPHICAL DIRECTORY

7.
PLANT SHED. 515 E. 72. Ch.: **10.**
RUTH BROOKS. 1138 3rd Av. Ch.: **7.**
SILK SURPLUS SCALAMANDRE. 843 Lexington Av. Ch.: **9.**

6 to 77
ARGUS APPLIANCES. 507 E. 80. Ch.: **1.**
DISCOUNT BOOKSHOP. 1448 1st Av. Ch.: **24.**
EUROPEAN LIQUIDATORS. 1404 2nd Av. Ch.'s.: **6, 7.**
FRENCH CONNECTION. 1091 Lexington Av. Ch.: **7.**
GIRLS CLUB THRIFT SHOP. 202 E. 77th at 3rd Av. Ch.'s.: **6, 7.**
IRVINGTON HOUSE THRIFT. 1534 2nd Av. at 80th. Ch.'s.: **6, 7.**
JENNIFER HOUSE CONVERTIBLES. 1530 2nd Av. Ch.: **12.**
MICHAEL'S RESALE DRESS. 1041 Madison Av. Ch.: **7.**
NORTHEAST FLOOR COVERINGS. 1492 1st Av. Ch.: **12.**
OK FURNITURE & CARPETING. 1504 1st Av. at 79th St. Ch.: **12.**
PAPERBACK EXCHANGES. 1437 1st Av. Ch.: **24.**
PLANT WORLD. 3rd Av. at 77th. Ch.: **10.**
SECOND AVE. 1046 Madison Av. Ch.: **5.**
S&T WOMEN'S SHOES. 1043 Lexington Av. Ch.: **7.**
S&T WOMEN'S SHOES. 1467 2nd Av. Ch.: **7.**
SUPER-THRIFT SHOP. 1437 2nd Av. Ch.'s.: **6, 7.**
WHAT'S NEW DISCOUNT. 1525 York Av. Ch.: **7.**
YORKVILLE LIQUORS. 1392 3rd Av. at 79th St. Ch.: **19.**

4-5-6 to 86
ALLIANCE ART GLASS. 169 E. 88. Ch.'s.: **15, 28.**
A-MARK COMMUNICATIONS. 218 E. 82. Ch.: **21.**
AMERICAN VISION CENTERS. 1276 Lexington Av. at 86th St. Ch.: **13.**
BARNES & NOBLE. 120 E. 86. Ch.: **24.**
CALL AGAIN THRIFT SHOP. 1735 2nd Av. Ch.'s.: **6, 7.**
CHRISTOS JEWELRY. 1260 Lexington Av. Ch.: **17.**
COZY BOUTIQUE. 200 E. 86. Ch.: **7.**
FRENCH CONNECTION. Madison at 87th. Ch.: **7.**
FRUGAL FROG. 1707 2nd Av. Ch.: **5.**
GOTHAM LIQUORS. 1543 3rd Av. Ch.: **19.**
GREAT NORTH WOODS. 160 E. 86. Ch.: **12.**
LEROY PHARMACY PRESCRIPTIONS. 1294 Lexington Av. Ch.: **13.**
LUMER'S LIQUORS. 1479 3rd Av. Ch.: **19.**
PAPERBACK EXCHANGES. 355 E. 86. Ch.: **24.**
STRAWBERRY. 147 E. 86. Ch.'s.: **7, 22.**
VALUE HOSIERY. 1653 2nd Av. Ch.: **7.**
YORKSHIRE WINES. 324 E. 86. Ch.: **19.**

6 to 96
FURNITURE WHOLESALE CO-OP. 1326 Madison Av. at 94th St. Ch.: **19.**
LEASE LIQUIDATORS. 1763 2nd Av. Ch.: **21.**
ONCE UPON A TIME. 171 E. 92. Ch.: **5.**
REDI-CUT CARPETS. 1833 1st Av. Ch.: **12.**
THE FISH FACTORY. 1825 2nd Av. Ch.: **11.**

1 to 66
GROUP NATIONAL CONTACT LENS. 1995 Broadway. Ch.: **13.**
LINCOLN TYPEWRITERS. 100 W. 67 at Columbus. Ch.: **21.**

1-2-3 to 72
ARTHUR M. EHRLICH LIQUORS. 222 Amsterdam Av. Ch.: **19.**
BARNES & NOBLE. 2105 Broadway. Ch.: **24.**
DESIGNER LIQUIDATORS. 2045 Broadway. Ch.: **7.**
FAIRWAY FOODS. 2127 Broadway. Ch.: **11.**
FASHIONS ALOFT. 208 W. 72. Ch.: **7.**
PAPERBACK EXCHANGES. 2145 Broadway. Ch.: **24.**
PATHMARK PHARMACIES. 2039 Broadway. Ch.: **13.**
SEVENTY-FOURTH ST. WINES. 291 Amsterdam Av. Ch.: **19.**
THE WORD CENTER. 150 W. 72. Ch.: **28.**
WEBER'S JOB LOT. 2064 Broadway at 71st. Ch.'s.: **8, 13, 15, 17, 18, 22, 28, 30.**

A-AA-B-CC to 72
THE WORD CENTER. 150 W. 72. Ch.: **28.**

1 to 79
A SECOND SPRING. 353 Amsterdam Av. Ch.: **7.**
HERTZ USED CARS. 210 W. 77 at Amsterdam. Ch.: **2.**
JRPS DISCOUNT. 2431 Broadway. Ch.: **13.**
WINFRED. 2183 Broadway. Ch.'s.: **7, 30.**
ZABAR'S FOR FOODS. 2245 Broadway. Ch.: **11.**
ZABARS UPSTAIRS. 2245 Broadway. Ch.: **8.**

1 to 86
ACKER, MERRALL LIQUORS. 2373 Broadway. Ch.: **19.**
AMERICAN VISION CENTERS. 2301 Broadway. Ch.: **13.**

A-AA-B-CC to 96
E.N.S. SHOP. 690 Columbus Av. Ch.: **7.**

1-2-3 to 96
BUY WELL HOSIERY. 2592 Broadway. Ch.: **7.**
F&G DISCOUNT. 2531 Broadway. Ch.: **13.**
FOWAD. 2554 Broadway at 96th St. Ch.'s.: **6, 7.**
JERRI'S SHOES. 2611 Broadway. Ch.: **7.**
LEROY PHARMACY PRESCRIPTIONS. 2507 Broadway. Ch.: **13.**
ORIGINAL HEALTH FOOD. 2530 Broadway. Ch.: **11.**
PATHMARK PHARMACIES. 2551 Broadway at 96th. Ch.: **13.**
S&S FASHION. 2496 Broadway. Ch.: **7.**
THE GRAB BAG. 2610 Broadway. Ch.: **7.**
THE SOPHISTICATE. 2618 Broadway at 99th St. Ch.: **7.**

1 to 103
DON RICARDO SHOES. 2691 Broadway. Ch.: **7.**
RODOS 104TH ST.. 2717 Broadway at 104th. Ch.: **12.**

1 to 110
BROADWAY WINES. 2780 Broadway. Ch.: **19.**
CROWN SEWING MACHINES. 2792 Broadway. Ch.: **1.**
HEUSTON COPY. 2879 Broadway. Ch.: **28.**

1 to 116
COLUMBIA RADIO. 1237 Amsterdam Av. Ch.: **1.**
COPYQUICK. 1211 Amsterdam Av. Ch.: **28.**

1 to 125
FRANKLIN & LENNON PAINT. 537 W. 125. Ch.: **15.**
LUCKY ROSE SHOES. 501 W. 125. Ch.: **7.**
OLD BROADWAY WINES. 574 W. 125. Ch.: **19.**

A-AA-B-CC-D to 125
LUCKY ROSE SHOES. 501 W. 125. Ch.: **7.**
RECORD KING. 314 W. 125. Ch.: **25.**
SMART SHOPPER'S LIQUORS. 268 W. 125. Ch.: **19.**

2-3 to 135
ABELSON BEER & SODA. 552A Lenox Av. Ch.: **19.**
FRIEDLAND WINES. 605 Lenox Av. Ch.: **19.**

A-AA-B-CC to 135
OZ LIQUORS. 2610 8th Av. at 139th St. Ch.: **19.**

A-AA-B-CC-D to 145
HUDGINS DISCOUNT LIQUORS. 1720 Amsterdam Av. at 145th. Ch.: **19.**

1 to 145
HUDGINS DISCOUNT LIQUORS. 1720 Amsterdam Av. at 145th. Ch.: **19.**

A-AA-B to 163
D. KALFIAN FOR REMNANTS. 475 Atlantic Av. Ch.: **12.**

A-AA-B-1 to 168-B'wy
WHOLESALE BEER & SODA. 2201 Amsterdam Av. Ch.: **19.**

A to 181
VALUE HOSIERY. 4225 Broadway. Ch.: **7.**

1 to 181
HEIGHTS LIQUORS. 547 W. 181. Ch.: **19.**
LYNN'S. 579 W. 181. Ch.: **7.**
STUART'S. 1420 St. Nicholas Av. Ch.'s.: **7, 30.**

1 to 191
BRITE GLO. 66 Nagle Av. Ch.: **11.**

A to 190
FINE WINES. 700 Columbus Av. Ch.: **19.**

A to 200-Dyckman
BRITE GLO. 66 Nagle Av. Ch.: **11.**
EVERYBODY'S WORLD LIQUORS. 148 Dyckman St. Ch.: **19.**
INTERNATIONAL GOURMET. 4791 Broadway. Ch.: **11.**

1 to Dyckman-200
EVERYBODY'S WORLD LIQUORS. 148 Dyckman St. Ch.: **19.**

1 to 207
FLAIR BEVERAGES. 3857 9th Av. Ch.: **19.**

A to 207

47: GEOGRAPHICAL DIRECTORY

ESPOSITO WINES, 608 W. 207. Ch.: **19**.
PATHMARK PHARMACIES, 4910 Broadway. Ch.: **13**.
REPLAY, 664 W. 204. Ch.: **5**.
VALUE HOSIERY, 4930 Broadway. Ch.: **7**.

6 to Morrison
PLUS DISCOUNT FOODS, 831 Rosedale Av. Ch.: **11**.

BRONX

6 to E. 177
C&R BEER BRONX, 1263 Wt. Plns. Rd. Ch.: **19**.
GIULIANO'S LIQUOR CITY, Bruckner Blvd. at Wt. Plns. Rd. Ch.: **19**.
H. ZIMMERMAN LIQUORS, 39 Hugh Grant Circle. Ch.: **19**.
LEROY PHARMACY PRESCRIPTIONS, 1448 Metropolitan Av. Ch.: **13**.

6 to E. Tremont
EXPECTATIONS, 24 Westchester Sq. Ch.: **7**.

6 to Buhre Av.
LEHIGH WINES, 2929 Westchester Av. Ch.: **19**.

2-5 to 3rd Av.
BEE HIVE, 2912 3rd Av. Ch.: **7**.
LYNN'S, 380 E. 150. Ch.: **7**.
RENARD PIANO, 3rd Av. at 159th St. Ch.: **20**.

2-5 to Freeman
VANKEITH LIQUORS, 1438 Boston Rd. Ch.: **19**.

2-5 to Allerton
ALLERTON LIQUORS, 693 Allerton Av. Ch.: **19**.

2-5 to Burke Av.
MERRI-JEAN'S FACTORY OUTLET, 3261 White Plains Rd. Ch.: **7**.

2-5 to Gun Hill Rd.
REDI-CUT CARPETS, 3545 Webster Av. Ch.: **12**.

2-5 to 225
WAKEFIELD WINES, 3965 Wt. Plns. Rd. at 225th St. Ch.: **19**.

2-5 to 233
CAL BEER, 740 E. 233. Ch.: **7**.
EDENWALD LIQUORS, 930 E. 233. Ch.: **19**.
RUSSO WINES, 4176 Wt. Plns. Rd. Ch.: **19**.

2-5 to 241
CITY LINE WINES, 4727 Wt. Plns. Rd. Ch.: **19**.
WAKEFIELD BEER, 857 E. 241. Ch.: **19**.

5 to Pelham Pkwy.
A&A DISTRIBUTORS, 1978 Williamsbridge Rd. Ch.: **7**.

5 to Gun Hill Rd.
GUN HILL BEER, 2850 Mickle Av. Ch.: **19**.

5 to Baychester
JO MISA COOKIE FACTORY, 1844 Givan Av. Ch.: **11**.
PALACE WINES, 117 Dreiser Loop. Ch.: **19**.

CC-D to 174
LIBEN-HANSEL FURNITURE, 1732 Webster Av. Ch.: **2**.

CC-D to Tremont
INDUSTRO BLDG. PRODUCTS, 1870 Webster Av. Ch.: **15**.

CC-D to Fordham Rd.
LYNN'S, 305 E. Fordham Rd. Ch.: **7**.
NORTH END LIQUORS, 2509 Webster Av. Ch.: **19**.
OK FURNITURE & CARPETING, 536 E. Fordham Rd. Ch.: **12**.
ROBBINS MEN'S WEAR, 279 E. Fordham Rd. Ch.'s: **6, 13, 27**.
RONALD'S HOSIERY, 2431 Grand Concourse. Ch.: **7**.
SMART SIZE, 111 E. Fordham Rd. Ch.: **7**.

4 to Fordham Rd.
LOEHMANN'S, W. Fordham Rd. at Jerome Av. Ch.: **7**.

CC-D to Kingsbridge
WEBSTER WALLPAPERS, 2737 Webster Av. Ch.: **15**.

CC-D to Bedford Pk. Blvd.
ABBOTT EXERCIZE EQT., 263 E. 204. Ch.: **27**.

4 to Bedford Pk. Blvd.
ABBOTT EXERCIZE EQT., 263 E. 204. Ch.: **27**.

D to 205
MOSHOLU WINES, 288 E. 204. Ch.: **19**.

1 to 231
RIVERDALE LIQUORS, 207 W. 231. Ch.: **19**.

VALUE HOSIERY, 271A W. 231. Ch.: **7**.

1 to 238
EMPIRE, 3765 Riverdale Av. Ch.: **7**.

BROOKLYN

B-D-F-M-N-QB to Coney Island
PLUS DISCOUNT FOODS, 1230 Neptune Av. Ch.: **11**.

B to Bay 50th
BOLAF WINES, 2997 Cropsey Av. Ch.: **19**.
BRANDS FOR LESS, 2615 W. 13th St. Ch.: **7**.

B to 25th Av.
PAGANO BEER, 2078 Stillwell. Ch.: **19**.
PETER PAN YARNS, 2347 86th St. Ch.: **9**.

B to Bay Pkwy.
C&S VARIETY, 2237 & 2271 86th St. Ch.'s: **5, 7**.
DEE & DEE STORES, 2159 86th St. Ch.'s: **6, 7**.
TREG'S DISCOUNT WINES, 8774 Bay Pkwy. Ch.: **19**.

B to 20th Av.
DISCOUNT BOOK STORE, 1908 86th St. Ch.: **24**.
EXPECTATIONS, 2038 86th St. Ch.: **7**.
JAY'S RUG SHOP, 1968 86th St. Ch.: **12**.
KLEIN DECORATORS, 1910 86th St. Ch.: **12**.
NAT SKOP, 1942 86th St. Ch.'s: **12, 15, 16**.
S&J STORES, 2029 86th St. Ch.: **13**.
TOP VALUE APPLIANCE, 1867 86th St. Ch.: **1**.
WORKER'S QUARTERS, 1940 86th St. Ch.: **6**.

B to 18th Av.
BRUCE SUPPLY, 8805 18th Av. Ch.: **15**.
HARRY'S DISCOUNTS, 8701 18th Av. Ch.: **1**.
TOZZI DISCOUNT LIQUORS, 8615 18th Av. Ch.: **19**.

B to 79th St.
MONA LISA BAKERY, 7713 13th Av. Ch.: **11**.
PETER PAN YARNS, 7609 18th Av. Ch.: **9**.

B to 71st St.
AUCTION OUTLET, 7305 New Utrecht Av. Ch.: **15**.
D'STILL FINE WINES, 6908 New Utrecht Av. Ch.: **19**.

N to Bay Pkwy.
CARLTON YARN, 1311 W. 7th St. Ch.: **9**.
GANIN TIRE, 6502 Bay Pkwy. Ch.: **2**.
MARBORO YARNS, 2178 Bay Ridge Av. Ch.: **9**.

N to 18th Av.
DOG DELIGHT, 6215 18th Av. Ch.: **23**.

B-N to 62nd St. & New Utrecht Av.
BORO BEVERAGE, 1675 63rd St. Ch.: **19**.
BRUCE SUPPLY, 6015 16th Av. Ch.: **15**.
ELEGANTE BRASS BEDS, 1460 65th St. Ch.: **12**.

B to 50th St.
BENNY'S IMPEX, 4717 13th Av. Ch.: **1**.
BENNY'S LOFT, 5012 New Utrecht Av. Ch.: **7**.
EASTSIDE CHINA, 5002 12th Av. Ch.'s: **8, 17**.
G & SONS DEPT. STORE, 4806 New Utrecht Av. Ch.'s: **13, 16, 27, 28, 29**.
HAMER'S SHOES, 5102 12th Av. Ch.'s: **5, 6**.
ODDS & ENDS SUNDRIES, 4809 New Utrecht Av. Ch.'s: **6, 7, 22, 29**.
QUALITY HEALTH FOODS, 4923 13th Av. Ch.: **11**.
RAINBARREL FACTORY OUTLET, 4610 13th Av. Ch.: **7**.
RAINBOW MIRROR, 4805 New Utrecht Av. Ch.'s: **5, 6, 7**.
SHOE ARCADE, 4801 New Utrecht Av. Ch.'s: **5, 6, 7**.
VALUE HOSIERY, 4615 13th Av. Ch.: **7**.
Y&T SODA AND PAPER, 4813 New Utrecht Av. Ch.: **16**.

B to Ft. Ham. Pkwy.
S&W FASHIONS, 4217 13th Av. Ch.: **7**.
BORO PARK LUMBER, 4601 13th Av. Ch.: **15**.
FOCUS ELECTRONICS, 4523 13th Av. Ch.'s: **1, 4**.
GOLDEN APPLIANCES, 4103 13th Av. Ch.: **1**.
KLEIN'S KIDDY KORNER, 4501 New Utrecht Av. Ch.: **12**.
LAMP WAREHOUSE, 1073 39th St. at Ft. Ham. Pkwy. Ch.'s: **12, 15**.
LOUIS BARGAIN CENTER, 4216 13th Av. Ch.: **9**.
QUALITY BROADLOOM & REMNANT, 4403 13th Av. Ch.: **12**.
YEEDL'S JUVENILE FURNITURE, 4301 13th Av. Ch.: **12**.

B to 9th Av.

47: GEOGRAPHICAL DIRECTORY

BENNY'S, 3804 13th Av. Ch.: **7**.
CARINI PASTRY, 3801 13th Av. Ch.: **11**.
LAMP WAREHOUSE, 1073 39th St. at Ft. Ham. Pkwy. Ch.'s: **12, 15**.
MODERN BAKERY, 3905 13th Av. Ch.: **11**.
SCOTTO'S BAKERY, 3807 13th Av. Ch.: **11**.

N to Ft. Ham. Pkwy.
ARGENTO BAKERY, 7114 Ft. Ham. Pkwy. Ch.: **11**.
CARINI PASTRY, 6213 Ft. Ham. Pkwy. Ch.: **11**.
MIKE'S BAKERY, 7005 13th Av. Ch.: **11**.
SCALA BROS. PASTRY, 7017 Ft. Ham. Pkwy. Ch.: **11**.

N to 8th Av.
OLSEN'S BAKERY, 5722 8th Av. Ch.: **11**.

RR to 86th St.
ANIMAL PANTRY, 699 86th St. Ch.: **23**.
AVRUTIS LIQUORS, 8702 5th Av. Ch.: **19**.
BAY RIDGE LIQUORS, 425 86th St. Ch.: **19**.
CENTURY 21, 472 86th St. Ch.'s: **5, 6, 7, 13**.
DEE & DEE STORES, 8515 5th Av. Ch.: **6, 7**.
RECORD FACTORY, 453 86th St. Ch.: **25**.

RR to 77th St.
BERGOS FABRICS, 8022 5th Av. Ch.: **9**.
KINGSBORO VENETAIN BLIND, 8002 3rd Av. Ch.: **15**.
RESRO PAINT, 7315 3rd Av. Ch.: **15**.

RR to Bay Ridge Av.
PETZINGER'S WINES, 123 Bay Ridge Av. Ch.: **19**.
P&G TRDG., 241 Bay Ridge Av. Ch.: **12**.

N-RR to 59th St.
LYNN'S, 5710 5th Av. Ch.: **7**.

N-RR to 53rd St.
DEE & DEE STORES, 5008 5th Av. Ch.'s: **6, 7**.
V.I.M. STORES, 5414 5th Av. Ch.: **7**.

B-N-RR to 36th St.
QUILTEX FACTORY OUTLET, 168 39th St. Ch.: **5**.

N-RR to Prospect Av.
AARON'S DRESS, 627 5th Av. Ch.: **7**.
ADCO DISTRIBUTING, 571 3rd Av. Ch.'s: **1, 15**.
BERGOS FABRICS, 637 5th Av. Ch.: **9**.
DEE & DEE STORES, 534 5th Av. Ch.'s: **6, 7**.
MURRAY SAFE, 92 19th St. Ch.: **21**.

F-N-RR to 9th St. & 4th Av.
DEE & DEE STORES, 534 5th Av. Ch.'s: **6, 7**.
VITA CHOW, 284A 9th Av. Ch.: **23**.
WALTER E. UMLA LUMBER, 180 6th St. Ch.: **15**.

B-N-RR to Pacific
D. KALFIAN FOR REMNANTS, 475 Atlantic Av. Ch.: **12**.
OMAHA FOOD DISCOUNT, 197 Ft. Greene Place.Ch.: **11**.

F to Av. X
EL-VEE OUTDOOR FURNITURE, 2425 McDonald Av. Ch.: **16**.
MAJOR TIRES, 2489 MacDonald Av. Ch.: **2**.

F to Kings Hwy.
KING'S PHARMACY, 472 Kings Hwy. Ch.'s: **13, 26**.
L&A PLUMBING SUPPLY, 519 Kings Hwy. Ch.: **15**.

F to Av. I
G.T. & SONS AUTO PARTS, 1219 McDonald Av. Ch.: **2**.
MCDONALD HOME CTR., 1258 McDonald Av. Ch.: **15**.
ROCKWELL SALVAGE, 1185 McDonald Av. Ch.: **16**.

F to Ditmas
JERRI'S LTD., 312 Ditmas Av. Ch.: **7**.
JET HANDBAG, 102 Cortelyou at McDonald. Ch.: **22**.
LYLE CARTRIDGES, 365 Dahill Rd. Ch.: **14**.
NORTHEASTERN TIRE SERVICE, 451 Dahill Rd. Ch.: **2**.

F to 7th Av.
SCHACHER LIQUORS, 322 7th Av. Ch.: **19**.

D-M-QB to Brighton Beach
NEPTUNE BEER, 257 Neptune Av. Ch.: **19**.

D-M-QB to Sheepshead Bay
AV. Z DISCOUNT LIQUORS, 1315 Av. Z. Ch.: **19**.
KING'S PHARMACY, 3082 Ocean Av. Ch.'s: **13, 26**.
LIQUOR WORLD, 3080 Ocean Av. Ch.: **19**.
LYNN RICHARDS HANDBAGS, 1664 Sheepshead Bay Rd. Ch.: **22**.

D-M-QB to Neck Rd.
HELEN WALTERS SPORTSWEAR, 2686 Coney Island Av. Ch.: **7**.

JOANN'S VARIETY STORE, 2209 Av. X. Ch.'s: **1, 13, 15, 16**.

D-M-QB to Av. U
ACE LEATHER, 2211 Av. U. Ch.: **22**.
AUCTION AL, 1221 Av. U. Ch.: **8**.
BROOKLYN ELTON PAINT, 2121 Av. U. Ch.: **15**.
D. COHEN PAINTS, 2415 Coney Island Av. Ch.: **15**.
HALF-PRICE STORE, 2962 Av. U. Ch.'s: **17, 30**.
HARMONY VIDEO, 2357 Con. Is. Av. Ch.'s: **1, 25**.
LESTER'S CHILDREN'S WEAR, 1110 Av. U. at Con. Is. Av. Ch.: **5**.
MANUFACTURER'S OUTLET, 1224 Av. U. Ch.: **7**.
MORRIS DISCOUNT, 1620 Av. U. Ch.'s: **13, 16**.
ROYAL BEAUTY SUPPLY, 1116 Av. U. Ch.: **13**.
THRIFTY THREADS, 2082 E. 13. Ch.: **5**.
TITUS OAKS RECORD EXCHANGE, 1928 Av. U. Ch.: **25**.
VARIETY STORE, 1402 Av. U. Ch.'s: **8, 16**.

D-M-QB to Kings Hwy.
AMERICAN VISION CENTERS, 1302 Kings Hwy. Ch.: **13**.
BRUCE SUPPLY, 2004 Coney Island Av. Ch.: **15**.
BYHOFF'S, 1322 Kings Hwy. Ch.: **27**.
GEMCO PAINT, 2001 Coney Island Av. Ch.: **15**.
H&E STORES, 1918 Kings Hwy. Ch.: **13**.
KING'S PHARMACY, 1110 Kings Hwy. Ch.'s: **13, 26**.
KING'S PHARMACY, 1928 Kings Hwy. Ch.'s: **13, 26**.
KINGSWAY CARPET, 907 Kings Hwy. Ch.: **12**.
KINGSWAY VIDEO, 1690 E. 15th St. Ch.: **1**.
MURRAY'S POTTERY, 802 Kings Hwy. Ch.'s: **8, 17**.
PAUL ASH'S MUSIKATALOG, 1669 E. 13. Ch.: **20**.
ROBBINS MEN'S WEAR, 1213 Kings Hwy. Ch.'s: **6, 13, 27**.
TIGHT END, 1309 Kings Hwy. Ch.: **13**.
WALLACH'S OUTLET, 1417 Kings Hwy. Ch.: **6**.
WARREN CAMERA, 1721 Kings Hwy. Ch.: **4**.

D-M-QB to Av. M
ADELMAN AUTOMOTIVE, 1539 Coney Is. Av. Ch.: **2**.
BARKOW'S YARN, 2636 Nostrand Av. Ch.: **9**.
CONSUMERS DISTRIBUTING, Av. U at Mill Av. Ch.'s: **2, 3, 8, 15, 16, 17, 27**.
DISCOUNT MATERNITY, 2663 Nostrand Av. at M. Ch.: **7**.
MIDWAY TIRE, 1755 Coney Is. Av. Ch.: **2**.
RAINBARREL FACTORY OUTLET, 1504 Coney Is. Av. Ch.: **7**.

D-M-QB to Av. J
CHEAP CHARLIE'S, 1362 Coney Is. Av. Ch.: **6**.
CITY OF BARGAINS, 1111 Av. J. Ch.'s: **16, 29**.
CLASSON TYPEWRITER, 1344 Coney Island Av. Ch.: **21**.
IRV-DAN-ACE WALLPAPER, 1464 Coney Island Av. Ch.: **15**.
LEE-OR DISCOUNT, 1113 Av. J. Ch.'s: **1, 16, 29**.
LUPU'S, 1494 Coney Island Av. Ch.: **7**.
MIDWOOD PAINT/WALLPAPER, 1327 Coney Island Av. Ch.: **15**.

D-M-QB to Newkirk
BROOKLYN PAINT FAIR, 1010 Coney Island Av. Ch.: **15**.
NEWKIRK STATION LIQUORS, 11 Newkirk Plaza. Ch.: **19**.

D-M-QB to Cortelyou
BROOKLYN BICYCLE, 715 Coney Is. Av. Ch.: **3**.
LEON'S HAND BAGS, 920 Cortelyou Rd. Ch.: **22**.
QUALITY BROADLOOM & REMNANT, 814 Coney Island Av. Ch.: **12**.

D-M-QB to Beverly
A&R NOVELTY, 1222 Flatbush Av. Ch.'s: **17, 28, 29**.
AUTOMOTIVE CITY, 555 Coney Is. Av. Ch.: **2**.
LOEHMANN'S, 19 Duryea Place. Ch.: **7**.

D-M-QB to Church
V.I.M. STORES, 1316 Flatbush Av. Ch.: **7**.
WORLD LIQUORS, 1711 Church Av. Ch.: **19**.

D-M-QB to 7th Av.
R. BORRELLO LIQUORS, 751 Bergen St. Ch.: **19**.

2-3-4 to Bergen
BERGEN TILE, 215 Flatbush Av. Ch.: **12**.
BERGEN TILE, 242 Flatbush Av. Ch.: **12**.

F-GG to Smith & 9th Sts.
PEARL BROS. TYPEWRITERS, 476 Smith St. at 9th St. Ch.: **21**.

F-GG to Bergen St.
AMERICAN BEVERAGE, 252 Court St. Ch.: **19**.
BEASTLY BITE, 140 Court St. Ch.: **23**.
COURT WHOLESALE, 244 Court St. Ch.'s: **11, 16**.

47: GEOGRAPHICAL DIRECTORY

GALDI INDUSTRIES, 290 Court St. at Douglass. Ch.'s: **12, 17.**

2-3 to Hoyt
AMERICAN VISION CENTERS, Albee Sq. Ch.: **13.**
BARNES & NOBLE, Albee Sq. Mall. Ch.: **24.**
BEE HIVE, 400 Fulton St. Ch.: **7.**
C&C BARGAINS, 400 Fulton St. at Gallatin Place. Ch.: **5.**
FACTORY OUTLET, 176 Livingston St. at Smith. Ch.: **7.**
LYNN'S, 545 Fulton St. Ch.: **7.**
ODD LOT TRDG., 503 Fulton St. Ch.'s: **8, 13, 28, 30.**
PATHMARK PHARMACIES, 376 Fulton St. Ch.: **13.**
SMART SIZE, Albee Sq. Mall. Ch.: **7.**
STRAWBERRY, 490 Fulton St. Ch.'s: **7, 22.**
V.I.M. STORES, 511 Fulton St. Ch.: **7.**
YOUNGWORLD, 452 Fulton St. Ch.: **5.**

2-3-4-5 to Nevins
C&C BARGAINS, 400 Fulton St. at Gallatin Place. Ch.: **5.**
YOUNGWORLD, 452 Fulton St. Ch.: **5.**

B-D-M-N-QB-RR to DeKalb
AMERICAN VISION CENTERS, Albee Sq. Ch.: **13.**
BARNES & NOBLE, Albee Sq. Mall. Ch.: **24.**
BEE HIVE, 400 Fulton St. Ch.: **7.**
C&C BARGAINS, 400 Fulton St. at Gallatin Place. Ch.: **5.**
LYNN'S, 545 Fulton St. Ch.: **7.**
SMART SIZE, Albee Sq. Mall. Ch.: **7.**
YOUNGWORLD, 452 Fulton St. Ch.: **5.**

A-CC-F to Jay St. & Boro Hall
MAJOR DEPT. STORE, 386 Fulton St. Ch.: **5.**
ROCKET DESK, 177 Tillary St. at Gold. Ch.: **21.**

A-CC to High St.
BROADWAY SUPPLY, 15 Cadams Plaza West. Ch.: **16.**

2-3 to Clark
BEASTLY BITE, 78 Henry. Ch.: **23.**
TOWNE LIQUORS, 73 Clark St. Ch.: **19.**

M-RR-2-3-4-5 to Borough Hall & Court St.
BARNEY'S CUT-RATE BROOKLYN, 76 Court St. at Livingston. Ch.'s: **13, 26.**
BEASTLY BITE, 140 Court St. Ch.: **23.**
BORO HALL LIQUORS, 105 Court St. Ch.: **19.**
BRUNO-SAM'S BIKES, 91 Court St. Ch.: **3.**
CAFE GALLERIA BAKERY, 174 Montague St. Ch.: **11.**
COBBLE HTS. BEER, 185 Atlantic Av. Ch.: **19.**
C.W. KEENAN INDUSTRIAL PAINTS, 27 Smith St. Ch.: **15.**
DAMASKUS BAKERY, 195 Atlantic Av. Ch.: **11.**
DISCOUNT FASHIONS, 129 Livingston St. Ch.: **7.**
ELIAS MALKO, 150 Atlantic Av. Ch.: **11.**
G. MALKO, 176 Atlantic Av. Ch.: **11.**
MALKO KARKANNI, 199 Atlantic Av. Ch.: **11.**
ORIENTAL PASTRY & GROCERY, 170 Atlantic Av. Ch.: **11.**
PATHMARK PHARMACIES, 376 Fulton St. Ch.: **13.**
SAHADI GIFT, 187 Atlantic Av. Ch.: **17.**
SAHADI IMPORTING, 187 Atlantic Av. Ch.: **11.**
SHAMMAS, 197 Atlantic Av. Ch.: **11.**
STEP 'N STYLE SHOES, 138 Montague St. Ch.: **7.**
VAN VLECK WINES, 116 Montague St. Ch.: **19.**
WOLF'S WHOLESALE, 126 Court St. at Atlantic. Ch.'s: **11, 26.**

3-4 to Flatbush Av.
DOLL HS. & MINIATURE FACTORY, 1871 Albany Av. Ch.: **29.**
EBA ASSOCIATES, 2329 Nostrand Av. Ch.'s: **1, 14, 16.**
ENGELHARD BAG & PAPER, 2358 Nostrand Av. Ch.: **16.**
OK FURNITURE & CARPETING, 1475 Flatbush Av. Ch.: **12.**

3-4 to Newkirk
LARRY'S PIANOS, 1787 Nostrand. Ch.: **20.**

3-4 to Beverly
A&R NOVELTY, 1222 Flatbush Av. Ch.: **17, 29.**

3-4 to Church
HAMMOND'S BAKERY, 1436 Nostrand Av. Ch.: **11.**
SCHAER BROS., 2602 Snyder Av. at Veronica Place. Ch.: **6.**

LL to Rockaway Pkwy.
GLENWOOD GIFT, 118 Conklin Av. Ch.'s: **8, 17.**
ODD LOT TRDG., 1166 E. 92nd St. Ch.'s: **8, 13, 28, 30.**

PENNSYLVANIA LUGGAGE, 7th Av. & 33rd St. Ch.: **22.**

LL to E. 105
CONSUMER FOOD OUTLET, 937 E. 107 at Flatlands. Ch.: **11.**

2 to New Lots
SML MEAT WAREHOUSE, Linden Blvd. & Ashford St. Ch.: **11.**
A&R NOVELTY, 1222 Flatbush Av. Ch.'s: **17, 28, 29.**

2 to Rockaway Av.
CASH WINES, 767 Rockaway Av. Ch.: **19.**

2 to Utica
KING MOTORCYCLE, 657 Utica Av. Ch.: **3.**

2 to Kingston
TROY-EAST LIQUORS, 300 Troy Av. Ch.: **19.**

LL to Sutter
EAST SIDE BEER, 431 Stone Av. Ch.: **19.**

LL to Atlantic
MIRANDA BEER, 2451 Dean St. Ch.: **19.**

LL-M to Myrtle & Wyckoff
CAROL-ANN SHOPPES, 56-47 Myrtle Av. Ch.: **7.**
CONSUMERS DISTRIBUTING, 54-30 Myrtle Av. Ch.'s: **2, 3, 8, 15, 16, 17, 27.**

LL to DeKalb
SIEB BEER, 418 Seneca Av. at Himrod. Ch.: **19.**

LL to Morgan
WILLIAM SCHMIDT BEER, 367 Johnson Av. Ch.: **19.**

GG-LL to Lorimer & Metropolitan
CHANDELIER WAREHOUSE, 40 Withers St. Ch.'s: **12, 15.**

GG to Greenpoint Av.
DEE & DEE STORES, 777 Manhattan Av. Ch.'s: **6, 7.**
E.Z. STEREO, 892 Manhattan Av. Ch.'s: **1, 14.**
INTERBORO WINES, 907 Manhattan Av. Ch.: **19.**

J-M to Marcy
BORO PARK LUMBER, 470 Kent Av. Ch.: **15.**
CO-OP SALES, 232 Broadway. Ch.'s: **1, 12, 17.**
HALF-PRICE TRASH BAG CO., 496 Wythe Av. at 9th St. Ch.: **16.**
KAHAN NATIONAL FURNITURE, 60 Broadway. Ch.'s: **12, 21.**
NATAN BORLAM, 157 Havemeyer St. Ch.: **5.**
WILLIAM WIESNER, 312 Roebling St. Ch.: **5.**

J-M to Lorimer
WALTON MIRROR WORKS, 61 Walton St. Ch.: **15.**

M to Central
AMENDOLARA BEER, 1377 DeKalb Av. Ch.: **19.**

M to Knickerbocker
AMENDOLARA BEER, 1377 DeKalb Av. Ch.: **19.**
HOCHBERG LIQUORS, 325 Knickerbocker Av. Ch.: **19.**
SHELMAR WINES, 1445 Myrtle Av. Ch.: **19.**
V.I.M. STORES, 428 Knickerbocker Av. Ch.: **7.**

A-CC to Franklin
RITTER WINES, 549 Classon Av. Ch.: **19.**

A-CC to Nostrand
BOB'S DISCOUNT LIQUORS, 627 Nostrand Av. Ch.: **19.**
THE PEOPLE'S BAKERY, 734 Nostrand Av. Ch.: **11.**

A-CC to Kingston-Throop
HARRY WEINSTEIN & SONS, 420 Tompkins Av. Ch.: **15.**
JACK LUCKNER SHELVING, 323 Herkimer St. Ch.: **21.**

A-CC to Rockaway Av.
SUN LIGHTING, 331 Rockaway Av. Ch.: **12.**

A-CC to Grant
GLOBE LIQUORS, 74-10 101st Av. Ch.: **19.**

J to Van Siclen
ATLANTIC TIRE SHOP, 2765 Atlantic Av. at Miller Av. Ch.: **2.**

A-CC to 80th St.
PAT'S SHOES, 1226 Liberty Av. Ch.'s: **5, 6, 7.**

A-CC to 88th St.
FERRARA BROS., 89-19 Liberty Av. Ch.: **15.**

QUEENS

47: GEOGRAPHICAL DIRECTORY

A-CC to Rockaway Blvd.
AUCTION OUTLET, 95-04 Liberty Av. Ch.: 15.
HENDEL PLUMBING SUPPLY, 98th St. at 95th Av. Ch.: 15.
ODD LOT TRDG., 103-54 94th St. Ch.'s: 8, 13, 28, 30.
TONY'S WINES, 93-08 Liberty Av. Ch.: 19.

A to 111th St.
AMERICAN BEDDING & FURNITURE, 109-03 Liberty Av. Ch.: 12.

A-CC to Howard Beach
MID-CITY LIQUORS, 155-12 Cross Bay Blvd. Ch.: 19.

J to Woodhaven Blvd.
DEEGAN'S DISCOUNT WINES, 95-19 Jamaica Av. Ch.: 19.
FAMILY BEER, 93-25 Jamaica Av. Ch.: 19.
ODDS & ENDS JOB-LOTS, 88-09 Jamaica Av. Ch.'s: 8, 13, 15, 16, 17, 25, 29, 30.

J to 102
PAT'S SHOES, 104-28 Jamaica Av. Ch.'s: 5, 6, 7.

J to 121
ROCKWELL SALVAGE, 120-05 Atlantic Av. Ch.: 16.

J to Metropolitan
BOUNDARY WHOLESALE FENCE, 131-02 Jamaica Av. Ch.: 15.
MAYBECK FLAGS, 134-16 Atlantic Av. Ch.: 15.

M to Seneca
PATHMARK PHARMACIES, 57-13 Myrtle Av. Ch.: 13.
ROBBINS MEN'S WEAR, 57-33 Myrtle Av. Ch.'s: 6, 13, 27.
VITO SANTORO BEER, 1820 Bleecker. Ch.: 19.

M to Forest Av.
QUEENS WINES, 59-03 71st Av. Ch.: 19.

M to Fresh Pond Rd.
CARPET DISCOUNT HOUSE, 61-01 Myrtle Av. Ch.: 12.
LYNN'S, 5609 Catalpa Av. Ch.: 7.

E-F to 179th St.
WARREN'S DISCOUNT LIQUORS, 175-25 Jamaica Av. Ch.: 19.

E-F to 169th St.
SHOE GIANT OUTLETS, 166-25 Jamaica Av. Ch.'s: 5, 6, 7.
SMART SIZE, 89-48 165th St. Ch.: 7.
V.I.M. STORES, 165-05 Jamaica Av. Ch.: 7.

E-F to Parsons Blvd.
BERGEN TILE, 153-05 Jamaica Av. Ch.: 12.
BERGEN TILE, 153-19 Jamaica Av. Ch.: 12.
FABULOUS JULIE'S, 77-40 164th St. Ch.: 5.
LYNN'S, 162-11 & 162-19 Jamaica Av. Ch.: 7.
ODD LOT TRDG., 162-03 Jamaica Av. Ch.'s: 8, 13, 28, 30.
RECORD EXPLOSION, 166-39 Jamaica Av. Ch.: 25.
SOFSAN, 159-29 Jamaica Av. Ch.'s: 8, 18.
SUN LIGHTING, 84-60 Parsons Blvd. Ch.: 12.

E-F to Sutphin Blvd.
HILLSIDE CYCLE, 139 Hillside Av. Ch.: 3.

E-F to Van Wyck Blvd.
COOPER ENTERPRISES, 114-41 Queens Blvd. Ch.: 28.

E-F to Union Tnpk.
AGE OF AQUARIUM, 116-06 Queens Blvd. Ch.: 23.
I. MARGULIS, 114-49 Queens Blvd. Ch.: 7.
MR. EXCITEMENT, 81-53 Lefferts Blvd. at Cuthbert. Ch.'s: 6, 30.

E-F to 75th Av.
I. MARGULIS, 114-49 Queens Blvd. Ch.: 7.
ODD LOT TRDG., 103-54 94th St. Ch.'s: 8, 13, 28, 30.
RENARD PIANO, 112-04 Queens Blvd. Ch.: 20.

E-F-GG-N to 71-Continental Avs.
BAGS 'N THINGS, 71-07 Austin St. Ch.: 22.
BARNES & NOBLE, 107-22 Continental Av. Ch.: 24.
BONNIE J, 71-07 Austin St. Ch.: 7.
CONSUMERS DISTRIBUTING, 107-18 70th Rd. Ch.'s: 2, 3, 8, 15, 16, 17, 27.
EMPIRE, 72-44 Austin St. Ch.: 7.
FOREST HILLS LIQUORS, 108-09 Queens Blvd. Ch.: 19.
GOLD STAR WINES, 103-05 Queens Blvd. Ch.: 19.
HARRIS'S WOMEN'S APPAREL, 70-44 Austin St. Ch.: 7.
LIVE WIRE ELECTRONICS, 107-21 Continental Av. Ch.'s: 1, 21, 25.
NATIONAL VIDEO DISCOUNT, 107-08 70th Rd. at Austin St. Ch.: 1.
PRESCRIPTION HEADQUARTERS, 106-24 71st Av. Ch.: 13.
VALUE HOSIERY, 107-10 Continental Av. Ch.: 7.

F-GG-N to 67th Av.
COMPUTER FACTORY, 100-17 Queens Blvd. Ch.: 21.
FOREST HILLS DISCOUNT BOOKS, 63-56 108th St. Ch.: 24.
TRYLON LIQUORS, 98-85 Queens Blvd. Ch.: 19.

F-GG-N to 63rd Dr.
BARETTA FASHIONS 1, 96-50 Queens Blvd. Ch.: 6.
BELL YARN, 95-16 63rd Rd. Ch.: 9.
CONSUMERS DISTRIBUTING, 97-10 Queens Blvd. Ch.'s: 2, 3, 8, 15, 16, 17, 27.
KING'S PHARMACY, 93-17 63rd Dr. Ch.'s: 13, 26.
LOEHMANN'S, 60-06 99th St. Ch.: 7.
NATIONAL BRANDS OUTLET, 95-24 63rd Rd. Ch.: 6.
PATHMARK PHARMACIES, 1 Lefrack City Plaza. Ch.: 13.
REGO DRIVE LIQUORS, 94-20 63rd Dr. Ch.: 19.
SHOE TOWN, 95-10 63rd Drive. Ch.: 7.

F-GG-N to Woodhaven Blvd.
HERMAN'S, 90-15 Queens Blvd. Ch.: 27.

F-GG-N to Grand Av.
ACE WINES, 85-10 Grand Av. Ch.: 19.
COMMUNITY BEVERAGE, 80-04 Grand Av. Ch.: 19.

F-GG-N to Elmhurst Av.
M.A.Z. TRDG., 81-19 Broadway. Ch.: 1.
M.&B. APPLIANCES, 83-15 Broadway. Ch.: 1.

E-F-GG-N-7 to 74th-B'wy & Roosevelt-Jack.Hts.
ABEHILL DISCOUNT II, 37-46 74th St. Ch.: 16.
ABEHILL STORES, 74-21 37th Av. Ch.: 13.
BROWN'S ARMY-NAVY, 74-17 Roosevelt Av. Ch.'s: 6, 27.
GANESH GROCERIES, 72-26 37th Av. Ch.: 11.
HOUSE OF SPICES, 76-17 Broadway. Ch.: 11.
JACKSON HTS. DISCOUNT BOOKS, 77-15 37th Av. Ch.: 24.
LONG ISLAND JANITOR SUPPLY, 75-15 Roosevelt Av. Ch.: 15.
ROOSEVELT DRUGS, 74-19 Roosevelt Av. Ch.: 13.
SAM & RAJ APPLIANCES, 37-12 74th St. Ch.'s: 1, 8.
SEA-TIDE FISH MARKETS, 75-11 Roosevelt Av. Ch.: 11.
SONA APPLIANCES, 37-42 74th St. Ch.: 1.

7 to 82nd St.
BROWN'S ARMY-NAVY, 83-18 37th Av. Ch.'s: 6, 27.
GENOVESE, 37-32 82nd St. Ch.: 13.
QUEENS DISCOUNT APPLIANCES, 40-16 82nd St. Ch.: 1.
SOPHISTICATE SECONDS, 83-07 37th Av. Ch.: 7.

7 to 90th St.
BUDGET USED RENTAL CARS, 91-01 Northern Blvd. Ch.: 2.
MIL AUTO PARTS, 37-65 88th St. Ch.: 2.

7 to Junction Blvd.
BERGEN TILE, 37-27 Junction Blvd. Ch.: 12.
ROBBINS MEN'S WEAR, 37-42 Junction Blvd. Ch.'s: 6, 13, 27.
SEA-TIDE FISH MARKETS, 95-31 Roosevelt Av. Ch.: 11.

7 to 111
FIRST COST, 46-20 108 St. Ch.'s: 5, 6, 7, 8, 11, 13, 15, 16, 17, 27, 29, 30.

7 to Main St.
BHARAT INDIAN FOODS, 42-71 Main St. Ch.: 11.
CAROL-ANN SHOPPES, 37-01 Main St. Ch.: 7.
CAROL-ANN SHOPPES, 37-11 Main St. Ch.: 7.
CARPET BAZAAR & REMNANTS, 136-16 Northern Blvd. Ch.: 12.
COLUMBIA APPLIANCES, 42-41 Main St. Ch.: 1.
C&R BEER, 133-31 32nd Av. Ch.: 19.
GENOVESE, 136-51 Roosevelt Av. Ch.: 13.
PLUS DISCOUNT FOODS, 144-29 Northern Blvd. Ch.: 11.
PRESCRIPTION HEADQUARTERS, 40-06 Main St. Ch.: 13.
ROBBINS MEN'S WEAR, 38-17 Main St. Ch.'s: 6, 13, 27.

47: GEOGRAPHICAL DIRECTORY

SPIRATONE LENSES/ACCESSORIES, 135-06 Northern Blvd. Ch.: **4**.

7 to 69th St.
MFR.'S UNIFORM OUTLET, 69-28 Queens Blvd. Ch.: **7**.

7 to 61st St.
ODDS & ENDS JOB-LOTS, 57-60 Woodside Av. Ch.'s: **8, 13, 15, 16, 17, 25, 29, 30**.
R.K. TRDG., 60-15 Roosevelt Av. Ch.: **1**.

7 to 46th St.
GENOVESE, 46-02 Greenpoint Av. Ch.: **13**.
PRINCIPE WINES, 45-22 46th St. Ch.: **19**.

7 to 40th St.
LOWERY DISCOUNT WINES, 40-14 Queens Blvd. Ch.: **19**.

7 to 33rd St.
CROWN DISCOUNT, 31-28 Queens Blvd. Ch.'s: **21, 28**.
D&E OUTLET, 32-02 Queens Blvd. Ch.: **7**.

F-GG-N to 65th St.
JOBBER JOE AUTO PARTS, 69-05 Northern Blvd. Ch.: **2**.

F-GG-N to Northern Blvd.
AMERICAN LECITHIN CO., 32-34 61st St. Ch.'s: **13, 23**.
OK FURNITURE & CARPETING, 54-05 Northern Blvd. Ch.: **12**.

F-GG-N to 36th St.
HERTZ USED CARS, 31-08 Northern Blvd. Ch.: **2**.

E-F-GG-N-RR-7 to Queens(boro) Plaza
ASE WINES, 28-18 Jackson Av. Ch.: **19**.
ASTORIA LUMBER, 29-70 Northern Blvd. Ch.: **15**.
CHEM-AROM, 39-15 28th St. Ch.: **13**.

7 to 45th Rd.
CROMEMCO COMPUTER, 21-55 44th Rd. Ch.: **21**.
PYRAMID STEEL SHELVING, 8-11 43rd Rd. Ch.: **21**.

E-F to Ely Av. & 23rd
CROMEMCO COMPUTER, 21-55 44th Rd. Ch.: **21**.

RR to Broadway
GENOVESE, 21-25 Broadway. Ch.: **13**.

RR to 30th Av.
BALLY WEAVE, 31-01 30th Av. Ch.'s: **6, 7**.
BENKERT'S BAKERY, 28-30 Steinway St. Ch.: **11**.
BIPHONIC ELEC., 28-13 Steinway St. Ch.: **1**.
GENOVESE, 30-09 Steinway St. Ch.: **13**.
GENOVESE, 30-14 30th Av. Ch.: **13**.
GRAND WINES & LIQUORS, 30-05 31st St. Ch.: **19**.
MADELINE'S HOSIERY, 30-14 Steinway St. Ch.: **7**.
ODD LOT TRDG., 28-32 Steinway St. Ch.'s: **8, 13, 28, 30**.
SCHATZ STEINWAY, 28-31 Steinway St. Ch.: **15**.

F-GG-N to Steinway St.
BENKERT'S BAKERY, 28-30 Steinway St. Ch.: **11**.
BERGEN TILE, 31-70 Steinway St. Ch.: **12**.
BIPHONIC ELEC., 28-13 Steinway St. Ch.: **1**.
FAIRWAY LUMBER, 34-35 Steinway St. Ch.: **15**.
GENOVESE, 30-09 Steinway St. Ch.: **13**.
LYNN'S, 40-17 31st Av. Ch.: **7**.
MADELINE'S HOSIERY, 30-14 Steinway St. Ch.: **7**.
M&M DISCOUNT LIQUORS, 38-09 Broadway. Ch.: **19**.
ODD LOT TRDG., 28-32 Steinway St. Ch.'s: **8, 13, 28, 30**.
QUEENS FLOOR COVERING, 30-74 Steinway St. Ch.: **12**.
ROBBINS MEN'S WEAR, 30-88 Steinway St. Ch.'s: **6, 13, 27**.
ROOSEVELT RUG & LINOLEUM, 31-74 Steinway St. Ch.: **12**.
SCHATZ STEINWAY, 28-31 Steinway St. Ch.: **15**.
SHOE GIANT OUTLETS, 31-13 Steinway St. Ch.'s: **5, 6, 7**.
SMART SIZE, 30-41 Steinway St. Ch.: **7**.
VALCO DISCOUNT, 32-40 & 32-62 Steinway St. Ch.'s: **3, 16, 27, 28, 29**.
WEINSTOCK LAMP, 34-30 Steinway St. Ch.: **12**.

RR to Astoria Blvd.
ATLANTIC EXPORT, 25-98 Steinway St. Ch.'s: **1, 8, 17**.
BILL ALLAN'S SPORTS, 25-77 Steinway St. Ch.: **27**.
DOMINICK'S WINES, 28-22 Astoria Blvd. Ch.: **19**.

RR to Ditmars
EXPECTATIONS, 20-10 Steinway St. Ch.: **7**.
GENOVESE, 31-09 Ditmars Blvd. Ch.: **13**.
ODD LOT TRDG., 19-40 37th St. Ch.'s: **8, 13, 28, 30**.
VACCARO BAKERY, 22-03 Astoria Blvd. Ch.: **11**.

ALL BOROUGHS NO SUBWAY

ABE'S HANDBAGS & LUGGAGE, 176-39 Union Tnpk. Ch.: **22**.
ABE'S RADIO, 1396 Rockaway Pkwy. Ch.: **1**.
AIDA'S LIQUORS, 2626 Hylan Blvd. Ch.: **19**.
AL'S SAMPLE NOOK, 179-05 Union Tnpk. Ch.: **7**.
ANYTHING & EVERYTHING, 2930 Av. X. Ch.'s: **11, 16, 23, 30**.
ARNOLD PLUMBING SUPPLY, 1254 Utica Av. Ch.: **15**.
AVIS USED RENTAL CARS, 48-05 Grand Av., Maspeth. Ch.: **2**.
BARNES & NOBLE, Kings Plaza. Ch.: **24**.
BAY TERRACE LIQUORS, 212-37 26th Av. Ch.: **19**.
BEER & SODA DISCOUNT, 1134 Hylan Blvd. Ch.: **19**.
BUY WISE LIQUORS, 79-05 Main St. Ch.: **19**.
CASTELLI WINES, 4334 Amboy Rd. Ch.: **19**.
CHEAP CHARLIE'S, 41-01 162nd St. Ch.: **7**.
CLEARVIEW LIQUORS, 205-17 35th Av. Ch.: **19**.
CONSUMERS DISTRIBUTING, 156-16 Northern Blvd. Ch.'s: **2, 3, 8, 15, 16, 17, 27**.
CONSUMERS DISTRIBUTING, 39-20 Bell Blvd. Ch.'s: **2, 3, 8, 15, 16, 17, 27**.
CROSS BAY COLD BEER, 164-44 Cross Bay Blvd. Ch.: **19**.
DISCOUNT PET FOODS, 1814 Hylan Blvd. Ch.: **23**.
EARL'S, 78-25 Metropolitan Av. Ch.'s: **5, 7, 12**.
EGAN WINES, 218-46 Hillside Av. Ch.: **19**.
ELIOT BEER, 60-03 Eliot St. Ch.: **19**.
EXPECTATIONS, 21-28 Main St. Ch.: **7**.
FINEST FOTO., 482 Sunrise Hwy. Ch.: **4**.
FIVE-L DISCOUNT WINES, 2312 Knapp St. Ch.: **19**.
FLUSHING DUPLICATING, 150-34 Northern Blvd. Ch.: **23**.
FOREST BEVERAGE, 2079 Forest Av. Ch.: **19**.
GANIN TIRE, 2360 Flatbush Av. Ch.: **2**.
GARO LEATHER, 98-18 Metropolitan Av. Ch.: **7**.
GENOVESE, 153-65 Cross Is. Pkwy. Ch.: **13**.
GENOVESE, 43-20 Bell Blvd. Ch.: **13**.
GOLDEN LIQUORS, 41-07 Bell Blvd. Ch.: **19**.
HABILD OF NEW DORP, 60 Winham Av. Ch.: **29**.
HERMAN'S, Kings Plaza. Ch.: **27**.
J&J LIQUORS, 71-06 Kissena Blvd. Ch.: **19**.
K-9 CATERERS & C&K, 89-50 Metropolitan Av. at Woodhaven Blvd. Ch.: **23**.
KINGS LIQUOR PLAZA, 2481 Flatbush Av. at U. Ch.: **19**.
KING'S PHARMACY, 2474 Flatbush Av. Ch.'s: **13, 26**.
LAWRENCE BEVERAGE, 1589 Hylan Blvd. Ch.: **19**.
LEISER LIQUORS, 41-30 162nd St. Ch.: **19**.
LEROY PHARMACY PRESCRIPTIONS, 61-28 Springfield Blvd. Ch.: **13**.
LIBEN-HANSEL TIRE. 44-10 Little Neck Pkwy. at Northern Blvd. nr. NYC line. Ch.: **2**.
LIQUOR CITY, 2239 Forest Av. Ch.: **19**.
LIQUOR GIANT, S.I. Convenience Mall. Ch.: **19**.
LIQUOR LOCKER, 172-10 46th Av. Ch.: **19**.
MAIN ST. FASHION WORLD, 67-09 Main St. Ch.: **7**.
MAJESTIC PLUMBING SUPPLY, 120-19 Rockaway Blvd. Ch.: **15**.
MANCINI'S LIQUORS, 106-31 150th St. Ch.: **19**.
MAR-PAT LIQUORS, 31-12 Farrington St. Ch.: **19**.
MEDCO SURGICAL, 220-30 Jamaica Av. Ch.: **13**.
MERCURY PAINT FACTORY, 4808 Farragut Rd. Ch.: **15**.
METRO INTERIORS, 3700 Nostrand Av. Ch.'s: **12, 17**.
MOST'S DEPT. STORE, 210-15 Horace Harding Blvd. Ch.'s: **5, 6, 7, 18**.
MYRTLE BEER, 255-47 Jamaica Av. Ch.: **19**.
NORMIE'S, 2102 Flatbush Av. Ch.: **7**.
OK FURNITURE & CARPETING, 210-06 Jamaica Av. Ch.: **12**.
PATHMARK PHARMACIES, 3823 Nostrand Av. Ch.: **13**.
PAY LESS BROOKLYN, 414 Av. U at E. 3rd St. Ch.: **13**.
PETE MILANO'S WINES, 1531 Forest Av. Ch.: **19**.
PLUS DISCOUNT FOODS, 1933 Victory Blvd. Ch.: **11**.
PLUS DISCOUNT FOODS, 2320 Ralph Av. Ch.: **11**.
PLUS DISCOUNT FOODS, 72-15 Kissena Blvd. Ch.: **11**.
PURITY MAID SPICES, 56-70 58th St. Ch.: **11**.
RAINBOW CHINA, 253-16 Northern Blvd. Ch.: **8**.

47: GEOGRAPHICAL DIRECTORY

REGO SMOKED FISH, 69-80 75th St. Middle Village. Ch.: **11.**
RIPLEY MARINE EQT., 66-00 Long Island Expwy. Ch.: **27.**
ROBERTS BICYCLE, 33-13 Francis Lewis Blvd. Ch.: **3.**
SAVEMART CLEARANCE, 317 E. 149. Ch.: **1.**
SIXTY-NINTH ST. BEER, 55-13 69th St. Ch.: **19.**
SKYVIEW LIQUORS, 5681 Riverdale Av. Ch.: **19.**
SMITH'S DONGAN LIQUORS, 1662 Richmond Rd. Ch.: **19.**
SOMERMAN DISCOUNT WINES, 78-17 Myrtle Av. Ch.: **19.**
SPRINGFIELD LIQUORS, 134-42 NY Blvd. Ch.: **19.**
STARRETT CITY WINES, 1370 Pennsylvania Av. Ch.: **19.**
THE PET NOSH, 254-11 Northern Blvd. Ch.: **23.**
TOPS LIQUORS, 2816 Av. U. Ch.: **19.**

48: INDEX

Abdominal Supports: Ch. 13
Accordions: Ch. 20
Accoustical Tiles: Ch. 15
Adding Machines: Ch.'s 1, 21
Adhesive Tapes: Ch.'s 1, 21
Adhesives: Ch. 15
Agates: Ch. 17
Air Brushes: Ch.'s 15, 28
Air Conditioners: Ch. 1
Air Mattresses: Ch. 27
Air Purifiers: Ch. 1
Airlines: Ch. 38
Airplanes, Model: Ch. 29
Alarms: Ch. 15
Amethysts: Ch. 17
Amplifiers: Ch.'s 14, 1
Andirons: Ch. 15
Animals: Ch. 23
Answering Mach.: Ch.'s 21, 1
Answering Svc.: Ch. 31
Antacids: Ch. 13
Antennas: Ch. 14
Apartments: Ch. 34
Aperatifs: Ch. 19
Appliances: Ch. 1
Aquariums: Ch. 23
Aquatic Plants: Ch. 23
Archery: Ch. 27
Army Surplus: Ch.'s 6, 27
Art: Ch. 17
Art-Supplies: Ch. 28
Ash-Trays: Ch. 16
Aspirins: Ch. 13
Attaches: Ch. 22
Automobiles: Ch. 2
Auto Alarms: Ch. 15
Auto Parts: Ch. 2
Auto Supplies: Ch. 2
Awards: Ch. 17

Axes: Ch. 15

Baby Clothes: Ch. 5
Baby Furnishings: Ch. 12
Back Packing: Ch. 27
Baked Foods: Ch. 11
Balls: Ch. 27
Bananas: Ch. 11
Bangles: Ch. 17
Banjos: Ch. 20
Banks: Ch. 32
Barbecues: Ch. 16
Barbells: Ch. 27
Barbers: Ch. 31
Barometers: 27
Bars: Ch.'s 12, 39
Baseballs: Ch. 27
Basketballs: Ch. 27
Bassinets: Ch. 12
Bassoons: Ch. 20
Bath Tubs: Ch. 15
Bathing Suits: Ch.'s 5, 6, 7
Bathrobes: Ch.'s 5, 6, 7
Bathroom Accessories: Ch. 18
Bathroom Vanities: Ch. 15
Batteries: Ch.'s 2, 14, 16
Beads: Ch. 17
Bean Pots: Ch. 1
Bean Curds & Sprouts: Ch. 11
Beans: Ch. 11
Beauty Aids: Ch. 13
Bed Sheets: Ch. 18
Bedding: Ch. 18
Beds: Ch. 12
Bedstands: Ch. 12
Beef: Ch. 11
Belts: Ch.'s 5, 6, 7

48: INDEX

Benches: Ch. 12
Bibles: Ch. 24
Bicycles: Ch. 3
Bikinis: Ch. 7
Billfolds: Ch. 22
Binoculars: Ch. 4
Bird Cages: Ch. 23
Birds: Ch. 23
Birth Control Pills: Ch. 13
Birthstones: Ch. 17
Blackboards: Ch. 28
Blankets: Ch. 18
Bleaches: Ch. 16
Blenders: Ch. 1
Blinds: Ch. 15
Blouses: Ch.'s 5, 7
Boa Constrictors: Ch. 23
Boats: Ch. 27
Book Cases: Ch.'s 12, 21
Books: Ch. 24
Boots: Ch.'s 5, 6, 7
Bottle Openers: Ch. 16
Bottles: Ch. 16
Bouquets: Ch. 10
Bowling: Ch. 27
Bowls: Ch. 8
Boxes: Ch. 16
Bracelets: Ch. 17
Brandies: Ch. 19
Bras: Ch. 7
Bread Boxes: Ch. 16
Breads: Ch. 11
Bricks: Ch. 15
Bridals: Ch. 7
Bridge Tables: Ch. 12
Brief Cases: Ch. 22
Briefs: Ch. 6
Briquets: Ch. 16
Broilers: Ch. 1
Brooches: Ch. 17
Brooms, Electrical: Ch. 1
Brooms, Manual: Ch. 16
Brushes: Ch.'s 15, 28
Buckles: Ch. 9
Bufferins: Ch. 13
Buffers: Ch. 15
Buffet Ranges: Ch. 1

Buffets: Ch. 12
Bugles: Ch. 20
Building Materials: Ch. 15
Bulbs, Light: Ch. 15
Bun Warmers: Ch. 1
Bunks: Ch. 12
Buns: Ch. 11
Burglar Alarms: Ch. 15
Business Cards: Ch. 28
Buttons: Ch. 9

Cabinets: Ch.'s 12, 21
Cabochons: Ch. 17
Cacti: Ch. 10
Cakes: Ch. 11
Calculators: Ch. 1
Cameos: Ch. 17
Cameras: Ch. 4
Camping Eqt.: Ch. 27
Can Openers: Ch.'s 1, 16
Candies: Ch. 17
Candle Snuffers: Ch. 8
Candlesticks: Ch. 8
Canes: Ch. 13
Canisters: Ch. 16
Canned Foods: Ch. 11
Canoes: Ch. 27
Canopies: Ch. 27
Canvases: Ch. 28
Caps: Ch.'s 5, 6
Car Radios: Ch. 1
Cars: See "Cars."
Carafes: Ch. 8
Carburetors: Ch. 2
Card Tables: Ch. 12
Cards, Greeting: Ch. 17
Cards, Playing: Ch.'s 16, 29
Carnations: Ch. 10
Carpet Cleaners: Ch.'s 1, 31
Carpet Sweepers: Ch. 1
Carpets: Ch. 12
Carriages: Ch. 12
Cars: Ch. 2
Cars, Rental: Ch. 38
Cartridges: Ch.'s 14, 25
Carts: Ch.'s 12, 21
Carving Boards: Ch. 8

48: INDEX

Cashews: Ch. 11
Casseroles: Ch 8
Cassettes: Ch. 25
Castanets: Ch. 20
Cats: Ch. 23
Caviars: Ch. 11
Ceiling Tiles: Ch. 15
Cellos: Ch. 20
Cement: Ch. 15
Chafing Dishes: Ch. 8
Chair Pads: Ch. 12
Chairs: Ch.'s 12, 21
Champagnes: Ch. 19
Chandeliers: Ch. 12
Changers: Ch. 14
Charms: Ch. 17
Cheeses: Ch. 11
Chemistry Sets: Ch. 29
Chess: Ch.'s 17, 29
Chests: Ch.'s 12, 17
Chicken: Ch. 11
Children's Clothes: Ch. 5
Children's Furniture: Ch. 12
Chimes: Ch. 12
Chimpanzees: Ch. 23
China: Ch. 8
Chocolates: Ch. 11
Cigarettes: Ch. 26
Cigars: Ch. 26
Cinder Blocks: Ch. 15
Clams: Ch. 11
Clarinets: Ch. 11
Cleaners: Ch. 31
Cleansers: Ch. 16
Clocks: Ch. 1
Cloths: Ch. 9
Clothes Dryers: Ch. 1
Clothing: Ch.'s 5, 6, 7
Coasters: Ch. 8
Coats: Ch.'s 5, 6, 7
Coffee Grinders: Ch. 1
Coffees: Ch. 11
Cognacs: Ch. 19
Colognes: Ch. 13
Colors: Ch.'s 15, 28
Comforters: Ch. 18
Commodes: Ch. 12

Commodities: Ch. 32
Compasses: Ch. 27
Components: Ch. 14
Compressors: Ch. 15
Computers: Ch. 21
Concertinas: Ch. 20
Concerts: Ch. 43
Concrete: Ch. 15
Condoms: Ch. 13
Contact Lenses: Ch. 13
Contact Papers: Ch.'s 15, 16
Convertibles: Ch.'s 2, 12
Cookies: Ch. 11
Cookware: Ch. 8
Copiers: Ch. 21
Copies: Ch. 28
Cordials: Ch. 19
Cork: Ch. 15
Corn Poppers: Ch. 1
Cornets: Ch. 20
Corsets: Ch. 7
Cosmetics: Ch. 13
Costume Jewelry: Ch. 17
Cots: Ch. 12
Cottons: Ch. 9
Couches: Ch. 12
Crafts: Ch. 17
Creams: Ch. 13
Credenzas: Ch.'s 12, 21
Cribs: Ch. 12
Croquet: Ch. 27
Crutches: Ch. 13
Crystal: Ch. 17
Cuff Links: Ch. 17
Cups: Ch. 8
Curlers: Ch. 13
Curtains: Ch. 18
Cushions: Ch. 12
Cuspidors: Ch. 8
Cutlery: Ch. 8

Dance: Ch. 43
Darts: Ch. 29
Decanters: Ch. 8
Decks: Ch. 14
Dehumidifiers: Ch. 1
Denture Cleaners: Ch. 13

48: INDEX

Deodorants: Ch. 13
Depth Finders: Ch. 27
Desks: Ch.'s 12, 21
Detergents: Ch. 16
Developers: Ch. 4
Diamonds: Ch.'s 17, 32
Diapers: Ch. 13
Dictionaries: Ch. 24
Dinettes: Ch. 12
Dinnerware: Ch. 8
Dioptases: Ch. 17
Direction Finders: Ch. 27
Discs: Ch. 25
Dishes: Ch. 8
Dishwashers: Ch. 1
Disinfectants: Ch.'s 13, 16
Disposers: Ch. 1
Diving Eqt.: Ch. 27
Dogs: Ch. 23
Dolls: Ch. 29
Doors: Ch. 15
Double Boilers: Ch. 8
Drafting Eqt.: Ch. 28
Dramas: 43
Draperies: Ch. 18
Drapery Fabrics: Ch. 9
Dress Fabrics: Ch. 9
Dress Forms: Ch. 9
Dressers: Ch. 12
Dresses: Ch.'s 5, 7
Dried Fruits: Ch. 11
Drills: Ch. 15
Drive-Away Cars: Ch. 38
Drop-Cloths: Ch. 15
Drugs: Ch. 13
Drums: Ch. 20
Dry Cleaners: Ch. 31
Dryers: Ch. 1
Duffle Bags: Ch. 27
Dungarees: Ch.'s 5, 6

Earrings: Ch. 17
Easels: Ch. 28
Edge Trimmers: Ch. 15
Editors: Ch. 4
Eggs: Ch. 11
Electronic Eqt.: Ch. 15

Encyclopedias: Ch. 24
Enlargers: Ch. 4
Envelopes: Ch. 28
Erasers: Ch. 28
Erector Sets: Ch. 29
Evening Gowns: Ch. 7
Exercizers: Ch. 27
Exposure Meters: Ch. 4
Extension Cords: Ch. 15
Eyeglasses: Ch. 15

Fabrics: Ch. 9
Facial Saunas: Ch. 1
Fans: Ch.'s 1, 15, 16
Faucets: Ch. 15
Fences: Ch. 15
Ferns: Ch. 10
Files: Ch.'s 15, 21
Film: Ch. 4
Films: Ch. 43
Findings: Ch. 17
Fire Extinguishers: Ch. 15
Fireplaces: Ch. 15
Firewood: Ch. 15
Fish: Ch.'s 11, 23
Fishing Eqt.: Ch. 27
Flags: Ch. 15
Flashlights: Ch. 16
Flatware: Ch. 8
Floor Coverings: Ch. 12
Floor Polishers: Ch. 1
Flours: Ch. 11
Flowers: Ch. 10
Fluorescents: Ch.'s 12, 15
Flutes: Ch. 20
Foam: Ch.'s 12, 15
Folk Dances: Ch. 43
Fondues: Ch. 8
Foods: Ch. 11
Footballs: Ch. 27
Footwear: Ch.'s 5, 6, 7
Foreign Car Parts: Ch. 2
Forks: Ch. 8
Formals: Ch. 6
Fowl: Ch. 11
Frames: Ch. 28
Frankfurters: Ch. 11

Freezers: Ch. 1
Fruits: Ch. 11
Frypans: Ch.'s 8, 1
Furniture: Ch.'s 12, 21
Furs: Ch. 7

Games: Ch. 29
Garbage Disposers: Ch. 1
Garden Eqt.: Ch. 15
Garden Furn.: Ch.'s 12, 16
Garden Supplies: Ch. 10
Garment Bags: Ch. 22
Gems: Ch. 17
Geodes: Ch. 17
Gessos: Ch. 28
Gifts: Ch. 17
Gins: Ch. 19
Girdles: Ch. 7
Glass: Ch. 15
Glassware: Ch.'s 8, 17
Globes, World: Ch. 28
Gloves: Ch.'s 5, 6, 7
Glues: Ch.'s 15, 16, 28
Goblets: Ch. 8
Goggles: Ch. 27
Gold: Ch.'s 17, 32
Goldfish: Ch. 23
Golf: Ch. 27
Gourmet Items: Ch.'s 8, 11
Grains: Ch. 11
Greeting Cards: Ch. 17
Griddles: Ch. 1
Grills: Ch.'s 1, 8
Grinders: Ch.'s 1, 8, 15
Guitars: Ch. 20
Gym Eqt.: Ch. 27

Hair Cutters: Ch. 1
Hair Dryers: Ch. 1
Hair Stylists: Ch. 31
Hairsprays: Ch. 13
Halvah: Ch. 11
Hammers: Ch. 15
Hams: Ch. 11
Handbags: Ch. 22
Handkerchiefs: Ch. 22
Handcrafts: Ch. 17

Hanging Baskets: Ch. 10
Hardware: Ch. 15
Harmonicas: Ch. 20
Hassocks: Ch. 12
Hatchets: Ch. 15
Hats: Ch.'s 5, 6, 7
Headboards: Ch. 12
Headphones: Ch. 14
Health Aids: Ch. 13
Health Foods: Ch. 11
Hearing Aids: Ch. 13
Heaters: Ch. 1
Heating Pads: Ch. 13
Hedge Trimmers: Ch. 15
Helmets: Ch. 27
Herbs: Ch. 11
High Chairs: Ch. 12
High Fidelity: Ch. 14
Hinges: Ch. 15
Hobbies: Ch. 29
Hockey: Ch. 27
Hollow Ware: Ch. 8
Honey: Ch. 11
Horns: Ch. 20
Horse Shoes: Ch. 20
Hosiery: Ch.'s 5, 6, 7
Hot Plates: Ch. 1
Hotels: Ch. 37
Housewares: Ch. 16
Humidifiers: Ch. 1
Hygrometers: Ch. 27

Ice Buckets: Ch. 8
Ice Crushers: Ch. 1
Inflatables: Ch. 27
Inks: Ch. 28
Insect Repellants: Ch. 28
Insecticides: Ch. 16
Insurance: Ch. 32
Intercoms: Ch. 1
Investments: Ch. 32
Ironing Boards: Ch. 16
Irons: Ch. 1

Jackets: Ch.'s 5, 6, 7
Jeans: Ch.'s 5, 6, 7
Jeeps: Ch. 2

48: INDEX

Jewelry: Ch. 17
Jigsaw Puzzles: Ch. 29
Jigsaws: Ch. 15
Joggers: Ch. 27
Jugs: Ch.'s 8, 16
Juicers: Ch. 1

Kettles: Ch. 8
Kitchenware: Ch. 8
Kites: Ch. 29
Knife Sharpeners: 1, 15, 16
Knitting Machines: Ch. 1
Knives: Ch.'s 8, 16, 27

Labels: Ch. 28
Laces: Ch. 9
Lacquers: Ch. 15
Ladles: Ch. 8
Lamb: Ch. 11
Lamp Parts: Ch. 15
Lamps: Ch. 12
Lanterns: Ch. 27
Lashes, Eye: Ch. 13
Lathes: Ch. 15
Lavabos: Ch. 12
Lawn Furniture: Ch.'s 12, 16
Lawn Mowers: Ch. 15
Layettes: Ch. 5
Lazy Suzans: Ch. 8
Leather Clothing: Ch. 6
Leather Furniture: Ch. 12
Lectures: Ch. 43
Lenses: Ch.'s 4, 13
Letter Openers: Ch. 28
Letterings: Ch. 28
Levels: Ch. 15
Licorice: Ch. 11
Life Jackets: Ch. 27
Light Bulbs: Ch. 15
Light Meters: Ch. 4
Lighters: Ch. 26
Lighting Fixtures: Ch. 12
Lighting Supplies: Ch. 15
Limousines: 38, 2
Linens: Ch. 18
Lingerie: Ch. 7
Linoleum: Ch. 12

Liquors: Ch. 19
Loans: Ch. 32
Lobsters: Ch. 11
Lockets: Ch. 17
Locks: Ch. 15
Lotions: Ch. 13
Loudspeakers: Ch. 14
Loungewear: Ch. 7
Luggage: Ch. 22
Lumber: Ch. 15

Magazines: Ch. 24
Manicure Sets: Ch. 1
Manicures: Ch. 31
Marimbas: Ch. 20
Marine Eqt.: Ch. 27
Markers: Ch. 28
Masking Tapes: Ch. 15
Masonry Supplies: Ch. 15
Massagers: Ch. 1
Mattress Pads: Ch. 18
Mattresses: Ch. 12
Meat Grinders: Ch.'s 1, 8
Meats: Ch. 11
Medals: Ch. 17
Medical Eqt.: Ch. 13
Medicine Chests: Ch. 16
Medicines: Ch. 13
Meters, Light: Ch. 4
Metronomes: Ch. 20
Microphones: Ch. 14
Microscopes: Ch. 4
Microwave Ovens: Ch. 1
Millinery: Ch. 7
Milk: Ch. 11
Minerals: Ch.'s 13, 17
Mirrors: Ch.'s 12, 15, 16
Mixers: Ch.'s 1, 8
Moccasins: Ch.'s 5, 6
Model Kits: Ch. 29
Monkeys: Ch. 23
Motion Pictures: Ch.'s 25, 43
Motor Scooters: Ch. 3
Motors: 15, 27
Movie Eqt.: Ch. 4
Movies: Ch.'s 25, 43
Moving Boxes: Ch. 16

Mowers: Ch. 15
Mufflers: Ch. 2
Mugs: Ch. 8
Musical Concerts: Ch. 43
Musical Instruments: Ch. 20

Nails: Ch. 15
Napkins: Ch.'s 16, 18
Necklaces: Ch. 17
Needlecraft: Ch. 9
Negligees: Ch. 7
Night Gowns: Ch. 7
Notions: Ch. 9
Nursery Furniture: Ch. 12
Nuts: Ch. 11

Oboes: Ch. 20
Office Eqt.: Ch. 21
Oils: Ch.'s 2, 11, 15, 28
Organs: Ch. 20
Oscilloscopes: Ch. 15
Ottomans: Ch. 12
Outboards: Ch. 27
Ovens: Ch. 1

Paint Sprayers: Ch. 15
Paints: Ch.'s 15, 28
Pajamas: Ch.'s 5, 6, 7
Palm Trees: Ch. 10
Pans: Ch. 8
Pants: Ch.'s 5, 6, 7
Panty Hose: Ch. 7
Paper: Ch. 28
Paper Towels: Ch. 16
Paprika: Ch. 11
Parakeets: Ch. 23
Party Supplies: Ch. 16
Patent Agents: Ch. 32
Patterns: Ch. 9
Peanut Butter: Ch. 11
Peanuts: Ch. 11
Pearls: Ch. 17
Peddle Cars: Ch. 3
Pencil Sharpeners: Ch. 28
Pencils: Ch. 28
Pendants: Ch. 17
Pens: Ch. 28

Pepper: Ch. 11
Percolators: Ch. 8
Perfumes: Ch. 13
Periodicals: Ch. 24
Personal Accessories: Ch. 22
Pet Foods: Ch. 23
Pets: Ch. 23
Pewter: Ch. 8
Pharmaceuticals: Ch. 13
Phono Cartridges: Ch. 14
Phonographs: Ch.'s 1, 14
Photo Copiers: Ch. 21
Photographic Eqt.: Ch. 4
Pianos: Ch. 20
Piccolos: Ch. 20
Pickles: Ch. 11
Picture Frames: Ch. 28
Pies: Ch. 11
Pillow Cases: Ch. 18
Ping Pong: Ch. 27
Pipes, Plumbing: Ch. 15
Pipes, Smoking: Ch. 26
Pitchers: Ch. 8
Place Mats: Ch. 18
Plants: Ch. 10
Plaques: Ch.'s 12, 17
Plaster: Ch. 15
Plate Glass: Ch. 15
Play Vehicles: Ch. 3
Playing Cards: Ch.'s 16, 29
Playpens: Ch. 12
Plays: Ch. 43
Plexiglas Furniture: Ch. 12
Pliers: Ch. 15
Plumbing Supplies: Ch. 15
Plywood: Ch. 15
Poetry Readings: Ch. 43
Poker: Ch. 29
Polishers: Ch.'s 1, 15
Polishes: Ch.'s 2, 16
Pool Tables: Ch. 27
Popcorn Makers: Ch. 1
Portfolios: Ch. 28
Posters: Ch. 24
Pots: Ch. 8
Pottery: Ch. 8
Powders: Ch.'s 13, 16

48: INDEX

Power Tools: Ch. 15
Prescriptions: Ch. 13
Pressure Cookers: Ch. 1
Printers: Ch. 28
Projectors: Ch. 4
Publications: Ch. 24
Pumps: Ch.'s 15, 27
Punchbowls: Ch.'s 8, 17
Purifiers: Ch. 1
Purses: Ch. 22
Puzzles: Ch. 29
Pythons: Ch. 23

Quilts: Ch. 18

Rackets, Tennis: Ch. 27
Radios: Ch. 1
Rafts: Ch. 27
Raincoats: Ch.'s 5, 6, 7
Range Hoods: Ch. 1
Ranges: Ch. 1
Razors: Ch. 13
Receivers: Ch.'s 14, 1
Recliners: Ch. 12
Record Players: Ch.'s 1, 14
Recorders: Ch.'s 1, 14, 20
Recordings: Ch. 25
Reels: Ch.'s 4, 25, 27
Refrigerators: Ch. 1
Rehabilitation Eqt.: Ch. 13
Religious Gifts: Ch. 17
Remainder Books: Ch. 24
Reptiles: Ch. 23
Restaurant Eqt.: Ch. 8
Restaurants: Ch.'s 39-42
Rice: Ch. 11
Rings: Ch. 17
Rockers: Ch. 12
Rocks: Ch. 17
Rodents: Ch. 23
Roofing Supplies: Ch. 15
Room Dividers: Ch.'s 12, 21
Ropes: Ch. 27
Roses: Ch. 10
Rotisseries: Ch. 1
Rubber Stamps: Ch. 28
Rubbers: Ch.'s 5, 6, 7, 13

Rubies: Ch. 17
Rugs: Ch. 12
Rum: Ch. 19

Safes: Ch. 21
Sailboats: Ch. 27
Salamis: Ch. 11
Salons, Hair: Ch. 31
Sand: Ch. 15
Sand Paper: Ch. 15
Sandals: Ch.'s 6, 7
Sanders: Ch. 15
Saphires: Ch. 17
Saunas, Facial: Ch. 1
Sausages: Ch. 11
Saws: Ch. 15
Saxophones: Ch. 20
Scales: Ch.'s 13, 16
Scarves: Ch. 22
Science Kits: Ch. 29
Scissors: Ch.'s 9, 16, 28
Sconces: Ch. 12
Scooters: Ch. 3
Scotch: Ch. 19
Screwdrivers: Ch. 15
Screws: Ch. 15
Secondhand: Ch.'s 5, 6, 7, 21
Septarians: Ch. 17
Services: Ch. 31
Sesame: Ch. 11
Sewing Aids: Ch. 9
Sewing Machines: Ch. 1
Shades: Ch.'s 12, 15
Shampooers, Rug: Ch.'s 1, 31
Sharpeners: Ch.'s 15, 28
Shavers: Ch. 1
Shears: Ch. 9
Sheet Metal: Ch. 15
Sheets: Ch. 18
Shelving: Ch.'s 21, 15
Shirts: Ch.'s 5, 6
Shock Absorbers: Ch. 2
Shoes: Ch.'s 5, 6, 7
Shopping Carts: Ch. 16
Shower Curtains: Ch. 18
Shower Stalls: Ch. 15
Shrimp: Ch. 11

Shrubs: Ch. 10
Shuffleboard: Ch. 27
Signal Generators: Ch. 15
Silks: Ch. 9
Silverware: Ch. 8
Sinks: Ch. 15
Skates: Ch. 17
Ski Wear: Ch.'s 6, 27
Skillets: Ch. 8
Skindiving: Ch. 27
Skirts: Ch.'s 5, 7
Skis: Ch. 27
Slacks: Ch.'s 5, 6, 7
Sleeping Bags: Ch. 27
Slicers: Ch. 1
Slippers: Ch. 6
Slips: Ch. 7
Smoke Detectors: Ch. 1
Smoking: Ch. 26
Snakes: Ch. 23
Sneakers: Ch.'s 5, 6, 27
Snorkels: Ch. 27
Soaps: Ch. 16
Soccer: Ch. 27
Socks: Ch.'s 5, 6
Sofas: Ch.'s 12, 21
Solderers: Ch. 15
Solvents: Ch. 16
Soy: Ch. 11
Speakers: Ch. 14
Spices: Ch. 11
Spoons: Ch. 8
Sporting Goods: Ch. 27
Spot Removers: Ch. 16
Sprayers: Ch. 15
Sprinklers: Ch. 16
Staplers: Ch.'s 15, 28
Station Wagons: Ch. 2
Stationery: Ch. 28
Steak: Ch. 11
Steel Shelving: Ch. 21
Steins: Ch. 8
Stemware: Ch.'s 8, 17
Stencils: Ch. 28
Stereos: Ch.'s 14, 1
Stethoscopes: Ch. 13
Stock Brokers: Ch. 32

Stockings: Ch.'s 5, 6, 7
Stones: Ch. 17
Stools: Ch.'s 12, 21, 28
Storm Windows: Ch. 15
Stoves: Ch. 1
Strollers: Ch. 12
Subscriptions: Ch. 24
Suitcases: Ch. 22
Suits: Ch.'s 5, 6, 7
Sun Glasses: Ch.'s 13, 22
Sun Lamps: Ch. 1
Surgical Appliances: Ch. 13
Surplus: Ch.'s 6, 27
Sweepers, Carpet: Ch. 1

T-Squares: Ch. 28
Tablecloths: Ch. 28
Tables: Ch.'s 12, 21, 28
Tackle: Ch. 27
Tahini: Ch. 11
Tankards: Ch. 8
Tanks: Ch. 23
Tape: Ch.'s 1, 15, 16, 25, 28
Tape Recorders: Ch.'s 14, 1
Tapestries: Ch. 12
Tarpaulins: Ch. 15
Teas: Ch. 11
Tel. Ans. Mach.: Ch.'s 21, 1
Telephones: Ch. 1
Telescopes: Ch. 4
Televisions: Ch. 1
Tennis: Ch. 27
Tents: Ch. 27
Terrariums: Ch. 10
Textbooks: Ch. 24
Textiles: Ch.'s 9, 18
Theatres: Ch. 43
Thermometers: Ch.'s 13, 16
Thermos Jugs: Ch.'s 16, 1
Threads: Ch. 9
Thrift Shops: Ch.'s 5, 6, 7
Ties: Ch. 6
Tiffanies: Ch. 12
Tiles: Ch. 15
Timers: Ch.'s 1, 16
Tires: Ch. 2
Tissue: Ch. 16

48: INDEX

Toasters: Ch. 1
Tobacco: Ch. 26
Toilet Seats: Ch.'s 15, 16
Toiletries: Ch. 13
Toilets: Ch. 15
Tone Arms: Ch.'s 14, 1
Tools: Ch. 15
Toothbrushes: Ch.'s 13, 1
Toothpastes: Ch. 13
Tote Bags: Ch. 22
Tourmalines: Ch. 17
Towel Racks: Ch. 15
Towels: Ch. 18
Toys: Ch. 29
Trains: Ch. 29
Trampolines: Ch. 27
Tranquilizers: Ch. 13
Trash Compactors: Ch. 1
Travel Agencies: Ch. 38
Trays: Ch. 8
Trees: Ch. 10
Tricycles: Ch. 3
Trimmings: Ch. 9
Trivets: Ch. 8
Trombones: Ch. 20
Trophies: Ch. 17
Trucks: Ch. 2
Trumpets: Ch. 20
Tubes: Ch. 14
Tumblers: Ch. 8
Tuners: Ch.'s 14, 1
Turntables: Ch.'s 14, 1
Tuxedos: Ch. 6
Typewriters: Ch.'s 21, 1

Umbrellas: Ch. 22
Underwear: Ch. 6
Unfinished Furniture: Ch. 12
Uniforms: Ch. 7
Upholstred Furn.: Ch. 12
Urns: Ch. 8
Used: 2, 5, 6, 7, 20, 21, 24

Vaccuum Cleaners: Ch. 1
Vaccuum Jugs: Ch.'s 16, 1
Valets: Ch. 12
Vanities: Ch. 22
Vaporizers: Ch.'s 1, 13
Vases: Ch. 8
Vaults: Ch. 21
Veal: Ch. 11
Vegetables: Ch. 11
Venetian Blinds: Ch. 15
Vests: Ch.'s 6, 7
Vibrators: Ch. 1
Video Tape Eqt.: Ch.'s 1, 25
Viewers, Slide: Ch. 4
Viewmasters: Ch. 29
Violins: Ch. 20
Vises: Ch. 15
Vitamins: Ch. 13
Vodkas: Ch. 19
Volleyballs: Ch. 27

Waffle Irons: Ch. 1
Walkers: Ch. 13
Walkie Talkies: Ch. 1
Wall Coverings: Ch. 15
Wallets: Ch. 22
Warmers: Ch. 1
Washing Machines: Ch. 1
Waste Baskets: Ch. 16
Waste Disposers: Ch. 1
Watches: Ch.'s 17, 1
Waterpiks: Ch. 1
Waterskiing: Ch. 27
Waxes: Ch.'s 2, 16
Wedding Favors: Ch. 16
Wheel Chairs: Ch. 13
Whiskies: Ch. 19
Wigs: Ch. 13
Window Shades: Ch. 15
Windows: Ch. 15
Wines: Ch. 19
Wood: Ch. 15
Wool: Ch. 9
Woolens: Ch. 9
Work Clothes: Ch. 6
Wreathes: Ch. 10
Wrenches: Ch. 15

Xerox Copies: Ch. 28
Xylophones: Ch. 20

Yachts: Ch. 27
Yarns: Ch. 9
Yo-yo's: Ch. 29

Zippers: Ch. 9
Zithers: Ch. 20

The author of this book Eric Zuesse, is available to address your organization or group concerning any of the subjects covered in BARGAIN FINDER. He also serves as a consultant to book publishers and self-publishers in saving money on producing and publicizing books. He may be reached at 242-0041.

He further holds monthly seminars on bargain-finding, as well as on the city's greatest bargain restaurants, and conducts periodic guided bargain finder's walking tours. For information regarding either of these seminars, or regarding the walking tour, contact The Learning Annex at 956-8800.

(continued from back cover)

For the first time, with this edition, *Bargain Finder* also makes specific product-recommendations, based on the research of its author, Eric Zuesse, who has culled through years of back-issues of dozens of consumer product-rating books and magazines, such as *Consumer Reports, The Car Book, Popular Photography, Audio, Modern Photography, Stereo Review,* and others, to identify those brands and manufacturers which have consistently scored highest in these ratings. However, he has not taken these rating-services as infallible authorities. Mr. Zuesse in addition spoke with repair-station personnel who know intimately from long personal experience, which manufacturers make the ruggedest products, and which have quality-control or hidden reliability problems. In addition, the author indicates when a commonly-available off-brand product is identical to, or otherwise better value than, the advertised brand-names.

Although everything in *Bargain Finder* is intended to be useful both to tourists and to newly-arrived New Yorkers, there are special sections of the book devoted to the unique needs of each.

If you're a visitor who came to the Big Apple not to see a lot of other tourists, but rather to explore this great and wonderful metropolis as the natives know the place, then you'll find *Bargain Finder* to be unique among all general New York guidebooks. It was written by a venturesome long-time Manhattanite, Eric Zuesse, the Director of New York's Consumers' Alliance, which he founded in 1971. The author knows the five boroughs of this City inside and out; and almost all of the places he recommends he has visited not just once but many times.

Bargain Finder takes you to all the exciting parts of town that New Yorkers love and that unfortunately few tourists ever get to see. For example, although tourists and travel agencies are well acquainted with Times Square and Rockefeller Center, neither place is nearly as beloved among the locals as are such less-touristed haunts as Canal St., Chambers St., Soho, Chinatown, Orchard St., Little Italy, or Brooklyn's Atlantic Avenue Arabic Quarter. Each of these neighborhoods is a world unto itself, yet distinctively and authentically *New York*. Many of the super-bargain stores and restaurants listed in *Bargain Finder* are in these—the most distinctive, atmospheric, and often beautiful—neighborhoods; and many of those shops will ship merchandise to your home-town or native country at a much lower price than you can purchase the same items where you live. The savings can more than pay for your entire NYC vacation.

Bargain Finder even has walking tours which take you through some of these great neighborhoods, and which indicate the terrific and yet inexpensive restaurants, and the marvelous discount stores. So you can get to experience the real New York, and you'll save bundles of money doing it.